PENGUIN BOOKS
INDIAN IDENTITY

An internationally renowned psychoanalyst and writer, Sudhir Kakar has been a visiting professor at the universities of Chicago, Harvard, McGill, Melbourne, Hawaii and Vienna, and a Fellow at the Institutes of Advanced Study, Princeton and Berlin. Currently, he is Adjunct Professor of Leadership at INSEAD in Fontainbleau, France. His many honours include the Bhabha, Nehru and National Fellowships in India, the Kardiner Award of Columbia University, the Boyer Prize for Psychological Anthropology of the American Anthropological Association, and Germany's Goethe Medal. The leading French magazine *Le Nouvel Observateur* listed him as one of twenty-five major thinkers of the world.

Sudhir Kakar's books, both non-fiction and fiction, have been translated into twenty languages. His non-fiction works include *The Indians: Portrait of a People*; *The Inner World: A Psychoanalytical Study of Childhood and Society in India*; *Intimate Relations: Exploring Indian Sexuality*; *The Analyst and the Mystic: Psychoanalytic Reflections on Religion and Mysticism* and *The Colours of Violence*. His three published novels are *The Ascetic of Desire*, *Ecstasy* and *Mira and the Mahatma*. He has also translated (with Wendy Doniger) Vatsyayana's *Kamasutra*.

SUDHIR KAKAR

INDIAN IDENTITY

Intimate Relations
The Analyst and the Mystic
The Colours of Violence

PENGUIN BOOKS

PENGUIN BOOKS
Published by the Penguin Group
Penguin Books India Pvt. Ltd, 11 Community Centre, Panchsheel Park, New Delhi
110 017, India
Penguin Group (USA) Inc., 375 Hudson Street, New York, New York 10014, USA
Penguin Group (Canada), 90 Eglinton Avenue East, Suite 700, Toronto, Ontario,
M4P 2Y3, Canada (a division of Pearson Penguin Canada Inc.)
Penguin Books Ltd, 80 Strand, London WC2R 0RL, England
Penguin Ireland, 25 St Stephen's Green, Dublin 2, Ireland (a division of Penguin
Books Ltd)
Penguin Group (Australia), 250 Camberwell Road, Camberwell, Victoria 3124,
Australia (a division of Pearson Australia Group Pty Ltd)
Penguin Group (NZ), 67 Apollo Drive, Rosedale, North Shore 0632, New Zealand
(a division of Pearson New Zealand Ltd)
Penguin Group (South Africa) (Pty) Ltd, 24 Sturdee Avenue, Rosebank, Johannesburg
2196, South Africa

Penguin Books Ltd, Registered Offices: 80 Strand, London WC2R 0RL, England

First published as *The Indian Psyche* in Viking by Penguin Books India 1996
This edition published in Penguin Books 2007

Copyright © Sudhir Kakar 1996

All rights reserved

10 9 8 7 6 5

ISBN-13: 978-0-14310-186-4   ISBN-10: 0-14310-186-2

Typeset in Times Roman by Interpress Magazines Pvt. Ltd, New Delhi
Printed at Chaman Offset Printers, Delhi

To the memory of Erik H. Erikson, shared with my two dear friends,
John Ross and Pamela Daniels.

CONTENTS

1. *A Personal Introduction* ix

2. Intimate Relations 1
3. The Analyst and the Mystic 125
4. The Colours of Violence 189
5. Notes 374
6. A Note from the Author 399
7. Index 400

A PERSONAL INTRODUCTION

In the memories of my childhood, the season is always summer. Blazing hot, dry, and invariably dusty, it is the special summer of small district towns in West Punjab, an area that now lies in Pakistan. Each of the towns—Dera Ghazi Khan, Multan, Lyallpur, Sargodha—where we would live for two to three years before my father was transferred to another town, indistinguishable from the one we had just left, have coalesced in my memory into one quintessential town. This is a town without character, neither old nor new, and no one is interested in its past history or its future prospects. Through the nostalgic haze of childhood, I can still summon up images of the town's cheerful dirtiness: its narrow, crowded bazaars lined with open, flowing gutters carrying children's pee, vegetable peelings and eggshells bobbing on the surface of the inky-black water. I can see the flies clustering on mounds of raw brown sugar in eating places where the chipped enamel plates with their blue borders are never clean enough and the smell of fried onions, garlic, cardamom, cloves and turmeric is embedded in the very walls.

The town is also the central market for surrounding villages. After the harvest, ox-carts loaded with gunny bags full of wheat or stacked high with sugarcane stream in. Their arrival is announced by the chiming of small bells that hang around the necks of the oxen drawing the cart, placidly ignoring the mangy, yelping dogs' attempts to provoke them. On market days the farmers are accompanied by their gaily-dressed women and excited children, giving the drab town a touch of shy festivity. These large family groups move deliberately from one shop to another, looking at the wares without expression, unhurriedly bargaining for their small luxuries—coloured glass bangles for the women, a piece of cloth for a child's shirt, a burnished copper pot and brass tumblers for the family kitchen.

As a child, I was as much an outsider to the bazaars as any child from the village. We lived a couple of miles away from the heart of the town in what was called the Civil Lines. The Civil Lines and its military counterpart, the Cantonment, were to be found in many towns. They were creations of the British whose rule was approaching its end in the period of which I write, the early 1940s. The houses in the Civil Lines, built at the end of the last century, were sprawling single-storeyed affairs with acres of ground and a number of servants' quarters. Lawns and flower beds, a vegetable garden, a pond or a well, groves of fruit-bearing trees (I particularly remember the blood-red oranges of the grove in Sargodha), were often a part of the estate. Not many Englishmen were now left in these towns. There was the deputy commissioner, of course, the chief representative of the Raj, a virtual lord over the half-a-million or so Indians who lived in the district. Then there was the superintendent of police and perhaps the chief medical officer, who were still Englishmen. All the other higher functionaries of the provincial government living in the Civil Lines, together with a couple of lawyers and doctors, were Indians. My father was one of these Indians, a magistrate dispensing justice in the district court and carrying out the tasks of civil administration in the villages.

Generally, I was content to play within the grounds of the house with my friends, mostly the servants' children. Climbing trees to eat unripe guavas that inevitably led to stomach-aches, trying to hit pigeons with pebbles from a slingshot, fishing in the pond for non-existent fish with a thread tied to a twig at one end and a bent pin at the other, the secret delights (and fears) of sexual games with Shanti, the sweeper's six-year old daughter in one town and Kishen, the washerman's precocious five-year old in another, kept me happy enough. The visits to the town's bazaars were outings I thoroughly enjoyed but did not desperately long for. Whenever I did go to the bazaar, though, accompanying a servant on a shopping errand, I quite liked being pampered by the shopkeepers, who all knew me as the magistrate sahib's son. I took this pampering for granted and confused it with the love I felt was my due as the only son of doting parents.

The pamperings continued in the village to which I often accompanied my father on his official tours. These tours, lasting from a week to a fortnight, were virtual expeditions. Bullock carts, and (in some districts) camels, loaded with tents, camping equipment and foodstuff, set off early in the morning while we followed more leisurely with a retinue of servants, policemen and court clerks. By the evening we would reach our destination, a village where my father would inspect the records, hear complaints and adjudicate disputes. In the falling darkness, which became magically alive with moving pinpoints of light given off by fireflies, cooking fires were lit, pleasantly scenting the air with the smoke from burning wood and buffalo-dung cakes. A stream of visitors and favour-seekers from the village would call on my father in our tent. From hundreds of years of experience as a conquered people, the villagers were well-versed in the arts of flattery, and making complimentary remarks about me was a part of their practised repertoire. By the age of six, I knew that the fawning I received from others in our retinue or from the villagers, was not always love, and that I was not the centre of everyone's world; of course, my sister had been born by then.

While my father worked during the day in his tent, I roamed about freely in the village, intensely curious about the other children whose lives seemed so different from my own. I longed to join in their games, yet we were all aware of the gulf dividing us that was only occasionally bridged. I might have felt myself a charmed being but there was little doubt that I was outside their charmed circle. Form the beginning, then, whether in town in village, I was the insider-outsider, the child who both belonged and yet did not.

The insider-outsider situation in my culture was very much a reflection of the life history of my parents. My father had grown up in the bazaars, though in his case they were the bazaars of Lahore, the capital city of Punjab. He came from a well-to-do family of merchants and contractors and had spent his childhood and youth in a typical Indian exended family—a sprawling noisy collection of parents, a dozen brothers and sisters, and assorted uncles and aunts on visits that in some cases could extend over a year. They all lived together in a dark three-storeyed house with little space but much warmth. My childhood impressions of life in my grandparents' house, where I often went for extended visits, is of swirling movement and excitement contained within secure boundaries of fierce loyalty and protection with which the family surrounded each individual member, whether child, man or woman. Moving from one part of the house to another, I could, within a few mintes, be witness to loud quarrels, heart-rending sobs, tender consolations, flirtatious exchanges, uproarious laughter, and sober business conversations. The kitchen full of women—daughters of the house, female relatives and visitors presided over by my strong-willed grandmother—was active from early morning, and except for a couple of hours' break in the afternoon closed late in the night. One ate whenever one liked and there was always a steaming hot delicacy that had just come out of the deep-bottomed frying pans. There were dozens of cousins and visiting children from the neighbourhood and we played everywhere—on the roof, from where we jumped on to the neighbouring roofs; in all the rooms of the house (there were no *private* spaces), as well as outside in the alley. All these spaces, inside and outside, were without boundaries, blending seamlessly into each other. Whenever I was tired, I'd find an empty bed, generally a mattress on the floor, and some woman would eventually drift over to put me to sleep. As the eldest son of the eldest son of the house, I had some privileges and could ask my favourite aunt to put aside her kitchen duties and tell me stories while I tried to fight my tiredness. The stories were usually from the Hindu epics but she also had a fund of exciting folktales about princes, princesses and magicians who turned them into birds and animals and back again into people.

My father had always been brilliant in his studies, effortlessly standing first in his class at school and in due course, he received a scholarship to study enonomics and political science at the college in Lahore. The family had placed great hopes in him. With his intellectual gifts, it was taken for granted that he would be the first one in the family to move out of the Indian world of the bazaar into the Indo-Anglian world of the Civil Lines. This move, barely a couple of miles in geographical distance but immense in cultural space, was the dream of most young men of his generation. The surest passport to this other world was by passing a competitive examination for the provincial civil service. The written examination, with an interview at its end, was very difficult; only four to five young men from all over the province were recruited for the service each year. The other routes to the Indo-Anglian world were through officer-training in the army, studies in law or medicine in England, or, through the most prestigious examination of them all, the Indian Civil Service which had been opened to Indians.

My father's family did not have enough money to finance years of study in England. The examination for the Indian Civil Service, for which too one ideally prepared in England, was beyond my father's cultural capabilities. To enter the service, the young man had to be at least the second if not the third generation out of the bazaar to possess the natural ease with Western manners and social sang-froid that upper-class English interviewers looked for in Indian recruits who were to be moulded into passable imitation of themselves. A short, dark man, not at all as ugly as he always thought himself to be, my father did not know how to eat with a knife and fork. He was sublimely unaware of the difference between a pink gin and a gin and tonic; indeed, having never touched alcohol, he would not have been able to distinguish whisky from rum. His acquaintance with the subtleties of cricket was slight. He neither rode, nor played tennis nor danced; he would have been tongue-tied in the presence of any young woman who was not a member of the family. What he loved was Indian-style wrestling on the banks of the river Ravi early in the morning and declaiming Sanskrit verse to admiring friends—the romantic poetry of Kalidasa in his youth and, later, when he grew older, the more cynical verses of Bharathari.

Though he had studied many of the classics of English literature and wrote a grammatically perfect though ponderous prose in the admired styles of Burke and Gibbon, he rarely spoke the language and was uncertain about the correct pronunciation of most words—a certain recipe for disaster in the ICS interviews. Later, when I, my sister or even my mother, all second-generation immigrants to the Indo-Anglian world, schooled in convents run by British missionaries of one persuasion or the other, teased him about his pronunciation of English words, his self-deprecating laughter did not quite hide his pride in the fact that he had made it possible for his children to fulfil his own 'lack'—to speak English as the British spoke it and with a minimum of the Indian lilt in its intonation. As an adult, when I was consciously trying to get a Punjabi lilt back into my spoken English (in contrast to many friends going in the opposite direction), there was always a slight twinge of guilt for having betrayed one of my father's cherished ideals.

My father did not have much difficulty in adapting his Indian background to the more Western lifestyle of the Civil Lines. Temperamentally incapable of being moved by religion or the beauty of Indian ritual, art or music, and with a strong belief in rationality as the ordering principle of human affairs, he was ready to identify with his British superiors whom he saw as valiant fighters against the decay of an Indian society ridden with 'magic' and 'superstition'. Any difficulties he may have experienced were more a matter of externals: giving up comfortable kurta-pyjamas for suits and ties, airy chappals for (given the realities of the Indian climate) smelly socks and constraining shoes. Eating porridge and toast for breakfast instead of his accustomed puri and halwa may also have given him twinges of cultural indigestion in the beginning. His readiness to adopt Western values had partly to do with his being a Punjabi and thus belonging to a people who, because of their geographical location at the gateway to India from the north-west, and historical circumstances that had made them live under a succession of alien rulers, were not as deeply anchored in traditional Hindu culture as people from most other parts of the country. The ease of his adaptation had also to do with his caste whose values and aspirations he could identify as being consonant with his own role as a civil servant of the British rule. Thus, many years later, he wrote me in a letter:

> As I could follow that Khatri (our caste) was a derivation from Kshatriya, the warrior and princely class of the Vedic and classical age, I have always thought of myself belonging to a *Herrenvolk* when compared to other castes. I used to take pride in the fact that Khatris are, by and large, good-looking and have a fair complexion, without bothering about the fact that I possessed neither. I know I do not possess any attributes of the warrior class, yet I cling to the dogma of being a warrior type of yore, of being a ruling type with all the obligations of conduct that go with it.

My mother's family had entered the Indo-Anglian world a generation earlier than my father's. Her father, hailing from a village, had been a brilliant student who had managed to go to England for higher studies in medicine. After his return to Lahore, he set up a practice as a surgeon that was flourishing by the time I was born. My mother, as also her sisters and brothers, was educated at English-speaking schools, and their house on Lawrence Road in Lahore was a grander version of the houses in the district towns where I spent my childhood. My memories of my maternal grandparents' house are quite different from those of my father's family. There was, of course, much more space in this house as also a greater order; there was more privacy for the individual family member, but also many more prohibitions. There was little of the indulgence and easy-going acceptance of children and their ways that was a characteristic of my father's family—my mother's father being a believer in strict discipline for the child and other such Western notions.

For me, the best part of the visits to my mother's family was provided by the circumstance that my grandmother's family owned a cinema in Lahore. With the help of a friendly usher who also doubled as an odd-job man around the house, I spent many delightful afternoons at the cinema, seeing a movie 15 to 20 times and thus beginning a love affair with the world of Hindi films that has continued to this day. Like everything else in India, from plants to men, the movies too were divided into a hierarchy. In the caste order of Hindi films, the Brahmin 'mythologicals' about the legends of gods and goddesses were at the top, followed by the Kshatriya 'historicals', while the Sudra 'stunt' films were at the bottom. My taste in movies, however, was catholic, consisting of indiscriminate adoration. As I sat there in the darkened hall, in the company of students giving their teachers a temporary breather and domestic servants prolonging their shopping errands, I felt no longer a small child from a provincial town but very much a man of the world. Watching flickering images on the screen portraying a love scene and trying to understand the loud remarks and double-entendres from the audience that were met by bursts of appreciative laughter in which I too joined, I felt tantalisingly closer to unravelling that secret of adulthood which every child yearns to understand. Now, in their familiar, unchanging plots and treatment, Hindu films keep the road to childhood open.

The cinema, the house on Lawrence Road and in the bazaar, were all lost during the Partition of the country in 1947. Caught up in the tidal wave of migration from Pakistan to India, the families of my parents were irrevocably scattered all over the country as individual members tried to fend for themselves and build new lives. My mother's father, for instance, went to the far eastern corner of the country—to Assam—to head a newly created medical college. My other grandfather, together with a couple of still unmarried aunts and an uncle, settled in Amritsar at the opposite end of the new country. The long and frequent visits to my parents' families, the closeness with uncles, aunts and cousins, became a thing of the past. From regular immersions into the river of extended family life, with its rituals and festivals, games and feasts, and rapidly shifting alliances of love and hate, my life became a narrow stream bounded by the world of Christian missionary schools on one side and of my parents and my sister on the other. For me the Partition of the country also effectively marked the end of my childhood.

The Independence of the country opened up avenues of 'getting on in the world' other than the traditional route through the civil service. The country was embarking on a process of modernisation and industrial development and it was accordingly decided, with my surgeon grandfather's vigorous support, that I would become an engineer. I was 17 when the decision was made, and like most Indian youth of the time, and perhaps even of today, I did not have much choice in the matter—even if I *had* shown a marked preference for a particular profession, which I did not. Unaware of what I really wanted to do with my life and with implicit confidence in the collective wisdom of family elders to look after my interests, I went off to study mechanical engineering at a college in Ahmedabad, north of Bombay, famous for its textile mills. In Ahmedabad I was to live with my mother's younger sister, Kamla, who was the head of the pyschological division of a research institute established by the textile industry.

Kamla was a remarkable woman who, like many other Indian women I came to know later, revealed unsuspected reserves of strength and depths of character when misfortune tore away the protective cocoon that enveloped Indian girls of her class. Married at the age of 18 to a man who had just returned from England after entering the Indian Civil Service, Kamla seemed set for a predictable life as the wife of a higher civil servant. Three months after her marriage, though, she became a widow in tragic cirumstances. Her husband had been posted to a town in the north-west, near the border of Afghanistan. In the course of his judicial duties, he had sentenced a man to prison. One evening, after being released, this man hid himself in the bedroom of the young couple's house. When Kamla awoke the next morning she found her husband lying dead next to her, shot in the head, flies buzzing over the brains spilled on his face. She had not heard a sound, the report of the gun transformed into exploding crackers in her dream.

Kamla did not remarry. She studied philosophy and then spent five years in the United States, acquiring a doctorate in psychology. By the time she returned to India, the country had been partitioned and she took up a job in distant Ahmedabad. She not only lived on her own, unusual for an Indian woman in those days, but openly took a married man as her lover, further scandalizing conservative Ahmedabad society. It was while living at Kamla's house that I encountered and took my first hesitant steps into the Western world. In her large library, I discovered European novels—Camus and Sartre, Huxley and Mann. I browsed through the philosophy of Schopenhauer and Russell and remember being fascinated by Freud's *Interpretation of Dreams* and *Psychopathology of Everyday Life*. I cannot pretend that I understood everything I consumed so voraciously. Reading the books was like travelling through a foreign country in a fast train, with glimpses of unusual landscapes where I might have liked to linger and of strange towns I might have wanted to explore further. I was still a shy and awkward adolescent, with no one to discuss the world I was discovering in these books. My studies had become a burdensome chore and though I did not know what I was going to do with myself I was certain I was not going to be an engineer.

The visitors to Kamla's house were a further revelation. As I listened to their animated talk, absorbing information, attitudes and ideas, I was also discovering the fascination of being an individual, of a person who did not need to think or behave only as a member of a group but could range beyond the traditional confines of family and caste. For, yes, however much I was later to long for the warmth of the family and community and return to a celebration of their virtues, I regarded them as wholly confining in those days. Through Kamla and her Westernised friends, I thought I caught glimpses of an Occident which, in my imagination, became the home of the 'heroic' individual following his desires and inclinations unencumbered by expectations and human ties. It was this caricature of the psychoanalytic man that enthralled me then and remained my model for many years.

I was 22 when I finished my engineering studies and began my journey to the West. The family had arranged for my further training in a shipyard in West Germany and, as usual, I had acquiesced in these plans. I embarked from Calcutta on a freighter that took a leisurely six weeks to reach Hamburg, loading and unloading at various Indian and African ports on the way. Each day at sea increased my newly-discovered feeling of freedom, and of escaping from the oppressiveness of a highly structured Indian society. I recall that I spent most of my time on board playing chess with any of the ship's officers that happened to be free, reading Victorian romantic novels borrowed from the ship's small library and, above all, daydreaming on the deck chair. They were the typical daydreams of a young man conquering the world except that they could not have been dreamt in India. My fantasies were of passionate love affairs, of drinking wine and of conversations late into the night with intellectual men and women with the world's knowledge of art and science; they were dreams of the success that excites the envy of men and the love of women. The reality, that I was a gangling provincial youth from an underdeveloped land, with nothing to offer but a bright-eyed enthusiasm and a puppy-tailed friendliness, on my way to an arrogant European country whose language I did not speak, did not affect the content of these daydreams in the least. I was 22 and everything was not only possible but capable of a magical transformation.

My first actions after I settled into my cheap lodgings in Hamburg, arranged for me by the shipyard, was to buy a large bottle of inexpensive red wine, enrol myself in a school for ballroom dancing, start on the first page of a novel, and write to my father that I had no intentions of going on further with engineering and would like to study philosophy instead. The consternation this later caused in the family must have been very great indeed. I got a quick reply from my father appealing to my reason, a reproachful how-much-I-was-hurting-her letter from my mother, and a thunderous missive recalling me to my duty towards the family from my surgeon-grandfather. With the relative safety of a 7,000-kilometer distance between us, I could afford to remain adamant. And while our letters went back and forth, I was discovering the attractions of a West that had been such a dominant counterpoint in all our personal and collective lives. I learnt German, though it was the slang German of docks and shipyards, full of interesting expletives. I learnt to dance the boogie-woogie and the cha-cha, the most popular dances of the time, and took music lessons on the clarinet. I heard my first Mozart, read my first Brecht, slept with my first woman.

It took eight months before my family finally relented—eight months in which I did a variety of jobs in the shipyard that further increased my distaste for engineering. I made sand moulds in the steamy, hot foundry, drinking enormous quantities of beer, and stood for hours at the drawing board in the design section, endlessly drawing pipes and waiting for the clock to strike five. Philosophy was out of the question, my father wrote. No one had ever made any money through the study or practice of philosophy and in any case it was a subject more suitable for the speculative Brahmins than for active Kshatriyas like us—just as playing the clarinet (as an uncle once wrote) was more the province of the low-caste musician than of the gun-wielding Khatri. If I insisted on studying further, then the compromise subject suggested, lying midway between philosophy and engineering, was economics. Still dependent on my family, both emotionally and financially, I agreed to this suggestion and went off to study economics, first at the University of Mainz and then at Mannheim, the choice of the university dictated more by the movements of a girl I was passionately in love with than by the reputation of either unversity's economics faculty.

I studied economics as I did engineering, with half my mind and with none of my soul. In my youthful love affair with the world I needed passion and surprise; engineering and economics had neither. In the five years of economics studies at Mannheim, I learnt some formal economics but collected a much greater store of an unsystematic knowledge of Western art, literature and philosophy. My teachers were less the remote Herr Professors of the university and more a group of budding painters and aspiring writers with whom I became close. I stayed up with these German friends almost every night of the week. Moving from one tavern to another as they closed for the night behind us, we drank vast quantities of beer, flirted with the waitresses and earnestly discussed Life and Art. Finally at daybreak, bleary-eyed with alcohol and replete with talk, we would end up in one of the sleazy joints near the wharves on the riverfront where we drank coffee in the company of incurious sailors and the last whores in town who were still awake. The Western artist given to creative excesses rather than the contemplative Indian mystic became my ideal, the hero of my personal myth and under the influence of these friends I began writing short stories in German that were occasionally published in the *feuilleton* section of the town's newspaper. When I now look at the yellowing newsprint of these early stories, I am struck by their intensity of longing for the life of provincial Indian towns where I grew up. For though my head was filled with the intellectual excitement of the West, India was still an overpowering emotional presence and these stories, crude in many ways, convey a deep and persistent undercurrent of nostalgia, almost sensual in character, for the sights, smells, tastes and sounds of the country of my childhood.

Like many other young men of my class who had discovered the West in India and who later went abroad to study, I too began to discover India while living in the West, understanding its history, culture and mythology primarily through the eyes of Western scholars. Without my being aware of it at the time, I was enthusiastically acquiring a certain perspective on the life I had lived and the tales and myths I had grown up with. In the German society of the early 60s, this perspective was very much informed by the modern enlightenment values of universality, objectivity, rationality and the notion of progress. Indian culture, though demanding respect for its past achievements, was—when compared to its modern Western counterparts—definitely on a lower rung of the ladder of human development. Not having sufficiently developed the 'scientific spirit', Indian society contained a greater share of ignorance, superstition, fanaticism, and oppression which crippled human effort and frustrated the search for timeless truths and rational self-direction. This was the heritage of all colonised minds, including that of my father, and it took a long time before I questioned these values and their underlying, unstated assumption that post-renaissance Europe marks the flowering of the human spirit and civilization. I travelled far on the road (on which Marx is an inevitable wayside stop) where the uniqueness of each human culture and the plurality of cultures is denied, where the myths of other cultures are considered false statements about reality—to be corrected by later rational scrutiny—rather than seen as embodying visions of the world as authentic as, for instance, Platonic philosophy. For too long a time I was enamoured by the quest for the construction of universal laws in human affairs and only much later in life gradually veered to the view that to understand anything was to understand it in its individuality and its development, in its concreteness rather than its abstraction. Indeed, my later attraction to Freud, who in many ways is also an epitome of the rationality of enlightenment, was less to his theoretical speculations or to his metapsychology than to his fascinating case histories, rich with individual detail. It is the latter model that I have tried to follow in my own recent work in the belief, bordering on conviction, that theories and insights must naturally emerge from the *narrative* and that for an understanding of human life one must never move far from the narration of human experience; much of modern social science writing, where narrative truth is missing, leaves me openly skeptical if not quite cold. I am, however, moving too far ahead of my own story.

I took my economics degree in 1964 and returned to India after an absence of five years. The return journey was a leisurely one by train through Turkey, Iraq and Iran. Somewhere on the way in Iraq my baggage was stolen and I arrived in Delhi with a three-week growth of beard and a cloth bag containing soiled underwear and a new toothbrush purchased in Baghdad. The warmth of the family's welcome, the delight on my parents' faces and the sight of my sister, now a beautiful young woman, were more than enough to compensate for the loss of clothes, books and records, and I had no difficulty in regressing to my former place in the family's life. Letting the waves of their love and concern wash over me, my recently acquired notions of independence and individual autonomy forgotten for the time being, I let myself be fed to bursting point by the women as they discussed proposals for my marriage received in my absence, and with equal pleasure I listened to my father, uncles and grandfather ponder over questions of my future career.

While in Germany, I had applied for an academic position at the newly established Institute of Management at Ahmedabad, one of the two such institutes modelled on American business schools that pioneered fashionable management studies in India. I was appointed research fellow in the faculty for the management of agricultural and rural development where my work involved collection of cases on leadership in rural institutions, cases that were later intended to be used in training administrators of development programmes. I travelled widely in rural India that year and during my travels, lost any idealizations I might

have had about the peace and harmony of Indian village life or, for that matter, about the new management 'science'. What for example, does one advise the village headman whose biggest problem is that the opposing faction expresses its dissent with his leadership by sending their womenfolk each morning and evening to pee against the wall of his house?

Travelling by train and bus to remote villages, I spent a great amount of time by myself. After the round of interviews in a particular village was complete, and I had made my notes on the day's work, there was nothing much to do in the evenings. The village normally went early to bed and I remember many nights lying out in the open, under the canopy of a sky packed densely with glittering stars, listening to the occasional barking of village dogs and to conversations that were taking place in my head on the future shape of my life. There were fantasies of my becoming a writer (but how would my family react and who had ever heard of anyone in India earning his livelihood through writing?), of applying to a film school for training as a movie director and of once again packing my bags and going back to Europe. Should I marry one of the three girls my parents had so carefully selected for me—all of them beautiful, accomplished and 'from a good family'—or should I, in Western fashion and in the tradition of its romantic literature to which I had become addicted, search for love and beauty and *the* great passion of my life? Of course, I now look back at my anguished 26-year-old self with affectionate irony. At the time, though, my tortured confusion about what I was and what I wanted to be was a serious affair that did not evoke indulgent smiles, either in me or in my parents. They could not understand why, after I had had my way and done (or almost done) what I had so stubbornly wanted, I could not now settle down to a career and to the raising of a family; I did not understand it myself. I needed help to fathom the depths of confusion gripping my soul. I needed to understand the ambivalence of my desires, to unravel my tangled perceptions of the world and assess the realistic possibilities it afforded for the fulfilment of my wishes. Looking back, I can see in this need the seeds of my later vocation as a psychoanalyst; I became a doctor because I could not be a patient at that time.

The help, when it came, was from an unexpected quarter—through a chance encounter with an elderly, European-born American scholar. The scholar was the psychoanalyst Erik Erikson, a professor of human development at Harvard, who was in India for a few months to work on his book on Gandhi. A tall, well-built man with almost shoulder-length white hair and a drooping Einsteinian moustache, Erikson and his wife Joan had rented my aunt Kamla's house while she was away on an extended visit to the United States. They became my neighbours since I lived in a small annexe on the grounds.

Erikson was very well known in the field of psychoanalysis, a field I only knew from rumours, but he was not yet the world famous figure he was to become later. He had complemented Freud's psychosexual stages of growth with his own theory of psychosocial stages of human development. Briefly, Erikson

had shown how significant relationships at various stages of life contribute specific strengths or pathologies to the self over the life cycle. Childhood and sexuality were vital but not completely determining for our personality and eventual fate. His contributions to other areas, such as psychology of religion and the initiation of a new field he called 'psychohistory', were to have a widespread impact on the study of humanities. Caught up in my own youthful turbulences, I was unaware of his stature and in fact confused his name with that of Erich Fromm.

I could therefore approach him naturally, without any inhibiting awe. Whenever I was back in Ahmedabad from my travels, I loved to go over to his house at sunset when he had finished his own work and we would sit out on the balcony overlooking the Sabarmati river. In companionable silence, we would sip at our cold drinks and contemplate the vista of an age-old life unfolding on the river bed: strings of small white Kathiawari donkeys, as mild and not bigger than sheep, carefully climbing up the river bank carrying bags of sand for the city's construction projects; wiry washermen clad in loin cloths and burnt black by the sun, beating cloth on flat-topped stones with loud rhythmic grunts; dyers with their steaming cauldrons practising an ancient craft, the freshly dyed five-yard long sarees strung between wooden stakes to dry in a riot of changing colours as the sun gradually sank below the horizon and the vermilion dusk deepened to grey.

We watched and talked of Gandhi and of the men and women whose lives he had transformed. Like Gandhi, Erik was no mean transformer himself. Erikson's sparse observations were full of wise insight and occasional gentle humour that completely captivated me. What struck me most about him was a benevolence singularly free from all traces of condescension—whether of the old towards the young, of the learned towards the ignorant, of the established scholar towards the novice or the famous towards the unknown. He had that rarest of gifts, a possession of the truly generous in spirit, of paying complete and total attention to the person he was with—even when what the person was saying was neither particularly original nor especially interesting.

I do not remember the details of those conversations but their life and spirit are still alive within me. The way he looked at people and events, with that indefinable quality called wisdom, was opening up my mind—and yes, my spirit—in a way I had never experienced before. It was the mental counterpart, rarely experienced, of the sudden opening up of senses and emotions in one's first, passionate love affair. It was not as if he talked a great deal. He was not one of those people infesting academic and public life who hold forth at great length, afflicting our ears and violating our sensibilities. Erik was quite capable of listening to my callow views on Gandhi and on life with a grave courtesy and responding in a way which never made me feel that he did not take them, or me, seriously. Many years later, when I was working with him at Harvard as his assistant, I saw this quality again and again in his seminars. Even if according to me, someone was spouting forth complete nonsense, Erik would paraphrase

the person in a way that made the contribution seem valuable, a value he added himself. Time and again, I saw the delighted surprise on the face of a student— 'Did *I* say this?' Everyone who attended a seminar with Erik or talked to him, went away with a sense of enhancement, never of being diminished. I believe it was this innate generosity of spirit which made him pay attention to me. I was lonely, desperately longing to return to Europe *and* stay in India, full of the most outrageous plans for my life, wanting to do so many things because I did not know what I wanted.

I read his writings, intially with curiosity and later with mounting excitement as I discovered that my own inner confusion was perhaps not a symptom of an idiosyncratic and pathological disorder (which I had secretly feared) but something many people have had at one or another time in their lives. My 'identity problems' (Erikson's concept of identity crisis was to become very well known in the next few years), though perhaps unduly prolonged, 'belonged' to a normative crisis of adolescence and young adulthood. The problems were, in addition, not only personal but located in my communal culture in the sense that they were a reflection of the contemporary crisis in the historical development of the Indian middle class, torn in its orientation between the East and the West, conflicted between European and Indian models and values.

Put simply, I was having an 'identity crisis'. It was my good fortune I could spend so many hours with a man who had coined the term. I recognized that an identity crisis is not a sickness but another chance to realign the shape of one's outer life with the core of one's being, with one's true self. What I really wanted, I discovered, was that special kind of life of the mind which I believed psychoanalysis could give me. I wanted to be like him.

The day Erikson left Ahmedabad for Delhi, on his way back to the United States, was also the day I discovered that what I wanted more than anything else was to work with him as an apprentice and, if possible, learn the psychoanalyst's craft. It became clear to me, as if in a sudden revelation, that he was the guru my Indian self was searching for. Unfortunately, there seemed to be no way of reaching him in time to give him the good news of his selection as my guru. The train journey to Delhi took 23 hours, by which time he would already have left India, and I could not afford to fly. Here, another piece of luck came my way. The chief representative of the Ford Foundation—one of the financial supporters of the Institute of Management—had come to Ahmedabad for a day and was returning to Delhi the same evening in the Foundation's private aircraft. All I had to do was ask him for a lift, a request to which he obligingly agreed. We reached Delhi airport at around ten in the night. I took a taxi straight to the hotel where the Eriksons were staying. After having said goodbye to me only the previous day, Erikson must have been surprised to see me. His face, however, did not betray any surprise as he listened to me pour out the news of my discovery. Courteously, and with his characteristic attention, he listened to what I wanted of him.

It was to his credit that he did not laugh out aloud when I told him of his adoption as my mentor and my intention to work with him when he returned to his job as professor of human development at Harvard. My degrees in engineering and economics were my only formal qualifications but I had published short stories in German, I told him. Gravely, but with a twinkle in his eye, he pointed out the vital flaw in my plans to teach in his course on the human life cycle. 'You have never studied psychology,' he said. I could only nod my assent to this intrusion of reality. 'It doesn't matter,' he said, 'neither have I'. For although later in life he was to be showered with honorary doctorates from universities all over the world, the culmination of his formal academic training remained a high school diploma. He had never studied at a university and had spent his 'wander-years' in Europe as a painter before he came to Freud in Vienna. 'I liked your stories, though. They show talent and a psychological-mindedness which is sufficient for me,' he said. 'I'll tell you what I'll do,' he went on to say, 'if you get your doctorate in the next two to three years, I'll try my best to get you an appointment at Harvard to work with me.' We shook hands as I once again bid him goodbye.

Humming to myself, I walked out into the sprawling Lodi Gardens next to the hotel. It was a clear night at the beginning of April, at the fag end of Delhi's tantalizingly short spring. The strong perfume of white narcissus that flowers in the night hung in the air. The gardens, with their imposing 800-year-old tombs of the grandees of a bygone empire, were quiet except for the rustle of a gentle breeze through the trees and the occasional cry of a parrot in uneasy sleep. The lights in the upper floor of the newly-built meteorological station next to the garden were still burning. I walked on the gravel path meandering between the mausoleums with a lightness in my step, feeling intensely active and alive. The confusion seemed to be over, the future stretching before me full of promise.

In the years to come, I would finish my doctoral studies at Vienna, work as Erikson's assistant at Harvard, and do my psychoanalytic training at Frankfurt. I would teach, practise, write books, marry and have children. I would know loneliness and sadness; but never again would I know the panic and confusion of the year I travelled through the villages with no idea of which direction I should turn, when I alternated between holding fast to a stubborn selfhood and a surrender to the family of which I was a part, when I spent many sleepless nights in the construction of private utopias that crumbled into nothingness.in the morning.

I whistled to myself as I walked through the garden on my way to my grandparents' house, where I would spend the night eagerly anticipating the expression of delighted surprise on my grandmother's face at my unexpected arrival.

INTIMATE RELATIONS

Exploring Indian Sexuality

For
Elisabeth and Manfred,
Anita and Vikram

CONTENTS

1 Introduction 5
2 Scenes from Marriages 12
3 Lovers in the Dark 24
4 The Sex Wars 38
5 Husbands and Others 56
6 Gandhi and Women 73
7 Masculine/Feminine: A View from the Couch 110
8 An Ending 120

ACKNOWLEDGMENTS

This book was largely completed during the two years I was the recipient of a Nehru Fellowship. Originally intended to be a study of family relationships in India through the medium of folktales, its focus soon narrowed to the relations between the sexes, yet also simultaneously expanded to include other narratives. I am grateful to the Jawaharlal Nehru Memorial Fund for their financial support. I am also happy to acknowledge a debt to Dr Renuka Singh for her sensitive and skilful interviews with women from Delhi slums, which form the basis of chapter 5.

Parts of this book have been presented at different forums in condensed versions. Chapters 2 and 3 were originally delivered as the George De Vos Lectures at the Department of Anthropology, University of California, Berkeley. Chapter 2 also formed the basis of a talk at the Department of Sociology,University of Delhi. Chapter 6 was presented in the Social Science Seminar at the Institute of Advanced Study, Princeton, the Department of Anthropology, Princeton University, and the Department of Political Science, Cornell University. I also wish to thank my friend John Ross for his comments and suggestions. Chapter 7 was presented at the Conference on Human Development, University of Chicago, the Swiss Psychoanalytic Society, Zurich, and the Second International Psychoanalytic Symposium at Delphi. It was published under the title 'The Maternal-Feminine in Indian Psychoanalysis.' in the *International Review of Psychoanalysis* 16(3), 1989, and I am grateful to the Institute of Psychoanalysis in London for their permission to reprint. Finally, I wish to thank Jayashree and R. Shankar at the Centre for the Study of Developing Societies for their help in the preparation of this typescript.

1

INTRODUCTION

This book is a psychological study of the relationship between the sexes in India. It is about men and women—lovers, husbands, and wives—living in those intimate states where at the same time we are exhilaratingly open and dangerously vulnerable to the other sex. It is about Indian sexual politics and its particular language of emotions. Such an inquiry cannot bypass the ways the culture believes gender relations should be organized nor can it ignore the deviations in actual behaviour from cultural prescriptions. Yet the major route I have selected for my undertaking meanders through a terrain hewn out of the *fantasies* of intimacy, a landscape whose contours are shaped by the more obscure desires and fears men and women entertain in relation to each other and to the sexual moment in which they come together, What I seek to both uncover and emphasize is the *oneiros*—the 'dream'—in the Indian tale of *eros* and especially the dreams of the tale's heroines, the women.

Tale, here, is not a mere figure of speech but my chosen vehicle for inquiry and its unique value for the study of Indian gender relations, as indeed for the study of any Indian cultural phenomenon, calls for some elaboraion.

The spell of the story has always exercised a special potency in the oral-based Indian tradition and Indians have characteristically sought expression of central and collective meanings through narrative design. While the 20th-century West has wrenched philosophy, history, and other human concerns out of integrated narrative structures to form the discourse of isolated social sciences, the preferred medium of instruction and transmission of psychological, metaphysical, and social thought in India continues to be the story.

Narrative has thus been prominently used as a way of thinking, as a way of reasoning about complex situations, as an inquiry into the nature of reality. As Richard Shweder remarks on his ethnographic experiences in Orissa, whenever an orthodox Hindu wishes to prove a point or convey what the world is like or ought to be like, he or she is more than likely to begin his exposition with that shift in the register of voice which is a prelude to the sentence, 'Let me tell you a story.'[1] The belief is widespread that stories, recorded in the culture's epics and scriptures or transmitted orally in their more local versions, reflect the answers of the forefathers to the dilemmas of existence and contain the distillate of their experiences with the world. For most orthodox Hindus, tales are a perfectly adequate guide to the causal structure of reality. The myth, in its basic sense as an explanation for natural and cultural phenomena, as an organizer of experience, is verily at the heart of the matter.

Traditional Indians, then, are imbedded in narrative in a way that is difficult to imagine for their modern counterparts, both Indian and Western. The stories they hear (or see enacted in dramas and depicted in Indian movies) and the stories they tell are worked and reworked into the stories of their own lives. For stretches of time a person may be living on the intersection of several stories, his own as well as those of heroes and gods. Margaret Egnor, in her work on the Tamil family, likens these stories to disembodies spirits which can possess (sometimes literally) men and women for various lengths of time.[2] An understanding of the person in India, especially the untold tale of his fears and wishes—his fantasies—requires an understanding of the significance of his stories.

What could be the reasons for the marked Indian proclivity to use narrative forms in the construction of a coherent and integrated world? Why is the preference for the language of the concrete, of image and symbol, over more abstract and conceptual formulations, such a prominent feature of Indian thought and culture? Partly, of course, this preference is grounded in the universal tendency of people all over the world to understand complex matters presented as stories, whereas they might experience difficulty in the comprehension of general concepts. This does not imply the superiority of the conceptual over the symbolic, of the paradigmatic over the narrative modes, and of the austere satisfactions of denotation over the pleasures of connotation. Indeed, the concreteness of the story, with its metaphoric richness, is perhaps a better path into the depths of emotion and imagination, into the core of man's spirit and what Oliver Sacks has called the 'melodic and scenic nature of inner life, the Proustian nature of memory and mind.'[3] For it may be, as Sacks further suggests, that the final form of the brain's record of experience and action is organized iconically and is, in fact, 'art', even if the preliminary forms of cerebral representation are computational and programmatic.[4]

Apart from any possible universal grounding in brain physiology, the Indian celebration of the narrative (and the dramatic) has its roots in one of the more enduring and cherished beliefs of the culture. This particular belief holds that there is another, higher level of reality beyond the shared, verifiable, empirical reality of our world, our bodies, and our emotions. A fundamental value of most schools of Hinduism and Buddhism, the belief in the existence of an 'ultimate' reality—related to ordinary, everyday reality in the same way as everyday reality is related to the dream—is an unquestioned verity of Hindu culture, the common thread in the teachings of the culture's innumerable gurus, swamis, and other mystics. This ultimate reality, whose apprehension is considered to be the highest goal and meaning of human life, is said to be beyond conceptual thought and indeed beyond mind. Intellectual thought, naturalistic sciences, and other passions of the mind seeking to grasp the nature of the empirical world thus have a relatively lower status in the culture as compared to meditative praxis or even art. Aesthetic and mystical experiences, as Robert Goldman has pointed out, are supposed to be closely related so that the aesthetic power of music and verse, of a well-told tale and a well-enacted play, makes them more rather than less real than life.[5] Moreover, since ultimate reality can only be apprehended experientially, its hue, flavour, and ramifications for ordinary life are best conveyed to the uninitiated mass of people in the culture through story—myth, fable, parable, and tale—thus further elevating the prestige of the narrative form. Little wonder that on occasion interrupting a story has been viewed as a sin equivalent to the killing of a Brahmin.[6]

With the declining fortunes of logical positivism in Western thought, the giving up of universalistic and ahistorical pretensions in the sciences of man and society, the traditional Indian view is not far removed from that held by some of the newer breed of social scientists. Many psychologists, for instance, believe that narrative thinking— 'storying'—is not only a successful method of organizing perception, thought, memory, and action but, in its natural domain of everyday interpersonal experience, it is the most effective.[7] Other thinkers are convinced that there is no better way to gain an understanding of a society than through its stock of stories, which constitute its dramatic resource.[8] The psychoanalyst, of course, whose practice has always consisted of helping the client construct a comprehensive self-narrative that encompasses previously repressed and disavowed aspects of the self, thus making better sense of his symptoms and behaviour, finds himself quite at home with the Indian insistence on story as the repository for psychological truth. At least in one influential view articulated by Ricouer, Habermas, Steele, and others, psychoanalysis is essentially telling and retelling the story of a particular life.[9] Explanation in psychoanalysis is then narrative rather than hypothetical-deductive. Its 'truth' lies in the confirmatory constellation of coherence, consistency, and narrative intelligibility. Whatever else the analyst and the analysand might be doing, they are also collaborators in the creation of the story of an individual life.

The larger story of gender relations I strive to narrate here is composed of many strands that have been woven into the Indian imagination. There are tales told by the folk and the myths narrated by family elders and religious story-tellers, or enacted by actors and dancers. These have, of course, been of traditional interest for students of cultural anthropology. Today, in addition, we also have popular movies as well as modern novels and plays, which combine the society's traditional preoccupations with more contemporary promptings. I have always felt, at least for a society such as India where individualism even now stirs but faintly, that it is difficult to maintain a distinction between folktales and myths as products of collective fantasy on the one hand and movies and literature as individual creations on the other. The narration of a myth or a folktale almost invariably includes an individual variation, a personal twist by the narrator in the omission or addition of details and the placing of an accent, which makes his personal voice discernible within the collective chorus. Most Indian novels, on the other hand, are closer in spirit to the literary tradition represented by such 19th-century writers as Dickens, Balzac, and Stendhal, whose preoccupation with the larger social and moral implications of their characters' experiences is the salient feature of their literary creations. In other words, it is generally true of Indian literature, across the different regional languages, that the fictional characters, in their various struggles, fantasies, unusual fates, hopes, and fears, seek to represent their societies in miniature. Indeed, one of the best known Hindi novels of the post-Independence era, Phanishwarnath Renu's *Maila Anchal*, goes even further in that it centres not on an individual but on a whole village. At the most, one could say that novels, films, folktales, and myths are ranged in order on a continuum which spans the expression of individual fate at one end and collective aspirations on the other. To a greater or lesser degree, the individual characters of each narrative form are symbolic revealers of a much larger universe.

In addition to drawing on the above-mentioned forms, I have also made use of other texts such as autobiography and clinical case history. In their use of imagination for the reconstruction of lives, combining facts and fiction to arrive at life-historical truth, they too are stories, strategically placed doorways into the arena of intimate relations.

My own narrative here is informed by the psychoanalytic perspective, which required a particular kind of imagination as well as a model for interpretation. Similar to the special competence of a literary critic which enables him to 'read' a poem by converting its linguistic sequences into literary structures and meanings, there is a specific kind of psychoanalytic reading—of the patient's utterances, a tale, or a myth—though, as we shall see later, not every type of narrative is read in exactly the same way. Developed through didactic analysis, clinical training, and experience, the 'psychoanalytic competence' as Donald Spence has called it, consists of certain conventions that affect the analyst's overall understanding of the material and his sense of the important units of meaning.[10] To mention some of these conventions: First, there is the convention of *thematic unity*, namely, that there is an underlying commonality among separate, discrete details, whether of the therapeutic hour or of the text. Second, there is the convention of *thematic continuity*, which holds that if a patient dramatically changes the subject, or presents more than one dream during the hour, we continue to listen to the original theme through the apparent discontinuities. In other words, in spite of the narrative's postponements and detours, we keep a lookout for the recurring theme. Third, there is the convention of *thematic significance*, which holds that significant problems are always under discussion no mater how trivial the details. This convention insists that the analyst pay attention to everything while, of course, continuing to mistrust the seemingly obvious implications of what he observes. (Another convention, namely of transference, which leads an analyst to hear a patient's utterance on at least two levels—as a statement about an obvious referent and as communication about the analyst-patient relationship—applies more to the clinical situation than to the nonclinical psychoanalytic reading of texts.)

The analytic competence, the method of loosening the text, works in tandem with interpretation, as a way of reorganizing it. Whereas there is a well-defined consensus in the psychoanalytic community on 'loosening,' on what consitutes competence, on *how* an analyst 'reads,' there is no longer a similar agreement on the psychoanalytic theory that should underlie the reorganization, i.e., on *what* he has read. Although psychoanalysis has not quite fragmented into several competing frameworks, it has begun to show greater tolerance for theories other than the classical instinctual drive theory. Of course, given Freud's stature and authority within the discipline, these theories—not unlike scholarship in the Hindu tradition which permitted innovation only under the guise of interpretation—have been at pains to proclaim their fealty to the intention and concerns of the founding father. Yet the fact remains that many of these later contributions diverge in critical ways from the assumptions of drive psychology, still considered by most people outside the field as the 'Freudian Theory'.

In general, most of the newer approaches are closer to a conception of psychoanalysis as a hermeneutic enterprise concerned with reasons rather than causes, explanation rather than prediction, a *Geisteswissenschaft* of meaning and configuration rather than a natural science of mechanisms employing the metaphors of physics or chemistry. Without going into specific details,it may be noted here that the focus of these 'relational' theories—to subsume the quite diverse work of theorists like Melanie Klein, Donal Winnicott, Margaret Mahler, Heinz Kohut, Erik Erikson, and Otto Kemberg, among others, under one label—is not on the derivatives of instinctual drives but on the mental representations of relationships with others which are assumed to build the fundamental building blocks of mental life.[11] There is a relative shift of emphasis in that the primary question being asked in a session changes from 'What infantile wishes does this material fulfil in the patient?' to 'What is the patient, as who, saying to the analyst, as whom, and from when—and why?'[12]

The theory I choose for my own work of interpretation is finally a matter of personal choice. The choice is dictated by how well the theory speaks to my own experience of the self and of others. In the last analysis, then, the criteria for selecting one theory over another are more 'aesthetic' than 'scientific'. They have to do with my relative attraction to the *Ur*-images conjured up by different theories. On Freud's screen, there is the whirling of imperious passions, the sharp stabbings of searching, burdensome guilt. On the next screen,a post-Freudian one, there is the voracious hunger of the urge to merge and the black empty despair in absence of the other. You look into your own soul, you pay your money (in fees of the training analyst), and you take your pick. Depending upon the context, I have used both kinds of theory in my own interpretations.

Besides the analytic competence and the choice of a theoretical framework, the interpretation of a literary text also needs a model which permits the equation, in some form or other,of the literary and the psychoanalytic enterprises. In other words, in contrast to the narrative produced in the analytic situation, the psychoanalytic interpretation of other narrative forms require, in addition, a model that allows us to regard these essentially literary and cultural narratives as if they were psychoanalytic ones.

The number of models available for our interpretative enterprise, at least as far as literary texts are concerned, is embarrassingly large. Depending upon one's attitude toward psychoanalysis and one's personal aesthetic preference for the baroque or the classical this can denote either the richness and success of psychoanalytic theorizing or its poverty and failure to recommend the best way of going about such efforts. Traditionally, the psychoanalysis of literature has followed one or the other of these models: first, the interpretation of the unconscious motivations of fictional characters; second, the psychogenesis of the text, i.e., a psychoanalytic study of the author's life history; and third, the psychodynamics of the reader's response. To this traditional triad of character, author, and reader, Lacan has added the text. In the literary criticism influenced by him, the narrative is viewed as a movement of desire, with arousals, expectation, surprises, reversals, delays, disappointments, transformations, and fulfilment.[13] More recently, Meredith Anne Skura's influential work has suggested the reorganization of analytic models of literary interpretation into five categories: literature as case history, as fantasy, as dream, as transference, and as psychoanalytic process.[14]

In my own analysis of the more literary texts, such as the novels, I have approached them as the raw material of family case histories. Here, in the flow of events and the flux of feeling, I try to draw out some of their characters; secrets which, psychoanalysts like to believe, the authors only half knew they knew. Indeed, what makes the man-woman relationship particularly fruitful for psychoanalytic inquiry is the fact, as Freud recognized long ago, that there is nothing about which our consciousness can be so incomplete or false as about the degrees of affection or dislike which we feel for another human being. If such an attempt involves approaching the fictional characters as if they were real men and women, we should not feel discomfitted. As Joyce Carol Oates observes,

> A serious author deals only with 'real' experiences and 'real' emotions, though they are usually assigned to people with fictional names. I cannot believe, frankly, that anyone could—or would want to—write about experiences the emotional equivalents of which he has not experienced personally. Writing is a far more conscious form of dreaming, and no one dreams dreams that are of no interest to him, however trivial and absurd they may appear to someone else.[15]

The narratives forming chapters of this book to which I have listened with the analyst's 'third ear,' possess a diversity matching that of the culture from which they originate and which, in its beliefs and attitudes toward gender relations, they seek to reflect. Modern fiction from North India, folk narratives, box office movie hits of the last 20 years, middle-aged women from the slums of Delhi recounting their lives and loves, Gandhi's autobiographical writings, case histories from the consulting rooms of Indian psychoanalysts, all have combined in the construction of the story of Indian love relations. The story is complex, played out in the cultural-psychological space that lies between universally shared wishes of the inner world and the specific restrictions placed on them by a particular society. The story's characters and the twists and turns of its plot are at times surprisingly familiar and at others utterly strange. But,then, each human culture is perhaps a kind of magical mirror for the others. Sometimes it appears to be an ordinary piece of glass coated with silver at the back which faithfully reflects the contours, planes, and details of our own familiar faces. At others, it throws up dark menacing visages, forceful intimations of our disavowed selves which we thought no longer existed. Through such a looking glass, crafted in India, let me tell a story.

2

SCENES FROM MARRIAGES

Ek Chadar Maili Si (*A Sheet, Somewhat Soiled*) by the Urdu writer Rajinder Singh Bedi, which has also recently been made into a film, narrates the story of a poor Sikh family in a village somewhere on the northern border of Punjab.[1] Rano, the heroine of the book, is a spirited young woman in her early 30s. Her husband Tiloka earns a meager living plying his tonga (horse carriage) for pilgrims who pass through the village on their way to the Vaishno Devi temple in the nearby hills. The couple has a daughter, just entering puberty, and two young sons. The rest of the family consists of Tiloka's old parents and his 20-year-old younger brother Mangla.

Tiloka is a layabout and a drunkard and Rano's struggle to ensure that he does not drink away the little money he earns is unremitting. Rano's attempts to prevent Tiloka from drinking whenever and wherever he chooses are perceived by him as an affront to his virility, a challenge to his overlordship as a male. The resulting quarrels are bitter and invariably end in physical violence. In these fights Rano, using her nails and teeth, tries to give as good as she gets, but Tiloka's superior strength ensures that she ends up bruised and battered.

One day, Tiloka abducts a young girl pilgrim and takes her to a shady hotel where she is raped by some of his disreputable friends. In a macabre revenge, the girl's temporarily crazed brother kills Tiloka, biting into his neck and drinking his blood. The village elders' council decides that it would be best for the community and the bereaved family if Mangla, who now drives the tonga and has otherwise taken his brother's place, also takes over his wife. He should, in the language of their community, 'cover her with a sheet'. Rano, who had brought up Mangla as her own son, giving him her breasts to suck when at the birth of her daughter the little boy too had insisted on being fed, is intially averse to the idea of this marriage. However, she soon overcomes her scruples. Although she views her turnabout as submission to the collective wish, Rano secretly welcomes the prospect of being the wife of someone who had often protected her against her drunken husband's onslaughts and toward whom she feels considerable tenderness.

Mangla, though, cannot bear the thought of a marriage with such a strongly incestuous colouring. As the time of ceremony draws near, he runs away in blind panic to hide in the fields. Hunted like a wild beast, he is caught and badly beaten by the village men. Half-senseless from the beating, he is dragged back to the house and compelled to cover Rano with a sheet.

Mangla now becomes quite withdrawn and barely goes through the motions of a family life. To Rano's considerable chagrin, and her friends' growing consternation, he refuses to consummate the marriage. One day, he finds an old bottle of liquor among his dead brother's personal effects. As he opens the bottle and as Rano makes her first protests in an eerie repetition of similar scenes with her former husband, she feels both fear and a fierce exhilaration. She dimly senses that in the impending violence Mangla will beat her like a husband and she will fight back like a wife, finally establishing a conjugal relationship which till now has only existed in the community's will. Afterwards, as she lies in bed, in excruciating pain from drunken blows, a repentant and tearful Mangla trying to staunch the flow of blood from a wound in her scalp received when he had flung her against a wall, Rano is filled with a deep satisfaction. In the preceding encounter, her body had ceased to be an object of avoidance. It had been man-handled, touched by Mangla as a husband. The marriage is consummated the same night and the couple begin to live together as husband and wife.

Rano's greatest worry now is the marriage of her daughter. The family's abysmal poverty makes it almost impossible to find a husband for the girl. Then one day, at the time of the annual festival of the local goddess, Rano is told of the arrival of a rich and handsome young man who has vowed that he will marry only Rano's daughter. The family is puzzled but nonetheless overjoyed at the good turn in their fortunes. When the procession of singing and dancing men passes by the house, the young suitor is conspicuous among them by the abjectness of his penitent mien and the frenzy of his devotion to the goddess. Rano recognizes in the man the killer of her husband, just recently released from prison. The procession stops in front of the house as if awaiting her decision. Rano is in a turmoil till her blind father-in-law tells her to regard the proposed marriage as the workings of fate, a play of unseen powers which rule over man's destiny and whose intent she should not even try to fathom. Rano consents to the nuptials of the daughter with the murderer of the girl's father, a version of the "wild man" of many an Indian tale, with whom the heroine has a sexual relationship.

Like the initial interview in clinical practice where the patient unconsciously presents his major conflict in a dramatized scene—produced by the characteristic way he uses the space of the therapist's office, the way he makes his entry and exit, the movements of his body, and his speech as he enters into a dialogue with the therapist—the novel's opening scene, too, dramatizes its main theme: the woman's wish to be valued by the husband as a woman and as a wife, that is, as *his* woman, and her longing for the tenderness such a valuation implies. The scene itself is quite short: It is late in the afternoon and the family's dog steps out into the street to find his favorite bitch lying dead. The dog sniffs at the carcass a couple of times and then unconcernedly ambles away. Rano has been watching the dog with a woman friend who remarks, 'The race of men! They are all the same.' Rano feels the tears smarting in her eyes but, controlling herself, attempts a mild jest. 'But *your* dog is not like that!'

In the reader's mind, this short scene sets up psychological eddies which gradually spread out into wider and wider circles. Some of the dimensions of struggle between Rano and Tiloka are already sketched on the very first pages. Behind the husband and wife conflict we can sense the perennial one between man and woman which, incidentally, is explicit in the novel as it is in much of Indian domestic life and folklore. Thus, for instance, Margaret Egnor reports from Tamil Nadu:

> Within the household, as well as in the domain of paid labour, there was a strong spirit of rivalry between many women and their husbands. Wives would not automatically accept submission. Neither would their husbands. Consequently, their relationship was often, from what I was able to observe, disputatious . . . . The eternal conflict between spouses is abundantly reflected in Indian mythology, especially Tamil which debates the issues of male vs. female superiority back and forth endlessly on a cosmic level in the form of battles and contests between deities or demons and their real or would-be mates.[2]

In folklore, Shiva and Parvati, for instance, argue interminably as to who is the better dancer, while Vishnu and Lakshmi need to descend to earth to find out which of them is the greater divinity.

Now in most regions of the country, male folk wisdom offers similar overt reasons for man's perennial war with woman. It agrees in portraying the female sex as lacking both sexual morality and intelligence. Punjabis and Gujaratis are of one mind that 'The intelligence of a woman is in her heels (*Strini akkal edi mā*).[3]' Tamils maintain that 'No matter how educated a woman is, her intelligence is always of the lowest order,' and Malayalis warn that 'One who heeds the advice of a woman will be reduced to beggary (*Penachollu kalkkunnavanu peruvali*). Folk sayings in the northern languages, however, place singularly greater emphasis on the employment of force and physical chastisement to correct perceived female shortcomings. 'The place of a horse and a woman is under the thighs (*ghoda aur aurat rān talē*)' we hear in Hindi. And in Gujarati, 'Barley and millet improve by addition of salt, women through a beating by a pestle (*Usī jawār bājrī musē nār pādhrī*)': 'Better to keep the race of women under the heel of a shoe (*Rāndni jāt khāsdane talē rākhelij bhalī*)'; (*Mūrkh nāri ne nagārā kutyani kāmnā*)'. The proverbs in the South Indian languages, on the other hand, convey more a man's sense of helplessness and resignation in the face of general female cussedness and constant provocation. 'Wind can be held in a bag, but not the tongue of a shrew,' is common to both Kannada and Telugu. 'Neither the husband nor the brother-in-law can control a pugnacious woman' goes another Telugu saying, while yet another admit even a king's helplessness in the face of female disputatiousness.

Like wives in other novels, Rano uses words, biting, scornful words that seek to humble male pretensions—to enrage an already furious spouse. She taunts the husband to do his worst as far as physical battering is concerned and then emerges bloody but triumphant, victorious in that she denied him her submission to his will.

Rano's chief weapon in her battle against Tiloka, a weapon she is constantly seeking to hone and make more effective, is her attempted control over Tiloka's sexual appetites. When she goes to the village *baba* (holy man) for a charm, it is for a spell which puts her husbands in her power—a charm even more coveted by the village women than the talisman for the birth of a child. The tablet which the *baba* gives is for the sexual enthralment of the husband. If it works, Rano fantasizes, she would refuse Tiloka all sexual access. Only after a long stretch of his begging and entreaty, his throwing himself at her feet in abject submission, rubbing his nose on the ground in repentant surrender, might she just allow him to approach her in carefully rationed doses.

Rano's need for the charm is far removed in intent from similar quests by women (for instance that of Sachi, Indra's wife) mentioned in the *Rig*-and *Atharva-vedas*, in which spells are sought to win the love of the husband from other co-wives.[4] Female sexuality for Rano and her friend is very much a utilitarian affair whose chief value lies in its capacity to redress a lopsided distribution of power between the sexes.

Finding a suitable object in her husband, Rano's hostility against the 'race of men' is split off from her erotic promptings. Without the tenderness of love to neutralize or transform it, her rage is rampant, unappeased even by Tiloka's murder. When she views Tiloka's corpse, Rano's first impulse is to celebrate by decking herself in all finery. She has to squeeze an onion into her eyes and remind herself of the miserable fate awaiting her as a widow before she can shed the tears expected of her. She can cry only for herself. Rano's love, both in its affectional and sensual currents, has to seek another object within the family.

Traditionally, this object has often been the husband's younger brother. For a time in Indian social history, the erotic importance of the brother-in-law—in the sense that he would or could have sexual relations with his elder brother's widow—was officially recognized in the custom of *niyoga*. The custom itself goes back to the times of the *Rig-veda* where a man, identified by the commentators as the brother-in-law, is described as extending his hand in promised marriage to a widow inclined to share her husband's funeral pyre.[5]

Though the custom gradually fell into disuse, especially with the prohibition of widow remarriage, surviving only among remote communities such as the hillsmen of Utter Pradesh, the psychological core of *niyoga*, namely the mutual awareness of a married woman and her younger brother-in-law as potential or actual sexual partners, is very much an actuality even today. The awareness is present in the chastest of mythical wives, Sita, who, in the *Ramayana*, accuses Lakshmana of hesitating to help her husband and his brother, Rama, because of his feelings for her. As Lakshmana later reports the conversation to Rama: 'Sita said to me, "Evil one, an excess of feelings for me has entered you. But if my husband is destroyed, you will not obtain me.'[6] Expressed in a certain tenderness, in erotically tinged banter, or cases of actual physical intimacy, the relationship is very much a part of a marriage's emotional space.[7] In clinical practice, I have found that women who are on terms of sexual intimacy with a brother-in-law rarely express any feelings of guilt. Their anxiety is occasioned more by his leaving home or his impending marriage, which the woman perceives as an end to her sensual and emotional life.

The disquieting murmurs of incestuous tensions have been the stuff of much drama and the distress of Rano and Mangla at their impending marriage are riveting for this reason alone. Mangla's suffering, however, in the face of a long-awaited denouement to the incestuous wish, the embodiment in the flesh of fantasy hitherto entertained in the imagination alone, is much greater than Rano's. He is like the boy who feels he bears the full culpability of being aroused by his mother. Beleaguered by his erotic yearnings for her, he does not truly conceive of hers for him. Rano, in contrast, is relatively more matter-of-fact and accepting of the paradoxes of the sexual realm. Perhaps like many other women, she seems better able to cope with the guilt of incestuous urgings than her 'son' who must first beat her for their impending transgression before he can accept his disturbing and dangerous sensual immersion.

Krishna Sobti's *Mitro Marjani*, another novel with a similar theme, is less a story than a portrait of a woman, with a lower-middle-class family life sketched in as the background.[8] The book is dominated by its heroine, a young Punjabi woman called Mitro. Her husband, the two brothers-in-law and their wives, the husband's old parents, are all bit players in the dramatization of her desire, existing only to enhance and provide counterpoints to Mitro's moods and actions.

As in *Ek Chadar*, the beginning of the novel features a violent quarrel between the husband and wife. Sardari, Mitro's husband, is hitting her while Mitro stands still, her eyes raised to his face in defiance. 'Will you lower your eyes or not?' the husband keeps asking her with each blow. A stubborn Mitro refuses to look down, denying him this token of her submission. The mother-in-law, a representative of the older generation of women, pleads with her, 'If he is stubborn, why don't *you* lower your gaze, daughter? How can we helpless women confront men who are our lords?'

The running battle between husband and wife, we learn later, is not only around the theme of dominance and submission, a trial of strength over the distribution of power between the two sexes. Mitro's husband suspects her of promiscuous tendencies, a belief the spirited young woman does nothing to dispel. Indeed, she underlines this impression by the evident pride she takes in the fullness and bloom of her body, the sexual banter she carries on with her brother-in-law, and the candid confession of her sexual hunger to her sister-in-law. 'Have you seen such breasts on another woman?' she asks in innocent yet deeply sensual self-satisfaction as she strips off her clothes. 'Your *devar* (younger brother-in-law, i.e., Mitro's husband) does not recognize my disease. At the most he approaches me once a week or fortnight . . . this body is so thirsty that it thrashes around like a fish out of water.' The sister-in-law, a good, conventional wife, is scandalized. For her, a woman's body is not an object of pride or pleasure but something that is made impure every day, an abode of sinfulness. Angrily, she counters Mitro's desires with the sanctimonious cultural definition of the woman's role in Hindu society: 'For daughters and daughters-in-law the ways of her home and household are like *Lakshmana-rekha.** Knowingly or unknowingly, if this line is ever breached . . . .', the unfinished sentence leaving behind in the trailing silence a stark intimation of disaster.

Mitro, however, is frankly open in the expression of her physical needs as a woman and in the mockery of her husband's inability to satisfy them. Once, when her mother-in-law mentions the pregnancy of her elder sister-in-law and seeks to console Mitro by saying, 'When you open up it won't be one but seven who will be playing around in the courtyard'. Mitro retorts:

If it was in my power I would bear one hundred *kauravas* (the 'evil' clan in the epic *Mahabharata*) but, mother, first do something about your son to produce some movement in that useless statue of stone.

The family, already reeling under the dishonest business dealings of the youngest son, who has left the house along with his wife, fear that Mitro's brazen behaviour will soon cause further scandal. They ask her to go to her mother's home for a while. Mitro, anticipating the freedom and ample opportunity for erotic liaison available at her mother's home—the mother is widely regarded as a fallen woman for her long-standing affair with a village official—is overjoyed at the prospect. Sardari, her husband, accompanies her on the visit. Mitro narrates her predicament to her mother who offers to help her out, to 'call a gardener for her garden' as she puts it. She even offers to keep a guard over the sleeping son-in-low's door and arranges for the daughter to visit her own lover. On the evening of the assignation, Mitro dresses like a dancing girl. In trying to make her husband drunk she behaves with the coquetry of an expensive whore in a high-class brothel, to the inebriated Sardari's early horror and eventual delight. When the husband sinks into a drunken stupor, Mitro is ready to go to the waiting man but is stopped by the weeping mother who has had second thoughts. Mitro goes back to her husband's room. When they wake up in the morning, she embraces him tightly and covers his face with kisses, expressing her affection for the husband as intensely as she had shown desire for adulterous sex in the previous evening.

My choice of *Ek Chadar* and *Mitro Marjani* has been dictated by my feeling, based on personal and professional experience, that their protrayal of the man-woman relationship has aspects with considerable potential for generalization. As with Freud's *Rat Man*, a single case history which later proved to be

* The line drawn by Lakshmana around Sita within which no harm could befall her.

psychodynamically representative for a host of other cases of obsessional-compulsive neurosis, fictional family histories too may illuminate significant themes in Indian marriages in situations quite different from their novelistic origins. That these themes relate to conflict in marriage, rather than to happiness and contentment, is of course embedded in the nature of the fictional enterprise itself. If happy families, as Tolstoy asserted, are all alike, then happy marriages have no history and consequently, 'They lived happily ever after' marks the end of the story rather than its beginning or middle. Of course, the abstraction of these themes from the novels in the form of generalizations must emerge through a careful engagement with other cultural-historical and social-anthropological materials dealing with marriages and the man-woman relationship in India. Fiction and what I like to call cultural psychology—the psychic representation in individuals of their community's history and social institutions—can reciprocally illuminate each other.

In her frank sexuality, and restlessness, and in her straining against the confines of cultural role she finds too restrictive, Mitro is certainly a woman unusual for her milieu and class. Superior to the role in life in which she finds herself struggling against a confining cultural fate, Mitro is the kind of troubled character who, all over the world, is a favorite of both novelists and healers of the soul. Like many women in India, in fiction and in life, she expresses her rage through words, or better, verbal barbs poisoned with ridicule and sharpened with the cutting edge of sarcasm. Yet even at the beginning of the story, we sense that Mitro's conflict, as she pushes against restraining cultural walls, is too deep to be bridged by creative coining of sarcastic phrases. We fear that if she is unable to get greater space for herself, she will become violent, self-destructive, or apathetic.

To me, *Mitro Marjani* is one of the more explicit renderings of a muted yet extremely powerful theme in Hindu marriages: the cultural unease, indeed, the fear of the wife as a woman, i.e., as a sexual being. More exactly, it is the age-old yet still persisting cultural splitting of the wife into a mother and a whore which underlies the husband-wife relationship and which explains the often contradictory Hindu views of the woman. The mother-whore dichotomy is of course a well-known Freudian syndrome which describes the separation of sexuality from tenderness, the object of desire from the object of adoration. Freud has described the psychodynamics of this occurrence in which a man idealizes one kind of a woman, generally of his own social class. She is seen as 'higher' and 'purer' than him, but he is impotent with her, while on the other hand he is capable of sexual relations with a woman of a lower social station, very frequently a prostitute.[9] This split can often be traced back to the anxiety surrounding incestuous imaginings, and with it, a horror of 'de-idealizing' a mother on whose image, in its purity, the man-boy still relies for nurturance and undying support. The splitting of the mother-image into the goddess and whore allows the man to have a modicum of sexual life without being overwhelmed by anxiety.

The mother-whore dichotomy or, in its Hindu version, the mother-whore-partner-in-ritual trichotomy, is crucial for understanding the culture's public and official attitudes toward women and wives. Manu, the Hindu law-giver, and his subsequent commentators, who have formulated the society's formal view of the other sex, have perhaps been unjustly branded as misogynists. A careful reading of their texts shows that misogyny as well as the praise of women follows a purely contextual course. In other words, a wife is not a wife in and for all seasons; it is the context which determines whether she is regarded as good, bad, or divine. As a partner to her husband in the prescribed sacrifices to ancestors and gods, that is, in the context of the ritual,the wife is a respected being. Manu can thus say, 'Where women are honored, there the gods are pleased; but where they are not honored, no sacred rite yields rewards.'[10] In her maternal aspect, actual or potential, a wife is again a person deserving of all reverence. 'Between wives who [are destined] to bear children, who secure many blessing, who are worthy of worship and irradiate [their] dwellings and between the goddesses of fortune [who reside] in the houses [of men], there is no difference whatever.'[11] It is only just as a woman, as a female sexual being, that the patriarchal culture's horror and scorn are heaped upon the helpless wife.

It is clear from its context that the oft-quoted verse. 'Her father protects her in childhood, her husband protects her in youth and her sons protect her in old age; a woman is never fit for independence,'[12] refers to a 'protection' not from external danger but from the woman's inner, sexual proclivities. Thus the previous verse talks of controlling her attachment to sensual enjoyments. The subsequent one calls reprehensible the father who does not give her away in marriage at puberty; the husband who does not approach her sexually when she is in her season(ritu); and the son who after his father's death does not protect the mother—from the attentions of other men and from her own urges, the implication is clear.

In fact the first 26 stanzas of the chapter 'Duties of Husband and Wife' in The Laws of Manu, which form the cornerstone of the culture's official view of women, can be read as a fantasy around the theme of the adult woman's possible sexual abandon and potential infidelity. The fantasy is very much that of the Oedipal boy who imagines the mother turning away from him and toward the father and his man-sized penis. She is a siren and has but seduced and abandoned him.

The fantasy thus starts with the wish to 'guard' a woman from her overwhelming sexual temptation and from the interlopers who would exploit it for their own and her pleasure. Yet guarding her by force is not realistically possible, and perhaps it is better to keep her throughly engaged in household work and thus fancy-free. 'Let the [husband] employ his [wife] in the collection and expenditure of his wealth, in keeping [everything] clean in [the fulfilment of] religious duties, in the preparation of his food, and in looking after the household utensils.'[13] On the other hand, even the dam of 'busy-ness' is really not enough to constrain her erotic turbulence and our Oedipal lover appeals to her conscience, the inner sentinel. 'Women confined in the house under trustworthy and obedient servants, are not (well) guarded, but those who of their own accord keep guard over themselves, are well guarded.'[14] Both the recourse to the external world and to the woman's own superego do not prove to be sufficient as the more primitive images in the jealous and disappointed lover's fantasy break through to the surface. 'Women ,do not care for beauty, not is their attention fixed on age; [thinking], "[It is enough that] he is a man," they give themselves to the handsome and the ugly.'[15] 'Through their passion for men, through their mutable temper, through their natural heartlessness, they become disloyal toward their husbands, however carefully they may be guarded in this [world].'[16] '[When creating them] Manu allotted to women [a love of their] bed, [of their] seat and [of] ornament, impure desires, wrath, dishonesty, malice, and bad conduct.'[17] Anger and retaliation now follow wherein the woman must atone for her lapse before she can again be resurrected as the pure and the needed mother. The mantra she needs to recite for the 'expiation of her sins' is not hers but in fact that of the son: 'If my mother, going astray and unfaithful, conceived illicit desires, may my father keep that seed from me.'[18] Punished and repentant, the whore finally disappears, to be replaced by the untainted mother who, in subsequent verses, is praised and equated with the goddess (of fortune).

The image of the wife as the needed mother and the feared whore is even today reflected in the proverbs of all the major Indian languages, a testimony to the cultural unity of the subcontinent in the way fundamental human relationships— between spouses, siblings and generations—are viewed.[19] As one would surmise, woman's infidelity is the major theme in the various proverbs seeking to grasp the nature of the feminine. 'Only when fire will cool, the moon burn or the ocean fill with tasty water will a woman be pure,' is one of the many Sanskrit pronouncements on the subject. 'A woman if she remains within bounds; she becomes a donkey out of them,' say the Tamils. The exceptional proverbs in praise of wives, for instance in Assamese and Bengali, invariably and predictably address their maternal aspect—'Who could belittle women? Women who bear children!' A Punjabi proverb puts the husband's dilemma and its resolution in a nutshell, 'A woman who shows more love for you than your mother is a slut.'

It is evident that with such a collective fantasy of the wife, the fate of sexuality *within* marriage is likely to come under an evil constellation of stars. Physical love will tend to be a shame-ridden affair, a sharp stabbing of lust with little love and even less passion. Indeed, the code of sexual conduct for the householder-husband fully endorses this expectation. Stated concisely in the *smritis* (the law codes), elaborated in the *Puranas* (which are not only collections of myths but also contain chapters on the correct conduct of daily life), modified for local usage by the various kinds of *religiosi*, the thrust of the message seems to be, 'No sex in marriage please, we're Indian.'

Consider: A husband should only approach a woman in her season (*ritu*), a period of sixteen days within a menstrual cycle. 'But among these the first four, the eleventh and thirteenth are [declared to be forbidden]; the remaining nights are recommended.'[20] The availability of ten nights a month for conjugal relations is only an apparent largesse. The Hindu counterparts of Blake's priests in 'black gowns, walking their rounds and binding with briars my joys and desires' have not yet finished with their proscriptions. Since the all-important sons are conceived only on even nights, while daughters are conceived on uneven ones, the number of recommended nights straightaway shrinks by a half. Then there are the *pravas*, the moonless nights and those of the full moon, on which sexual relations lead either to the 'hell of faeces and urine' (*Vishnu Purana*) or to the birth of atheist sons (*Brahma Purana*). In addition, there are many festival days for gods and ancestors which are forbidden for any erotic transports. Thus the likelihood that most of the remaining five nights are sexually safe decreases greatly. Moreover, it is not a matter of permitted and forbidden nights (sex during the day is, of course, beyond the pale). The question is of a general disapproval of the erotic aspect of married life, a disapproval which is not a medieval relic but continues to inform contemporary attitudes. This is quite understandable since changes in sexuality occur at a more gradual pace than transformations in the political and social sphere; sexual time beats at a considerably slower pace than its chronological counterpart.

Sexual taboos, then, are still so strong among some Hindu communities that many women, especially from the higher castes, do not have a name for their genitals, At the utmost, the genitals are referred to obliquely—for instance 'the place of peeing,' though even this euphemism carries a strong affective charge. One patient, educated in England, did not have any trouble in mentioning her sexual parts as long as she could do so in English. If asked to translate the words into her mother tongue, the language nearer her early bodily experience, she would either 'forget' the appropriate words or freeze into a long silence which all her conscious efforts could not break. Ignorance, of course, thrives in the socially generated pall of silence. One college-educated patient believed well into her late teens that menstrual blood, urine and babies all came out through the urethra. Another woman, brought up in a village and presumably more familiar with the 'barnyard' facts of life, realized with deep consternation only when giving birth to her first child that babies were not born through the anus as she had believed. Writing on Indian sexuality some 2000 years after the *Kamasutra*, I still cannot say to its author—'Elementary, dear Vatsayana'.

Of course, the modern notion of sexuality diverges in essential ways from that of Vatsayana, a change to which psychoanalysis has significantly contributed. Sexual need in the psychoanalytic sense is not a need for coitus, and sexuality is neither equated with genitality nor with the expression of a biological drive. The psychoanalytic concept of sexuality is far more than simple genital conjunction or a question of 'fit' in organ sizes. A mental absence of satisfaction can exist where there is no lack of normal sexual intercourse. Sexuality, in psychoanalysis, is a system of conscious and unconscious human fantasies, arising from various sources, seeking satisfaction in diverse ways, and involving a range of excitations and activities that aim to achieve pleasure that goes beyond the satisfaction of any basic somatic need.

What we are talking of here is the cultural impact on psychosexuality in Indian marriage. Cultural injunctions perhaps do not affect the act of coitus or regulate its transports. What they can do, though, is to increase the conflicts around sexuality, sour it for many, and generally contribute towards its impoverishment. This can effectively block many men and most women from a deep full experience of sexual love and the mutual cherishing of bodies, the only containers we have of our souls. Cultural injunctions become significant for the family since a fundamental aspect of the relationship between the parents involves the meaning of each child in terms of the parents' conscious and unconscious fantasy around the act that produced the conception. And if one agrees with Winnicott, as I do, that the way we arrange our families practically shows what our culture is like, just as a picture of the face portrays the individual, then beliefs and norms around sexuality in marriage gain a wider significance for the understanding of culture.[21]

The considerable sexual misery is not only a postulate inferred from Hindu cultural ideals and prohibitions relating to sex in marriage or deduced from interpretations of modern fiction. Even discounting the sexual woes of a vast number of middle-and upper-class women who come for psychotherapy as being an unrepresentative sample, there are other, direct indications that sexual unhappiness is also widespread in the lowest castes whom the upper sections of society have always imagined to be free of the culture's restrictive mores. Thus interviews with low-caste, 'untouchable' women from a poor locality in Delhi, most of them migrants from villages of Uttar Pradesh, revealed sexuality pervaded by hostility and indifference rather than affection and tenderness. Most women portrayed even sexual intercourse as a furtive act in a cramped and crowded room, lasting barely a few minutes and with a marked absence of physical or emotional caressing. Most women found it painful or distasteful or both. It was an experience to be submitted to, often from a fear of beating. None of the women removed their clothes for the act since it is considered shameful to do so. Though some of the less embittered women still yearned for physical tenderness from the husband, the act itself was seen as a prerogative and need of the male—'*Admi bolna chahta hai* (man wants to speak)'.

If we agree with Lokoff and Johnson that human thought processes are largely metaphorical, that we understand and experience things and concepts in the network of their metaphorical affinities, then it is instructive to look at other metaphors used by this group of women for what in English is called 'love-making.'[22] '*Hafte mein ek bar lagwa lete hain* (I get it done to me once a week),' has in its original Hindustani the connotations of a weekly injection, painful but perhaps necessary for health. The most common expressions for intercourse are *kaam* and *dhandha*, work and business. Sexual intercourse for these women (and men) seems to be structured in terms of contractual and impersonal exchange relations, with the ever-present possibility of one party exploiting or cheating the other.

The conflict between the sexes in marriage, which I have charted out in this chapter, is not devoid of moments of tenderness between the spouses and, especially for the women, the feelings of loss and mourning at its absence. Mitro's occasional gestures of physical affection and of financial generosity toward Sardari when the family is in deep financial trouble, or Rano's deeply felt anguish and regret as she tells Mangla that the war between the sexes is like that of the *Mahabharata*, are just two illustrative scenes from our novels. Indeed, Rano's analogy of the Kurukshetra battle is an apt characterization of the basic struggle between husbands and wives. The war is between antagonists who know each other well, even have loyalty and admiration for one or another member of the enemy host, and where regular pauses in the daily hostilities do take place.

What these novels only hint at and which becomes an overwhelming issue in fiction (and patients) from (and of) the middle- and upper-middle-class social milieu is the profound yearning of a wife, as a woman, for a missing intimacy with the husband—as a man. Generally fated for disappointment, the fantasy of constituting a 'couple,' not in opposition to the rest of the extended family but within this wider network, is a dominant theme running through women's lives, actual and fictional. Connecting the various stages of a woman's adulthood, from an expectant bride to a more sober grandmother, the intense wish to create a two-person universe with the husband where each finally 'recognizes' the other, is never far from her consciousness. It stands as a beacon of hope amidst the toil, drudgery, fights, disappointments, and occasional joys of her stormy existence within the extended family. In contrast to much of popular Western fiction, the Indian 'romantic' yearning is not for an exploring of the depths of erotic passion, or for being swept off the feet by a masterful man. It is a much quieter affair, with the soul of a Mukesh-song, and when unsatisfied this longing shrivels the emotional life of many women, making some go through life as mere maternal automatons. Others, though, react with an inner desperation where, as one woman put it, even the smell of the husband is a daily torture that must be borne in a silent scream. The desired intimacy, forever subduing the antagonism between husband and wife, inherent in the division of sexes and culturally exaggerated, is the real *sasural*— the husband's home—to which a girl looks forward after marriage and which even a married woman keeps on visiting and revisiting in the hidden vaults of her imagination.

3

LOVERS IN THE DARK

When I was growing up in the 1940s, going to the cinema, at least in the Punjab and at least among the middle- and upper-classes, was regarded as slightly dissolute, if not outright immoral, and the habit was considered especially dangerous to the growing sensibilities of young children. Of course not all films were equally burdened with disapproval. Like everything else in India—from plants to human beings—there was (and is) a strict hierarchical classification. In the movie caste system, stunt films, the Indian version of Kung Fu movies, were the low-caste Shudras at the lowest rung of the ladder while the Brahmin 'mythological' and the Kshatriya 'historical' vied for supremacy at the top. The only time I was admitted to the owner's box of Prabhat Talkies—the cinema owned by a grand-uncle in Lahore—was to see an eminently forgettable mythological called *Kadambari*. In childhood, stunt films were my favourite, although my taste was quite catholic, consisting as it did of indiscriminate adoration. With the complicity of a friendly doorman who doubled as an odd-job man in my grand-uncle's adjoining house, I was in the fortunate position of being able to indulge my secret passion for films whenever we visited Lahore. I use the word 'passion' literally and not as a metaphor, since my craving for movies was insatiable and my consumption equally remarkable; I saw *Ratan* 16 times, *Shikari* 14 times, and even *Kadambari* three times after that first viewing from the owner's box.

I remember my movie-going with a nostalgia which cloaks childhood events, at least the good ones, in a unique glow of permanence and ephemerality. In the anonymity of a darkness pierced by the flickering light which gave birth to a magical yet familiar world on the screen, I was no longer a small boy but a part of the envied world of adulthood, although I sensed its rituals and mysteries but dimly. I always joined in the laughter that followed a risqué comment, even if its exact meaning escaped me. I too would hold my breath in the hushed silence that followed a particularly well-enacted love scene, and surreptitiously try to whistle with the O of the thumb and the index finger under the tongue, in imitation of the wolf-whistles that greeted the obligatory scene in which the heroine fell into the water or was otherwise drenched. Recently, when in *Satyam Shivam Sundaram* Miss Zeenat Aman's considerable charms were revealed through her wet and clinging saree at the receiving end of a waterfall, I felt grateful to the world of Hindi movies for providing continuity in an unstable and changing world. When I was a child, the movies brought the vistas of a desirable adulthood tantalizingly close; as an adult, I find that they help to keep the road to childhood open.

I have described my engagement with the world of Hindi films at some length, not in order to claim any vast personal experience or specialized knowledge but to stress the fact of an enduring empathic connection with the world of Indian popular cinema. Today, this cinema, which draws upon images and symbols from the traditinal regional cultures and combines them with more modern Western themes, is the major shaper of an emerging, pan-Indian popular culture. Though its fixed repertoire of plots, with which the audience is presumably thoroughly familiar, has striking parallels with traditional folk theatre, the popular culture represented by the cinema goes beyond both classical and folk elements even while it incorporates them.

The appeal of the film is directed to an audience so diverse that it transcends social and spatial categories. Watched by almost 15 million people every day, popular cinema's values and language have long since crossed urban boundaries to enter the folk culture of the rural-based population, where they have begun to influence Indian ideas of the good life and the ideology of social, family, and love relationships. The folk dance of a region or a particular musical form such as the devotional *bhajan*, after it has crossed the portals of a Bombay or Madras studio, is transmuted into a film dance or a film *bhajan* by the addition of musical and dance motifs from other regions as perhaps also from the West, and is then relayed back in full technicolour and stereophonic sound to decisively alter the original. Similarly, film situations, dialogue, and decor have begun to colonize folk theatre. Even the traditional iconography of statues and pictures for religious worship is paying homage to film representations of gods and goddesses.[1]

My own approach to popular cinema is to think of film as a collective fantasy, a group daydream. By 'collective' and 'group' I do not mean that Hindi film is an expression of a mythic collective unconscious or of something called a group mind. Instead, I see the cinema as the primary vehicle for shared fantasies of a vast number of people living on the Indian subcontinent who are both culturally and psychologically linked. I do not use 'fantasy' in the ordinary sense of the word, with its popular connotations of whimsy, eccentricity, or triviality, but as another name for that world of imagination which is fuelled by desire and which provides us with an alternative world where we can continue our longstanding quarrel with reality. Desire and fantasy are, of course, inexorably linked. Aristotle's dictum that there can be no desire without fantasy contains even more truth in reverse. Fantasy is the *mise-en-scène* of desire, its dramatization in a visual form.

The origins of fantasy lie in the unavoidable conflict between many of our desires, formulated as demands on the environment (especially on people), and the environment's inability or unwillingness to fulfil our desires, where it does not proscribe them altogether. The power of fantasy, then, comes to our rescue by extending or withdrawing the desires beyond what is possible or reasonable, by remarking the past and inventing a future. Fantasy, the 'stuff that dreams are made of,' is the bridge between desire and reality, spanning the chasm between what is asked for and what is granted. It well deserves psychoanalyst Robert

Stoller's paean as 'the vehicle of hope, healer of trauma, protector from reality, concealer of truth, fixer of identity, restorer of tranquillity, enemy of fear and sadness, cleanser of the soul.'[2] Hindi films, perhaps more than the cinema of many other countries, are fantasy in this special sense.

The sheer volume of unrelieved fantasy in one film after another is indeed overwhelming, and it is disquieting to reflect that this exclusive preoccupation with magical explanations and fairy-tale solutions for life's problems could be an expression of a deep-seated need in large sections of Indian society. Some may even consider such a thorough-going denial of external reality in Indian cinema to be a sign of morbidity, especially since one cannot make the argument that fantasy in films fulfils the need for escapism of those suffering from grinding poverty. In the first place, it is not the poor who constitute the bulk of the Indian film clientele. In the second, one does not know the cinema of any other country which, even in the worst periods of economic deprivation and political uncertainty, dished out such uniformly fantastic fare. Neither German cinema during the economic crisis of the 1920s nor Japanese cinema in the aftermath of the Second World War elevated fantasy to such an overwhelming principle. And if one considers that neorealism even flourished in Italy during the economic chaos following the Allied victory, then one must acknowledge that economic conditions alone cannot explain the fantasia permeating Indian films.

The reason for the ubiquity of fantasy in the Hindi cinema, I suspect, lies in the realm of cultural psychology rather than in the domain of socio-economic conditions. Now, as in other cultures, we too have our film addicts. These are the unfortunate people who are pressed in childhood to view reality in an adult way and now need the fantasy of the film world to fill up the void left by a premature deprivation of magic in early life. Leaving aside this group, no sane Indian believes that Hindi films depict the world realistically, although I must admit I often feel that our willingness to suspend disbelief is relatively greater than in many other cultures. This is not because the thought processes of Indians are fantasy-ridden. The propensity to state received opinion and belief as observation, to look for confirmation of belief rather than be upon to disturbing new knowledge, to generally think in a loose, associative rather than a rigorous and sequential way, is neither Indian, American, Chinese, Japanese, or German, but common to most human beings. However, I would hypothesize, without passing any value judgment, that, relatively speaking, in India the child's world of magic is not as far removed from adult consciousness as it may be in some other cultures. Because of a specific thrust of the culture and congruent childrearing practices which I have described in detail elsewhere, the Indian ego is flexible enough to regress temporarily to childhood modes without feeling threatened or engulfed.[3] Hindi films seem to provide this regressive haven for a vast number of our people.

If, as I have indicated above, I regard the Indian cinema audience not only as the reader but also as the real author of the text of Hindi films, what is the role played by their ostensible creators—the producers, directors, scriptwriters, music directors, and so on? In my view, their functions are purely instrumental and akin to that of a publisher who chooses, edits, and publishes a particular text from a number of submitted manuscripts. The quest for the comforting sound of busy cash registers at the box office ensures that the filmmakers select and develop a daydream which is not idiosyncratic. They must intuitively appeal to those concerns of the audience which are shared; if they do not, the film's appeal is bound to be disastrously limited. As with pornography, the filmmakers have to create a work which is singular enough to fascinate and excite, and general enough to excite many. Moreover, in their search for the 'hit,' the ten to 15 films out of the roughly 700 produced every year which evoke the most enthusiastic response, the filmmakers repeat and vary the daydreams as they seek to develop them into more and more nourishing substitutes for reality. Under the general rubric of fantasy, which can range all the way from the most primal images in dreams to the rationalized misinterpretations of reality in everyday life, the Hindi film is perhaps closest to the daydream. Indeed, the visual landscape of these films has a strong daydream quality in that it is not completely situated outside reality but is clearly linked to it. As Arjun Appadurai and Carol Breckenridge point out, while the landscape of the popular films contains places, social types, topological features, and situations which are reminiscent of ordinary experience, these elements are transformed or transposed so as to create a subtly fantastic milieu.[4] Even film speech is reminiscent of real speech. Thus the frequently heard admonition in 'Indinglish,' 'Don't *maro filmi* dialogues, *yaar,*' (Don't spout dialogues from films at me, friend), is often addressed to someone expressing highly inflated sentiments of friendship, love, or hostility which typify exchanges between the characters of Indian cinema.

Like the adult daydream, Hindi film emphasizes the central features of fantasy— the fulfilment of wishes, the humbling of competitors and the destruction of enemies. The stereotyped twists and turns of the film plot ensure the repetition of the very message that makes, for instance, the fairytale so deeply satisfying to children— namely, that the struggle against difficulties in life is unavoidable, but if one faces life's hardships and its many, often unjust impositions with courage and steadfastness, one will eventually emerge victorious.[5] At the conclusion of both films and fairytales, parents are generally happy and proud, the princess is won, and either the villains are ruefully contrite or their battered bodies satisfactorily litter the landscape. Evil in film, too, follows the same course it does in fairy tales; it may be temporarily in ascendance or usurp the hero's legitimate rights, but its failure and defeat are inevitable. Like the temptations of badness for a child who is constantly forced to be good, evil in Hindi cinema is not quite without its attractions of sensual licence and narcissistic pleasure in the unheeding pursuit of the appetites. It is usually the unregenerate villain who gets to savour the pleasures of drinking wine and the companionship, willing or otherwise, of sexy and attractive women.

Another feature common to both Hindi films and fairy tales is the oversimplification of situations and the elimination of detail, unless the detail is absolutely essential. The characters of the film are always typical, never unique, and without the unnerving complexity of real people. The Hero and the Villain, the Heroine and Her Best Friend, the Loving Father and the Cruel Stepmother, are never ambivalent, never the mixed ticket we all are in real life. But then, unlike in novels, the portrayal of characters in film is neither intended to enhance our understanding of the individual complexities of men and women nor to assist our contemplation of the human condition. Their intention is to appeal to the child within us, to arouse quick sympathies and antipathies, and thus encourage the identifications that help us to savour our fantasies more keenly.

When dogmatic rationalists dismiss Hindi films as unrealistic and complain that their plots strain credibility and their characters stretch the limits of the believable, this condescending judgment is usually based on a restricted vision of reality. To limit and reduce the real to that which can be demonstrated as factual is to exclude the domain of the psychologically real—all that is felt to be, enduringly, the actuality of one's inner life. Or, to adapt Bruno Bettelheim's observation on fairytales, Hindi films may be unreal in a rational sense but they are certainly not untrue. Their depiction of the external world may be flawed and their relevance to the external life of the viewer remote; yet, as we shall see, in their focus on the unconsciously perceived fantasy rather than the consciously perceived story, the Hindi film demonstrates a confident and sure-footed grasp of the topography of desire. The stories they tell may be trite and limited in number, with simple, recognizable meanings which on the surface reinforce rather than challenge cultural convention. yet beneath the surface, the fantasies they purvey, though equally repetitious, are not so trite and add surprising twists to the conscious social understanding of various human relationships in the culture.

Having described the relationship between Indian cinema, culture, and psyche is some detail, let me now turn to the cinema audience's internal theatre of love as they watch the images flicker by on the screen. The composite love story I seek to present here is culled largely from a score of the biggest box office hits of the last 20 years.[6] Since it would be impossible as well as tedious to narrate the plots of all these films, I will take as my illustrative text only one film. Raj Kapoor's *Ram Teri Ganga Maili (Rama, Your Ganga Is Polluted)*, the top box office hit for the year 1986. I shall then use examples from other films to amplify and otherwise complete the prototypical love story of Hindi cinema.

Narendra, the hero of the film is a student of a Calcutta college and the son of a rich, thoroughly corrupt businessman. His father is a close associate of Bhag Choudhary, a villainous politician, whose only daughter, Radha, is romantically interested in our young hero. Narendra, however, is unaware of Radha's feelings for him. He ignores her not-so-subtle advances and generally treats her in a friendly asexual fashion.

Narendra goes on a college trip to Gangotri, the source of the sacred river Ganges, in the Himalayan hills. He has promised to bring his doting grandmother pure Ganges water from the river's very source, since the water is polluted by the time it reaches the sea at Calcutta. He clambers down a mountainside to reach the stream, but the pitcher he has brought with him slips from his hand and rolls down the slope. As Narendra seeks to retrieve the pitcher, he is saved from falling over a cliff by a shouted warning from the heroine of the movie, Ganga. Ganga is a pretty, young girl of the hills, unspoilt and innocent, and frankly expresses her liking for the city boy. Often enough, she takes the initiative in their budding relationship. She leads him by the hand on their excursions through the mountains, barefooted and impervious to the cold while he both stumbles and shivers. During their courtship they sing duets in meadows full of wild flowers and frolic through streams which, of course, make Ganga's thin white sari wet and cling revealingly to her well-formed breasts. Narendra saves Ganga from being raped by one of his college friends, which deepens the girl's feelings for the boy and increases their mutual attachment.

Although Ganga has been promised in marriage to one of her own people, she decides to break the engagement and marry Narendra. The marriage ceremony is preceded by a rousing (and arousing) folk dance and is succeeded by the wedding night. While inside the room, Narendra undresses Ganga with the gravity and devotion of a priest preparing the idol of the goddess for the morning worship, Ganga's brother and her enraged ex-fiance are engaged outside in a murderous fight which will end in both their deaths.

Narendra goes back to Calcutta, promising to send for Ganga as soon as he has informed the family of his marriage. There he discovers that his grandmother has betrothed him in his absence to Radha, the politician's daughter, a match welcomed by both the families. After many emotional scenes involving the boy and his parents, in the course of which his grandmother suffers a heart attack and eventually dies. Narenda, defying his parent's wishes, sets out for the hills to fetch Ganga. By virtue of the political influence exercised by Choudhary, he is forcibly taken off the bus by the police before he can reach her village in the hills and is brought back to Calcutta.

In the meanwhile, a letter by Narendra's grandmother to her grandson reaches Ganga, from which she learns of the family's plans for Narendra's betrothal; Ganga believes her husband now to be married to another woman. Their wedding night, however, has had consequences and Ganga gives birth to a child. Since, in Hindu tradition children belong to the father, Ganga nobly decides to take the infant son to far off Calcutta and hand him over to Narendra. It is now that the perils of Ganga begin. Alighting from the bus at the foot of the hills and looking for the train station from where she can take the train to Calcutta, Ganga is instead guided to a cheap whorehouse. There she is sold to a customer who would rape her but Ganga manages to escape with the baby clutched to her breast. She then approaches an old priest for directions to the station. He, too, turns out to be lecherous. Ganga is saved from his attentions by the timely arrival of the police. Finally put on the train to Calcutta by a kindly police officer—who for a change does not try to rape her—Ganga is kidnapped on the way by a pimp who brings her to a *kotha* in Benares, a brothel whose customers are first entertained by song and dance in the traditional style of the Indian courtesan. Ganga becomes a well-known dancing girl though all the while retaining her mysterious purity, that 'purity of the Ganges which lies in a woman's heart and which makes a man attracted to her, merge into her.'

Ganga is now sold by the owner of the *kotha* to Choudhary who has come to Benares to find a girl to keep him company in his declining years. Choudhary, her husband's future father-in-law, installs the girl in a house in Calcutta and one day brings Narendra's father along with him to show off the girl's charms. He promises to share Ganga with him once the marriage of their children has been solemnized. On the day of the marriage, Ganga is called upon by Choudhary to entertain the wedding guests. As she sings and dances, Narendra recognizes her and without completing the marriage rites rushes to her side. His father and especially Choudhary and his goons try to stop him but Narendra and Ganga are finally united. Together with their infant son, they go away from the corruption of a degraded older generation toward a hopeful new future.

Superficially, *Ram Teri Ganga Maili* is a syrupy tale of the eternally pure woman whose devotion and innocence triumph over the worst efforts of lustful (mostly older) males to enslave and exploit her. As the third ear is deemed essential for listening in the analytic hour, similarly the analyst may need a third eye to break up the cloying surface of the film into less obvious patterns. Unlike Shiva's third eye which destroys all reality, the Freudian one merely cracks reality's stony surface to release its inner shape of fantasy. Like the dreamer who is not only the author, producer, and director of his dream but often plays all the important leads himself, the creator-audience of the film, too, is not limited to existing within the skin of the hero or the heroine but spreads out to cover other characters. The analyst may then reassign different values to the characters of the story than what has been the dreamer's manifest intent. He will, for instance, be mindful that besides experiencing the overt pity aroused by the hapless Ganga, the audience may well be deriving secret pleasure in the sexual villainy as well as surreptitiously partaking of the masochistic delight of her ordeals. Moreover, the third eye also destroys the very identities of the film's characters, replacing them with those of a child's internal family drama. Thus Ganga's screen image, with the infant clutched perpetually to her breast, becomes the fantasized persona of the mother from a particular stage of childhood. The faces of the various villains, on the other hand, coalesce into the visage of the 'bad' aggressive father, forcing the poor mother to submit to his unspeakable desire. It is then with the third eye that we look at Indian men and women as lovers and at some of the situations and spaces of love they project on the screen.

Bearing a strong resemblance to another girl from the hills, Reshma, played by Nargis in Raj Kapoor's first film *barsaat* four decades ago, Ganga is the latest reincarnation of the heroine who is totally steadfast in her devotion to a hero who is passive, absent, or both. Independent and carefree before being struck by the love-god Kama's flowery arrows, all that love brings her is suffering and humiliation, particularly of the sexual kind. Indeed, her suffering, like that of such legendary heroines as Laila and Sohni, seems almost a punishment for breaking social convention in daring to love freely. Rape, actual or attempted, is of course the strongest expression, the darkest image of the degradation she must undergo for her transgression.

The question why rape is a staple feature of Indian cinema where otherwise even the kiss is taboo, why the sexual humiliation of the woman plays such a significant role in the fantasy of love, is important. That this rape is invariably a fantasy rape, without the violence and trauma of its real-life counterpart, is evident in the manner of its visual representation. Villains, mustachoied or stubble-chinned, roll their eyes and stalk their female prey around locked rooms. With deep-throated growls of gloating, lasciviously muttering a variant of 'Ha! Your cannot escape now,' they make sharp lunges to tear off the heroine's clothes and each time come away with one more piece of her apparel. The heroine, on the other hand, retreats in pretty terror, her arms folded across her breasts to protect her dishevelled modesty, pleading all the while to be spared from the fate worse than death. As in the folk theatre presentations of the scene from the *Mahabharata* where Dushasana is trying to undrape Draupadi, what is being enjoyed by the audience is the sado-masochistic fantasy incorporated in the defencelessness and pain of a fear-stricken woman.

Now masochism is usually defined as the seeking of pain for the sake of sexual pleasure, with the qualifiction that either the seeking or the pleasure, or both, are unconscious rather than conscious. The specific locus of the rape fantasy for men is the later period of childhood which I have elsewhere called the 'second birth,' when the boy's earlier vision of the mother as an overwhelming feminine presence is replaced by her image, and that of woman generally, as a weak, castrated, suffering, and humiliated being. This is less a consequence of the boy's confrontation with female reality in the Indian family setting and more a projection of what would happen to him if he sexually submitted to the father and other elder males. As the boy grows up into a man, this fantasy needs to be repressed more and more, banished into farther and farther reaches of awareness. In the cavernous darkness of the cinema hall, the fantasy may at last surface gingerly and the associated masochistic pleasure be enjoyed vicariously in the pain and subjugation of the woman with whom one secretly identifies.

The effect of the rape scene on the female part of the audience, even if the movie rape is highly stylized and eschews any pretence to reality, is more complex. On one hand the sexual coercion touches some of her deepest fears as a woman. On the other hand, we must note the less conscious presence of a sexual fantasy due to the fact that the raping 'baddies' of Indian cinema are very often older figures on whom the woman is dependent in some critical way: employers, *zamindars* (landlords), and so on. The would-be rapists in *Ram Teri Ganga Maili*, apart from the anonymous brothel customer, are the priest and the powerful Choudhary, the future father-in-law of Ganga's husband. In many other movies, the face of the father behind the rapist's mask is more clearly visible. Thus in *Karz*, a box office hit of 1979, the heroine's step-father stages a mock rape of his step-daughter to test the suitability of the hero as her future spouse. Wendy O'Flaherty has linked the power of this particular scene to the ancient myth in which the father-god (Brahma, Prajapati, or Daksha) attempts to rape his own daughter until she is rescued by the hero, Shiva.[7] She points out that this well-known myth is tolerated and viewed positively in Hindu texts which tell of the birth of all animal life from the incestuous union of father and daughter. I would, on the other hand—a case of cultural psychology complementing mythology—trace the woman's allurement in the fantasy of rape by the villainous father-figure to many an Indian woman's adolescence. This is perhaps the most painful period of a girl's life, in which many renunciations are expected of her and where her training as an imminent daughter-in-law who must bring credit to her natal family is painfully stepped up. Psychoanalysis regularly brings up the powerful wish from this period for an intimacy with the father in which the daughter is simultaneously indulged as a little girl and treated as a young woman whose emerging womanhood is both appreciatively recognized and appropriately reacted to. In part, this is a universal fantasy among women, arising from the fact that a father often tends to withdraw from his daughter at the onset of puberty, feeling that he should not longer exhibit physical closeness, doubtless also because of the sexual feelings the daughter arouses in him. The daughter, however, learning to be at home in a woman's body and as yet insecure in her womanly role, may interpret the father's withdrawal as a proof of her feminine unattractiveness. The wished for father-daughter intimacy becomes a major fantasy in India because of the fact that in the Indian family the father's withdrawal from his daughter is quite precipitate once she attains puberty. The daughter is completely given over to the woman's world which chooses precisely this period of inner turmoil to become increasingly harsh. The rape by the father is then the forbidden, sexual aspect of her more encompassing longing for intimacy. The fearful mask worn by the father is a projection of the daughter's own villainous desire which frees her from the guilt for entertaining it.

Narendra, the hero of the movie, is a passive, childlike character, easily daunted by his elders who put obstacles in the path of the lovers' union. He is a pale shadow of the more ubiquitous romantic hero who suffers the despair of separation or disappointment in love with a suprahuman intensity (by which I mean less that of an inconstant god than of the faithful child lover). Such a hero used to be very popular in Indian films until about 20 years ago. Since in India nothing ever disappears, whether religious cults, political parties, or mythological motifs, the romantic lover too lives on, though at present he is perhaps in the trough rather than at the crest of the wave. For my generation, however, the images of this lover, as played for example by Dilip Kumar in *Devdas* or Guru Datt in *Pyasa*, remain unforgettable.

The Majnun-lover, as I would like to label this type after the hero of the well-known Islamic romance, has his cultural origins in a confluence of Islamic and Hindu streams. His home is as much in the Indo-Persian *ghazal* (those elegies of unhappy love where the lover bemoans the loss, the inaccessibility, or the turning away of the beloved) as in the lover's laments of separation in Sanskrit and Tamil *viraha* poetry—of which Kaildasa's *Meghaduta* (*The Cloud Messenger*) is perhaps the best-known example.

Elsewhere, I have discussed the psychological origins of the Majnun-lover as part of the imperious yet vulnerable erotic wishes of infancy.[8] His is the wish for a total merger with the woman; his suffering, the wrenching wail of the infant who finds his budding self disintegrating in the mother's absence. What he seeks to rediscover and reclaim in love is what is retrospectively felt to be paradise lost—the postpartum womb of life before 'psychological birth,' before the separation from the mother's anima took place. These wishes are of course part of every man's erotic being and it is only the phallic illusion of modern Western man which has tended to deny them legitimacy and reality.

All soul, an inveterate coiner of poetic phrases on the sorrows and sublimity of love, the romantic lover must split off his corporeality and find it a home or, rather, an orphanage. The *kotha*, the traditional style brothel, is Hindi cinema's favorite abode for the denied and discarded sexual impulses, a home for vile bodies. Sometimes replaced by the shady night club, a more directly licentious import from the West, the *kotha* provides the alcohol as well as the rhythmic music and dance associated with these degraded impulses. Enjoyed mostly by others, by the villain or the hero's friends, for the romantic lover the sexual pleasures of the *kotha* are generally cloaked in a pall of guilt, to be savored morosely in an alcoholic haze and to the nagging beat of self-recrimination.

The Krishna-lover is the second important hero of Indian films. Distinct from Majnun, the two may, in a particular film, be sequential rather than separate. The Krishna-lover is physically importunate, what Indian-English will perhaps call the 'eve-teasing' hero, whose initial contact with women verges on that of sexual harassment. His cultural lineage goes back to the episode of the mischievous Krishna hiding the clothes of the *gopis* (cow-herdesses) while they bathe in the pond and his refusal to give them back in spite of the girls' repeated entreaties. From the 1950s Dev Anand movies to those (and especially) of Shammi Kapoor in the 1960s and of Jeetendra today, the Krishna-lover is all over and all around the heroine who is initially annoyed, recalcitrant, and quite unaware of the impact of hero's phallic intrusiveness has on her. The Krishna-lover has the endearing narcissism of the boy on the eve of the Oedipus stage, when the world is felt to be his 'oyster.' He tries to draw the heroine's attention by all possible means—aggressive innuendoes and double entendres, suggestive song and dance routines, bobbing up in the most unexpected places to startle and tease her as she goes about her daily life (Jeetendra is affectionately known as 'jack in the box'). The more the heroine dislikes the lover's incursions, the greater is his excitement. As the hero of the film *Aradhana* remarks, 'Love is fun only when the woman is angry.'

For the Krishna-lover, it is vital that the woman be a sexual innocent and that in his forcing her to become aware of his desire she get in touch with her own. He is phallus incarnate, with distinct elements of the 'flasher' who needs constant reassurance by the woman of his power, intactness, and especially his magical qualities that can transform a cool Amazon into a hot, lusting female. The fantasy is of the phallus—Shammi Kapoor in his films used his whole body as one—humbling the pride of the unapproachable woman, melting her indifference and unconcern into submission and longing. The fantasy is of the spirited androgynous virgin awakened to her sexuality and thereafter reduced to a grovelling being, full of a moral masochism wherein she revels in her 'stickiness' to the hero. Before she does so, however, she may go through a stage of playfulness where she presents the lover a mocking version of himself. Thus in *Junglee*, it is the girl from the hills—the magical fantasy-land of Indian cinema where the normal order of things is reversed—who throws snowballs at the hero, teases him, and sings to him in a good-natured reversal of the man's phallicism, while it is now the hero's turn to be provoked and play the reluctant beloved.

The last 15 years of Indian cinema have been dominated, indeed overwhelmed, by Amitabh Bachchan who has personified a new kind of hero and lover. His phenomenally successful films have spawned a brand new genre which, though strongly influenced by Hollywood action movies such as those of Clint Eastwood, is neither typically Western not traditionally Indian.

The Bachchan hero is the good-bad hero who lives on the margins of his society. His attachments are few but they are strong and silent. Prone to quick violence and to brooding periods of withdrawal, the good-bad hero is a natural law-breaker, yet will not deviate from a strict private code of his own. He is often a part of the underworld but shares neither its sadistic nor its sensual excesses. If cast in the role of a policeman, he often bypasses cumbersome bureaucratic procedures to take the law in his own hands, dealing with criminals by adopting their own ruthless methods. His badness is not shown as intrinsic or immutable but as a reaction to a development deprivation of early childhood, often a mother's loss, absence, or ambivalence toward the hero.

The cultural parallel of the good-bad hero is the myth of Karna in the *Mahabharata*. Kunti, the future mother of the five Pandava brothers, had summoned the Sun when she was a young princess. Though her calling the Sun was a playful whim—she was just trying out a mantra—the god insisted on making something more of the invitation. The offspring of the resulting union was Karna. To hide her shame at Karna's illegitimate birth, Kunti abandoned her infant son and cast him adrift on a raft. Karna was saved by a poor charioteer and grew up into a formidable warrior and the supporter of the evil Duryodhana. On the eve of the great battle, Kunti approached Karna and revealed to him that fighting on Duryodhana's side would cause him to commit the sin of fratricide. Karna answered:

It is not that I do not believe the words you have spoken, *Kshatriya* (warrior caste) lady, or deny that for me the gateway to the Law is to carry out your behest. But the irreparable wrong you have done me by casting me out has destroyed the name and fame I could have had. Born a *Kshatriya*, I have yet not received the respect due a baron. What enemy could have done me greater harm than you have? When there was time to act you did not show your present compassion. And now you have laid orders on me, the son to whom you denied the sacraments. You have never acted in my interest like a mother, and now, here you are, enlightening me solely in your interest.[9]

Karna, though, finally promised his mother that on the battlefield he would spare all her sons except Arjuna—the mother's favourite.

The good-bad Bachchan hero is both a product of and a response to the pressures and forces of development and modernization taking place in Indian society today and which have accelerated during the last two decades. He thus reflects the psychological changes in a vast number of people who are located in a halfway house—in the transitional sector— which lies between a minuscule (yet economically and politically powerful) modern and the numerically preponderant traditional sectors of Indian society. Indeed, it is this transitional sector from which the Bachchan movies draw the bulk of their viewers.

The individual features of the good-bad hero which I have sketched above can be directly correlated with the major psychological difficulties experienced by the transitional sector during the course of modernization. Take, for instance, the effects of overcrowding and the high population density in urban conglomerations, especially in slum and shanty towns. Here, the lack of established cultural norms and the need to deal with relative strangers whose behavioural cues cannot be easily assessed compel the individual to be on constant guard and in a state of permanent psychic mobilization. A heightened nervous arousal, making for a reduced control over one's aggression, in order to ward off potential encroachments, is one consequence *and* a characteristic of the good-bad hero.

Then there is bureaucratic complexity with its dehumanization which seems to be an inevitable corollary of economic development. The cumulative effect of the daily blows to feelings of self-worth, received in a succession of cold and impersonal bureaucratic encounters, so far removed from the familiarity and predictability of relationship in the rural society, gives rise to fantasies of either complete withdrawal or of avenging slights and following the dictates of one's personal interests, even if this involves the taking of the law into one's own hands. These, too, form a part of our hero's persona.

Furthermore, the erosion of traditional roles and skills in the transitional sector can destroy the self-respect of those who are now suddenly confronted with a loss of earning power and social status. For the families of the affected, especially the children, there may be a collapse of confidence in the stability of the established world. Doubts surface whether hard work and careful planning can guarantee future rewards of security. The future itself begins to be discounted to the present.[10] The Bachchan hero, neither a settled family man nor belonging to any recognized community of craftsmen, farmers, etc., incorporates the transitional man's collective dream of success without hard work and of life lived primarily, and precariously, in the here-and-now.

The last feature of the portrait is the core sadness of the good-bad hero. On the macro level, this may be traced back to the effects of the population movements that take place during the process of economic development. The separation of families, the loss of familiar village neighbourhoods and ecological niches, can overwhelm many with feelings of bereavement. Sometimes concretized in the theme of separation from the mother, these feelings of loss and mourning are mirrored in the Bachchan hero and are a cause of his characteristic depressive detachment, in which the viewers, too, can recognize a part of themselves.

As a lover, the good-bad hero is predictably neither overly emotional like Majnun nor boyishly phallic like the Krishna lover. A man of controlled passion, somewhat withdrawn, he subscribes to the well-known lines of the Urdu poet Faiz that 'Our world knows other torments than of love and other happinesses than a fond embrace.' The initial meeting of the hero and heroine in *Deewar*, Bachchan's first big hit and widely imitated thereafter, conveys the essential flavour of this hero as a lover. The setting is a restaurant-night club and Bachchan is sitting broodingly at the bar. Anita, played by Parveen Babi, is a dancer—the whore with a golden heart—who comes and sits next to him. She offers him a light for his cigarette and tells him that he is the most handsome man in the bar. Bachchan, who must shortly set out for a fateful meeting with the villian, indifferently accepts her proffered homage as his due while he ignores her sexually provocative approach altogether. Indeed, this narcissistically withdrawn lover's relationships with his family members and even his best friend are more emotionally charged than with any woman who is his potential erotic partner. Little wonder that Shashi Kapoor, who played the hero's brother or best friend in many movies, came to be popularly known as Amitabh Bachchan's favourite heroine!

Afraid of the responsibility and effort involved in active wooing, of passivity and dependency upon a woman—urges from the earliest period of life which love brings to the fore and intensifies—the withdrawn hero would rather be admired than loved. It is enough for him to know that the woman is solely devoted to him while he can enjoy the position of deciding whether to take her or leave her. The fantasy here seems of revenge on the woman for a mother who either preferred someone else—in *Deewar*, it is the brother—or only gave the child conditional love and less than constant admiration.

The new genre of films, coexisting with the older ones, has also given birth to a new kind of heroine, similar in some respects to what Wolfenstein and Leites described as the masculine-feminine girl of the American movies of the 1940s and

1950s.[11] Lacking the innocent androgyny of Krishna's playmate, she does not have the sari-wrapped femininity (much of the time she is clad in jeans anyway!) of Majnun's beloved either. Like the many interchangeable heroines of Bachchan movies, she is more a junior comrade to the hero than his romantic and erotic counterpart.

Speaking a man's language, not easily shocked, she is the kind of woman with whom the new hero can feel at ease. She is not an alien creature of feminine whims, sensitivities and susceptibilities, with which a man feels uncomfortable and which he feels forced to understand. Casual and knowing, the dull wholesomeness of the sister spiced a little with the provocative coquetry of the vamp, she makes few demands on the hero and can blend into the background whenever he has more important matters to attend to. Yet she is not completely unfeminine, not a mere mask for the homosexual temptation to which many men living in the crowded slums of big cities and away from their women-folk are undoubtedly subject. She exemplifies the low place of heterosexual love in the life of the transitional man, whose fantasies are absorbed more by visions of violence than of love, more with the redressal of narcissistic injury and rage than with the romantic longing for completion—a gift solely in the power of a woman to bestow.

Having viewed some dreams in Indian popular cinema with the enthusiast's happy eye but with the analyst's sober perspective, let me reiterate in conclusion that *oneiros*—dream, fantasy—between the sexes and within the family, does not coincide with the cultural propositions on these relationships. In essence, *oneiros* consists of what seeps out of the crevices in the cultural floor. Given secret shape in narrative, *oneiros* conveys to us a particular culture's versions of what Joyce McDougall calls the Impossible and the Forbidden,[12] the unlit stages of desire where so much of our inner theatre takes place.

4

THE SEX WARS

There is a certain kind of popular narrative in India which neither consists of the folk version of stories from the pan-Indian epics nor of legends based on local events and motifs. Widespread over large linguistic regions, this narrative has a specific form, where the mundane is not separated from the supernatural.[1] With a frame-tale as its starting point, the narrative comprises loosely connected stories within stories, a format made famous by *A Thousand And One Nights*.

In spite of a profusion of magical happenings, these narratives are closer in spirit to the folktale than to the myth. They too fulfil the folktale's psychological function of neutralizing the archaic, alloying ambivalence with humor, alleviating anxiety through playfulness, and demonstrating clear-cut pedagogical intentions. The last is accomplished by portraying specific patterns of behaviour which are registered unconsciously by the reader or the auditor till a corresponding situation arises in his life. Recalling the story, he can then recognize the pattern as it applies to his own predicament, thus enhancing his feeling of conscious mastery and expanding the borders of his observing ego.[2]

Printed in cheap paperbacks in thousands of copies every year, and easily available at the pavement bookstalls of bazaars in both small towns and larger cities, these books are also a part of the literary offerings at well-known temple complexes where they routinely jostle Hindu theogonies, prayer collections, descriptions of rituals, and shiny scrolls with coloured illustrations of the various tortures of hell. Sporting a jacket cover of pure kitsch, generally in faded reds, blues, and yellows which have run into each other on the low-quality paper used for their production, these books are printed in an unusally larger type—known as Bombay type in the Hindi-speaking heartland and *periya elutta* (literally 'large script') in Tamil—for the instruction and entertainment of men and women at the edge of literacy and also uncertain of the availability of sufficient illumination at night.

Exclusively focusing on the relationship between the sexes, *Kissa Tota Myna* or *The Story Of The Parrot And The Starling* is one such popular collection of 14 tales in Hindi. Although of poor literary quality, *Tota Myna* may nonetheless claim a noble ancestry in *Sukasaptati*, a 12th-century collection of tales on the unfaithfulness of women, told by a parrot to a merchant's wife to guard her chastity while her husband was away. Like its counterparts in other languages, for instance *Matankamarajan Katai* in Tamil, *The Parrot And The Starling* has an abundance of magical and supernatural trappings and eschews decription and reflection in favour of a fast forward (and sideward) movement of the story. Its characters are preeminently princes, princesses, and courtiers from kingdoms of never-never lands. Its language, though undemanding, is nevertheless ornamented with well-known couplets and folk sayings from both Hindi and Urdu, reflecting the interpenetration of Hindu and Muslim streams in the mass culture of northern and central India from which this narrative derives.

The frame tale of *Kissa Tota Myna* is of a parrot who alights upon the branch of a tree one evening seeking a place to rest for the night. The tree is home to a starling, militantly feminist in her own way, who demands that the parrot fly off immediately. The starling cannot bear the thought of sharing her night abode with a member of a sex she hates for its cruel and unfaithful nature. The exhausted parrot defends the male sex and levels counter-allegations against the female of the species. As evidence for their respective positions, each bird then tells a succession of tales which, taken together, last for 14 nights. The following story, eighth in the series, is quite typical for both the literary poverty and the cultural-psychological richness of the whole collection.

The parrot said 'O Myna! A city called Kanchanpura was ruled by a king Angadhwaja and his queen Chandraprabha. The queen was virtuous and devoted to her husband. One day a brahmin came to Angadhwaja and gave him two pieces of paper. On the first piece it was written, 'A king who stays awake all night achieves great results.' On the second; 'Whoever honours an enemy has all his transgressions forgiven.'

'King Angadhwaja put both pieces of paper in his pocket and sent away the brahmin after honouring him with a gift of money. After a few days the king wanted to test the truth of the brahmin's words. One night, after finishing all his work, he decided to stay up till the morning. While the king was awake in his palace, he heard a woman crying outside. The king felt great pity for the woman and thought to himself that there were unhappy people dwelling in his city. "I must go at once and find the cause of her unhappiness," he said to himself. For the *dharma* of the ruler demands that he take part in the sorrows and pleasures of his subjects, punish according to the crime and look after his people as if they were members of his own family.'

'Arming himself fully the king walked towards the sound of weeping and found a 100-year-old woman sobbing loudly. "O Mother! What makes you so unhappy that you are crying at midnight?" the king asked.

"O traveller! Why do you interfere? Go your way. The cause of my suffering cannot be removed by the Creator himself let alone by a man," the woman answered.

"At least tell me what makes you so sad," said the king.

"I'll tell you only if you never repeat it to anyone for otherwise you'll be turned into stone," the old woman replied.

'The king agreed to this condition and the old woman said, "Son, tomorrow night at ten, Angadhwaja, the king of this city, will be bitten by a snake and die.

That is why I'm crying. Where will we ever again find such a virtuous king?"

"'O mother, just as you have told me the reason for your weeping, kindly also tell me from where this snake will çome," the king said.

"'Son, outside the western gate of this city there is temple of Shiva. Near the temple there is a banyan tree and the snake lives in a hole at the root of the tree. The snake is an enemy of the king from its previous birth and now wishes to avenge itself for the earlier enmity," the old woman said.

"'Mother, tell me also why the snake is an enemy of the king?" the king asked.

"'Son, this king was a merchant called Manisen in his last incarnation and his wife was named Kesar. She was 20 years old and very beautiful. One day Manisen went off to a distant land on business leaving Kesar at home with an 18-year-old servant. In his absence the lord of love, Kama, sorely afflicted Kesar's body and her fancy turned toward the young servant. She called the boy, asked him to sit on the bed with her and frankly expressed her desire for him. The boy folded his hands and said, "O merchant's daughter! I shall never perform the act with you since I have heard from elders that a person who feeds and clothes you is like a parent and a man who does the bad act with his mistress goes to hell." Hearing the boy, Kesar said, "It will go badly with you if you do not make love to me." She threatened him in various ways but the boy was adamant. After some days when Manisen returned, the wife thought that she would get into trouble if the boy ever told the husband what had transpired while he was away. So she thought of something which would both protect her and punish the boy for the insult he had offered her.

'When Manisen came home he found his wife sad. "O Beloved! why are you lying listless today?" "O Lord! you have returned. Now take care of your house because I am going to kill myself," Kesar replied. "What is your unhappiness that you want to give up on life?" Manisen asked. "Lord, I have no sorrows for your glory has given me all possible happiness. But in your absence your servant did me grievous injury and you must punish him, otherwise I shall die," Kesar said. "What did he do to you? Tell me frankly," Manisen said.

"'O Lord! One night as I was sleeping on the roof he climbed up on my bed, seated himself on my breasts and wanted to do the bad act with me. But I awakened and seeing him astride my body I cried out aloud and only then did he leave me. On hearing my screams people came up, but out of shame I could say nothing to them. Only God protected my virtue that night," Kesar said. Hearing this, Manisen became red with anger and said, "O my beloved! Why be unhappy? Have your bath, eat, and enjoy yourself. The boy shall be punished this very night for what he has done to you." When night fell, Manisen stabbed the boy repeatedly with a knife and buried the body in his courtyard. Manisen has been now reborn as the king and that boy is reborn as a snake who seeks vengeance.'
On hearing this the king went back to his palace.

The parrot said, 'O myna! Think about it. What was the poor boy's fault that the woman did not have any pity on him and had him murdered?' The starling replied, 'In this affair both the man and woman are at fault since the man killed the youth merely on the say-so of his wife without further inquiring into the matter.' The parrot said, 'O Myna! I have already said earlier that when a woman in her attractive form embraces a man and infatuates him with her sweet words and desire's arrows then the man loses all his reflective power.'

'Let me reply to that,' said the starling.

'First let me finish my story and then you may give your reply,' said the parrot.

'When the king returned to his palace he could not fall asleep because of worry. His hand went to his pocket and he found the second piece of folded paper given to him by the brahmin. He opened this and read therein that one's enemy should be honoured. He said to himself, "What the brahmin wrote down on the first scrap of paper certainly came true. Let me also try out his second piece of advice. At the moment I have no other enemy than the snake so I must show him all respect." In the morning he called his chief minister and other courtiers and told them that a snake would come to bite him that night. "So you should clean up the road from my bed to the snake's hole. Sprinkle the whole way with perfume and rose petals and line it with cups of perfumed milk," he instructed.

'When the time came, the snake, full of anger, emerged from its hole and started moving towards the king's palace. But it was completely captivated by the perfume and the rose petals lining its way. In whichever direction it turned there was delicious milk to be drunk. In its contentment the snake said to itself, "The king, knowing me to be his enemy, still looks after me so well. I shall not bite him. I must go and tell him that I have forsworn my revenge." When the snake entered the king's bed chamber the minister reached for his sword. But the king forbade him from drawing the weapon. He then extended his had and said, "O Lord Serpent! Now take your revenge by biting me."

'"Glory be to you, O king, and glory to the parents who have sired such a courageous and virtuous son. I am very pleased with you and shall not harm you." So saying the snake went away.

'On seeing all this the people were amazed. Then the queen addressed her husband thus, "O King! Please tell me how you knew about the snake?"

'"O Queen! I cannot do so because the person who told me warned me that I shall be turned to stone if I ever revealed the secret," the king replied. "Whether you turn into stone or not, you must tell me the story otherwise I shall give up my life," said the queen. The king was very upset for he loved his wife dearly and could not bear to be without her for even a moment. He was so blinded by his love that he did not reproach her for her stubbornness and only said, "Well, if I must turn into stone I shall do so at the banks of the river Ganges. Then, as a stone, I shall at least lie in the sands of the holy water."

'The king then prepared to proceed to the Ganges. The king's servants and many others from the city accompanied him on his journey. His minister tried to reason with him saying. "If there is life you'll get many other queens. You are otherwise so sensible yet are bent on losing your life because of a woman's whim." But the king was so infatuated that he did not heed this wise counsel. Then the minister went to the queen and said, "O Queen! Renounce this wilfulness so that the king's life may be saved. If he reveals the secret and turns into a stone where will you again find such a king? Will his successor give you any respect? Every headstrong woman has always suffered for her wilfulness."

"'Which woman has paid for her stubbornness? Tell me the story of even one such woman." said the queen.

'The minister said, "O Queen! there was a city called Srusen ruled by King Rupadutta, who was very handsome. His wife, Chandrakanta, was very beautiful, but she had become immoral even before her marriage. When she came to her husband's home after marriage she brought her lover along with her in the guise of an eunuch. During the king's absence in his court she enjoyed herself with the lover. One day the king came to know this and he tried to reason with the queen. But the queen said, 'I have given my heart to my lover. You can do what you like but I shall never give him up.' The king had both her ears and her nose cut off and banished her from his city while the eunuch was hanged. The woman who does not listen to her husband always comes to a bad end. Now leave this stubbornness of yours because your husband is a king and no one can ever be sure of a king's moods. Some poet has rightly said:

A king, a yogi, fire, and water
Have a contrary nature
One should always avoid them
For their affections are uncertain.

But the queen remained adamant in her wish to know the king's secret and the hapless minister retreated.

'In the morning they all left the city and at noon came to a river where the king rested. He went to the river to wash himself and saw a herd of goats come to the stream to drink water. All the goats left after slaking their thirst except for one who saw a fruit floating on the current. The goat wanted the fruit badly. When the billy goat saw that one goat remained behind, he asked her the reason for not joining the others. The goat answered, "If you get me the fruit from the river I'll come with you otherwise I shall not move."

"'What if I drown?" asked the billy goat.

"'Whatever happens I will not move without the fruit," was the reply. The billy goat was furious. Eyes red with anger, it said, "You don't know me well enough. I am not a fool like King Angadhwaja who, infatuated with a woman, goes to the Ganges to lay down his life." It then started butting the goat till she rejoined the herd.

'The billy goat's remarks went straight to the king's heart, who said to himself, "I am even lower than a goat in my infatuation. Today I realize that the queen whom I love so much is hungry for my very life. Some poet has indeed rightly remarked:

A woman is a mother to give birth
A girl, for intercourse
A goddess, to receive worship
And death, to take life back."

The king said to himself, "I am a big fool. Fie on my intelligence! Fie on women who control men by their sweet words and fie on those men who lose everything and become slaves to these bundles of wickedness!" He then called his minister and the queen and said, "O Queen! I shall now tell you the secret and then become a stone. What is your wish?"

"'O King! whatever may happen, you must tell me the secret," the queen answered. The king then picked up a whip and thrashed the queen. She begged forgiveness but the king was implacable. He called his executioners and told them to pluck out the queen's eyes and leave her in the jungle. The executioners followed the orders and the queen received due punishment for her deeds.'

The parrot said, 'O Myna! The race of women is indeed not to be trusted.'

The starling answered. 'O Parrot! Do not exaggerate, I too can tell you of the unfaithfulness of men.'

The next night, in reply, the starling tells the story of four princes who got lost while hunting in a forest. When they finally emerged from the forest they came to a city inhabited by sorcerers. After wandering around in the city the princes sought out an inn where they could rest for the night. The innkeeper was a sorceress who had four beautiful daughters. The girls were infatuated with the princes and at night had them carried to their rooms through their magic. The three older girls turned three princes into sheep whom they fed well during the day and then transformed back into men at night for the purpose of sexual enjoyment. The youngest daughter, however, fell in love with the youngest prince and kept him as a man without employing any magic spells at all. Their love grew so much that they could not stay apart for a moment. One day, the youngest prince became very sad as he sorely missed his parents. On being asked the cause for his sadness he told the girl about the unhappiness being caused to his parents at the separation from all their sons. He asked her to employ her skills in sorcery so that the brothers could be released from their enthralment and go back to their parents. He further suggested that she too accompany him back to his father's kingdom where they would be married and she become a princess. In her devotion to the man, the young sorceress followed his wishes, thus earning the wrath and vengefulness of her sisters. She fled the city together with her lover and his brothers. On the way to the prince's kingdom, while resting for the night in a forest, the youngest prince deserted the sleeping girl. After many tribulations, the sorceress reached her lover's city and wanted to be together with him again. He, however, threw her into prison for the night and had her hanged in the morning.

Of the many narrative forms, the folktale, it seems to me, is closest in reflecting the concerns of the ego of the Freudian tripartite model, an ego which mediates between the instinctual desires of the id and the imperatives of the superego. In the folkale, the primitive aspects of the id and the superego are relatively underplayed. The analysis of the folktale would then ideally keep closer to the surface of the text. In addition, the analyst would look for a single fantasy (in contrast to the novel where fantasies are generally multiple) which would help him structure the surface elements of the tale into a new pattern, revealing a new emphasis.

A major feature of the *Tota Myna* stories is the marked lack of any tender feeling or mutuality between men and women who move across their pages as if they were members of different species altogether. At the conclusion of each tale, one of the lovers is routinely mutilated, stabbed,thrown alive in a well, or decapitated by the other, with the female more likely to meet a bloodier end than the male. The stories can be more correctly described as erotic fantasies of hatred than love, the hostility and aggression between the sexes far outweighing any affectionate promptings.

In the tales, the male perception of the woman as an erotic partner is of a sexually voracious being who is completely ruled by the dictates of her body. Especially vulnerable to the power of eros, the phrase *jab uske sharir ko kamdeva ne sataya* ('when her body was sorely troubled by the god of love') is used solely in connection with a woman, never a man. She is the initiator of sexual advances and loses all sense of proportion and moral constraints when in the grip of erotic passion. At such times, in her quest for sexual satisfaction, she would blithely sacrifice her parents, husband, or children. When sexually intoxicated, the woman takes one lover after another without discriminating between young and old, handsome and ugly, rich and poor. In many tales, women perversely favour fakirs and yogis as lovers, doubtless also because the dishevelled 'holy' men, with their unkempt beards and matted hair, are fantasized by Hindus and Muslims alike to be possessors of great virility, capable of satisfying the most insatiable of women. It goes without saying that women are also deceitful and unpredictable, with motivations that are an enduring puzzle to men. As one of the folk proverbs in a story puts it, *Triya charitra na jane koye, Khasam mar ke sati hoye.* ('No one knows the character of a woman; she will first kill her husband and then mount the funeral pyre as a sati.')

Elsewhere, I have traced this view of the woman's rampant, heedless sexuality to the 'sexual mother' of early childhood.[3] She is a figure of male imagination, constructed from the boy's perception of an actual maternal eroticism, heightened in the Indian context, combined with the projection of his own desire toward her.

The sorceress who uses the prince for sexual enjoyment at night while she turns him into a helpless sheep during the day—night being the diurnal home of fantasy and imagination—the merchant's wife who, Phaedra-like demands that the servant boy gratify her desire or risk severe retribution, are two of the many masks of the 'sexual mother' which women wear in these tales. The 'Oedipal' fantasy of many stories is further underscored by the lovers women serve or choose in preference to and in betrayal of the hero. Often enough the lover is a fakir and yogi who, as Robert Goldman suggests in the case of the guru in legends from Sanskrit epics, may well be a substitute for the father who lays sexual claim to the mother.[4]

Although most stories mark the passage of the Freudian mother in the man's fantasy, there are also a couple of tales which herald the appearance of the Kleinian one; the defence against the anxiety around genital sexuality being replaced by reassurance against the earlier 'oral' fears of devouring and being devoured by the mother. In one story, for example, a goddess fires a king in oil every night, eats his flesh and then the next morning sprinkles nectar (amrita) on the bones by which he is resurrected in his original form. In return for this service, the king daily receives a large quantity of gold from the gratified goddess.

The female perception of man in Tota Myna is of a creature of shortlived passions whose only experience of love is lust. Once erotic passion retreats and lust is satisfied, the man is revealed as a being full of guilt who will unceremoniously desert the woman he has loved to distraction only a short while earlier. The man's guilt is chiefly toward the parents for his desertion of them in order to initiate adult sexual relations. In one story after another, the hero proves to be vastly more attached to his parents than to the beloved. Given the perception of the man as someone who is infantile in his attachments, volatile in his affections, and cruel in his anger, the woman's choice in love, the stories seem to suggest, is limited to appeasement and masochistic surrender.

Serpents as Lovers and Spouses

In literature, folklore, myth, ritual, and art, the snake and especially the cobra (nag) plays a prominent role in Hindu culture. Born of one of the daughters of Prajapati, the Lord of Creation, snakes are carried by Shiva, the Destroyer, around his neck and arms, while there is no more popular representation of Vishnu, the Preserver of the Hindu trinity, than of his reposing on the Sesha, the seven-headed cobra. Sculpted into the reliefs of Buddhist, Jain, and Hindu temples, snakes, both single and entwined, are a ubiquitous presence in Indian sacred space. On a more mundane level, nag is a popular name among both men and women and Naga-Panchami, the festival of snakes on the fifth day of the Bhadon month in the rainy season, is celebrated all over India with the ritual worship of the cobra.

One would therefore expect that the motif of the snake lover, of both men and women, is widespread in popular Indian narrative, and this expectation is not belied. This motif can trace its antiquity to the myths of the *Mahabharata* where the great ascetic Jaratkuru married the sister of Vasuki, the king of snakes. The redoubtable warrior-hero Arjuna, too, married Ulipi, Vasuki's sister, and bedded a serpent princess during the one year of his banishment.[5] The first tale of the snake lover that I would like to narrate and interpret here is the second part (quite unconnected with the first) of the story of Princess Standing Lamp. This story, well-known as a folktale in other parts of South India, is part of a Tamil collection of tales mentioned earlier in the chapter, *Matankamarajan Katai—The Story of King Matanakama*—and my version is condensed from the English translation of Kamil Zvelebil.[6] The section of the story I reproduce here commences after the marriage of the princess and the prince, a time when they should have 'lived happily ever after.' But it so transpires that the prince becomes infatuated with another woman with whom he spends his days and nights, completely neglecting his young bride.

For three years, things went on like this. Then one day an old woman who happened to be the neighbour of the princess came to see her and said: 'Dear child! You are quite young and pretty, and yet your husband is a whoremonger! What kind of wife is she who is unable to control her husband?'

'What can I do, mother?' complained Standing Lamp. 'Since Brahma has created me like this, nothing can be done against it!'

'So, Brahma has created you like this, has he?' answered the old woman in mockery. 'Don't say foolish things! It is your own fault that you suffer! But if you listen to my advice you won't regret it!' And when the princess agreed to listen, the old woman proceeded: 'Here, take this magic drink and mix it with the *rasam* (spiced lentil soup) prepared for your husband! He won't leave you for a second!'

Taking the magic drink with apprehension, the princess thought: 'I wish I knew how this works! If she is right, we will be happy as before. But suppose that it harms him. What shall I do?' And, being unable to make up her mind, Standing Lamp went out and spilt the magic drink in her backyard, serving her husband an innocent usual *rasam*.

A snake lived in an old anthill in the backyard, and a few drops of the *rasam* mixed with the love potion fell on its head. As a result, the snake became infatuated with the princess. As soon as her husband left for the house of the *dasi* (female servant), the enamoured serpent tapped at Standing Lamp's door. She went to see who it was. As she opened the door, she was happy to behold her husband come back! The snake had taken the form of the prince. Without further hesitation, she gave herself to the snake, who enjoyed her fully in its embrace.

The princess carried on thus with the serpent for some time, and as a result became pregnant. When the snake came to know of her condition he felt a desire to tell her the truth. The serpent said: 'Woman! I am not your real husband! Your husband is at this moment in the house of the *dasi*. I am the five-hooded snake living at the back of your house. The love potion which your neighbour, the old woman, gave you the other day, fell on me, and as a result I came to love you. But now I am going to break the infatuation which your husband feels for the *dasi* who plays the role of his wife.'

After a short time, the prince, still infatuated with the *dasi*, found out that his wife was with child. He ran to his father-in-law and complained that his wife, the princess, must have been unfaithful to him, since although he had not touched her for some two years, she was pregnant!

The king sent a few maids to bring his daughter to his presence. Standing Lamp sought the advice of the snake.

The serpent, coiled in the bed of the princess, laughed and said: 'Your bad days are over. When the king, your father, asks about your condition, tell him without any fear whatsoever that your husband alone is the father of your child. If there should be any doubt, turn to the members of the court and tell them that you are willing to undergo any test in the temple or before any deity. Don't be afraid! Or better still, say this: Bring a pot and let in a serpent. I'm willing to put my hand into the pitcher with the snake to retrieve a gold coin placed inside! In this way, no one will doubt your word. I shall of course manage to be the snake in the pitcher!' And the serpent left.

As soon as the sun rose, the princess got up, dressed in her best attire and jewels, and appeared in the hall of audience of the royal palace. The king turned to his son-in-law and said: 'Well! Why don't you ask her what you wanted to ask her?'

'Sir,' said the prince-husband, 'how is it that when it is two or three years since I last touched her, this woman is now bearing a child?'

Standing Lamp addressed the gathering of councillors: 'I am indeed pregnant, and no one else but my husband is the father. If you have any doubt, I am willing to undergo the ordeal by snake!' The king and the prince and the members of the council agreed, and a snake-catcher was immediately sent for and asked to produce a suitable corbra.

The snake-catcher came and started to play his flute. The five-hooded snake king subdued all other snakes, and entered the pitcher that had been prepared, with a golden coin dropped inside.

The princess had a bath, and as soon as the returned she went round the pot and uttered the following words: 'The one whom I touched on my wedding day was truly my husband; today I shall truly touch the serpent.' Then she removed the seal from the pot, thrust her hand inside, took out the snake, threw it round her neck like a garland, removed the gold coin, deposited it on a golden platter— and the father and the husband, and the ministers cheered her, shouting: 'She is indeed a *maha pativrata*, utterly chaste and faithful and a great lady!' All of them praised her virtue, while she returned home, and the prince had no more doubts that he must be the father of the child.

The *dasi* was curious; she sent her servants to the princess with the request that she should bring her child for her to see. 'Our mistress must see your baby! Please, give it to us!' Standing Lamp told them to come on the next day. The servant girls returned without the baby, and the offended *dasi* reported to the prince what had happened. 'What? I send for my son and she dares to refuse? What is this?' And he promptly complained to his father-in-law the king about the conduct of his wife.

That night Standing Lamp called the serpent and asked him: 'The *dasi* asked for our son. What shall I do? Shall I send him to her?'

The snake replied: 'Finally it has happened. Good days are ahead of you now. Your husband will return to you, and the *dasi* will this time lose his affection. Deck the child with all ornaments and send him to your father. When they come to fetch him, weigh the child along with jewels. Tell them that they should return him precisely as he is. If the weigh will be less, the *dasi* will not only have to make good the loss but also become your slave. The jewels of the child will be made of *nagaratna*, the snake-gems, and even your father's entire treasury will not equal them in value. I'll come, and snatch away the jewels. Don't be afraid, and send the child without worry!'

Next morning, the king's servants came to the princess: 'Lady, your father our lord the king wants to see you.' The princess took the child and appeared in the king's presence. 'Daughter,' said the king, 'your husband wishes to see his son!' When she remained silent, he went on: 'Why haven't you sent the child to him?' Standing Lamp answered: 'Sir, I have no objection to send my boy to the house of the *dasi*. All I fear is that he may be robbed of his precious jewels. I therefore humbly submit that he is weighed here and now along with his jewels. If he is returned intact and in the same weight, I shall be satisfied. However, if something is missing, I insist that the *dasi* be dispossessed and become my slave. If she agrees to this, I'm willing to send my child along.'

The king summoned his son-in-law and the *dasi*. They accepted the conditions. The princess placed her son in a cradle, in another cradle she placed the jewels and she had them weighed so that everyone could see and have no doubt. The *dasi* then took the boy and the jewels to her house, fondled the child, caressed it, played with it, fed it with milk, and kept it with her for the night.

In the dead of the night, the serpent crawled in, and in utter secrecy stole away some of the most precious jewels.

In the morning, Princess Standing Lamp insisted that the child and the jewels be weighed in the presence of the king and the councillors. It was at once revealed that the weight of the jewels had diminished! The councillors watched everything carefully and decided: 'The *dasi* is guilty of a crime. The jewels have been stolen. The *dasi* must act according to the agreement.' Without the least contradiction the *dasi* became a servant in the household of the prince. The princess was happy. After some time, she was restored to her husband's affection, and while the *dasi* took their orders as their domestic slave, they enjoyed life to the full.

In this new-found joy, the princess completely forgot the snake. The snake thought: 'Ah! Oh! Because of us, the princess has found new happiness, and now she has forgotten us! However if we bite and kill her, there won't be any joy in that for us! We cannot make love to her now. All that is gone. The best solution for us is to commit suicide!' And it decided to strangle itself with a lock of Standing Lamp's hair.

So, one night, the snake crawled into her bed, and entangling itself in a lock of her hair, died on the spot.

The next morning, at sun-rise, the young ruler woke up and was horrified to find a dead snake in his wife's hair! As he woke her up, her head was heavy with the weight of the dead snake, so large was it. She was afraid even to move, but she felt terrible remorse and sadness. She realized why it had killed itself. 'Why do you weep?' asked the husband. 'O lord of my soul! This is our home snake. I had prayed to him and offered *puja* (worship) to him for your return to me! But when you did return, I forgot all about him! That's why he came, and died!' And she added: 'Please, take the boy, and perform the rites, and have the snake cremated prayerfully with due obsequies.'

The prince agreed. With the assistance of the boy, he performed obsequial ceremonies for the snake and had it burnt. They worshipped the snake regularly. From them on, Princess Standing Lamp, the young king, and the boy lived happily together.

This shows that women are not to be trusted in this world! They are a tricky and deceptive lot.

The serpent as a lover of the human female virtually *demands* an interpretation of the snake's symbolic significance. This demand cannot be evaded even when we know that it is the area of symbolism which has earned psychoanalysis its greatest opprobrium and harshest criticism. Viewed by some as akin to a crankish medieval bestiary, the Freudian theory of symbols has been accused by its critics of ignoring the all-important context in its quest for ferreting out a universal sexual significance of natural objects and artifacts. The accusation has some substance although it was Wilhelm Stekle rather than Freud who introduced the notion of one-to-one correspondence between the symbol and the symbolized. Taken over by Freud and incorporated in the second and subsequent editions of *The Interpretation Of Dreams*, the notion of universal symbolism, in fact, contradicts, Freud's own dream theory.[7] Whatever its uneasy place in theory, we know that in his clinical work, an analyst, of whatever persuasion, proceeds from and remains closely connected to the uniqueness of his patient's 'text.' There is neither a straightforward application of theory from a cookbook of interpretations nor any culling out of facile equivalencies from some lexicon of universal symbols that can help the analyst understand and interpret the meaning of the analysand's communications.

The impression that the psychoanalytic theory of symbolism is based on a kind of invariance and is indifferent to context perhaps stems from its historical evolution where, in the early years, the Oedipal period was regarded as the fulcrum, both of mental life and of symbol formation. Thus the child's use of the representation of his own body parts to symbolize his conflicted relationship with a parent—the cutting off of hair to symbolize castration anxiety, to take an example, is then limited to analytical material from the Oedipal context. In later periods of development, the 'castration anxiety' may be expressed in symbols of loss of identity or of humiliation which do not necessarily involve a mutilation of body parts. Conversely, one symbol may express more than one idea and it is the various details minutiae of the context which determine whether a given image is symbolic and what exactly it is symbolic of.

The caution is especially necessary in the case of the snake, which traditionally has been a symbol with multiple meanings. In religious beliefs around the world, the snake is both accursed and worshipped. Repository of all mysteries, representative of the chthonic powers of the underworld, epiphany of the moon, a symbol both of immortality and the threatening powers of death, symbolically the snake occupies a unique position in the animal world.[8]

Psychologically, too, depending upon the context, the snake can symbolize a variety of meanings.[9] Because of some of its real or perceived characteristics—extending itself, swelling and rearing up the head (cobra), penetrating into holes and crevices in the earth, secreting a fluid, evoking the tacky and clammy sensation associated with genitals—the snake has been traditionally considered the most important symbol of the male organ. There are, however, other contexts in which the snake is not a phallic symbol. Evoking its hidden aspects and the more python- rather than cobra-like associations of enveloping, strangling, incorporating, and swallowing small creatures, the snake can come to symbolize a devouring vagina, a dangerous femininity; its poison—a death in the coital embrace. In yet other contexts, it can be equated with the umbilicus which is a bridge to the womb, while its characterstic of sloughing off the old sin in exchange for a new one can come to represent change and transformation, the hope of psychic rebirth in therapy. It is then through the configuration of three contexts—of the narrative, of the culture, and of the symbolism associated with the snake, that we can arrive at a more careful interpretation of the serpent lover of our tale.

The situation in which a newly married bride competes with another woman for the affections of her husband is not particularly novel in narratives of Indian gender relations. The theme of the *souten*, a co-wife or a mistress who rules the man's heart and must be dislodged from this position, is the subject of many folktales as well as songs. In most tales, we are told the wife wins back her husband's love by being patient, virtuous, and clever.[10] She tricks her rival into revealing her flaws which puts her own attractiveness in sharp relief. The fantasy of the serpent lover, however, involves deeper layers of the woman's psyche. In psychoanalytic parlance, it contains more id than ego material, which is generally true in folktales. The serpent lover appears in reaction to Princess Standing Lamp's grievous disappointment in the prince at the beginning of their married life. The snake provides her with the status of motherhood which, for an Indian girl, consolidates her identity as a woman and can mean a significant improvement in her position in the politics of joint family life. The snake is the elusive fulfilment of both a romantic and social quest. It is the 'good penis,' the idealized phallus of the woman's fantasy. This interpretation is fully consistent with the cultural symbolism of the snake where the worship of god-like *naga* deities is closely linked to sexuality and reproduction and is also supported by the serpent's more universal phallic significance. We can see some of the underlying dynamics in this fantasy in a clinical vignette.

A 25-year-old woman has been deeply worried about her husband's evident romantic interest in another woman. She dreams that the man tells her he is going to spend the weekend with the woman. She protests violently, but her protestations have no effect on the man who goes off on his tryst. A group of gods, dressed as bandits, of whom she is not sure whose side they are on, follow the man. When she comes to the house where the husband has gone, she finds him lying dead on a hospital bed, his body badly mutilated, evidently killed by the bandit gods. Sitting on the man's body is a wonderful snake, glistening, glittering, and studded with diamonds, and toward whom she feels a strong attraction.

In the story, of course, the murderous rage felt by Princess Standing Lamp toward her philandering husband is completely absent, whereas in the dream it is half-heartedly sought to be disavowed by the device of the bandit-gods who may or may not be on the woman's side, that is, may or may not be a part of her. Yet the outcome in both the dream and the story, the replacement of the disappointing real-life husband by an idealized serpent lover, is strikingly similar.

· The snake lover of our story differs significantly from the animal groom tales of Western folklore which have been a subject of psychological analysis by Bruno Bettelheim.[11] In a reversal of the Indian pattern, the Western sexual partner is first experienced as an animal, a human being who has been turned into a loathsome beast by a sorceress. He is not a product of the heroine's disappointment in marriage. She is forced to join him while still a maiden because of her love or obedience to the father, and it is her devotion to her animal lover that disenchants him and gives him back his human form. Bettelheim interperts the European fairy tale as a message for the girl that to achieve a happy union the female has to overcome her view of sex as loathsome and animal-like. In my own interpretation of the snake lover as an idealized phallus, it may well be that idealization helps the girl overcome her childhood fears of the adult male organ which can lacerate and 'bite' into her inside. The 'good penis' helps her in the acceptance of a violation of her body's boundaries, a violence inherent in the sexual act. The snake, after all, figures prominently in threats of chastisement directed toward the female child in some parts of India. But more important, given the radical changes in a girl's situation brought about by marriage and the overwhelming nature of demands made on her by her new family, coupled with an inattentive or straying husband, the private yet culturally shared fantasy of the idealized phallus both consoles and eases her transition.

The psychic transformation required in giving up the dreams of girlhood and settling into the reality of married womanhood then require the unconscious fantasy of the 'good penis.' Whoever this phallus may ultimately belong to—the father, a god, the ideal male—it can only serve as a transitional object. The snake, strangled in her tresses at night while she sleeps, must die as must her earlier dreams of love and passion before she can settle into conjugal domesticity and motherhood. Both the snake and the 'good penis'—the one is the other—are then perpetually mourned in the secret recesses of her heart, their memory now incorporated in the son.

My story of the snake *wife* derives from the arena of popular, mass culture. It is the 1987 movie, *Nagina*, said to be an all-time top grosser in the history of Indian cinema. Raju, the 21-year-old hero of the movie, returns home after a 15-year sojourn in England. He is the only son of a wealthy mother—his father having died while he was away—who was sent to England as a child to be treated there for inexplicable anxiety attacks. Raju was cured and stayed on with his uncle in London, where he grew up and went to school.

During his absence, the family's considerable estates were looked after by a friend of his father's, the movie's first villain, who would like his daughter to be married to Raju. Encouraged by the mother, who is not averse to this proposal, the young man takes the girl out on a buggy ride. On the way he narrowly misses being bitten by a cobra which, coiled around the rear axle of the buggy, follows him home and is witness to the mother's love and distress at the danger her son has just escaped.

The next day Raju visit the ruins of the house in which he had spent the first six years of his life. Here, among the ruins which have a powerful emotional impact upon him, he hears a female voice singing a song with the refrain: 'A forgotten story is remembered. An old memory surfaces again.' Through the mist which swirls among the ruins, Raju gets tantalizing glimpses of the singing woman—the back of her head, a shoulder, a foot tapping in rhythm to a dance—and he follows her. Finally, he comes face to face with a beautiful young woman who tells him that they had spent a lot of time together in the ruined house in the past. Raju, in spite of his best efforts, cannot remember. He continues to meet Rajni ('Night'), which is her name, and duly falls in love with her.

In the meanwhile, the villain has received Raju's mother's consent to the hero's marriage to his daughter. Raju, though, protests and persuades his mother to change her decision in favor of Rajni. The villain vows revenge for this slight. He sends one of his henchmen to murder Rajni, but two cobras, who are the girl's protectors, kill the would-be assassin. The villain then arranges for a gang of bandits to attack Raju's house on the day of his wedding to Rajni, but cobras bar the bandits' way and the marriage takes place as scheduled.

The villain now refuses to hand back Raju's property; the documents in which he had acknowledged Raju's ownership have been misplaced. But Rajni, who the audience by now knows is an *ichhadhari* cobra—a snake who, in India serpent lore, as a reward for many hundred years of ascetic practices, can assume any form at will—locates the missing documents through her paranormal vision. The villain and his men waylay Raju with the intention of killing him. Rajni again protects her husband and the villain dies, bitten by the cobra.

Much more dangerous to the couple, however, is the arrival of the family's guru, an evil *tantrik* (the practitioner of an esoteric Hindu cult) who possesses formidable occult powers. Immediately on entering the family mansion, he discerns the presence of a cobra and recognizes Rajni to be a snake woman. However, before he can do anything he is ordered out of the house by the unsuspecting Raju who looks down upon *tantriks* and gurus as purveyors of old-fashioned religious mumbo jumbo.

The guru sends his own pet cobra to bite Raju, who is convalescing in a hospital room from injuries received in the fight with the villain. Rajni, who is watching over her sleeping husband, resumes her snake from and kills the guru's cobra after a fierce struggle. She then warns the guru from trying to harm Raju, maintaining that her powers gained through her devotion to her husband are as great as the guru's undoubted ones.

The guru now informs Raju's mother about the real nature of her daughter-in-law. He tells her to keep a close watch on Rajni who must resume her original snake form once every 24 hours. The old woman does so and sees for herself Rajni changing into a cobra at night. She rushes to the guru for help. The evil guru tells her that she should get her son out of the way on the day of the snake festival, when he would come to their home and carry away the snake bride whom he needs for his own purposes. She is his lead to a *nagmani*, the mythical snake ruby supposedly found in the head of a rare *ichhadhari* cobra, whose possession will make him the most powerful man on earth.

Rajni, who knows of her mother-in-law's visit to the *tantrik*, seeks to dissuade her from seeking the guru's help. She tells Raju's mother that she has come to their home to love and protect the son and means the family no harm. In a series of flashbacks, she reminds Raju's mother of the day when her son was bitten by a snake on his sixth birthday. The boy was dead but was revived by the *tantrik* guru, who took out the snake's life and put in into Raju's body. The snake who thus died in return for the child's life was Rajni's husband and she had vowed revenge. But on seeing the closeness between mother and son, she had relented and decided on Raju as a husband. The frightened mother-in-law, however, chooses to follow the guru's wishes and on the day of *Naga-Panchami* sends Raju away from home on some pretext.

Now follows what has been popularly regarded as the movie's highlight: Rajni's 'snake dance.' Clad in saffron robes, a string of beads around his neck, the guru enters the hallway along with four of his similarly attired disciples. They start playing the *been*, the thick wooden flute pipes used by snake charmers, whose sound is supposed to be irresistible, drawing out snakes from the most hidden nooks and crannies. In an upstairs room we see Rajni dressed in a sequined, tightfitting white dress which emphasizes her large breasts and swelling hips. As the strains of the *been* come floating into the room, Rajni feels impelled towards the sound in a snake-like slithering movement. Her hands cupped over her head in a cobra's hood, she sashays down the spiral staircase. Dancing toward and away from the men, all jiggling breasts and writhing hips, the *been* of the men looming large over her body in close-ups and then retreating, the guru's face reflecting a cold, determined lust, Rajni is dancing her way into an apparently reluctant yet clearly willing sexual surrender. The spell is broken by the unexpected return of Raju who slaps his wife for her 'shameless' dancing. Rajni runs away to the ruins, followed by the guru who, in turn, is followed by a furious Raju. There is a long drawn-out fight between the two men, in which Raju's mother is killed while protecting her son. The guru is finally bitten by the cobra but before dying repents of his evil desires and prays to Shiva to release Rajni from her snake incarnation into a human one. The prayer is granted and both Raju and Rajni live happily ever after.

Nagina is, of course, also a traditional folk narrative, though with many additions and modifications to suit contemporary Indian conditions which encompass certain modern, essentially Western, elements. Just as many scholars claim that in India, in contrast to Europe, there are no hard and fast boundaries between folk and classical traditions, both of which share a common base and thus are different aspects of the same tradition rather than separate traditions,[12] similarly I believe Indian popular mass culture also cannot be clearly delimited from its folk and classical counterparts. Popular culture, too, exists in continuity, almost a flux, with other cultural forms, and a part of the same basic tradition to which it provides fresh subject matter and new impetuses.

The story of *Nagina* can be 'read' from many perspectives. A more sociological reading, for instance, will perhaps emphasize the critique of modernity implicit in the persona of the naive hero whose Western style rationality is utterly ignorant of the hidden mysteries of the occult realm accessible only to traditional knowledge. Our more psychological reading, though, focuses exclusively on the symbolic reverberations of the snake woman figure, both in the plot of the movie and in the larger tale of Indian gender relations.

Raju's first encounter with the snake woman already points in the direction we should look for her meaning. Singing of forgotten, that is, repressed memories in the ruins of the house where Raju had spent the first six years of his childhood and which he feels impelled to visit again and again, emerging from and retreating into mists of the past, the snake woman, I would suggest, incorporates a particular 'vision' of the mother from the earliest years of the boy's life. She is not a passive, long-suffering paragon of maternal love, which is the way the real mother is portrayed in the movie and the way 'Mother' is consciously perceived by men in most Indian narratives. A more unconscious construction, this mother is utterly sensual yet fiercely protective. She is both the seductive dancer and the hissing, spitting cobra fighting to protect the boy from all who would harm him. She is the desired mother of the six-year-old's wilful fantasy to whom a villainous father, in the shape of the guru, also lays sexual claim, and whose adult virility she can barely (and perhaps does not even want to) resist. Saved from the 'evil' designs of the man by the boy, she helps the son vanquish the father so that they can live blissfully united together in an age-old boyhood dream.

HUSBANDS AND OTHERS

To cynics, love, the core of gender relations, is the opiate of the privileged classes; its relevance for lives of the destitute, locked in a struggle for sheer survival, minimal. Suspicious of romanticism, old or new, they believe that the 'culture of poverty' (to use Oscar Lewis's telling phrase), generates its own compulsions in the very poor, which override the ideals, values, and prescriptions of the traditional culture of the society which in any case is preeminently an elite creation.

The following autobiographical accounts from the slums of Delhi try to give voice to the hopes, wishes, fantasies and conflicts of two women who belong to a group which is otherwise ignored and rarely heard from in the largely middle- and upper-class discourse on the relationship between the sexes. The self-narratives of Janak and Basanti are vibrant tales whose allusions and nuances can only be imperfectly conveyed in any English translation of their tape-recorded interviews. In narrating their first-person stories, my primary intent is to recreate a sense of the 'who' in the lives of two individual women enmeshed in a web of relationships. As an analyst who is also professionally aware of the fate that befalls an interrupter of tales, I would ideally have the reader fully enter Janak and Basanti's stories before I come in with my own interpretations. My endeavor is to guard against the reader's *experience* of the two women being prematurely foreclosed by *explanation*.

Yet going beyond their individual fates, the women's tales invariably also tell us something about gender relations in Indian lower-class life and in the culture of the larger society to which they both belong. Before letting them speak in their own voices, I shall abstract some of the features they share with other lower-class Indian women and compare them with other women, both in the higher strata of Indian society and in the urban slums of some other parts of the world.

Together with many others from the 'resettlement colony,' home to some of the poorest of the poor of Delhi, Janak and Basanti have a gift for self-description, even self-dramatization, once their initial mistrust of a stranger is replaced by a confidence in the stranger's empathic intentions. They are neither inarticulate nor does their language operate according to a 'restricted code' (as compared to a supposedly more 'elaborate' code of middle-and upper-class language) which is said to be the characteristic of lower class speech in the West.[2] Often crude **and vulgar** by middle-class standards, their language reflects accurately the women's animation and their utter involvement in the drama of their own lives. With a marked lack of preparation in utterance, there is yet a kind of zany fluency in the language which is liberally sprinkled with analogies, allusions, and proverbs from the dominant Hindu culture from which the women have not been separated by poverty. Thus when Janak, talking of what she swears are her husband's unjustified suspicions about her sexual morals, says 'I wished the earth would split open to swallow me,' she is referring to the well-known episode from the *Ramayana* where the epic's heroine, Sita, placed in a similar predicament, called upon her mother Earth, to open up and take her innocent daughter back into herself.

The culture penetrates many other areas of their lives. Janak and Basanti are not strangers to the rituals and the *vratas* (the ritual days of fasting) prescribed for Indian women, and have followed the Hindu blueprint for a woman's dealings with the supernatural, for instance, when one is possessed by a spirit or a goddess.

The stamp of the traditional culture is clearest in shaping their ideals of the 'good' woman, especially in relationship to a man. They share with women of the higher classes the feelings of being loved and approved of by a watchful inner sentinel when conforming to this ideal, and stabbings of guilt when they deviate, as sometimes they must. The 'good' woman, of course, is a daughter whose premarital chastity and steadfastness to the monogamous ideal in thought, word, and deed is the repository of her parental family's honor (*izzat*). The 'good' woman is naturally fertile, particularly in the matter of giving birth to all-important sons. Her failure in this regard can lead to banishment from hearth and home, a punishment which may be resented yet is also accepted as just for her betrayal of the ideal.

Above all, in the ideals of the traditional culture, the 'good' woman is a *pativrata*, subordinating her life to the husband's welfare and needs in a way demanded of no other woman in any other part of the world with which I am familiar. The *pativrata* conduct is not a mere matter of sexual fidelity, an issue of great importance in all patriarchal societies. We can understand the underlying male concerns when in the *Mahabharata*, the goddess Uma, laying down the guidelines of right conduct for women describes a *pativrata* as one, 'who does not cast her eyes upon the Moon or the Sun (both male in Hindu cosmology) or a tree that has a masculine name.' The goddess, however, goes further.

> Devotion to her lord is a woman's merit; it is her penance; it is
> her eternal heaven. Merit, penances, and Heaven become hers who
> looks upon her husband as her all in all, and who endowed with
> chastity, seeks to devote herself to her lord in all things. The
> husband is the god which women have. The husband is their
> friend. The husband is their high refuge. Women have no refuge
> that can compare with their husband, and no god that can compare

with him. The husband's grace and Heaven, are equal in the
estimation of a woman; or, if unequal, the inequality is very trivial.
O Maheshwara, I do not desire Heaven itself if thou are not
satisfied with me. If the husband that is poor or diseased or
distressed were to command the wife to accomplish anything that
is improper or unrighteous or that may lead to destruction of life
itself, the wife should without any hesitation accomplish it.[3]

This 'right conduct' for the wife, repeated over and over again in the major
repositories of the cultural tradition, builds a part of the Hindu woman's 'ideology
of the superego.' With varying degrees of intensity it cuts through all strata of
Indian society. The echoes of the *pativrata* wife will also be heard in the accounts
of women from the slums who often invoke the name of Sita, the personification
of the *pativrata* ideal, and allude to one or another episode of her mythological
life.

The problem, of course, is that unlike the spouse of most women in the
higher classes, the slum husband is apt to be shiftless. For all practical purposes,
the lower-class woman frequently finds herself abandoned and in charge of the
family even if her abandonment does not reach the degree and proportions met
with in the ghetto families of, say, New York. The imperatives of physical
protection, economic support, and the quieter need for male companionship lead
her to establish more or less permanent liaisons with other men. Such unions
and consensual marriages inevitably force cracks in her inner image of the good
woman, faithful to one man not only through this life but in all subsequent ones.
Sexual promiscuity is not a consolation or a compensation she readily permits
herself for her many deprivations, unlike her sisters from slums of some other
parts of the world. Like other Indian women, she too recoils from seeking a
sexual remedy for injuries inflicted by life.

The woman from the Delhi slum is like her counterparts in other slums of
the world in that there is a high degree of physical violence in her relationships
with men; mutual suspicions of sexual infidelity being the apparent cause for
frequent explosions. She, too, is more tolerant of hedonistic entrancements
(except those of sex) which make spontaneity and enjoyment still possible in the
daily grind for survival. She, too, has developed a fortitude and an ability to
cope with problems that would leave women from the middle-and-upper-classes
helpless.

Where she differs from women of other urban slums is in an enduring intimate
connection with the traditional culture in her inner life and in her close, tangible
ties with the natal family. Indeed, the support she receives from her parents,
brothers and sisters, would be the envy of other Indian women who are expected
to forego this source of aid and succour and deal with the exigencies of married
life on their own. Thus the slum woman rarely feels marginal, isolated, or
dependent, and only occasionally helpless.

Her connectedness to the cultural tradition and the family also help in shielding her from the realities of her situation when these become too grim. It provides her raw material for fantasy in her poignant yet determined struggle to maintain self-respect as a 'good' woman. One major fantasy, protecting her from feelings of depression and rage, is of the heroine, battered by fate and men, finally triumphing both through her suffering and her commitment to virtue. In the last act which fantasy obligingly conjures up on her inner screen, the man will be abjectly contrite as he realizes her true worth, his brutishness transformed into adoration. The grown-up children, mindful of the mother's sacrifices on their behalf, will be devoted to her needs and welfare. And in the heavenly aisles the gods, no longer indifferent, will give her a standing ovation as they shower her with flowers and looks of pride.

[The translations of the following narratives are my own.]

Janak

We have lived in Madangir since the last 17-18 years. Earlier we stayed in Gandhinagar. We were three sisters and two brothers. After coming to Delhi from Pakistan as refugees we stayed with relatives. My father was very poor. We ate two *rotis* (North Indian bread) in the evening and then went to sleep. There was never a third one. When we sisters wore clothes or plaited our hair, people used to say, 'There father is so poor. Where do they get money for clothes?' We wore clothes only when someone gave us old ones. My father was mostly unemployed. I was the eldest child in the house. When my father came home in the evening he was always in a bad state. My heart ached for him. The other sisters did not care.

When I was in the tenth class in school, a man used to visit our house. I asked him to get me a job as a village welfare worker. (I have never told this to anyone before but am telling you now.) He said he would do it. This man used to deal in girls from an office in front of the Irwin Hospital. I was clever and alert from the very beginning. He took me to the office and around seven in the evening brought me to a deserted spot in Shahadra where there is now a cremation ground. God saved me. The man said, 'Take off your clothes.' I took off my new sandals which I had got from Lucknow. Then I said to him, 'I will take my clothes off'. I had to trick him. I said, 'Step back a little, so I can strip without shame.' He thought he had trapped me. I untied the string of my trousers, dropped them and ran. Wearing just a shirt I came back home naked, but he had not succeeded in touching me. I cried and cried. My parent's honour was almost plundered that day and it was only God who gave me the strength to save it. The man brought my sandals and my trousers back because he knew my father was poor. My parents collapsed on the floor. In those days I kept all the *vratas*—

and went to the temple every day.

For the training as a village welfare worker, I went to Durgapur near Simla. I did not even have a uniform. A contractor I had come to know said he would buy me one. But his eye was evil. Look, if a person is poor then everyone looks at her with bad intentions. He brought me two saris, a pair of shoes, and blouses. I had to travel alone that night. The contractor asked me to marry him because his wife was not a good woman. I told him. 'I have called you "brother" so I cannot look at you in that way.' Then I got on the train but felt sad during the whole journey.

I wanted to help my father financially. I felt homesick in Durgapur. I contracted smallpox and my skin erupted with boils. After a year I came back home. Mother had taken to bed. The other sisters did not look after her, so after returning I got her treated. I was very fond of my brother and sisters. I would have liked them to be educated but they wanted to take the evil path. The parents were respectable people, but the children betrayed their trust.

Now I am 50 years old. I was 17 when I was married to Premnath in Gandhinagar. He is a distant relative and in those days he was in the army in Allahabad. Once when he visited our home my father asked him to look me up in the village near Nainital since I was living alone in foreign parts. When he finally found me I welcomed him with great respect. His looks changed then. He thought he'd be happy if he could marry me. Such a thought never entered my head. Then he went back to Allahabad and wrote me a letter, asking me to marry him. But I said this was not possible since we were related.

Should I tell you the truth? I went to Allahabad to meet him. When he came to the station to see me off he cried and cried. He was very handsome in those days and I like handsome men. His complexion was fair and he spoke so sweetly and softly that if a third person was sitting nearby he couldn't make out what the man was saying. He had so much politeness. I forgot everything after meeting him. I said to myself that I must have him for my very own. His mother had died when he was a child. He wept often, saying he had no one. I forgot everything after seeing his loneliness. I did not see any of his inner qualities. I thought about him day and night. We both used to write verses and songs to each other in our letters. We said we couldn't live without each other.

When I came home for a vacation I told my mother about him. He took leave from his job and came to our house one day and just sat there. He said if he couldn't get married to me he would knife everyone. My father took off his turban and placed it on my feet and said 'Child, keep my honour and refuse him. He is a very bad man. He will ruin your life.' I said 'No, if he is a bad person then it is in my hands to make him good.' I said to my father, 'So what if he kills me! You'll carry my corpse to the cremation ground on your shoulders.' My father married me off but when I was about to leave home he hid himself. He said, 'She has done this against my will, she has not listened to me. I will not see her when she leaves. She was the one who was my son, but she has now betrayed me.' So my *doli** went to my sister's house since my husband had no money for us to go anywhere else.

When he left me to go to Allahabad he promised to send money. My parents began to hate him. They said he has got married and left his wife which is a matter of great dishonour. So they also harassed me. I wrote him a worried letter and without letting him know came to Allahabad. We took a room from one of his friends and spent a very good year. We were together all the time: I never slept alone for even one night. Then I became pregnant. My health worsened. The vomiting would not stop. So in the eighth month he brought me back to my mother. My baby was about five weeks old when he ran away from the army but said that he had come on leave. One day passed, two days passed. Whenever the girl cried he would say, 'Come, let's throw her into the Jamuna river. Throw the sister-fucker into the river!' Neither the child nor I had anything to eat. At home the parents would say, 'What was the great pleasure in getting married when there is no money. He is nothing but a naked, starving beggar!' I could not tolerate this and so we shifted to my sister's shanty in Link Road. We got a hut of our own but did not have enough money even for milk for the child. By this time he had started beating me with a whip.

The baby became very weak and died when it was four months old. We brought her to Irwin Hospital and they put four bottles of glucose into her but she could not be saved and died by the morning. He began to be upset with our lack of money. I would tell him, 'I will always be with you. I have left my parents, I have left my brothers and sisters, left all my relatives, I am with you.' Then my sister got him a job in Eros Cinema for a hundred rupees a month.

One night what happens is that he has gone to the cinema. Taking my younger sister—she died sometime ago—we looked for him the whole night. When he came home at four in the morning he was drunk. I said to him, 'Listen, I searched for you the whole night.' He did not say anything. He took off his boots and hit me hard with one of them. Four, five times, on the head. Who was I to question him if he had been with a woman! When a man's character goes bad he will always hit the woman. He locked me in the hut and went off. The same day the police came to demolish our huts. They loaded us and our belongings in trucks and threw us out here in Madangir which was then just an empty, dusty plain. I was alone. When my brothers came to know, they came looking for me. They asked what had happened. I told them that their brother-in-law had left me. They spent the whole day clearing up a space, digging foundations, making a hut for me.

Eventually, he came back. Everyday he would harass me, beat me. By this time I had another child, almost 15 months old. He would take a knife out in front of the child and say that he'd kill me. My mother often said, 'Leave him,

---

*The groom's carrying away of the bride from her father's home in a ritual procession.

his character is bad. You will weep your whole life.' But I said, 'No, I have taken hold of his hand. He is my consort. You may all leave me but I shall never leave him.' He made scenes. Abuses, beatings, staying away from home. When I was sick he'd never ask whether I needed a cup of tea or milk. He'd often say, 'I will throw you down the roof.' But he is my husband. And then my son died when he was a year and a half old.

You know, when I was a child my father told me many stories. Two of these stories have stayed in my mind. In a village the daughter of a brahmin and the son of another brahmin loved each other. The brahmin boy asked the girl to run away with him and one night they took off. On the way they stopped to rest in the veranda of a house. Two thieves who had just robbed a house came to the place where the couple was sleeping. They were followed by the villagers who cornered them in the veranda. The villagers asked the girl which one was her husband. The brahmin boy was a weakling while one of the thieves was a strong and handsome young man. Besides, he also had money and jewellery. The girl did not take a moment to change her mind. Ignoring the brahmin boy, she identified the thief as her husband and went away with him. On the way they came to a river and wondered how to cross it. The thief said, 'Let me first go and leave the bag on the other side and then I will come back and carry you across.' When he reached the other shore the girl called him to come back and take her with him. He said 'When after choosing a man you left him so easily, how can I trust you to stay with me?' So my father told that a woman belongs to one man only. If she is going to get happiness then it is only from him, never from someone else. A husband is God.

Another story I liked a great deal is about a king who had five daughters. he made them sit in a row and asked, 'Who gives you the food you eat?' All the daughters except one said, 'Father, you give us the food.' The fifth daughter said, 'Father, I eat what is given by God, what is given by my *karma*.' The king was furious. He called a leper, bleeding from his sores, married this daughter to him and turned her out of the palace in rags. While leaving the girl said, 'O Father! This is the husband of my *karma*—this husband is my god!'

She began begging to feed her husband, patiently broke pieces of bread and put them in his mouth. He would ask her not to waste her youth on him and to marry someone else. 'God has made me to serve you,' she always replied. One day, leaving him in the jungle, she went off to the town to beg. A bird came and sat on the tree under which the leper was resting. The bird said to the leper, 'My prince, there is a pond nearby. If you bathe in its waters your leprosy will disappear.' The man dragged himself to the pond and put one leg in the water. It was cured instantly. He put in another leg which also became clear of all disfigurement. he dipped his whole body and came out clean, like a golden king. When the girl came back, she did not believe this handsome man was her husband. He convinced her by putting his little finger, which had not touched the water earlier, in the pond and showing her that it had become clean. The bird came again and said 'If you boil two cans of oil and put the oil in the pond, the water will part and you will find at the bottom treasures buried by ten kings.' The couple followed the bird's instructions and built a big palace for themselves from the gold and the gems.

One day the husband said to the wife, 'We must call your father for dinner'. When the king came the daughter served him, wearing a new dress and jewellery with every dish. When the king finished eating she came out with the rags in which her father had turned her out. She then presented her husband to him and said, 'These are the clothes you gave me and you have seen the clothes given by my *karma*. You gave me a leper for my husband and this is the man *karma* has given me.'

Look, no one can erase even one line of what *karma* has written down in your book. My man could not be mine. I do not understand why. But my lack of understanding does not mean that I should leave good *dharmic* (according to the law) thoughts and embrace bad ones. You can get peace only from your own man, not from others.

We had been hiding in shanties for five years while the warrants for his arrest for desertion from the army were out. One day, finally, the police came and took him away to Banga in Punjab. I followed him to the police station, crying all the way. They took him to jail in the military cantonment in Jullundhar. I stayed there for 21 days and went to see him each day. He would abuse me every time I came and I would cry.

I love him. I love him so much that mother-father, sisters-brothers, the whole world was of less worth to me than my man. I could not leave him. I said if he is sent far away from me I will die. They gave him a three-month sentence and took him to Lucknow jail. I came back to Delhi. The house was lying unattended and there was a child in my womb. My husband was jailed for three months. When he came back I was delivered of a boy. He had been given 350 rupees by the army which we spent on the baby, but he died.

Afterward, the same story started all over again. Drinking, beating, filthy abuses, suspicions. He would say 'Why does this man come, why does that one come?' I'd answer. 'I have given up everyone for you. I have given you my all, don't accuse me falsely.' He'd pick up sticks, take out knives, and I would keep silent out of fear.

Then I gave birth to four daughters, one after another. After the fourth daughter he did not even let me rest. The third day after I gave birth he sent me to work in the kitchen. He had not let anyone from my family come and help me at the time of delivery. When the fifth child was about to come I said, 'God, give me a son otherwise this man won't let me live.' But those whose habits are bad do not change even if they have ten sons!

Gradually, we built a small house in Mehrauli and shifted there with our five daughters. I thought perhaps being among good people he might change. We also kept our hut in Madangir. But his habits worsened. He would beat me and tell me to get out of the house. But I thought of the future of my daughters, of their marriages. If I left the house, people would say I was a bad woman who has run off with a lover. There was a woman who lived next to us in Mehrauli. She did some black magic which made my eldest daughter very sick. I went to all the hospitals. Then someone sent me to the *baba* (holy man) of the Mehrauli tomb. Baba asked me not to worry and gave me some water in a bottle. The water cured my daughter. Baba also intimated that the neighbouring woman had been responsible for the illness. So I talked my husband not to visit her. She turned him completely against me. She would make him drink and tell him that in this absence other men visited me.

One night, coming home drunk, he really wanted to kill me. With the children in tow I climbed up the rear wall and hid in a neighbour's house while he was out in the street looking for us with a drawn knife. We ran barefoot through the jungle at night and came to my sister's house. In the morning I went to the police station and got them to write down that I have left with my five daughters and nothing else so that he does not accuse me of theft. The next day I sent word to him through my sister's daughter. He told her in front of everyone that I should send our daughters out on the street, earn money by making them whores. I went to Eros Cinema, where he worked, and asked him why he was making such a spectacle out of his family. He started beating me in front of a big crowd till my body was blue with bruises. But I did not fall down. When some taxi drivers intervened to save me, he ran away. We came back to Madangir and I started working. He would turn up every other day and abuse all of us 'Sister-fuckers, whores, bastards, even prostitutes are better than you. Go and do your work in the streets.' He called me such filthy names that I wished the earth would split open and take me in. After three months we all returned to Mehrauli.

Someone stole a lot of money from the cinema theatre where he worked. He was also implicated in the theft, lost his job, and was arrested. I spent all my money running from one court to another, hiring a lawyer, finding the jail he was in and arranging bail. When they released him all he said was 'Bitch, why did you spend all that money?'

My brother, my sister, and her children came to visit us. I cried a lot that day for my own sister betrayed me. I cannot bear to tell you. When a man becomes bad, women take advantage of him. First they asked me to cook for them and then I served them liquor. I also drank some but then went to sleep. Only heaven knows what he did that night. Three bottles of liquor had been consumed. My daughter woke up in the night and she saw my husband and my sister doing the work that is done between man and woman. My whole body trembled. I said to myself. 'Now my house is ruined.'

I told my mother She is a frank woman and cannot tolerate any harm done to me. She went to my sister's house. 'Why are you destroying that poor woman's home?' she said to her. When my sister discovered that I knew, she came to meet me. I did not say anything. I did not want to create a scene in front of the whole world. My sister only said, 'Brother-in-law gave me some *roti* to eat and exacted its price.'

Look, when a man is drunk, he does not distinguish between his wife, sister or even mother. He will fuck even his mother. When he came home in the evening I abused him roundly. I said 'She may be my sister, she may be anyone. But if that woman crosses the threshold of my house, I will set her on fire and also burn myself.'

One day he called me for 'business' and when I took off my clothes, he said, 'You can now get out of the house.' I felt so humiliated. If I had had a tin of kerosene in front of me that night. I would have set myself on fire.

Look, there is one kind of love which makes the woman blind and lose her senses. There is another kind of love which is true and yet another which is false. A woman understands everything about the differences in the kinds of love. The woman may not speak but she understands. True love has a lot of *rasa* (literally 'juice,' 'flavor'). False love is dry. The third one makes the woman blind so that she does not ask which other woman her man visits. These are the three kinds of love. He used to call me to bed once in ten or 15 days only to make me blind.

Look, I didn't want him to feel any lack in love. If he called me 20 times, I went to him 20 times. If he called me ten times, I went ten times. A man goes out of the house only if he is not getting enough. So I never let him remain hungry. In the early days of the marriage he used to call me two to four times a day.

I drink sometimes. Liquor intoxicates in many ways. I am talking about myself. When a woman drinks she needs a man. Every woman will say that. She wants new men. It is natural to feel that way. My husband had no idea of intercourse in the beginning. He didn't even know about a woman's monthly periods. I taught him everything. I had such strength that even if he called me to bed 20 times it was too little for me. Now he has ruined my body. When I walked people used to say, 'There comes the police inspector!' But the strength is gone now. Well, the strength is still there and will come out if he does not abuse me and shares his life with me. If he'd still love me I would forget everything. Earlier he used to call me 'wrestler' and then he called me 'head woman.' Now it has come down to 'bitch,' 'whore,' and *'badmash'* (bad character). Once when he came home early and I was not there, for I had to attend a programme of religious singing in our alley, he took out two tins of kerosene and said, 'Before burning yourself arrange to have the news brought to me in the cinema. I will come to throw your corpse away.'

Then one day he went to work and met with an accident on the way. My sister's son brought him back, all bandaged and stitched. When I saw him I forgot all the woe he had caused me. My heart ached for him. I had eaten his salt and was true to him. When I brought him milk, he said, 'Sister-fucker, go and give the milk to your parents to drink.' Still in bandages, he went to work the next day and brought back papers for divorce. He told me to sign them. I said 'First get well and then get the divorce.' The children and I came back to Madangir. He stayed away for 12 days and then came home.

None of my wishes have been fulfilled. Before marriage I thought I will wear nice clothes and jewels and most of all that I will get love. I thought if our two hearts met and became one we could cross the span of this life together. For the first few years I kept the *vrata* of *Karwachauth* (a day of fasting by married women for the welfare of their husbands). He said, 'Why are you making this show? Why are you playing a role in a drama?' I said, 'I have true love for you in my heart.' How he has made me suffer!

They say there was once a bad man. People asked him why good men die but the bad ones don't. He replied that God doesn't take bad men because He knows that in heaven too the bad men will bring their filth in. See, Sita also suffered under great cruelties but she passed her time on earth for the love of one man. I too tolerated everything because I loved him. I couldn't live without him even if he abused me thousands of times. But a man who abuses and beats you in public, why should I love him? Now my love is slowly dying from inside. I only think of the children. He doesn't even know in which class the children are studying or whether they even go to school. In fact he now has his eyes on our third daughter who has just turned 14 and I have to watch him carefully.

My health has been affected and my heart it affected. Sometimes I become mad. If a woman can talk then she remains sane, otherwise there is something inside her which keeps on pressing. By talking one can take the pressure out. I often talk to myself or start talking in front of children in the alley. Once in a while my children call me mad. In spite of all this I don't get angry. The children say, 'Mother, you are made of stone.' Despite saying all the filthy things to me over the years, he too has been defeated. But I have no anger. If he can get women from outside, we can also get other men. But to do so goes against my *dharma* and when I die only my *dharma* will go with me. They say that the man who spits on the sun gets the spit back on his own face. So he is the one whose face will be smeared with spittle. The love of a man and a woman is very strange. No one can give woman the love which a man can. A woman who loves a man from inside is hungry only for him. Now I would like to renounce the world and go away to a forest. I have hopes in my children but perhaps like my mother no one will care for me. It would have been better if I had married a blind man. At least I could have served him, been rewarded for performing good deeds. What did I get marrying someone with eyes—ruin, filth, and abuse.

Basanti

Before marriage, I lived happily with my parents in our village in Bihar. We were three brothers and three sisters. A brother was the eldest and I was the next in line. Two brothers and a sister are still unmarried.

I got along well with my parents but I loved my father best. I did all his work. Mother used to beat me. The whole day she abused me because I did not work and was busy playing. Two or three times a week I would get beaten by her. Because a mother teaches you to work, she also hits you more. I don't remember my childhood much except that I was happy, laughing even after being abused. We all loved each other but didn't talk much. I remember the festivals we celebrated. On *Holi* (the spring festival of colours) we worshipped liquor. We made liquor from rice then put it in a brass dish with some *sal* leaves, worshipped it and then drank it. We also worshipped a chicken. We took out its blood and drank one drop. Everyone fasted for two to three days and then ate and drank. Then there was the worship of Kali (the fierce mother goddess) every year. Two days we fasted and the goddess would enter one of the women. While the goddess was in her no one went near her, not even her own children. Afterwards, we would go to the temple, offer milk, water and flowers for her worship and then bathe. But ever since I came to Delhi I left all the rituals because I took the wrong path. Every year we also went to see the play about Rama and Sita though I did not understand it much. Now I go to see it only because of the children.

When I became mature my parents married me off at 15. After marriage I went to live in Calcutta with my husband. We spent a very happy six years. I stayed at home while he worked. My husband treated me well and we did not lack anything. He talked lovingly to me and we laughed a lot. Twice a night we did 'work.' In the beginning it was very painful, but then I liked it. We slept apart only at the times of my period. At those times he would not even take water from my hands. Before sleeping we would drink, chew *pan* (betel leaf) and smoke cigarettes.

I was young in years and perhaps that is why I could not conceive. When the body is ready, the child too comes. After a while, I fell sick. There were dizzy spells, bouts of fever, and I became as thin as a stick. I couldn't even walk and my hearing was affected. I went to the doctor, daily drank coconut water for four months, and didn't eat. Perhaps Calcutta's water did not suit me. But because we were both so happy, even the fact that I couldn't conceive did not bother us. I thought, we two beings are together in a foreign land and when I get well we will go back to the village and perhaps it will happen there.

After returning to the village, I was quite unhappy. We sold our fields. He earned money by working as a labourer, and I supplemented the income by making and selling rice liquor. When I did not get a child he said there was no point in his keeping me. I said to him, 'Only God can help us. If we don't have a child what can I do? Let's wait another four, five years.' He started talking like this seven years after marriage. When my sister-in-law came to visit us she said, 'Why are you sad? When God is ready to give you a child, he will do so.' I said, 'But your brother has to understand this. Otherwise how will I live in his house?' Then my husband together with my mother-in-law stopped giving me food. I would also be beateen My body became black and blue, with swellings and scars all over it. My husband would kick me and hit me with a stick.

He then said to me, 'If you want to stay in my house you can do so, but only if you get me married for a second time.' I said, 'I will get you married but then I won't stay here. I will only get unhappiness. When you beat me so much now how can you treat me well after your second marriage?' He said he would keep his word. 'You can live here in comfort and I will marry again.' I gave him 500 rupees of my own, three dresses and got him married. Though we all lived together for two years I was not happy. My husband slept between the two of us. Sometimes he would love one woman and sometimes the other.

One day he said, 'Leave the house. I don't want to keep you.' I walked off to commit suicide by throwing myself under a train. A boy from the village stopped me and said, 'Why do you want to die? You are still young and all your limbs are strong and healthy. Why die?' I said, 'I have no one now in this world. So why should I live?' When my husband heard about this he came immediately. I was sitting under a tree and he asked me to come home. I said 'You drink liquor every day, you beat me. I won't go back with you.' The other wife said, 'Elder sister, if you won't stay then I will also leave the house. I will go anywhere, go away with any man, beg for my food but you should not leave. I would be very unhappy if you left.'

My mother-in-law was a very bad. woman. She would hit and kick me. She'd snatch away bread from me. When my man gave me a *roti* she would say, 'Why are you giving her food? Don't give her anything to eat.' When a-person gets very unhappy only then does she leave her home. I was dejected that I was not conceiving and my man was also unhappy because of this, so I decided to go away. But before leaving, I broke everything in the house in my anger. I destroyed everything. I said 'You want to destroy my home. So there! I will do it myself!' Before leaving I did not even take the 3000 rupees I had saved up. The other wife found it in the rice storage bin after I left. Afterwards, my husband would admiringly say to others, 'How did she save so much money though we had so little!' He also said of me that she is very wise and he cannot understand why I broke everything and ran away.

Then my parents said, 'You shouldn't worry. Earn for yourself. Take it easy and go wherever fate takes you. Go to the festivals, go to see the dances.' But when the *jodi* (pair) is broken, how can one be happy! I was constantly with the women in the household and traded in rice like a merchant. Then I thought, 'What happiness do I get in my parents' home?' When the brothers marry and bring their wives they might not want to keep me any longer! I told my father, 'While you are alive I will work and use up all my strength. But when you die

I will be feeble and no one will look after me. If had a son or a daughter it might have been all right, but otherwise there will be no one to ask about my welfare.' So I decided to come to Delhi because two of my brothers and a sister were already in this city. I came with a group of 30 to 40 men and women who were coming to work on construction sites. My father put me on the train.

After reaching Delhi I stayed with my brothers and sister in Sultanpur and began to work as a sweeper. There I met my second husband, who was a contractor and who gave my father 1500 rupees to marry me. After marriage, Mannu's father (the second husband) said, 'I have made a mistake in getting married. But don't be afraid, I will look after your needs till the end.' His wife had died six years ago and he had children. Because his children objected, he told me to stay separately by myself. I said, 'Fine, but you should keep on meeting me sometimes.' Now his children are grown up and even they come to visit me. I tell my husband, 'Do whatever you like. Keep another wife. Just provide me with food.' But now he doesn't give me anything.

I work and earn myself. I have three children, two boys and a girl. My sister's two children are also with me because she is dead. Sometimes my mind tells me to marry again. My brother-in-law says he will take his children away. I say, 'Let them be with me. Listen to me, otherwise you will regret it. Earn here and feed them here.' Now we are going to fight the case of my sister because she was murdered. I used to be visited by the Goddess but I passed Her on to my sister because it exhausted me. The Goddess has now gone into the murderer. When the Goddess used to come into me my whole body would tremble. Now I am often sick. To take care of the visits of the Goddess one has to do a lot of things like not touching dirty utensils, cleaning the hut immediately with cowdung and so on. I cannot serve her now. I have to earn my living. As long as I am alive I will earn, feed the children, and when there are difficulties we will see what happens.

At the time of marriage I had no worry. God had created a good pair from the two of us. No old people to interfere. But when I think of the mistake he made by turning me out I feel my heart collapsing. How well I lived! Now I live in a shanty. God knows what will happen though I have stopped believing in Him. I don't know whether I will be happy or unhappy; whether I will get happiness when the children grow up. But for now they have to be sent to school.

There is no profit in getting married, no advantage at all. When the children grow up, at least they will say she has brought us up by working so hard. People and relatives tell me to marry, but I don't want to extend my hand to anyone anymore. I don't want to go anywhere. Wherever there is a place for me I will stay.

I sometimes think that Mannu's father is old and about to die. I also feel ashamed to be with him. Mannu's father also beat me once. He said, 'You talk to other men.' I said, 'When someone asks about my welfare then I have to reply. And then you make me unhappy. If you kept me happy I would not talk to other men.' He kept quiet. I don't say any of this to my brothers and sisters because his honour would be smirched. I tell them that we live well, eat, and drink. For three years he hasn't given me anything. Not even a rag. Only for the children did he once take out a hundred rupees. I said, 'If these are your children get clothes for them.' So he brought them some rotten stuff.

I often don't remember my earlier married life. I am quite alone. No fucker cares for me. I only think of the children and get some happiness from them. Or occasionally my family members come for a visit, and we laugh and joke together and I get some happiness that way. Relatives bring me peace.

I have thought of drowning myself, but then think of the children. Sometimes I cry inside myself. I don't want to quarrel with anyone but if someone says untrue things about me I get into a rage. Here when people say that I'm a whore, that when working in the bungalows I get fucked in the ass, then I get furious. Where do I have the time for all that stuff? I don't even have time to sit.

There is another thing which makes me angry. This is the matter of love. There is a man here who must have given me some kind of potion to drink, which has trapped me in his love. I thought of him as a brother but then he did the bad work with me. If he still loved me, it would have been fine. But he neither talks to me nor wants me to talk to anyone else. He doesn't even talk to the children anymore. I feel so unhappy, and even the heart can stop beating with so much pain.

He doesn't talk to me because of that milk (seller) woman. 'If you have done that mistake with me then I will go with you,' I say. I won't marry him, but I won't let him get away from me. He is scared so he doesn't come. For six years he kept me, but now he doesn't care anymore. My husband knows about it. He says I am a young woman and he doesn't mind. Earlier, my lover looked after me well. Whenever he needed me at night, he took me to his hut. The children also called him 'papa.' But now he says he'll watch me from afar and that I shouldn't joke around with other men. He would have had an affair with the milk woman but I came between them. I told him that if he'd so much as touched her, I'd skin him alive. One day I saw them together. I pulled him away and took out my sandal to hit him. I said, 'We have been lovers for six years but I have never taken out my sandal to hit you. But today you must decide. Tell me what is you relationship with this woman, otherwise I will beat you. You have ruined my life and I shall not spare you.'

There were four or five other men standing there. The milk woman called me a whore. Then she kept quiet and I too calmed down. But from inside I feel a great anger. When I fight with him I feel a little relieved, but what can I do? If my pair (*jodi*) had not broken up I wouldn't be in this situation. I have gone from one man to another and ended up by loving three men. Now I shall never love or marry again. I'll earn and bring up my children. My daughter is maturing and I have to arrange her marriage. I have to save money for that . . . . But love causes me sadness from within. they say when insects burn in the forest everyone can see, but when one's heart is burning no one comes to know of it. I cannot even go to the temple because I have taken the wrong path. In our area they don't let women get on the wrong track. She may not talk unnecessarily even to her relatives. As long as she is unmarried she has some freedom, but after marriage she can only go with her husband. She may not talk to other men. I have come away from all that and so I am suffering.

The squalor of slum life, as the narratives of Janak and Basanti reveal, does nothing to dim the luminosity of their romantic longing. On the contrary, the abysmal material conditions and the struggle against poverty arouses their 'sense of life according to love' to its fullest wakefulness. The dream of the transforming power of love, of what the woman might have been if she were well and truly loved, is tenaciously clung to amidst (and perhaps because of) all the suffering and pathos of her existence.

The central image of this dream is of the *jodi*, the pair. The pair, of coure, exerts a universally powerful pull on human imagination. To adopt Dostoevsky's observation on the lover's vision, in the pair we may sometimes see the other, and ourselves, as God might have done so. In Janak and Basanti's fantasy of the pair, there are echoes of another universal myth: of the philandering husband, and the abandoned wife faithfully preserving the sanctity of the marriage bed. Its Indian versions have tales of Parvati's anger and jealousy as Shiva continues on a path of unremitting seduction; of Radha alternately wrathful and pining away in solitude while Krishna dallies with other *gopis* (cow herdesses). Indeed, Jungians will see in the women's yearning for containment in a couple a manifestation of the 'pairing instinct' which they would ascribe to the feminine aspects of the soul.[4] The women's pain, rage, jealousy, vengefulness and despair are then aroused less by the fact of the man's infidelity than in his denying her fulfilment of the need for completion in the pair.

Freudians, on the other hand, would try to pinpoint individual, life-historical needs in the woman's (or the man's) fantasy of the couple. The partner, according to Freud's view of what he called 'object choice,' is a replacement for an earlier counterplayer from infancy—usually the father, mother, or a sibling—who will compensate for the loss, disillusionment, and pain experienced in the earlier wishful pairing. The partner in the couple may thus fulfil one or more of a variety of needs. He may provide nutrients for the woman's sense of the self through his 'mirroring' of her, reflecting back with favour and with a confirming glow in his eyes all her acts of relationship. He may, on the other hand, be an incorporation of the idealized Other in whom the woman seeks to merge, hoping therein to find a way to build cohesiveness and strength into her own self. The man can also be needed as a container for all the despised and disavowed aspects of the self. He may thus be an incarnation of the woman's negative identity—of all she fears she might be (or become) but dares not acknowledge. Here the partner can either be the repository of the woman's unacceptable sexual or aggressive impulses, living out her 'wickedness,' which then allows her to keep her 'goodness' and 'purity' intact, or, he may take over the weaker part of her self; the woman can then afford to be strong and energetic as long as her hidden conviction that she is their opposite, finds an expression in the man's manifestation of weakness and passivity.

I have little doubt that one or another or many of the Jungian and Freudian motivations also go into the construction of Janak and Basanti's dream of the *jodi*. Yet besides universal archetypes and individual fantasies, I believe there is also a cultural image which comes through sharply in the woman's yearning for the couple. Iconically, this cultural image is represented by the *ardhanarishwara*—'the Lord that is half woman'—from of the God Shiva. Displaying the attributes of both the sexes, with the right side male and the left female, this form of the god shows his body merged with that of his consort, Uma and Parvati.

The *ardhanarishwara* then represents the wished-for oneness of the divine couple rather than the twoness of mortal spouses. The husband is not simply a partner, however intimate, for that would still highlight his separate, bounded, individuality. Instead, the cultural ideal visualizes the *jodi* as a single two-person entity.

Perhaps the psychological concept that comes closest to representing the woman's ideal in marriage is what the psychoanalyst Heinz Kohut has called the 'selfobject.'[5] A seemingly odd apparition, a selfobject neither coincides with the contours of the self nor is unreservedly the other but leads a nomadic existence in the intermediate space between the two. According to Kohut, the selfobjects of early childhood, of which the parental caretakers are the foremost, constitute the stuff of the self through a process of 'transmuting internalization.' In adult life, they provide the self with its vital nutrients.

The *jodi*, then, is a 'cultural selfobject'—making a Hindu invoke Sita Ram and not Sita *and* Ram—Radhakrishna and not Radha *and* Krishna—which connects the woman to the community of Indian women and thus helps to maintain the vitality and continuity of her identity. Despite the realities of life in the slums, of wife-beating husbands and reluctant lovers, of adulterous liaisons and consensual marriages, it is the contribution of this ideal to maintaining a sense of the self which helps us to understand the tenacity with which Janak and Basanti, as also women from other strata of Indian society, cling to the notion of the indissolubility of the couple. The persistence and importance of the *jodi* for the woman's sense of identity helps us comprehend better why many women, in spite of their economic independence, choose to suffer humiliation rather than leave an oppressive husband; why some women, in times of extreme marital stress and a burning rage toward the spouse, exercise the option of suicide rather than separation.

GANDHI AND WOMEN

Continuing my search for facets of the man-woman relationship in India, I turn to the autobiographical writings of one of the greatest men of the 20th century. Although my task of psychoanalytic deconstruction, the activity of taking a text apart by bringing out its latent meanings, remains the same, Gandhi's fame and status as a culture hero makes this enterprise both easier and more difficult.

The task is easier in that the retrospective narrative enrichment engaged in by every autobiographer—who consciously or otherwise selects and orders details of his life so as to create a coherent and satisfying story, explaining and indeed justifying his present situation for the particular audience he has in mind—is capable of correction and modification through the accounts of other actors involved in the hero's epic.[1] The inconsistencies and the omission of vital details which may otherwise mar the symmetry of the hero's unconscious myth about himself, are easier to detect in the case of a man like Gandhi who has attracted so much biographical attention, both contemporary and posthumous. I may, though, add here that Gandhi's autobiographical writings, *The Story of My Experiments With Truth* the foremost among them, are marked by a candour and honesty which, if not unique, are certainly rare in the annals of self-narration. In his quasi-mystical preoccupation with 'truth,' the blame for any distortions in the story of his self-revelation can be safely laid at the door of the narrator's unconscious purposes rather than ascribed to any deliberate efforts at omission or concealment.

The work of deconstruction is made more difficult as Gandhi is the foremost culture-hero of modern India. For an Indian child, the faces of Gandhi and other heroes like Nehru and Vivekananda are identical, with the masks crafted by the culture in order to provide ideals for emulation and identification. Every child in India has been exposed to stock narratives that celebrate their genius and greatness, the portraits utterly devoid of any normal human blemish such as envy, anger, lust, ordinariness, pettiness, or stupidity. The Indian analyst, also a child of his culture, is thus bound to have a special kind of 'counter-transference' towards the culture-hero as a biographical subject. In other words, the analytic stance of respectful empathy combined with critical detachment, difficult enough to maintain in normal circumstances, becomes especially so in the case of a man like Gandhi. His image is apt to merge with other idealized figures from the biographer's own past, who were loved and admired yet secretly rebelled against. The analytic stance must then be charted out between contradictory hagiographic and pathographic impulses that seek constantly to buffet it.

For the analyst, the story of a man's relationship with women inevitably begins ('and also ends,' sceptics would add) with his mother. Yet we know the mother-son dyad to be the most elusive of all human relationships. Located in the life space before the birth of languge, the effort to recapture the truth of the dyad through words alone can give but teasing intimations of the hallucinatory intensity of a period when the mother, after giving the son life, also gave him the world. With some exceptions, like that of Nabokov, a mother cannot speak to her son through memory alone.[2] *Her* truth lies in the conjunction, indeed confabulation of imagination, symbols and reality through which she was earlier perceived and through which she may be later conjured, the latter being a rare artist's gift. For others, including Gandhi, the truth of the dyad we once built with our mothers is but fragmentarily glimpsed in various maternal proxies—from inanimate objects ('part' or 'transitional' objects in analytic parlance) which a child endows with her vital spirit, to the woman who will later attract and hold him. Like all mothers, Putlibai, whose favourite Gandhi was by virtue of his being the youngest child and whose special object of care and concern he remained because of his sickly constitution, is an abiding yet diffuse presence in her son's inner life, an intensely luminous being albeit lacking definition. We will discover her chimerical presence in Gandhi's relationships with various other women in whom she was temporarily reincarnated, his wife Kasturbai the foremost among them.

In his autobiography, written over a five-year period during his mid-50s, Gandhi begins the account of his sexual preoccupations and struggles with his marriage at the age of thirteen. He had been betrothed to Kasturbai Nakanji, the daughter of a well-to-do merchant in his hometown of Porbandar, since they were both seven years old. Now, with the two children entering puberty, the families decided that the time for the nuptials had finally arrived.

In Kathiawar, on the west coast of India, the region where Gandhi grew up and where his father was the prime minister of a small princely state, such child marriages were the norm rather than the exception. Writing 43 years after the event, Gandhi could still recall the details of the marriage festivities. His elder brother and a cousin were to be married at the same time in one big ceremony and young Mohandas was excited by the prospect of new clothes, sumptuous wedding feasts, and the evenings and nights full of music and dance. During the ceremony itself, whenever the couple was required to hold hands for a particular rite, Mohandas would secretly give Kasturbai's hand a squeeze which she, in turn, eagerly reciprocated.

The excitement of the wedding was marred by one jarring incident. On his way to the celebrations, Mohandas's father had a serious accident when the horse-carriage he was travelling in overturned, and he arrived late for the ceremony, with bandages covering his arms and back. The young boy was much too excited by what was happening to him to pay attention to the injured father, a fact that the older man notes with shame. 'I was devoted to my father but I was equally devoted to sensuality. Here by sensuality I do not mean one organ but the whole realm of sensual enjoyment.'[3]

Looking back at his younger self, Gandhi feels that sex became an obsession with the adolescent Mohandas. At school, his thoughts were constantly with his wife, as he impatiently waited for the night to decend when he could go to her. He was also consumed by a raging jealousy. He wanted to know of every move his wife made in his absence and would forbid her to go out alone to the temple, on household errands or to meet girlfriends. Kasturbai was not the sort of girl to accept such unreasonable restrictions and accusations based on unfounded jealousy with any degree of equanimity. Small in staure, she was an attractive girl with glossy black hair, large dark eyes set deep in an oval face, a well-formed mouth, and a determined chin. She was by no means a female creature subservient to male whims and could easily be self-willed and impatient with her young husband. They had violent quarrels, dissolved in the love-making of the night, only to reemerge with the light of day.

Later in life, Gandhi, regretting his treatment of Kasturbai during the first 15 years of their married life, gave two causes for his jealousy, The first was the projection of his own turbulent sexual wishes and fantasies onto his wife—'I took out my anger at her for my own weakness'—while the second was the influence of Sheikh Mehtab, the intimate friend of his youth. Physically strong, fearless, and rakishly handsome, while Mohandas was none of these, Sheikh Mehtab has been portrayed by Gandhi as his evil genius, the tempter whose blandishments Mohandas was incapable of resisting. The breacher of taboos and values Mohandas held dear, Sheikh Mehtab introduced the vegetarian lad to the guilt-ridden pleasures of eating meat, and was the organizer of their joint visit to a brothel. Mehtab constantly fueled Gandhi's suspicions with regard to Kasturbai's fidelity. Reading about their youthful transgressions a hundred years later, to us Mehtab does not appear especially evil. He is neither more nor less than an average representative of the world of male adolescence, with its phallic displays and the ethic of a devil-may-care bravery. For a 13-year-old (and from all accounts, including his own) 'mama's boy,' dealing with the sexual upsurge of adolescence at the same time as the demand for establishing an emotional intimacy with a strange girl, Sheikh Mehtab must have been a godsend. He provided Mohandas with the adolescent haven where young men can be both dismissive and fearful of women and heterosexual love, where in the vague homoeroticism of masculine banter and ceaseless activity a youth can gradually come to terms with the femininity within and without him. Little wonder that, in spite of the family's strong disapproval and Mohandas's own conscious view of their relationship as one between a reformer and a rake, their friendship remained close and lasted for almost 20 years. During his sojourn in England Gandhi sent Mehtab money from his meagre allowance, voluntarily sought him out again after his return to India and later took his friend with him when he sailed for South Africa.

Two circumstances, Gandhi writes, saved him from becoming an emotional and physical wreck during the initial phase of his marriage. The first was the custom among the Hindus, wisely aware of the consuming nature of adolescent passion, of separating the husband and wife for long periods during the first years of marriage. Kasturbai was often away on extended visits to her family and Gandhi estimates that in the first six years of their married life they could not have lived together for more than half of this period.

The second saving circumstance was Gandhi's highly developed sense of duty, both as a member of a large extended family, with an assigned role and definite tasks, and as a son who was especially conscientious and conscious of his obligation to an ageing and ailing father. After coming home from school, Gandhi would first spend time with his father, massaging his legs and attending to his other needs. Even when he was thus engaged, his mind wandered as he impatiently waited for the filial service to come to an end, his fantasies absorbed by the images of his girl-wife in another room of the house. As all readers of his autobiography know, the conflict between sexual desire and his sense of duty and devotion to the father was to load the marriage, especially its physical side, with an enormous burden of guilt. We shall briefly recapitualate the incident that has often been reproduced either as a cautionary moral tale or as a choice text for psychoanalytical exegesis.

Gandhi's father had been seriously ill and his younger brother had come to look after him, a task he shared with the son. One night around 10-30 or 11, while Gandhi was massaging his father's legs, his uncle told him to rest. Happily, Gandhi rushed off to the bedroom to wake up his pregnant wife for sexual intercourse. After a few minutes, a servant knocked at the bedroom door and informed the couple that the father had expired. Gandhi talks of his life-long feeling of remorse that blind lust had deprived him of the chance of rendering some last service to his father and thus missing the patriarch's 'blessing' which was instead received by the uncle. 'This is the shame I hinted at in the last chapter,' he writes,

> my sexual obsession even at the time of service to my father. Till today I have not been able to wash away this dark stain. I cannot forget that though my devotion to my parents was boundless and I could have given up everything for them, my mind was not free of lust even at that critical moment. This was an unforgivable lack in my service to my father. This is why in spite of my faithfulness to one woman I have viewed myself as someone blinded by sexuality. It took me a long time to free myself of lust and I have had to undergo many ordeals before I could attain this freedom.
>
> Before I close this chapter of my double shame I also want to

say that the child born to my wife did not survive for more than a couple of days. What other outcome could there have been?[4]

Sexual passion endangers all the generations, Gandhi seems to say, not only the parents to whom one is morally and filially obliged, but the children conceived in sexual union.

At the age of 18, Mohandas left his wife and family behind (a son had been recently born) as he sailed for England to study law. He faced a good deal of opposition to his plans from his family and his community, which propounded the orthodox view that a man could not remain a good Hindu if he went abroad. Gandhi could leave for England with his family's consent (the community was not so easily mollified and declared him an outcaste) only after he made a solemn vow to his mother to avoid scrupulously the three inflamers of passion, 'wine, women, and meat'—the anxious Hindu counterpart of the more cheerful 'wine, women, and song'—during his sojourn in that distant island.

Gandhi's account of his three-year stay in England is striking in many ways. V.S. Naipaul has pointed out Gandhi's intense self-absorption, which made him oblivious to all the externals of his surroundings.[5] Gandhi does not mention the climate or the seasons. He does not describe London's buildings and streets, nor touch upon its social, intellectual, and political life.

What he immerses himself in and passionately discovers are fringe groups and causes which the mainstream English society would have unhesitatingly labeled 'eccentric.' An active member of the London Vegetarian Society and the 'Esoteric Christian Union' (many years later in South Africa he would proudly identify himself as the agent for these Societies on his letterhead), he was also a fervent admirer of Annie Besant, the heir of the Russian mystic Madame Bavatsky, and a self-declared 'bride of Christ.'

Knowing that till very recently (and again in the future) the crore of Gandhi's self-absorption was his concern with his sexuality, the meagre space he devotes to the stirring of sexual desire is even more striking. In the full flush of youth, learning such English graces as dancing, and becoming somewhat of a dandy, this passionate young man—a (however reluctant) sensualist—tells us very little about how he dealt with his desires and their inevitable stimulation in a society where the sexes mingled much more freely that in his native Kathiawar. The only exception to this silence is an incident near the end of his stay, when Gandhi was attending a conference of vegetarians in Portsmouth and stayed with a friend at the house of a woman, 'not a prostitute but of easy virtue.' At night, while the three of them were playing cards, there was much sexual banter in which Gandhi enthusiastically participated. Gandhi was ready, as he says, 'to descend from speech into action,' when his friend reminded him of his vows.

I was embarrassed, I came to my senses. In my heart I was grateful to the friend. I remembered my vow to my mother I was trembling when I reached my room. My heart was racing. My condition was that of a wild animal who has just escaped the hunter. I think this was the first occasion I was 'possessed by passion' for a woman not my wife and desired to 'make merry' with her.[6]

This is the only explicit event in which higher duty opposed and conquered sexual temptation that is reported in this part of Gandhi's autobiography. The earlier sexual preoccupation, I would surmise, went underground, to reemerge in two different streams which on the surface seem quite unrelated to genital sexuality. One of these streams is Gandhi's increasing preoccupation with religious and spiritual matters. He tells us of his visit to theosophists, conversations with Christian clergymen, the reading of inspirational and religious literature. At times, Gandhi seems to be quite aware of the connection betwen his sexual struggles and his spiritual interests. Thus he notes down the following verses from the *Bhagavad Gita*:

If one
Ponders on objects of the senses there springs
Attraction; from attraction grows desire,
Desire flames to fierce passion, passion breeds
Recklessness; then the memory—all betrayed—
Lets noble purpose go, and saps the mind,
Till purpose, mind, and man are all undone.

'These verses,' he says, 'made a deep impression on my mind, and they still ring in my ears.'[7]

The other stream is his obsession with food, an obsession that was to remain with him for the rest of his life. Page after page, in dreary detail, we read about what Gandhi ate and what he did not, why he partook of certain foods and why he did not eat others, what one eminent vegetarian told him about eggs and what another, equally eminent, denied. The connection between sexuality and food is made quite explicit in Gandhi's later life when his ruminations about his celibacy would almost invariably be followed by an exhaustive discussion of the types of food that stimulate desire and others that dampen it. Again, we must remember that in the Indian consciousness, the symbolism of food is more closely or manifestly connected to sexuality than it is in the West. The words for eating and sexual enjoyment, as A.K. Ramanujan reminds us, have the same root, *bhuj*, in Sanskrit, and sexual intercourse is often spoken about as the mutual feeding of male and female.[8]

On his return to India, Gandhi was faced with the necessity of making a living as a lawyer, a task for which he found himself both professionally and personally ill-equipped. A section of his caste was still hostile to him, having never forgiven him for his defiance of its mandate not to go abroad. There were further difficulties in his adjustments to the norms and mores of life in an Indian extended family—and in the family's adjustments to the newly acquired habits and values of its somewhat Anglicized member. Today, with infinitely larger numbers of people moving across cultural boundaries and back again, the urbane Indian might indulgently smile at the tragicomic aspects of this reverse cultural shock. Tea and coffee, oatmeal porridge and cocoa were introduced to the breakfast table of the Gandhi household. Boots, shoes—and smelly socks—were to be worn in the burning heat of Kathiawar. Indeed, as a colonial subject, his indentification with the British overlord was so strong that when some years later he was to sail for South Africa, he insisted on his sons being dressed like English public school boys with Etonian collars and ties. Poor Kasturbai was to dress up as a British lady—corset, bustle, high lace collar, laced shoes, and all. Her vehement protests and perhaps the absurdity of it all made him finally relent, though Kasturbai still had to dress up as a Parsi lady, a member of the community most respected by the British.

The marriage was still tempestuous, his driven genital desire the cause of these storms. His stay in England had neither reduced the strength of Gandhi's jealousy nor put an end to the nagging suspicions about his wife's fidelity. At the egging on of his old friend Sheikh Mehtab, Gandhi went so far as to break Kasturbai's bangles—to an Indian girl the dreaded symbol of widowhood—and to send her back to her parents' house. It took him a year before he consented to receive her back and over four years before his suspicion was stilled.[9] Purists can be cruel, especially to those dependent women who threaten to devour their virtue.

Economic, social, and familial conflicts, besides the perennial erotic one, seem to have spurred Gandhi's travels on the spiritual path. In this journey he now acquired a guide, Raichandra, a young jeweller. Raichandra was a man after Gandhi's own heart, more interested in *moksha* (the release from the cycles of birth and death which Hindus believe govern the wandering of the individual soul) than in diamonds. The two men met often to discuss spiritual topics and the depth of Raichandra's sincerity, purpose, and knowledge of Hindu thought and scriptures made a deep impression on Gandhi's mind. Of the three men, he says, who had to greatest influence on his life (the others were Tolstoy and Ruskin), Raichandra was the only one with whom he had a long personal asociation. Indeed, the young jeweller who talked so eloquently about *moksha* was the nearest Gandhi came to having a guru, and 'In my moments of inner crisis, it was Raichandra with whom I used to seek refuge.'[10]

Unforunately, in spite of the vast amount written on his life (over 400 biographical items), and the wealth of material contained in the 90 volumes of Gandhi's collected works, we know very little of the subjects of these talks, the letters they exchanged, or the kind of guidance Gandhi sought for his inner turbulence. From the available references, scattered in Gandhi's writings, it is evident that a central concern of their earnest exchanges was the relationship of sexuality to 'salvation,' the transformation of sexual potency into psychic and spiritual power—the core issue, in fact, of much of Hindu metaphysics and practice. Gandhi notes that the idea that 'milk gives birth to sexual passions is something which I first learnt from Raichandrabhai,' and he ascribes to the jeweller the predominant role in his decision to become a celibate.[11]

In 1893, at the age of 24; Gandhi left for South Africa where he had been engaged as a lawyer by an Indian businessman. With brief interruptions for home visits, he was to stay there for the next 22 years.

Gandhi's years in South Africa, especially from 1990 to 1910, roughly spanning the fourth decade of his life, were crucial for the formation of Gandhi's historical persona. During these years Gandhi remade himself in that final image which is now evoked by his name. The first great nonviolent political campaigns for the rights of Indians living in South Africa, which introduced and refined the instrument of *Satyagraha* (literally, insistence on truth), took place during this period, at the end of which the would become well-known in many parts of the world. Equally important for our purposes is the fact that it was also during these years that he defined for himself the kind of personal life he would lead, and developed his ideas on the desired relationship between the sexes which would form the foundation for his own marriage with Kasturbai.

Founding and living in communes with disciples and seekers who shared his vision, radically experimenting with food and alternative systems of healing such as nature cure, generally embracing an ascetic lifestyle, the cornerstone of his personal life was *brahmacharya* or celibacy. Indeed *brahmacharya* was one leg of a tripod of which the other two were nonviolence (*ahimsa*) and truth (*satya*), which he adopted as the conscious basis for his adult identity and about which he would later write: 'Nonviolence came to me after a strenuous struggle, *brahmacharya* I am still struggling for, but truth has always come naturally to me.'[12]

The decision for sexual abstinence was taken in 1901, the year in which Raichandra died and in which Gandhi had just become a father for the fourth time (Devdas, the youngest son, was born in 1900). Both these circumstances must have contributed to Gandhi's resolve to renounce sexuality. The birth of the son, as we know from the account of the fateful night of the father's death and the newborn who did not survive because of *his father's* accursed lust, was a reminder of Gandhi's despised genital desires and therefore a stigma. To give them up was an offering made at the altar of Raichandra's (and, we would conjecture, his father's) departed soul. Kasturbai had not been consulted and Gandhi confesses that for the first few years he was only 'more or less successful' in his practice of self-restraint.[13] Gandhi had left for India with his family in November 1901 and returned to South Africa the next year after promising his wife that she would soon follow. Yet once he was back in South Africa, Gandhi was reluctant to have Kasturbai join him. Paramount in his decision must have been the fact that his resolve to abstain from sexual intercourse was still fragile. The monetary argument he advances in the letters to his relatives, where he asks their help in persuading his wife to remain behind for two to three years, namely, that the savings he could make in South Africa would enable her and the children to lead an easy life in India,[14] neither jibes with the realities of running a household alone nor with Gandhi's character and temperament. Only a few months earlier, while leaving for India, he had gifted all the gold and diamond jewellery presented to him by a grateful Indian community to a trust, maintaining, 'I feel neither I nor my family can make any personal use of the costly present,' and that what he valued was their affection and not money.[15]

Gandhi finally took the vow to observe complete celibacy in 1906 when he was 37 years old, on the eve of his first nonviolent political campaign in South Africa. The preceding five years of attempted abstinence he felt, had only been a preparation for what would amount to a total and irrevocable renunciation of sexuality. The example of Tolstoy further deepened his resolve. As he writes in 1905, 'He (Tolstoy) used to enjoy all pleasures of the world, kept mistresses, drank and was strongly addicted to smoking. . . . He has given up all his vices, eats very simple food and has it in him no longer to hurt any living creature by thought, word or deed.'[16] Tolstoy's ideas on chastity, not only for the unmarried but also for the married, outlined in the *Kreuzer Sonata* (1889), were combined with the Hindu notions on *brahmacharya* to form Gandhi's own vision of the 'right' relationship between men and women. More than a personal code of conduct, these ideas regulated the life of all those who lived with him in his various communes (*ashrams*) in South Africa and India. Briefly summaried in his own words, this doctrine on the relationship between a couple holds that

The very purpose of marriage is restraint and sublimation of the sexual passion. Marriage for the satisfaction of sexual appetite is *vyabhichara*, concupisence. . . if they come together merely to have a fond embrace they are nearest the devil.

The only rule that can be laid down in such instances (if a child is not conceived) is that coitus may be permitted once at the end of the monthly period till conception is established. If its object is achieved it must be abjured forthwith.

There is not doubt that much of the sensuality of our nature, whether male or female, is due to the superstition, having a religious sanction, that married people are bound to share the same bed and the same room. But every husband and wife can make a fixed resolution from today never to share the same room or same bed at night, and to avoid sexual contact, except for one supreme purpose which it is intended for in both man and beast.[17]

Whatever its other consequences, there is little doubt that Gandhi's vow of celibacy distinctly improved his marriage, perhaps because poor Kasturbai was no longer perceived as a seductive siren responsible for his lapses from a longed-for ideal of purity. Ever since they had been in South Africa, there was much bickering and quarreling between the two. They had fought over her desire to keep her ornaments while Gandhi sought to convince her of the virtues of nonpossession. There was a major explosion, in which Gandhi almost turned her out of the house, over his wish that she clean up after an untouchable Christian visitor, a task abhorrent to a traditional Hindu woman with her deeply ingrained taboos about pollution. There was a running battle between the couple over their eldest son Harilal's wish that he grow up like other boys of his age and be allowed to avail of formal schooling. Gandhi's radical views on education would not allow the son to be sent to school, while Kasturbai was obstinate in the advocacy of her firstborn's cause.

From all accounts, before the vow of *brahmacharya*, Gandhi was an autocrat with his wife, 'completely steel,' as he tried to bend her to his will and get her to embrace what must have appeared to her as eccentric notions that endangered the present and future welfare of the family.

After 1906, their relationship improved steadily and Gandhi could write with some justification that 'I could not steal into my wife's heart until I decided to treat her differently than I used to do, and so I restored to her all her rights by dispossessing myself of any so-called rights as her husband.'[18] In their later years, though there were occasional disagreements, generally with respect to the children and Kasturbai's discomfort with the many women in the various *ashrams* who jostled each other to come closer to Gandhi, the marriage was marked by deep intimacy and a quiet love which impressed everyone who witnessed the old couple together.

For Gandhi, celibacy was not only the sine qua non for *moksha*, but also the mainspring of his political activities. It is from the repudiation, the ashes of sexual desire, that the weapon of nonviolence which he used so effectively in his political struggle against the racial oppression of the South African white rulers and later against the British empire, was phoenix-like born. As Gandhi puts it :

> *Ahimsa* (nonviolence) means Universal Love. If a man gives his love to one woman, or a woman to one man, what is there left for the world besides? It simply means, 'We two first, and the devil take all the rest of them.' As a faithful wife must be prepared to sacrifice her all for the sake of her husband, and a faithful husband for the sake of his wife, it is clear that such persons cannot rise to the height of Universal Love, or look upon all mankind as kith and kin. For they have created a boundary wall round their love. The larger their family, the farther are they from Universal Love. Hence one who would obey the law of *ahimsa*

cannot marry, not to speak of gratification outside the marital bond.[19]

As for those who are already married,

> If the married couple can think of each other as brother and sister, they are freed for universal service. The very thought that all women in the world are his sisters, mothers and daughters will at once enable a man to snap his chains.[20]

The truth of Gandhi's assertion that sexual love limits rather than expands personal concerns and that the narrow role of a husband is antithetical to the larger identity of one who would husband the world is not at issue here. Our intention for the moment is to elucidate Gandhi's conflict in the way he viewed it—in this case, the imperatives of desire straining against the higher purpose of unfettered service to community. Yet another of his pansexualist formulations of the conflict has it that the gratification of sexual passion vies with a man's obligation to enhance personal vitality and psychic power. 'A man who is unchaste loses stamina, becomes emasculated and cowardly,'[21] is a sentiment often echoed in his writings as is the reiteration that his capacity to work in the political arena was a result of the psychic power gained through celibacy. Still another, later formulation is put in religious and spiritual terms—sexuality compromises his aspiration to become 'God's eunuch.' Reminiscent of Christ's metaphors of innocent childhood to describe would-be entrants to the kingdom of heaven and Prophet Mohammed's welcoming of 'those made eunuchs,' not through an operation but through prayer to God, Gandhi too would see sexual renunciation as a precondition for self-realization and, Moses-like, for seeing God 'face to face.'

Like his communes, which are a combination of the *ashrama* of the ancient sages described in the Hindu epics and the Trappist monastery in South Africa which so impressed him on a visit, Gandhi's views on the importance and merits of celibacy too seem to be derived from a mixture of Hindu and Christian religious traditions. Where Gandhi proceeded to give these views a special twist, going much beyond the cursory juxtaposition of sexuality and eating made in his culture, was in emphasizing, above all, the relation of food to the observance of celibacy. Experiments with food, to find that elusive right combination which would keep the libido effectively dammed, continued right through to the end of his life. In South Africa, as reported by an admiring yet detached disciple, there were months of cooking without salt or any condiments. Another period witnesses the absence of sugar, dates, and currants being added for sweetening purposes. This was followed by a period of 'unfired' food served with olive oil. 'Food values were most earnestly discussed, and their effect upon the human body and its moral qualities solemnly examined. For a time a dish of raw chopped onions, as a blood purifier, regularly formed part of the dinner meal. . . . Ultimately Mr Gandhi came to the conclusion that onions were bad for the passions, and so onions were cut out. Milk, too, Mr Gandhi said, affected the "passion" side of human life and thereafter milk was abjured likewise. "We talk about food quite as much as gourmands do," I said on one occasion to Mr Gandhi. "I am sure we talk about food more than most people; we seem to be always thinking of the things we either may or may not eat. Sometimes, I think it would be better if we just ate anything and did not think about it at all."[22] But for Gandhi food was a deathly serious business.

> Control of palate is very closely connected with the observance of
> *brahmacharya* (celibacy). I have found from experience that the
> observance of celibacy becomes comparatively easy, it one acquires
> mastery over the palate. This does not figure among the
> observances of time-honoured recognition. Could it be because even
> great sages found it difficult to achieve. Food has to be taken as
> we take medicine, without thinking whether it is tasty or otherwise,
> and only in quantities limited to the needs of the body. . . . And
> one who thus gives up a multitude of eatables will acquire self-
> control in the natural course of things.[23]

The above passage is reminiscent of St Augustine who, too, would take food as physic, strive daily against concupiscence in eating and drinking, and assert that "the bridle of the throat then is to be held attempered between slackness and stiffness."[24] St Augustine's attitude toward food, though, is part of his attempt to gain a general freedom from the grip of sensuality, including 'the delights of the ear (that) had more firmly entangled and subdued me '[25] Augustine treats imbibition as he does all sensory input. Gandhi, on the other hand, makes of food a primary regulator of the genital impulses. 'A man of heightened sexual passion,' he writes, 'is also greedy of the palate. This was also my condition. To gain control over the organs of both generation and taste has been difficult for me.'[26]

A radical cure for his epicurean disease is, of course, fasting, and Gandhi was its enthusiastic proponent. 'As an external aid to *brahmacharya*, fasting is as necessary as selection and restriction of diet. So overpowering are the senses that they can be kept under control only when they are completely hedged in on all sides, from above and from beneath.'[27] Remembering Gandhi's great fasts during his political struggles, we can see how fasting for him would have another, more personal meaning as a protector of his cherished celibacy and thus an assurance against the waning of psychic, and, with it, political power.

Battle, weapons, victory and defeat are a part of Gandhi's image in his account of a life-long conflict with the dark god of desire, the only opponent he did not engage nonviolently nor could ever completely subdue. The metaphors that pervade the descriptions of this passionate conflict are of 'invasions by an insidious enemy' who needs to be implacably 'repulsed'; while the perilous struggle is like 'walking on a sword's edge.' The god himself (though Gandhi would not have given Kama, the god of love, the exalted status accorded him in much of Hindu mythology) is the 'serpent which I know will bite me,' 'the scorpion of passion,' whose destruction, annihilation, conflagration, is a supreme aim of his spiritual strivings. In sharp contrast to all his other opponents, whose humanity he was always scrupulous to respect, the god of desire was the only antagonist with whom Gandhi could not compromise and whose humanity (not to speak of his divinity) he always denied.

For Gandhi, defeats in this war were occasions for bitter self-reproach and a public confession of his humiliation, while the victories were a matter of joy, 'fresh beauty,' and an increase in vigour and self-confidence that brought him nearer to the *moksha* he so longed for. Whatever may be his values to the contrary, a sympathetic reader, conscious of Gandhi's greatness and his prophetic insights into many of the dilemmas of modern existence, cannot fail to be moved by the dimensions of Gandhi's personal struggle—heroic in its proportion, startling in its intensity, interminable in its duration. By the time Gandhi concludes his autobiography with the words:

> To conquer the subtle passions seems to me to be far harder than
> the conquest of the world by the force of arms. Ever since my
> return to India I have had experiences of the passions hidden
> within me. They have made me feel ashamed though I have not
> lost courage. My experiments with truth have given, and continue
> to give, great joy. But I know that I must traverse a perilous path.
> I must reduce myself to zero,[28]

no reader can doubt his passionate sincerity and honesty. His is not the reflexive, indeed passionless moralism of the more ordinary religionist.

How did Gandhi himself experience sexual desire, the temptations and the limits of the flesh? To know this, it is important that we listen closely to Gandhi's voice describing his conflicts in the language in which he spoke of them— Gujarati, his mother tongue. Given the tendency toward hagiolatry among the followers of a great man, their translations, especially of the Master's sexual conflicts, are apt to distort the authentic voice of the man behind the saint. The English translation of Gandhi's autobiography by his faithful secretary, Mahadev Desai, in spite of the benefit of Gandhi's own revision, suffers seriously from this defect, and any interpretations based on this translation are in danger of missing Gandhi's own experience. Take, for instance, one famous incident from Gandhi's youth, of the schoolboy Gandhi visiting a prostitute for the first time in the company of his Muslim friend and constant tempter, Sheikh Mehtab. The original Gujarati version describes the incident as follows:

I entered the house but he who is to be saved by God remains pure even if he wants to fall. I became almost blind in that room. I could not speak. Struck dumb by embarrassment, I sat down on the cot with the woman but could not utter a single word. The woman was furious, gave me a couple of choice abuses and showed me to the door [my translation].[29]

The English translation, however, is much less matter-of-fact. It is full of Augustinianisms in which young Gandhi goes into a 'den of vice' and tarries in the 'jaws of sin.' These are absent in the original. By adding adjectives such as 'evil' and 'animal' before 'passions,' the translation seems to be judging them in a Christian theological sense that is missing in Gandhi's own account. St Augustine, for instance—with whose *Confessions* Gandhi's *Experiments* has much in common—was rent asunder because of the 'sin that dwelt in me,' by 'the punishment of a sin more freely committed, in that I was a son of Adam.'[30] Gandhi, in contrast, uses two words, *vishaya* and *vikara*, for lust and passion respectively. The root of *vishaya* is from poison, and that is how he regards sexuality—as poisonous, for instance, when he talks of it in conjunction with serpents and scorpions. The literal meaning of *vikara*, or passion, is 'distortion,' and that is how passions are traditionally seen in the Hindu view, waves of mind that distort the clear waters of the soul. For Gandhi, then, lust is not sinful but poisonous, contaminating the elixir of immortality. It is dangerous in and of itself, 'destructuralizing' in psychoanalytic language, rather than merely immoral, at odds, that is, with certain social or moral injunctions. To be passionate is not to fall from a state of grace, but to suffer a distortion of truth. In contrast to the English version, which turns his very Hindu conflict into a Christian one, Gandhi's struggle with sexuality is not essentially a conflict between sin and morality, but rather one between psychic death and immortality, on which the moral quandary is superimposed.

We can, of course, never be quite certain whether Gandhi was a man with a gigantic erotic temperament or merely the possessor of an overweening conscience that magnified each departure from an unattainable ideal of purity as a momentous lapse. Nor is it possible, for that matter, to evaluate the paradoxical impact of his scruples in intensifying the very desires they opposed. Both fuelled each other, the lid of self-control compressing and heating up the contents of the cauldron of desire, in Freud's famous metaphor, their growing intensity requiring ever greater efforts at confinement.

Gandhi himself, speaking at the birth centenary of Tolstoy in 1928, warns us to refrain from judgments. While talking of the import of such struggles in the lives of great *homo religiosi*, he seems to be asking for empathy rather than facile categorization:

The seeming contradictions in Tolstoy's life are no blot on him or

sign of his failure. They signify the failure of the observer. . . .
Only the man himself knows how much he struggles in the depth
of his heart or what victories he wins in the war between Rama
and Ravana.* The spectator certainly cannot know that.³¹

In judging a great man, Gandhi goes on to say, and here he seems to be talking
as much of himself as Tolstoy,

> God is witness to the battles he may have fought in his heart and
> the victories he may have won. These are the only evidence of his
> failures and successes. . . . If anyone pointed out a weakness in
> Tolstoy though there could hardly be an occasion for anyone to do
> so for he was pitiless in his self-examination, he would magnify
> that weakness to fearful proportions. He would have seen his lapse
> and atoned for it in the manner he thought most appropriate before
> anyone had pointed it out to him.³²

This is a warning we must take seriously but do not really need. Our intention
is not to 'analyze' Gandhi's conflict in any reductionist sense but to seek to
understand it in all its passion—and obscurity. Gandhi's agony is ours as well,
after all, an inevitable by-product of the long human journey from infancy to
adulthood. We all wage wars on our wants.

A passionate man who suffered his passions as poisonous of his inner self
and a sensualist who felt his sensuality distorted his inner purpose, Gandhi's
struggle with what he took to be the god of desire was not unremitting. There
were long periods in his adulthood when his sensuality was integrated with the
rest of his being. Old movie clips and reminiscences of those who knew him in
person attest to some of this acceptable sensuality. It found expression in the
vigorous grace of his locomotion; the twinkle in his eye and the brilliance of his
smile; the attention he paid to his dress—even if the dress was a freshly laundered,
spotless loincloth; the care he directed to the preparation and eating of his simple
food; the delight with which he sang and listened to devotional songs; and the
pleasure he took in the daily oil massage of his body. The Christian St Augustine
would have been altogether shocked. Here, then, the Indian ascetic's path diverges
from that trod by the more austere and self-punishing Western monk. Here, too,
from Gandhi's sensuous gaiety, stems his ability to rivet masses of men not by
pronouncement in scripture but by his very presence.

In Gandhi's periods of despair, occasioned by real-life disappointments and
setbacks in the sociopolitical campaigns to which he had committed his life, the
integration of his sensuality and spirituality would be threatened and again we
find him obsessively agonizing over the problem of genital desire. Once more he

* The good and evil protagonists of the Indian epic, *Ramayana*.

struggled against the reemergence of an old antagonist whom he sought to defeat by public confessions of *his* defeats.

One such period spans the years between 1925 and 1928, after his release from jail, when he was often depressed, believing that the Indian religious and political divisions were too deep for the country to respond to his leadership and that Indians were not yet ready for his kind of nonviolent civil disobedience. There was a breakdown with a serious condition of hypertension and doctors had advised him long rest. Interestingly, this is also the period in which he wrote his confessional autobiography, where he despondently confides, 'Even when I am past 56 years, I realize how hard a thing it (celibacy) is. Every day I realize more and more that it is like walking on the sword's edge, and I can see every moment the necessity of continued vigilance.'[33] His ideals and goals failing him, Gandhi finds sublime purpose and intent crumbling, exposing desires held in abeyance. These then become prepotent. The psychoanalyst would speak in this instance of the disintegration of 'sublimations'—conversions of base wishes into socially sanctioned aspirations—and the lonely, painful regression which ensues.

In the copious correspondence of the years 1927 and 1928, the two longest and the most personally involved letters are neither addressed to his close political co-workers and leaders of future free India such as Nehru, Patel or Rajagopalachari, nor do they deal with vital political or social issues. The addressees are two unknown young men, and the subject of the letters is the convolutions of Gandhi's instinctual promptings. Responding to Balakrishna Bhave, who had expressed doubts about the propriety of Gandhi placing his hands on the shoulders of young girls while walking, Gandhi conducts a characteristic, obsessive search for any hidden eroticism in his action.[34] The other letter, to Harjivan Kotak, deserves to be quoted at some length since it details Gandhi's poignant struggle, his distress at the threatened breakdown of the psycho-sensual synthesis.

> When the mind is disturbed by impure thoughts, instead of trying to drive them out one should occupy it in some work, that is, engage it in reading or in some bodily labour which requires mental attention too. Never let the eyes follow their inclination. If they fall on a woman, withdraw them immediately. It is scarcely necessary for anyone to look straight at a man's or woman's face. This is the reason why *brahmacharis*, and others too, are enjoined to walk with their eyes lowered. If we are sitting, we should keep them steady in one direction. This is an external remedy, but a most valuable one. You many undertake a fast if and when you find one necessary. . . . You should not be afraid even if you get involuntary discharges during a fast. *Vaids* (traditional doctors) say that, even when impure desires are absent, such discharges may occur because of pressure in the bowels. But, instead of believing that, it helps us more to believe that they occur because of impure

desires. We are not always conscious of such desires. I had involuntary discharges twice during the last two weeks. I cannot recall any dream. I never practised masturbation. One cause of these discharges is of course my physical weakness but I also know that there are impure desires deep down in me. I am able to keep out such thoughts during waking hours. But what is present in the body like some hidden poison, always makes its way, even forcibly sometimes. I feel unhappy about this, but am not nervously afraid. I am always vigilant. I can suppress the enemy but have not been able to expel him altogether. If I am truthful, I shall succeed in doing that too. The enemy will not be able to endure the power of truth. If you are in the same condition as I am, learn from my experience. In its essence, desire for sex-pleasure is equally impure, whether its object is one's wife or some other woman. Its results differ. At the moment, we are thinking of the enemy in his essential nature. Understand, therefore, that so far as one's wife is concerned you are not likely to find anyone as lustful as I was. That is why I have described my pitiable condition to you and tried to give you courage.[35]

A 'hidden power,' an 'enemy to be expelled'—in such circumstances the body becomes a strange land inhabited by demons of feeling and impulse divided from the self. With setbacks in unity of intent, there is a further fragmenting of the self. The moral dilemma stirs conflicts of a primeval order, when early 'introjects'—those presences bound to desire out of which we construct our primary self—are awakened, taste blood or better, poison, and threaten our identity—our sense of wholeness, continuity, and sameness.

Another emotionally vulnerable period comprises roughly 18 months from the middle of 1935 onwards, when Gandhi was almost 66 years old. Marked by a 'nervous breakdown,' when his blood pressure went dangerously out of control, Gandhi was advised complete rest for some months by his doctors. He attributed this breakdown to overwork and especially mental exhaustion brought on by the intensity of his involvement and emotional reactions to the personal problems of his co-workers. He considered these as important as those pertaining to the country's independence, regretting only that he had not reached the Hindu ideal, as outlined in the *Gita*, of detachment from emotions. Gandhi used this enforced rest for introspection and decided to give up his practice of walking with his hands on the shoulders of young girls. In 'A Renunciation,' an article he wrote for his newspaper during this time, he traced the history of this particular practice, reiterated the purity of his paternal intentions towards the girls involved, acknowledged that he was not unaware of the dangers of the liberty he was taking, and based his renunciation on the grounds of setting a good example to the younger generation.[36]

What is more significant is that in the very first article he was allowed to write by his doctors, Gandhi, meditating on the causes of his ill-health, comes back to the question of his celibacy. He mentions an encounter with a woman during the period of convalescence in Bombay, which not only disturbed him greatly but made him despise himself. In a letter to Prema Kantak, a disciple and confidante in his Sabarmati *ashram*, he elaborates on this incident further.

I have always had the shedding of semen in dreams. In South Africa the interval between two ejaculations may have been in years. I do not remember it fully. Here the time difference is in months. I have mentioned these ejaculations in a couple of my articles. If my *brahmacharya* had been without this sheding of semen then I would have been able to present many more things to the world. But someone who from the age of 15 to 30 has enjoyed sexuality (*vishya-bhog*)—even if it was only with his wife— whether such a man can conserve his semen after becoming a *brahmachari* seems impossible to me. Someone whose power of storing the semen has been weakened daily for 15 years cannot hope to regain this power all at once. That is why I regard myself as an incomplete *brahmachari*. But where there are no trees, there are thorn bushes. This shortcoming of mine is known to the world.

The experience which tortured me in Bombay was strange and painful. All my ejaculations have taken place in dreams; they did not trouble me. But Bombay's experience was in the waking state. I did not have any inclination to fulfil that desire. My body was under control. But in spite of my trying, the sense organ remained awake. This experience was new and unbecoming. I have narrated its cause.* After removing this cause the wakefulness of the sense organ subsided, that is, it subsided in the waking state.

In spite of my shortcoming, one thing has been easily possible for me, namely that thousands of women have remained safe with me. There were many occasions in my life when certain women, in spite of their sexual desire, were saved or rather I was saved by God. I acknowledge it one hundred percent that this was God's doing. That is why I take no pride in it. I pray daily to God that such a situation should last till the end of my life.

To reach the level of Shukadeva is my goal.** I have not been

---

* By remaining inactive and eating well, passions are born in the body.
** Son of Vyasa, Shukadeva is the mythical reciter of the *Bhagavatapurana*. In spite of having married and lived the life of a householder (like Gandhi, he was the father of four sons), in later life he succeeded in conquering his senses to an extent that he rose up to the Heavens and shone there like a second sun.

able to achieve it. Otherwise in spite of the generation of semen I would be impotent and the shedding will become impossible.

The thoughts I have expressed recently about *brahamacharya* are not new. This does not mean that the ideal will be reached by the whole world or even by thousands of men and women in my lifetime. It may take thousands of years, but *brahmacharya* is true, attainable and must be realized.

Man has still to go a long way. His character is still that of a beast. Only the form is human. It seems that violence is all around us. In spite of this, just as there is no doubt about truth and nonviolence similarly there is not doubt about *brahmacharya*.

Those who keep on burning despite their efforts are not trying hard enough. Nurturing passion in their minds they only want that no shedding of semen take place and avoid women. The second chapter of *Gita* applies to such people.

What I am doing at the moment is purification of thought. Modern thought regards *brahmacharya* as wrong conduct. Using artificial methods of birth control it wants to satisfy sexual passion. My soul rebels against this. Sexual desire will remain in the world, but the world's honour depends on *brahmacharya* and will continue to do so.[37]

Further self-mortification was one of his responses to what he regarded as an unforgivable 'lapse.' Even the ascetic regimen of the *ashram* now seemed luxurious. Leaving Kasturbai to look after its inmates, he went off to live in a one-room hut in a remote and poverty-stricken, untouchable village. Though he wished to be alone—a wish that for a man in his position was impossible of fulfilment—he soon became the focus of a new community.

Another dark period covers the last two years of Gandhi's life. The scene is India on the eve of Independence in 1947. A Muslim Pakistan is soon to be carved out of the country, much against Gandhi's wishes. His dream of Hindus and Muslims living amicably in a single unified state seems to be shattered beyond hope. Gandhi would even postpone Independence if the partition of the country could be averted, but his voice does not resonate quite so powerfully in the councils where the transfer of power is being negotiated. The air hangs heavy with clouds of looming violence. Hindus and Muslims warily eye each other as potential murderers . . . or eventual victims. The killings have already started in the crowded back-alleys of Calcutta and in the verdant expanses of rural Bengal, where the 78-year-old Mahatma is wearily trudging from one village to another, trying to stem the rushing tide of arson, rape, and murder that will soon engulf many other parts of the country. The few close associates who accompany him on this mission of peace are a witness to his despair and helpless listerers to the anguished cries of '*Kya karun, kya karun*? (What should I do?

What should I do?)' heard from his room in the middle of the night.[38] 'I find myself in the midst of exaggeration and falsity,' he writes, 'I am unable to discover the truth. There is terrible mutual distrust. Oldest friendships have snapped. Truth and *Ahimsa* (nonviolence) by which I swear and which have to my knowledge sustained me for 60 years, seem to fail to show the attributes I ascribed to them.'[39]

For an explanation of his 'failures' and sense of despair, Gandhi would characteristically probe for shortcomings in his abstinence, seeking to determine whether the god of desire had perhaps triumphed in some obscure recess of his mind, depriving him of his powers. Thus in the midst of human devastation and political uncertainty, Gandhi wrote a series of five articles on celibacy in his weekly newspaper, puzzling his readers who, as his temporary personal secretary, N.K. Bose, puts it, 'did not know why such a series suddenly appeared in the midst of intensely political articles.'[40]

But more striking than this public evidence of his preoccupation were his private experiments wherein the aged Mahatma pathetically sought to reassure himself of the strength of his celibacy. These experiments have shocked many and have come to be known as 'having naked young women sleep with him when he was old,' although their intent and outcome were far removed from the familiar connotations of that suggestive phrase. In the more or less public sleeping arrangements of his entourage while it rested in a village for the night, Gandhi would ask one or another of his few close women associates (his 19-year-old grandaughter among them) to share his bed and then try to ascertain in the morning whether any trace of sexual feeling had been evoked, either in himself or in his companion.[41] In spite of criticism by some of his close co-workers, Gandhi defended these experiments, denying the accusation that they could have ill effects on the women involved. Instead, he viewed them as an integral part of the *Yagna* he was performing—the Hindu sacrifice to the gods—whose only purpose was a restoration of personal psychic potency that would help him to regain control over political events and men, a control which seemed to be so fatally slipping away. Again he exploits his desires (and, admittedly, women) for the sake of his cause—the prideful vice of an uncompromisingly virtuous man.

Two Women

In his middle and later years,, a number of young women, attracted by Gandhi's public image as the Mahatma, his cause, or his fame, sought his proximity and eventually shared his *ashram* life. These women, who in many cases had left their well-appointed middle- and upper-class homes to take upon themselves the rigors of an ascetic lifestyle, were all else but conventional. Some of them were not only 'highstrung' but can fairly be described as suffering from emotional crises of considerable magnitude. Like their counterparts today who seek out well-known gurus, these women too were looking for the therapist in Gandhi as much as the Mahatma or the leader embodying Indian national aspirations. If toning down the intensity of a crippling emotional disturbance and awakening latent productive and creative powers that neither the individual nor the community 'knows' he or she possesses is the mark of a good therapist then, as we shall see later, Gandhi was an exceptional one. From women who were a little more than emotional wrecks, he fashioned energetic leaders directing major institutions engaged in the task of social innovation and actively participating in the country's Independence movement.

Gandhi's relationships with these women are fascinating in many ways. First, one is struck by the trouble he took in maintaining a relationship once he had admitted the woman to a degree of intimacy. Irrespective of his public commitments or the course of political events, he was puncitilious in writing (and expecting) regular weekly letters to each one of his chosen women followers when they were separated during his frequent visits to other parts of the country or his lengthy spells of imprisonment. Cumulatively, these letters build up a portrait of the Mahatma which reveals his innermost struggles, particularly during the periods of heightened emotional vulnerability, and the role played therein by Woman, as embodied in the collectivity of his chosen female followers.

At their best, the letters are intensely human, full of wisdom about life and purpose. Even at times of stress, they are invariably caring as Gandhi encourages the women's questions, advises them on their intimate problems, and cheerfully dispenses his favorite dietary prescriptions for every kind of ailment. As he writes to one of them: 'Your diagnosis is a correct one. The pleasure I get out of solving the *ashram's* problems, and within the *ashram* those of the sisters, is much greater than that of resolving India's dilemmas.'[42]

The second striking characteristic of these letters is what appears to be Gandhi's unwitting effort simultaneously to increase the intimacy with the correspondent and to withdraw if the woman wished for a nearness that crossed the invisible line he had drawn for both of them. The woman's consequent hurt or withdrawal is never allowed to reach a point of breakdown in the relationship. Gandhi employed his considerable charm and powers of persuasion to draw her close again, the hapless woman oscillating around a point between intimacy and estrangement, nearness and distance. The emotions aroused, not only in the women (who were also in close contact with each other) but to some degree in Gandhi, simmered in the hothouse *ashram* atmosphere to produce frequent explosions. In accordance with our narrative intent, let us look at the stories of two of these women, making of them brief tales rather than the novel each one of them richly deserves.

Prema Kantak belonged to a middle-class family from a small town in Maharashtra. She was still a schoolgirl when she heard about Gandhi and the wonderful work he had done for the cause of Indians in South Africa. An only daughter among five sons, she was a favourite of her father and enjoyed more than the usual freedom for a girl of her class and times.

As Prema grew into youth, she was gripped by the fervour of nationalist politics and agonized over personal spiritual questions, interests which Gandhi too combined in his person. Had he not maintained that 'politics without religion is dangerous?'

Her first encounter with the great man took place when Gandhi came to address students of her college at Poona. After the talk, she remembers going up to the platform where he was sitting so as to touch his feet in the traditional Indian gesture of respect. Since Gandhi was sitting cross-legged, his feet were tucked under his body. Prema reports:

> Without any mental reservations I touched his knee with my finger and saluted him. With a start he turned to look at me, reciprocated the greetings and looked away. If he but knew that by touching him my heart had blossomed forth with incomparable pride! With the pure touch an electric current ran through my body and I walked home lost in a world of bliss![43]

Sensitive and emotional, intelligent and idealistic, Prema refused to follow the traditional life plan of an Indian girl and get married, perhaps also because of a problematic (most analysts would say 'classically hysterical') attitude toward sexuality. 'Once, when I was 16, I was reading the *Bhagavata*,' she writes, 'when I came to the conversation between Kapila and Devahuti,* I learnt how babies come into world. I remember that my hair stood up on end. I visualised my own conception and was seized with disgust toward my parents and my body! My life seemed dirty! This disgust remained with me for may years.'[44] After a bitter quarrel between the daughter and her beloved father, Prema left home to live in a women's hostel. She earned her livelihood by tutoring children while she continued her studies toward a Master's degree.

Prema's fascination for Gandhi and her decision to go and live with him in the *ashram* is quite understandable. In the very nature of the *ashram* life and its ideals, there is a promised protection from disgusting sexuality. In her wishful imagination Gandhi looms up as the ideal parent who will soothe the hurt caused by the disappointment in the real-life one. He is also tthe admired mentor for Prema's political and spiritual interests, who is capable of comprehending the deeper needs of her soul.

---

* Kapila is the legendary expounder of the Samkhya system of Hindu philosophy. Devahuti is Kapila's mother.

At the age of 23, then, bubbling with innocent enthusiasm, Prema found herself in Ahmedabad in the Mahatma's presence. As was his wont, at first Gandhi discouraged her. He described to her in detail the hard physical work, the chores of cutting vegetables, grinding grain, cooking meals, cleaning utensils and toilets which awaited her if she adopted the *ashram* life. Prema, exultant in her youthful vitality and idealism, dismissed his cautions as trifles. 'I want to do something tremendous!', she exclaimed on one of her very first nights in the *ashram*. With wry humour, Gandhi tried to temper her exuberance without crushing her spirit. 'The only tremendous thing you can do just now is go to sleep,' he said.[45]

At the start of her stay, when Gandhi was out of town for a few days, Prema had the following dream. She is a little girl reclining in Gandhi's lap. From his breast, a stream of sweet, good milk is flowing straight into her mouth. Prema is drinking the milk and the Mahatma is saying, 'Drink, drink, drink more.' Prema is replete but the milk continues to flow and Gandhi keeps insisting that she drink more. Prema's clothes and body are thoroughly soaked in milk but the stream is unending. She wakes up in alarm.[46]

On narrating her dream to Gandhi and asking for an interpretation, Gandhi replied, 'Dreams can have the quality of purity (*sattvik*) or of passion (*rajasik*). Your dream is a pure one. It means that you feel protected with me.'[47] From the orthodox Freudian view, the interpretation cannot be faulted. An instinctive psychoanalyst, Gandhi provides reassurance to the patient and encourages her to give him her trust at this stage of their relationship. Unwittingly following the technical rule of proceeding from the surface to the depths, his interpretation could have been as easily made by an analyst who, for the time being, would have kept his hypotheses on the deeper imports of the dream images—of the symbolic equivalence of milk and semen, Prema's greedy voraciousness, her possible fantasy regarding the persecuting breast and so on—quietly to himself.

In the *ashram*, the competition among women for Gandhi's attention was as fierce as it is in any guru's establishment today. When he went for his evening constitutional, Gandhi would walk with his hands around the shoulders of the *ashram* girls. There was intense jealousy among them as each kept a hawk's eye for any undue favouritism—the number of times a girl was singled out for the mark of this favour, the duration of time a girl had Bapu's hands on her shoulder and so on. At first Prema felt aggrieved when other girls teased her, 'Prema—*ben*, Bapuji does not put his hands on *your* shoulders!' 'Why should he? I am not like you to push myself forward!' Prema would reply spiritedly. 'No, he never will. The *ashram* rule is that he can keep his hands only on the shoulders of girls who are younger than 16.'[48]

Prema felt her deprivation acutely and approached Gandhi who asked her to get the *ashram* superintendent's permission if she wanted him to treat her like the younger girls. Prema's pride was hurt and she responded angrily, 'Why should I hanker after your hand so much that I have to go and get permission?'

and stalked off. One night, however, Gandhi had gone to the toilet since he was suffering from diarrhoea because of one of his food experiments. He had fainted from weakness and Prema, who had heard him fall, reached his side. Gandhi walked back leaning his body against her for support and she even lifted him onto the bed. From that night onwards she often accompanied him on his evening walk, with his hand on her shoulder, while she, I imagine, looked around her with the pride of the chosen one, a victor in the secret struggle among the women. In her elation at being closer to him, she tells us, she once kissed his hands saying. 'The hand that has shaken the British throne is resting on my shoulders! What a matter of pride!' Gandhi had laughed, 'Yes, how proud we all are!' and, clowning, he threw out his chest and strutted about in imitation of a stage emperor.[49]

In 1933, when she was 27 years old, Gandhi begged Prema to give him as *bhiksha* (meritorious alms) a life-long vow of celibacy. Prema wrote back that there was no difficulty in her compliance with his wish as celibacy was in any case her ideal. In unreflected arrogance she added, 'I may sleep with any man on the same bed during the whole night and get up in the morning as innocent as a child.' Touched on a sore spot, Gandhi reprimanded her on a pride unbecoming a celibate. From mythology he gave examples of those whose pride in their celibacy had gone before a grievous fall. She was no goddess (*devi*), he said, since she still had her periods. For Gandhi believed that in a really celibate woman menstruation stopped completely, the monthly period being but a stigmata of *vikara*, of the sexual distortions of a woman's soul.[50]

Gradually, Prema was trusted with greater and greater responsibilities in running the *ashram*, though her constant struggle, like those of most other women, was for an intimate closeness with Gandhi. He would try to turn her thoughts toward the *ashram* community, instruct her to regard herself as belonging to the community and vice versa. 'You are dear to me, that is why "your" *ashram* is dear to me. Love wants an anchor, love needs touch. It is human nature that not only the mind needs an anchor but also the body and the sense organs,' she would argue back.[51] He would ask her to sublimate her emotions, affectionately call her hysterical, explaining that by hysterical he meant someone under an excessive sway of emotions. He would berate her for her lapses and then coax and cajole her back if she showed any signs of withdrawal. Prema felt that the 'Old Beloved,' her affectionate name for him, had ensnared her. Gandhi replied,

> I do not want to snare anyone in my net. If everyone becomes a
> puppet of mine then what will happen to me? I regard such efforts
> as worthless. But even if I try to trap someone you shouldn't lose
> your self-confidence. Your letters prove that you are on guard. Yes,
> it is true that you have always been fearful of being caught in my
> net. That is a bad sign. If you have decided (to throw in your lot

with me) then why the fear? Or perhaps it is possible that we
mean different things by the word 'ensnare'?[52]

Feeling trapped—by the frustration of her own unconscious wishes in relation
to Gandhi, the analyst would say—Prema sought to detach herself from him.
She fought with him on what in retrospect seem minor issues. Remaining a
devoted follower of Gandhi and his ideals, she was aware of a degree of
estrangement from the Mahatma. Prema finally went back to Maharashtra in
1939 and set up an *ashram* in a small village. It was devoted to the fulfilment of
Gandhi's social agenda—uplift of the poor and the untouchables, education of
women, increasing the self-sufficiency of the village community, and so on. Like
the portentous dream after their initial meeting, the separation too is the occasion
for a significant dream. In this dream Prema is alone on a vast plain which
meets the sky at the horizon. She is sitting in a chair in the middle of this plain
with green grass all around her. Behind the chair, she senses the presence of a
man. She cannot see him but has no doubt that the man is her protector and her
companion. Suddenly four or five beautiful, well-dressed boys come running up
to her with bouquets of flowers in their hands. She begins to talk to the boys.
More and more children now appear with bouquets. From the sky, flowers begin
to rain down upon her. She wakes up with a start. After waking up, when she
thinks of the dream, she is convinced that the man standing behind her is Gandhi
and that his blessings will always remain with her.[53]

As I reflect on the dream and its context, I cannot help musing (which is less
an interpretation of the dream than my associations to it) that perhaps the dream
fulfils some of Prema's contradictory wishes. Once again restored to the centre
of her world with Gandhi, from which she has been recently excluded, she is the
celibate *devi* of Hindu mythology on whom gods shower flowers from heaven as
a sign of their approbation and homage. On the other hand, she has also become
the life-companion of the Mahatma, bearing him not only the four sons Kasturbai
had borne but many, many more adoring and adorable children.

Since it was the man rather than what he stood for who was the focus of her
emotional life, Prema gradually drifted back to her earlier spiritual interests after
Gandhi's death. As she consorted with yogis and mystics, the memory of the
Mahatma and the years she had spent with him would become locked up in a
corner of her mind, to be occasionally opened and savoured privately, a secret
solace in times of distress.

In many ways, Madeline Slade was one of the more unusual members of Gandhi's
female entourage. Daughter of an admiral in the British Navy who had been a
commander of the East Indies Squadron, she was a part of the British ruling
establishment, which both despised and feared Gandhi as an implacable foe.
Brought up in the freedom of an upper-class English home of the era, Madeline

had been dissatisfied and unhappy for years, and tells us that everything had been dark and futile till she discovered Gandhi and left for India when she was in her early 30s.[54] A great admirer of Beethoven—she had thought of devoting her life to the study of his life and music—her plans underwent a drastic change after she read Romain Rolland's book on Gandhi (*Mahatma Gandhi*, 1924). Not wishing to act hastily, she first prepared herself for the ordeal of *ashram* life in India. Madeline went about this task with her usual single-minded determination. She learned spinning and sitting cross-legged on the floor; she became a teetotaller and a vegetarian and learned Urdu. She then wrote to Gandhi expressing her wish and received a cordial reply inviting her to join him.

A tall, strapping woman, handsome rather than pretty, Madeline took avidly to the ascetic part of the *ashram* life. She clung to Gandhi with a ferocity which he found very unsettling, perhaps also because of feelings which her strong need for his physical proximity in turn aroused in him. During the 24 years of their association, Gandhi would repeatedly send her away to live and work in other *ashrams* in distant parts of the country. She would have nervous breakdowns as a consequence of these separations and 'struggles of the heart' (as she called them) or 'spiritual agony' (as Gandhi put it), impetuously rush back to wherever Gandhi was only to be again banished from his presence. He tried to redirect her from her single-minded concentration on him as a person to the cause they both served.

> The parting today was sad, because I saw that I pained you. I want you to be a perfect woman. I want you to shed all angularities . . . .
>
> Do throw off the nervousness. You must not cling to me as in this body. The spirit without the body is ever with you. And that is more than the feeble embodied imprisoned spirit with all the limitations that flesh is heir to. The spirit without the flesh is perfect, and that is all we need. This can be felt only when we practise detachment. This you must now try to achieve.
>
> This is how I should grow if I were you. But you should grow along your own lines. You will, therefore, reject all I have said in this, that does not appeal to your heart or your head. You must retain your individuality at all cost. Resist me when you must. For I may judge you wrongly in spite of all my love for you. I do not want you to impute infallibility to me.[55]

Madeline, now appropriately renamed Mira by Gandhi after the 16th-century Indian woman-saint whose infatuation with Krishna was not much greater than Madeline's own yearing for the Mahatma, was however a battlefield of forces stronger than those amenable to reason. She was like the women described by the psychoanalyst Ralph Greenson, who come to analysis not to seek insight but to enjoy the physical proximity of the analyst.[56] Such patients relate a history of achievement and an adequate social life but an unsatisfactory love life characterized by wishes for incorporation, possession, and fusion. Gandhi's attitude to Mira, like that of the analyst with the patient, combined sympathetic listening with the frustration of wishes for gratification—a certain recipe, the mandrake root, for intensifying and unearthing ever more fresh capacities for love in her.[57] It further enhanced what analysts would call her transference to the Mahatma, a type of intense love felt for people who fulfil a role in our lives equivalent to the one fulfilled by parents in our childhood.

The presumption that their relationship was not quite one-sided and that Mira too evoked complex 'counter-transference' reactions in Gandhi is amply supported by his letters to her. Once, in 1927, when Mira had rushed to Gandhi's side on hearing that he was under severe strain, and had promptly been sent back, Gandhi wrote to her:

> I could not restrain myself from sending you a love message on reaching here. I felt very sad after letting you go. I have been very severe with you, but I could not do otherwise. I had to perform an operation and I steadied myself for it. Now let us hope all would go on smoothly, and that all the weakness is gone.[58]

The letter was followed the next day with a post card: 'This is merely to tell you I can't dismiss you from my mind. Every surgeon has a soothing ointment after a severe operation. This is my ointment. . .'[59] Two days later, yet another letter followed:

> I have never been so anxious as this time to hear from you, for I sent you away too quickly after a serious operation. You haunted me in my sleep last night and were reported by friends to whom you had been sent, to be delirious, but without any danger. They said, 'You need not be anxious. We are doing all that is humanly possible.' And with this I woke up troubled in mind and prayed that you may be free from all harm. . .[60]

From prison, where he was safe from her importunate physicality, Gandhi could express his feelings for her more freely. While translating a book of Indian hymns into English for her, he wrote: 'In translating the hymns for you I am giving myself much joy. Have I not expressed my love, often in storms than in gentle soothing showers of affection? The memory of these storms adds to the pleasure of this exclusive translation for you.'[61] As with his other women, Gandhi could not let Mira get away further than the distance he unconsciously held to be the optimal for his own feelings of well-being.

Like the child on his first explorations of the world who does not venture further from the mother than the length of an invisible string with which he seems attached to her, Gandhi too would become anxious at any break that threatened to become permanent and would seek to draw the woman closer to him.

> Chi. Mira,
> You are on the brain. I look about me, and miss you. I open the *charkha* (spinning wheel) and miss you. So on and so forth. But what is the use? You have done the right thing. You have left your home, your people and all that people prize most, not to serve me personally but to serve the cause I stand for. All the time you were squandering your love on me personally, I felt guilty of misappropriation. And I exploded on the slightest pretext. Now that you are not with me, my anger turns itself upon me for having given you all those terrible scoldings. But I was on a bed of hot ashes all the while I was accepting your service. You will truly serve me by joyously serving the cause. Cheer, cheer, no more of idle.

To this, Mira added the commentary, 'The struggle was terrible. I too was on a bed of hot ashes because I could feel the Bapu was. This was one of the occasions when, somehow or other, I managed to tear myself away.'[62]

In 1936, when Gandhi was recovering from his breakdown and had decided to leave Sabarmati to go and live by himself in a remote village, Mira thought she finally had a chance to fulfil her deepest longing, to live with Bapu in the countryside. Gandhi, however, was adamant. He would stay in the village Mira lived in only if she herself shifted to a neighbouring one. 'This nearly broke my heart, but somehow I managed to carry on, and when Bapu finally decided to come and live in Seagaon,' she writes, 'I buried my sorrow in the joy of preparing for him his cottage and cowshed. For myself I built a little cottage a mile away on the ridge of Varoda village, and within a week of Bapu's coming to live in Seagaon I departed for the hut on the hill where I lived alone with my little horse as my companion.'[63] Even this relative nearness was not to last long as political events inexorably pulled Gandhi away on his travels.

In 1948, at the time of Gandhi's death, Mira was living in her own *ashram* near Rishikesh in the foothills of the Himalayas, devoting herself to the care of cattle in the nearby villages. Starting one *ashram* after another, deeper and deeper into the Himalayas, she was to live in India till 1958 when she decided to return to Europe, almost 35 years after she had first left home in search of Gandhi. I visited her with a friend in 1964, in the forests above Baden near Vienna where she now made her home in an isolated farmhouse with a dog and an old Indian servant from Rishikesh. Gracious but reserved, she offered us tea and biscuits and perfunctorily inquired about current events in India. She refused to talk about Gandhi, claiming that he did not interest her any longer. What animated her exclusively and what she enthusiastically talked about was Beethoven whom she saw as the highest manifestation of the human spirit. He had been her first love before she read Romain Rolland's book on Gandhi that was to change her life. Working on a biography of Beethoven and with his music as her dearest companion she had come back to the composer after a 35-year detour with Gandhi. Somewhat disappointed, we left her to her new love. Walking toward our car parked a few hundred yards away from the farmhouse, we saw the servant come running up to us, desperation writ large on his lined face: 'Sahib, I don't want to live here. I want to go home. Please take me home.' I mumbled our apologies for being unable to help and left him standing on the grassy meadow, peering after us in the mild afternoon sun as we drove away.

To place Gandhi's sexual preoccupations in their cultural context, we should remember that sexuality, whether in the erotic flourishes of Indian art and in the Dionysian rituals of its popular religion, or in the dramatic combat with ascetic longings of yogis who seek to conquer and transform it into spiritual power, has been a perennial preoccupation of Hindu culture. In this resides the reason, puzzling to many non-Indians, why in spite of the surface resemblances between Jungian concepts and Indian thought, it is Freud rather than Jung who fascinates the Indian mind. Many modern Indian mystics feel compelled, in fact, to discuss Freud's assumptions and conclusions about the vagaries and transfigurations of libido while they pass over Jung's work with benign indifference. Indian spirituality is preeminently a theory of 'sublimation.'

Indian 'mysticism' is typically intended to be an intensely practical affair, concerned with an alchemy of the libido that would convert it from a giver of death to a bestower of immortality. It is the sexual fire that stokes the alchemical transformation wherein the cooking pot is the body and the cooking oil is a distillation from sexual fluids. The strength of this traditional aspiration to sublimate sexuality into spirituality, semen into the elixir Soma, varies in different regions with different castes. Yet though only small sections of Indian society may act on this aspiration, it is a well-known theory subscribed to by most Hindus, including non-literate villagers. In its most popular form, the Hindu theory of sublimation goes something like this.

Physical strength and mental power have their source in *virya*, a word that stands for both sexual energy and semen. *Virya*, in fact, is identical with the essence of maleness. *Virya* can either move downward in sexual intercourse, where it is emitted in its gross physical form as semen, or it can move upward through the spinal chord and into the brain, in its subtle form known as *ojas*. Hindus regard the downward movement of sexual energy and its emission as semen as enervating, a debilitating waste of vitality and essential energy. Of all emotions, it is said, lust throws the physical system into the greatest choas, with every violent passion destroying millions of red blood cells. Indian metaphysical physiology maintains that food is converted into semen in a 30-day period by successive transformations (and refinements) through blood, flesh, fat, bone, and marrow till semen is distilled—40 drops of blood producing one drop of semen. Each ejaculation involves a loss of half an ounce of semen, which is equivalent to the vitality produced by the consumption of 60 pounds of food.

In another similar calculation with pedagogic intent, each act of copulation is equivalent to an energy expenditure of 24 hours of concentrated mental activity or 72 hours of hard physical labour.[64] Gandhi is merely reiterating these popular ideas when he says that

> Once the idea, that the only and grand function of the sexual
> organ is generation, posesses men and women, union for any other
> purpose they will hold as criminal waste of the vital fluid, and
> consequent excitement caused to men and women as an equally
> criminal waste of precious energy. It is now easy to understand
> why the scientists of old have put such great value upon its strong
> transmutation into the highest form of energy for the benefit of
> society.[65]

If, on the other hand, semen is retained, converted into *ojas* and moved upwards by the observance of *brahmacharya*, it becomes a source of spiritual life rather than cause of physical decay. Longevity, creativity, physical and mental vitality are enhanced by the conservation of semen; memory, will power, inspiration—scientific and artistic—all derive from the observation of *brahmacharya*. In fact, if unbroken (*akhanda*) *brahmacharya* in thought, word, and deed can be observed for 12 years, the aspirant will obtain *moksha* spontaneously.

These ideas on semen and celibacy, I have emphasized above, are a legacy of Indian culture and are shared, so to speak, by Hindu saints and sinners alike. Indeed, the very first published case history in Indian psychoanalytic literature sounds like a parody of Gandhi.

> The patient is a married young man and is the father of several
> children. He is of religious bent and his ideal in life is to attain
> what has been called in Hindu literature *Jivanmukti*, i.e., a state of
> liberation from wordly bondages and a perfect freedom from all
> sorts of passions whether bodily or mental. The possibility of the
> existence of such a state and of its attainment is never doubted by
> the patient as he says he has implicit faith in the Hindu scriptures
> which assert that the realization of *brahma* or supreme entity,
> results in such a liberation. (He believes). . . that the only thing he
> has to do is to abstain from sex of all sorts and liberation will

come to him as a sort of reward . . . Since one pleasure leads to another it is desirable to shun all pleasures in life lest they should lead to sex. The patient is against forming any attachment whether it be with his wife or children or friend or any inanimate object. He is terribly upset sometimes when he finds that in spite of his ideal of no-attachment and no-sex, lascivious thoughts of the most vulgar nature and uncontrollable feelings of love and attraction arise in his mind . . . In spite of his deep reverence for Hindu gods and goddesses filthy sexual ideas of an obsessional nature come into his mind when he bows before these images.[66]

The 'raising' of the seed upwards,' then, is a strikingly familiar image in the Indian psycho-philosophical schools of self-realization commonly clumped under the misleading label of 'mysticism.' As Wendy O' Flaherty remarks: 'So pervasive is the concept of semen being raised up to the head that popular versions of the philosophy believe that semen originates there.'[67] The concept is even present in the *Kamasutra*, the textbook of eroticism and presumably a subverter of ascetic ideals, where the successful lover is not someone who is overly passionate but one who has controlled, stilled his senses through *brahmacharya* and meditation.[68] Indian mythology, too, is replete with stories in which the gods, threatened by a human being who is progressing toward immortality by accruing immense capacities through celibacy and meditation, send a heavenly nymph to seduce the ascetic (even the trickling down of a single drop of sexual fluid counting as a fatal lapse), and thereby reduce him to the common human, carnal denominator.

Of course, given the horrific imagery of sexuality as cataclysmic depletion, no people can procreate with any sense of joyful abandon unless they develop a good deal of scepticism, if not an open defiance, in relation to the sexual prescription had ideals of the 'cultural superego.' The relief at seeing the ascetic's pretensions humbled by the opulent charms of a heavenly seductress is not only that of the gods but is equally shared by the mortals who listen to the myth or see it enacted in popular dance and folk drama. The ideals of celibacy are then simultaneously subscribed to and scoffed at. Whereas, one the one hand, there are number of sages in the Indian tradition (Gandhi is only the latest one to join this august assemblage), who are admired for their successful celibacy and the powers it brought them, there are, on the other hand, also innumerable folktales detailing the misadventures of randy ascetics. In the more dignified myths, even the Creator is unable to sustain his chastity and is laid low by carnality.

The heavenly nymph Mohini fell in love with the Lord of Creation, Brahma. After gaining the assistance of Kama, the god of love, she went to Brahma and danced before him, revealing her body to him in order to entice him, but Brahma remained without passion. Then Kama struck Brahma with an arrow. Brahma wavered and felt desire, but after a moment he gained control. Brahma said to Mohini, go away, Mother, your efforts are wasted here. I know your intention, and I am not suitable for your work. The scripture says, 'Ascetics must avoid all women, especially prostitutes.' I am incapable of doing anything that the Vedas consider despicable. You are a sophisticated woman, look for a sophisticated young man, suitable for your work, and there will be virtue in your union. But I am an old man, an ascetic Brahmin; what pleasure can I find in a prostitute? Mohini laughed and said to him, 'A man who refuses to make love to a woman who is tortured by desire—he is an eunuch. Whether a man be a householder or ascetic or lover, he must not spurn a woman who approaches him, or he will go to Hell. Come now and make love to me in some private place,' and as she said this she pulled at Brahma's garment. Then the sages bowed to Brahma, 'How is it that Mohini, the best of celestial prostitutes, is in your presence?' Brahma said, to conceal his scheme, 'She danced and sang for a long time and then when she was tired she came here like a young girl to her father.' But the sages laughed for they knew the whole secret, and Brahma laughed too.[69]

The piece of gossip that Gandhi 'slept with naked women in his old age' has therefore resounding echoes in the Indian cultural tradition. It arouses complex emotions in both the purveyor or and the listener, namely a malicious relief together with an aching disappointment that he may indeed have done so.

The ultimate if ironic refinement of celibacy is found in the tantric version, where the aspirant is trained and enjoined to perform the sexual act itself without desire and the 'spilling of the seed,' thus divorcing the sexual impulse from human physiology and any conscious or unconscious mental representation of it. The impulse, it is believed, stirs up the semen in this ritual (and unbelievably passionless) sexual act and evokes energetic forces that can be rechanneled upwards. This and other *tantric* techniques were familiar to Gandhi, whose own deeply held religious persuasion, Vaishnavism, was pervaded by many such tantric notions. On the one hand, as we have seen, Gandhi often sounds like Chaitanya, the 15th-century 'father' of North Indian Vaishnavism, who rejected a disciple for paying attention to a woman, saying: 'I can never again look upon the face of an ascetic who associates with women. The senses are hard to control, and seek to fix themselves on wordly things. Even the wooden image of a woman has the power to steal the mind of a sage. . . .'[70] On the other hand, however, Gandhi in his sexual experiments seems to be following the examples set by other famous Vaishnavas like Ramananda and Viswanatha. Ramananda, Chaitanya's follower and companion, used to take two beautiful young temple prostitutes into a lonely garden where he would oil their bodies, bathe, and dress them while himself remaining 'unaffected.'[71] The philosopher Viswanatha, it is said, went to lie with his young wife at the command of his guru: 'He lay with her on the bed, but Viswanatha was transformed, and he did not touch her, as it had been his custom to do. He lay with his wife according to the instructions of his guru. . . . and thus he controlled his senses.'[72]

There are germs of truth in the signal importance Indian cultural tradition attaches to sexuality. The notion, arising from this emphasis, that sexual urges amount to a creative fire—not only for procreation but, equally, in self-creation— is indeed compelling. Further, a tradition that does not reduce sexual love to copulation but seeks to elevate it into a celebration, even a ritual that touches the partners with a sense of the sacred, and where orgasm is experienced as [a symbolic blessing of man by his ancestors and by the nature of things,' is certainly sympathetic.[73] My concern here has to do with the concomitant strong anxiety in India surrounding the ideas of the 'squandering of the sperm' and 'biological self-sacrifice.' Such ideas and the fantasies they betray cannot help but heighten an ambivalence toward women that verges on misogyny and phobic avoidance. As for self-realization through renunciation of sexual love, I would tend to side with Thomas Mann when he observes:

It is undeniable that human dignity realizes itself in the two sexes, male and female; so that when one is neither one nor the other, one stands outside the human pale and whence then can human dignity come? Efforts to sustain it are worthy of respect, for they deal with the spiritual, and thus, let us admit in honour, with the preeminently human. But truth demands the hard confession that thought and the spirit. come badly off, in the long run, against nature. How little can the precepts of civilization avail against the dark, deep, silent knowledge of the flesh! How little it lets itself be taken in by the spirit![74]

How would Freud, who in his mid-life also chose to become celibate, have regarded Gandhi's celibacy and its intended efficacy? In general, Freud was understandably skeptical about the possibility that sexual abstinence could help to build energetic men of action, original thinkers, or bold reformers. Yet he also saw such attempts at the sublimation of 'genital libido' in relative terms:

The relationship between the amount of sublimation possible and the amount of sexual activity necessary naturally varies very much from person to person and even from one calling to another. An abstinent artist is hardly conceivable; but an abstinent young savant is certainly no rarity. The latter can, by his self-restraint, liberate forces for his studies; while the former probably finds his artistic achievements powerfully stimulated by his sexual experience.[75]

It is quite conceivable that Freud would have conceded the possibility of successful celibacy to a few extraordinary people of genuine originality with a self-abnegating sense of mission or transcendent purpose. In other words, he would have agreed with the Latin dictum that 'what is allowed to Jove is forbidden to the ox.' The psychoanalytic question is, then, not of sublimation but why Gandhi found phallic desire so offensive that he must, so to speak, tear it out by the very roots.

Some of Gandhi's uneasiness with phallic desire has to do with his feeling that genital love is an accursed and distasteful prerogative of the father. In his autobiography, in spite of expressing many admirable filial sentiments, Gandhi suspects his father of being 'oversexed' since he married for the fourth time when he was over 40 and Putlibai, Gandhi's mother, was only 18. In his fantasy, we would suggest, Gandhi saw his young mother as the innocent victim of a powerful old male's lust to which the child could only be an anguished and helpless spectator, unable to save the beloved caretaker from the violation of her person and the violence done to her body. In later life, Gandhi would embrace the cause wherein the marriage of old men with young girls was adamantly opposed with great zeal. He wrote articles with such titles as 'Marriage of Old and Young or Debauchery?' and exhorted his correspondents who reported such incidents to fight this practice. The older men he respected and took as his models were those who shared his revulsion with genital sexuality. These were the men who (like Tolstoy and Raichandra) had sought to transform sexual passion into a more universal religious quest or (like Ruskin) into a moral and aesthetic fervour.

If phallic desire was the violent and tumultuous 'way of the fathers,' genital abstinence, its surrender, provided the tranquil, peaceful path back to the mother. Here Gandhi was not unlike St Augustine, who, too, inwardly beheld celibacy garbed in soothing, maternal imagery:

> . . . . there apeared unto me the chaste dignity of Continence,
> serene, yet not relaxedly gay, honestly alluring me to come and
> doubt not; and stretching forth to receive and embrace me, her
> holy hands full of multitudes of good examples; there were so
> many young men and maidens here, a multitude of youth and
> every age, grave widows and aged virgins; and Continence herself
> in all, not barren, but a fruitful mother of children of joys. . . .[76]

More specifically, the psychobiographical evidence we have reviewed above is compelling that Gandhi's relationships with women are dominated by the unconscious fantasy of maintaining an idealized relationship with the maternal body. This wished-for oneness with the mother is suffused with nurturance and gratitude, mutual adoration and affirmation, without a trace of desire which divides and bifurcates. Replete with wishes for fusion and elimination of differences and limits, Gandhi 'perceived' sexual desire, *both* of the mother and the child, as the single biggest obstacle to the preservation of this illusion. Many of his attitudes, beliefs, and actions with regard to women can then be understood as defensive manoeuvres against the possibility of this preception rising to surface awarenes.

Since the mother is a woman, a first step in the defensive operations is to believe that women are not, or only minimally, sexual beings. 'I do not believe that woman is prey to sexual desire to the same extent as man. It is easier for her than for man to exercise self-restraint,'[77] is an opinion often repeated in his writings. Reflecting on his own experiences with Kasturbai, he asserts that 'There was never want of restraint on the part of my wife. Very often she would show restraint, but she rarely resisted me, although she showed disinclination very often.'[78] Whereas he associates male sexuality with unheeding, lustful violence, female sexuality, where it exists, is a passive, suffering acceptance of the male onslaught. This, we must again remember, is only at the conscious level. Unconsciously, his perception of masculine violence and feminine passivity seem to be reversed, as evident in the imagery of the descriptions of his few erotic encounters with women. In his very first adolescent confrontation, he is struck 'dumb and blind,' while the woman is confident and aggressive; in England, he is trembling like a frightened wild animal who has just escaped the (woman) hunter.

The solution to the root problem between the sexes is then, not a removal of the social and legal inequalities suffered by women—though Gandhi was an enthusiastic champion of women's rights—but a thoroughgoing desexualization of the male-female relationship, in which women must take the lead. 'If they will only learn to say "no" to their husbands when they approach them carnally. . . . If a wife says to her husband: "No, I do not want it," he will make no trouble. But she has not been taught. . . . I want women to learn the primary right of resistance.'[79]

Besides desexing the woman, another step in the denial of her desire is her idealization (especially of the Indian woman) as nearer to a purer divine state and thus an object of worship and adoration. That is why a woman does not need to renounce the world in the last stage of life to contemplate God, as is prescribed for the man in the ideal Hindu life cycle. 'She sees Him always. She has no need of any other school to prepare her for Heaven than marriage to a man and care of her children.'[80] Woman is also

> the incarnation of *Ahimsa*. *Ahimsa* means infinite love, which, again means infinite capacity for suffering. Who but woman, the mother of man shows this capacity in the largest measure? Let her transfer that love to the whole of humanity, let her forget she ever was, or can be, the object of man's lust. And she will occupy her proud position by the side of the man as his mother, maker and silent leader.[81]

Primarily seeing the mother in the woman and idealizing motherhood is yet another way of denying feminine eroticism. When Millie Polak, a female associate in the Phoenix *ashram* in South Africa, questioned his idealization of motherhood, saying that being a mother does not make a woman wise, Gandhi extolled mother-love as one of the finest aspects of love in human life. His imagery of motherhood is of infants suckling on breasts with inexhaustible supplies of milk. For example, in a letter explaining why the *Gita*, the sacred book of the Hindus, is called Mother, he rhapsodizes,

> It has been likened to the sacred cow, the giver of all desires (sic!). Hence Mother. Well, that immortal Mother gives all the milk we need for spiritual sustenance, it we would but approach her as babies seeking and sucking it from her. She is capable of yielding milk to her millions of babies from her exhaustless udder.
>
> In doing the Harijan (untouchable) work in the midst of calumny, misrepresentations and apparent disappointments, her lap comforts me and keeps me from falling into the Slough of Despond.[82]

Whereas desexualizing, idealizing, and perceiving only the 'milky' mother in the woman is one part of his defensive bulwark which helped in preserving the illusion of unity with the maternal body intact, the other part consists of efforts at renouncing the gift of sexual desire, abjuring his own masculinity. Here we must note that the Hindu Vaishnava culture, in which Gandhi grew up and in which he remained deeply rooted, not only provides a sanction for man's feminine strivings, but raises these strivings to the level of a religious-spiritual quest. In devotional Vaishnavism, Lord Krishna alone is the male and all devotees, irrespective of their sex, are female. Gandhi's statement that he had mentally become a woman or that he envied women and that there is as much reason for a man to wish that he was born a woman, as for women to do otherwise, thus struck many responsive chords in his audience.

If Gandhi had had his way, there would be no art or poetry celebrating woman's beauty.

> I am told that our literature is full of even an exaggerated apotheosis of women. Let me say that it is an altogether wrong apotheosis. Let me place one simple fact before you. In what light do you think of them when you proceed to write about them? I suggest that before you put your pens to paper think of woman as your own mother, and I assure you the chastest literature will flow from your pens, even like the beautiful rain from heaven which waters the thirsty earth below. Remember that a woman was your mother, before a woman became your wife.[83]

Although Gandhi's wished-for feminization was defensive in origin, we cannot deny the devlopment of its adaptive aspects. Others, most notably Erik Erikson, have commented upon Gandhi's more or less conscious explorations of the maternal stance and feminine perspective in his actions.[84] In spite of a welter of public demands on his time, we know of the motherly care he could extend to the personal lives of his followers, and the anxious concern he displayed about their health and well-being, including solicitous inquiries about the state of their daily bowel movements.[85] We also know of the widening of these maternal-feminine ways—teasing, testing, taking suffering upon oneself, and so on—in the formulation of his political style and as elements of his campaigns of militant nonviolence.

We have seen that for Gandhi, the cherished oneness with the maternal-feminine could not always be maintained and was often threatened by the intrustion of phallic desire. His obsession with food at these times, evident in the letters and writings, not only represented a preparation for erecting physiological barriers against desire, but also the strengthening of his psychological defences, and thus a reinforcement of his spiritual armamentarium. In other words, in his preoccupation with food (and elimination), in his persistent investment of edible physical substances with psychological qualities, Gandhi plays out the 'basic oral fantasy,' as described by the psychoanalyst Donald Winnicott—'when hungry I think of food, when I eat I think of taking food in. I think of what I like to keep inside and I think of what I want to be rid of and I think of getting rid of it'—whose underlying theme is of union with the mother. His experiments with various kinds of food and a reduction in its intake—in his later years, he abjured milk completely so as not to eroticize his viscera—appear as part of an involuted and intuitive effort to recover and maintain his merger with his mother.

Gandhi's relationship with women and the passions they aroused are, then, more complex than what he reveals in his own impassioned confession. Nor does a recourse to traditional Hindu explanations and prescriptions for their 'diagnosis and cure' reflect adequately the depths of the inner life in which his desires found their wellsprings. Beset by conflicts couched in moral terms familiar to Christian and classical psychoanalyst alike, he struggled with the yearnings aroused by the goddess of longing besides the passions provoked by the god of desire. Or, to use a well-known Indian metaphor in which a woman is said to have two breasts, one for her child, another for her husband, Gandhi's unconscious effort to shift from the one breast to the other—from man to child—was not always successful. He was a man in spite of himself. We know that the sensuality derived from the deeply felt oneness with a maternal world, a sensuality that challenges death, energized Gandhi's person, impelled his transcendent endeavours, and advanced him on the road to a freedom of spirit from which India, as well as the world, has profited. Yet we have seen that throughout his life, there were profound periods of emotional turmoil when this original and ultimately illusory connection broke down, emptying him of all inner 'goodness' and 'power'.

MASCULINE/FEMININE:
A VIEW FROM THE COUCH

On 11 April 1929, Girindrasekhar Bose, the founder and first president of the Indian Psychoanalytical Society, wrote to Freud on the difference he had observed in the psychoanalytic treatment of Indian and Western patients:

> Of course I do not expect that you would accept offhand my reading of the Oedipus situation. I do not deny the importance of the castration threat in European cases; my argument is that the threat owes its efficiency to its connection with the wish to be female [Freud in a previous letter had gently chided Bose with understating the efficiency of the castration threat.] The real struggle lies between the desire to be a male and its opposite, the desire to be a female. I have already referred to the fact that the castration threat is very common in Indian society but my Indian patients do not exhibit castration symptoms to such a marked degree as my European cases. The desire to be a female is more easily unearthed in Indian male patients than in European.... The Oedipus mother is very often a combined parental image and this is a fact of great importance. I have reason to believe that much of the motivation of the maternal deity is traceable to this source.

Freud's reply is courteous and diplomatic:

> I am fully impressed by the difference in the castration reaction between Indian and European patients and promise to keep my attention fixed on the opposite wish you accentuate. The latter is too important for a hasty decision.[1]

In another paper, Bose elaborates on his observations and explains them through his theory of opposite wishes:

> During my analysis of Indian patients I have never come across a case of castration complex in the form in which it has been described by European observers. This fact would seem to indicate

that the castration idea develops as a result of environmental conditions acting on some more primitive trend in the subject. The difference in social environment of Indians and Europeans is responsible for the difference in modes of expression in the two cases. It has been usually proposed that threats of castration in early childhood days, owing to some misdemeanour is directly responsible for the complex, but histories of Indian patients seem to disprove this.[2]

Bose then goes on to say that though the castration threat is extremely common—in girls it takes the form of chastisement by snakes—the difference in Indian reactions to it are due to children growing up naked till the ages of nine to ten years (girls till seven) so that the difference between the sexes never comes as a surprise. The castration idea, which comes up symbolically in dreams as decapitation, a cut on a finger, or a sore in some part of the body, has behind it the 'primitive' idea of being a woman.

Indeed, reading early Indian case histories, one is struck by the fluidity of the patients' cross-sexual and generational identifications. In the Indian patient, the fantasy of taking on the sexual attributes of both the parents seems to have a relatively easier access to awareness. Bose, for instance, in one of his vignettes tells us of a middle-aged lawyer who, with reference to his parents, sometimes

took up an active male sexual role treating both of them as females in his unconscious and sometimes a female attitude, especially towards the father, craving for a child from him. In the male role sometimes he identified himself with his father and felt a sexual craving for the mother, on the other occasions his unconscious mind built up a composite of both the parents toward which male sexual needs were directed; it is in this attitude that he made his father give birth to a child like a woman in his dream.[3]

Another young Bengali, whenever he thought of a particular man, felt with a hallucinatory intensity that his penis and testes vanished altogether and were replaced by female genitalia. While defecating he felt he heard the peremptory voice of his guru asking, 'Have you given me a child yet?' In many of his dreams, he was a man whereas his father and brothers had become women. During intercourse with his wife he tied a handkerchief over his eyes as it gave him the feeling of being a veiled bride while he fantasized his own penis as that of his father and his wife's vagina as that of his mother.[4]

In my own work, 50 years after Bose's contributions of which till recently I was only vaguely aware, I am struck by the comparable patterns in Indian mental life that we observed independently of each other, and this in spite of our different emotional predilections, analytic styles, theoretical preoccupations, geographical locations, and historical situations. Such a convergence further strengthen my belief, shared by every practicing analyst, that there is no absolute arbitrariness in our representation of the inner world. There is unquestionably something that resists, a something which can only be characterized by the attribute 'psychical reality,' which both the analyst and the analysand help discover and give meaning to.

It is the ubiquity and multiformity of the 'primitive idea of being a woman' and the embedding of this fantasy in the maternal configurations of the family and the culture in India, which I would like to discuss in my own observations. My main argument is that the 'hegemonic narrative' of Hindu culture as far as male development is concerned, is neither that of Freud's Oedipus nor of Christianity's Adam. One of the more dominant narratives of this culture is that of Devi, the great goddess, especially in her manifold expressions as mother in the inner world of the Hindu son. In India, at least, a primary task of psychoanalysis, the science of imagination or even (in Wallace Steven's words) 'the science of illusion' (can one call it *Mayalogy?*)[5]—'The great Illusion'—as the goddess is also called. Of course, it is not my intention to deny or underestimate the importance of the powerful mother in Western psychoanalysis. All I seek to suggest is that certain forms of the maternal-feminine may be more central in Indian myths and psyche than in their Western counterpart. I would then like to begin my exposition with the first 15 minutes of an analytic session.

The patient is a 26-year-old social worker who has been in analysis for three years. He comes four times a week, with each lasting 50 minutes and conducted in the classical manner with the patient lying on the couch and the analyst sitting in a chair behind him. He entered analysis not because of any pressing personal problem, but because he thought it would help him professionally. In this particular session, he begins with a fantasy he had while he was in a bus. The fantasy was of a tribe, living in the jungle, which unclothes its dead and hangs them on the trees. M., the patient, visualized a beautiful woman hanging on one of the trees. He imagined himself coming at night and having intercourse with the woman. Other members of the tribe are eating part of the hanging corpses. The fantasy is immediately followed by the recollection of an incident from the previous evening. M. was visiting his parents' home, where he had lived till recently before he married and set up his own household. This move was not only personally painful but also unusual for his social milieu, where sons normally brought their wives to live in their parental home. An older cousin, with her three-year-old son, was also visiting at the same time. M. felt irritated by the anxious attention his mother and grandmother gave the boy. The grandmother kept on telling the child not to go and play out of the house, to be careful of venturing too far, and so on. On my remarking that perhaps he recognized himself in the nephew, M. exclaimed with rare resentment, 'Yes, all the women (his mother, grandmother, his father's brother's wife, and his father's unmarried sister who lived with them) were always doing the same with me.'

Beginning with these 15 minutes of a session, I would like to unroll M.'s conflicts around maternal representations and weave them together with the central maternal configurations of Indian culture. Because of this particular objective, my presentation of further material from M.'s analysis is bound to be subject to what Donald Spence has called 'narrative smoothing.'[6] A case history though it purports to be a story that is true is actually always at the intersection of fact and fable. Its tale quality, though, arises less from the commissions in imagination than from omissions in reality.

Born in a lower-middle-class family in a large village near Delhi, M. is the eldest of three brothers and two sisters. His memories of growing up, till well into youth, are pervaded by the maternal phalanx of the four women. Like his mother, who in his earliest memories stands out as a distinct figure from a maternal-feminine continuum, to be then reabsorbed in it, M, too, often emerges from and retreats into femininity. In the transference, the fantasies of being a woman are not especially disturbing; neither are the fantasies of being an infant suckling at a breast which he has grown onto my exaggeratedly hairy chest. One of his earliest recollections is of a woman who used to pull at the penises of the little boys playing out in the street. M. never felt afraid when the woman grabbed at his own penis. In fact, he rather liked it, reassured that he had a penis at all or at least enough of one for the woman to acknowledge its existence.

Bathed, dressed, combed, and caressed by one or the other of the women, M.'s wishes and needs were met before they were even articulated. Food, especially the milk-based Indian sweets, were constantly pressed on him. Even now, on his visits to the family, the first question by one of the women pertains to what he would like to eat. For a long time during the analysis, whenever a particular session was stressful, because of what he considered a lack of maternal empathy in my interventions, M. felt compelled to go to a restaurant in town where he would first gorge himself on sweets, before he returned home.

Besides the omnipresence of women, my most striking impressions of M.'s early memories is their night setting and their primarily tactile quality. Partly, this has to do with the crowded, public living arrangements of the Indian family. Here, even the notions of privacy are absent, not to speak of such luxuries as separate bedrooms for parents and children. Sleeping in the heat with little or no clothes next to one of his caretakers, an arm or a leg thrown across the maternal body, there is one disturbing memory which stands out clearly. This is of M.'s penis erect against the buttocks of his sleeping mother and his reluctance to move away as he struggled against the feelings of shame and embarrassment that she might wake up and notice the forbidden touch. Later, in adolescence, the mothers are replaced by visiting cousins sharing mattresses spread out in a room or on the roof, furtive rubbings of bodies and occasional genital contact while other members of the extended family are in various stages of sleep.

Embedded in this blissful abundance of maternal flesh and promiscuity of touch, however, is a nightmare. Ever since childhood and persisting well into the initial phase of the analysis, M. would often scream in his sleep while a vague, dark shape threatened to envelop him. At these times, only his father's awakening him with the reassurance that everything was all right helped M. compose himself for renewed slumber. The father, a gentle, retiring man, who left early in the morning for work and returned home late at night, was otherwise a dim figure hovering at the outskirts of an animated family life.

In the very first sessions of the analysis, M. talked of a sexual compulsion which he found embarrassing to acknowledge. The compulsion consisted of travelling in a crowded bus and seeking to press close to the hips of any plump, middle-aged woman standing in the aisle. It was vital for his ensuing excitement that the woman have her back to him. If she ever turned to face M., with the knowledge of his desire in her eyes, his erection immediately subsided and he would hurriedly move away with intense feelings of shame. After marriage, too, the edge of his desire was often at its sharpest when his wife slept on her side with her back to him. In mounting excitement, M. would rub against her and want to make love when she was still not quite awake. If, however, the wife gave intimation of becoming an enthusiastic partner in the exercise, M. sometimes ejaculated prematurely or found his erection precipitately shrivel.

It is evident from these brief fragments of M.'s case history that his desire is closely connected with some of the most inert parts of a woman's body, her hips and buttocks. In other words, the desire needs the woman to be sexually dead for its fulfilment. The genesis of the fantasy of the hanging corpse with whom M. has intercourse at night has at its root the fear of the mother's sexuality as well as 'the anger at their restraint of his explorations of the world. My choice of M.'s case, though, is not dictated by the interest it may hold from a psychoanalytical perspective. The choice, instead, has to do with its central theme, namely the various paths in imagination with M. traverses, in the face of many obstacles, to maintain an idealized relationship with the maternal body. This theme and the fantazied solutions to the disorders in the mother-son relationship are repeated again and again in Indian case and life histories. Bose's observation on the Indian male patient's 'primitive idea of being a woman' is then only a special proposition of a more general theorem. The wish to be a woman is one particular solution to the discord that threatens the breaking up of the son's fantasized connection to the mother, a solution whose access to awareness is facilitated by the culture's views on sexual differentiation and the permeability of gender boundaries. Thus, for instance, when Gandhi publicly proclaims that he has mentally become a woman or, quite unaware of Karen Horney and other deviants from the orthodox analytic position of the time, talks of man's envy of the woman's procreative capacities, saying, 'There is as much reason for a man to wish that he was born a woman as for woman to do otherwise,' he is sure of a sympathetic and receptive audience.[7]

In the Indian context, this particular theme can be explored in individual stories as well as in the cultural narratives we call myths, both of which are more closely interwoven in Indian culture than is the case in the modern West. In an apparent reversal of a Western pattern, traditional myths in India are less a source of intellectual and aesthetic satisfaction for the mythologist than of emotional recognition for others, more moving for the patient than for the analyst. Myths in India are not part of a bygone era. They are not 'retained fragments from the infantile psychic life of the race,' as Karl Abraham called them,[8] nor 'vestiges of the infantile fantasies of whole nations, secular dreams of youthful humanity' in Freud's words.[9]

Vibrantly alive, their symbolic power intact, Indian myths constitute a cultural idiom that aids the individual in the construction and integration of his inner world. Parallel to patterns of infant care and to the structure and values of family relationships, popular and well-known myths are isomorphic with the central psychological constellations of the culture and are constantly renewed and validated by the nature of subjective experience.[10] Given the availability of the mythological idiom, it is almost as easy to mythologize a psychoanalysis, such as that of M., as to analyse a myth, almost as convenient to elaborate on intrapsychic conflict in a mythological mode as in a case historical narrative mode.

Earlier, I advanced the thesis that myths of Devi, the great goddess, constitute a 'hegemonic narrative' of Hindu culture. Of the hundreds of myths on her various manifestations, my special interest here is in the goddess as mother, and especially the mother of the sons, Ganesha and Skanda. But before proceeding to connect M.'s tale to the larger cultural story, let me note that I have ignored the various versions of these myths in traditional texts and modern folklore—an undertaking which is rightly the preserve of mythologists and folklorists—and instead picked on their best-known, popular versions.

The popularity of Ganesha and Skanda as gods—psychologically representing two childhood positions of the Indian son—is certainly undeniable. Ganesha, the remover of obstacles and the god of all beginnings, is perhaps the most adored of the reputed 330 million Hindu gods. Iconically represented as a pot-bellied toddler with an elephant head and one missing tusk, he is proportionately represented as a small child when portrayed in the family group with his mother Parvati and father Shiva. His image, whether carved in stone or drawn up in a coloured print, is everywhere: in temples, homes, shops, roadside shrines, calendars. Ganesha's younger brother, Skanda or Kartikkeya, has his own following, especially in South India where he is extremely popular and worshipped under the name of Murugan or Subramanya. In contrast to Ganesha, Skanda is a handsome child, a youth of slender body and heroic exploits who, in analytic parlance, may be said to occupy the phallic position.

Ganesha's myths tell us one part of M.'s inner life while those of Skanda reveal yet another. Ganesha, in many myths, is solely his mother Parvati's creation. Desirous of a child and lacking Shiva's cooperation in the venture, she created him out of the dirt and sweat of her body mixed with unguents. Like M.'s fantasies of his femininity, Ganesha too is not only his mother's boy but contains her very essence. Even when indubitably male like Skanda, M. is immersed in the world of mothers which an Indian extended family creates for the child. Skanda, like M., is the son of more than one mother; his father Shiva's seed, being too powerful, could not be borne by one woman and wandered from womb to womb before Skanda took birth. M.'s ravenous consumption of sweets to restore feelings of well-being has parallels with Ganesha's appetite for *modakas,* the sweet wheat or rice balls which devotees offer to the god in large quantities 'knowing' that the god is never satisfied, that his belly empties itself as fast as it is filled.[11]

The lean M., like the fat god, craves sweets as a lifeline to the mother's breast; his hunger for the mother's body, in spite of temporary appeasements, is ultimately doomed to remain unfulfilled. M. is further like Ganesha in that he, too, has emerged from infancy with an ample capacity for vital involvement with others.

In the dramatization of M.'s dilemma in relation to the mother, brought to a head by development changes that push the child toward an exploration of the outer world while they also give him increasing intimations of his biological rock-bottom identity as a male, Ganesha and Skanda play the leading roles. In a version common to both South India and Sri Lanka the myth goes as follows:

> A mango was floating down the stream and Uma (Parvati) the mother, said that whoever rides around the universe first will get the mango. (In other versions, the promise is of *modakas* or wives.) Skanda impulsively got on his golden peacock and went around the universe. But Ganesha, who rode the rat, had more wisdom. He thought: 'What could my mother have meant by this?' He then circumambulated his mother, worshipped her and said, 'I have gone around my universe.' Since Ganesha was right his mother gave him the mango. Skanda was furious when he arrived and demanded the mango. But before he could get it Ganesha bit the mango and broke one of his tusks.[12]

Here Skanda and Ganesha are personifications of the two opposing wishes of the older child at the eve of the Oedipus stage. He is torn between a powerful push for independent and autonomous functioning, and an equally strong pull toward surrender and reimmersion in the enveloping maternal fusion from which he has just emerged. Giving in to the pull of individuation and independence, Skanda becomes liable to one kind of punishment—exile from the mother's bountiful presence, and one kind of reward—the promise of functioning as an adult, virile man. Going back to the mother—and I would view Ganesha's eating of the mango as a return to feeding at the breast, especially since we know that in Tamil Nadu, the analogy between a mango and the breast is a matter of common awareness[13]—has the broken tusk, the loss of potential masculinity, as a consequence. Remaining an infant, Ganesha's reward, on the other hand, will be never to know the pangs of separation from the mother, never to feel the despair at her absence. That Ganesha's lot is considered superior to Skanda's is perhaps an indication of Indian man's cultural preference in the dilemma of separation-individuation. He is at one with his mother in her wish not to have the son separate from her, individuate out of their shared anima.[14]

For M., as we have seen, the Ganesha position is often longed for and sometimes returned to in fantasy. It does not, however, represent an enduring solution to the problem of maintaining phallic desire in face of the overwhelming inner presence of the Great Mother. Enter Skanda. After he killed the demon Taraka, who had been terrorizing the gods, the goddess became quite indulgent toward her son and told him to amuse himself as he pleased. Skanda became wayward, his lust rampant. he made love to the wives of the gods and the gods could not stop him. On their complaining to the goddess, she decided to take the form of whatever woman Skanda was about to seduce. Skanda summoned the wife of one god after another but in each saw his mother and became passionless. Finally, thinking that 'the universe is filled with my mother,' he decided to remain celibate forever.[15]

M., too, we saw, became 'passionless' whenever in the bus the motherly woman he fancied turned to face him. But instead of celibacy he tried to hold on to desire by killing the sexual part of the mother, deadening the lower portion of her trunk, which threatened him with impotence. Furthermore, the imagined sexual overpoweringness of the mother, in the face of which the child feels hopelessly inadequate, with fears of being engulfed and swallowed by her dark depths, is not experienced by M. in the form of clear-cut fantasies, but in a recurrent nightmare from which he wakes up screaming.

Elsewhere, I have traced in detail the passage of the powerful, sexual mother through Hindu myths, folk beliefs, proverbs, symptoms, and the ritual worship of the goddess in her terrible and fierce forms.[16] Here, I shall only narrate one of the better-known myths of Devi, widely reproduced in her iconic representations in sculpture and painting, in order to convey through the myth's language of the concrete, of image and symbol, some of the quality of the child's awe and terror of this particular maternal image.

The demon Mahisasura had conquered all the three worlds. Falling in love with the goddess, he sent a message to make his desire known to her. Devi replied that she would accept as her husband only someone who defeated her in battle. Mahisasura entered the battlefield with a vast army and a huge quantity of equipment. Devi came alone, mounted on her lion. The gods were surprised to see her without even armour, riding naked to the combat. Dismounting, Devi started dancing and cutting off the heads of millions and millions of demons with her sword to the rhythm of her movement. Mahisasura, facing death, tried to run away by becoming an elephant. Devi cut off his trunk. The elephant became a buffalo and against its thick hide Devi's sword and spear were of no avail. Angered, Devi jumped on the buffalo's back and rode it to exhaustion. When the buffalo demon's power of resistance had collapsed, Devi plunged her spear into its ear and Mahisasura fell dead.

The myth is stark enough in its immediacy and needs no further gloss on the omnipotence and sexual energy of the goddess, expressed in the imagery of her dancing and riding naked, exhausting even the most powerful male to abject submission and ultimately death, decapitating (i.e., castrating) millions of "bad boys" with demonic desires, and so on. The only feature of the myth I would like to highlight, and which is absent both in M.'s case vignette and in the myths narrated so far, is that of the sword- and spear-wielding Devi as the phallic mother. In the Indian context, this fantasy seems more related to Chasseguet-Smirgel's notion of the phallic mother's being a denial of the adult vagina and the feelings of inadequacy it invokes rather than allowing its traditional interpretation as a denial of castration anxiety.[17] In addition, I would see the image of the goddess as man-woman (or, for that matter, of Shiva as *ardhanarishwara*, half man-half woman), as incorporating the boy's wish to become a man without having to separate and sexually differentiate from the mother, to take on male sexual attributes while not letting go of the feminine ones.

The myth continues that when Devi's frenzied dancing did not come to an end even after the killing of the buffalo demon, the gods become alarmed and asked Shiva for help. Shiva lay down on his back and when the goddess stepped on her husband she hung out her tongue in shame and stopped. Like M.'s gentle and somewhat withdrawn father, who was the only one who could help in dissipating the impact of the nightmare, Shiva too enters the scene supine, yet as a container for the great mother's energy and power. In other words, the father may be unassuming and remote, yet powerful. First experienced as an ally and a protector (or even as a covictim), the father emerges as a rival only later. The rivalry, too, in popular Indian myths and most of my case histories, is less that of Oedipus, the power of whose myth derives from the son's guilt over a fantasized and eventually unconscious parricide. The Indian context stresses more the father's envy of what belongs to the son—including the mother—and thus the son's persecution anxiety as a primary motivation in the father-son relationship. It is thus charged with the fear of filicide and with the son's castration, by self or the father, as a solution to the father-son competition. Shiva's beheading of Ganesha, who on the express wish of his mother stood guard at her private chambers while she bathed, and the replacement of his head by that of an elephant, the legends of Bhishma and Puru, who renounced sexual functioning in order to keep the affections of their father intact, are some of the better-known ilustrations.[18] But the fate of fathers and sons and families and daughters are different narratives; stories yet to be told, texts still to be written.

Cultural ideas and ideals of masculinity and femininity, then, manifested in their narrative form as myths, pervade the innermost experience of the self. One cannot therefore speak of an 'earlier' or 'deeper' layer of the self beyond cultural reach. As a "depth psychology,"[6] psychoanalysis dives deep, but in the same waters in which the cultural river too flows. Preeminently operating from within the heart of the Western myth, enclosed in the *mahamaya* of Europe—from myths of ancient Greece to the 'illusions' of the Enlightenment—psychoanalysis had had little opportunity to observe from within, and with empathy, the deeper import of other cultures' myths in the working of the self.

The questions relating to the 'how' of this process are bound up with the larger issue of the relationship between the inner and outer worlds, which has been of perennial psychological and philosophical interest. It is certainly not my intention to discuss these questions at any length. I would only like to point out that apart from some notable exceptions, such as Erik Erikson, who both held aloft and significantly contributed to the vision of a 'psychoanalysis sophisticated enough to include the environment,'[19] most theorists generally underestimated the impact of culture on the development of a sense of identity—the construction of the self, in modern parlance. Freud's 'timetable' of culture, entering the psychic structure relatively late in life as the 'ideology of the supergo,' has continued to be followed by other almanac makers of the psyche.[20]

Even Heinz Kohut, as Janis Long has shown, does not quite follow the logical implications of his concept of 'selfobject.'[21] These are, of coure, the aspects of the other which are incorporated in the self and are experienced as part of one's own subjectivity. Kohut, too, follows Freud in talking of a 'culture selfobject' of later life, derived in part from cultural ideals, which helps in maintaining the integrity and vitality of the individual self.[22] Yet the idea of selfobject which goes beyond the notion of a budding self's relatedness to the environment, to the environment's gradual transmutation into *becoming* the self, implies that '*what* the parents respond to in a developing child, *how* they respond and what they present as idealizable from the earliest age'[23]—surely much of it a cultural matter—will be the raw material for the child's inner construction of the self, including the gender self.

In other words, a caretaker's knowing of the child, a knowing in which effect and cognition are ideally fused, is in large part cultural and forms the basis of the child's own *knowing* of him-or herself. The notion that the construction and experience of the self is greatly influenced by culture from the very beginning does not imply that there is no difference between individual faces and cultural masks, no boundary between inner and outer worlds. The tension between the two is what gives psychoanalysis and literature much of their narrative power. All I seek to emphasize here is that this boundary cannot be fixed either in time or psychic space. It is dynamic, mobile, and constantly subject to change.

8

AN ENDING

This book has presented the viewpoints of the actors involved in the drama of the sexes in India. Each chapter was, so to speak, a site report, an account of intimate relations as perceived and defined by the participants. For a long time, the ruling orthodoxy in social sciences devalued such personal testimony as 'subjective.' It preferred to see individual feelings, desires, and fears as an epiphenomena of macro forces located in genes, culture, history, social or sexual division of labour. Conflicts between the sexes could then be attributed to one of the many theories in vogue: 'programmed genetic traits,' 'system of patriarchy,' 'mode of production,' and so on.[1]

The intent of this study has been to avoid conceptualizing Indian gender relations in such abstract terms and to eschew the overobjectification of human behaviour that this kind of theorizing entails. Instead, I have tried to highlight the personal and the 'storied' nature of relations between the sexes. I have then interpreted these stories in a way which circumvents the second common weakness of most social theories— their lack of appreciation of the role of sexuality and the irrational in human affairs.

As portrayed in various narratives, from films to folktales, from autobiographies to case histories, gender relations seem impelled more by hostility than tenderness or love. The fantasies entertained by each sex in relation to the other are pervaded as much by hatred and fear as by desire and longing. Partly, this has to do with the very nature of the narrative enterprise. It is difficult to conceive of a tale which will hold our attention and grip our imagination if it is totally devoid of conflict between its sexual protagonists. Somewhere along the course of the story, men and women must misunderstand, mistrust, or hurt each other, given if the chasm that opens up between them is temporary and will be ultimately spanned. Stories in which lovers continue to dwell in a blissful paradise with nary a serpent to intrude upon the stillness of their repose, dramas that show couples in complete harmony undisturbed by the slightest tremor, are understandably rare.

Apart from the needs of the narrative form, our cultural conditioning makes us unwilling to accept the existence of a fundamental hostility between the sexes. For its own reproduction, each society has to focus on the positive aspects of this most basic of all human relationships. Official spokesmen of a culture, the apologists and sentimentalists of its tradition, must necessarily hold up affirmative models. In India, for instance, the images of the *pativrata* wife and the couple that is like the *ardhanarishwara*, have been held up as the immanent reality of the relations between the sexes. Hostility and rage will tend to be dismissed as pathological episodes, avoidable occurrences which are neither an integral part of the sexual drama nor inherent in the man-woman connection.

Yet we know from psychoanalysis that sexual desire which compels men and women toward each other in promised fulfilment of a timeless yearning has another darker face. In desire, the body's wanting and its violence, the mind's yearning for sexual pleasure but also the need to rid itself of ancient pain and noxious hate, the excitement of orgasm and the fierce exultation of possession, all flow together.[2] Forces of selfishness, destruction, and ambivalence always accompany the quest for sexual pleasure and spiritual union. In the coming together of the sexes, we resent the violation of the body's boundaries even while we want nothing more than to transcend them. We fear sexuality's threat to the tenuous order we have carved out for ourselves during the course of our development—even as we long for its dissolution into a veritable *mahabhava*, a 'great feeling' that will allow us esctasy and exaltation rather than the small joys and dribbles of pleasure we extract from our inner order.

Little wonder, then, that theories of gender relations, especially as they pertain to the oppression of women, founder on the ambiguities and ambivalences of sexuality. Although oppressed in many societies, women still cannot be likened to any other exploited group, such as the blacks in South Africa or the 'untouchable' castes in India. Blacks and whites, low and high castes do not have to deal with the conscious and unconscious exigencies of a mutual desire which is both a promise of self-enhancement, even transcendence, and a threat of disintegration to the self. Nor do they, or any other pairing of the oppressor and the oppressed, need each other—in Plato's comment on his myth of the origin of sexes—for 'reuniting our original nature, making one of two, healing the state of man.'[3]

Coming back to Indian gender relations, we saw that in plumbing the fantasies of men and women we reached a common bedrock in human imagination. Here, the similarities in the ways the sexes perceive each other—within the culture and between cultures—seems to outweigh differences, at least as far as patriarchal societies are concerned. This universality springs from our infantile discovery, struggling against wishes and fears which would have it otherwise, that we are either one sex or the other— as are our beloved and hated caretakers and siblings. In other words, the universally shared features in the portrayed amalgamation of fact, fantasy, and folklore men call 'woman' and women 'man', spring from a common psychical reality and are relatively independent of my looking at these portraits from an 'essentialist' psychoanalytic perspective.

Universality is not synonymous with uniformity. Within global clusters of human longings and anxieties, cultures can and do accentuate certain elements more than others. In India, too, the dominant Hindu culture has created its own brand of sexual mythology through the fantasies it has chosen to underscore in its narratives. Thus, for instance, it is generally true that the public discourse of all patriarchal societies stresses motherhood as the primary if not the sole reason of woman's existence whereas, ironically, it underplays the importance of fatherhood for a man. Hindus, too, share this widespread orientation wherein the image of woman as mother is sought to be superimposed upon and thereby to obliterate the picture of woman as a sexual being. Yet during the superimposition, and this is the most salient feature of male fantasy in India, what emerges is a composite image of the sexual mother. As we saw, she is an overwhelming presence in man's perception of woman, a being to whom one is in danger of ceding both genitals and the self. She pervades Gandhi's agonizings but also looms large in clinical case histories, myths, and in popular narratives.

Following on the sexual mother's heels, her features somewhat more amorphous and blurred, is the unfaithful mother. We saw her appear prominently in the story of the snake woman, although her visage is also glimpsed in other narratives as well as in proverbs and pronouncements of ancient law-givers. In her willing or 'unwilling' sexual submisison to the 'father,' she is the universal betrayer of a boy's first love and primordial passion. A favorite heroine of psychoanalytic stories for over eight decades, there is nothing more one can say about her and she need not detain us further here.

The dread of the sexual mother and the rage at the unfaithful one are dealt with in our stories in certain specific ways. In other words, the culture highlights some defences more than others. Whereas viewing women as dangerous antagonists to be subdued through violence or denying their existence altogether in a misogynous turn to the world of men are responses common enough across partiarchies, Indian fantasy seems to favour one particular defensive mode. This is desexualization, either of the self or of the woman. In the former, a renunciation of the awareness of sexual differentiation is sought in ascetic longings or in the quiescence of the infant at the breast. In the latter, the woman is unsexed, à la Hindi movies, by turning her into a maternal automaton, a dispenser of emotional pap, or into an androgynous virgin.

Similarly, the women in the universe of our stories share many characteristics of their counterparts in other patriarchal societies. We see the same private protest, at every level of society, against a socialization which has emphasized the mother and housewife as the woman's primary gender roles. As in the marriage scenes from North Indian novels, there is a constant struggle, waged through the bickerings of household life, for a redressal of the uneven balance of power between the sexes. In the sexual metaphors availed of by fantasy, the woman would wrest the phallus—the symbol of male power—or have one of her own in the male child she therefore craves and subsequently invests with the full might or her emotions.

Yet what strikes me most in the Indian woman's fantasy, as reflected in the narratives, is less a burning rage than an aching disappointment. Her imagination seems propelled by the longing for a single two-person universe—which the women from the slums called a *jodi*—where the affirmation of her female body and the recognition of her feminine soul take place simultaneously. The longing is for an idealized phallus which will serve as a 'transitional object' in the consolidation of her feminine identity. To elaborate upon what was earlier mentioned only in passing, I would speculate that this yearning has its roots in the course taken by the girl's interactions with adult men in the family, especially the father. We know that a girl's sexual awakening depends to a considerable extent upon the seductive attention paid to her by the 'father,' an entity who, according to the family type, can mean a single individual or the collectivity of paternal men. Within the space demarcated by the incest taboo, the father must make the girl conscious of his masculine appreciation of her femininity, especially at various critical periods of her development, such as early childhood and adolescence.[4] Without this 'normal seduction,' the daughter's desire may remain relatively inhibited. If, however, after early demonstrations of erotically tinged interest, the father withdraws or otherwise absents himself from the girl's life, she will be deprived of a sustained experience of a more normal father-daughter relationship, which would have helped her gradually to desexualize the father. A sense of rejection of her eroticism and a fixing of her inner state of aroused desire on the paternal phallus of early childhood may then be a few of the consequences which constitute an area of vulnerability in the women's psyche.

What gives this particular developmental sequence in individual women's lives a wider cultural significance is the structure of relationship between the sexes in the family, especially 'father' and 'daughter,' in large sections of Hindu upper castes. After the first four or five years of a child's life, the father progressively (and at puberty, even precipitately) withdraws from interaction with the growing girl, who is taken over and assimilated into the community of women at an early age. Although the entrance into the women's community mitigates the slights and shields the girl from humiliation at the hands of the surrounding patriarchal order, it also has the result of isolating her from the 'father.' This increases the longing for the idealized paternal phallus which is manifested in various ways, including the menacing movie images of rape by father figures.

Leaving the question of origins aside, the stories make it abundantly clear that in contrast to the fear and dread pervading men's fantasies of women, anger and disappointment are a large part of women's feelings in relationship to men.

At the end, we will do well to remember that the Indian tale of intimate relations, or for that matter that of any culture, has many renderings. The sober, dark version recounted here, in which the dream of intimacy verges on a nightmare and where the sexual union of man and woman becomes a zone of genital combat, is preeminently a psychoanalytic story. As such it is only one building block in that imposing and mysterious edifice we call love, and which houses our soul in a more essential way than the buildings of straw and mud, bricks and mortar, sheltering our bodies.

THE ANALYST AND THE MYSTIC

Psychoanalytic Reflections on Religion and Mysticism

For
Wendy Doniger
in friendship and admiration

CONTENTS

Preface   128

1   Ramakrishna and the Mystical Experience   131
2   The Guru as Healer   160
3   Psychoanalysis and Religion Revisited   177

PREFACE

Two years ago, I was invited by the Divinity School of the University of Chicago to deliver its Haskell Lectures in the area of comparative religion. I accepted this invitation with alacrity. It encouraged me to return to a field which I had reconnoitered in an earlier work on the healing function of religion and of such religious 'functionaries' as shamans and mystics. After a decade-long intellectual exploration into the vagaries of sexual love, I welcomed the chance to once again engage with this other major area of human transcendence.

In retrospect, it seems inevitable that the focus of these lectures would be ecstatic mysticism, which signifies both a continuity with the departure from my preceeding preoccupation with eroticism. Like the lover, the emotional mystic too strives for the transcendence of personal boundaries in an ineffable union with the other, though in the case of the latter the other is spelled with a capital "O". The fervour of erotic passion, we know, only recognizes the spontaneity of religious passion as its equal and, in some cultures and at certain historical periods, even as its superior. I thus came to ecstatic, emotional mysticism with a curious sense of familiarity which I hoped would permit me access to its strangeness.

Mysticism for me is not something that lies outside the vast spaces of the human mind. Its insights, experiences, and yearnings are a heritage of our condition as human beings; they are a part of our humanity. Shorn of religious trappings, the mystical quest is not apart from the dailiness of life but pervades and informs life in its deepest layers.

I have approached the mystic as a psychoanalyst approaches a subject in the clinical encounter, with empathy, respect, and a sense of the complexity and wonder of human life. My intention has not been to pursue any reductionistic agenda, to 'shrink' the mystic, but rather to expand our understanding of his mystery and, ultimately, of the working of our own selves. Of course, given the nature of my discipline, the understanding of mysticism and mystical experiences I aim for is necessarily in a psychological mode. The psychological understanding, I hope, complements other kinds of understanding; it does not replace them. A psychological appropriation of mysticism is certainly not the intention of these reflections. Yet, if my endeavour, like those of the analyst before me, brings the mystic down from the level of 'divine' to that of human, I console myself with the thought that it may also help in raising the rest of us by making us more aware of our own sensuous and psychic potentials.

Traditionally, psychoanalysis has viewed art and science as valuable sublimatory creations. On the other hand, it has often seen in mysticism in particular and religion in general a regressive return to the protective beings (and being) of infancy and early childhood. Mysticism, I try to show in this book, is a radical enhancement of the capacity for creative experiencing, of the ability to experience 'with all one's heart, all one's soul, and all one's might.' It requires that the mystic undergo a creative immersion in the deepest layers of his or her psyche, with its potential risk of phases of chaos and lack of integration. The mystical regression is akin to that of the analysand, an absorbing and at times painful process at the service of psychic transformation. It differs from most analyses in that the regression is deeper. Where the mystical ability to experience profoundly is sought to be enhanced within a master-disciple relationship, as in most schools of Hinduism, Buddhism, and Sufism, the potential mystic may be better placed than the analysand to connect with—and perhaps correct—the depressive core at the base of human life which lies beyond language. Psychically, he or she is also more endangered. Mystical techniques in the master-disciple relationship, compared to those of psychoanalysis, are thus designed to foster radical regression, and the role of the master—*guru, pir, roshi*—is better understood by taking recourse to the concepts of the more 'relational' analysts such as Donald Winnicott and Heinz Kohut, rather than by remaining within the paradigm of classical psychoanalytic theory with its motivational emphasis on drives and defences.

The illustrative examples for my arguments are preeminently drawn from the Hindu religious tradition. Following a time-honored psychoanalytic usage where one strives for an in-depth understanding of a single case history in the hope that it may later prove to be representative for a host of other similar cases, I have tried to organize my observations and understanding of mysticism around the person of a single mystic, the 19-century Hindu saint, Shri Ramakrishna. I have sought to discuss in detail three interacting factors in his story—particular life historical experiences, the presence of a specific artistic or creative gift, and a facilitating cultural environment—which I believe may well go into the making of a mystic, at least of the ecstatic variety.

The first chapter of this book was also presented as an invited talk to the Canadian Psychoanalytic Association in Montreal. The comments of my Canadian colleagues were most helpful. I am especially thankful to the discussant of the paper, Dr Eva Lester, for her helpful input which I have incorporated gratefully into the text.

1

RAMAKRISHNA AND THE MYSTICAL EXPERIENCE

Of the many ways of inner transformation known to man, the mystical path is perhaps one of the most ancient, universal, and highly regarded, even when its practitioners have often lived in an uneasy truce, if not in frank antagonism, with the established religions of their societies.

The mystical path may be one but has many forks. Scholars of religion have distinguished them in various ways. Nathan Söderblom talks of 'mysticism of the infinite,' an elevation of awareness where the unifying experience with the suprahuman eliminates perception of the concrete and abstract elements from the sensate world. He contrasts this to 'mysticism of personal life' where the experience is not rooted in ecstatic rapture, but in a meeting with God in the midst of life's problems and struggles, a meeting experienced at a deep level of faith within normal waking consciousness.[1] Martin Buber and John of the Cross would be two exemplars of Söderblom's mysticism of personal life. Of course, such distinctions are more sign posts rather than sharp dividers since shades of both 'infinity' and 'personality' will exist in every mystic.

Mysticism of the 'infinite', my own focus of interest, has also been variously categorized—nature mysticism, theistic mysticism, and monistic or soul mysticism—although it is doubtful whether the categories are any different at the level of inner experience. Yet another distinction is the one made by William James between sporadic and cultivated mysticism, which corresponds to Arthur Deikman's separation between untrained-sensate and trained-sensate mystical experiences.[2] Ramakrishna was of course, a 'career' mystic, and though his initial forays into mysticism may have been sporadic and untrained, the latter half of his life was marked by regular and frequent mystical experiences of the cultivated, trained-sensate kind.

A mystical experience may be mild, such as a contact with a 'sense of Beyond' among completely normal people, or it may be extreme with ecstasies and visions. We know from survey studies that more or less mild mystical experiences are widespread, even in countries without an active mystical tradition and where the intellectual climate is not particularly conducive to mystical thought. In the United States, for instance, 35 per cent of the respondents in a large sample study by Andrew Greeley in 1975 reported having mystical experiences, a finding which has been since confirmed by other, comparable studies. It is significant that those who had such experiences were more educated than the national average and in 'a state of psychological well-being' unmarked by any obvious neurotic difficulties.[3]

My focus here, though, is mysticism of the extreme variety and especially ecstatic mysticism. Most dramatically manifested in visions and trances, psychologically it is characterized by an expansion of the inner world, by a consciousness suffusing the whole of the body from inside. The expanding consciousness also fills the external world which appears to be pervaded by a oneness of existence.

The overwhelming feeling is of the object of consciousness, the world, having at last become transparent and more real than its conventional reality. All of this is accompanied by heightened intrapsychic and bodily sensations, culminating in a great feeling of pleasure which eliminates or absorbs all other experience.[4] Variously called cosmic consciousness, peak experience (Maslow), *mahabhava*, ecstatic mystical experience seems to differ from one where consciousness and its object, the world, become one and subject-object differentiations vanish. The *samadhi* of the Hindus, *satori* of Zen masters, and *fana* of the Sufis are some of the terms for this particular mystical experience. Again these distinctions are not either/or categories, the former often leading to the latter, as in the case of Ramakrishna, though not all mystics need to have spanned the whole gamut of mystical experience, each with its specific degree of ineffability and noesis—the conviction of knowing.

We must also remember that Ramakrishna was an heir to the Hindu mystical tradition which in spite of many similarities to the mysticism of other religious faiths, also has its own unique context. First, mysticism is the mainstream of Hindu religiosity, and thus Hindu mystics are generally without the restraints of their counterparts in monotheistic religious traditions such as Judaism, Islam, and to a lesser extent, Christianity, where mystical experiences and insights must generally be interpreted against a given dogmatic theology.[5] A Hindu mystic is thus normally quite uninhibited in expressing his views and does not have to be on his guard lest these views run counter to the officially interpreted orthodoxy. Second, God as conceived in the monotheistic religions does not have the same significance in two major schools of Hindu mysticism. Upanishadic mysticism, for instance, is a quest for spiritual illumination wherein a person's deepest essence is discovered to be identical with the common source of all other animate and inanimate beings. Yogic mysticism strives to realize the immortality of the human soul outside time, space, and matter. Through intensive introspection and practice of disciplines that lead to mastery of senses and mental processes, it seeks to realize the experience of one's 'soul' as an unconditioned, eternal being, distinct from the 'illusory' consciousness of the conditioned being. In both Upanishadic and Yogic mysticism there is no trace of love of or yearning for communion with God, which is considered the highest manifestation of the mystical mood in both Christian and Islamic traditions and without which no *unio mystica* is conceivable.

In these two Hindu schools, mystical liberation is achieved entirely through the mystic's own efforts and without the intervention of divine grace. It is only in *bhakti* or devotional mysticism—Ramakrishna's preferred form—where love for the Deity creeps in, where the mystic's soul or 'self' is finally united with God (or Goddess) in an ecstatic surrender, that Hindu mysticism exhibits a strong family resemblance to the mysticism of monotheistic faiths.

Let me state at the outset that given the theoretical uncertainties in contemporary psychoanalysis which threaten its basic paradigm, the earlier equation of the mystical state with a devalued, if not pathological, regression comparable to a psychotic episode is ripe for radical revision. Many analysts interested in the phenomenon would now agree that in spite of superficial resemblances, the mystical retreat is neither as complete nor as compelling and obligatory as psychotic regression. Moreover, in contrast to the psychotic, the mystic's ability to maintain affectionate ties remains unimpaired when it does not actually get enhanced. Given the analyst's commitment to Freud's dictum that the capacity 'to love and work' is perhaps the best outer criterium for mental health, then the mystic's performance on both counts is impressive—that is, if one can succeed in emancipating one's self from a circumscription of the notions of love and work dictated by convention. In short, the full force of the current flowing through the psyche that leads to short circuit in the psychotic may, and indeed does, illuminate the mystic.

Some of the more recent work in psychoanalysis recognizes that mystical states lead to more rather than less integration of the person.[6] The mystics insight into the workings of his or her self is more rather than less acute. Although consciousness during the mystical trance may be characterized by 'de-differentiation' (to use Anton Ehrenzweig's concept)[7], that is, by the suspension of many kinds of boundaries and distinctions in both the inner and outer worlds, its final outcome is often an increase in the mystic's ability to make ever-finer perceptual differentiations. In other words, the point is not the chaotic nature of the mystical experience, if it is indeed chaotic, but the mystic's ability to create supreme *order* out of the apparent chaos. In fact, what I would like to do here is address the question Romain Rolland, in writing of Ramakrishna's initial trances, posed for 'physicians both of the body and of the mind,' namely, 'There is no difficulty in proving the apparent destruction of his whole mental structure, and the disintegration of its elements. But how were they reassembled into a synthetic entity of the highest order?'[8] To put it differently, how does the mystic become master of his madness and of his reason alike whereas the schizophrenic remains their slave?

The timing of my attempt to formulate some kind of answers to these questions is not inopportune. Today, psychoanalysis is in a relatively better position of *adequatio* (adequateness) in relation to mystical phenomena as well as other states of altered consciousness, such as the possession trance. The *adequatio* principle, of course, states that the same phenomenon may hold entirely different sets of meaning for different observers.[9] To a dog, a book belongs to a class of object which can be played with but not eaten. To the illiterate, it may be just a book, ink markings on paper he cannot decipher. To the average educated adult, the book is an impenetrable scientific tome. To the physicist, the volume is a brilliant treatise on relativity which makes him question some of the ways he looks at the universe. In each case the level of meaning is a function of the *adequatio* of the observer. As far as mysticism is concerned, psychoanalysts today are neither dogs nor even illiterates but are, perhaps, just moving beyond the stage of the average educated adult.

The increase in the level of analytical *adequatio* has not come about because of any analyst's personal experience of training in the mystical disciplines (as far as I know). In part, this higher *adequatio* is due to the increased availability of analytically relevant information which is no longer limited to the writings or biographical and autobiographical accounts of a few Western mystics such as Teresa of Avila and John of the Cross. In the last 15 years, we have had access to psychodynamically informed interviews with members of mystical cults who have travelled varied distances on the mystical path and have experienced various states of altered consciousness, including the ecstatic trance.[10] In addition, we have at least two detailed case histories of intensive psychoanalytic therapy with patients who had both mystical proclivities and trance experiences.[11]

More than the availability of additional information, the greater *adequatio* of psychoanalysis in relation to mysticism stems from the work of many writers—Erik Erikson, Donald Winnicott, Wilfred Bion, and Jacques Lacan come immediately to my mind—who, in spite of their very different theoretical concerns, pursued a common antireductionistic agenda. The cumulative effect of their writings has been to allow the adoption of what Winnicott, in talking of transitional phenomena, called 'a particular quality in attitude', with which I believe mystical states should also be observed. In other words, my own enhanced feeling of *adequatio* reflects the presence of an unstated project in contemporary psychoanalysis in which the copresence of different orders of experience is tolerated and no attempts are undertaken to explain one in terms of the other without reciprocity. As we shall see later, in their separate efforts to develop a phenomenology of creative experiencing, Winnicott, Lacan, and Bion are directly relevant for a reevaluation and reinterpretation of mystical phenomena.[12] Of the three, whereas Winnicott was more the poet, Lacan and Bion, in their explicit concern with questions of ultimate reality, its evolution and reflection in psychic life, may fairly be described as the mystics of psychoanalysis. (As someone who spent his childhood in India, it is quite appropriate than Bion is radically sincere in his approach to 'O', his symbol for ultimate reality, whereas Lacan, I like to think, as befitting a Frenchman talking of the Real, is more an ironic mystic.)

The psychoanalytic understanding of any phenomenon begins with the narrative, with the echoes and reverberations of individual history. The individual I have selected for my own explorations is the 19th-century Bengali mystic Sri Ramakrishna. Together with Ramana Maharishi, Ramakrishna is widely regarded as the preeminent figure of Hindu mysticism of the last 300 years, whatever preeminence may mean in the mystical context. He is a particularly apt choice for a psychoanalytic study of ecstatic mysticism since Freud's observations on the mystical experience, on what he called the 'oceanic feeling', an omnibus label for all forms of extreme mystical experience, were indirectly occasioned by Ramakrishna's ecstasies.

It was the biography of Ramakrishna which Romain Rolland was working on at the time when he wrote of Freud in 1927, saying the though he found Freud's analysis of religion (in *The Future of an Illusion*) just, he would ideally have liked Freud to 'make an analysis of spontaneous religious feelings, or more exactly, religious sensations which are entirely different from religion proper and much more enduring.'[13] Rolland went to call this sensation oceanic, without perceptible limits, and mentioned two Indians who had such feelings and 'who have manifested a genius for thought and action powerfully regenerative for their country and for the world.'[14] Rolland added that he himself had all his life found the oceanic feeling to be a source of vital revival. Freud's response to Rolland, his analysis of the 'oceanic feeling,' was then spelled out in *Civilization and its Discontents*. It is highly probable that the term 'oceanic feeling' itself is taken from Ramakrishna's imagery to describe the ineffable. For instance, one of Ramakrishna's oft-repeated metaphors is of the salt doll which went to measure the depth of the ocean: 'As it entered the ocean it melted. Then who is there to come back and say how deep is the ocean?'[15]

Of course, ocean as a symbol for boundless oneness and unity in which multiplicities dissolve and opposites fuse not only goes back to the Upanishads in the Hindu tradition, but is one of the preferred metaphors of devotional mystics for the melting of ego boundaries in the Buddhist, Christian and Muslim traditions as well.[16] Christian mystics, for instance, have been greatly fond of the metaphor. 'I live in the ocean of God as a fish in the sea.'

Freud's response to Ramakrishna, as generally to 'Mother India,' was of unease. Although of some professional interest, Ramakrishna's florid ecstasies were as distant, if not distasteful, to his sensibility as jumbled vision of flesh, the labyrinth flux of the animal, human, and divine in Indian art. In his acknowledgement of Rolland's book about Ramakrishna, Freud writes, 'I shall now try with your guidance to penetrate into the Indian jungle from which until now an uncertain blending of Hellenic love of proportion, Jewish sobriety, and Philistine timidity have kept me away. I really ought to have tackled it earlier, for the plants of this soil shouldn't be alien to me; I have dug to certain depths for their roots. But it isn't easy to pass beyond the limits of one's nature.'[17]

We are, of course, fortunate that the last four years of Ramakrishna's life, from 1882 to 1886, were recorded with minute fidelity by a disciple, Mahendranath Gupta, or M as he called himself with modest self-effacement.[18] In the cases of most mystics throughout history, we have either had to rely on doctrinal writing that is formal and impersonal, or on autobiographical accounts from which intimate detail, considered trifling from transcendental heights, has been excised. M, on the other hand, with the obsessive fidelity of a Bengali Boswell, has left an enormously detailed chronicle of the daily life and conversations of Ramakrishna— his uninhibited breaking out in song and dance, his frequent and repeated ecstasies, his metaphysical discourses full of wisdom and penetrating insight, his parables, jokes, views, anxieties, and pleasures, the times he slept and ate and what he ate— which is rare in hagiographical literature. Let me then begin with the outer scaffolding of the story, a brief narration of events of Ramakrishna's early life. And though we can never know what *really* happened in his or anyone else's infancy and childhood, the former forever beyond the reach of memory, I have no hesitation in extending a qualified belief to Ramakrishna's own version of his life story. Yet, of course, it is not solely his version. As a reteller of his tale, I cannot help but also bring to bear a psychoanalytic sensibility in the choice of events I emphasize and others that I must have underplayed. The biographies by his direct disciples, on the other hand, are shaped by the traditional Hindu religious idiom, while the narration by Romain Rolland is moulded by his more universalistic, spiritual concerns, in the sense of what Adlous Huxley called the 'perennial philosophy.'

Ramakrishna was born in 1836 in a Brahmin family in the village of Kamarpukur in Bengal. The parents were pious and very poor, but what I find exceptional about them in the context of 19th-century village India is their ages at the time of Ramakrishna's birth. At a time when the average longevity was less than 30 years, maternal death during childbirth fairly common, and the sexually reproductive years of the woman over by her early 30s, Ramakrishna's father was 61 and his mother 45 years old when he was born. In the family there was a brother 31 years older, a sister 27 years older, and another brother 11 years older. Yet another sister was born when Gadhadhar, that was his given name, was four years old.

Ramakrishna later remembered his mother Chandra as a simple soul without a trace of worldliness who could not even count money. She said whatever came to her mind, without obfuscation or concealment, and people even called her a 'simpleton.' Devoted to her youngest son, the fruit of old loins, she was nevertheless, as elderly parents often tend to be, inordinately anxious about any harm befalling him when he was not within her ken. A curious and lively child, intent on exploring the world, Ramakrishna did not exactly help in allaying his mother's anxieties. She sought to master these by daily prayers to the family deity wherein she besought the continued welfare of her little boy. Perhaps Ramakrishna's later anxiousness whenever he was physically incapacitated, his almost hypochondriacal concerns at such times, can be directly traced to the elderly mother's anxieties about her youngest son.

The incident given as an example of the boy's wilfulness, which sometimes ignored the conventional rules of conduct, concerns his hiding behind a tree and peeping out at women while they washed clothes and bathed at the village tank. One of the women complained to Chandra who then admonished the boy that all women were the same as his mother. Shaming them was shaming her, insulting their honour was insulting hers. We are told that the mortified boy never again repeated his behaviour. To us post-Freudians, the incident embodies a child's natural sexual curiosity which the mother dampens by associating it with incestuous anxiety. Interestingly, in later life, Ramakrishna would use a mythological version of this personal experience, wherein the incestuous urgings and fears are much more explicit, to explain a part of his attitude toward women. One day, during his childhood, the god Ganesha saw a cat which, as some boys are apt to do, he proceeded to torture in various ways till the cat finally made its escape. When Ganesha came back home he saw to his surprise the bruises and marks of torture on his mother's, the goddess Parvati's body. The mother revealed to her son that all living beings in female form were part of her and whatever he did to any female he did unto his mother. On reaching marriageable age, Ganesha, lest he marry his mother, decided to remain a celibate forever. 'My attitude to women is the same,' was Ramakrishna's final comment.[19]

Khudiram, Ramakrishna's father, was a gentle man who is reported to have never scolded his son. He took a quiet pride in the boy's evident intelligence and phenomenal memory, which were further displayed to advantage when he started attending the village school at the age of five. However, though good at school (but bad at arithmetic), what the boy most enjoyed was painting pictures and spending time with the village potters learning how to make clay images of gods and goddesses. The artistic streak in Ramakrishna was strongly developed, and it seems appropriate that his first ecstasy was evoked by the welling up of aesthetic emotion; an episode of 'nature' mysticism, it was the consequence of an aesthetically transcendent feeling: 'I was following a narrow path between the rice fields. I raised my eyes to the sky as I munched my rice. I saw a great black cloud spreading rapidly until it covered the heavens. Suddenly at the edge of the cloud a flight of snow white cranes passed over my head. The contrast was so beautiful that my spirit wandered far away. I lost consciousness and fell to the ground. The puffed rice was scattered. Somebody picked me up and carried me home in his arms. An excess of joy and emotion overcame me. . . . This was the first time that I was seized with ecstasy.'[20]

Ramakrishna's father, who had been ill for awhile, died when the boy was around eight years of age. The effect of the father's death was to make Ramakrishna withdrawn and fond of solitude. His attendance at school became fitful. He drew closer to his mother and spent much time in helping her with her household duties and her daily prayers to the gods. He became very fond of listening to discourses on spiritual matters and spent hours at a pilgrimage house where wandering ascetics found a bed for a night or two before they resumed their wanderings. The latter activity alarmed his mother who feared that her son might decide to leave home and embrace the renunciant's life.

There were other fainting spells, as on the way to the temple of a goddess or when acting the part of Shiva in a play he lost all external consciousness. He later attributed these states to spiritual stirrings although his family suspected a physical malady and refrained from forcing him to go to school which by now he quite disliked.

The gradually deteriorating condition of the family after Khudiram's death worsened with the marriage of Ramakrishna's second brother. With the advent of the new daughter-in-law, quarrels and bickerings in the household increased markedly, a situation which the family's worsening economic circumstances, driving it to the edge of subsistence, did not help improve. The daily clamour and strife, I imagine, perhaps added its own impetus in pushing the sensitive and artistic boy more and more away from the distasteful discord of everyday reality and toward transcendental, spiritual matters and religious life. The latter too coursed through the village, as it does to great extent even today in rural India, in a powerful stream. There were the many rituals in which everyday life was embedded, frequent recitals from the Puranas, and the religious plays and festivals in which Ramakrishna participated by singing and dancing with fervid abandon. And, above all, there were the sudden inward, abstracted states, brought on at the oddest of times by outer stimuli such as listening to a song in praise of a god or to snatches of devotional music.

The young daughter-in-law died in childbirth when Ramakrishna was 13 years old, and the burden of running the household once again fell on the aging shoulders of Ramakrishna's mother. To help alleviate the poverty, his eldest brother left for Calcutta to run a small Sanskrit school. His position as the head of the family now devolved on Ramakrishna's second brother who was temperamentally disinclined to take over responsibilities for his siblings and was in any case much too busy scrounging around for work.

Thus at the beginning of adolescence, Ramakrishna was left to his own devices, without the paternal guiding voice of his father or eldest brother. School became even more occasional. When he was not an enthusiastic participant in the village's religious life, he was at home with his mother, helping her with household tasks and sharing with her the rhythm of her woman's days. The village women who dropped in on his mother for a visit during the day seem to have adopted him as one of their own. They would ask him to sing—he had a very sweet singing voice—or to tell stories from the *Puranas*, of which he had an enormous stock. He performed scenes from popular plays for their amusement, playing all the parts himself. He listened to their secrets and woes and would attempt to lift the spirits of a dejected woman by acting out a rustic farce.

He loved putting on women's clothes and ornaments. Dressed thus, with a pitcher under his arm to fetch water from the tank like other village women, he would pass in front of the men and felt proud that no one suspected he was not a woman. Once, disguised as a poor weaver girl, he spent a whole evening in the closely guarded women's quarters of the village shopkeeper's house taking part in their conversation, without being discovered. In his mature years, talking to his disciples, there was a certain wry pride with which he related, and occasionally enacted to their surprised delight, incidents from his youth which showed his ability to mimic women's gestures and movements to perfection.

A fantasy from this period has Ramakrishna imagining that were he to be born again he would become a beautiful child widow with long black hair who would not know anyone else except Lord Krishna as a husband. The girl widow would live in a hut with an elderly woman as a guardian, a spinning wheel, and a cow which she would milk herself. During the day, after finishing household work, she would spin yarn, sing songs about Krishna, and after dusk ardently weep for the god, longing to feed him sweets made from the cow's milk. Krishna would come in secret, be fed by her and go away, his daily visits taking place without the knowledge of others.[21]

In the meantime, Ramakrishna's eldest brother Ramkumar was doing well in Calcutta, running his small school and performing religious services for some rich families. He called the 17-year-old Ramakrishna over to the city to assist him in his priestly duties. Soon after, a new opportunity opened up when a rich woman built and consecrated a temple to the goddess Kali outside Calcutta and employed Ramkumar as its full-time priest. Ramkumar, who had been ailing for some time, found the task arduous and handed over his duties to Ramakrishna, the younger brother. He died a year later.

Ramkumar's death was to have a profound effect on Ramakrishna. Thirty-one years older, he had looked after Ramakrishna like a father after Khudiram's death. 'Who can say,' Ramakrishna's disciple-biographer asks, 'how far his brother's death contributed to the kindling up of the fire of renunciation in the Master's pure mind, by producing in him a firm conviction about the transitoriness of the world?'[22] In any case his behaviour changed markedly as he became more and more engrossed in the worship of the Mother Goddess. As her priest he had to wake her up early in the morning, bathe and dress her, make garlands of flowers for her adornment. At nine he had to perform her worship, offer her food, and escort her to her silver bed at noon where she rested for the afternoon. Then came the evening worship. For Ramakrishna, these were no longer duties but heartfelt services. He became so absorbed in each one of them that he had to be reminded when it was time to go on to the next ritual.

After the closing of temple at midday and midnight, Ramakrishna shunned all company and disconsolately roamed around in the jungle at the edge of which the temple was located. All he yearned for with all his soul, he was to later tell us, was a vision, the personal *darshan* of the Mother. The spiritual thirst, the clinician would observe, was embedded in all the signs of a full-fledged depression. There was a great restlessness of the body, sleepless nights, loss of appetite in which eating was reduced to the bare minimum, eyes that filled up often and suddenly with tears. The nephew who looked after him became alarmed for his sanity when at night he saw Ramakrishna sitting under a tree naked, having flung off his clothes and even the sacred thread of a Brahmin, or, when he saw him put the leavings from leaf plates from which beggars had eaten to his mouth and to his head. But now, as we come to a culmination of his 'dark night of the soul,' we need Ramakrishna's own words. 'There was then an intolerable anguish in my heart because I could not have Her vision. Just as a man wrings a towel forcibly to squeeze out all the water from it, I felt as if somebody caught hold of my heart and mind and was wringing them likewise. Greatly afflicted by the thought that I might not have Mother's vision, I was in great agony. I thought that there was no use in living such a life. My eyes suddenly fell upon the sword that was in the Mother's temple. I made up my mind to put an end to my life with it that very moment. Like one mad, I ran and caught hold of it, when suddenly I had the wonderful vision of the Mother, and fell down unconscious. I did not know what happened then in the external world—how that day and the next slipped away. But in my heart of hearts, there was flowing a current of intense bliss, never experienced before . . . . It was as if the house, doors, temples, and all other things vanished altogether, as if there was nothing anywhere! And what I saw was a boundless infinite conscious sea of light! However far and in whatever direction I looked, I found a continuous succession of effulgent waves coming forward, raging and storming from all sides with great speed. Very soon they fell on me and made me sink to the abysmal depths of infinity.'[23]

Those familiar with mystical literature will recognize many elements in Ramakrishna's vision which are known to us from similar descriptions from all over the world, especially the feeling of being flooded by light. In the still controversial studies of near-death experience, 'seeing the light' and 'entering the light' are said to be the deepest and most positive parts of that particular experience. The incident has not only universal but also cultural aspects. It is a very Hindu story of a man forcing the Goddess to appear by threatening to decapitate himself. This is an old theme, found both in religious and secular literature, for instance in the well-known story which has been so brilliantly retold for Western readers by Thomas Mann in his *The Transposed Heads*.

Unlike similar accounts of the first vision in the lives of most mystics, this particular vision, to which we will come back later and to which all his boyhood experiences seem like forerunners, was not sufficient to take him out of the 'valley of the shadow of death.' Its aftertaste but whetted an appetite for repeated blissful salvings. Even for the pious visitors to the temple, accustomed to a wide range in manifestation of religious fervour, Ramakrishna's behavior appeared bizarre. He would decorate his own person with the flowers and sandalwood paste brought for the worship of the goddess. He would feel the statue of the goddess breathing, try to feed her stony mouth, and carry on playful conversations as to who, the goddess or her priest, should eat first. Any diminution in the sense of her presence made him throw himself and roll violently on the ground, filling the temple with loud wailings at her absence. At such times his breath would almost stop, and he appeared to struggle for his very life. When he again received a vision of the goddess, he would beam with joy and become a different person altogether. The consensus of his employers and others was that he had become insane. Romain Rolland calls this a necessary period of hallucination, and even Ramakrishna referred to it as a passing phase of *unmada* (insanity), leaving it unambiguous—something he was not wont to do in respect of the visions in his later life— that the 'madness' was less divine intoxication than human disintegration, however necessary it may have been as a prelude to the former. Later in life, he would wonder at some of his behaviour during this phase—worshipping his own phallus as that of Shiva, being seized by ecstatic visions while he defecated, and so on.

The prescribed medical treatment for 'insanity' did not have the desired effect. Finally, he was taken to his village home where his worried mother had him ministered to by both an exorcist and an Ayurvedic doctor. Slowly, he regained his normal state of health. To safeguard the apparent gains the family arranged his marriage, a step, which I know from professional experience, is even today considered as the best antidote to threatened or actual psychic breakdown. Of course, as far as Ramakrishna was concerned, there was never any question of the marriage being consummated. From the very beginning, in relation to his girl bride, he saw himself either as a woman or, in his ecstatic state, as a child. In the former case, the husband and wife were both girlfriends (*sakhis*) of the Mother Goddess while, in the latter, the wife was envisioned as the Goddess herself.

At the age of 24, Ramakrishna, now accompanied by his wife, returned to Calcutta to resume his priestly duties at the Kali temple. There was a relapse in his condition, though in an attenuated form. Whereas his initial visions had been untutored and spontaneous, intiated by the passionate intensity of his longing for *darshan* of the Goddess, during the next eight years he systematically followed the prescribed practices laid down by the different schools of Hindu mysticism. The disciplines were undertaken under the guidance of different gurus who were amazed at his natural facility and speed in reaching the goal of *samadhi*, a capability they themselves had acquired only after decades of strenuous effort.

First, there were the esoteric meditations of Tantra, fierce and fearful, under the tutelage of a female guru, Brahmani Bhairavi. This was followed by the nondualistic way of Vedanta, of concentration and contemplation techniques which seek to discriminate the Real from the Non-Real, a discipline without the need for any divinity or belief in God, till in the attainment of the *samadhi* all distinctions between I and the Other vanish. Then there were the various ways of Vaishnava mysticism, full of love and devotion for Rama or Krishna, the incarnations of Vishnu, and of Shakta mysticism where the supreme deity is Shakti, the primordial energy and the great Mother Goddess. All of these, the Vaishnava and Shakta ways, are essentially affective, and to which he felt personally most attuned. Whatever the discipline, his mystical genius was soon recognized by laymen and experts alike. Disciples gathered. Pandits—the theologically learned—came to visit and to partake of his clear insight into the whole gamut of Hindu metaphysics, a product of lived experience rather than scriptural proficiency; in any conventional sense, he was more or less illiterate. Ramakrishna would convey this experience simply yet strikingly through devotional songs, Puranic myths, analogies, metaphors, and parables fashioned out of the concrete details of the daily life of his listeners. Most of all, they were attracted by his riveting presence, even when he absented himself in ecstatic trances many times a day, with a few lasting for several days.

The *samadhis* did not now come unbidden but when his constantly receptive state crossed a certain threshold either in song or abandoned dance, in contemplation of a natural phenomena or absorption in the image of a divinity. He had become both a great teacher and a great mystic without losing his childlike innocence and spontaneity, which extended well into his final days. At the end of his life, dying of throat cancer, his disciples pleaded with him to ask the Mother Goddess for an easing of his disease so that he could eat some solid food rather than continue to subsist on a little barely water which had been his only nourishment for six months. Ramakrishna reluctantly agreed. On the disciples' inquiry as to the fate of their request, Ramakrishna answered: 'I said to the Mother, "I canot eat anything on account of this (showing the sore in his throat). Please do something that I can eat a little." But the Mother said, "Why? You are eating through all these mouths (showing all of you)." I could speak no more for shame.'[24]

In my attempt to understand the meaning of Ramakrishna's inner states, let me begin with Ramakrishna's own version of his experience. Anthropologically speaking, I shall start with the 'native's point of view' on the phenomenology of mystical states.

Although Ramakrishna had successfully practised the 'higher' Vedantic disciplines of monotheistic, soul-mysticism his own personal preference was for devotional, theistic mysticism of the Vaishnava and Shakta varieties. Ultimately, of course, both roads lead to the same destination. The impersonal soul of the Vedantic seer and the God or Mother Goddess—the primordial energy—of the devotee are identical, like fire and its power to burn. At first one may take the *neti, neti* (not this, not this) road of discrimination in which only Brahman is real and all else is unreal. Afterwards, the same person finds that everything in the universe, animate and inanimate, is God himself—he is both the reality and the illusion of the *Maya*. The negation is followed by an affirmation.

Ramakrishna felt that the classical disciplines of Yoga were very difficult to follow for most human beings since the identification of the self with the body, which these disciplines seek to undo, was too deeply embedded for any easy sundering. For those who could not get rid of the feeling of 'I,' it was easier to travel on the devotional path where one could instead cherish the idea that 'I am God's servant' (or child, or friend, or mother, or lover, as the case may be). He illustrated this point through the example of the monkey god Hanuman, symbol of *dasa* (servant) devotionalism, who when asked by Rama, by God, how he looked at Him replied, 'O Rama, as long as I have the feeling of 'I', I see that you are the whole and I am a part; you are the Master and I am your servant. But when, O Rama, I have the knowledge of truth, then I realize that You are I and I am You.'[25]

Even the passions—lust, anger, greed, inordinate attachment, pride, egoism—which have been traditionally held as obstacles to spiritual progress, do not need to be vanquished in devotional mysticism. The *vairagya*, the renunciation or rather the depassioning, can take place equally well by changing the object of these passions, directing them toward God rather than the objects of the world. 'Lust for intercourse with the soul. Feel angry with those who stand in your way toward God. Be greedy to get Him. If there is attachment, then to Him; like *my* Rama, *my* Krishna. If you want to be proud, then be like Vibhishana [Ravana's brother in the epic of *Ramayana*] who says, "I have bowed before Rama and shall not bow to anyone else in the world."'[26] Devotional mysticism does not demand an elimination of a sense of individual identity, of I-ness, which can instead be used to progress along the spiritual path. Thus in *vatsalya* devotionalism, the attitude of a mother toward God, Ramakrishna gives the example of Krishna's mother as the ideal to be emulated. 'Yashoda used to think, "Who will look after Gopala (Krishna's name as child) if I do not? He will fall ill if I do not look after him." She did not know Krishna as God. Udhava said to Yashoda, 'Mother, your Krishna is God Himself. He is the Lord of the Universe and not a common human being." Yashoda replied, "O who is talking about your Lord of the Universe? I am asking how *my* Gopala is. Not the Lord of the Universe, *my* Gopala."'[27]

Ramakrishna's preferred mystical style did not need ascetic practices, yogic exercises, or a succession of ever more difficult meditations. What it required of the aspirant was, first , a recovery of a childlike innocence and freshness of vision, a renunciation of most adult categories. 'To my Mother I prayed only for pure devotion. I said "Mother, here is your virtue, here is your vice. Take them both and grant me only pure devotion for you. Here is your knowledge and here is your ignorance. Take them both and grant me only pure love for you. Here is your purity and here is your impurity. Take them both Mother and grant me only pure devotion for you. Here is your *dharma* (virtue) and here is your *adharma*. Take them both, Mother, and grant me only pure devotion for you."'[28] And at another place, 'Who can ever know God? I don't even try. I only call on him as Mother . . . . My nature is that of a kitten. It only cries "Mew, mew." The rest it leaves to the Mother.'

Being like a child in relation to the Divinity does not mean being fearful, submissive, or meek, but of existing in the bright-eyed confidence of continued parental presence and *demanding* its restoration when it is felt to be lacking or insufficient. 'He is our Creator. What is there to be wondered if He is kind to us? Parents bring up their children. Do you call that an act of kindness? They must act that way. Therefore we should force our demands on God. He is our Father and Mother, isn't He?[29] Being a child, then, meant the joy of total trust, of being in the hands of infinitely powerful and infinitely beneficient forces. The power of this total trust is tremendous; its contribution to reaching the mystical goal vital. One of Ramakrishna's illustrative stories went that Rama who was God Himself had to build a bridge to cross the sea to Lanka. But the devotee Hanuman, trusting only in Rama's name, cleared the sea in one jump and reached the other side. He had no need of a bridge.

But perhaps the most important requirement of devotional mysticism, in all its varieties, was the intensity of the aspirant's yearning to be with God, whether in the dyad of mother-child, or as friend or as servant, or as lover. The longing had to be so intense that it completely took over body and mind, eliminating any need for performing devotions, prayers, or rituals. Ramakrishna illustrated this, his own yearning, through the parable of a guru who took his disciple to a pond to show him the kind of longing that would enable him to have a vision (*darshan*) of God. On coming to the pond, the guru pushed the disciple's head underwater and held it there. After a few seconds he released the disciple and asked, 'How do you feel?' The disciple ansered, 'Oh, I felt as if I was dying! I was longing for a breath of air!' 'That's exactly it,' said the guru.[30] Like other kinds of mysticism, affective mysticism too has its developmental stages. Devotion (*bhakti*) matures into (*bhava*), followed by *mahabhava, prema*, and then attainment of God in the *unio mystica*. Since the distinctions between *bhava, mahabhava* and *prema* seem to me to lie in their degrees of intensity rather than in any fundamental qualitative difference, let me try to understand the nature of only one of the three states, *bhava*, a term which Ramakrishna uses constantly to describe states of consciousness which preceded his visions and ecstatic trances.

Literally translated as 'feeling,' 'mood,' *bhava* in Vaishnava mystical thought means a state of mind (and body) pervaded with a particular emotion. Basing his illustrations on Hindu ideals, Ramakrishna lists the *bhavas* in relation to God as *shanta*, the serenity of a wife's devotion to her husband, *dasya*, the devoted submissiveness of the servant, *sakhya*, the emotion of friendship, *vatsalya*, the feeling of mother towards the child, and *madhurya*, the romantic and passionate feelings of a womam toward her lover. Ramakrishan felt that the last, symbolized in Radha's attititude toward Krishna, included all the other *bhavas*. Indeed, the discourse of passionate love is conducted in many *bhavas*. At times idealizing the lover makes 'me' experience the loved one as an infinitely superior being whom I need outside myself as a *telos* to which or whom 'I' can surrender and obey in *dasya*. At other times, there is the contented oneness of *vatsalya* as the lover becomes as a babe on the breast, not in quiescence, a complacence of the heart, but in voluptuous absorption and repose. At yet other times, there is the serene tranquillity of *shanta*, the peace of the spouses in an ineffable intimacy, a state which the eighth-century Sanskrit poet Bhavabhuti lets Rama, with Sita asleep across his arm, describe as 'this state where there is no twoness in response of joy or sorrow/where the heart finds rest; where feeling does not dry with age/

where concealments fall away in time and essential love is ripened.'[31] Besides the compulsions of possessive desire, all these *bhavas* too are at the core of man's erotic being.

Vaishnava mysticism, being a mysticism of love, does not consider awe as a legitimate *bhava* in relation to the Divine. Thus there are no feelings of reverence, of the uncanny, or of mystery. Nor are there the degrees of fear associated with awe where, in extremity, terror and dread can reign. Awe is perhaps the central *bhava* of what Erich Fromm called authoritarian religion. Vaishnava devotionalism, on the other hand, would consider awe as an obstacle in the mystical endeavour. It distances and separates rather than binds and joins.

I am aware that Ramakrishna's immersion in the various *bhavas* at different times in which he even adopted their outward manifestations can make him appear an outrageous figure to unsympathetic and prosaic observers. Practising the *madhurya bhava* of Radha towards Krishna, he dressed, behaved, and lived as a girl for six months. At another time, going through the *dasya bhava* of Hanuman, he attached an artifical tail to his posterior in an effort to resemble the monkey god. When living in the motherly *bhava* of Yashoda toward Krishna, he had one disciple, who felt like a child toward him, lean against his lap as if suckling at his breast while the mystic talked or listened to the concerns of his other disciples.

I have mentioned *mahabhava* and *prema* as the higher, more intense states of *bhava* which most aspirants never manage to reach. *Mahabhava* shakes the body and mind to its very foundations, and Ramakrishna compared it to a huge elephant entering a small hut. *Prema*, on the other hand, which makes visions of the Divine possible, was in his analogy a rope by which one tethered God. Whenever one wanted a *darshan*, one had merely to pull the rope, and He appeared.

Psychologically speaking, I would tend to see *bhavas* as more than psychic looseners that jar the soul out of the narcissistic sheath of normal, everyday, self-limiting routine. They are experiences of extreme emotional states which have a quality of irradiation wherein time and space tend to disappear. We know of these feeling states from our experience of passionate love where, at its height, the loved one's beauty is all beauty, the love canot be conceived as not being eternal, and where the memories of all past loves dim so precipitately as to almost merge into darkness. We also know *bhava* from our experience of grief which, beginning with a finite loss, irradiates all the world at its height. The world becomes empty, and all that is good is felt to be lost forever. We even know of the quality of *bhava* from states of extreme fear when the smallest sound, the minutest changes of light and shade, the quivering shapes of objects in the dark, all take on an air of extreme menace. The threat becomes eternal, with nary a thought that it might ever end.

Bhava, then, is a way of experiencing which is done 'with all one's heart, all one's soul, and all one's might.' The *bhava* fills the ecstatic mystic, as it did Ramakrishna, to the brim. He is not depleted, and there is no need for that restitution in delusion and hallucination that is the prime work of insanity. In a *bhava*, Ramakrishna rekindled the world with fresh vision, discovering or rather endowing it with newfound beauty and harmony. *Bhava* animated his relation with nature and human beings, deepened his sensate and metaphysical responsiveness.

Bhava, then, is creative experiencing, or rather the ground for all creativity—mystical, artistic, or scientific. The capacity for *bhava* is what an ideal analysis strives for, an openness toward experiencing, a capacity for 'experiencing experience' as Bion would call it. All the other gains of analysis—insight into one's conflicts, the capacity to experience pleasure without guilt, ability to tolerate anxiety without being crippled, development of a reliable reality testing, and so on—are secondary to the birth of the analytic *bhava*. Of course, the analytic *bhava*, the total openness to the analytic situation manifested in the capacity to really *free*-associate, is not simply a goal to be reached at the end of analysis, but a state to strive for in every session. In the language of the traditional drive-defence analytic model, if we divide defences into creative and uncreative, the latter by definition pathological, then the capacity for *bhava* is perhaps the most creative of defences and needs a place of honour beside and even beyond sublimation.

From *bhava*, the ground of mystical creativity, let us turn to *darshan*, vision, the mystic's primary creative product, his particular non-material creation or mystical art. Ramakrishna's explanation of visionary experience is simple, heartfelt, and sensuous. 'God cannot be seen with these physical eyes. In the course of spiritual discipline (*sadhana*) one gets a love's body endowed with love eyes, love ears, and so on. One sees God with these love eyes. One hears His voice with these love ears. One even gets a penis and a vagina made of love. With this love body one enjoys intercourse with the soul.'[32]

In my own explorations, I prefer to use the religious term vision rather than its psychiatric counterpart hallucination for the same reason that I have talked of mystical *ecstasy* rather than of euphoria, namely the connotations of psychopathology associated with psychiatric categories. The distinction between the two, though, is not very hard and fast, their boundaries constantly shifting. Both can be produced by severe depression or manic excitement, toxic psychosis due to exhaustion or starvation or sensory deprivation or simply a febrile illness. What is important in distinguishing them is their meaning and content and not their origin.

Visions are like hallucinations in that they too are images, such as flashes of light, which are visually perceived without the external stimulation of the organ of sight. They are, however, not hallucinations in that they occur during the course of intense religious experience rather than during a psychotic episode. They are thus less bizarre and less disorganized. Visions belong more to the realm of perceptions that take place say, during a dream, while falling asleep (hypnagogic) or when awakening (hypnopompic). None of these can be called a consequence of psychic impairment. Visions are, then, special kinds of dreams which find their way into waking life. To have vision is in itself as much a manifestation of mental disorder as is the corresponding process of real events being drawn across the barrier of sleep into the formation of dreams. Freud recognized the special nature of visions when, in an aside on the psychology of the mystic, he remarked, 'It is easy to imagine, too, that certain mystics may succeed in upsettting the normal relations between the different regions of the mind, so that, for instance, perception may be able to grasp happenings in the depths of the ego and in the id which were otherwise inaccessible to it.'[33] Ramakrishna's visions, as perhaps those of other mystics, do not constitute a unitary phenomenon. They span the whole range from what can be fairly described as hallucinations in the psychiatric sense, through more or less conscious visions, to what I would call 'unconscious visions' (or 'visions of the unconscious'?) which cannot be described since the observing ego is absent. These are the ineffable 'salt doll' visions which comprise a small, though perhaps the most striking part of the total mystical repertoire.

Before we discuss the various kinds of visions, let us note their central common feature: the intense affect they generate, an affect that endows them with their characteristic sense of noesis. The affect, so strong that it is experienced as *knowing* partakes of some of the quality of the symbiotic state in infancy when the child knew the mother through an interchange of their feelings, when affect and cognition were not differentiated from one another.[34]

The affects are also manifested in the body, and Ramakrishna's visions had certain well-defined physical correlates. At times, he would shudder while tears of joy streamed unchecked down his cheeks. At other times, his eyes would become half-closed and unfocused, a faint smile playing around the mouth while his body became completely rigid and had to be supported by a disciple lest he fall and hurt himself. The accompaniment to certain other trance states was a flushed chest or a strong burning sensation all over the body. Ramakrishna reports that once when in such a state, Brahmani, his tantric guru, tried to lead him to his bath. She could not hold his hand, so hot was his skin, and she had to wrap him in a sheet. The earth that stuck to his body while he was lying on the ground became baked. Then there is the feeling of being famished—one wonders, spiritual receptivity with a bodily analogue (or is it vice versa)? Or there are the bouts of gluttony in which he consumed enormous quantities of food, generally sweets. The craving for a particular dish or a sweet would come upon Ramakrishna unexpectedly, at any time of night or day. At these moments, Ramakrishna would be like a pregnant woman who is dominated by her obsession and cannot rest till the craving is satisfied.

From inside the tradition, all these manifestations are some of the 19 bodily signs of the mystical experience. To the analyst, however, they are a further confirmation of the mystic's access to a period in early life—'oral' in the classical nomenclature—when the boundary between psyche and soma was much more porous than is the case in adulthood. His is the reclamation of a truly dialogical period wherein engendered affects were discharged through the body while physical experience found easy expression in affective states. Ramakrishna's longing for the Mother, accompanied by breathlessness of a kind where he feels he is about to die, for instance, is akin to a certain type of asthmatic bodily manifestation of damned-up urge for the mother's succour.

Coming back to the various types of visions, the hallucinations, unbidden and unwelcome, belong to his period of insanity (*unmada*): 'I would spit on the ground when I saw them. But they would follow me and obsess me like ghosts. One the day after such a vision I would have a severe attack of diarrhoea, and all these ecstasies would pass out through my bowels.'[35]

These hallucinations, or better, nightmarish visions, are not alien but perhaps as much a part of Ramakrishna's personality as are his artistic sensibility or his more elevated, mystical visions. Their essential linkage may be better understood if we take recourse to Ernst Hartmann's work on nightmares.[36]

In his study of nonpsychiatric volunteers who suffered from nightmares since childhood, Hartmann found that these subjects were usually sensitive people with a strong artistic bent and creative potential. More important, they demonstrate what he calls 'thin boundaries of the mind,' a permeability between self and object, waking/sleeping, fantasy/reality, adult/child, human/animal, and other such boundaries, which are relatively fixed for most people. The thin boundary of the mind, Hartmann tries to show, is at the root of both their artistic sensibility and potential for nightmares. It is tempting to speculate that Ramakrishna, and perhaps most other mystics, have a genetic biological predisposition, reinforced by some early experiences to which we will come later, to thin boundaries, also between nightmarish and ecstatic visions.

The second class of visions are the conscious ones. Welcomed by a prepared mind, they fall on a receptive ground. Conscious visions may be symbolic representations of an ongoing psychic process, the symbols taken from the mystic's religious and cultural tradition. This is true, for instance, of Ramakrishna's vision of his 'enlightenment,' which he 'saw' in the traditional yogic imagery of *Kundalini*, the coiled serpent energy rising through the different centres (*chakras*) of his body and opening up the 'lotuses' asociated with these centres, a specifically Hindu metaphor for mental transformation and the opening up of the psyche to hitherto inaccessible psychic experience. 'I saw a 22, 23-year-old, exactly resembling me, enter the Sushumna nerve and with his tongue 'sport' (*raman*) with the vulva-(*yoni*) shaped lotuses. He began with the centre of the anus, through the centres of the penis, navel, and so on. The respective four-petaled, six-petaled, and ten-petaled lotuses which had been dropping, rose high and blossomed. I distinctly remember that when he came to the heart and sported with it with his tongue, the 12-petaled lotus which had been dropping rose high and opened its petals. Then he came to the 16-petaled lotus in the throat and the two-petaled one in the forehead. And last of all, the 1000-petaled lotus in the head blossomed.'[37] This particular vision, in which self-representation is split into observing and participating aspects, can also be seen through psychiatric glasses as a heutroscopic depersonalization which occurs particularly among individuals with tendencies toward self-contemplation and introspection. Yet in the absence of any associated painful or anxious affect and the fact that this kind of vision was only one among Ramakrishna's vast repertoire of visions with very different structures and qualities, I would tend to see its ground in a creativity, akin to the heightened fantasy of an artist or a writer, rather than in pathology. Goethe and Maupassant are two instances of creative writers who also experienced the phenomenon of their doubles.[38]

Other conscious visions are visual insights, images full of conviction and sudden clarity, couched either in a universal-mystical or in a particular, cultural-historical idiom. Some examples of the former would be seeing the universe filled with sparks of fire, or glittering like a lake of quicksilver, or all its quarters illuminated with the light of myriad candles. Such visions of light, we mentioned earlier, have been reported by mystics throughout the ages, and, indeed, seeing the divine light has been a central feature of many mystical cults, including 17th-century Quakerism. Another visual insight of the universal variety is seeing everything throbbing with consciousness: 'Sometimes I see the same consciousness playing in small fish that is animating the world. Sometimes I see the world soaked with consciousness in the same way as the earth is soaked with water during the rains.'[39]

The full import of the more culturally constituted visions, on the other hand, can only be appreciated if we keep in mind that Ramakrishna was a Hindu Brahmin living at a time—the 19th century, and place—rural Bengal—in which the ideas of pollution and polluting substances were strong, caste taboos strict, and the threatened loss of caste a horror of the first magnitude. Visions dissolving religious distinctions and caste taboos, such as the ones on touching forbidden substances or taking food from forbidden persons, were thus primarily expressed in a cultural imagery relevant to Ramakrishna's community. For instance, 'Then I was shown a Muslim with a long beard who came to me with rice in an earthen plate. He fed other Muslims and also gave me some grains to eat. Mother showed me there exists only one and not two.'[40] 'Another day I saw excrement, urine, rice, vegetables, and other foods. Suddenly the soul came out of my body and, like a flame, touched everything: excrement, urine, everything was tasted. It was revealed that everything is one, that there is no difference.'[41] Or, when on the repeated egging on by his nephew, he asked the Goddess for occult powers and saw a middle-aged prostitute come up, squat on her haunches with her back to him, and proceed to evacuate. The vision revealed that occult powers were the shit of that whore.

There is another class of visions, or strictly speaking, mystical illusions, since these rest on a transmutation of external stimuli into creations which are nearer to those of the artist. Thus the way an English boy leans against a tree is transformed into a vision of Krishna; a prostitute walking toward him is changed into a vision of the Mother Goddess—-both images irradiate his body and mind with beneficence. In Blake's words, these illusions are 'auguries of innocence' enabling the mystic 'to see a world in a grain of sand, and a heaven in a wild flower.'

And finally, there are the indescribable, unconscious visions. 'You see,' Ramakrishna once said to diciples, 'something goes up creeping from the feet to the head. Consciousness continues to exist as long as this power does not reach the head; but as soon as it reaches the head, all consciousness is completely lost. There is no seeing or hearing anymore, much less speaking. Who can speak? The very idea of "I" and "You" vanishes. While it (the serpent power) goes up, I feel a desire to tell you everything—how many visions I experience, of their nature, etc. Until it comes to this place (showing the heart) or at most this place (showing the throat) speaking is possible, and I do speak. But the moment it goes up beyond this place (showing the throat) someone forcibly presses the mouth, as it were, and I lose all consciousness. I cannot control it. Suppose I try to describe what kind of vision I experience when it goes beyond this place (showing the throat). As soon as I begin to think of them for the purpose of description the mind rushes immediately up, and speaking becomes impossible.'[42]

His feelings during these visions could then only be expressed in metaphors— 'I feel like a fish released from a pot into the water of the Ganges.' Ramakrishna, however, does not seem to have been overly enamoured of these states which have been so often held as the apex of the mystical experience. He consciously tried to keep a trace of the observing ego—a little spark of the big fire—so as not to completely disappear, or disappear for a long time, into the *unio mystica* with its non-differentiation of 'I' and the 'Other.' 'In *samadhi*, I lose outer consciousness completely, but God generally keeps a little trace of the ego in me for the enjoyment [here he uses a deliberately sensual metaphor, *vilas*] of intercourse. Enjoyment is only possible when "I" and "You" 'remain.' As he maintained, 'I want to taste sugar, not become sugar.' Yet in spite of himself he was often the salt doll that went into the ocean.

The unconscious visions, irreducible to language. are different from other visions which are ineffable only in the sense that their description can never be complete. The unconscious visions are a return to the world before the existence of language, visions of 'reality' through the destruction of language that the particular mystical act entails. As Octavio Paz puts it,'Language sinks its roots into this world but transforms its juices and reactions into signs and symbols. Language is the consequence (or the cause) of our exile from the universe, signifying the distance between things and ourselves. If our exile were to come to an end, languages would come to an end.'[43] The salt doll ends exile, writes a *finis* to language.

The vicissitudes of separation have been, of course, at the heart of psychoanalytic theorizing on mysticism. The yearning to be reunited with a perfect, omnipotent being, the longing for the blissful soothing and nursing associated with the mother of earliest infancy (perhaps as much an adult myth as an infantile reality), has been consensually deemed the core of mystical motivation. What has been controversial is the way this longing has been viewed and the value placed on it by different analysts.

The traditional view, initiated by Freud, sees this yearning as reactive, a defence against the hatred directed towards the Oedipal father. For writers influenced by Melanie Klein, the longing for the blissful 'good' mother is a defensive denial of her terrifying and hated aspects.[44] Given the limitation that Ramakrishna did not spend any time on the couch (but, then, neither have other theorists had mystics as patients), I can only say that there is no evidence in the voluminous record of his conversation, reminiscences, and accounts of his visions which is remotely suggestive of any strong hostility toward the Oedipal father. The evidence for the denial of the dreaded aspects of the mother is slightly greater, namely through a plausible interpretation of some elements of his vision in the Kali temple when he had taken up a sword to kill himself. However, seen in the total context of a large number of visions of the Mother Goddess, the ambiguous evidence of one particular vision is not enough to compel an acceptance of the Kleinian notions on mystical motivation.

Paul Horton has advanced a more adaptive view of mystical yearning and mystical states, especially during adolescence.[45] He sees them as a consequence of the pangs of separation in which the felt reality of being utterly and agonizingly alone is *transiently* denied. The mystical experience is then a transitional phenomenon which soothes and reassures much as a baby is soothed by a blanket, a child by a stuffed toy or fairytale, an adult by a particular piece of music—all these various creations, material and nonmaterial, providing opportunities for the controlled illusion that heals.

There is much to be said for the hypothesis that experiences of separation and loss spurred Ramakrishna onto the mystical path. We know that Ramakrishna's first quasi-mystical ecstasy when he became unconscious at the sight of white cranes flying against a background of dark clouds took place in the last year of his father's final illness (according to one place in Ramakrishna's reminiscences, two years after his father's death), that is, at a time of an impending loss. And I have described the marked change that came over Ramakrishna is not unlike some of the Christian mystics in whose lives too, as David Aberbach has demonstrated, one could hypothesize a link between personal loss and their mystical calling.[46] Teresa of Avila's life in the church began with the death of her mother when Teresa was 12 years old. The loss of a parent or parent-surrogate may also be an early one, heightening a later sense of abandonment and the subsequent search for the 'eternal Thou,' as perhaps in the examples of St John of the Cross, whose father died a few months after his birth, or of Martin Buber, whose mother deserted him when he was three.

The mystical path is then also a way of lessening the agony of separation, mitigating the grief at loss, reducing the sadness of bereavement. In my own interviews with members of a mystical cult in India, loss was the single most important factor in their decision to seek its membership. The very embarkation on the mystical path had a therapeutic effect by itself, while any experience of a mystical state had a further marked effect in altering the person's dysphoric state of mind.[47] In contrast to the person's previous feelings of apathy and depression, the turn to mysticism had the consequence of his dealing with grief in a more orderly and more detached, though in a more transcendent, manner. Perhaps T.S. Eliot is correct in observing that 'A man does not join himself with the universe so long as he has anything else to join himself with.'[48]

Of course, Ramakrishna's two actual experiences of loss are not sufficient to explain the totality of his mysticism, the intensity of his yearning throughout life to end the state of separation from the Divine, and the acuteness of his distress at the absence of the Mother. The motivational skein of mysticism, as of any other psychic phenomenon, is composed of many strands. One could speculate that the advanced age of his mother at his birth, his family's poverty and thus his mother's added preoccupations with household tasks, the birth of another sibling when he was four, may have led to the emotional unavailability of the mother at a phase of the child's development when his own needs were driving him closer to her. In other words, the suggestion is that in the crucial 'rapprochement' phase (which occurs later in India than in psychoanalyst Margaret Mahler's timetable), the mother was unavailable at a time when his anxiety about separation, and its convergent depression, were at their apex. This would fix separation and its associated anxiety as the dominant theme of his inner life. Each feared or actual loss would reactivate separation anxiety together with a concomitant effort at combating it by reclaiming in fantasy an adored and adoring intimacy with the maternal matrix. The unity Ramakrishna aimed for is, then, not the mergerlike states of the infant at the breast, though these too prefigured his trances, but the ending of separation striven for by the toddler. It is a state in which both mother and child have boundaries in relation to each other while another boundary encloses their 'double unit' from the rest of the world. Here the enjoyment of the mother's presence is deeply sensuous, almost ecstatic, and informs Ramakrishna's selection of words; images and metaphors that describe his experiences.

Together with the speculated impact of early mother-child interaction in Ramakrishna's psychic life, admittedly a construct derived from analytic theory rather than a reconstruction based on compelling psychobiographical evidence, I would tend to attribute his acute sensitivity to the theme of separation to the mystical gift (or curse) of a specific kind of creative experiencing. This can be understood more clearly, if we take recourse to some ideas of the 'metaphysical' analysts mentioned earlier.

Lacan, for instance, has postulated that man's psychic life constantly seeks to deal with a primordial state of affairs which he calls the Real. The Real itself is unknowable, though we constantly create myths as its markers. Perhaps the principal myth involves the rupture of a basic union, the separation from the mother's body, leaving us with a fundamental feeling of incompletion. The fantasies around this insufficiency are universal, governing the psyche of both patients and analysts alike. In the psyche, this lack is translated as desire, and the human venture is a history of desire as it ceaselessly loses and discovers itself in (what Lacan calls) The Imaginary and, with the advent of language, The Symbolic order. Born of rupture, desire's fate is an endless quest for the lost object; all real objects merely interrupt the search. As the Barandes put it, 'It is the task of the *neotenique* [i.e., immature, even foetalized being] being separated from its original union by its fall into life and into time, to invent detours for itself, deviations of object as well as means and aims. Its condition is inexorably perverse—if perversions must be.'⁴⁹ The mystical quest seeks to rescue from primal repression the constantly lived contrast between an original interlocking and a radical rupture. The mystic, unlike most others, does not mistake his hunger for its fulfilment. If we are all fundamentally perverse in the play of our desire, then the mystic is the only one who seeks to go beyond the illusion of The Imaginary and, yes, also the *maya* of The Symbolic register.

One of Ramakrishna's more 'private' vision attempts to paint the issue of separation with crude yet compelling brushstrokes. As Bion would say, here he is like the analyst who knows that emotional truth is ineffable, available only in intimations and approximations. Like the Bionian analyst, the mystic too is compelled to use terms from sensuous experience to point to a realm beyond this experience. 'Let me tell you a very secret experience. Sitting in a pine grove, I had the vision of a small, hidden [literally 'thief's door'] entrance to a room. I could not see what was inside the room. I tried to bore a hole with a nail file but did not succeed. As I bored the hole it would fill up again and again. And then suddenly it made a big opening.' He kept quiet and then started speaking again. 'These are all higher matters. I feel someone is closing my mouth. I have seen God residing in the vagina. I saw Him there at the time of sexual intercourse of a dog and a bitch.'⁵⁰

Ramakrishna's vision, followed by an associative sequel, does not need extended analytic gloss. The small secret opening to a room into which he cannot see and which he tried to keep open, the seeing of God in the genitals of a bitch in intercourse, do not encode the mystical preoccupation with opening a way back to the self-other interlocking in any complex symbolic language. This interlocking, the mystical unity, is not unitary. As we saw in Ramakrishna's case, it extends in a continuum from the foetalized being's never having known separation from the mother's insides, an expulsion from her womb, through the satiated infant's flowing feelings of merger at the breast, to the toddler being pulled back to the mother as if held at one end of an invisible string.

What I am emphasizing, however, is not the traditional analytic agenda of pathological, defensive, or compensatory uses of these various degrees of dyadic unity in mystical experiencing. As Michael Eigen has elaborated in a series of papers, for Freud, ideal experiencing, that is, states or moments of beatific (or horrific) perfection, in which I would include the mystical states, usually involved something in disguise—mother, father, sex, aggression and so on.[51] Lacan, Winnicott and Bion (and implicitly also Erikson), on the other hand, look at ideal experiencing in its own right, as a spontaneously unfolding capacity for creative experiencing. This capacity can be deployed defensively as has been spelled out in detail in the Freudian literature, but it is not conterminous with defence.

All these authors emphasize the positive, regenerative aspects of this experiencing not as idealists but as empirical analysts who chart out its developmental vicissitudes from early infancy onward. The experiencing itself, they maintain, should not be confused with the introjection of the mother and father images or functions. These only foster or hamper this capacity. 'If one reads these authors carefully, one discovers that the *primary object of creative experiencing is not mother or father but the unknowable ground of creativeness as such*. Winnicott, for example, emphasizes that what is at stake in transitional experiencing is not mainly a self or object (mother) substitute, but the creation of a symbol, of symbolizing experiencing itself. The subject lives through and toward creative immersion (including phases of chaos, unintegration, waiting).'[52] What we should then pay equal attention to is not only the conflicts of the mystic that threaten to deform or disperse his creative experiencing, but the experiencing itself—its content, context, and evolution.

Most of us harbour tantalizing 'forgotten' traces of this kind of experiencing, an apperception where what is happening outside is felt to be the creative act of the original artist (or mystic) within each of us and recognized as such with (in Blake's word) *delight*. For in late infancy and early childhood we did not always see the world as something outside ourselves, to be recognized in detail, adapted, complied with, and fitted into our idiosyncratic inner world, but often as an infinite succession of creative acts.

Mystical experience, then, is one and—in some cultures and at certain historical periods—the preeminent way of uncovering the vein of creativity that runs deep in all of us. For some, it is the throes of romantic love that gives inklings of our original freshness of vision.

Others may strive for creative experiencing in art or in natural science. In the West, the similarities between mystics and creative artists and scientists have been pointed out since the beginning of the century. Evelyn Underhill in her path-breaking work on mysticism emphasized the resemblance between artistic geniuses and mystics—though one should hesitate to use the terms as interchangeable—while James Leuba pointed out the similarity at a more mundane level in creative phenomena of the daily kind and at a lower level of intensity.[53] In China, we know that it was the mystical Taoists stressing spontaneity, 'inaction,' 'emptying the mind,' rather than the rational Confucians, who stimulated Chinese scientific discovery. In India, too, in different epochs, the striving for mystical experience through art, especially music, has been a commonly accepted and time-honoured practice. And Albert Einstein writes of his own motivations for the scientific enterprise, 'The most beautiful, the most profound emotion we can experience is the sensation of the mystical. It is the fundamental emotion that stands at the cradle to true art and science.' Einstein goes on to say that there is a need 'to escape from everyday life with its painful crudity and hopeless dreariness, from fetters of one's own shifting desires.' Instead the scientist and the artist creates his own reality, substituting it for the world of experience and thus overcoming it: 'Each makes his own cosmos and its construction the pivot of his emotional life, in order to find in this way peace and security which he cannot find in the narrow whirlpool of personal experience.'[54] Here it seems to me that Einstein is not talking as someone who is depressed but with a creative individual's clear-sighted and inevitable response to the world as it is. When Buddha, as the young Siddhartha confronted with illness, old-age, and death proclaims '*Sabbam dukham* (All is suffering)', he too is not depressed but in perfect attunement with the reality principle. To see the world with a creative eye but a sober perspective is perhaps our greatest adaptation to reality— a state where Buddha, Freud and Ramakrishna come together.

Sexuality and the Mystical Experience

Ramakrishna was one with other Vaishnava mystics in his insistence that sexuality, by which he meant male sexuality, phallic desire, constituted the biggest obstacle to mystical experiencing. This is a formulation with which psychoanalysts will not have any quarrel. For both male and female infants, the differentiation between self and object is achieved and ego boundaries constituted by a gradual detachment from the mother. The presence of the father is vital for this process. Whereas the masculinity of the father makes it possible for the boy to overcome his primary femininity, the presence of the paternal phallus also helps to protect the little girl from fusional tendencies with the mother. Male sexuality and male desire may thus be viewed as obstacles in the path of fusion, the phallus as the prime symbol of boundaries the mystic seeks to transcend.

The renunciation of adult masculinity is not only a feature of Hindu devotional mysticism but is also a feature of Christian emotional mysticism of medieval and early modern Europe. Affective prayer or Bernardine mysticism, as it has often been called after the influential sermons of the 11th-century saint Bernard of Clairvaux, possesses a striking affinity to its Hindu counterpart. Femininity pervades both. In the case of medieval Europe, most of the practicing mystics were women. But even the outstanding male mystics—St John of the Cross, Francois de Sales, Fenelon—show strong feminine identifications and produced their most important ideas under the direct influence of women.[55] The psychological stance of Christian ecstatic toward Divinity, paralleling that of the Vaishnava mystics, is either that of the infant toward a loving maternal parent, or of a woman toward a youthful lover. Like the Hindus, the Christian mystics too disavowed or overthrew the paternal phallus as they divested the Judeo-Christian God of much of his original masculinity and sternness, virtually relegating him to the role of a grandfather. The message of the European emotional mystics seems to be the same as that of Ramakrishna: the actual gender of the mystics is not important for his practice. It is, however vital that the mystic accept and cultivate his or her femininity to the point that the female-self part becomes dominant in his or her inner psychic reality.

Of the many mystical disciplines, the one Ramakrishna could never practise was the 'heroic' one of *tantra* where, at its culmination, God as a female is sought to be pleased—or perhaps I should say, pleasured—as a man pleases a woman through intercourse. In his own *tantric* training, he had escaped the demand for ritual sex by going into an ecstatic state just before he had to actually 'perform'. He repeatedly warned his disciples against *kamini-kanchani* (literally, woman and gold), and his advice to novices on the mystical path was to avoid the female sex altogether, the whirlpool in which even Brahma and Vishnu struggle for their lives. For a renunciant, he felt, to sit with a woman or talk to her for a long time was a kind of sexual intercourse of which there were eight kinds. Some of these were to listen to a woman, to talk to her in secret, to keep and enjoy something belonging to a woman, to touch her, and so on. Given the fact that a vast majority of widely known mystics, at least in medieval Christian and devotional Hindu traditions, have been celibates, one wonders whether celibacy, with its profound influence on hormonal balance, is not an important physiological technique for mystical ecstasy.

The prescribed avoidance of women was only for beginners. Once mystical knowledge was gained, sexual differentiation too vanished: 'Then you don't have much to fear. After reaching the roof you can dance as much as you like, but not on the stairs.' Yet though Ramakrishna constantly reiterated that he looked at the breasts of every woman as those of his mother, that he felt as a child or as another woman with women, his male awareness of women as sexual beings, and of the dangers of a desire that separates and bifurcates, never quite disappeared as his biographers would have us believe. He felt uncomfortable with female devotees sitting in his room and would ask them to go and visit the temple as soon as he could decently get rid of them. Being touched by a woman was not a matter of unconcern but evoked strong physical reactions. 'If a woman touches me, I fall ill. That part of my body aches as if stung by a horned fish. If I touch a woman my hand becomes numb; it aches. If in a friendly spirit I approach a woman and begin to talk to her, I feel as if a curtain has come down between us.'[56] However minimal his sexual conflict, even a great mystic seems to retain at least a vestigial entanglement with the world of desire. In his normal nonecstatic state, Ramakrishna too was never quite free of the sexual *maya* free from the delight, wisdom, beauty, and pain of the 'illusion' which so beguiles the rest of us.

Ramakrishna's attempted renunciation of male sexual desire is the subject of one vision, although as someone who claimed to never having even dreamt of intercourse with a woman, the *conscious* promptings of desire could not have been too peremptory. 'During the *sadhanas*, I vividly perceived a heap of rupees, a shawl, a plate of sweets and two women. "Do you want to enjoy any of these things?" I asked my mind. "No," replied the mind. I saw the insides of those women, of what is in them; entrails, piss, shit, phlegm and such things.'[57] We can, of course, try to understand the contents of this vision in biographical terms. Money, shawl, and sweets embody overpowering temptations for a boy who grew up in a poor family whose dire financial straits allowed but the most spartan of fare. Similarly, one posible cause for the hankering after sexual purity in his youth could be a deep feeling of shame he associated with the sexual act. In a country and at a time where women not infrequently became grandmothers in their late 20s, where sexual activity has always been considered a prerogative of the young—sexual desire of older men and women occasioning derisive laughter—Ramakrishna's birth itself (followed by that of the sister) is the sign of a tainted and deeply mortifying sexuality of his old parents. We have already seen how Ramakrishna's enduring wish to be a woman, expressed variously in dressing and moving his limbs like one, his fantasy of being a girl widow who secretly trysts with Krishna every evening, fitted in well with a tenet of Vaishnava mysticism that all mankind is female while God alone is male. Ramakrishna would approvingly cite the opinion that irrespective of biological gender everyone with nipples is a female. Arjuna, the heroic warrior of the *Mahabharata,* and Krishna are the only exceptional males since they do not have nipples. In the *madhurya bhava*, Ramakrishna had even tried to engender in himself female erotic feelings. Moved by an intense love for Krishna, 'such as a woman feels for her lover,' he had stretched out his arms to embrace the Lord's stone idols.

Just as the writings of medieval European female mystics, wherein they wax rhapsodic over their ecstatic union with Jesus, portrayed as an exceedingly handsome and loving bridegroom of the human soul, have been analyzed as expressions of a pathological, hysterical sexuality, it would not be difficult to diagnose Ramakrishna in traditional Freudian terms as a secondary transsexual. He would seamlessly fit in with Robert Stoller's description of the secondary transsexual as being someone who differs from his primary counterpart in that he does not appear feminine from the start of any behavior that may be classed in gender terms.[58] Under the surface of masculinity, however, there is the persistent impulse toward being feminine, an urge which generally manifests itself in adolescence. The most obvious manifestation of these urges is the wish for the actual wearing of women's clothes. Though these urges may gather in strength and last for longer and longer periods, the masculine aspects of identity are never completely submerged.

Ramakrishna's open espousal and expression of his feminine identifications as a boy, however, also have to do with the greater tolerance of his community and its culture towards such identifications. His urge toward femininity did not meet an unyielding opposition or strenuous attempts at suppression by an enforced participation in masculine play. Any transsexual or homosexual labels may obscure his sense of comfort and easy familiarity with the feminine components of his self. It may hide the fact that the freeing of femininity from repression of disavowal in man and *vice versa* in a woman may be a great human achievement rather than an illness or a deviation. The deviation may actually lie, as in one view of the etiology of homosexuality, in the *inability* to come to terms with the opposite sexual personality in one's self.[59]

Summarizing, I would say that the male-self part of Ramakrishna's personality was split off in early childhood and tended to grow, if at all, rather slowly. In contrast, the female-self part of his personality dominated his inner psychic reality. Ramakrishna's girl-self was neither repressed nor disassociated but could mature to an extent where psychically he could even possess female sexual equipment and enjoy female sexual experience.

Yet even a celebratory avowal of secondary femininity in a male mystic may not be enough to exhaust the mystery of the link between sexuality and mysticism. For if, together with 'infant-likeness,' secondary femininity and female bodily experience—breastpride, absence of male external genitalia, the presence of vulva and womb—are important for affective mysticism, then women will be seen as having a head start in this particular human enterprise. They naturally are what male aspirants must become. This may be true though it has yet to be demonstrated that gender makes a substantial difference in the making of a mystic. What is perhaps essential in mysticism is not the presence of secondary but of 'primary" femininity—the 'pure female element' (not the female person) in Winnicott's sense of the term. In his theory of the life of male and female elements in a person, the purely male element, in both man and woman, presupposes separateness and trafficks in terms of active relating, or being passively related to, and is backed by the whole apparatus of instinctual drives.[60] The female element, on the other hand, relates to the other—the breast, the mother (both with a small and capital 'm')—in the sense of an identity between the two. When this element finds the other, it is the self that has been found. It is the female element that establishes the simplest, the most primary of experiences, the experience of *being*. Winnicott remarks, 'psychoanalysts have perhaps given special attention to this male element or drive aspect of object relating and yet have neglected the subject-object identity to which I am drawing attention here, which is at the basis of the capacity to be. The male element *does* (active-passive) while the female element *is* (in males and females) and concludes 'After being—doing and being done to. But first *being*.'[61]

Looking at Ramakrishna's sexuality in relation to his mystical experience in terms of oral, anal, and phallic stages of development or of identifications with mother, father and so on, as in classical analytic discourse, is then to forget that this discourse itself may be based on the life of the male element. Our psychology has still little to say of the distilled female element, the primary femininity, at the heart of emotional mysticism. The pure female element, in both men and women, continues to testify to the category of mystery as a basic dimension in which we all, and especially the mystic, live. As analysts, however, we cannot look at mystery as something eternally beyond human comprehension, but as a phenomenon to which we repeatedly return to increase our understanding. As our perspectives change, our earlier views do not get replaced but are subsumed in an ever-widening set of meanings.

2

THE GURU AS HEALER

The contemporary images of the Indian guru, the sacred centre of Hindu religious and philosophical traditions, are many. He is that stately figure in spotless white or saffron robes, with flowing locks and beard, to all appearances the younger brother of a brown Jehovah. To be approached in awe and reverence, he is someone who makes possible the disciple's fateful encounter with the mystery lying at the heart of human life. He is also the Rasputin look-alike, with piercing yet warm eyes, hypnotic and seductive at once, a promiser of secret ecstasies and radical transformations of consciousness and life. The guru is also the venerable guardian of ancient, esoteric traditions, benevolently watchful over the disciple's experiences in faith, gently facilitating his sense of identity and self. He can also be (to use the imagery of Pupul Jayakar, the biographer of the Indian sage Jiddu Krishnamurti), 'the silent, straight-backed stranger, the mendicant who stands waiting at the doorways of home and mind, holding an invitation to otherness,' evoking 'passionate longings, anguish and a reaching out physically and inwardly to that which is unattainable.'[1]

In the above snapshots we find little trace of the old polarity which characterized the guru image. This polarity consisted of the worldly, orthodox teacher guru at one end representing relative, empirical knowledge, and the otherworldly, mystic guru at the other pole who was the representative of esoteric, existential knowledge. In Hindu terms, the dominant image of the guru seems to have decisively shifted toward the *moksha* (liberation) guru rather than the *dharma* (virtue) guru, toward the *bhakti* (devotional) guru rather than the *jnana* (knowledge) guru or, in tantric terms, toward the *diksha* (initiation) guru who initiated the novice into methods of salvation rather than the *shiksha* (teaching) guru who taught the scriptures and explained the meaning and purpose of life.[2]

This was, of course, not always the case. In Vedic times (1500-500 B.C.), when man's encounter with the sacred mysteries took place through ritual, the guru was more a guide to their correct performance and an instructor in religious duties. A teacher deserving respect and a measure of obedience, he was not yet a mysterious figure of awe and the venerated incarnation of divinity.

In the later Upanishadic era (800-500 B.C.), the polar shift begins in earnest as the person of the guru starts to replace Vedic rituals as the path to spiritual liberation. He now changes from a knower and dweller in Brahman to being the only conduit to Brahman. Yet the Upanishadic guru is still recognizably human—a teacher of acute intellect, astute and compassionate, demanding from the disciple the exercise of his reason rather than exercises in submission and blind obedience. When, in the seventh-century A.D., the great Shankara, in his project of reviving the ancient Brahminical tradition, seeks to resurrect the Upanishadic guru, he sees in him a teacher who 'is calm, tranquil, childlike, silent and free from distracting motivations. Although learned he should be as a child, parading neither wisdom, nor learning, nor virtue itself. . . . He is a reservoir of mercy who teaches out of compassion to the multitude. he is sympathetic to the conditions of the student and is able to act with empathy towards him.'[3] In the disciple's spiritual quest, Shankara's guru places reason on par with scriptural authority and constantly exhorts the student to test and verify the teachings through his own experience. Every student needs to discover anew for himself or herself what is already known, a spiritual patrimony which has to be earned each time for it to become truly one's own. Here, the ideal of the Hindu guru was not too far removed from the Buddhist master who, too, constructed near-experience situations to illustrate a teaching and who saw the master-disciple relationship as one of perfect equality in self-realization, with radical insight as its goal. The relationship between the guru and disciple was of intimacy, not of merger. Both the guru and disciple were separate individuals, and potential equals, though striving for ever-greater closeness.

From the seventh-century onwards, the swing away from the teacher image of the guru received its greatest momentum with the rise of the *bhakti* cults in both North and South India. Devotional surrender on the part of the disciple, with such features as ritualistic service to the guru, the worship of his feet, bodily prostration and other forms of veneration, and divine grace (*prasada*) on the part of the guru, mark the guru-disciple relationship: 'Guru and Govind [i.e., Lord Krishna] stand before me,' says the 15th-century poet-saint Kabir, and asks, 'Whose feet should I touch?' The answer is, 'The guru gets the offering. He shows the way to Govind.'[4] The operative word is now love rather than understanding. To quote Kabir again:

> Reading book after book, the whole world died
> And none ever became learned
> He who can decipher just a syllable of 'love'
> is the true learned man (pandit)[5]

With the spread of *tantric* cults around 1000 A.D., the guru not only shows the way to the Lord, but is the Lord. 'There is no higher god than guru,' *tantric* texts tell us, 'No higher truth than the guru.' 'The guru is father, the guru is mother, the guru is the God Shiva. When Shiva is angry, the guru is the Saviour. But when the guru is angry, there is no one who can save you.'[6] The guru is now an extraordinary figure of divine mystery and power, greater than the scriptures and the gods, and all that the disciple requires to realize his own godlike nature, his extraordinary identity as Lawrence Babb puts it, is to merge his substantial and spiritual being with that of the guru.[7] The ambiguities of thought and the agonizings of reason can be safely sidestepped since the way is no longer through a complete and wilful surrender—the offering of *tana, mana*, and *dhana* (body, mind, and wealth) in the well-known phrase of North Indian devotionalism. The responsibility for the disciple's inner transformation is no longer that of the disciple but of the guru. 'One single word of the guru gives liberation,' says a tantric text. 'All the sciences are masquerades. Only the knowledge flowing out of the guru's mouth is living. All other kinds of knowledge are powerless and causes of sufferings.'[8]

The combined forces of the *bhakti* and *tantra* pushed toward an ever-increasing deification of the guru, a massive idealization of his mystery and power. The 13th-century Marathi saint Jnaneshvara writes of the guru:

As for his powers,
He surpasses even the greatness of Shiva,
With his help,
The soul attains the state of Brahman;
But if he is indifferent,
Brahman has no more worth than a blade of grass.[9]

Complementary to the movement of the guru from man to god is the shift in the disciple from man to child. The favoured, the ideal disciple is pure of heart, malleable of character, and a natural renouncer of all adult categories, especially of rational inquiry and of the sexual gift. These images of the guru and disciple and their ideal relationship pervades the Hindu psyche to a substantial extent even today. 'Guru is Brahma, guru is Vishnu, guru is Maheshwara,' is a verse not only familiar to most Hindus but one that evokes complex cultural longings, that resonates with what is felt to be the best part of their selves and of the Hindu tradition.

Let me not give the impression that the triumphant procession of the liberation/salvation guru in Hindu tradition has gone completely unchallenged. In traditional texts there are at least two instances questioning the need for a guru, admittedly an insignificant number compared to hundreds of tales, parables, and pronouncements extolling him. The first one is from the *Uddhavagita* in the sixth-century text of *Bhagvata Purana* where Dattareya, on asked to account for his self-possession and equanimity, lists elements of nature, the river, certain animals, and even a prostitute (from whom he learned autonomy from the sensual world) as his 24 gurus. The parable of Dattareya ends with the exhortation, 'Learn, above all, from the rhythms of your own body.' The second incident is an episode from the *Yogavasistha*, a text composed between the ninth and 12th-centuries in Kashmir, wherein Princess Cudala, setting out on her inner journey of self-exploration, deliberately eschews all gurus and external authorities, and reaches her goal through a seven-stage self-analysis.

In more recent times, beginning in the 19th-century, there have been reformers who have sought to revive Vedic rituals and Upanishadic religion. They would at the most sanction the teacher guru, such as the socially engaged intellectual swami of the Ramakrishna Mission or of the 19th-century reformist movement, Arya Samaj. There have been also reluctant gurus, such as Krishnamurti, who vehemently denied the need for a guru and in fact saw in him the chief obstacle to spiritual liberation. For him and some modern educated Indians the guru institution as it exists today is a focus of all the anti-intellectual and authoritarian tendencies in Hindu society.[10] Yet for the great mass of Hindus, the mystical, charismatic, divine guru image continues to be a beacon of their inner worlds. The all-pervasiveness of this image is due to more complex reasons than the mere victory of irrationality over reason, servility over autonomy, or of a contemporary dark age over an earlier golden era.

What I am suggesting here is that the shift from the teacher to the master image is inevitable given the fact that perhaps a major, if not the most significant, role of the guru is that of a healer of emotional suffering and its somatic manifestations. This psychotherapeutic function, insufficiently acknowledged, is clearly visible in well-known modern gurus whose fame depends on their reported healing capabilities, rather than deriving from any mastery of traditional scriptures, philosophical knowledge, of even great spiritual attainments. Of course, in cases of international gurus, the healing is tailored to culture-specific needs. In India there will be more miracles and magical healing, while in the West there will be a greater use of psycho-religious methods and techniques which are not unfamiliar to a psycho-therapeutically informed population.[11]

The importance of the healing guru comes through clearly in all available accounts. Ramakrishna's disciple-biographer writes:

> The spiritual teacher has been described in the *Guru-Gita* and other books as the 'physician of the world-disease.' We did not at all understand that so much hidden meaning was there in it before we had the blessing of meeting the master. We had no notion of the fact that the guru was indeed the physician of mental diseases and could diagnose at first sight the modifications of the human mind due to influence of spiritual emotions.[12]

Perhaps the most vivid recent account of the therapeutic encounter between a guru and a disciple is contained in Pupul Jayakar's moving description of her first one-to-one meeting with Krishnamurti. The narration could very well also have been of an initial interview with a good analyst. In her early 30s, outwardly active and successful, yet with intimations of something seriously wrong with her life, Jayakar is apprehensive and tries to prepare for the meeting. She begins the interview by talking of the fullness of her life and work, her concern for the underprivileged, her interest in art, her desire to enter politics. As the first flow of words peters out, Jayakar gradually falls silent.

> I looked up and saw he was gazing at me; there was a questioning in his eyes and a deep probing. After a pause he said, 'I have noticed you at the discussions. When you are in repose, there is a great sadness on your face.'

> I forgot what I had intended to say, forgot everything but the sorrow within me. I had refused to allow the pain to come through. So deep was it buried that it rarely impinged on my conscious mind. I was horrified of the idea that others would show me pity and sympathy, and had covered up my sorrow with layers of aggression. I had never spoken of this to anyone—not even to myself had I acknowledged my loneliness; but before this silent stranger all masks were swept away. I looked into his eyes and it was my own face I saw reflected. Like a torrent long held in check, the words came.[13]

Jayakar talks of her childhood, of a sensitive lonely girl, 'dark of complexion in a family where everyone was fair, unnoticed, a girl when I should have been a boy.' She talks of her pregnancies, in one case the baby dying in the womb, in other the birth of a deformed child, a girl who dies in childhood. She tells Krishnamurti of the racking pain of her beloved father's death and the tearing, unendurable agony she feels as she talks. 'In his presence the past, hidden in the darkness of the long forgotten, found form and awakened. He was as a mirror that reflected. There was an absence of personality, of the evaluator, to weigh and distort. I kept trying to keep back something of my past but he would not let me. He said, "I can see if you want me to." And so the words which for years had been destroying me were said.'[14]

Krishnamurti is one of the most 'intellectual' of modern gurus, with a following chiefly among the most modern and highly educated sections of Indian society. It is nonetheless the news of his 'miracle' cures—deafness in one instance, an acute depression in another—which spreads like wildfire through the *ashrams* all over the country. Crowds of potential disciples gather at his talks, striving to touch his hand, to share in his benediction. 'These incidents and the vastness of his silent presence impressed people tremendously,' Jayakar writes somewhat ruefully. 'The teaching, though they all agreed it was grounded in a total nonduality, appeared too distant and too unattainable.'[15]

In my own work with gurus and disciples, I found that many of the latter shared a common pattern in their lives that had led them to a search for the guru and to initiation in his cult.[16] Almost invariably the individual had gone through one or more experiences that had severely mauled his sense of self-worth, if not shattered it completely. In contrast to the rest of us, who must also deal with the painful feelings aroused by temporary depletions in self-esteem, it seems that those who went to gurus grappled with these feelings for a much longer time, sometimes for many years, without being able to change them appreciably. Unable to rid themselves of the feelings of 'I have lost everything and the world is empty,' or 'I have lost everything because I do not deserve anything,' they had been on the lookout for someone, somewhere, to restore the lost sense of self-worth and to counteract their hidden image of a failing, depleted self—a search nonetheless desperate for its being mostly unconscious. This 'someone' eventually turned out to be the particular guru to whom the seekers were led by events—such as his vision—which in retrospect seemed miraculous. The conviction and the sense of a miracle having taken place, though projected to the circumstances that led to the individual's initiation into the cult, actually derived from the 'miraculous' ending of a persistent and painful internal state, the disappearance of the black depressive cloud that had seemed to be a permanent feature of the individual's life. Perhaps a vignette from a life history will illustrate this pattern more concretely.

Harnam was the youngest of four sons of a peasant family from a North Indian village who had tilled their own land for many generations. As the 'baby' of the family, Harnam had been much indulged during his childhood, especially by his mother. She had died when he was 18, and ever since her death, he said, a peculiar *udasinta* (sadness) had taken possession of his soul. Though he had all the comforts at home, enough to eat and drink, and an abundant measure of affection from his father and elder brothers, the *udasinta* had persisted. For 15 long years, he said, his soul remained restless, yearning for an unattainable peace. His thoughts often dwelt upon death, of which he developed an exaggerated fear, and he was subject to crippling headaches that confined him to the darkness of his room for long periods. Then, suddenly he had a vision in a dream of the guru (he had seen his photograph earlier), who told him to come to his *ashram* to take initiation into the cult. He had done so; his sadness had disappeared as did his fear and headaches, and he felt the loving omnipresence of the guru as a protection against their return.

Besides cultural encouragement and individual needs, I believe there are some shared developmental experiences of many upper caste Hindu men which contribute to the intensification of the fantasy of guru as healer. In an earlier work, I have described the male child's experience of 'second birth,' a more or less sudden loss of a relationship of symbiotic intimacy with the mother in late childhood and an entry into the more businesslike relationships of the world of men.[17] Two of the consequences of the 'second birth' in the identity development of Hindu men are first, an unconscious tendency to 'submit' to an idealized omnipotent figure, both in the inner world of fantasy and in the outside world of making a living, and second the lifelong search for someone, a charismatic leader or a guru, who will povide mentorship and a guiding worldview, thereby restoring intimacy and authority to individual life. I would interpret the same phenomena more explicitly in terms of self psychology. Since I believe some of the concepts of self psychology to be of value in illuminating the healing process in the guru-disciple relationship, these concepts may first need a brief elucidation.

The major focus of the Kohutian psychology of the self is what he called a selfobject.[18] One exists as a person, a self, because a significant other, the selfobject, has addressed one as a self and evoked the self experience. Selfobjects, strictly speaking, are not persons but the subjective aspect of a function performed by a relationship. It is thus more apt to speak of selfobject experiences, intrapsychic rather than interpersonal, which evoke, maintain, and give cohesion to the self.[19] The very emergence and maintenance of the self as a psychological structure, then, depends on the continued presence of an evoking-sustaining-responding matrix of selfobject experiences. Always needed, from birth to death, the absence of these experiences leads to a sense of fragmentation of the self, including, in extreme states of narcissistic starvation, the terrors of self dissolution.

The mode of needed selfobject experiences, of course, changes with age from the simple to the more complex. In a child, the required selfobject experience occurs primarily, though not exclusively (remember the importance of the glow in the mother's eye and of the affirmative timbre in her voice), through physical ministrations. In the adult, symbolic selfobject experiences supplied by his culture, such as religious, aesthetic, and group experiences, may replace some of the more concrete modes of infancy and childhood. In the language of self psychology, the guru is the primary cultural selfobject experience for adults in Hindu tradition and society. For everyone whose self was weakened because of faulty selfobject relations during crucial developmental phases or for those who have been forced into defensive postures by the self's fragility where they are cut off from all normal sustaining and healing selfobject responses, the guru is the culture's irresistible offer for the redressal of injury and the provision of selfobject experiences needed for the strengthening of the self.

It is the immanence of the healing moment in the guru-disciple relationship which inevitably pushes the guru image toward that of a divine parent and of the disciple toward that of a small child. Western psychiatrists have tended to focus more on the pathology and the malevolent regression unleashed by the psychic shifts in the images of the self and the guru when therapeutic expectations of the disciples take firm hold.[20] They have talked of the extreme submissiveness of the disciples, of a denial of strong unconscious hostility, of the devotee's deepest desire being of oral dependence on the mother, and so on.

I believe the Western psychiatric emphasis on the pathological and regressive— 'bad' regressive—aspects of the guru-disciple relationship does it injustice. However one may prefer the Enlightenment virtues of reason and ideological egalitarianism, the universal power exercised by what I would call the guru fantasy is not to be denied. By guru fantasy I mean the existence of someone, somewhere, who will heal the wounds suffered in the original parent-child relationship. It is the unconscious longing for the curer of the 'world-disease,' a longing which marks all potentially healing encounters whether they are or not officially termed as such. This fantasy invariably exerts its power in changing the self-image of the seeker and of the healing Other in the directions I have described above.

My own profession, psychoanalysis, in its theories of cure has not escaped from the ubiquitous power of this fantasy. Patients, of course, have always approached analysis and analysts with a full-blown guru fantasy. Analysts, on the other hand, tended at first to believe with Freud that healing took place through knowledge and an expansion of conscious awareness. Yet beginning with one of the most original of the first generation of analysts, Sandor Ferenzci, there has been a growing body of opinion which holds the person of the analyst and his interaction with the patient, in which the analyst counteracts the specific pathogenic deficit of the parent-child relationship, as the prime carriers of the healing moment. Franz Alexander was perhaps the most outright advocate of the analyst adopting corrective postures, but the stress on the role of the analyst as someone who makes up in some fashion or other for a deficient nonempathic parent is met with again and again in analytical literature, especially in the school of object relations. Winnicott, for instance, believed that with patients who suffered from not-good-enough early maternal environment, the analytic setting and the analyst, more than his interpretations, provided an opportunity for the development of an ego, for its integration from ego nuclei. Kohut's self psychology with its stress on the curative powers of the analyst's empathy moves further in the same direction. As Ernst Wolf states the self psychological position, 'It is not the content of the information conveyed to the patient, not the substance of the interpretations and interventions made, not the correctness of the therapist's conjectures, not even the therapist's compliance with demands to 'mirror' the patient or to be his or her ideal that is pivotal: It is decisive for the progress of the therapeutic endeavour that the patient experience an ambience in which he or she feels respected, accepted and at least a little understood. . . . The person who is the therapist then becomes as crucial a variable as the person who is the patient.'[21]

Many years earlier, Sacha Nacht had captured this shift in the psychoanalytic view of healing when he said 'It is of more value from the curative point of view, to have a mediocre interpretation supported by good transference than the reverse.'[22] In interviews with devotees, the unconscious expectation that the guru will counteract specific parental deficits becomes manifest in the way an individual selects a particular guru. It seems to be a fact that often the Master who is experienced as an incarnation of the Divine by his own disciples leaves other seekers cold. In the politics of gurudom, reverence and worship by your own devotees does not ensure that you are not a figure of indifference, even of derision and contempt, to other gurus and members of *their* cults. Let me illustrate.

Amita, a 30-year-old woman who is a lecturer in Hindi in a local college, is one of the closest disciples of a contemporary female guru, Nirmala Devi. Born into an orthodox middle-class Brahmin family, she has been engaged in the 'search' ever since childhood. 'My mother used to worship 560 million gods every day,' she says in a bitter, contemptuous voice, 'but it didn't change her a bit. She was a hot-tempered, dried-up woman with little human sympathy or kindness. So what was the use of observing all the rites and praying to the gods?' As Amita talks of her past, it is clear that she has been in a hostile clinch with her mother all her life. Amita went to see many gurus but was dissatisfied with every one of them till one day, a few years ago, she attended one of Mataji's public meetings. Her conversion was instantaneous and she has remained a devoted disciple ever since. 'Mataji is like the cloud that gives rain to everyone,' she says. I am struck by the juxtaposition of her imagery in which mother is dry while Mataji brims over with the rain of love.

For Amita, then, Mataji's parental style has elements of both the familiar and the strange. The familiarity is in Mataji's fierceness, the 'hot temper'; the difference, and this is indeed crucial, is in the preponderance of warmth and love in Mataji as compared to Amita's early experience of the indifference of her mother's style. A guru like the late Maharaj Charan Singh of the Radhasoami sect, I would suggest, is too remote from Amita's central conflict, while the late Bhagwan Rajneesh, of Oregon and Pune fame, would be too threatening to the moral values of a girl brought up in an orthodox, middle-class Brahmin family. Mataji's parental style, on the other hand, dovetails with Amita's selfobject needs and social experience.

That the guru-disciple relationship is in important ways an extension of the parent-child relationship, constituting a developmental second chance for obtaining the required nutrients for the cohesion, integration, and vigorousness of self, is implicit in some of the older devotional literature and is often explicitly stated by modern gurus. Basava, the 12th-century founder of the Virsaiva sect, identifies the guru god with a particular aspect of the mother:

As a mother runs
Close behind the child
With his hand on a cobra
or a fire
The lord of meeting rivers
Stays with me
Every step of the way
And looks after me.[23]

In his instructions to disciples a contemporary guru, Swami Satyanand Saraswati, tells us, 'Now in relation with the guru, the disciple chooses and *bhava* (emotional state) for himself, according to his personality and needs, and develops that to its fullest potential. If he feels the need for a friend, he should regard the guru as his friend. Or, if he has been lacking parental love, the guru can be his father and mother. . . . It all depends on your basic needs and which area of your personality is the most powerful. Sometimes in adopting a certain *bhava* toward the guru, the disciple tends to transfer his complexes and neurosis too. If he has become insecure due to the suffering meted out to him by harsh parents, then in relationship with the guru too, he feels insecure.'[24]

Swami Satyanand's remarks also tell us of the difficulties in the path of *surrender* to the guru, an emotional experience which is indispensable for mutative changes in the disciple's self.

If there is one demand made by the guru on the disciple, it is of surrender, an opening up and receptivity of the latter's psyche which is sometimes sought to be conveyed through (what men imagine to be) the imagery of female sexual experience. Saraswati writes, 'When you surrender to the guru, you become like a valley, a vacuum, an abyss, a bottomless pit. You acquire depth, not height. This surrender can be felt in many ways. The guru begins to manifest in you; his energy begins to flow into you. The guru's energy is continuously flowing, but in order to receive it, you have to become a womb, a receptacle.'[25]

Surrender of the self is, of course, ubiquitous in the religious traditions of the world. In his *The Varieties of Religious Experience*, William James called it regeneration by relaxing and letting go, psychologically indistinguishable from Lutheran justification by faith and the Wesleyan acceptance of free grace. He characterized it as giving one's private convulsive self a rest and finding that a greater self is there. 'The results, slow or sudden, great or small, of the combined optimism and expectancy, the regenerative phenomenon which ensues on the abandonment of effort, remain firm facts of human nature.' He added, . . . 'You see why self-surrender has been and always must be regarded as the vital turning point of religious life. . . . One may say the whole development of Christianity in inwardness has consisted in little more than greater and greater emphasis attached to this crisis of self-surrender.'[26]

In Sufism, too, surrender to the master is a necessary prerequisite for the state of *fana fil-shaykh* or annihilation of oneself in the master. Of the *iradah*, the relationship between the Sufi master and his disciple, the Sufi poet says: 'O heart, if thou wanted the Beloved to be happy with thee, then thou must do and say what he commands. If he says, "Weep blood!" do not ask "Why?"; if He says, "Die!" do not say "How is that fitting?"'[27]

In terms of self psychology, surrender is the full flowering of the idealizing transference, with its strong need for the experience of merging into a good and powerful, wise and perfect selfobject—the guru. 'This is the secret of the guru-disciple relationship,' says one guru. 'The guru is the disciple, but perfected, complete. When he forms a relationship with the guru, the disciple is in fact forming a relationship with his own best self.'[28] The disciple, in experiencing his or her self as part of the guru's self, hearing with the guru's ears, seeing with the guru's eyes, tasting with the guru's tongue, feeling with the guru's skin, may be said to be striving for some of the most archaic selfobject experiences.

Ramakrishna, the arch example of the Indian penchant for using narrative form in construction of a coherent and integrated world, of his preference for the language of the concrete, of image and symbol over more conceptual and abstract forms, tells us the following parable.

One day while driving with Arjuna (the warrior hero of the epic *Mahabharata*), Krishna (who is both God and Arjuna's guru) looked at the sky and said, 'See, Friend, how beautiful is the flock of pigeons flying there!' Arjuna saw it and immediately said, 'Yes, friend, very beautiful pigeons indeed.' The very next moment Krishna looked up again and said, 'How strange, friend, they are by no means pigeons.' Arjuna saw the birds and said, 'Quite so, my friend, they are not pigeons at all.' 'Now try to understand the matter,' Ramakrishan exhorts us. 'Arjuna's truthfulness is unquestionable. He could have never flattered Krishna in agreeing with him both the times. But Arjuna's devotional surrender to Krishna was so very great that he actually saw with his own eyes whatever Krishna saw with his.'[29]

Devotees come to the guru, as do patients to the analyst, in a conflicted state. On the one hand, there is the unconscious hope of making up for missing or deficient selfobject responses in interaction with the guru. On the other hand, there is the fear of evoking self-fragmenting responses through the same interaction. The omnipresence of fears of injury to the self and of regression into early primitive states of self-dissolution is what forces the devotee to be wary of intimacy. It prevents the desired surrender to the guru, however high the conscious idealization of the values of surrender and letting go might be. Gurus are of course aware of the conflict and in their various ways have sought to reassure the disciples about their fears. Muktananda, for instance, writes, 'There are only two ways to live: One is with constant conflict, and the other is with surrender. Conflict leads to anguish and suffering. . . . But when someone surrenders with understanding and equanimity, his house, body and heart become full. His former feeling of emptiness and lack disappears.'[30] And one of his disciples puts it in a language which the modern self psychologist would have no hesitation in acknowledging as his own: 'We live in countless fleeting relationships, always seeking, finding and losing again. As children and adults, we learn through these relationships. We learn by taking into ourselves our loved ones' thoughts and voices, absorbing our loved ones' very presence along with their knowledge.'[31] Gurus, gurus have always emphasized, are not human beings, not objects in the inelegant language of psychoanalysis, but functions. They are the power of grace in spiritual terms and intense selfobject experiences in the language of self psychology.

The psychological term 'intense selfobject experience' of course transfers the location of the fount of 'grace' from the person of the guru to the psyche of the devotee. It is a grace we have all experienced as infants when the mother's various ministrations transformed our internal world from states of disintegration to one of feeling integrated, from dreaded intimations of fragmentation to blissful experiences of wholeness. The persistent search for this inner metamorphosis in adult life is what makes the guru in India—to use Christopher Bollas' concept—a primary 'transformational object.'[32] He is the culturally sanctioned addressee of a collective request for the transforming experience which goes beyond healing in its narrow sense. The guru's grace is, then, the devotee's recollection of an earlier transformed state. It is a remembrance, Bollas reminds us, which does not take place cognitively but existentially through intense affective experience, even when the latter is not on the same scale as in early life. The anticipation of being transformed by the guru inspires the reverential attitude toward his person, an attitude which in secular man, especially in the West, is more easily evoked by the transformational objects of art than those of religious faith.

The idealizing transference, leading to the merging experience, is thus the core of the healing process in the guru-disciple relationship. The healing is seen in terms of an alchemical transformation of the self: 'When iron comes in contact with the philosopher's stone, it is transmuted in gold. Sandalwood trees infuse their fragrance into the trees around them.'[33] Psychoanalysts, of the object relations and self psychology schools, will have no quarrel with this formulation of the basis of healing. Their model of the healthy person, however, requires an additional step—of reemergence; the drowning and the resurfacing are both constituents of psychological growth, at all developmental levels. In Kohut's language, healing will not only involve an ancient merger state but a further shift from this state to an experience of empathic resonance with the selfobject.

Gurus are generally aware of the dangers of self-fragmentation and the disciple's defences against that dreaded inner state. Modern gurus, like Muktananda, talk explicitly about the agitation and anxiety a disciple may feel when he is close to the guru. The training required en route to surrender is hard and painful. Merger experience, they know, takes place not at once but in progressive stages as, for instance, depicted in Jnaneshvara's description of the unfolding of the guru-disciple relationship in the imagery of bridal mysticism.[34] They are aware of the resistances and the negative transferences, the times when the devotee loses faith in the guru, and doubts and suspicions tend to creep in. Do not break the relationship when this is happening, is the general and analytically sound advice. The development of inimical feelings toward the guru are part of the process of healing transformation. What is important about the feelings toward the guru is their strength, not their direction. Whether devoted or hostile, as long as the disciple remains turned toward the guru, he will be met by total acceptance. Muktananda describes the ideal guru's behavior: 'A true guru breaks your old habits of fault-finding, of seeing sin, of hating yourself. He roots out the negative seeds that you have sown as well as your feelings of guilt. . . . You will never hear the guru criticize you. Instead, when you are in his company, you will never be found guilty in the guru's eyes. You will find in them only the praise of your hidden inner God.'[35]

The 'ambience of affective acceptance' provided by the guru and his establishment, the *ashram,* will, the master knows, make the disciple feel increasingly safe, shifting the inner balance betweeen need and fear toward the former. Old repressed and disavowed selfobject needs will rewaken and be mobilized, making the transference more and more intense. Or, put simply, as the conflict between need and fear recedes, the guru, like the analyst, will become the focus for the freshly released, though old, capacities for love, which push strongly toward a merger with the beloved.

If there is a second word besides surrender with which the guru-disciple relationship can be captured, it is intimacy. As Lawrence Babb remarks of his interviews with the devotees of Sai Baba, 'What emerges as one general theme in these accounts is the same kind of visual, tactile and alimentary intimacy that is so central to devotional Hinduism in general. The devotees long to see him, to hear him, to be near him, to have private audiences with him, to touch him (especially his feet) and to receive or consume, or use in other ways, substances and objects that have been touched by him or that originate from him.'[36] This striving for intimacy not only marks the disciple's response to the devotional, but also to the knowledge, guru. Pupul Jayakar, in talking of her response to the 'intellectual' Krishnamurti, says 'I was driven by the urge to be with him, to be noticed by him, to probe into the mysteries that pervaded his presence. I was afraid of what would happen, but I could not keep away.'[37]

The sought-for intimacy is of an archaic nature, before the birth of language which separates and bifurcates. In the intimacy scale of the 16th-century north Indian saint Dabu:

> The guru speaks first with the mind
> Then with the glance of the eye
> If the disciple fails to understand
> He instructs him at last by word of mouth
> He that understands the spoken word is a common man
> He that interprets the gesture is an intiate
> He that reads the thought of the mind
> Unsearchable, unfathomable, is a god.[38]

In the desired preverbal intimacy with the guru, Jnaneshvara highlights the devotee's infantile quiescence.

> To say nothing is your praise
> To do nothing is your worship
> To be nothing is to be near you.[39]

Analysts are, of course, familiar with the regressive movements in the patient's psyche occasioned by the growing transference toward the analyst. The regression gives the patient a double vision, both in relation to himself and to the analyst. Within the transference, he 'sees' the analyst as a parental selfobject; in the real relationship as a helpful doctor. The two images, in flux over time, constantly condition each other. Because of the copresence of the patient's adult self, the illusion in relation to the analyst, though it waxes and wanes, remains more or less moderate.[40]

The patient's illusion of the analyst corresponds to another illusion in relation to the self. Patients in analysis often report feeling childlike, even childish, also outside the analytic setting. They imagine themselves at times to be smaller and more awkward than their actual adult selves. The infantile and the adult in relation to the self shape each other and are often in a state of partial identity. In the guru-disciple relationship, the identity between the actual and the infantile selves of the disciple on the one hand and the real and parental representations of the master on the other overlap to a much greater extent and for longer periods of time than in psychoanalysis. The double vision in relation to both self and guru representations tends to become monocular. In other words, the guru-disciple interaction touches deeper, more regressed layers of the psyche which are generally not reached by psychoanalysis. The devotee, I believe, is better (but also more dangerously) placed than the analysand to connect with—and correct—the depressive core at the base of human life from which a self first emerged and which lies beyond words and interpretations.

The healing techniques of the guru are thus designed to foster deeper regressions than those of the analyst. Elsewhere, I have talked of the importance of looking and being looked at as a primary technique of the master-disciple intercourse.[41] I discussed the identity-giving power of the eyes that recognize, that is, of their self-evoking and self-sustaining functions. Taken in through the eyes, the guru as a benign selfobject opens the devotee's closed world of archaic destructive relationships to new possibilities. The technical word, used in scriptural descriptions of the initiation process, is *darshanat*, 'through the guru's look' in which, as Muktananda observes, 'you are seen in every detail as in a clear mirror.'[42] To the utter clarity of the look he might have added its absolute love and complete forgiveness. To adapt Dostoyevski's remark on the lover's vision, in *darshanat* the devotee is looked at, and is enabled to look at himself or herself, as God might have. Even gurus with thousands of disciples, whose devotees might conceivably doubt that a one-to-one recognition by the guru is taking place at regular intervals, are at pains to confirm the operation of *darshanat* in spite of the large numbers involved. To quote Muktananda again: 'Many people become angry with me out of love. They say "Baba did not look at me," or "When Baba looked at me, he didn't smile!" People who say these things do not understand that when I sit on my chair I look at everyone once, silently and with great joy. . . . True love has no language. If I look at someone, silently emitting a ray of love, that is sublime. This is true and should be understood: love is a secret ray of the eyes.'[43]

What about the guru's words, the discourses to which the devotees listen with such rapt attention? To someone reading such a discourse or listening to it apart from a devotee group, it may seem trite, repetitious, and full of well-known homilies. The power of the guru's speech, however, lies not in its insight, but has a different source. 'I did not understand but I came away with the words alive within me' is a typical reaction.[44] The psychological impact of the words is not through their literal meaning but their symbolic power, through the sound which conveys the experience of the guru's presence within the psyche. They are a form of early human contact, much as the experience of a child who is soothed by the mother's vocalizations even when he is physically separated from her and cannot feel her arms around him. In psychoanalysis, a patient will sometimes comment on the quality of the therapist's voice when he feels it as a psychological bridge which joins the two or when he feels it as distancing and evoking a self-fragmenting response. Susan Bady has suggested that it is not only the psychological reaction to the therapist's voice but its virtual ingestion by the patient in a concrete way which is significant.[45] Taken into one's vocal chords, the pattern and rate of breathing, the movement of the diaphragm, the relaxed and self-assured voice of the therapist or the guru will calm his agitation, infuse hope and courage into his own timid and hesitant voice.

The concrete physical and psychic manifestations of the guru's speech and sound are immeasurably enhanced by the group setting in which a disciple normally hears his words. To quote from my own experience of listening to a guru in a large crowd: 'At first there is a sense of unease as the body, the container of our individuality and the demarcator of our spatial boundaries, is sharply wrenched from its habitual mode of experiencing others. For as we grow up, the touch of others, once so deliberately courted and responded to with delight, increasingly becomes ambivalent. Coming from a loved one, touch is deliciously welcomed; with strangers, on the other hand, there is an involuntary shrinking of the body, their touch taking on the menacing air of invasion by the other. But once the fear of touch disappears in the fierce press of other bodies and the individual lets himself become a part of the crowd's density, the original apprehension is gradually transformed into an expansiveness that stretches to include the others. Distances and differences—of status, age and sex—disappear in an exhilarating feeling (temporary to be sure) that individual boundaries can indeed be transcended and were perhaps illusory in the first place. Of course, touch is only one of the sensual stimuli that hammer at the gate of individual identity. Other excitations, channelled through vision, hearing and smell, are also very much involved. In addition, as Phyllis Greenacre has suggested, there are other, more subliminal exchanges of body heat, muscle tension and body rhythms taking place in a crowd. In short the crowd's assault on the sense of individual identity appears to be well-nigh irresistible; its invitation to a psychological regression—in which the image of one's body becomes fluid and increasingly blurred, controls over emotions and impulses are weakened,critical faculties and rational thought processes are abandoned—is extended in a way that is both forceful and seductive.'[46]

Other techniques employed in the guru-disciple interaction perform a similar function of psychic loosening and fostering deep regression—an increasing surrender to the selfobject experience of the merging kind. The taking in of *prasada*, food offerings touched or tasted by the guru, drinking of the water used to wash his feet, helps in a loosening up of individual bodily and psychic boundaries, transforming the experience of the guru from that of a separate Other to one of comingling with a selfobject. Gurus and devotees have always known that meditation on the guru's face or form or the contemplative use of his photograph, as required in some cults, will contribute to and hasten the merging experience. As Muktananda observes: 'The mind that always contemplates the guru eventually becomes the guru. Meditation on the guru's form, immerses the meditator in the state of the guru.'[47]

In a sense, my use of the term guru-disciple interaction has been a misnomer since it has had the disciple's rather than the guru's inner state as its focus. Perhaps this is as it should be given the fact that ostensibly the disciple is the one in search of healing, and that we know infinitely more about the inner processes of disciples than those of the gurus. Yet an analyst has to wonder how a guru deals with the massive idealizing transferences of so many disciples. Negative transferences and malignant projections are of course easier to handle since they cause severe discomfort, compelling us to reject them by discriminating inside between what belongs to us and the alien attributes that have been projected onto us. This painful motivation for repelling the invasion of the self by others does not exist when projections are narcissistically gratifying, as they invariably are in case of the adoring followers.

The problem is further complicated by the fact that for the self-sustaining and self-healing responses to be evoked in the follower (or in the patient), the guru (and the analyst) must accept being the wiser, greater, and more powerful parent. To accept and yet not identify with the disciple's parental representation demands the guru remain in touch with his own infantile self. The best of the gurus, as we saw in the case of Ramakrishna, clearly do that; their own relationship to the Divine keeps intact self-representations other than those of the omniscient parent. But for many others, I would speculate, the temptation to identify with the disciple's projected parental self is overwhelming. As the parent and the stronger figure in the parent-child relationship, it is easier to unload one's conflicts and the depressive self onto the child. In the case of the analyst's countertransference, as Michael Moeller points out, the identification with the parental role is a source of twofold relief: one, in the transferential repetition of the relationship with the patient the analyst is the stronger and the less incriminated parent, and two, in reality he is not that parent at all.[48] The empirical finding on the antidepressive effect of the psychoanalytic role also applies to the guru. His calm, cheerful, loving mien is perhaps a consequence rather than a cause of his role as the healer.

I have mentioned above that the dangers of the guru role lie in the disciples' massive parental projections which the guru must process internally. Although the guru shares this danger with the analyst, or more generally, with any healer, the intensity of these projections, their duration, and the sheer number of devotees involved are vastly greater than in the case of his secular counterparts. These idealizing projections are subversive of the guru's self-representation, constitute an insidious assault which a few gurus—again like some therapists—are not able to successfully resist. A regression to an omnipotent grandiosity is one consequence, while in the sexual sphere a retreat into sexual perversion has been reported often enough to constitute a specific danger of the guru role. It is sad to hear or read reliable reports about 70-year-old gurus who become Peeping Toms as they arrange, with all the cunning of the voyeur, to spy on their teenaged female disciples (generally Western) undressing for the night in the ashram. The promiscuity of some other gurus, pathetically effortful in the case of elderly bodies with a tendency to flag, is also too well known to merit further repetition.

The sexual aberrations, however, have not only to do with pathological regression in stray individual cases, but are perhaps also facilitated by the way the fundamentals of healing are conceptualized in the guru-devotee encounter. For instance, given the significance of a specific kind of intimacy, there is no inherent reason (except cultural disapproval) why intimacy between guru and devotee does not progess to the most intimate encounter of all and be seen as a special mark of the guru's favour; why the merger of souls does not take place through their containers, the bodies. If substances which have been in intimate contact with the guru's body are powerful agents of inner change when ingested by the devotee, then the logic of transformation dictates that the most powerful transforming substance would be the guru's 'purest' and innermost essence—his semen.

3

PSYCHOANALYSIS AND RELIGION REVISITED

In conclusion, as I take up the wider issue of the relationship between psychoanalysis and religion, I do not propose to dwell overly long on Freud's well-known and essentially hostile view of religion. Freud believed that the common theme running through different aspects of religion—knowledge, belief, ritual, religious experience and feelings, ethical consequences in values and conduct— was an expression of the infantile in mental life. Religion was the way man defended himself against anxiety and the afflictions of an incomprehensible fate. Given Freud's stature and authority within the field, his views were to have a decisive influence on the way psychoanalysis, especially in its fledgling years, approached religion. Occasionally Freud might have tried to relativize his position, as in his letter to Oskar Pfister on *The Future of an Illusion:* 'Let us be quite clear on the point that the views expressed in my book form no part of analytic theory. They are my personal views, which coincide with those of many non-analysts and pre-analysts, but there are certainly many excellent analysts who do not share them. If I drew on analysis for certain arguments—in reality one argument—that need deter no one from using the non-partisan method of analysis for arguing the opposite view.'[1] At another place Freud admitted that his study of religious belief was limited to that of the common man, and that he regretted having ignored 'the rarer and more profound type of religious emotion as experienced by mystics and saints.'[2] In this brief book, I have in a sense tried to address the outstanding psychoanalytic agenda on religion. By concentrating on the 'more profound type of religious emotion' experienced by the mystic, I have attempted to complement Freud's analysis of the meaning of religion for the 'common man' with the meaning it has for the saint.

Freud's rare disclaimers, perhaps attempts at protecting the sensitivities of his more spiritually inclined friends and admirers, did not prevent the emergence of a dominant psychoanalytic interpretation of religion. If there were disagreements among the early analysts with the master, they were on details rather than the essence of Freud's theoretical approach. Basic to this approach, of course, was the analogy between religious and psychopathological phenomena.

Religious *ideas,* for instance, the Judeo-Christian cosmogonies, were dubbed as illusory wish fulfilments. Their hold on man's imagination was seen as derived from the child's helplessness in the face of a threatening external world on the one hand and his ambivalent feelings toward a father who is both a source of protection and fear on the other.[3]

Religious *rituals* were scathingly indicted through psychiatric diagnostic labels after Freud began the process by comparing the practices of the devout to the self-imposed restrictions of the obsessional neurotic.[4]

Religious *experience*, of which the mystical, 'oceanic' feeling is widely held to be the standard bearer, we already saw in the first chapter, was a regression to the limitless primary narcissism of the infant united with the mother at the breast. Or, in more libidinal terms, Wilhelm Reich interpreted mystical experience as a misinterpretation of sexual feelings. The mystical response was a distorted sexuality which did not allow the perception of sexual excitation and precluded orgastic release.[5] (Let me add here that a Hindu *tantric* in describing a vital part of his own practice would be in substantial agreement with Reich's formulation.) The inner world of religious *belief* too did not escape psychopathological analogy in being compared to amentia, a state of blissful, hallucinatory confusion.[6]

Well into the adult years of psychoanalysis as a discipline, many analysts would continue to follow Freud's lead. To give only one notorious instance: Franz Alexander, seeking a psychological understanding of the stages of meditation in Buddhism, discerned in them successive clinical pictures of melancholia, catatonic ecstasy, apathy, and schizophrenic dementia.[7] For him what motivates the Buddhist meditator is the attempt to regress to a condition of intrauterine existence. Even today, more than 80 years after Freud's first foray into religion in his 1907 article 'Obsessive Actions and Religious Practices,' the efforts by psychoanalysts to move the religious world with the lever of psychopathology have not been given up. In Jeffrey Masson's 1980 study of Indian religious traditions, for example, much of Buddhism was seen as a massive defence against depression while the Hindu *tantric's* desire for stillness, echoing Wilhelm Reich, was traced to early fears of sexual excitement.[8]

There are numerous other instances within psychoanalytic literature where the significance of the analogy between religious and psychopathological phenomena is not questioned. The writers share Freud's original assumption that the meaning of the likeness between the two is unambiguous. But as the French philosopher Paul Ricouer remarks, 'Analysis does indeed throw some light on what we have called the birth of idols; but it has no way of deciding whether that is all that faith is; whether ritual is originally, in its primordial function, obsessional ritual; whether faith is merely consolation on the childhood pattern. Analysis can reveal to the religious man his caricature, but it leaves him the task of meditating on the *possibility* of not resembling his distorted double.'[9] From within the ranks of the analysts, Erik Erikson voices a similar concern when in speaking of religious striving he rhetorically asks, 'But must we call it regression if man thus seeks again the earliest encounters of his trustful past in his efforts to reach a hoped for and eternal future?'[10]

Even in the early years, besides apostates like Jung, there were the so-called revisionist, neo-Freudians like Erich Fromm and Karen Horney who tried to bridge the gulf between analysis and religion. To them the convergence between the two, the common agenda of both psychoanalysis and religion, lay in the healing of man's soul. After all, as Bruno Bettelheim has demonstrated, Freud's writings in their original German, though excised in English translation, are full of references and matters pertaining to the soul—its nature and structure, its development and attributes, and the way the soul reveals itself in all we do and dream.[11] Freud's own text is full of rich ambiguities, his terminology often open-ended and allusive, his tone personal and conversational. In the translation such qualities are played down for the sake of an abstract, medicalized 'scientific language' using ancient Greek and Latin words. As a *Seelenartzt*, not a doctor of the mind or of the *Nerven*, what the analyst clearly does is minister to the soul. Of course, the Freudian analyst, first and foremost a psychologist of love, conceives of the soul in a particular, erotic way that is akin to the mythic psyche of the Greeks, a butterfly eternally pursued by an indefatigable Cupid.

For Fromm, who was part of a stubborn nonmedical tradition within psychoanalysis which persists to this day, though perhaps less in the United States than in other countries, what a successful and effective analysis achieved above all was to awaken the patient's sense of wondering and questioning. Ideally, it brought to life a capacity for being genuinely bewildered, called forth an engagement with what the theologian Paul Tillich called 'ultimate concern.' The neurotic, in the view of both Horney and Fromm, passionately concerned with the fulfilment of his own desires, always aimed at the absolute, the unlimited, and the infinite. In this he was the antithesis of the truly religious man for whom everything is possible only for God. As Horney put it, 'The neurotic is the Faust who is not satisfied with knowing a great deal, but has to know everything.'[12] He is at the opposite pole from the well-functioning man—religious and psychoanalytic—who has a vision of possibilities while at the same time he realizes the limitation of necessities, and of the concrete.

The convergence of the psychoanalytic and the religious man requires, of course, a particular vision of religion (and of psychoanalysis) which Fromm called 'humanist religion.'[13] He professed to see it pervading early Buddhism, Taoism, and Jewish and Christian mysticism. In contrast to what he termed 'authoritarian' religion, the aim of humanist religion is fullest self-realization and the achievement of greatest inner strength. Authoritarian religion, on the other hand, wanted man to submit and surrender to a transcendent power. It extolled obedience, reverence, and worship of a higher entity. In advancing the ideals of knowledge, brotherly love, reduction of suffering, independence, and responsibility, Freud articulates the ethical core of humanist religion. Jung, on the other hand, according to Fromm, though apparently a greater friend of religion, emphasized man's helplessness and seizure by powers higher than himself and is thus at best a spokesman for authoritarian religion.

The distinction between two kinds of religion, the one a mature faith with which psychoanalysis has no quarrel and whose aims it even shares, and the second a system of infantile belief and neurotic ritual, continued to be made in essentially similar terms by a few writers on the psychology of religion. Abraham Kaplan's contrasting of infantile religion with a mature version which emphasizes responsibility rather than dependency, anxiety, and guilt, Harry Guntrip's description of mature religiosity based on the experience of meaningful human relationships, and Peter Homans' opposition between 'transference God' and a nonpathological religion of transcendence, all are sóme examples.[14] In the same vein, Ricouer has contrasted infantile and idolatrous consolation with a consolation 'according to spirit' which, evoking shades of Horney, is free of all narcissism and self-seeking.[15] Though in no way providing a refuge from the harshness of existence, the consolation according to spirit is acquired in extreme obedience to reality—the psychoanalytic God—and can only emerge from the ashes of the first consolation.

Starting from the late 1950s, there have been voices within the mainstream of Freudian psychoanalysis which too have attempted to articulate a new approach to religion. Instead of harping on the resemblance between unconscious id impulses and elements of religious myths and ritual, these analysts sought to elaborate on the ways religion strengthens and supports the ego and thus serves adaptive rather than defensive purposes in human maturation. Sympathetic to or associated with the American school of ego psychology, which emphasizes adaptation and not only conflict, their approach was closer to that of anthropology where in spite of a few reports that describe anxiety-generating aspects of ritual or the dysphoric impact of religious participation, the leitmotif within the field has been the psychologically integrative function of religion. The ego psychologists interested in religious phenomena, Jacob Arlow and Erik Erikson being perhaps the foremost, recognized that religious knowledge incorporated in myths provided the ego opportunities for mastery through a healing identification with the central figures of the myth.[16] Rituals were viewed as communal experience of special import, 'ceremonial dreams of great recuperative value' as Erikson called them,[17] which support the ego in its struggle against id impulses.

The influence of the ego psychologists, however, has remained confined to the United States, and here too it has made itself felt more in scholarly disciplines outside psychoanalysis. Freud's legacy, which holds that gods, both in the inner world of the individual and in the cultural universe of communities, have clay feet and that psychoanalysis, if it is to remain psychoanalysis, must of necessity be iconoclastic in its encounter with religion, has remained much too strong to be modified in any significant way.

Even while acknowledging iconoclasm as the specific contribution of psychoanalysis to the study of cultural phenomena, one is puzzled by the inconsistencies in its application. For instance, again following Freud, the respect accorded to art and the combination of benevolence and admiration with which the artist is regarded in psychoanalytic writings, even while his deeper motivations are being scrutinized, is strikingly absent from studies of religion and the *homo religiosi*. Creativity is granted to the writer and the painter while all psychoanalytic virtue is denied to the mystic.

The harshness of the psychoanalytic discourse toward religion, especially in the early years of its establishment as a clinical method and intellectual discipline, has two roots. The first goes back to the person of the founder of psychoanalysis and the second to the intellectual compulsions and ideologies of the historical era in which psychoanalysis was born and struggled to establish itself as a profession. Freud has taught us that an individual's passionately held ideas and convictions are not autonomous from his unconscious needs and conflicts, and analysts have not hesitated to apply this lesson to Freud's own views and complex relationship with religion. Gregory Zilboorg, for instance, comes to the conclusion that Freud struggled with unresolved religious conflict and that his vehement denouncements revealed repressed, deeply religious convictions.[18] Others too have discerned in Freud a deep ambivalence toward religion which might lead some to conclude that Freud was more a closet than a godless Jew.

Freud himself was too much of an analyst to ignore the possibilitiy of the existence of a relationship between his conception of religion and his deeper motivations, though he chose to pass over the possible connections without conducting a searching public examination. Thus in a letter to Pfister he writes, 'Of course it is very possible that I might be mistaken on all three points, the independence of my theories from my disposition, the validity of my arguments on their behalf, and their content. You know that the more magnificent the prospect the lesser the certainty and the greater the passion—in which we do not wish to be involved—with which men take sides.'[19]

The focal unconscious conflict which some students of Freud believe to have identified is his ambivalence toward the mother of the earliest years of his life and the persistence of preoedipal influences and residues in his inner world.[20] These are also reflected in the directions taken by his work. Till well into the mid-1930s, Freud's writings did not take the infant's early experience of its mother fully into account, though toward the end his recognition of the impact of the mother on mental life was coming closer to conscious toleration. The ambivalence toward the maternal feminine began to ease as he was inexorably pulled into the embrace of the *ewigweibliche*, the eternal feminine. Irving Harrison relates Freud's pivotal conflict to the first three years of his life when he lived with his parents in a one-room house.[21] Here, in cramped quarters, following Sigmund's birth, two siblings were conceived and born, and one died. The exposure to the intense stimulation of the first three years, not only in the repeated excitement at being a witness to the primal scene but also through the contagious effect of strong emotions experienced by the parents, including the grief at the death of a child, moulded Freud's particular area of psychic vulnerability.

On the one hand, this psychic space is filled with the diffuse, yet abiding and beckoning, presence of the adoring mother who bequeaths to her favourite son what Nabokov in his memoirs called 'unreal estate,' the special pleasures of childhood, the minutiae of utterly precise sensations, especially piquant and intense because they are as yet uncategorized, without the conceptual order that levels novelty into predictability. 'A child's emotional impulses,' Freud was to write, 'are intensely and inexhaustibly deep to a degree quite other than those of an adult; only religious ecstasy can bring them back.'[22] Yet perhaps for Freud the emotions associated with the preoedipal mother to be brought back to awareness also meant the rising to the surface of the 'horror of abandonment, the awareness of siblings as occupying his mother and contributing to that abandonment and the raging wish that all sources of such terror cease to be.'[23]

In some of his writings on religion, for example, in *Moses and Monotheism*, it has been suggested that Freud's focal conflict is reflected in his stubbornly held notion of an archaic heritage of primeval parricide which obscures and bypasses the maternal aspects of monotheistic religions.[24] And if religious feeling begins with the wonder, magic, and maternal awe of the child's early years, to ripen into the mature faith of adulthood that can engage with 'ultimate concern,' then Freud's private religion remained at an archaic level. A fascination with the occult, with mysterious psychical phenomena and a tendency toward what is called superstition, accompanied him through a major part of his life. In his biography, Ernst Jones noted that Freud once wrote but then forgot and later denied: 'If I had my life to live over again I shoud devote myself to psychical research rather than psychoanalysis.'[25] We also know that despite his dismissal of mysticism, Freud was strongly attracted toward men with a mystical bent—Jung, Rolland, and even Flies with his numerological theories—extending to them a reverence he normally reserved for creative artists. Harrison links Freud's personal conflict, his treatment of religion, and the birth of psychoanalysis even more intimately when he observes, 'How tempting to any man harbouring such latent potential for terrors and rages must be the mystical vision of regaining total bliss—of the ocean as a womb! And psychoanalysis, for all its selective inattention to that theme, may have been born of Freud's resolute determination to resist just that temptation.'[26]

I have attributed the second reason for the analytic antagonism toward religion to the historical origins of psychoanalysis. Its pioneers were steeped in a European culture where the sense of the sacred was fast disappearing and *disenchantment*, as Max Weber called the loss, had spread far and wide in the wake of capitalism and the industrial revolution. In fact, Peter Homans has directly linked the very origins of psychoanalysis to the creative response of Freud and other early analysts to this loss, to their ability to mourn the withering away of traditional forms of community life and long-cherished values, including, after the carnage of the First World War, the values of German liberalism.[27]

In any event, the birth of psychoanalysis took place 'under a planetary constellation' (an astrologically inclined Hindu would say) when rationalism was the preeminent current of the intellectual climate and the ideology of positivism reigned unchallenged in the sciences. Though religion and psychoanalysis may have looked at a similar universe, the former, according to Freud, was a mythological view of the world while the psychoanalytic *Weltanschauung* was modern and scientific. Freud was hopeful of replacing religious knowledge by the psychological science he was in the process of forging.

In point of fact I believe that a large part of the mythological view of the world which extends a long way into most modern religions is nothing but psychology projected into the external world. The obscure recognition [the endopsychic perception] of psychical factors and relations in the unconscious is mirrored in the construction of a supernatural reality, which is destined to be changed back once more by science into the psychology of the unconscious. One could venture to explain in this way the myths of paradise and the fall of man, of God, of good and evil, of immortality, and so on, and to transform metaphysics into metapsychology.[28]

The respectability and recognition as a positivistic science which psychoanalysis claimed for itself was not to be won so easily in spite of the analogies and metaphors from the physical sciences that peppered Freud's writings. Its practice, the healing of *Seelenstorungen*—disturbances of the soul—was too near that of the numerous occultists and faith healers who operated at the fringes of the established churches. For intellectuals, scholars, and men of science, psychoanalysis was not so far removed from the animal magnetism of another Viennese healer with an international reputation, Franz Anton Mesmer, or from the endeavours of various spiritualists—phrenologists, Christian Scientists, and others—who sought to cloak religious concerns in scientific trappings. As late as 1932, Stefan Zweig, a great admirer of Freud, apologetically wrote in the introduction to his book *On Mental Healers* (*Die Heilung Durch Den Geist*) that he hopes he won't be 'accused of being a Mesmerist or a Christian Scientist or a devotee of psychoanalysis.'[29]

There were other, more concrete manifestations in the practice of psychoanalysis which appeared to be directly derived from religious practices. For instance, the setting of psychoanalysis, with the analyst sitting outside the visual field of the patient, was uncomfortably similar to that of the priest hearing confession. The importance of the doctor establishing a good rapport with the patient had been earlier stressed by St Ignatius of Loyola, the founder of the order of the Jesuits, as vital for the work of an effective spiritual director.

A traditional Hindu or Buddhist, on the other hand, would point out even more parallels. In the practice of psychoanalysis he would see a modern form of the master-disciple relationship which has the personal transformation of the disciple as its goal. In its method of free association he would discern a rational meditation, with goals different from its religious counterpart and striking only insofar as the meditation is more joint than solitary. He may even go so far as to characterize psychoanalysis as 'a secular Western counterpart to *tantra*.' He may also acknowledge that psychoanalysis has developed a specific and a most elaborate theory of *karma*—the influence of the past on the present—which has no rival in his own traditional canons either in subtlety or in sophistication.

Coming back to the Judeo-Christian tradition, the method of psychoanalysis, an introspective free association, was too close to older techniques of introspection and self-interrogation which drew their sustenance from religion and which were in the process of withering away. Many scientists and other educated men would have agreed with George Steiner's comment that 'It [psychoanalysis] provides a secular, though heavily mythological surrogate for an entire range of introspective and elucidatory disciplines extending from private meditation to the metaprivacies of the confessional.'[30] It then becomes understandable that psychoanalysis would seek to sharply demarcate its boundaries and differentiate its methods from comparable religious techniques which antedate it so vastly in the history of human consciousness. It also becomes understandable that there may have been lingering fears of psychoanalysis being taken over by religion. Of his book *The Future of an Illusion*, Freud would write that in this work he wished to protect psychoanalysis from the priests and entrust it 'to a profession that doesn't yet exist, a profession of secular ministers of soul who don't have to be physicians and must not be priests.'[31]

Today, in the last decade of the 20th century, the compulsions I have described and which shaped the relationship of psychoanalysis to religion have largely disappeared. First, there is no longer the same concern with establishing psychoanalysis as a science in the positivist sense. There is an acceptance among analysts, of all persuasions, that psychoanalytic theory cannot be proven by experimental means and that research methods which take psychoanalysis out of its natural context cannot but distort its essence. There is growing consensus that accurate predictions about a multidetermined human behaviour cannot be made. Like the quantum universe of physics and unlike its Newtonian predecessor, the universe of psychoanalysis is of the interconnection between the subjectivities of the analyst and the analysand, and it is precisely the analyst's participation which makes it impossible to speak of either the absolute subjectivity or the absolute objectivity of the discipline. Whereas Freud, forced by the prevailing view of science which made a sharp demarcation between subject and object, felt compelled to distinguish between fantasy and reality, between *Dichtung* and *Wahrheit*, we no longer need to make this distinction quite so sharply and in fact, as we shall see, must not even formulate the question in the same way.

If today psychoanalysis aspires to be scientific at all it is only through keeping alive a questioning, searching attitude that would ideally breakfast every morning on a discredited theory. It is scientific in its continuous struggle, not always successful, to avoid falling prey to dogmas, irrespective of the authority or charisma of their propounders. No longer afraid to be called a hermeneutic enterprise, a *Geisteswissenschaft* of meaning rather than a natural science of causation, that is, a soul physics, psychoanalysis can contentedly exist in the boundary space between science and art and religion without feeling the need to accede to any one of them. Today, as Bion has observed, 'it is as absurd to criticize a piece of psychoanalytic work on the ground that it is "not scientific" as it is to criticize it because it is "not religious" or "not artistic".'[32]

The bypassing of the preoedipal mother which perhaps gave Freud's writings on religion their particular slant has since been amply rectified. In the work of many post- Freudians—such as Klein, Winnicott, Mahler, Kohut, Erikson—the Great Mother looms so large as not only to complement Freud's awesome father but to almost set up a parallel regime. In the 'relational' models of the post-Freudians, it is not the derivatives of instinctual drives but the mental representations of relationships with others which constitute the fundamental building blocks of mental life.[33] Fragments of experiences with parents and other adults, images and fantasies of one's self in relation with others, and inner voices derived from these real and imagined experiences become the stuff of the self.

The pivotal relationship in the many relational theories, the basic building block of the self, is the infant-mother dyad at the beginning of life. Religion then gets connected to the origins of sentient life and the preoedipal experience. Winnicott, for in stance, links religion to what he calls transitional phenomena in mental life.[34] These begin with the infant's transition from a state of being merged with the mother to a state of being in relation to the mother as something outside and separate. They are located in an intermediate space between inside and outside, between the subjective and what is objectively perceived, between the baby's inability and growing ability to recognize and accept reality. Winnicott sees transitional space as a resting place for the individual engaged in the perpetual human task of keeping inner and outer reality separate yet interrelated.

Relational theorists who seek to describe the ineffability of our earliest experience before language is born are often poetical—even Melanie Klein with her violent surrealistic images of breasts that persecute or/are filled with urine and feces. Winnicott calls transitional phenomena 'the substance of illusion,' the realm which is allowed to the infant and in adult life is inherent in art and religion. 'The intermediate area of experience,' Winnicott writes, 'unchallenged in respect of its belonging to inner or external (shared) reality, constitutes the greater part of the infant's experience and throughout life is retained in the intense experiencing that belongs to the arts, and to religion and to imaginative living, and to creative scientific work.'[35] By 'unchallenged' Winnicott means that an essential part of the formulation of transitional phenomena is 'that we agree never to make the challenge to the baby: did you create this object, or did you find it conveniently lying around? That is to say, an essential feature of transitional phenomena and objects is a *quality in our attitude* when we observe them.'[36]

The presence of this particular 'quality in attitude' in observation of religious phenomena distinguishes most relational theorists from their more classical predecessors and contemporaries. Eriskon is not being reductionist when he links one face of religion to a dim nostalgia for a hallucinatory sense of unity with the maternal matrix and for a supply of benevolently powerful substances.[37] Noting man's wish for transcendence he does not proceed to reduce transcendence, but elevates the status of the wish. Nor does Kohut subscribe to a deterministic scientism when he would have religion as a cultural selfobject which provides vital nutrients for the maturation and maintenance of the self.[38]

Similarly, relational theories would interpret other areas of religion, such as methods of religious healing, quite differently from the classical drive model. For instance, taking an example from Hinduism, let us look at the silent 'looking' of *darshan*, which I have described in the previous chapter as the most important form of interaction between the guru and the disciple, the chief healing technique if you will.[39] The classical analytic understanding of the self and an insight into its workings in the analytic situation is through verbalization. Words are the carriers of the knowledge that heals. Silence and quiescence are most often interpreted as resistance, defensive inhibition, or an ego disturbance of shorter or longer duration.

In the relational models, where the avoidance of a sense of estrangement and abandonment is deemed to be one of the primary motivational thrusts in the individual, the identity-giving powers of the eyes that *recognize* are at least as crucial as words that explain and integrate diffuse experience. In the silent affirmation of every *darshan*, the individual experiences in the guru the caretaker of his 'prehistoric' era and a brief but regular fulfilment of a profound human need for mutual recognition. Taken in through the eyes, the guru is gradually internalized as a benign figure who is different from the disciple's bad inner objects and who opens the disciple's closed world of archaic and destructive object relationships to new possibilities.

That the silence of *darshan* works better in India than in the West may have to do with the caretaking patterns of the culture. In most Western societies, a large part of reassurance against the separation anxiety of childhood is provided by the mother's voice, for instance, at bedtime. Sleep itself means darkness, silence and—in most middle-class sleeping arrangements—separation from the mother so that silence becomes associated with the fear of her absence. In India, on the other hand, the child is almost constantly carried on the mother's body and sleeps at night with the mother in the same bed. Silence and quiescence may well be associated with the mother's presence and a union with the deep rhythms of her body. The analyst of relational models will thus admit to a certain affinity with the guru in that they share recognizable features of a common ancestry based on what evolution has created: human development embedded in a web of human connectedness, the self as a locus of relationships.

With greater awareness of the meaning and function of its own rituals, psychoanalysis can now appreciate religious ritual in a way more differentiated than was possible in Freud's early formulations. Every analyst is keenly cognizant of the importance of keeping the analytic atmosphere and setting constant. He or she is aware of the feeling of fragmentation in the patient, even if mild and fleeting, when the rituals of greeting and leave-taking are varied or the regularity of the sessions disturbed. Analytic ritual, when good, repeatedly confirms the personal bond between the patient and the analyst. It thus allows the patient to approach conflict and contradiction within an environment whose familiar interdependency has been stressed again and again. Like Thomas Mann's sartorial advice to the imaginative writer to dress like a bank clerk, the outer formalization of the analytic session fosters inner spontaneity. Of course, when the ritual, analytic or religious, is 'bad', that is, when its repetiveness has become forced, rigid, and bereft of all spontaneity, it is then that Freud's analysis of ritual regains a certain validity.

Besides suggestive parallels and interesting convergences between religious ritual, spiritual techniques of self-interrogation, and psychoanalysis, what can push psychoanalysis away from its current habitat in the boundary space between science, art, and religion and toward declaring its alliance with religion is its mythic core. By this I do not mean that myths, such as that of Oedipus, which for most people now is more a Freudian than a Greek myth, build the core of psychoanalytic theory. Nor do I wish to highlight the concerns with origins, transformations, shifting realities—basically with meaning—that psychoanalysis shares with mythology. By mythic, of course, I do not mean fictional, the common meaning of myth in every European language since Plato pronounced it to be so. Mythic refers more to a certain structure of thought and reflection which serves to organize inner and outer experience. This particular structure, both at the heart of mythology and psychoanalysis, has fantasy as its foundation. Fantasy is again not used in the ordinary sense of the word with its popular connotations of whimsy, eccentricity, or triviality, but as another name for that world of imagination which seeks to give meaning to experience. Fantasy, 'the stuff that dreams are made of,' is to different extents and in different forms also the stuff out of which works of art, scholarly discourses, and scientific theories are constructed.

The intricate encasement of fantasy by symbolism, metaphor and analogy— the mythic structure of thought—is the source of the power of psychoanalytic theories as also its practice where it pervades the interweaving of the patient's productions with the analyst's responses, his interpretations. Ava Siegler has suggested that Freud's extensive use of metaphor and analogy in the development and expression of his ideas is not incidental but necessary to the explanatory power of his theories.[40] 'Metaphor and analogy enable possibilities for complex orderings of knowledge. They can be used to help explain perception that would be difficult to explain otherwise. . . . Additionally, metaphor and analogy share an attribute of ambiguity. It is in their very nature to participate in and transfer excess or surplus meaning from one perception to another, enriching our understanding of subtle and intricate human experiences.'[41]

Metaphor and analogy are not only integral to psychoanalytic theory but also to its practice. Even the conveying of analytic insight through interpretation, I believe, must not be crystal clear but to some extent overlapping and overinclusive.

Like myths, the truly transmuting analytic insights exceed the language used to convey them, setting up resonances that reveal ever more hidden depths. Contrary to Freud's expectations, it is not the scientific worldview with its language of denotation, but the mythological *Weltanschauung* with connotation marking *its* language, which is a better path into the depths of emotion and imagination—the subject of psychoanalysis. Corresponding more to that which Oliver Sacks suggests is the iconical and 'artistic' organization of the final form of the brain's record of experience and action, the mythic is truer to the melodic and scenic nature of inner life, to the Proustian nature of memory and mind.[42]

In summary, then, my own stance acknowledges the many significant similarities between psychoanalysis and religious healing and ordains the adoption of a different 'quality in attitude' in the observation of religious phenomena. It certainly does not go as far as Wilfred Bion, a cult figure for many analysts, especially in Latin America, for whom the goals of psychoanalysis are mystical goals, and who deliberately takes recourse to religious terminology to describe what happens in a psychoanalysis. Bion would not rest content with the analysand's *knowing* of the phenomena of his real self but would ideally have him or her pass from knowing to *being* the real self.[43] This gap, Bion would say, can only be bridged by the 'godhead' of the analysand consenting to be incarnated in his or her person. He would ideally suspend memory and desire to promote the exercise of the aspects of psyche that have no background in sensuous experience.

Though attracted and intrigued, I would prefer to remain with sensuous experience and the body, the only container we have of our souls. I would agree that the goal of analysis is setting free and greatly increasing the capacity for 'experiencing experience' but would not ignore the sensual nature of experience, of having consciousness suffuse every part of one's body. To adapt one of Bion's own metaphors, I would be content to grow, dig out, and eat potatoes, intensely and sensuously, while admiring from afar, without doubting it, the mystic's ability to sing potatoes.

THE COLOURS
OF
VIOLENCE

For my daughter Shveta, also because she asked.

CONTENTS

Preface 192

Acknowledgements 194

1 The Setting 195
2 The Riot 216
3 The Warriors 240
4 Victims and Others: I. The Hindus 271
5 Victims and Others : II. The Muslims 299
6 A New Hindu Identity 320
7 The Muslim Fundamentalist Identity 345
8 Conclusion: Religious Conflict in the Modern World 359

Appendix I 370
Appendix II 372

PREFACE

This book is a psychoanalyst's exploration of what is commonly known as religious conflict. The hesitations—'psychoanalyst's' instead of 'psychoanalytic', the qualifier 'commonly known as'—are due to an awareness that such conflicts are complex phenomena, involving the interaction of political, economic, cultural and psychological forces. To reduce their complexity exclusively to psychoanalytic notions is to engage in a psychological imperialism which has been deeply offensive to practitioners of other disciplines—history, political science, and sociology among others—who have traditionally engaged in the study of social conflict.

My own aspirations in this book are modest. They are to provide a way of looking at conflict—the psychoanalyst's way—so as to deepen the understanding provided by other disciplines. To their insights, I wish to add my own discipline's characteristic way of reflecting on issues involved in religious conflict. Taking the Hindu-Muslim violence of 1990 in the south Indian city of Hyderabad as my case-study, I have tried to bring out the subjective, experiential aspects of conflict between religious groups, to capture the psychological experience of being a Hindu or Muslim when one's community seems to be ranged against the other in a deadly confrontation. This means working with a notion of the group aspect of identity which is constituted of a person's feelings and attitudes toward the self as a member of an ethnic/religious/cultural collectivity. This particular self-image is transmitted from one generation to the next through the group's mythology, history, ideals and values, and shared cultural symbols. Group identity is an extended part of individual self-experience, although the intensity of this experience varies across individuals and with time. It can range from feelings of nominal affiliation with the group to a deep identification or even to feelings of fusion, where any perceived harm to the group's interests or threats to its 'honour' are reacted to as strongly as damage to one's own self. I have then tried to describe the ways in which social-psychological forces in a particular period of history bring out latent group identities and turn them to violent ends. With evidence drawn from interviews with men, women, and children, psychological tests and speech transcripts of Hindu and Muslim 'fundamentalists', I have sought to analyse the fantasies, social representations, and modes of moral reasoning about the out-groups—'them'—that motivate and rationalize arson, looting, rape, and killing.

Chapter 1 describes the context of Hindu-Muslim violence: personal, social, and historical. After trying to understand the emotional reverberations of the Hyderabad riot of 1990, the central event of my study, I give a brief account of its setting—a social and historical portrait of the city of Hyderabad—before going on to trace the contested and contentious history of Hindu-Muslim relations.

Chapter 2 begins with my own memories of the violence between Hindus and Muslims on the eve of the partition of the country in 1947. It examines the nature of such memories and the ways they are transmitted from one generation to another. It discusses the morphology of religious group violence, the sequence of steps leading to the formation of riotous mobs, the psychology of such mobs, and then briefly summarizes events leading to the 1990 riot.

Chapter 3 turns our attention to the 'activists' of violence. These are the 'strong men', the pehlwans and the dadas who take over the direction and organization of violence once the riot begins. The chapter views religious violence through their eyes and tries to identify some common themes in their psychological make-up and professional socialization.

Chapter 4 looks closely at one set of victims of the riot—the Pardis of Shakkergunj, a small Hindu community in an old part of the city who have been repeated victims of religious violence. Through interviews with members of one extended Pardi family, we see the different ways in which men and women experience this violence and understand how the Hindu image of Muslims is constructed. The chapter concludes with a discussion of children's representation of Hindu-Muslim violence.

Chapter 5 describe Hindu-Muslim relations and violence from the viewpoint of a poor Muslim family from Karwan in the old part of the city. The chapter analyses the different 'victim' responses of Indian Muslims and concludes with a discussion of the morality of violence, that is, with the ways Muslims and Hindus evaluate their various interactions with members of the other community, including such riot-time 'interactions' as arson, rape, and murder.

Chapter 6 discusses the social-cultural impact of modernization and globalization in fostering fundamentalist and revivalist group identities. Its centrepiece consists of the analysis of a speech by a Hindu demagogue which shows the psychological steps through which such an identity is sought to be constructed.

Chapter 7 is, so to speak, the Muslim counterpart of the preceding chapter. It analyses the speech transcript of the mullahs, the most conservative spokesmen of the community, to describe the psychological construction of Muslim fundamentalist identity.

In conclusion, Chapter 8 summarizes the various identity-threats arising from the social-cultural arena that bring the latent group aspect of our identity to the forefront. It traces the development of this aspect of personal identity, the conditions necessary for the release of its potential violence, and the role played by religion in its facilitation.

ACKNOWLEDGMENTS

I gratefully acknowledge the support of the John D. and Catherine T. MacArthur Foundation which made long periods of fieldwork in Hyderabad and other cities possible. A National Fellowship of the Indian Council of Social Science Research enabled me to work on the preliminary aspects of study. Most of all, I am grateful to my friend Vikram Lal for his support when it mattered the most.

I am thankful to Sujata Patil for her assistance in collecting the materials on the Pardis and for the many discussions on the project. I owe a special debt of gratitude to Sahba Hussain for her interviews with the Muslims of Karwan. Without her deep involvement and courage in locating and arranging interviews with the 'killers', this study would have lost an essential intimacy with the violence of the conflict. I am also grateful for the assistance of my dear friend Ali Baquer and the help given by Mehdi Arslam and Javed Alam.

Institutionally, the Committee on Human Development and the Divinity School at the University of Chicago have been generous hosts for an academic quarter each year for many years, and that is where the plans for this work first took shape. I also owe a debt of gratitude to the Institute of Advanced Study in Berlin where a fellowship allowed me to complete the writing of the book. Colleagues at the Institute, especially George Lowenstein and Aziz al-Azmeh, were generous with their time and helpful with their comments and criticisms. Chapter Six was first prepared for K. Basu and S. Subhramanyan (eds.) *Nationalism and Communalism* and is reprinted with the permission of the publishers, Penguin, India.

1

THE SETTING

The face of the two-year-old girl has come to occupy a permanent corner of my mind. Every now and again it rises to the surface of my consciousness. Some of these occasions are predictable. There is little mystery when the disfigured face flashes across an inner screen while I am reading about, or seeing on television, episodes of violence between racial, religious, or language groups in different parts of the world. I can also understand, even as I resent, the little girl demanding attention whenever people talk of Hyderabad, whenever they are praising its old-world charm and the deliciousness of its cuisine or lamenting its lost feudal glories. The connection of the face with other contexts is more obscure. Why does it suddenly bob up when a man in therapy is telling me of a painful encounter with his boss at work or a female patient weeps as she recalls memories of her humiliation at the hands of an elder sister? I know I will have to go through a long chain of association to lift this veil of obscurity. I am rarely in the mood to make this effort since the girl is not a welcome tenant. She is a squatter.

I first saw the face in the newspaper photograph accompanying a report on the Hindu-Muslim riots in Hyderabad in December 1990. When I finally began this study in the following year, I encountered this particular photograph again and again in newspaper and magazine clippings. It had become the dominant image of that particular carnage. I do not know whether the girl is a Hindu or a Muslim, although a Telugu paper, championing the Hindu cause, identifies her as a Hindu. What you see in the photograph is the unkempt hair, matted with dust, of a child from the slums and then, shockingly, the deep gash of the scythe across the top of her face. The wound, not yet healed into a scar, starts at the right temple, cleaves the corner of the eyeballs and the bridge of a rather flat nose, to peter out in the sands of the left cheek. The stitches are not the careful job of a well-paid professional. They bespeak a harried resident doctor trying to cope with an overflow of the wounded and the dying in the emergency room of a run-down government hospital. The stitches are uneven crosses across the face, hasty scrawls of someone anxious to get over with a silly game of noughts and crosses. One arm of the girl is around a cushion, seeking comfort without finding it. The right side of the face and and the injured eye rests against the edge of the cushion as she looks out through the left eye at the camera, the world, and, if I am not careful, at me.

There is an unfathomable numbness in her expression, the aftermath of a cataclysm that has shaken the little body and soul to a depth unimaginable for me. I try to look through the child's eyes at what must have appeared as a phalanx of giants, with black strips of cloth covering the lower halves of their faces, come crashing through the splintered front door. She sees one of the men raise an axe and club her father down, the sharp edge of the weapon catching him in the back of his neck as he turns and tries to flee. She sees him disappear as he falls, and the men close in with knives, scythes, and wooden clubs. She sees her mother standing transfixed and then hears her make a sound between a sharp cough and a scream as a spear slices through the base of her throat. The girl takes a step toward her mother when the scythe is swung. There is a burning pain beyond all her experience of pain. Blood streams into the eye and, then, oblivion.

I imagine, in that particular moment when her consciousness began the distinctive spiral which ends in the loss of all accustomed moorings, that the universe revealed its secret to the little girl. She caught a glimpse of the immeasurably vast stretch of indifference surrounding the pinpoint of light we call a human life and from whose odds and ends—birth, death, bodily functions, sexual feelings, relationships with parents, siblings, children—we desperately keep on trying to construct a meaning.

I shake my head to free myself of these fantasies and again turn to the photograph of the child with a stony face and one uncomprehending eye. I am aware that my flight of imagination is a failure rather then a success of empathy. The sheer magnitude of the violence done to her is too oppressive for me to employ that crucial tool of my trade, without which no psychoanalyst can grasp and make sense of what is going on within another person. Perhaps this is so because the child is so patently a victim. She is pathetic because she has been flattened by fate. Empathy requires its addressee to be tragic, someone who has helped to bring fate upon herself and was thus fate's active even if unwitting collaborator rather its passive victim. Tragedy at least preserves a memory of one's agency and therefore holds out the hope of its eventual recovery. The unmitigated passivity of pathos, on the other hand, is a dead weight that tugs down at the spirit of everyone who comes in its contact. I cannot empathize with the child because I must defend myself against her pathos. It is far easier for me to pity her. Pity is distant. The girl's face, then, is not haunting but nagging, like a child beggar or a leper with his insidious whine, evoking an angry guilt that will not let you shout at the wretch, 'Disappear! Die!'

At the outset, then, I am apprehensive whether I will be able to bring the essence of psychoanalytic sensibility to bear upon my conversations with the victims of the riots, as well as to my interviews with the agents of violence, the men who stab, bludgeon, and burn. It is not enough for me to take up the clinician's stance and, for instance, speculate upon the little girl's eventual fate: namely, if she survives the poverty and the neglect of a disfigured orphan (who is female to boot) and grows up into and adult, she will become fearful of expressing any anger, will be easily startled by any physical surprise, and will have incomprehensible impulses to injure herself. I want to do more but am afraid that I will do much less as I leave my accustomed clinical moorings to enter the world of social violence with nothing more than what is called a psychoanalytic sensibility.

The core of the analyst's sensibility does not lie in clinical expertise or in a specific way of observing and interpreting people's words and actions. It does not even lie in a perhaps easier acceptance of the gulf between people's ideals and their behaviour, in the analyst's greater difficulty in summoning up righteous indignation or his reluctance to carry out a lover's quarrel with the world. The core is empathy. Empathy is the bridge between the serene reserve of the clinician striving for objectivity and the vital, passionate and vulnerable person who inhabits the clinician's body. Empathy makes me, as an analyst or scholar, step out of the anonymity of an impersonal enterprise and constantly recognize myself in it as a human being of flesh and blood. Without its vital presence I fear that the creative tension between objectivity and impassioned involvement, between the stoic and the emotionally responsive perspectives, will be lost.

Shifting Perspectives

I began this study with a description of the reaction evoked in me by the title victim of the Hyderabad riot in the conviction that not only the observer but also his state of consciousness belongs to the description of the phenomenon he seeks to describe and understand. The father, with his new polaroid camera, photographs the child. As he holds up the print, the child is first pleased and then puzzled. "But, Father," the child asks, "where are *you* in the picture?" The father could at least have extended a leg to get his foot into a corner of the photograph.

Whereas quantum physicists realized the importance of the interaction of subject and object in the comprehension of reality—"We cannot describe the world as if we did not belong to it," was the credo of the poineers[1]—this recognition has not generally taken place in the social sciences. Most social scientists have continued to exclude their own subjectivity from descriptions of psychological and social reality. They have not felt the need for putting imaginative flesh on academic bones. Subjectivity has been regarded as irrational. At best, it is irrational not in the sense of being against reason or constituting the not-understood but of being outside reason.

Perhaps the social scientists were unwittingly forced to choose a more convenient strategy when they kept the subject strictly separate from the object, since an attempt to grasp a more holistic world, the "really real", through the inclusion of their own subjectivity would have led to a degree of complexity which could have bordered on chaos. Psychoanalysts, however, were compelled to abandon this Cartesian stance because of the very nature of their discipline. Whereas in the early years of psychoanalysis, the feelings aroused in the analyst by the patient—countertransference—were thought to contaminate the analyst's objectivity, to be eliminated through a rigorous self-analysis, it was soon realized that the analyst's subjectivity was an essential source of information about the patient. In other words, the analyst understands the patient only in so far as he or she understands the disturbance the patient evokes in himself or herself. As the analyst follows the patient's productions and their effects the analyst must be both an observer and the object of observation. Whether it is the individual patient or large collectivities, we still see with our experiences, hear through our memories, understand with our bodies. In my own account of religious violence, it is these different yet interdependent modes of engaging with the persons and events of this study, the keeping alive of the tension between the immersive and reflective parts of my self, the quest not to let the experiencing self get buried under the agenda of a self that would rather organize and interpret the experience, that I seek to capture in my writing of this book.

The City: 'Unparalleled in the World'

The city of Hyderabad was conceived of as the new capital of the Deccan Kingdom of Golconda after the old fortress city a few miles away became congested and unhygienic due to an acute shortage of water.[2] Mohammed Quli Qutub Shah, the founder of the city, named it Bhagnagar after his beloved Hindu mistress, Bhagmati. Officially renamed Hyderabad after her death—Hyder being the title give to her by the king—Bhagnagar continued to retain its popular name. Even a hundred years after its founding in 1589, travellers' accounts continued to refer to Hyderabad by the name of Mohammed Quli's beloved Hindu mistress.

Four hundred and two years old at the time of this writing, Hyderabad was envisaged by its founder to be a city 'unparalleled anywhere in the world and a replica of heaven on earth'. The benevolent ruler, with artistic sensibilities and literary tastes, who liked to flaunt his sensual excesses in verse, had the good sense to entrust the task of giving his vision a concrete shape to his prime minister, Mir Momin. The minister, who had grown up in the garden city of Isfahan in Persia, planned the new capital on the lines of the city he had loved as a child and brought in architects and builders from Persia to carry out the grand design. Mir Momin's plan favoured a gridiron pattern with two main intersecting roads, each sixty feet wide, which divided the city into four quarters. The north-western quarter adjacent to the intersection was reserved for the royal palaces and the eastern quarter for the residences of the prime minister and the nobles of the realm.

For the houses of the commoners, twelve main zones, spread over an area of ten square miles, were allocated. Each of these mohallas had schools, hospitals, mosques, inns, and gardens—with vegetable and fruit markets at the periphery—in an effort to make every mohalla self-sufficient. Later, during the short period Hyderabad came under Mughal rule, the construction of a protective wall around the city was started. Completed by Asaf Jah in 1740, the wall had twelve gates which closed nightly at eight and opened at the crack of dawn.

The main roads were lined with 14,000 double-storeyed shops, and there were separate areas earmarked for state offices, public buildings, and foreign embassies. The pride of the public buildings were the Jami mosque and the Char Minar ("four minarets")—a square edifice with four broad and lofty arches and a minaret, 220 feet high, at each corner—which has come to symbolize old Hyderabad and the faded glory of its Islamic heritage. Located at the centre of the walled city, at the intersection of the two main highways, it was from Char Minar that the imperial power of the Qutub Shahis emanated outwards.

The French merchant and celebrated traveller Jean-Baptiste Tavernier came to Hyderabad in April 1641, during the reign of Abdulla Qutub Shah, who succeeded his father Mohammed Quli to the throne of Golconda in 1611 and ruled till 1672. Tavernier describes the city thus:

A larger river bathes the walls of the town on the south-west side, and flows into the Gulf of Bengal close to Masulipatam. You cross it at Bhagnagar by a grand stone bridge [Purana Pul], which is scarcely less beautiful than the Pont Neuf at Paris. The town is nearly the size of Orleans, well built and well opened out, and there are many fine large streets in it, but not being paved—any more than are those of all other towns of Persia and India—they are full of sand and dust; this is very inconvenient in summer. . . .

When you have crossed the bridge you straightaway enter a wide street which leads to the King's palace. You see on the right hand the houses of some nobles of the court, and four or five *caravan sarais*, having two storeys, where there are large halls and chambers, which are cool. At the end of this street you find a large square, near which stands one of the walls of the palace, and in the middle there is a balcony where the King seats himself when he wishes to give audience to the people. The principal door of the palace is not in this square, but in another close by, and you enter at first into a large court surrounded by porticoes under which the King's guards are stationed. From this court you pass to another of the same construction, around which there are several beautiful apartments, with a terraced roof, upon these, as upon the quarter of the palace where they keep the elephants, there are beautiful gardens, and such large trees, that it is a matter of astonishment how these arches are able to carry such a weight. . . .

On the other side of the town, from whence one goes to Masulipatam, there are two large tanks, each of them being a coss in circuit, upon which are some decorated boats intended for the pleasure of the King, and along the banks many fine houses which belong to the principal officers of the court.[3]

Hyderabad was cast in the mould of other medieval cities of the Islamic world. Imposing public buildings and palaces were to line its main streets. Secondary streets then led to self contained neighbourhoods or mohallas, with their narrow winding lanes often ending in blind alleys, small open squares, and densely packed low-rise houses with inner courtyards, many of them surprisingly spacious. The city was also Islamic both in population and in its mainstream culture which had roots in Arab, Turkish, and, especially, Persian ways of life. Since the Qutub Shahis were Shias, with strong links with their coreligionists in Iran, a great number of Persians streamed into Hyderabad over the years to seek their fortunes. The most important positions in the administration of the kingdom were held by Persians who had a tremendous impact on the art, architecture, literature, and culture of Hyderabad for nearly 200 years after its foundation. With the establishment of the Asaf Jahi rule, Persian influence declined a little but nevertheless continued to shape the Hyderabadi way of life, at least among the upper classes. Tavernier notes the fair countenance and good stature of its Muslim inhabitants as compared to the dark complexion of the surrounding peasantry, presumably Hindu, who had their assigned, mostly humble, places in the feudal order and whose native Telugu culture existed only at the fringes of the dominant Islamic ethos. In the cultural pecking order, the Persians were right at the top, followed by Turks and other central Asian immigrants. Native-born Indian Muslims felt inferior to both and were keen to establish the existence of Persian or Turkish blood in their lineage, a mind-set which has persisted till very recently. The anthropologist S.C. Dube quotes Hindus in the villages of Shamirpet outside Hyderabad in the 1960s saying: 'A Hindu untouchable of yesterday becomes a Muslim today: and tomorrow he will start proclaiming that his forefathers lived in Arabia!'[4] Because of the Brahminical notions of pollution, the few Hindus who aspired to share the dominant cultural ethos could do so only on a limited basis.

The Perso-Islamic domination of Hyderabad's cultural and social life does not mean that Hindus were excluded from administrative positions and from a share of political power. Talented Brahmins and later the Kayasths could rise to high positions in the court. Another French traveller, Francois Martin, tells us of the heartburn among the Persian, Pathan, and Deccani nobles at the elevation of the Brahmin Madanna, who had become the most powerful minister of the king at the time of his visit.[5] Hindus were to hold high positions in the civil and revenue administration of the state well into the early period of the Asaf Jahi dynasty in the 18th century.

As the construction of the new capital gathered pace and the grand design of the city began to unfold, Mohammed Quli could not have imagined that the lowly Hindus would one day threaten its Islamic cultural suzerainty or that the city's decline was already presaged by an insignificant event taking place at the outer edges of his dominions. I refer, of course, to the entry of what would later be called the 'modern West' through the East India Company, which began setting up a 'factory' in the port city of Masulipatam in 1611.

For almost a hundred years, the city flourished in an approximation of Mohammed Quli's vision. Even making allowances for travellers' hyperbole, Hyderabad seems to have deserved the accolades that come its way as not only a great but also a gracious city, with considerable hedonistic charm. Its Islamic ethos was not of the puritan kind but of the more pleasure-loving Persian variety. Martin gives appetizing details of his dinner on the evening of 28 June 1681 with a persian noble at Hyderabad's court—in fact, the brother-in-law of the king.[6] The number and quality of the dishes served on this memorable occasion far surpassed the fare of the court feasts in Turkey. Every quarter of an hour, at the ringing of the bell, fresh glasses of wine were served. Female dancers entertained the guests and were offered as companions for the night as farewell gifts by a generous host.

Martin's evening, however pleasant for the participants, is not particulary remarkable. Irrespective of the period of history or region of the world, sensual indulgence has been a hallmark of the wealthy and the powerful, of what soap television today calls "the lifestyles of rich and the famous". What is more interesting about Hyderabad is the percolation of hedonism into the lower strata of the city's population and its satisfactory partnership with the ends of commerce as well as the interests of the state. Tavernier, an epicure who loved good food and wine tells us:

> There are so many public women in the town, the suburbs and in the fortress, which is like another town, that it is estimated there are generally more than 20,000 entered in the Darogha's [the commissioner of police] register, without which it is not allowed to any woman to ply this trade. In the cool of the evening you see them before the doors of their houses, which are for the most part small huts, and after the night comes they place at the doors a candle or a lighted lamp for a signal. It is then, also, that the shops where they sell *tari* [palm toddy] are opened. The king derives from the tax which he places on this *tari* a very considerable revenue, and it is principally on this account that they allow so many public women, because they are the cause of the consumption of much *tari*.[7]

Another Frenchman, Thevenot, notes the liberty enjoyed by the women of Hyderabad. Their marriage contracts had a clause that the wife would retain complete freedom of movement and could even drink *tari* if that was her desire!

In 1685, Hyderabad was plundered by the Mughals. Two years later, it was annexed to the Mughal empire by Aurangzeb, but the period of its relative obscurity was brief. In 1725, Nizam ul mulk, the Mughal's viceroy in the Deccan, made himself virtually independent of his nominal overlord. Hyderabad again became the capital of a dynasty, this time that of the Asaf Jahis ("equal in dignity to Asaf, the minister of King Solomon"), the title given to Nizam ul mulk by the hapless emperor of a rapidly unravelling Mughal empire.

The threat to the fortunes of the walled city (the walls themselves were demolished in the 1920s to relieve traffic congestion), however, did not arise from the quick changes what were taking place on India's political map during the 18th and 19th centuries. The impending danger was more from the process of modernization which picked up pace in the wake of the British conquest of India. Although the Nizam's suzerainty over his dominions was spared—he became a subordinate ally of the British in 1978—the political, economic, and administrative importance of the old city was now fatefully set on a course of slow erosion. With the coming of the railway in 1974 and the establishment of an incipient industrial base through the setting up of railway repair workshops and a textile mill, it was clear, at least in hindsight, that the northern part of the city outside the fortified walls held the key to Hyderabad's future.

The shift northward, across the Musi river, was accelerated by the floods of 1908 and the plague of 1911 which led the Nizam to move his residence and administrative offices out of the walled city to the north of the river. The ruler's example was soon followed by most of his nobility. The final blow to old Hyderabad was, of course, the integration of the state with the Republic of India after the country's independence from British rule. This meant not only the dismantling of the Nizam's administrative machinery but also the disappearance of the feudal economic base on which most of the old city's population had subsisted. In addition, many of the Muslim elite fled out of Hyderabad, mostly to Pakistan. The old city was well on its way to becoming a ghetto. As Ratna Naidu in her sociological study of Hyderabad has observed, "Deprived of economic opportunities with the dismantling of the feudal structure, and deprived of its elite, who are usually the powerful spokesmen for the enhancement of civic amenities, the walled city as an area languishes in multiple deprivation."[8] The deprivation is not only material but also psychological and cultural.

Culturally, the history of Hyderabad is witness to a process of ever increasing heterogenization. Although the Hindus were always a part of what was essentially a Muslim city, their native Telugu culture was clearly a subordinate, 'low' culture in the preeminently Islamic scheme of things. In the 18th and 19th centuries, many cultural groups migrated to Hyderabad from other parts of the country and even, as in the case of Arabs, from as far away as the Middle East. The Arabs, like the Marathas, came to Hyderabad to soldier in the Nizam's army. The trading communities of the Muslim Bohras from Gujarat and the the Hindu Marwaris from Rajasthan became prominent in the city's commercial life. Then there were the

Kayasths and the Khatris from north India, traditionally the backbone of many an Indian state's administration, who played a similar role in the Nizam's affairs of state. These groups tended to cluster together in separate enclaves where they could follow their own ways of religious and community life. This is not to say that individuals did not leaven their traditional lifestyles with the dominant Perso-Islamic culture. Many (especially the Kayasths, who are well known for their identification with the masters they have so ably served, whether the ruler be British or Muslim) would cultivate an appreciation of Urdu poetry or adopt the sartorial style of sherwani, the long buttoned-up coat with a high round collar and gumi topi, a cousin of the Turkish fez. They would prefer Hyderabad's distinctive cuisine and its gracious modes of public address and speech. Yet, on the whole, the lifestyles of the various groups in the rest of the population—their customs, mores, architectural styles, food habits—remained distinctive. In the 17th century, for instance, in the inns set up by the Qutub Shahis for poor travellers, Muslims received a dole of bread, rice, or vegetables already cooked whereas 'the idolaters, who eat nothing which has been prepared by others, are given flour to make bread and a little butter and as soon as their bread is baked they cover it on both sides with melted butter.'[9] As in the rest of the country, in the medieval period, Hindus and Muslims shared activities and experiences in the public realm 'even though in private they were completely segregated, almost opposed to each other.'[10] In short, it was a multicultural coexistence rather than any merger into a single, composite culture; Hindus and Muslims lived together separately. They were more than strangers, not often enemies, but less than friends.

After Hyderabad's integration with independent India, the heterogenization percolated even into the mohallas as Hindus began to replace the Muslims who had left for Pakistan. Thus from 1951 to 1961, the Muslim population of the old city declined from 69 per cent to 50 per cent while the Hindu population increased from 21 per cent to 40 per cent, a trend which began to be reversed only after the violence between the two communities became endemic. The recurrent bloodletting in the past 15 years has had the demographic consequence that Muslims from the outlying areas began to flee to the old city as if to a fortress while the Hindu exodus was in the reverse direction. Currently, the Muslim population of the old city is estimated at around 70 per cent.

Contemporary Hyderabad is certainly not a city for those with a partiality for nostalgia. The Musi river is now a stinking sewer without the sewer's saving grace of flowing water which at least keeps the garbage moving. It is but a marshy tract between the old and the new cities, with slime-covered puddles and a sewage-borne creeping, crawling, and buzzing life which, to me, makes Hyderabad the mosquito capital of India. Like the river, there is no longer an 'old city' of medieval Islam. Leprous beggars asking for alms in the name of Allah are still to be found but the nobles, taking the evening air dressed in flowing muslin robes, are long gone. There are no carriages clattering on the unpaved streets or groups of veiled women, hinting at supressed laughter and whispered assignations, gliding through the brightly lit bazaars redolent with strong flowery perfumes and the smell of fresh horse droppings, the shops stocked with choice wares from Persia, Arabia, and the rest of Hindustan.

Today, the old city is barely one step ahead of being a vast ghetto of over a million people, living in settlements, bastis and mohallas, that are homogeneous in their religious and caste compositions. Small houses stacked side by side line winding alleys which are negotiable only by foot or bicycle. Goats, dogs, and chickens, coexisting in the harmony of the chronically hungry, rummage through the refuse littering the open spaces. Unemployed young men stride purposefully through the lanes, even if the purpose is only to buy a cigarette from a corner shop or to impress any hidden female watcher with their purposeful mien. Children play the staple games of the poor—hopscotch for the girls while the boys run after an old bicycle tyre, kept rolling in a wobbly motion as much by their excitement as by the strokes of the stick propelling it forward.

The economic picture of the walled city, described by Naidu, is dismal.[11] The working population is around 30 per cent of the total number of inhabitants. The largest number, about a third, are skilled and semiskilled artisans engaged in the traditional occupation of weaving, pottery, sandal making, and food preparation. About a quarter of the working population earns its livelihood from casual daily wage work, as pushcart vendors of vegetable and fruit, hawkers of trinkets, pullers of rickshaws, scavengers, and other low-prestige occupations such as watchmen and messenger boys in government offices. The fabled earnings of the Muslims who went to work in the Arab countries of the Persian Gulf have brought only minor changes into the lives and the living standards of their families. They have provided only a temporary respite from pervasive economic hardship. The Gulf connection of the Muslims has had more social and cultural rather then economic consequences; for instance, it has resulted in the greater pan-Islamic pride which is visible in the sleek new mosques that have recently been built in the Muslim-dominated areas of the walled city.

The city is poor, but its poverty is more a general unkemptness and disorder than drabness. Economic deprivation has not smothered Hyderabad's vitality or dulled its desire for vivid definition. Even in destitute mohallas there are startling splashes of colour. Here, only the front door has been painted; there, the wooden shutters of a small window. Green, the colour of the faithful, is the most preferred. It ranges in hue from a bilious green to the freshly planted paddy green of those gleaming new mosques of the last two decades. Occasionally, there is a swathe of sunflower yellow across a house front, but another universal favourite of both the Hindus and the Muslims appears to be a cheap metallic blue, the colour of the sky on glossy religious posters. Hyderabad's bazaars and the houses of its well-to-do citizens favour ornamental wrought iron grills for the shutters of their shops and gates. The work is intricate and distinctive, giving the impression of swirling curlicues and scimitars, of Persian calligraphy cast in iron.

Hindus and Muslims: Versions of the Past

My aim here is not to write a history of Hindu-Muslim relations in Hyderabad during the preceding 300 years. It is both more modest and in some ways more ambitious. It is modest in that I would like to get for myself and convey to the readers a general impression of the way Hindus and Muslims or, in other, more psychological words, whenever overarching religious identities have become salient and dwarfed other group identities through which individuals also experience themselves. It is difficult because historians are of little help in an enterprise which is so contentious and where the interpretation of historical dates is so inseparable from the historian's own political aims, ideological commitments, and the strong emotions these commitments often generate. Yet some sense of this past is utterly necessary for my enterprise, considering the myriad reflections in which I was to encounter it in the present. In an ancient country like India, where collective memories reach back thousands of years, cultural psychology can never be as ahistorical as it may be in a young country like the United States. Cultural psychology in India must necessarily include the study of the psychic representations of collective pasts, the way collective memories are transmitted through generations, and the ways the past is used as a receptacle for projections from the present.

The chief protagonists of the debate on the past of Hindu-Muslim relations which excites so much contemporary passion are the secularist (both Hindu and Muslim) on the one side and the Hindu nationalist on the other, with the Muslim fundamentalist and the Hindu revivalist on the sidelines, trying to inject their particular brand of venom into the proceedings. The debate has momentous consequences, its winner aiming at nothing less than the capture of India's political soul and the chance to shape its destiny in the coming decades.

The secularist faction—framer of India's constitution and politically ascendant since the time of Nehru—comprises most of the Western-educated liberal and leftist intelligentsia and is greatly influential in academia.[12] Hindu and Muslim, the secularist avers, are relatively recent categories in Indian history. Before the late 19th century, overarching religious entities and identities such as Hindu and Muslim did not exist. Among the Hindus, there were various sects frequently at odds with each other; nor did Indian Muslims constitute a monolithic Islamic collectivity. The secularist goes on to draw a picture of widespread Hindu-Muslim symbiosis of the precolonial and early colonial periods and the development of a syncretic popular religion, especially at the village level, which borrows elements both from Islamic practice and Hindu ritual while it reveres Muslim saints as much as Hindu holy men.

The secularist view makes a clear-cut distinction between the terms 'religious' and 'communal', the latter is not used in its Anglo-American lexical sense, meaning someone who is altruistic and civic-minded, but in its specifically Indian meaning of one whose exclusive attachment to his or her community is combined with an active hostility against other communities which share its geographical and political space. Whereas religion is seen solely as a matter of personal faith and reverence for a particular set of icons, rituals, and dogmas, communalism is a more collective affair which involves a community's politics and economics as much as its faith. Communalism not only produces an identification with a religious community but also with its political, economic, social and cultural interests and aspirations. This identification is accompanied by the strong belief that these interests not only diverge from but are in actual conflict with the interests of other communities.

In this view, the precolonial and early colonial period conflicts between Hindus and Muslims were rare. Whenever they occurred, they were essentially religious in nature, that is, the conflicts were over religious symbols such as the route or form or mosques, and so on. Twentieth-century conflicts, on the other hand, have been initiated by communal ideologies and are basically over clashing economic interests. In the secularist view, even the religious persecution of Hindus by such 18th-century monarchs as the Mughal emperor Aurangzeb or, later, by Tipu Sultan in south India, were dictated by reasons of state rather than the communal ideology of any particular ruler. Aurangzeb's discrimination against Hindus and the destruction of their temples is interpreted as an attempt to reformulate the ideological basis of the late Mughal state, while Tipu's attacks on Hindu temples and the Hindu culture of the Kerala Nayars was more a deliberate act of policy rather than of religious fanaticism.[13]

The secularist holds that communalism, and the consequent large-scale violence between Hindus and Muslims, began to spread in the late 19th century chiefly because of colonialism.[14] To counter a growing Indian nationalism, he argues, the British followed a 'divide and rule' policy by deliberately strengthening Muslim communalism. The rapid diffusion of 19th-century Hindu revivalism and of pan-Islamism in the following century, again the products of Asia's colonial encounter with the imperial West, was another reason for the rise of communalism. Yet another factor was the decline of the syncretic warrior of the 18th century, who had been forged in the mixed bands of soldiers, Hindu and Muslim, who served various kings, again Hindu or Muslim, or foraged on their own in the anarchic political conditions which prevailed in India as the Mughal empire unravelled.

The basic fabric of India, though, remains syncretic, a commingling of Islamic influences with Hindu traditions. Hindus and Muslims are not divided along any cultural or social-psychological lines except in the narrow area of personal faith.

The Hindu nationalist argues that a fundamental divide between Hindus and Muslims is a basic fact of Indian history which is ignored by the secularist.[15] The Hindu nationalist would support the contention of the French anthropologist Marc Gaborieau, that Hindus and Muslims found their identity in the deepest sentiments of opposition between the two, sentiments that are traceable throughout the nine centuries of Indo-Muslim history, from the writings of the Arab traveller Al-Beruni in the 11th century to Jinnah, the founder of Pakistan in the 20th.[16] The Hindu nationalist is thus in basic agreement with Pakistani historians who too support the 'two nations' theory and label Akbar, the syncretic Mughal monarch who is a hero to the secularist, as an apostate to Islam.

In the Hindu nationalist view, the conflict between Hindus and Muslims is squarely religious, indeed theological. Its roots lie in Islam's exclusive claim to truth and its refusal to grant equal status to Hindu beliefs and doctrines. Islam's division of people into believers and infidels and the world into arenas of peace—*dar-ul-Islam*—and of conflict—*dar-ul-harb*—which led to terrible cruelties against the Hindu infidel's person and religious shrines over hundreds of years, cannot be erased from the Hindu collective memory. Moreover, the Hindu nationalist maintains, the Muslim continues to persist in intolerance, in the belief that all that is outside the *Qur'an* is an error if not an abomination. The Hindu nationalist avers that secularists seem to direct their arguments and appeals only toward the Hindus since they are firmly rejected by the Muslims who seek identity in their own religious tradition and personal laws even when those go against the very fundamentals of a secular state. The roots of Hindu-Muslim conflict lie in Muslim religious intolerance, Muslim failure to outgrow a medieval bigotry, and the inability to learn, in the absence of guidelines in the *Qur'an*, how to live in a state which is not Muslim-controlled.

To summarize: the story of Hindu-Muslim relations takes on different hues depending upon the colour of the ideological lenses through which it is viewed. For the liberal historian or one with leftist leanings, the story is bathed in a roseate glow of the precolonial golden age of Hindu-Muslim amity. For these storytellers, the tale is of a commingling and flowering of a composite cultural tradition, especially in art, music, and architecture.[17] It is the story of a gradual drawing closer of Hindus and Muslims in the forms of their daily lives and of an enthusiastic participation in each other's festivals. In this vision, there is little room for conflict between the communities. Sporadic outbreaks of violence needing some explanation are almost never religious in their origin but dictated by local economic interests and political compulsions. To the conservative Hindu nationalist, on the other hand, for whom the Hindu saffron and the Muslim green do not mix to create a pale pink, the rift between the two communities is a fundamental fact of Indian history. They see Hindu-Muslim relations framed by a thousand-year-old 'civilizational' conflict in which the Muslims, militarily victorious and politically ascendant for centuries, tried to impose Islamic civilization on their Hindu subjects through all means from coercion to bribery and cajolery, and yet had only limited success. The composite civilization, according to this view, was limited to small sections of the population around the Muslim courts and to court-patronized arts like music and architecture. It also included some Hindus who adopted the Persian-inspired language and ways of life of their rulers. The vast majority of Hindus kept their civilzational core intact while they resentfully tolerated the Muslim onslaught. In this view, the outbreaks of violence between the two communities were inevitable whenever Muslim dominance was threatened; the rage of the denigrated Hindu, stored up over long periods of time, had to explode once historical circumstances sanctioned such eruptions.

Between Enemy Lines

To look critically at any aspect of Hindu-Muslim relations today is a task fraught less with difficulty than with trepidation. As political passions run high, a commitment to either the secularist or the Hindu nationalist view is considered almost mandatory. Any critique which is seen as deviating from the one or the other easily invites the epithets of 'cryptofascist' from one side and 'pseudosecularist' from the other. Both 'crypto-' and 'pseudo-' are angry words, the former connoting a base veiling of real intent, the latter alluding to a fake or malicious deception. Yet, as important as it is to stand up and be counted, there is still a place for standing aside and counting, something I intend to do when examining the two different views of the Hindu-Muslim past. For, ideally, the psychoanalyst is essentially an onlooker and commentator on the worlds of love and hate. Still somewhat starry-eyed after so many years in the profession, I see the psychoanalyst standing outside the fray, unmoved by the violent passions that swirl all around: his only intellectual commitment to a questioning that does not seek answers but encourages reflection, his suspicion evoked by ideals excessively noble and ideas particularly *en vogue*, his interest aroused by all that is tabooed. It is comforting for me to remember—to counteract my guilt at not being able to live up to the ideal—that an analyst is also compassionate toward ideals which one falls short of, including his own, since I know my own emotional involvement in the issue will not always allow me the neutrality I may strive for.

Let me begin with the fallacies of the secularist position which, I believe, has understimated the extent of the historical rift between Hindus and Muslims and has thus invited a backlash to its Panglossian view of the past. In other words, the secularist has tended to downplay the dark side of Hindu-Muslim relations in India. Scholars sympathetic to this viewpoint have pointed out that Hindu-Muslim conflicts are not only a product of the colonial period but also occurred in precolonial times and were often also communal—in the secular understanding of the term—rather than religious.[18]

In the medieval period, even the Sufis, the Islamic mystics who are so often held up as examples of 'composite culture', the syncretic Muslims *par excellence*, had serious limits to their tolerance. In the question of faith they were unequivocal about the superiority of Islam and the hellish fate in store for the Hindu infidels on judgement day. As Muzaffar Alam puts it: 'Indeed, in relation to Hindus, often it is difficult to distinguish between an orthodox theologian [the obstreperous mullah of Hindu imagination] and a liberal mystic.'[19] Many a Sufi was openly hostile to the religion and social practices of the Hindus, paranoid—even at the zenith of Muslim power—that the Hindus would obliterate Islamic laws, Islam, and the Muslim community if they ever captured political power. Alam summarizes the Muslim side of the Hindu-Muslim equation thus: 'An average literate Muslim believed that Islam and Hinduism belonged to two radically diverse traditions and that the twain would never meet.'[20] To emphasize the sense of separate identities, of the distance between the two communities, even common social practices came to be known as Hinduwani and Muslamani.[21] Thus although Hindu and Muslim identities were not as fixed and continuous over time as the Hindu nationalist believes, neither were these identities absent as claimed by the secularist. In the medieval period, for large sections of people, Hindu and Muslim identities were intermittent rather than continuous, occasionally flowering rather than perpetually in full bloom, evoked whenever religious symbols and sentiments moved to the forefront of conscious concern, which was mostly when they were perceived to be threatened or under actual attack.

The secularist underestimation of the aversion between Hindus and Muslims and the denial of the existence of any kind of collective, cultural identities in the past derives, I believe, from the reliance of many historians and political scientists on objective rather than subjective experiential data, which is more often mined by the anthropologist. To illustrate this, let me take the earlier example of Tipu Sultan, whose destruction of some Hindu temples and persecution of certain Hindu groups are objectively considered as motivated by his suspicion of the loyalty of these groups and of the temple priests' close ties to the Hindu house of Wodiyar which Tipu and his father had replaced. Tipu did not go on any general anti-Hindu rampage and in fact even supported some temples with donations from the state coffers.

There is another, unwritten verison of these incidents which has gone into the making of what I would call the 'cultural memory' (a term I prefer to 'collective memory') of many Hindus. Cultural memory is the imaginative basis for a sense of cultural identity. For isn't imagination a memory of vital moments of life freed from their actual, historical context? Cultural memory, too, is a group's history freed from rootedness in time—it is as much imagination as the actual events that go into its construction. The cultural memory of Tipu's actions (as of Aurangzeb's) has a markedly different flavour from that which one reads in history texts. A very different realm of experience and distinctive emotion is evoked in a believing Hindu who reads or hears about Tipu forcibly circumcising Brahmins and compelling them afterwards to eat cow's flesh as an unequivocal token of their loss of caste. That Hindu shares the indignation of his 17th-century compatriots at Tipu's destruction of the temple and their relief when they are finally rid of 'the yoke of this tyrant'.[22] Indeed, it would be odd to expect, as the secularist sometimes seems to do, that such a deeply religious people as the Hindus would have understood the mysterious workings of Tipu's *raison d'etat* and not reacted with disgust and horror to what clearly seemed to be a brazen attack on their religious sentiments and cherished symbols of faith.

The ethnographers of the 17th, 18th, and 19th centuries, who were also the cultural psychologists of their eras, are preeminently the European travellers. Generally looking down upon India and its peoples from the heights of European superiority, the travellers are especially contemptuous of the Hindus, who are mostly referred to as idolators or Gentiles, whereas the Muslims, clearly identified as such, are more familiar to the Christian and thus less an object of mystery or scorn. Lacking in any knowledge of the country's religious traditions, the travellers' interest is excited by what appear to them as strange Hindu ceremonies, rituals, and customs—with an emphasis on the temple courtesans, burning of widows, and orgiastic religiosity.

From the travellers, then, we can only get pointers to Hindu-Muslims relations by paying attention to casual observations and throw-away remarks that are adjunct to the European's main interest in describing to countrymen at home the political and economic situation of India and the unfamiliar manners and mores of its inhabitants. Thus, for instance, we get the following observation from the French traveller, Francois Bernier, who travelled in the Mughal empire between 1656 and 1668:

> The tenth incarnation (of Vishnu), say the Gentiles, will have for its object the emancipation of mankind from the tyranny of the Mahometan, and it will take place at a time when according to our calculation, Anti-Christ is to appear; this is however but a popular tradition, not to be found in their sacred books.[23]

Such scattered remarks, lacking the necessary context, cannot be taken as an accurate description of Hindu-Muslim relations. They do, however, make us doubt the picture of widespread amity, while pointing to the existence of many sullen Hindus resentful of Muslim rule, if not of the 'Mahometans'.

The exception to most other travellers is Abbe Dubois, a French missionary who spent thirty years (1792-1823) in the south of India. As a man of the cloth, the Abbe is naturally convinced of the superiority of his faith over the religions of India. Yet he also displays a compassionate understanding for the customs of the people he observed so closely for so long. Most of the time he is remarkably fair. Abbe Dubois is a natural ethnographer, with a stance toward his 'fieldwork' which would meet the approval of any graduate school of anthropology.

At first glance, Dubois's work seems to support the secularist contention that the conflict between the Hindu and Muslim was not communal but religious, no different from the quarrels between various Hindu sects. And indeed it is true that relgious strife is as Indian as mango pickle. Yet when we compare the internecine strife of Hindu sects with the violence between Hindus and Muslims, the difference between the two is obvious. Here, for instance, is the Abbe's description of a 'riot' he observed between the followers of Vishnu and those of Shiva:

> According to Vishnavites it is the height of all abomination to wear the *lingam* [the sign of Shiva]. According to their antagonists whoever is decorated with the *naman* [the sign of Vishnu] will be tormented in hell by a sort of fork similar in form to this emblem. These mutual recriminations often end in violent altercations and riots. The numerous bands of religious mendicants of both sects are specially apt to provoke strife. One may sometimes see these fanatics collected together in crowds to support their opinion of the super-excellence of their respective doctrines. They will overwhelm each other with torrents of abuse and obscene insults, and pour forth blasphemies and imprecations, on one side against Shiva, on the other Vishnu; and finally they will come to blows. Fortunately blood is seldom shed on these battle fields. They content themselves with dealing each other buffets with their fists, knocking off each other's turbans, and much tearing of garments. Having thus given vent to their feelings, the combatants separate by mutual consent.

> That these religious dissensions do not set the whole country ablaze, occasion those crimes of all kinds which were for centuries the result of religious fanaticism in Europe and elsewhere, is due no doubt to the naturally mild and timid character of the Hindus, and especially to the fact the greater number compound with their consciences and pay equal honour to Vishnu and Shiva. Being thus free from any bias towards either party, the latter serve as arbitrators in these religious combats and often check incipient quarrels.[24]

The description of this riot reveals a ritualized, gamelike quality which combines passion with restraint. It is a ritualization of antagonisms, what Erik Erikson called 'a creative formalization' which helps to avoid both impulsive excess and compulsive self-restrictions.[25] The Vaishnavites and the Shaivites engage each other in both interplay and combat, practising 'a form of war which can occur only among those who are at peace.' In contrast, the Hindu-Muslim conflicts have no such playlike quality, pervaded as they are by deathly intent, with the burning down of houses, demolition of temples, mosques, and shrines.[26] Their vocabulary is of mortal enmity, victory, and defeat, a combat that must lead to humiliation and grievous wounds to the collective self of one group or the other.

I have already mentioned that the Hindu nationalist may well be overestimating (in contrast to the secularist under-estimation) the existence and strength of overarching Hindu and Muslim religious identities in India's precolonial past. The Hindu nationalist is, I believe, also overestimating the role of doctrinal differences between Islam and Hindu beliefs for the difficulties in the relations between the two communities. To me the Hindu-Muslim rift appears as much the consequence of a collision between two collective narcissisms, between two equally grandiose group selves, each convinced of its civilizational superiority, as of differences in matters of faith. Abbe Dubois brings out clearly the injuries to group narcissism, the wounds to collective vanity sustained in the Hindu-Muslim encounter:

> The Brahmins in particular cherish an undying hatred against the Mahomedans. The reason for this is that the latter think so lightly of the pretensions of these so-called gods of earth; and, above all, the Mahomedans do not scruple to display hearty contempt for their ceremonies and customs generally. Besides, the haughty Mussulmans can vie with them in pride and insolence. Yet there is this difference: the arrogance of a Mussulman is based only on the political authority with which he is invested, or on the eminence of the rank he occupies; whereas the Brahmin's superiority is inherent in himself, and it remains intact, no matter what his condition in life may be. Rich or poor, unfortunate or prosperous, he always goes on the principle ingrained in him that he is the most noble, the most excellent, and the most perfect of all created beings, that all the rest of mankind are infinitely beneath him, and that there is nothing in the world so sublime or so admirable as his customs and practices.[27]

The Hindu nationalist may also be overestimating the depth of the Hindu's historical aversion to the Muslim which was perhpas more prevalent in the upper castes where Muslim religious intolerance came up against the Brahminical conviction of Hindu superiority. Dubois remarks:

> But if Brahmins cannot with any justice be accused of intolerance in the matter of religion, the same can certainly not be said in regard to their civil usage and customs. On these points they are utterly unreasonable. . . . Though they have had to submit to various conquerors who have proved themselves to be their superiors in courage and bravery, yet in spite of this, they have always considered themselves infinitely their superior in the matter of civilization.

> The Mahomedans, who can tolerate no laws, no customs, and no religion but their own, used every advantage which conquest gave them in a vain attempt to force their religion on the people who had succumbed to them almost without resistance. But these same Hindus, who did not dare to complain when they saw their wives, their children, and everything they held most dear carried off by these fierce conquerors, their country devastated by fire and sword, their temples

destroyed, their idols demolished, these same Hindus I say, only displayed some sparks of energy when it came to changing their customs for those of their oppressors.[28]

What excited Hindu hostility was as much the Muslim assault on his lifestyle as on his idols. As we shall see later, the Hindu's shocked disgust, for example, at the Muslim eating of beef, then as now, is a far more potent factor in Hindu-Muslim relations than Islam's reputed intolerance.

The Hindu nationalist, I believe, also overemphasizes the impact of ten centuries of Muslim domination. The explanation for the Hindu's negative sentiments toward the Muslim as lying in a subjugated people's 'natural' resentment is not wholly convincing if we remember that such aversion was negligible in the case of the British. In spite of the fact that the Raj was economically exploitative, funneling wealth out of the country, whereas during the Muslim rule wealth stayed within, the latter evokes a hostility not due to the former. Political subjugation and economic exploitation, it seems, played less of a role in determining the Hindu reaction because the Hindu collective identity, however nebulous, was crystallized around shared religious symbols rather than based on political or economic structures. Muslims were perceived to be outragers of Hindu religious sentiment and mockers of their faith whereas the British were, at worst, indifferent. Granted that the British too ate beef—a practice deeply repugnant to most Hindus—but they were too few and carried out their private lives holed up in bungalows and barracks which were shielded from public scrutiny by high walls and thick hedges. In contrast, the Muslim lived cheek by jowl with the Hindu. This proximity created the potential for the emergence of new cultural and social forms but also occasioned simmering resentment and nagging friction. The British beef-eater was remote, almost abstract. The Muslim butcher in his blood-flecked undervest and lungi, wielding a huge carving knife, was a very visible part of a town's life, a figure of awe and dread for the Hindu child and of a fear-tinged repulsion for the adult. The Englishman remained a stranger, the Muslim became the Other.

Looking at the Hindu-Muslim encounter as decisively coloured by the facts of dominance and subordination, by aggression and resistance, by the zero-sum game of winners and losers, the Hindu nationalist pays homage to the influential paradigm in contemporary historical, anthropological, and political science writing which considers power as the main axis around which all relations between groups are structured. The impressive work that has resulted through the emphasis on power, especially on the inequality of colonial and imperial relations, has been invaluable. But as Raymond Grew points out, this very emphasis also tends to obscure and often ideologize the processes of assimilation, transformation, reassertion, and recreation, which too are inherent in all cultural encounters.[29] The Hindu-Muslim encounter has been no exception.

The gulf between the two opposing views of the Hindu-Muslim encounter is not a matter solely of interest to scholars and political propagandists but is reflected in and vitally influences many facets of contemporary consciousness. Much of the Indian heritage—monuments, art, music, legends, history—which people of an earlier generation were accustomed to regard as noncontroversial has suddenly become hotly contested. As an example, let me take the legend of the founding of Hyderabad. For those subscribing to the syncretic school, this legend is the narrative embodiment of an essential Hindu-Muslim amity in the past. The story itself is a *mythos*, seeking to convince through the power of aesthetics and symbolism, and is a counterpoint to the *logos* of formal thought on Hindu-Muslim relations which is routinely employed by the social scientist. The tale goes thus:

> Sultan Mohammed Quli Qutub Shah (1580-1612) was the grandson of Sultan Quli Qutub Shah, founder of the Qutub Shahi dynasty. In 1579, when still a prince and just 14 years old, he fell in love with Bhagmati, a commoner [and a Hindu], an extraordinarily talented and beautiful dancer. She lived across the river Musi in the village of Chichlam, some distance away from the royal fortress at Golconda. Every evening when dusk fell, the prince stole away from the palace grounds to meet his beloved across the river. One day a terrible storm broke and the river was in spate. Fearing that his lover might drown, the prince braved the turbulent rising waters and saved Bhagmati. Compelled to accept his son's choice, the king, Sultan Ibrahim, had a large stone bridge built across the Musi to enable Mohammed Quli to court the dancer. Known today as the Purana Pul ['old bridge'], it stands mute witness to this story. On his accession to the throne, Mohammed Quli married Bhagmati and in her honour built a splendid new city on the site of the village Chichalam. He called the city 'Bhagnagar' or the 'City of Good Fortune'. Bhagmati later took the name of Hyder Mahal and Mohammed Quli renamed the city as Hyderabad.[30]

It is not surprising that, whereas history discerns the origins of Hyderabad in the mundane facts of congestion and lack of water in the old fortress capital of Golconda, legend attributes the founding of the city to the sublimity of a prince's love for a commoner. What is more relevant to our purpose, however, is the way Hindu nationalists interpret the legend today. They see in the tale yet another illustration of the fundamental Hindu-Muslim divide. 'All the story tells us,' says a militant Hindu, active in the campaign to have Hyderabad revert back to its original name of Bhagnagar, 'is that the Mussulman has always fucked our women whenever he has wanted to, as he has fucked us over the centuries. If he deigned to take one of our women into his harem, he could not tolerate her remaining a Hindu but forced her to convert to Islam. Where are the stories of Hindu princes marrying Muslim wives?' This particular interpretation of the legend is not about how a youth's erotic obsession for a girl flowered into the deep love of a mature man, or about an era of close Hindu-Muslim relations which permitted, even when they did not encourage, love across religious persuasions. For the Hindu nationalist, the legend is about Hindu defeat and a collective shame wherein the community's most beautiful and accomplished women had to be ceded to the Muslim conqueror.

Finally, what is the truth? As far as I can see the truth is that there are two overarching histories of Hindu-Muslim relations—with many local variations—which have been used by varying political interests and ideologies and have been jostling for position for many centuries. In times of heightened conflict between the two communities, the Hindu nationalist history that supports the version of conflict between the two assumes preeminence and organizes cultural memory in the particular direction. In times of relative peace, the focus shifts back to the history emphasizing commonalities and shared pieces of the past. Many of the cultural memories which were appropriate during the conflict will retreat, fade, or take on new meaning, while others that incorporate the peaceful coexistence of Hindus and Muslims will resurface. And so it goes, on and on.

2

THE RIOT

My first personal experience of Hindu-Muslim violence was at the time of the partition of the country in 1947, when ferocious riots between the two communities engulfed many parts of the subcontinent, especially in the north. I was nine years old at the time and we lived in Rohtak, a small town some 50 miles west of Delhi, where my father was an additional district magistrate, 'the ADM Sahib'. As the killings and looting raged uncontrolled in the villages and towns of Punjab, more and more members of his extended family poured into Rohtak as refugees from the cities of Lahore, Lyallpur, and Sialkot, where they had lived for many generations and which now lay in the freshly created state of Pakistan. The rooms and verandas of our house became sprawling dormitories, with mats and durries spread close to each other on the floor as uncles, aunts, and cousins of varying degrees of kinship lived and slept in what for a child was an excitingly intimate confusion. The kitchen, over which my mother had willingly abdicated all control, hummed the whole day with the purposeful activity of women, and there was not a time of day when a few bodies were not seen huddled in nooks and corners in various stages of sleep.

With the loss of their homes and places of work, with the snapping of long-standing friendships and other social ties, there was little for the refugees to do in our house except seek comfort from the sharing of each other's riot experiences. This they did in groups which continuously changed in their membership as they shifted from one room of the house to another. As a small boy, yet privileged as the son of a father who gave them food and shelter, I could sit in on any group of adults, though at its edge, without being shooed away and told to go and play with other children. I became aware of their bitterness about the leaders of a newly independent India, Nehru and especially Gandhi by whom they felt most betrayed. Gandhi was the pet object of my grandmother's aversion, and many of my uncles and aunts shamelessly encouraged her as she held forth in her toothless, gummy voice, surprisingly similar to the Mahatma's own, on Gandhi's many affronts to Hindu sentiment and advanced salacious speculations on the reasons for his love of the 'Mussulman'.

It was also the first time I became aware of the Hindu hate of the Mussulman— the destroyer of temples, devourer of cow flesh, defiler of Hindu womanhood, rapers and killers all! Mussulmans were little better than animals, dirty and without self-control, who indulged all the demands of the senses, especially the violence of the body and pleasures of the flesh. Up to this time I had known Muslims as occasional colleagues of my father, some boys in school and, especially, as indulgent servants. In Sargodha, where my father was posted before he was transferred to Rohtak, I was particularly fond of Imtiaz, his Muslim orderly, who took me on forbidden bicycle rides to the bazaar. Once, seeing him get his forearm covered with an elaborate tattoo, I too had insisted on one—to the subsequent shocked disapproval of my parents. Then there was Fatima, a teenaged girl who looked after me from the ages of four to seven, and who was almost on par with my mother as the object of my first desires and longings. Fatima was a patient and very often a willing participant in the games I invented for both of us. She was a valiant liar on my behalf whenever one of my undertakings ended disastrously. Half girl, half woman, Fatima delightfully forgot to be consistently one or the other when she was with me. Hitching up her salwar, she would scamper up a guava tree to pluck the best fruit from the top branches. Her maternal persona taking over once she was back on ground, she would clean the guavas for me and hold the salt in the open palm of her hand while I ate. Fatima was an indispensable assistant on our fishing expeditions to the small pond that lay in the grounds of the house. She helped me make the fishing rod from a twig, a piece of string and a bent pin. She kneaded the dough we brought and made it into small pellets which were used as bait. In spite of my never catching any fish she did not destroy my illusion that there were indeed some lurking under the scummy green film that covered the pond.

It is not as if I were unaware that the Muslim were somehow different, although I do not recollect ever hearing the statement, 'He [or she] is a Mussulman,' as a marker of a person's identity in our home. I knew Imtiaz and Fatima could not enter the kitchen where Chet Ram, the Brahmin cook, held sway, because they were Muslims. The Muslim parts of Sargodha were subtly different from the Hindu mohallas concentrated around the bazaar. In the early evening, the coooking smells wafting out into the alleys were more pungent—the odour of mutton fried with onion, garlic, and ginger paste, with coriander and cumin, seemed embedded in the very walls of the houses. Old men with henna-dyed beards sat out on stringed cots, smoking their hookahs and murmuring their incessant gossip. The women, covered from head to toe in flowing white and black veils, glided silently through the alleys, followed by small children scurrying to keep up. There were also fewer stray dogs in the alleys, the ritually unclean animal being far less tolerated by the Muslim than by the indifferent Hindu.

As a little child, I had registered the differences but never felt the need to either evaluate or explain them to myself. It was only now, in Rohtak, that the family's 'war stories' from the riot-torn towns of Pakistan began to retrospectively shape my early observations in the direction of prejudice. Two of these I recount below. For a time these stories threatened to become the core of my memory of the 'Muslim' although, in the end, I like to believe, they did not overlay the child's love for Imtiaz and Fatima, did not replace it with fear, anger, and aversion. When I was carrying out this study in a Muslim locality in Hyderabad and engaging groups of Muslims in conversation, I became aware that within myself 'the Muslim' was still somewhat of a stranger. The strangeness was not due to my ignorance of him but due to my being singularly affected by someone I did not know. The ambivalence of fear and fascination from my past with which I had regarded Muslims had not vanished; I was no indifferent to the subjects of my study. I became aware that my first impulse was to defend myself against the threat the Muslims posed to my boundaries by strengthening and fortifying them as a Hindu. Then, in a kind of reaction formation, my tendency was to move in the opposite direction by consistently placing a more positive, 'humane' gloss on Muslim statements and actions than on Hindu ones. Ambivalence, however, also has a positive aspect. It prevents the crystallization of ideological convictions and an approach to the study with preconceived notions firmly in place. Convictions, as Nietzsche remarked, are more damaging to truth than lies. '

The Story of a Cousin Told by His Elder Brother

Sohan Lal killed himself on the way to Rohtak. He threw himself in front of a train. I could not stop him. We had made all the arrangements for the escape from Lyallpur. A Muslim truck driver was ready to drive the 300 miles to the border for 600 rupees. Sohan Lal had been married for only five months. He had a very pretty wife.

On the day of our departure we went out to make the final arrangements with the truck driver. The house was attacked in our absence. When we came back we hid on the roof of a Hindu neighbour's vacant house. We watched five husky Muslims in our courtyard. They had long butcher's knives stuck in their lungis. They were methodically looting the house. The corpse of our youngest brother—we were three—lay in the courtyard, the head completely severed from the trunk. One of the Muslims sat on a chair in front of the corpse directing the looters. They were bringing out the packed trunks from inside the house and throwing them in front of him on the ground. The ground was cluttered with wedding sarees and coloured silk blouses. I can still see the shining brass pots lying on their side reflecting the rays of the afternoon sun. We could not move. I was transfixed by the sight of the leader's hairy torso of which every inch was covered by a thick black fur. Then two of the Muslims went inside the house and brought out Sohan Lal's wife and the leader pulled her to him. She sat on the man's lap, naked to the waist, her petticoat ripped open, and the Muslim's hairy hand, like a giant black spider, covered her thigh. After laying her on the ground next to our brother's corpse, where drops of blood still oozed from the severed neck, they raped her in turn. I was holding Sohan Lal fast, my palm covering his mouth. If he had made the slightest sound the Muslims would have discovered us. But I do not think Sohan Lal would have done anything. His legs were buckling under him and I had to hold him up. After they finished, they ripped open her belly. Sohan Lal never said a word after it was all over and the Muslims had gone. In the day it took us to cross the border he remained mute. I tried my best to make him talk, ot make him shed some of his grief in tears but his soul remained far away. He killed himself just before we reached Rohtak.

The Cousin from Lahore

We did try to retaliate, at least the younger Sangh [Rashtriya Swayamsevak Sangh] members like me. And of course the Sikhs. A police inspector told me of going to a Sikh village where there was a reported massacre of the Muslims. As the police entered the village they passed under a kind of welcoming arch which was a rope strung out between the poles. To this rope, attached with short pieces of string, were the circumcised penises of all the Muslim men who had lived in the village, hanging there as if they were small eels drying in the sun. In our own neighbourhood there were three Muslim houses. Two of the families went away, leaving only Gul Mohammed behind. He was a silversmith, a quiet graying man who kept to himself and did not really have any friends among his Hindu neighbours, although he had lived in the same street for over 15 years. We knew him and his family—a wife and three young children—cursorily, nodding to him as we passed by his shop located on the ground floor of his house. In his faded, embroidered skull cap, often working late into the night, his head bent down in concentration as he fashioned silver bracelets or ornamental anklets with delicate strokes of a hammer, he was a familiar figure to all of us. The young men from our street who went out during the riots to join Hindu mobs operating in other parts of the city, averted their eyes when they passed by his shop. They had left Gul Mohammed alone, not because of any particular affection for him but because of the established pattern among the rioters, both Hindu and Muslim. A mob always foraged wide from its home base, killing and plundering in other distant parts of the town, leaving people of the other community living in its own area unharmed. It is easier to kill men who are strangers, to obliterate faces which have not smiled on one in recognition. It is easier to burn houses which have never welcomed one as a guest. So we kept inside our houses when a Hindu mob from Anarkali came to our alley for Gul Mohammed. Later, I was told they broke open the door and one by one, Gul Mohammed's family was dragged out into the alley where they were trussed up with ropes and left lying on the ground. From the open windows of the house, string cots, low wooden stools, and sleeping mattresses were thrown out onto the ground where they were gathered into a pile. The doors and window shutters of the house were chopped into kindling and added to the heap which was set on fire. One by one, the children were picked up and thrown into the burning pyre. Gul Mohammed's wife was the last one to be burnt alive, having been first forced to watch her husband and children die in the agony of the flames. The shop was then broken into and methodically stripped of the silverware. Within an hour our alley was silent again, only a charred and still smoking heap left to mark the end of Gul Mohammed's family. Whenever possible, this is the way Hindu mobs preferred to kill Muslims—by burning them alive. A Muslim who is burnt and not buried after death is automatically consigned to hellfire.

Even as I retell the stories of my relatives from memory, I know I cannot trust that they adhere strictly to facts. I am, of course, aware of the small embellishments I have made for the purposes of making the narratives more aesthetically compelling. I wonder if in the original stories there were details from other accounts of riots, incorporated by the teller to increase the emotional impact of his or her own story. In their first versions, some of the more gruesome details were prefaced by 'I am told', a qualification which disappeared in the retellings. My later, adult experience of riot accounts has taught me that the *talk* of atrocities which one was told about (and then even personally witnessed) is much more than their actual occurrence. The importance of the rhetorics of violence, as the British psychologist Peter Marsh has observed, is not necessarily that they illuminate actual action but that they substitute for it.[1]

I am also unsure how much I can trust my own memory not to make additions from its store of images, picked up from narratives of riots, even as I tell the tale. The truth of these stories, then, lies in the archetypal material they contain rather than in the factual veracity of particular details. The riots brought to the surface (as they continue to do every time they occur in a fresh edition), both at the level of action and of imagination, certain primitive fantasies of bodily violence which are our heritage from infancy and childhood. Prominent among these fantasies are those relating to sexual mutilation—the cutting off of male genitals, and the sadistic fury directed against female breasts which are hit repeatedly by iron rods, stabbed with knives, and lopped off by scythes and swords. At one level, the castration of males and the cutting off a female breasts incorporate the more or less conscious wish to wipe the hated enemy off the face of the earth by eliminating the means of its reproduction and the nurturing of its infants. At another, more unconscious level, in the deep regression and the breakdown of many normal defences occasioned by the widespread violence and the fear of one's own imminent death, the castration of the enemy may be viewed as a counterphobic acting out of what psychoanalysis considers one of the chief male anxieties, that is, it is a doing unto others— castration—what one fears may be done to one's self. The mutilation of the breast may be similarly derived from the upsurge of a pervasive infantile fantasy—the fantasy of violent revenge on a bad, withholding breast, a part of the mother whose absence gives rise to feelings of disintegration and murderous rage.

Sexual violence undoubtedly occurred during the Partition, although far below the level enshrined in collective memory. On a more sociological level, the chief reason for the preponderance of specifically sexual violence in the Partition riots in the north is that, as compared to many other parts of the country, the undivided Punjab was (and continues to be) a rather violent society. Its high murder rate is only one indication of a cultural endorsement of the use of physical force to attain socially approved ends such as the defence of one's land or of personal and family honour. There is now empirical evidence to suggest that the greater the legitimation of violence in some approved areas of life, the more is the likelihood that force will also be used in other spheres where it may not be approved. In this so-called cultural spillover effect there is a strong association between the level of nonsexual violence and rape, rape being partly a spillover from cultural norms condoning violent behaviour in other areas of life.[2] Given this violent tradition and its associated cultural norms, the riot situation further undermined, if it did not completely sweep away, the already weak norms curbing male aggression. It is then quite understandable that sexual violence during the Partition riots could reach levels of brutality which have rarely been approached in subsequent riots in other parts of the country.

It is only now that I can reflect more composedly, even tranquilly, and give a psychological gloss to the stories of the riots. At the time I heard them, their fearful images coursed unimpeded through my mind which reverberated wildly with their narrators' flushes of emotion. There was a frantic tone to the stories, an underlying hysteria I felt as a child but could only name as an adult. After all, my uncles, aunts, and cousins had not yet recovered from the trauma of what had befallen them. The Partition horrors stalked their dreams. They were still not free of the fear of losing their lives, a fear that had clutched them for weeks. They had lost their homeland, where they had been born and lived, which constitutes such an important, albeit unconscious, facet of our identity. With the loss of their homes, their sense of personal identity was tottering—had become 'diffused' in Eriksonian terms[3]—while they had yet to begin the process of adapting this fragmenting identity to a new homeland.

It is sobering to think of hundreds of thousands of children over many parts of the subcontinent, Hindu and Muslim, who have listened to stories from their parents and other family elders during the Partition and other subsequent riots, on the fierceness of an implacable enemy. This is a primary channel through which historical enmity is transmitted from one generation to the next as the child, ignoring the surface interpretations and rationalizations, hears the note of helpless fury and impotence in the accounts of beloved adults and fantasizes scenarios of revenge against those whose have humiliated his family and kin.[4] The fantasies, which can later turn from dimly conscious images to concrete actions during communal conflagrations, are not only a vindication of the parents and a repayment of the debt owed them but also a validation of the child-in-the-man's greater strength and success in overpowering those who had shamed his family in the distant past. Given the strong family and kinship ties all over the country, a

Hindu's enmity towards the Muslim (and vice versa) is often experienced by the individual as a part of the loyalty due to or (in the case of a more conflictful parent-child relationship) imposed by the parents. Later, as the child grows up, the parental message may be amplified by the input of one or more teachers. As Rajesh, one of the subjects of this study whom we will encounter later, remarked: 'We had a history teacher in school. He was the type who loved his subject. He would keep the text book aside and teach us the lesson extempore—like stories. When he used to tell us about the inhuman atrocities committed by Muslim invaders on the Hindus, I remember I used to get so angry that I felt like walking out of the class and beating up a few Muslim boys.'

Leaving aside the stories, I am uncertain whether even my direct childhood memories of the riots, with their vivid images which carry such an intense charge of *noesis*, the certainty of knowing, can be completely trusted to represent reality or are even wholly mine. For instance, I 'remember' going with my father to the railway station one night. Was it Rohtak? Hindu and Sikh refugees from Pakistan were camped on the station platform. Many had moaned in their sleep and a couple had woken up screaming (I now imagine) to escape from their persistent nightmares. We had walked through the sea of uneasy sleepers, their faces discoloured by the dim violet glow of the neon tubes hanging high above the platform. Sitting silently among empty canisters and tattered bedrolls, shrinking at our approach, the children did not cry and rarely whimpered, their large dark eyes full of a bewildered hurt and (again I imagine) the memories of stabbed and hacked bodies lying in the streets of towns and villages which now belonged to Pakistan. One particular image has become permanently etched: a four-year-old boy with a running nose, the yellow-green mucous, a thin plaster of salted sweat on the upper lip, dense with buzzing files which the child did not lift his hand to drive away, afraid perhaps of giving offence to even the smallest of living creatures.

I never personally witnessed the kinds of violence described in the family stories during the few days of rioting in Rohtak. For we lived at the outskirts of the town, in Civil Lines, where the spacious bungalows of the sahibs of the Raj and a few elite non-officials were located. The Civil Lines families rarely went into town, preferring the company of each other. Our social life was focused on the Rohtak Club and was carried out in its high-ceilinged rooms with their covered padded chairs, the wooden dance floor, and books on big game hunting and mores of obscure Indian tribes lying unread on the shelves of teak bookcases. Sometimes in the evening, when children were not allowed in, I had watched my father and his friends sitting outside on the lawn from behind the cactus hedge surrounding the club. In their white drill trousers and their cotton bush shirts, they looked fresh and cool, radiating an aura of peace and quiet authority which made me feel safe and quietly sleepy. A part of this effect was achieved through the sensory background of their setting—the settling dusk, the smell of freshly watered grass, the low murmurs of waiters gliding between the clubhouse and the widely spaced bridge tables bearing iced lemon and orange squashes. And as they sat there, the upright garden lamps transforming the lawn into a dull yellow island surrounded by the brilliant Indian darkness from which only moths and fireflies ventured in as intruders, the silence disturbed only by the occasional dream cry of a peacock, they had looked remote from the dust, the colour, and the noise of the town they administered. I remember well the night the riot started. From the terrace, where most of the family gathered on hearing a continuous, muffled roar break the stillness of the night, I counted at least 20 separate fires within the span of an hour as Muslim homes and shops were burnt on that first night. By midnight, the night had the shimmering glow of a slow-burning coal fire, the overcast sky beginning to have the ragged crimson edge of an uneven and unnatural dawn. Although on the following days the sounds of the riot coming from the town were blended into a low-pitched buzzing, not unlike the one near a beehive, I sometimes imagined I could distinguish the distant shouts of the mobs roaming the bazaars from the panic-filled screams of their victims.

We had enough company that night. The roof terraces of our neighbouring bungalows were crowded with whole families come up to watch the distant fires. Angry cries of babies awoken from sleep mingled with excited shouts of discovery as fresh fires were sighted. There were animated exchanges across the roofs as to the exact location of a new fire and the possible reactions of the Muslims. On the whole, the onlookers were in a gay mood; there was a feeling of respite from the petty concerns of daily life, a kind of relaxation which comes from the release of long pent-up tensions. 'This is a lesson the Muslims needed to be taught! We should have put them in their places long ago!' was the general consensus.

Although the night air began to be permeated by the acrid smell of smoke, the fires were far away and the possibility of any danger to our own homes and lives remote. At the most, the distant threat gave all of us a tingling sense of excitement which heightened the gaiety of what was fast turning into a festive occasion.

For the children, and perhaps for the adults too, that first night of the riot thus had a quality akin to the day of the kite-flying festival at the onset of spring, when people throng the roofs and the clear blue of the sky is profusely dotted with kites in all their bright colours; the town resounds to the battle cries of children as the men compete against each other, trying to cut the string holding a rival kite entangled with their own. The duels taking place in the town that night did not use paper kites as weapons, and the battle cries we heard so faintly were no mere expressions of childish exuberance but declarations of deadly intent. Yet, in the safety of our house and surrounded by the family, an uncanny impression of the riot as macabre festival persisted throughout the hours I spent on the roof.

When the riots were brought under control after three days, I remember that my father gave in to my persistence and promised to take me into the town the next morning to see the aftermath. I remember waking up early that day and looking out at the speckled dawn as the sun struggled with the first clouds of the season. The monsoon was a few days away and, my elbows resting on the window-sill of my parents's bedroom, I watched its foreunners, dark fluffy clouds racing across the sky as imperious heralds. The morning had been different from others, smelling not only of the sun's warmth but also of budding grass shoots and the dark, far away thunder. The walk through Rohtak's bazaars with my father was disappointing. I had expected to see smouldering heaps, amputated limbs, cut-off breasts—which I pictured as pale fleshy balls without a trace of blood. The reality was oddly disappointing Except for an occasional house with charred doors, missing windows, and smoke scars on its front, the bazaars presented the unchanging vista of a provincial town awakening to another day. There were the men vigorously (and loudy) chewing on marigossa twigs to clean their teeth and clearing their throats with much hawking and spitting. Others murmured their prayers as they bathed under the cool streams of water from public hydrants. The women hissed encouragement over naked babies held up above the gutter. Older children squatted by themselves, with that faraway look which be speaks of an inward absorption in the working of one's bowels, a trance occasionally broken as they bent down to contemplate their own dirt.

Almost 20 years later, in 1969, when I was again a witness to another Hindu-Muslim riot, this time in Ahmedabad in the western state of Gujarat, I was surprised to hear essentially the same rumours I had heard as a child in Rohtak. Thus we heard (and in Rohtak believed) that milk vendors had been bribed by the Muslims to poison the milk in the morning. Four children were said to be lying unconscious and two dogs had died after having drunk of the poisoned milk. Apparently, most of the servants in Civil Lines who went into the town frequently, had personally seen the dogs in the throes of death. Women had hurried to empty out the pails of milk; sticky patches of white soon spread to plaster the cobbed stones of the streets. We heard that Muslims had broken into grocery shops in the night and mixed powdered glass with the salt. A police van with a loudspeaker was said to be driving around the town, warning people not to buy salt. Both in Rohtak and Ahmedabad there was talk of large stocks of weapons, acid and other materials needed for manufacturing bombs, put in a cache in the underground cellars of mosques; of prior Muslim preparations for a slaughter of the Hindus being forestalled by the riot. In Ahmedabad there was the additional rumour of armed Pakistani agents seen parachuting into the city at night. Its Rohtak counterpart was the imminent attack by thousands of armed Meo tribesmen making a detour to the town on their way to Pakistan.

The fact that rumours during a riot take such dramatic and fanciful turns is not surprising. In a study of the ratio of rumours to actual events such as killing, rape, beating, harassment, property violation, and inconvenience among the Asians expelled from Uganda by Idi Amin, the relationship was strikingly linear.[5] That is, the more threatening and dramatic the experience, the more likely it was to be a wellspring of rumour. At the high point of a riot, the content of the rumours is at its most threatening and the speed at which they circulate at its highest. For it is at this particular time when three of the four conditions for the generation and transmission of rumours—personal anxiety, general uncertainty, and topical importance—are at their highest level. The fourth condition, credulity, is no longer in operation since at high levels of anxiety, disbelief in rumour is suspended, that is, rumours will be believed regardless how far-fetched.[6]

Rumours, of course, also serve some less conscious purposes. Deriving from and reinforcing the paranoid potential which lies buried in all of us, they were the conversational food which helped in the growth of a collective Hindu body. They sharpened our awareness of our own kind and many, who though they lived in the same bazaar were relative strangers earlier, became brothers overnight. They made misers discover a forgotten generosity as they offered to share food with those who had none; neighbours who had little use for each other now enquired daily about each other's well-being. There is little doubt that rumours are the fuel and riots the fire in which a heightened sense of community is also forged. If I remember the Rohtak riots so vividly it is not only because I was an impressionable child but also because of the deep sense of communion I felt with my family and the wider, although vague, entity of 'the Hindus'. The riots generated emotions which expanded my boundaries. They gave rise to exhilarating feelings of closeness and belonging to something beyond myself which I desperately wanted to keep. My memory of the Rohtak riots, I recognize, is not free from a shame-faced nostalgia for a shining flower which sprang from the mean soil of decaying corpses and ashes left behind by arsonists' fires.

In undermining our familiar controls over mental life, a riot is often experienced as a midwife for unfamiliar, disturbing fantasies and complex emotions, such as both disgust and overwhelming sexual attraction for a member of the enemy community. The overcharged atmosphere of violence breathed day in and day out by a person lifts the lid on the cauldron of instinctual drives as civilized sensibility threatens to collapse before the press of instinctuality in both its sexual and violent aspects. Accounts of sexual violence during a riot, for instance, not only evoke the publicly acceptable reaction of horror but may also release the more hidden emotion of a shameful excitement which bespeaks instinctual desire in its rawer form. Besides the expression of moral outrage, riot violence can be subjectively used for an unwanted but wished for vicarious satisfaction of sadistic impulses, for the fulfilment of one's urge to utterly subjugate another human being, to reduce his or her consciousness to a reactivity of the flesh alone.

In fiction, this complex flow of subjectivity during a riot has been brilliantly captured by the Hindi writer Krishna Baldev Vaid in his novel *Guzra Hua Zamana* (*A Bygone Era*). Biru, the teenaged hero of the novel, together with his parents, his sister Devi, and Kumari, the young wife of a neighbour, whom Biru has always lusted after with the innocence and ancient knowledge of a boy on the verge of manhood, have been given shelter by a Muslim friend, Bakka, during the Partition riots in a small town in Punjab. As the marauding Muslim mob, consisting of many men Biru knows well, including Bakka himself, roams the streets at night in an orgy of looting, killing and rape, the Hindu family cowers in the small dark room and a terrified Biru's thoughts flow in a full, barely controllable stream.

Even if I survive it will be as a cripple. Before pushing us out, Bakka will first cut an ear off everyone. Devi and Kumari will also have a breast chopped off. Perhaps he will also break one of my legs. What if all the others are killed and I survive! I will commit suicide. I know how to. Somewhere here there must be a rope. What if I am killed and the others live? Mother will surely kill herself. Or she will become mad. She will go around asking, have you seen my Biru? My innocent, naive Biru? What will probably happen is that we will all die and only Kumari will be left alive. Bakka will take her as his wife. Or as his slave. He will change her name. Sakina or Hafiza. I like Muslim names and Muslim women. When Bakka comes to kill me I will say, don't kill me I like Muslim names and Muslim women. He will be so surprised by my courage that his uplifted hand will remain suspended in air. I'll say, I am half a Muslim. When I hear the call for prayers from the mosque I shiver all over. He will think I am making fun of Islam but I am really telling the truth. . . .

The killer will agree that I am a Muslim at heart. But this will not stop him from striking. If I was in love with a Muslim girl would I have converted for her sake? I certainly would have become a Muslim if she had asked. Lovers have faith not religion. . . .

The accounting will start once it is morning. The counting of corpses. How many Hindus, how many Sikhs. There must be a few Muslims too. The intention of killing ten of us for every one of them. On the other side (the Muslims would say) so many of ours were killed, why so few of them here? There they took out processions of our naked women, why has that not happened here? Strip off the clothes of their women! Tear apart their bodies too. In front of their men. And then parade them in the bazaar! In front of their impotent men! At least they will learn to fear God! There, we hear, they cut off the breasts of our women, their hair too. We also will not let them get away intact. Chop one off everyone! Shave their heads! And then kick them in the arse! These are the ones who would not let us touch them. they would not eat from our hands. Now force them to eat everything. Stuff it into their mouths! And say, go to your Hindustan! Why are so few orphans here? Why are the heaps of rubble so small? Do not rest till all these accounts are settled. Avenge blood with blood! For a hurled brick, retaliate with a stone! Take vengeance on the son for the deeds of the father!. . . .

And this cycle will continue, for centuries. It is better if it remains dark. Because the darkness of the day will be unbearable. Because when morning comes no one will be ashamed. No one will embrace. No one will console.[7]

Territory and Passion

The Partition violence is commonly agreed to have been the most momentous event in the shaping of Hindu-Muslim relations in independent India. It is not as commonly recognized that it may not have been the memories of this violence which have been passed down through the generations—traumatic as the violence was in its scale and intensity—but the *division* of the country into two states of India and Pakistan which has had the stronger psychological impact on many Hindus. The Partition of India sharpened, if not gave birth to, the distinction between the secularist and the nationalist Hindu. As often happens, even for the same set of memories, the lessons drawn were quite contradictory. The secularist looked confidently to the country's future polity once this regrettable business of dividing the country was over. One of the most respected political figures of the post-Independence era, Jai Prakash Narain, argued that it had been like two brothers fighting for separation. Once the separation had taken place and the parental assets were divided, the brothers would live in amity and fraternal harmony.[8] The secularist was convinced that the burning embers of the Partition conflagration were permanently extinguished. Its memories were gone forever and perhaps existed only in the nightmares of an older generation which would soon disappear. 'It can never happen again,' was the common refrain in the first 20 years after Independence. The gates to religious violence were securely locked, and the riots which took place occasionally were regarded like the fall of small pebbles in the aftermath of the big landslide. Men of goodwill among both Hindu and Muslims echoed the poet Iqbal's famous line, 'Religion does not teach mutual enmity.' Others maintained that it was only because of the machinations of the British that the Partition riots took the gruesome turn that they did.

Most of all, the secularist pinned hopes about the end of Hindu-Muslim conflict on economic development. The stand taken by Nehru, which for many years produced a remarkable consensus within India's political class and the Westernized intelligentsia fascinated by Marxism, was that industrialization of the country and the spread of the 'scientific temper' through modern education would undermine the religious outlook of the people and consolidate secular values. Implied in this 'modernity project'—a catch-all term for political democracy, scientific rationality, and philosophical individualism—were the notions that the tasks of economic development would absorb all the energies of the people, and any conflicts which arose as a consequence of this enterprise would be taken care of by the democratic processes.

For the Hindu nationalist, politically weak till the remarkable ascent of the Bharatiya Janta Party (BJP) and its Hindutva movement in the last few years, the Partition, with Jinnah's Muslim League successfully insisting on a separate state for the Muslims, was the final proof that Hindus and Muslims were really two different nations as Jinnah had claimed. There was a basic opposition between Islam and Indian nationalism, and, given the right circumstances, Indian Muslims will want yet another separate state for themselves. As we shall see later, 'They [the Muslims] want to create another Pakistan', is an emotionally powerful appeal in contemporary Hindu nationalist discourse.

There was, of course, a third Hindu, probably in a large majority till at least a few years ago. This was the indifferent Hindu for whom the Hindu-Mulsim problem and the national identity question were simply not salient. Such Hindus continued to live in their faith with a traditional indifference—often confused with tolerance— toward the Other sharing their space, whether the Other was the Mussulman or the Isai (Christian).

National identities, we are told by political scientists, can be based on several defining principles of collective belonging: territory (e.g., Switzerland), ethnicity (e.g., Japan), religion (e.g., Pakistan), and ideology (e.g., the United States).[9] Although territory is invariably a part of the idea of the nation-state, it does not have to be the defining principle in all cases. For instance, the notions of ethnicity in Germany or religion in Iran evoke greater political passions than territory. In India, the political scientist Ashutosh Varshney suggests, for both the secularist and the Hindu nationalist, the defining principle in the idea of national identity is territory; 'national unity' and 'territorial integrity' are thus highly charged phrases in the Indian political discourse.[10] In the secular imagination, the territorial notion of India, emphasized for 2500 years since the times of the *Mahabharata*, is of a land stretching from he Himalayas in the north to Kanya Kumari (Cape Comorin) in the south, from the Arabian Sea in the west to the Bay of Bengal in the east. These boundaries are coterminous with the 'sacred geography' of the Hindu nationalist whose hallowed pilgrimage sites mark off essentially the same boundaries of the country, although the Hindu nationalist would go back much further into mythic history than two and a half millennia to date the origin of these sites. Varshney remarks:

> Since the territorial principle is drawn from a belief in ancient heritage, encapsulated in the notion of 'sacred geography,' and it also figures in both imaginations [secularist and nationalist], it has acquired political hegemony over time. It is the only thing common between the two competing nationalist imaginations. Therefore, just as America's most passionate political moments concern freedom and equality, India's most explosive moments concern its 'sacred geography', the 1947

partition being the most obvious example. Whenever the threat of another break-up, another 'partition', looms large, the moment unleashes remarkable passions in politics. Politics based on this imagination is quite different from what was seen when Malaysia and Singapore split from each other, or when the Czech and Slovak republics separated. Territory not being such an inalienable part of their national identity, these territorial divorces were not desecrations. In India, they become desecrations of the sacred geography.[11]

Later we shall look in some detail at the psychological processes involved in the arousal of political passions around the issue of territorial integrity which, the Hindu revivalist seeks to convince the indifferent Hindu, is under grave threat from all Indian Muslims and not just from those clamouring for secession in Kashmir.

Profile of a Riot

As I now look back at the Partition riots, I am aware that perhaps there are very few people who reflect on the past with the professional historian's perspective. For most of us, as the sociologists Howard Schuman and J. Scott have remarked, it is only the intersection of personal and national history that provides the most vital and remembered connection to the times we have lived through.[12] If the Partition is a significant source of collective memory it is only because the origin of a nation is emotionally a particularly charged time. As Maurice Halbwachs has observed, not all emotion-provoking events are memorable, only those which require considerable psychological adaptation.[13] The Partition events were not only unique and provoked strong emotional reactions but also required profound changes in the behaviour and beliefs of those affected by them.

Yet the memory of the deep experiences of those days grows dim as I write, like a dream which loses its experiential charge even as it is recollected and retold. Recollections of all I have heard and read about other Hindu-Muslim riots come rushing in to make my unique event part of a category, with the dulling of individual detail and highlighting of similarities which mark the birth of a category.

As a category, communal riots in India differ from other kinds of riots— student riots, caste riots, language riots, agricultural and labour rioting—in that they are the most violent and most difficult to control. They are the most virulent because the particular conflict, generally a blend of religious, political and economic aims, becomes imbued with religious ultimacy. In other words, the issues at stake become life and death issues through an arsenal of ideational and ritual symbols. Moreover, as we saw in the last chapter, both Hindu and Muslim religious cultures have a long tradition in specifying 'the enemy' and, as in other religious cultures, their violent champions have an acceptable, even admired rationale for the violence unleashed in 'defence'. Communal riots also differ from other riots in that they rarely remain confined to one location so that within a few days or (given the speed and reach of modern communications) hours, they can engulf many parts of the country.

Leaving aside the difficult and contested question of their ultimate cause, the eruption of a riot is always expected and yet takes everyone by surprise, By eruption I do not mean that a riot is spontaneous and involves no degree of planning or preparation, but only that it generally takes place after a considerable degree of tension between the two communities has been built up. To change the metaphor, the riot is then the bursting of a boil, the eruption of pus, of 'bad blood' between Hindus and Muslims which has accumulated over a few days or even weeks in a particular location. In some cities and towns—Ahmedabad and Hyderabad come immediately to mind—where the boil is a festering sore, the tension never really disappears but remains at an uncomfortable level which is below that of violent eruption.

Besides the ultimate cause, then, a riot has a period of *immediate tension* and a *precipitating incident* which have received much less attention than the more glamorous search for 'ultimate' causes. The build-up of immediate tension occurs when religious identities come to the forefront because of a perceived threat to this particular social identity. The threat, a collective distortion of the meaning of a real event, makes members of the community demonstratively act through words and actions as Hindus, or as Muslims. In turn, the demonstration of this religious identity threatens members of the other community who, too, begin to mobilize their identity around their religious affiliation. Thus begins a spiral of perceived (or misperceived) threats and reactive counterpostures which raises the tension between Hindus and Muslims. To give examples from some major riots: The recent demolition of the Babri mosque was perceived as a threat to Muslim religious identity—a chain of mental associations leading from the razing of an unused mosque to the disappearance of Islam in India—which was then openly demonstrated against and, in turn, reacted to by a further consolidation and demonstration of a militant Hindu identity. The 1969 riot in Ahmedabad was preceded by a period of tension when members of the Rashtriya Swayamsevak Sangh (RSS) began a campaign demanding the 'Indianization' of Muslims and thus initiating a similar chain of mental associations and actual events. We saw that the threat to Hindus is generally around the issue of the country's territorial integrity which the Muslim seems to threaten either through a demonstrative identification with pan-Islamic causes or in the demand for a separate cultural identity, expressed through the insistence on maintaining Islamic personal law or in demanding a greater role for Urdu. Here the Hindu distortion of the threat takes place through an associative chain where such Muslim actions are imagined as precursors to a separate Muslim enclave, the creation of another Pakistan and, ultimately, the dreaded revival of medieval Muslim rule. For instance, the immediate tension which led to the Ranchi riots in 1967 was initiated by the state government's plan to raise the official status of Urdu which was perceived by the Hindus as a step down the road of Muslim separatism.

'Tension', of course, is too general a term to convey more than the most superficial of meanings. We need to further explore the contents and processes of this 'tension' in our specific context of Hindu-Muslim rioting. What happens in the period of tension is that individuals increasingly think of themselves as Hindus or Muslims. In the more psychological language of the 'social identification' theory, associated with Henri Tajfel and his coworkers, when group salience becomes high, an individual thinks and behaves in conformity with the stereotypical characteristics of the category 'Hindu' (or 'Muslim') rather than according to his or her individual personality dispositions.[14] In a period of rising social tension, social identity dominates, if it does not altogether replace, personal identity as individuals perceive members of the Other group purely in terms of the former. As Hindu and Muslims increasingly see each other as stereotypes, there follows an inevitable homogenization and depersonalization. Individual Hindus or Muslims become interchangeable, perceiving each other in terms of shared category characteristics rather than their personal, idiosyncratic natures. Conversations couched in terms of group categories increase markedly: 'Look at what the Hindus are doing!' 'The Muslims have crossed all limits!' The stereotypes attributed to one's own and the adversarial group, we shall see later, take their shape from popular history, orally transmitted through generations.

The immediate tension at the eve of the riot is not merely a matter of cognitive functioning according to a social identity. The tension is also constituted of strong affects and emotions, 'raw passions' if one will. The somewhat bloodless formulations of social identity theory are not completely sufficient to explain a process which will end up being so bloody. Here we need to add psychoanalytic insights on the intertwining of the individual and the group from earliest childhood onward and a revival of the associated emotions in the current situation.

In the first years of life, it is only gradually that the child learns to integrate dichotomous 'good' and 'bad' images of the self—the angry and the loving baby—as well as opposing representations of caretakers who both gratify and frustrate. The child also learns that to have hostile impulses directed toward those on whom it depends is dangerous to its own well-being and that these negative feelings must be disowned. One of the main ways of disowning 'bad', hateful representations is to externalize them, first on to inanimate objects or animals and then to people and other groups. In a given cultural group, mothers and other adults usually offer the same targets of externalization, or 'reservoirs', as the psychiatrist Vamik Volkan calls them.[15] The Hindu (and associated cultural symbols) is thus an emotionally charged target of externalization for the Muslim's own 'bad' representations and angry feelings (and vice versa) from an early period of life, a convenient reservoir also for the subsequent rages which grow out of thwarted needs and private hurts. Together with this creation of the enemy, which is neither 'merely' real nor 'merely' projection',[16] there is also a process of identification with one's group taking place. The child is assimilating within itself images of family and group members, thus coming to resemble them more and more while increasing its emotional investment in the group's shared symbols and traditions.

In the period of immediate tension, when the salience of one's religious-cultural group increases markedly, the feelings of love connected with the early identifications revive, as do the hate and rage associated with the targets of externalization. Since the enemy is also a reservoir of our own unwanted selves and negative feelings, it is important it be kept at a psychological distance. Consciously, the enemy should never be like us. Even minor differences between 'us' and 'them' are therefore exaggerated as unbridgeable chasms in what Freud called the 'narcissism of minor differences'[17] which evoke stronger hostility and hate than do wide disparities. There is a special quality to the enmity I feel for a person who resembles me most but is not me. Next to my brother, it is my neighbour the Ten Commandments enjoin me to love as I do myself, precisely because my neighbour is the one I am most likely to consider as a rival. The stereotyping of the enemy group involves a progressive devaluation which can extend to the point of dehumanization where 'they' come close to the child's earliest, nonhuman targets of externalization. Making the enemy nonhuman is to avoid feeling guilt about destroying 'it' in the riot that is imminent.

To summarize: the heightened salience of social identity, fuelled by a revival of strong childhood emotions that arise from the intertwining of the self and the cultural group, together with the fact that the groups involved are religious ones, thus imbuing the conflict with religious ultimacy, are the distinctive markers of the tension immediately preceding a riot.

Among the various precipitating incidents, there are two which occur with such regularity in reports of riots that they may fairly be called archetypes. One of them has to do with Muslim violence toward the cow while the other pertains to disputes over religious processions. Whereas riots around the former are specific to India, riots provoked by religious processions have been common in the history of religious violence.[18] Both incidents are archetypal in the sense that, irrespective of their factual veracity in a particular case, they are perceived as legitimate causes for violence to begin—shots from the starter's gun, so to speak. There is thus an unarticulated expectation that an incident around a cow or a religious procession should belong to the account of a Hindu-Muslim riot even if such an incident did not actually take place. Historically speaking, this expectation is not unjustified. Consider, for instance, the precipitating incidents of communal riots in the Punjab in a single year in the last century.

In 1886, riots occured in Ambala, Ludhiana, Hoshiarpur, and Delhi. In Ambala, the precipitating incident was a change, insisted upon by the Muslims, in the route of the Hindu procession on the festival of Bawan Sawadasi. It was also widely rumoured that the Muslims intended to bring large quantities of beef into the city the next day on the occasion of Eid. In Ludhiana, the riot began with the report that a cow had been sacrificed in a Muslim's house. In Hosiarpur, the Muharram procession of the Muslims had passed a major part of its route when a bull suddenly appeared amidst it. The processionists were already involved in an argument with the Hindus over the entanglement of the *tazia* in the branches of a *pipal* tree, held sacred by the Hindus, which the Muslims wanted to cut. The Hindus objected to the Muslims' beating of the bull and the riot was on. In Delhi, the riots began with the clash between Muslim and Hindu processions whose routes crossed each other.[19] It is thus not surprising to read 80 years later that one of the worst riots of post-Independence India, the 1969 riot in Ahmedabad, was set off by a Muslim vegetable seller who hit a cow which had stopped at its stand for a munch. Fisticuffs with the Hindu cowherd followed and 'the treatment of the cow (which was not seriously injured), greatly magnified out of all proportion, spread through the city and touched off further incidents. The rioting continued in various parts of Gujarat for some ten days.'[20]

The precipitating incident is immediately followed by the aggrieved group taking out a procession—when the procession itself is not the incident. A procession is necessary for the creation of what I call a 'physical' group. A physical group is a group represented in the bodies of its members rather than in their minds, a necessary shift for a group to become an instrument of actual violence. For if we reflect on our own experiences of various groups we become immediately aware of a significant difference between, say, my experience of my cultural identity as a Hindu and my psychic processes when I am taking part in a religious assembly. In other words, belonging to a relatively abstract entity, the Hindu, touches a very different chord of the self than the one touched by being a member of a physical group, such as a tightly packed congregation in a Hindu temple. The self-experience of the latter is determined more by concrete, bodily communication and physical sensations in the press of other bodies. The self-experience of the cultural-group identity, on the other hand, is evoked more, and differently, by shared cultural symbols and history—heavily mythological—which is shaped by the group's hopes and fears and distorted by its ambitions and ideals.

The information I receive sensorially and sensually, linguistically and subliminally in a physical group and which influences the experience of my self at that particular moment, is of another order, and is processed differently, than the information received as member of a cultural group. In a crowd—an example of a physical group—the very nature of the situation with many people in close bodily contact brings a considerable sensual stimulation through channels of touch, vision, hearing, and smell which are simultaneous and are intensified by the multiplicity of their sources.[21] There is also a communication of body heat, muscle tensions, and, sometimes, of body rhythms. The individual is practically wrapped up in the crowd and gets continuous sensual pounding through all the avenues that his body can afford. The consequence is a blurring of the body image and of the ego, a kind of self-transcendence that is reacted to by panic or exhilaration as individuality disappears and the 'integrity', 'autonomy', and 'independence' of the ego seem to be wishful illusions and mere hypothetical constructs. That the physical and cultural groups sometimes coincide and that it is the endeavour of those who use and manipulate symbols of cultural identity to bring the cultural group closer to the psychological state of a physical group is a subject which I will not pursue here.

I do not find the argument convincing that, as personal identity disappears in a crowd, the residue is some regressed, primitive state where the violent side of human nature is unleashed, as has been postulated in both the Freudian and the Jungian traditions. Such formulations need to be relativized and seen in the context and framework of a particular place and period in history—Europe between the two World Wars—when extremist ideologues of the Left and Right were creating mass movements imbued with messianic fervour. Building on the classical notions of crowds described by Gustave Le Bon (whose own ideas, in turn, were framed by the dread the French upper classes felt in relation to the revolutionary masses), Freud's reflections on the psychology of crowds as well as Jung's observations on mass psychology were not free of the ideological concerns of their time, namely the liberal fear of the loss of individual autonomy in a collectivity and the socialist concern about how to make the desired collectivities more tolerable and tolerant.

Identity in a crowd only gets refocused.[22] This refocusing is certainly dramatic and full of affect since a crowd amplifies all emotions, heightening a feeling of well-being into exaltation, fear into panic. The loss of personal identity in a crowd, however, makes individuals act in terms of the crowd's identity, for instance, according to the behaviour 'expected' of an anti-Hindu or anti-Muslim mob. The individual is not operating at some deeply regressed, primitive level of the psyche but according to the norms of the particular group. The violent acts are thus not random but represent the expression and adaptation to a novel situation of a historical tradition of anti-Hindu or anti-Muslim mob violence.

It is paradoxical that religious processions, presumably with spiritual aims, perhaps produce the most physical of all groups. Rhythms of religious ritual are particularly effective in breaking down social barriers between the participants. The produce a maximum of mutual activation of the participants and a readiness for action, often violent. This is why violence, when Muslim-initiated, often begins at the end of Friday afternoon prayers when congregants, who have turned into a congregation, stream out of the mosque into the street in a protesting procession. Processions at Muharram for the Muslims and Dussehra (and increasingly Ganesh Chaturthi) for the Hindus are almost a certain recipe for violence when they are preceded by a period of tension between the communities and when a precipitating incident has just occurred.

Whereas internally a procession must transform itself into a physical group, externally it should demonstrate the community's strength. As the political scientist Sarah Moore points out, the success of the procession depends not only upon the number of people taking part but also on the route it takes.[23] Routes are valued differently. To take a procession near or through an area inhabited by the adversary is more valued than taking a route which avoids potential confrontations. A procession which can pass through known trouble spots and major traffic arteries is considered more successful than one which slinks through back alleys. The number of chaperoning policemen, protecting processions which are going to cause the very trouble the police are trying to prevent, is another indicator of success.

Normally, the first two to three days of a major riot are the most violent when a majority of the casualties take place. As the police regain control of the situation, the riot settles down to a low-level intensity of violence. Isolated incidents of stabbing, looting, and arson take place in the narrow alleys and twisting bylanes rather than in the major bazaars. Gradually, peace returns, although some kind of curfew and orders prohibiting the gathering of more than five persons may remain in force for many weeks. The official end of the riot is marked by the state appointing a commission of inquiry headed by a retired judge who is asked to detemine the sequence of events leading up to the riot, name those who were responsible, tally the losses, and offer suggestions to prevent future riots. The sole result of such an inquiry, besides offering temporary employment to he judge, is the transfer of a few hapless police officers who are held culpable for not having taken adequate precautions. Police officers, of course only the dishonest, have long since calculated the monetary value of this occupational risk and have made it a part of the compensation they feel entitled to, above and beyond the miserly salary they are paid by the state.

Hyderabad: December 1990

The Hyderabad riot of December 1990, the central event of my study, occured after a period of relative peace between the Hindus and Muslims, the last riot in the city having taken place in 1984. Before that, riots had been an annual feature since 1978, the year of the first major communal conflagration since 1948 when Hyderabad became a part of independent India.

The 1978 riot was triggered off by the rape of a Muslim woman. Rameeza Bi, and the murder of her husband, Ahmed Hussian, in the Nallakunta police station. In the beginning the mobs protesting police brutality included Hindus, but soon the situation took a turn where the two communities became pitted against each other. The incident sparking off the antagonistic postures was, as usual, the tiniest of sparks: some Hindus beat up a Muslim boy, the Muslims retaliated, the Hindus retaliated against the retaliation, and so on in an ever increasing escalation. The riots were centred around Subzimandi, the central vegetable market, which is also one of the two locations of this study. Given the general propensity of the students of Hindu-Muslim relations to explain the violence between the two in economic terms, the hidden agenda of these riots is said to be an economic offensive by the Muslims designed to recapture Subzimandi from Hindu traders.[24] Destitute for almost three decades, most of the wealthier members of their community having migrated to Pakistan or other countries, the Muslims of the old city had suddenly come into money through remittances from the Arab countries of the Gulf, where the economic boom in the late Seventies had created a big market for Muslim labour from Hyderabad. After having suffered a rapid economic decline within a decade of Hyderabad's integration with India, the Muslims again sought to regain control of the city's vegetable trade which they had lost to the Hindus.

After 1978, there was at least a riot a year, sometimes more, usually at the time of major religious festivals. The tension in the city is especially palpable during Ganesh Chaturthi of the Hindus, when clay idols of the Hindu god are taken out in procession through the streets to be immersed in the Musi river, and Muharram of the Muslims, when the Shias march through the city bewailing the martyrdom of Hussein, the Prophet's grandson. The riots also erupted on many other pretexts: Hindu shopkeepers refusing to close their shops in the strikes called by the Majlis (to protest against the takeover of the Kaaba in Mecca by a man claiming to be the Mehdi), the burning of the Al Aqsa mosque in Jerusalem, the removal of a chief minister perceived as sympathetic to one community. Between 1978 and 1984, over 400 people lost their lives and thousands more were injured in the communal riots. A common thread in some of these riots (as in riots elsewhere) is the assumption of the state's role by the mobs of one or the other community. Like the 16th-century Catholic-Protestant riots in France described by Natalie Davis, the Hindu or Muslim mob perceives itself as doing what the state should have done in the first place; it is helping the political authorities get over their failure in fulfilling their duties, thus providing itself with a certain legitimacy.[25]

Coming back to the 1990 violence, the countdown for the Hyderabad riot began when L.K. Advani, the president of the Bharatiya Janata Party (BJP), began his *rath yatra* from the temple of Somnath on the west coast to Ayodhya in the Hindi heartland of the north. The stated purpose of the *yatra*, which was to take Advani through a large part of the country in 30 days and over 10,000 kilometers, was the construction of the Rama temple at the legendary birth site of the god where stood a mosque constructed in 1456 by the founder of the Mughal dynasty. The Toyota van in which the BJP leader travelled was decorated to make it resemble the chariot of the legendary hero Arjuna, as shown in the immensely popular television serial of the *Mahabharata*. Advani's chariot aroused intense fervour among the Hindus. Crowds thronged the roads to catch a glimpse of the *rath*, showered flower petals on the cavalcade as it passed through their villages and towns, and the vehicle itself became a new object of worship as women offered ritual prayer with coconut, burning incense, and sandalwood paste at each of its stops. In a darker, more sombre aftermath, there were incidents of violence between Hindus and Muslims at many places in the wake of the *rath yatra*.

Like a pond choked with lotus stalks during the monsoon, this religious-political exercise was replete with symbols. The symbolism began with the 'chariot': a large lotus, the symbol of the BJP, was painted on the front grill of the Toyota. The painted lotus and the chariot is one of the most Hindu of the universal symbols and is ubiquitous in India's religious iconography. Various lotuses are associated with different gods and goddesses, e.g., the eight-petaled lotus is the dwelling place of Brahma. The lotus on the van—the chariot—was therefore highly significant. In the Hindu mind, influenced by tales from the *Mahabharata* and the visuals of popular poster and calender art, the chariot is the vehicle of gods and mythical heroes going to war. Above all, the chariot is associated with Arjuna, with Lord Krishna as his charioteer, as he prepares for a just, *dharmic* war against an evil though intimately related foe, the Kauravas. Arjuna's horses were white, signifying his purity; Advani's Toyota-chariot, which the newspapers were soon to call the 'Juggernaut of Hindutva,' was also white.

Somnath, the starting point of the *yatra* and the location of an ancient Shiva temple, is also the greatest symbol of Hindu defeat and humiliation at the hands of Muslims. The legend of Somnath, which has entered Hindu folklore over large parts of the country, tells us that in the 11th century Somnath was the richest and the most magnificent temple of Hindu India. One thousand Brahmins were appointed to perform the daily worship of the emblem of Shiva, 13½ foot *lingam*, four-and-a-half feet in circumference. Three hundred men and women were employed to sing and dance before the lingam every day and the temple treasury possessed vast riches in gold, silver, and precious gems, accumulated over the centuries. Mahmud, the sultan of the central Asian kingdom of Ghazni, who swept over the north India almost every year like a monsoon of fire and was famed far and wide as the great destroyer of temples and a scourge of the Hindus, came to know of the Hindu belief that he could destroy so many of their temples only because the deities of those temples had forfeited Somnath's support. With a view to strike at the very root of the Hindus' faith in their gods, and tempted by the prospect of plundering the temple's treasures, Mahmud marches to Somnath. The Hindus were complacent in their belief that Shiva had drawn Mahmud to Somnath only to punish the sultan for his depredations. Hoping for a manifestation of Shiva's divine wrath, the Hindu resistance to Mahmud was unorganized and offered much too late. According to legend, hundreds of thousands of Hindus perished in the ensuing slaughter—50,000, according to nationalist historians. The temple was razed to the ground. The Shiva *lingam* was broken to pieces and together with the temple's plundered treasure transported to Ghazni where its fragments were fashioned into steps at the gate of the chief mosque. The Hindu historian, acknowledging Mahmud's skill as a general and the fact that Muslim chroniclers regard him as one of the most illustrious kings and a great champion of Islam, adds: 'By his ruthless destruction of temples and images he violated the most sacred and cherished sentiments of the Indian people, and his championship of Islam therefore merely served to degrade it in their eyes such as nothing else could.'[26] Somnath and Mahmud of Ghazni have become intimately associated over the following centuries. Today, among Hindus, the name of the temple conjures up less the image of Shiva than the memory of one of the most rapacious and cruel of Muslim invaders. In choosing to start the *rath yatra* from Somnath, the symbolic reverberations of the act were well calculated; the righteous Hindu chariot was setting forth to avenge ancient humiliations, to right old historical wrongs.

For the Hindus, Somnath is indeed what Volkan calls a 'chosen trauma', just as the demolition of the Babri mosque at Ayodha in December 1992 fairly bids to become one of the chosen traumas of the Indian Muslim.[27] The term 'chosen trauma' refers to an event which causes a community to feel helpless and victimized by another and whose mental representation becomes embedded in the group's collective identity. Chosen trauma does not mean that either the Hindus or the Muslims chose to become victims but only that they have 'chosen' to mythologize, psychologically internalize, and thus constantly dwell upon a particular event from their history. A chosen trauma is reactivated again and again to strengthen a group's cohesiveness through 'memories' of its persecution, victimization, and yet its eventual survival. In the late 19th centry, Swami Vivekananda had 'remembered' Somnath thus: 'Mark how these temples bear the marks of a hundred attacks and hundred regenerations continually springing up out of the ruins rejuvenated and strong as ever.'[28] At the beginning of the last decade of the 20th century, Advani was to summon up the Hindu chosen trauma again from the depths of cultural memory.

If the *yatra* began in Somnath it was symbolically symmetrical for it to end in Ayodhya, the birthplace and capital of the kingdom of Lord Rama and thus the site of the Hindu's chosen glory. For many Hindus, the story of Rama is the most resplendent moment of India's history. The revival of its memory, commemorated annually in the Ram Lila, makes the collective chest swell with pride. The chosen glory, too, is psychologically internalized and is as salient for a group's cultural identity as its chosen trauma; both constitute landmarks on the terrain of a group's cultural memory.

Advani's cavalcade, of symbols as much as of people, came to a halt when on 23 October he was arrested in Bihar before he could start on the last lap of his journey to Ayodhya, where the BJP and its allied organizations, the *sangh parivar*, had promised to start the construction of the Rama temple on 9 November. The already high political passions were now nearing the point of explosion. The spark was provided by the chief minister of Uttar Pradesh Mulayam Singh Yadav, who had vowed that to prevent the construction of the temple he would not 'let even a bird enter Ayodhya'. The well-oiled machine of the *sangh parivar*, however, had succeeded in smuggling in thousands of *kar-sevaks* from all over the country for the task of construction. On 9 November, Yadav ordered the police to open fire on the *kar-sevaks* who had broken through the police barriers and were intent on the demolition of the Babri mosque as a prelude to the building of the temple.

Scores of *kar-sevaks* died in the police firing. Their bodies were cremated on the banks of the river Saryu and the ashes taken back by the BJP workers to the villages and towns in different parts of the country from which the dead men hailed. There they were eulogized as martyrs to the Hindu cause. Soon, Hindu-Muslim riots erupted in many parts of the country.

In Hyderabad, more than a thousand miles to the south of Ayodhya, the riots began with the killing of Sardar, a Muslim auto-rickshaw driver, by two Hindus. Although the murder was later linked to a land dispute between two rival gangs, at the time of the killing it was framed in the context of rising Hindu-Muslim tensions in the city. Muslims retaliated by stabbing four Hindus in different parts of the walled city. Then Majid Khan, an influential local leader of Subzimandi who lives and flourishes in the shaded space formed by the intersection of crime and politics, was attacked with a sword by some BJP workers and the rumour spread that he had died. Muslim mobs came out into the alleys and streets of the walled city, to be followed by Hindu mobs in their areas of strength, and the 1990 riot was on. It was to last for ten weeks, claim more than 300 lives and thousands of wounded. One of the wounded was the two-year-old girl in the photograph.

3

THE WARRIORS

....In my heart there are furies and sorrows.
Quevodo

Majid Khan survived the attack. When I met him two-and-a-half years later, he was especially keen to show me the scar from the sword blow which had split his balding head in the middle. The thick ragged scar, many shades darker than the nut-brown scalp it traversed before meandering down into the fringe of wispy black hair at the back of his neck, was displayed as a proud badge of honour, a battlefield decoration from an old war. The murderous assault had made him, as Majid Khan put it,'the hero of Hyderabad'. 'Thousands of people gathered at the hospital when they heard the news about the attack,' he recollected with pride as he looked in the direction of two young men in the room for their choral confirmation. 'Thousands every day,' the men obligingly responded. 'Nothing united the Muslim nation of this city as much as that cowardly blow,' said Majid Khan. 'Absolutely true. Hyderabad has never seen anything like it before,' both the men confirmed, this time with greater enthusiasm as they warmed up to their roles.

I took the men, in their early 30s, to be his *chamchas*, the fawning, all-purpose factotums who hang around politicians and film stars, catering to their physical and especially to their narcissistic needs. Majid Khan was not yet a political star of the kind who would be surrounded by a whole group, by what I would call a *katori* (cup), the modest local version of the *coterie* which has traditionally built up around prime ministers.

Majid Khan's political fortunes have nonetheless soared since the riots, and the visiting card he gave me was testimony to his importance in the Majlis. Printed in English, his name in cursive red letters riding many lines of different-sized letters in green, like the miniature flag of a new Islamic nation, the card informed me that Abdul Majid Khan was a council member of the all India Majlis-e-Itehad-ul-Muslimeen, a director of Sarussalam Urban Cooperative Bank, had two telephone numbers and a residential adderess in Karwan Sahu, the part of the city where he owned a house and an eatery (which may be called a restaurant but which is respectfully referred to as a hotel.)

I think we took him by surprise when we walked unannounced into the anteroom of his house around 11 in the morning of a hot, late April day. If he was inconvenienced by our intrusion, his deep-set eyes in a dark round face did not betray annoyance. Interrupting his conversation with the *chamchas* to greet us warmly, he inquired about Sahba's health and expressed his great pleasure in seeing her again, before turning to me in courteous regard. A middle-aged, barrel-chested man of medium height, with a short thick neck that took its function of joining the head to the trunk more seriously than of separating the two, Majid Khan, even in his undervest and crumpled green-and-black checked lungi, dominated the room with a miasma of raw power. One of the walls of the room was covered with mounted black-and-white photographs which showed him garlanding state and national politicians and being garlanded in turn by more local ones. As expected, the tall, cadaverous leader of the party, Sultan Owaisi, was a gravely benign presence in most of the photographs. Another wall was fully papered by over by coloured, grainy photographs of a wooden Swiss chalet standing at the edge of an icy cool stream and outlined against an impossibly blue sky, the colour of the sky highlighted by two fluffy light grey clouds. Spring trees cast dark velvet shadows on sun-dappled grass. Plump European cows with silky sheens and pink udders grazed in the gently rolling meadow. Outside, the morning was steadily getting hotter. The temperature had crossed the 100 degree mark, yet the boiling sun had only begun its inexorable ascent.

Majid Khan's discomfort as we exchanged further courtesies while he inquired about the purpose of my visit, was not due to the heat or the sheen of perspiration on his bald scalp that periodically coalesced into large drops of sweat which then trickled down his forehead. He seemed to be more bothered by the informality of his attire and our meeting place. For someone aspiring to be a political figure of more than local significance, Majid Khan naturally wanted to present himself in more appropriate surroundings and suitably dressed for the role. Excusing himself, he asked one of his men to take us to the party office located about a hundred yards from his house above his restaurant where we were to wait for him.

The office itself was spanking new but looked bare and unused. Along one wall, painted in what I have come to regard as Hyderabad blue, there was a brown rexine-covered sofa. The only other furniture was a table with a formica top and a white plastic cane chair. The sofa, the table, and the chair were covered with a fine layer of dust. There were no cupboard, boxes of files, pens, pencils, paperclips, notepades, or other paraphernalia which bespeak of an office where work is done. We were asked by our companion to step into the adjoining room which was more luxuriously, even garishly appointed, in a lower-class fantasy of aristrocratic splendour as shaped by Hindi cinema. The peach-coloured plush-covered sofa could easily seat six while the divan, with two cylindrical pillows encased in dark pink satin covers and in an exultant floral design, was equally spacious. A gleaming new Mirzapur carpet in loud blue with an intricate dark red Persian motif covered the full area of the floor. Majid's man politely asked us if we would care to look at the Sahib's photographs, an offer we accepted with equal politeness. The man came back after a few mintues, carrying two bulging cardboard shoe boxes and followed by a younger man, the *chamcha's chamcha*, bearing two bottles of cold lemonade. As we sipped the oversweet lemonade, we were taken on a photographic tour of Majid Khan's life which highlighted his political career and the social status he had achieved. There was genuine awe and admiration in the *chamcha's* voice as he pointed out the burly figure of his patron in various situations: here he is in the welcoming committee receiving the former Chief Minister Sahib, there he is next to Sultan Sahib in the reception for the Governor Sahib, there he is in the front of the group garlanding Sultan Sahib at the opening ceremony of the bank.

As we murmured our involvement with subdued 'oohs!', 'ahs!' and increasing 'uh-huhs!' Majid Khan came into the room followed by one of the young men we had earlier met at his home. Majid Khan was now clad in the politician's uniform of fresh, lightly starched white kurta-pyjamas and matching white leather sandals. He apologized elaborately for keeping us waiting and then took out a remote control device from his pocket with which he tried to switch on the vertical fan standing next to the divan. The blades completed one full circle before coming to a halt. The remote control button was pressed again and the fan made another effort. This was repeated a couple of times before an almost imperceptible nod to the *chamcha* galvanized him into switching on the fan manually. During the play with the fan, Majid Khan kept on talking to the young man about how everything was now sorted out with the police and that there was no longer any cause for concern. I had the distinct feeling that this conversation had already taken place earlier in the house and on the way to the office. It seemed to me that the highlights were now being repeated for our benefit; Majid Khan was introducing himself. Without appearing to be overtly boastful, he was conveying through the conversation the extent of his power, the breadth of his concern, and the degree of his importance in the life of his community and the mohalla where he lived. Someone, it seems, had reported to the police that a bomb and a revolver were hidden in a house in the neighbourhood. A police party came to Karwan in the evening, took away everyone in the house to the police station for questioning, and some of the men were roughed up. A young man, who worked in a factory, was the only member of the family who was not at home at the time of the police raid. He came running to Majid Khan for help. Majid went to the police station and arranged for the release of the young man's family, a task made easier by the fact that the house search had not yielded any weapon. After the young man left, Majid Khan procceded to deliver a lengthy monologue on the ever increasing *zulm*, the oppression of the Muslims, by the police. The *chamcha* took up the narrative by telling us of other incidents where Majid Khan had also starred as the helper and saviour of the oppressed poor, fearlessly confronting police high-handedness, facing down armed policemen who were ready to fire into Muslim crowds during a riot.

For me, it was difficult to reconcile the image of this courteous, confident man whose zeal in the service of his community could not be a total pretence, with the one projected by Hyderabad's English language newspapers and the police for whom Majid Khan was a well-known goonda. Most of the urban elite know the goonda in his caricatured form from Hindi movies as the villainous, dark-skinned, usually unshaven, solidly muscled tough in tight sweatshirts and jeans (or in a checked lungi, if Muslim), with a knotted scarf around the neck and a gold 'chain nestling in the chest fur. The Hyderabad police have a special name for them. In their records such men are listed as 'rowdies'; a rowdy, the Oxford English Dictionary informs us, is a 'rough, disorderly person; one addicted to quarrelling, fighting or disturbing the peace'. Although the word itself is of American origin, today a rowdy conjures up more the image of a British soccer fan wreaking mayhem in a European football stadium than a knife-wielding tough in the back alleys of Hyderabad. The police also call them 'history sheeters', which refers to the sheets of paper in police files where, year after year, a history of their unlawful activities is carefully recorded from the surveillance and surmise of plainclothes officers, together with the noting of arrest records and any subsequent trial verdicts.

In the mohallas where Majid Khan and others of his kind live, there are not too many who would go along with their characterization as goondas by the police and upper middleclass sentiment. Unsurprisingly, the men do not have a name for themselves, although they would prefer a descriptive phrase such as 'friend of the poor' or 'protector of the oppressed'. A name would categorize them, separate them from the rest of the community, take them out of the ocean in which they swim as big fish but nonetheless constitute a vital part of the ocean's ecology. The only name they are not reluctant to accept and which is also acceptable to others, including the police, is pehlwan. Specifically, pehlwan is a wrestler, but generally it may also mean a 'strong man'; the purpose for which the strength is employed is left ambiguous and open to the interpretation of different groups. So let me call them pehlwans (rather than goondas, hooligans, rowdies, history sheeters), whether or not they have actually trained as wrestlers or bodybuilders, although a surprisingly large number have done so. Indeed, it is the culture of traditional Indian wrestling, which I will discuss later, which has had a profound influence in the formation of their personalities and which constitutes the most distinctive marker of their identities.

Strictly speaking, then, Majid Khan is not a pehlwan although he went through a few years of training as a wrestler, the taleem, as a boy. His younger brother is the well-known Mumtaz pehlwan and many of the young men who hang around him, *his* men, are aspiring pehlwans who follow the wrestler's daily regimen. He is, though, a great admirer of the whole wrestling ethos which he feels builds character and prevents young men from going astray. He feels distressed that traditional wrestling is coming to an end in Hyderabad, and young men are drawn more to such imports as judo and karate. The Japanese martial arts are just that, arts to be picked up without the necessity of being steeped in and internalizing the culture which underlies them. The reasons for the decline of wrestling are many. Primarily, economic deterioration makes it difficult for a family to let one of their sons turn into a pehlwan, since he would then need an expensive diet of pistachios, almonds, choice cuts of meat, and litres of milk every day. Then the Hindu-Muslim tensions have led the police to ban wrestling matches in the city, since a bout between a Hindu and a Muslim wrestler can easily ignite a riot between the two commmunities. 'Only ten per cent of the pehlwans are involved in violence,' Majid said. 'In fact, becoming a pehlwan improves the character and disposition of many young men who are otherwise inclined to be violent and intemperate. When four people respectfully salute you as pehlwan as you walk down the street, you would hold your head high and wouldn't do anything to lose that respect.'

Majid describes his own role in the riots primarily in terms of a peacemaker, an older mentor with some influence on young hotheads of the Muslim community, especially in Karwan. He is generally successful in calming violent passions and excited crowds. 'It is not so easy to control these boys,' he says in mock sorrow as he indulgently smiles at the adoring young *chamcha*. 'Without any provocation, these young men are taken in by the police during a riot, who register murder cases against them. Released on bail, they come out swaggering, as if they really are killers and have become equal to the pehlwans. The police have notarized them as killers and what better credentials can they have?' Majid Khan believes a major part of his role during the riot lies in curbing young 'killers' who want to show off their killing prowess; he prevents the consolidation of a killer identity, as the psychologist would say in the discipline's language. Personally, Majid Khan said, he has never experienced any kind of blood lust even during the worst course of religious violence. This does not mean that he is some kind of a believer in nonviolence when there are riots between the Hindus and the Muslims. He is not a fanatic either way as far as violence is concerned. He has a 'healthy' attitude toward the mutual slaughter, an outlook he states as the following: 'Riots are like one-day cricket matches where the killings are the runs. You have to score at least one more than the opposing team. The whole honour of your nation (*qaum*) depends on not scoring less than the opponent.'

The other part of his role during a riot consists in liaising with the police and the administration on behalf of the community and in organizing and distributing relief supplies on behalf of his party, the Majlis. Although some accuse him of pilferage ('of ten bags of rice he keeps seven') and thus of enriching himself on the misery of others, Majid Khan is sincerely eloquent on the great human suffering caused by every riot and about his own modest efforts at its relief. I have the impression that Majid Khan feels much more comfortable talking about human suffering than violence, about the fellowship of misery than the divisions of murderous ethnocentrism. Losing loved ones, seeing one's house and meagre belongings go up in flames, the whimpering of children in hunger and fear, is a shared experience of Muslims and Hindus alike and, after all, he is talking to me, a Hindu. Talk of suffering during the riots brings the two of us closer in mutual human sympathy whereas an elaboration on the violence will divide, will keep reminding us of our potential as deadly enemies.

In an earlier meeting with Sahba, who is a Muslim, there had been an absence of constraints imposed by my alien Hindu presence, and Majid Khan had talked freely about his more Muslim sentiments. The Muslims never initiated any attacks; they only defended themselves. They are discriminated against in every field and the police oppresion is making the whole community mutinous (*baghi*). One day they will rise up to fight, even against the modern weapons of the police. After all, there are only four fighting communities in India: Sikhs, Marathas, Rajputs, and Muslims. Even badly outnumbered Muslims can hold their own against a far superior Hindu host as long as the police do not turn their guns against them. But this situation too will change. There is nothing like a riot to unite the community and strengthen its collective will for the fight ahead of it.

Testing the Tigers

The Giessen Test (*Appendix 1*) is one of the most widespread test instruments in clinical use in Germany today.[1] Constructed on psychoanalytic and psychosocial considerations, its 40 statements are divided into six scales: social response, dominance, self-control, underlying mood, permeability, and social potence. Using it to systematically tap the self-image of the pehlwans, the characteristics each ascribed to himself, I found the test to be a particularly useful interview tool which helped me gain a more comprehensive view of the 'warriors' in a relatively short period of time. The pehlwans often did not restrict themselves to just marking off an alternative on a statement but would generally elaborate, offering anecdotes from their lives as illustrations. Thus, for instance, in response to a statement, Majid Khan did not simply say, 'I am very patient' but went on to add: 'I had to learn patience, the hard way,' and then narrated an incident from his life where he had suffered because he could not control his temper.

In the first area, social response, which has to do with the person's effect on his environment—whether one is narcissistically gratified or frustrated in social interactions—Majid Khan sees himself as evoking positive responses on the social stage. He finds it easy to attract others and believes people are highly satisfied with his work. He cares greatly about looking nice and feels he has been successful in achieving his aims in life.

In the area of dominance, which on one side has to do with aggressiveness, impulsiveness, stubbornness, and authoritarian tendencies, and the other with an incapacity for aggression, patience, willingness to conform and the tendency to submit, Majid Khan comes across as particularly dominant and self-willed although he tries hard to control his impatience in public life.

As far as self-control is concerned, Majid Khan is more uncontrolled than compulsive, but not to an extent that would signal delinquency or sociopathic tendencies. It is, however, evident that Majid Khan has a problem in dealing with his aggressive impulses. He has a tendency to let out his anger easily which he struggles to control, lest it break out in episodes of unchecked rage and bouts of violence.

Although Majid lets out his anger and is not at all timid, there are strong indications of an underlying depressive mood. He tends to worry a good deal about personal problems, lets outer changes greatly affect his emotional state, and is often depressed. Coupled with his difficulties with self-control and the fact that he finds it very easy to get into high spirits, I would suspect a disposition where hyperactivity compensates for and sometimes alternates with a dysphoric mood and where there is a marked tendency to blow a fuse in tense situations.

As far as permeability is concerned—the fundamental ways in which the outer world is experienced and how open or closed the person is in interaction with others—Majid Khan sees himself as very trusting and experiences strong feelings in love. Yet he also finds it very hard to come out of his shell, gives away very little of himself, and avoids getting close to another person. The fact that this is true only of personal relations and does not happen in the public sphere, where he can work well with others, would lead one to suspect disturbances in the development of his sense of basic trust and in an openness to his own feelings. It is as if the early contacts with the world were not positive, generating a fear of a hostile environment which led to a defensive closing up and guarding of the core self. I sense in Majid Khan an anxiety about being exploited and abused if he ever opened himself fully to another human being. This way, though he may remain emotionally isolated, he also cannot be destroyed by others. This hypothesis is supported by his responses to other statements in the questionnaire such as that he finds it relatively hard to feel tied to someone for long, that is, he is fearful of personal commitment. He thus comes across as someone who mimics trust and affection without deeply feeling them, something he does quite successfully in his public life since he confesses to being very good at acting and not too particular about truth.

The Violent Poet

Unlike Majid Khan, Akbar is a true pehlwan, He has been trained as a wrestler since the age of ten and comes from a family where for the last four generations the men have all been wrestlers. Among the Hindus, he is notorious as a killer while many Muslims approvingly acknowledge his role in the organization of the community's violence during the riots. Living in a large house with four wrestler brothers and their families, a widowed mother, and three wives, Akbar is a prosperous man who owns a hotel and three *taleemkhanas*, as the wrestling gymnasiums are called in Urdu. Like most other pehlwans, the chief source of his income is what the pehlwans delicately describe as 'land business'.

Baldly stated, 'land business' is one of the outcomes of India's crumbling legal system. Since landlord and tenant disputes as well as other disputes about land and property can take well over a decade to be sorted out if a redress of grievance is sought through the courts, the pehlwan is approached by one of the party. The dispute being thus 'settled' the pehlwan receives a large fee for his services. In the case of well-known pehlwans with *taleemkhanas* (or the Hindu *akharas*) and thus a large supply of young toughs as students and all-purpose assistants, land business can be very profitable. Many of the pehlwans do not need to use strong-arm methods any longer. The mere fact that a famous pehlwan like Akbar has been engaged by one of the parties is enough for the opponent to back down and reach a settlement to the dispute. In some cases, and these are on some increase, if the second party also employes a pehlwan to protect its interests, then the two pehlwans generally get together and come to a mutually satisfactory solution which, because of the fear they arouse, they can impose on their clients. Built on the threat of physical violence, overt violence is rare in this informal system where a black legality, like a black economy, runs parallel to the state's legal system, and violence occurs only when new pehlwans try to muscle into the territories of established 'tigers', as the pehlwans also like to call themselves, threatening their vital interests and inviting swift reprisals. At least among the Muslim pehlwans, Akbar is a tiger's tiger, a well-respected man who is a figure of awe for his prowess as a wrestler, success in the land business, and the high esteem in which he is held by his community. A political career is on the cards. Akbar has been asked to and plans to stand for the state legislature election on the platform of the Muslim party.

The history sheet of the police, though, is not a respecter of success or sentiment. It goes on to call him a chronic 'rowdy' and to list a succession of dates, beginning in the early 1960s, and a few laconic lines in front of the date for the offence committed. Akbar was first convicted of sexual harassment when he was 20 years old—'Eve teasing of a girl'—as the police history sheet puts it—and was fined ten rupees by the court. A few months later, he came to the attention of the police on a charge of physical assault; the complainant failed to press charges because, the police suspect, Akbar intimidated the victim. He was then suspected of snatching a gold chain, but the first serious crime for which he was sentenced to a couple of years in prison was assaulting a special police party, 'causing grievous injury'. There follows a succession of charges of assault, stabbing, kidnapping, and wrongful confinement, most of them in connection with land deals, although he is acquitted every time either because the witnesses or the complainant or both are too scared to give evidence against him in court. A long list of arrests, orders of externment and removal from the city for specified periods, and short jail sentences (many of which he circumvented by getting himself admitted to the prison hospital) follows in monotonous detail.

What is now striking about his record are his increasing confrontations with the police. Abuse of police personnel, threats, and a couple of assaults on police officers are actions which the Hyderabad police, like the police of any other city in the world, view with particular disfavour and on which they come down severely. What is not mentioned in the records is that these confrontations with the police are often in the context of Hindu-Muslim violence where Akbar is seen to be defending Muslim interests in a clear-cut and unambiguous manner by putting his body on the line. This wins admirers in the community, especially among the young. And then something strange happens. The rowdy is recruited into the police ranks, undergoes training and is appointed as a police constable in the armed police, something which can only happen as one of the minor fallouts of a political deal struck by the Majlis with the ruling Congress party at that particular time. Akbar's police career is cut short when he is dismissed for threatening to kill an assistant police commissioner during one of the riots in the Seventies. He assaulted a police inspector and landed in jail again, this time for one year of imprisonment. He spent a large part of this sentence in the prison hospital where he continued to be active. Cases of wrongful confinement, assault, and extraction of money are registered as having been organized by Akbar from his hospital bed.

For about a decade now, though, Akbar's history sheet is clean. Akbar is becoming increasingly busy in the political arena and is no longer personally involved in any of the street and mohalla violence. He is no more a soldier but is suspected of being a general and one of the chief organizers of Muslim violence during a riot. The police, in their written summary which reveals an aversion to pronouns, concede: 'Is very popular. Called pehlwan in his locality. Has earned a lot of money in land business. Many local people approach for settlement of domestic problems and civil disputes which he settles amicably. Has car and properties and income from house rents and hotels. Trains many people of locality, in wrestling. Of late not involved in any criminal cases. However, close watch is being maintained on his activities.'

Akbar questioned Sabha closely when she first met him. He wanted to know the names of the people who had mentioned his name, how she knew his student who had brought her to him, the number of visits she had made to the Karwan area and what the people had said about politics, religion, and violence. He was guarded at first and reluctant to talk, asking why it was necessary to interview him and why he should believe that Sabha was a Muslim except that her dress, face, and way of carrying herself and talking gave her away as a Muslim. After all his bitter experiences in life, he found it difficult to trust people. If people knew about him it was because of the good work he had been doing to uphold the honour (*izzat*) of the Muslim nation. Once his suspicions were lulled, however, Akbar talked to Sabha freely about himself and his view of Hindu-Muslim relations.

'I am proud to be a Muslim. It is this pride which has carried me through many wrestling competitions I won. My aim in wrestling has not been to achieve fame for myself but to make a name as a Muslim I always felt thrilled when large numbers of Muslim boys bought tickets because I was fighting in the arena. Each time I defeated a Hindu wrestler, I felt I had not only made a name for myself but for the entire Muslim community, which looked up to me for its honour and fame.

I train a lot of Muslim boys in my *taleemkhanas*. I visit the *taleemkhanas* occasionally since I have trained others to do the job. But it is done under my close supervision. Apart from wrestling, the boys are also trained to protect themselves from attack by the enemy. They are trained on the condition that they will never misuse the training to unnecessarily harm someone.

'I also teach my disciples to be good Muslims—to respect their parents, elders, neighbours and women. A wrestler's life is not easy. He has to observe certain rules very strictly. Besides eating a good diet, he must go to bed early and wake up very early in the morning. Alcohol, cigarettes, and *pan* are absolutely prohibited. He must not drink tea and loaf around on the streets. I myself have strictly followed these rules and even today I do not drink alcohol or tea, smoke or eat *pan*. To become an example to others, I have undergone a lot of hardship. Today my disciples are very attached to me. If I were to tell them to kill themselves, they would not hesitate for a moment. But they know that their *ustad* will never ask them for their lives. He only works for their welfare. He wants them to be brave.'

Akbar was now leaning forward, his voice swelling with pride.

'Your list of pehlwans has more Muslims than Hindu names because Muslims are stronger than Hindus. The Muslim has God's strength in him. A Muslim reflects the strength of the nation. Muslims are united and one. The other nation (Hindu) does not have this unity. They are divided. We know our immense strength, given to us by God. A true Muslim is never afraid. The only fear in his heart is of God. The wooden stave of a Muslim or only the cry "Allah-u-Akbar (God is Great)" is more than ten Hindu swords. Whatever is happening today is a test the Muslims have to go through. The *Qur'an* says very clearly that it is a sin to oppress others but an even greater sin to bear oppression. A good Muslim can never tolerate oppression. Today I am a pehlwan because our society, government, and police have forced me to be one. I have faced a lot of *zulm* but have never submitted to it. I have always fought it.

'I was myself a policeman once but I quit the service after I witnessed police brutality. I saw the atrocities they commit on innocent people. One day I openly took on the police in public. I beat up a policeman very badly. Later they ransacked my house and destroyed my hotel. I was charged with assault and jailed for one year. It was solitary confinement. In this one year I changed a lot. My sentiment for God and my love for the nation awakened. I also read the *Qur'an* and prayed regularly. I decided to dedicate my life to the well-being of my community.

'On my return, I received a hero's welcome. People were so happy to see me back. I did a lot of work for the poor of the community. I am satisfied that I am doing good work—not for myself or for my own good but for others, for my people. A pehlwan does not get strength from the building of the body but from the blessings of the poor and the grace of Allah to whom he prays. To pray to God in the early hours of the morning when others are sleeping is the best. He is not distracted by the prayers of so many others who are still asleep.'

There was no trace of banter now, only a deadly seriousness.

'I believe in equality for everyone. There should be no divide between the rich and the poor. I have the communist way of thinking. I am religious and communist at the same time. You might think I am a hypocrite because I own such a big house, a hotel, property. But even in Russia the leaders had everything. I am talking about beliefs and ideas. I hate the rich, their vulgar lifestyle, and the show of wealth. I also hate the whites because they exploit the dark races not only in Africa but all over the world. I also hate the police whose uniform gives them the licence to commit such horrible crimes. Today the Muslim's fight is not only against the other nation but also against the police.

'I feel very happy when young Muslim boys are tortured by the police. They should be beaten up even more. My prayer to God is for the police to commit unlimited atrocities on young Muslims. Whenever I hear about Muslim boys being tortured, I feel like dancing with joy. Unless these boys directly experience oppression on their bodies, they will never be able to stand up against it. When they are victims of police brutality they become tigers who join my army. Today, because of God's grace there are hundreds of these young disciples who are spread all over the city.' There was no hysteria as he spoke now, just a cold fanatic dedication.

'The impression is false that in every riot more Muslims than Hindus are killed. I can say with complete confidence that at least in Hyderabad this is not ture. Here the Muslims are very strong and completely united. More Hindus than Muslims are killed in every riot.

'In another ten to 15 years the Hindus will be finished as a political force and not only politically. It is important to remember that many Muslim men marry more than once and have large families with many children. Every other Muslim house has at least five to six childern. Imagine only two boys in every family growing up to be tigers and it is these tigers who will take them on without fear. Then the Hindus have the caste sytem in which poor Hindus are exploited. It has happened many times in the past that lower caste Hindus have converted to Islam or Christianity. This is going to happen in a big way now. There won't be many Hindus left.'

His expression was again relaxing, a seductive light coming back into his eyes and in the hint of a smile.

'During the riots or at the time of curfew, I often go away from home. Because whenever there is disturbance this is the first place where the police land up. I get the work I have to do during the riots done but never out of my own house. For the last many years the police have been unable to nab me. I do my land business the same way. I buy and sell land but I am not a land grabber like others. All my land dealings are done at home. No one ever sees me at a site and my signature is never found on any document.

'When you came to meet me, you must have had a certain image of me as a pehlwan. But I am sure you will go back thinking differently of Akbar pehlwan. I am not like the others.'

Sahba's account of her meeting with Akbar had whetted my curiosity. She had been impressed with the dignity with which he carried himself, his elegance and his chaste idiomatic Urdu, liberally sprinkled with couplets from well-known poets. His courtly ways, coupled with the air of menace around him because of his reputation, made him an intriguing figure. Akbar was like the soft paw of a big cat, the talons retracted and almost invisible in the silken fur, a Damascus-steel sword sheathed in a velvet scabbard. I thus went to our meeting with Akbar, which was to take place in his hotel in the late afternoon, with much anticipation.

The rickshaw driver who took us to the meeting place did not need an address more elaborate than our simple instructions to take us to 'Akbar pehlwan's hotel'. The hotel was located near a bus terminal where buses from all over Andhra Pradesh as well as the neighbouring states disgorge pilgrims bound for the temple of Tirupathi, one of the holiest of Hindu shrines. Families from far-flung villages, often led by wizened women, bent with age yet shuffling along, sprightly with faith, stream out of the buses to stretch their legs, use the toilets and perhaps eat before they take the connecting buses for Tirupathi. I found it ironical that Akbar's hotel advertised itself as serving special vegetarian meals for Hindu pilgrims. This time, though, 'hotel' was not a misnomer since on one side of the restaurant, there was a flight of stairs leading up to the first floor which had six rooms lined along a narrow corridor. At the end of the corridor, recessed into a wall, there was a sort of, well, reception desk. Behind it, barely visible in the shadows, were three strapping young men. We asked for Akbar and one of the youths, disengaging himself from his companions, told us we were expected. Akbar would be with us in 20 minutes and in the meanwhile to please follow him.

He led us through the corridor to the last room, motioned us inside, and went away. All the other rooms seemed empty and the corridor was silent, with only the subdued late afternoon street noises filtering through its closed windows barred with iron grills. The room was stuffy and dingy, without a single window, the weak whirring of the fan churning the same stale air over and over again. There were two chairs, a twin bed, a television set on a low stool and a red telephone on a table. Otherwise the room was bare without even a poster or a print to mar the uniformity of its ugliness. Above the bed, there was a red bulb sticking out of the wall, baffling as to its purpose. I could feel the stream of perspiration thickening all over my back and my chest as molecules of sweat sought each other to form drops which trickled down to enter the pyjamas at the waist. The fan wheezed slowly, dispensing its miserly breeze only to someone who sat right under it, a space both Sahba and I were too polite to occupy by moving our chairs. The sheets on the bed were washed though they still looked soiled, covered with a profusion of patches, a cheap detergent having changed the colour of the original stains to various shades of grey. There were oil stains on the pillows from the heads of guests who believed a daily smearing of coconut oil not only kept the hair thick and healthy but acted as a coolant for the head and tonic for the body. I could not help wondering what the hotel was used for and how many customers rented its rooms for periods shorter than a night's stay.

Half an hour went by but there was no sign of Akbar or, for that matter, anyone else. There was a palpable sense of unease, even fear, as we waited in the room, with the only exit out of the empty hotel leading through a narrow corridor which was blocked at the end by the three young toughs who, like his other disciples, Akbar had told us, were ready even to kill at the merest nod of the master's head. We tried to keep our fearful fantasies at bay through an exchange of light banter, punctuated by loud nervous laughter.

'How much do you think a room in this hotel costs?'

'Oh, you think they rent it by the night?'

'If they try to rape you,' I tell Sahba, 'keep your protests down to a minimum. I don't want them to get enraged and kill both of us. On the other hand, if they do have their way with you, I doubt whether any of us will be left alive to bear witness.'

'They throw the bodies under the bridge, remember?' says Sahba.

The red telephone rings. For a few moments we sit rooted to our chairs, staring, before Sahba picks up the receiver. 'He will be here in another 15 minutes,' she says.

The minutes pass, very slowly. We have lapsed into silence, alone with our disquieting thoughts. I think of the room as a set from a movie with Ajit, the villain of old Hindi films whose drawl has spawned a whole industry of Ajit jokes.

'Raabert,' says Ajit.

'Yes, baas,' answers the henchman.

'In the room there is a red bulb.'

'Yes, bass.'

'There is also a red telephone which will ring.'

'Yes, baas.'

'Pick up the phone. I will be at the other end of the line.'

'How will I know it is you baas?'

Akbar entered the room, leaving my creation of an Ajit joke unfinished. (Frankly, although successful in dealing with my anxiety, I don't think the joke was really going anywhere.) A powerfully built man of less than medium height, he wore a white kurta pyjama, the kurta having a faint pink and yellow floral design, so subdued that it was barely noticeable from a distance of ten feet. He was wearing white sandals, the front of the sandals narrowing down to thin strips which curved up like the ends of a proud warrior's moustache. His own moustache was a thin line on an otherwise clean-shaven face. His hair dyed a jet black, it was apparent that Akbar took great care of his grooming and appearance.

After the exchange of obligatory courtesies, Akbar turned his attention to me, his eyes bright and sharp. He asked me about the study, what exactly I wanted to achieve through it, what exactly I did for a living, where I lived in Delhi and so on. My answers were frequently followed by a witty comment from him which had the intention of mocking my earnestness and exposing my ignorance of the really real life. I complied with the direction in which he wanted to take our meeting, exaggerated my naivete, pretended to greater stupidly than I feel I am naturally endowed with. My weak laughter at his sallies, a tribute to his easy victories, began to relax him as he often turned to Sabha to receive her appreciative smiles which further sealed his triumph.

He continued in this vein with the Giessen Test. Instead of answering a question, he would toy with me, ask me how I thought he would answer a particular question. With mock humility, he would turn to Sabha, sometimes discoursing on the subject of the question—on patience or strong feelings in love, for instance—with quotes from Urdu poetry, while I waited on the sidelines for an answer I could use for the purpose of the test. There was a coquettishness about him, especially in the way he played with his eyes. He would be looking normally at her while talking and then suddenly the look would become bold, charged with sexual complicity, the boldness further underlined by the briefest flash of a smile before both the look and the smile vanished.

I felt I could sense Akbar's dilemma in relation to me. Clearly, he was far superior in bodily strength, physical courage, and fighting skills. And as for matters of heart, or soul, was he not a better man here too? After all, he was a poet. Was not a man all about strength and sentiment, both of which he possessed in abundance? Yet he could not dismiss me lightly, this 'doctor' from Delhi, who could come to his city for a 'study' with a modern Muslim woman as his assistant, a woman who boldly walked in the city's mohallas with her face unveiled and talked to men on equal terms. I had better access to the modern world, to its systems of knowledge, and to its new relationships between the generations and the sexes. In terms of his own civilization, Akbar was far above me; yet he could not be easily dismissive of the modern world whose values I understood better and whose symbols I could perhaps manipulate more easily. At that particular moment, it seemed to me, Akbar and I were more than just two men warily circling each other, jousting for advantage; in our individual frames, we also incorporated the collective fastes of the Indian Muslim and the Hindu at the end of the 20th century.

Once I had given up, closed the questionnaire in apparent bafflement and given Akbar the opportunity to remark to Sabha that he had succeeded in making the psychiatrist mentally confused, Akbar became magnanimous in his victory. He was now ready to go through the statements in the Giessen Test with more sincerity.

As I expected, Akbar, unlike Majid Khan, did not give many extreme responses to the statement, further underlining the image of cautiousness which I had formed of him. The only exception was on statements relating to the social response scale where Akbar believed that he evoked a very positive response. He felt people were very satisfied with his work. He was easily liked, found it easy to attract others, and was confident that people thought highly of him. Akbar's uncharacteristic emphasis on his social attractiveness made me wonder about his narcissistic vulnerability, whether there was not a strong need for continuous narcissistic gratification which sought to counteract a depressive tendency revealed by his responses to some other statements. Akbar stated that he consistently suppressed his anger and was often depressed. He felt very strongly in love, yet gave away little of himself, found it hard to come out of his shell or to trust others. The cautious and controlled impression he gave also seemed to be an aspect of a tendency toward compulsivness, manifested in his dealings with money, tidiness, and concentration ability. I wondered whether the control he sought over his inner world and the domination of others exercised in the outer were not aspects of the same defence which guarded against the fragmentation of a self threatened by strong sexual and aggressive impulses; a self in danger of losing its cohesiveness and thus to the outbreak of a full-scale depression.

In brief, Akbar's presentation of the self was of the 'strong, silent man' with unsuspected pools of deep feelings which are guarded and bounded by high fences and almost never revealed to a casual emotional visitor or even to those who would like to be close to him. By the time the long interview was over, Akbar was regarding me with a certain distant friendliness. He wanted to give me one of his poems, he said, and I should please write it down.

Do not trouble to test me
I am always in the forefront
When it comes to bearing
The burden of grief.

When they talked of constancy in her mehfil
I turned out to be the one
Who was faithless
In an otherwise constant world.

In these times
Both of us have achieved fame
I, in creating her
She, in destroying me.

A broken mosque
Can be rebuilt in four days
It takes a lifetime, though,
To knit sundered hearts together.

The wines of yore are there no longer
The drinkers too are gone
In the wine houses
They drink blood now.

Akbar, guard the mirror
Of your heart with care
It will break
If you show it around everywhere.

'You will put me in a book,' he said resignedly after I had expressed an appreciation of his poetic talent. The final victory will not be his but mine, he meant, for it will be my version of him that will be taken as his reality by the larger world outside Hyderabad. The line in his poem on handling the mirror of the heart with care was also directed at me, a plea which he was too proud to be aware of and would never have dreamt of making openly.

Young Tigers and Pussy Cats

Nissar is one of the soldiers, a 28-year-old man, a young tiger, who reveres Akbar and other famous Muslim pehlwans. He is a handsome young man with broad tapering shoulders, a narrow waist, shoulder-length hair, and a pleasant face with high cheekbones. He wears a thin moustache fashionable among Muslim youth who do not like to sport the beards favoured by their elders. Nissar is dressed flamboyantly in a blue shirt of some satiny material, printed with large red flowers and is wearing tight, lemon green trousers. There is a certain reserve in his demeanour, a combination of hauteur and shyness which sometimes cracks when he is youthfully boastful about importing whole bales of cloth from the United States for his shirts or when he coyly asks us to guess the number of people he has killed. It is not eight, the number of murder cases registered against him by the police. Some of them are false, he says, but then with a modest but obvious delight adds that, of course, there are other killings of which the police are unaware. Nissar likes to tell war stories; tales of Muslim throats being cut by the Hindu enemy in underground blood sacrifices to its obscene gods and goddesses, of corpses thrown into the river under the bridges at the dead of the night. Akbar and the other pehlwans are the protectors of Muslim lives, yes, but also the guardians of a boy's sleep and tranquillity in the face of such fearful fantasies.

His admiration for the old tigers is proportionate to the number of Hindus they are reputed to have killed. For Nissar they are the fighter pilots whose fame in serving the nation depends on the number of enemy planes each one has shot down. Indeed, it is the military analogy which is most useful in understanding the tigers, young and old. A riot is a battle, an outbreak of hostilities in a long simmering war where the killings do not involve moral qualms or compunctions. On the contrary, to kill under such circumstances is a moral duty higher than the patriotism of a soldier serving a modern nation-state since the killing of Hindus in a riot is in service of the nation of one's faith. Indeed, an outbreak of violence in

Hindu-Muslim conflict should no longer be called a riot, with the anarchical connotations of the word. Less planned than a battle yet more organized than a riot, communal violence lies somewhere between the two. The analogies used by Majid Khan, Akbar, Nissar (and as we shall see later, Mangal Singh) which highlight the warrior aspect of their religious identity should not be surprising. It would be an error to discern in them mere rationalizations for their killings and other acts of violence. As Samuel Klausner has pointed out, riot, assassination, massacre, and terrorism are victim-defined spheres of violence.[2] From the viewpoint of the instigator and the perpetrator, they are defence of faith, crusade, just war, act of purification.

'These are the real people who serve the Muslim nation. All the others are useless, interested in making money and sticking to the chair. The next time a Majlis leader enters this alley he will be thrown out bodily. Our second slogan will be, kill the police. At least 200 policemen must be eliminated. They have done so much *zulm* on the Muslims. In jail we were so thirsty and hungry, but never received any water or food. After leaving the jail, when I went to the Majlis office, the leader said, "Why are you upset? You are not dead—you are still alive." When Hindus get arrested, a BJP leader immediately arrives and gets them released on bail. We keep rotting in jail. The Majlis is of no use to us. The leaders fight among themselves. They collect money in the name of poor Muslims like me and then eat it up themselves. They have opened a medical college but the number of Muslim students in the college are only five paise to a rupee (5 per cent). Where do they have money for the fees? The college benefits the Hindus more. Actually the biggest school in the world is the mother's lap. The child will grow up to be as capable as the education given by the mother. My mother was a complete illiterate and look at my sorry state!'

Nissar was married, with four children, and sold vegetables from five to eight in the morning. On a good day he could earn as much as a hundred rupees. He also does land business whenever he is called by a senior pehlwan to go and negotiate a deal. He is usually paid a commission of 5 per cent. He is very proud of his activities as a 'soldier' in the service of the Muslim nation. 'Our work is to serve the nation [the Muslim *qaum*] and protect our mothers and sisters. We never look at their [Hindu] sisters but their bravery is limited to raping and killing our mothers and sisters. I decided to work for the nation after all I saw during the riots following Rameeza Bi's case. It is always the Hindus who start the trouble. Earlier, we felt very scared. We were often abused when we walked through their alleys. But today I am proud that when I walk through a Hindu lane, the heads bow down. They know me as Nissar *dada*.'

Dada ('elder brother') is not yet a pehlwan, but someone who may become one, someone who is high enough in the heirarchy of strong men. As a *dada*, Nissar is not a poverty-stricken vegetable seller, a poor Muslim who needs to defer to the well-off Hindus, but someone who demands and receives respect. Having been trained as a wrestler for many years in different *taleemkhanas*, he stopped the training after he was married since he felt he could not afford the diet of huge quantities of milk, nuts and meat, required by a wrestler. Now he serves the nation through *chaku-bazi*, wielding of the knife. 'If I hear that two of our poeple have been attacked and killed at the wooden bridge it takes me just five minutes to knife five of them.' Because of Sabha's expression of open interest (obviously, he would not have revealed himself in this way if I, a Hindu, had also been present), Nissar elaborated on his professionalism. 'There is a way to kill with the knife. Once I stab with a knife nd I do not need to turn and look. I am sure the man is dead even as he is falling. Then, on a street, I never make a mistake between a Hindu and a Muslim. We recognize the religion from the face. If I saw you somewhere else, in a different dress, I would know immediately you are a Muslim. It is clear from your very face.

'Most of the time the police are not able to catch us. We move very fast. All they can do is to suspect. Sometimes we dump the bodies under some bridge and they are discovered disfigured after three to four days. Sometimes dogs eat up parts of the body which is then very difficult to identify. We always make sure that if Hindus kill two of our people, we should kill at least four of theirs. This is to scare them away. They must not think we are helpless, frightened or unarmed.

'Personally, I don't take away a weapon with me when we go out to kill Hindus during a riot. I only have a wooden stave (*lathi*) but I do have a strategy. I make sure that the first person I confront on the other side is the one with a sword. I disarm him with my *lathi* and then kill him with his own sword. It is easy.

'Scared? What an idea! Once the decision to serve the nation is made where is the room for fear? One has to be brave. Cowards die quietly. Instead of dying inside the house it is better to be martyred outside. Allah is with us. He knows that we are doing good work and He protects us.

'I have told my wife never to worry about me or stop me from my work. I have told her not to wait for me more than three or four days in times of trouble. Where will she look for me? We go everywhere wherever there are disturbances. She should simply break her bangles (the sign of widowhood) and feel proud that I have become a martyr.'

Nissar's wife, though, is less worried about his heroics or eventual martyrdom. She complains bitterly about her own situation, about Nissar's attitude towards women that does not allow her to step out of the house. To run their home, she has to depend on her old father to buy groceries, medicines, and other essentials. He never takes her out since he is embarassed to be seen with a dark-skinned wife. 'If I was fair he would take me out everywhere,' the killer's wife sighs in bitter regret. Another man, Aslam, a sullen middle-aged vegetable seller, unemployed for most of the day, who sits across the street wrapped in a mantle of sardonic gloom and has watched our interest in the *dadas* and pehlwans, gives his own assessment of the young tigers. Pointing to his chapped, dusty feet with grotesque toes and discoloured nails, he says: 'The police pulled the nails out one by one when they took me to jail during the last riot. I have to keep my feet in water whenever I want to clip the nails. All this tiger business is nonsense, except that they pocket three-fourths of the relief supplies which go through their hands. Otherwise, when the police take them, every tiger turns into a pussy cat.'

Spreading the Wind

Mangal Singh is a well-known Hindu pehlwan. In many ways he is the Hindu counterpart of Akbar although he does not possess any of Akbar's old-world graces. He belongs to the Lodha community, economically one of the fastest rising groups in Hyderabad, whose prosperity, observers say, rests on illicit liquor distillation. Brewed in the backyards of houses and stills near the riverbed, the raw liquor is a potent brew which drastically lowers the life expectancy of its hapless consumers. Basically distilled from jaggery and the grey oxide powder used to coat the insides of brass utensils with tin (and which can easily dissolve lead), the liquor is expectedly severe on stomach linings. It is believed that anyone who daily consumes half a bottle of the liquor, the *pauwa*, will not survive for more than a year. In the poor neighbourhoods of the city where the liquor is mostly consumed, it is not an unfamiliar sight early in the morning to see a corpse or two lying on the street near an *adda* where the liquor is clandestinely sold.

The reputation of the Lodhas is of a mercurial and violent people who are always in the forefront of a riot from the Hindu side, 'They will kill as many people in two hours as the rest will in a week,' says an old Hyderabad resident who has studies the community closely. They claim to be Rajputs, the traditional martial caste and the sword arm of Hindu society although this claim is often disputed by others. In spite of their taking a leading part in religious violence, their economic ties with Muslims are close. Muslims are the main customers of their lethal brew, both as retailers and, together with the Dalits, the poverty-stricken Hindu outcastes, as its consumers. Even socially, they have adopted some Muslim customs. Although they regard Muslims as their chief enemy, it does not prevent them, for example, from regularly visiting Muslim shrines, the dargahs, in a spirit of devotion.

Mangal Singh's house is in one of the crowded localities of Hyderabad where there is a large concentration of Lodhas. The bazaar running through it has shops stocking somewhat more expensive goods but in essence differs visually from other similar bazaars of the city only in one curious particular. This is the occasional sight of two to three men on bicycles wearing very loose clothes, emerging from one of the alleys and, with a look of determined concentration, furiously pedalling away to turn and disappear into another alley. These are the liquor carriers, wearing bicycle tyre tubes full of the illegal stuff tied around their bodies, on their way to various distribution centres in the city.

A young-looking 40, Mangal Singh is a handsome man who laughs easily and has a kind of manic charm about him. He walks with the compact, swaggering gait of a wrestler, with shoulders swinging like a young woman's hip, as he proudly shows us around his house and his *vyamshala*, the gymnasium, both of which are situated in a large compound just off the road and very near the river. The gymnasium, which trains more than a hundred boys and young men, consists of two rectangular halls adjacent to each other. The first hall is used for weight training. There are wooden dumbbells, iron tyres to be put around the neck to strengthen the neck muscles, parallel bars, ropes hanging down from iron rings in the ceiling, and many other contraptions for the pulling, pushing and lifting of weights. The whitewashed walls are lined with coloured lithographs and posters. There is a lithograph of the reclining god Vishnu, his face shaded by the hoods of the hydra-headed snake, Sheshnag. There is a poster of one of his incarnations, the God Rama in his heroic pose with a long bow and a quiver of arrows visible above his shoulders. There is the portrait of the goddess Durga in her ferocious form, in the act of killing the buffalo demon, Mahisasura. Threre are portraits of the Hindu heroes Shivaji and Rana Pratap, who have come to epitomize Hindu resistance to the Mughals; there is also the reproduction of a popular painting of Nehru looking down from the ramparts of Delhi's Red Fort, the Indian national flag flying proudly behind him as he pensively faces a large crowd, the faces of the leaders of India's Independence movement—Patel, Rajagopalachari, Kripalani, Maulana Azad—clearly recognizable in the forefront.

The other wall, too, is covered with pictures. There are three large portraits of wrestlers, one of them Mangal's own guru. The other two are famous wrestlers from the Thirties and Forties, each in a loincloth and standing with his feet and arms a little apart, in the pose where they are ready for grappling. Pointing to one of the pehlwans, who has very close-cropped hair and a thick moustache, Mangal Singh informs me that this man was the prime accused in Hyderabad's first major riot between the Hindus and the Muslims in 1938, when the state was ruled by the Nizam. This pehlwan, I forget his name, had killed one of the leading members of the Razakars, the Nizams's unofficial Muslim militia, and then disappeared. He is still believed to be alive and living in a remote area of Nepal where he now pactises the austerities of a holy man.

There are many coloured lithographs of scenes from the Independence movement—Gandhi leading a long line of volunteers on his march to the sea, the Jallianwala Bagh massacre where British soldiers are shown firing into the trapped crowd, men caught in the act of falling down, clutching at their chests from which blood is spurting out, open-mouthed in silent screams. Then there are lithographs depicting scenes from earlier periods of history: small Hindu children being thrown up and impaled on the spears of the Razakars, Indian soldiers being blown up from the mouths of cannons by the British after the failure of India's first war of independence, the Sepoy Mutiny as British historians called it. Pointing to the Razakar picture, Mangal Singh informs me, 'This is what used to happen all the time in those days in Hyderabad. Hindu girls were picked up from the streets or the fields at any time at the will of Muslim nobles and raped. That is why our girls started marrying so early. If a girl had a *mangalsutra* around her neck and *payals* around the ankles (the signs of marriage), she was not kidnapped.'

There is a further series of pictures depicting Muslim atrocities from the long period of Islamic rule: Banda Bairagi and his followers being beheaded by Muslim soldiers, the martyrdom of the Sikh Gurus, Mahmud of Ghazni destroying the famous temple of Somnath as shaven-headed Brahmin priests look up with bulging eyes and mouths open in iuncomprehensible horror. Next we come to a photograph of Subhash Chandra Bose, the stormy rebel of the national movement who sought an alliance with Hitler's Germany and Tojo's Japan during the war to violently overthrow the British empire in India. Next to it is a full-sized wooden statue of Gandhi which is overturned and lies on its side, facing the wall. 'There was a high wind a few days ago and Gandhiji toppled over. He has his back to this country,' Mangal Singh jokes.

'How is it that you have Gandhiji, the apostle of nonviolence, together with the violent Hindu heroes next to each other?' I venture to ask.

'First, I talk like Gandhiji,' he replies with a smile. 'Only when talk fails, I use force like Shivaji or Bose.'

The second hall is dominated by the *akhara* where the actual wrestling takes place. About four feet under the floor level, the *akhara* is a flat smooth rectangle of reddish coloured mud mixed with oil and finely threshed stalks of wheat, covering about half the area of the hall. Presiding over it is a Shiva *lingam*; a garland of fresh white jasmine flowers and sticks of burning incense bear witness to its daily morning worship. On the other side of the room, next to the wall, there is a small temple of Hanuman, the ascetic patron god of Hindu wrestlers. The idol is smeared with red paste, flowers are strewn around its feet, and incense sticks burn from between the toes. On the wall itself there are photographs of famous wrestlers—I recognize Guru Hanuman from Delhi among them—as well as photographs clipped from Western bodybuilding magazines and pasted to the walls. The slightly fading photographs show off the oily sheen of bulging biceps, thundering thighs, and sculpted pectorals. One entire side of the hall is without a wall and opens out to the river and a peaceful scene of dark-skinned women with sarees tied above their knees, whirling wet clothes above their shoulders and bringing them down with rhythmic thuds on flat stones to clean them of dirt. Mangal Singh draws my attention back to the gym when he points to the corner next to the temple where some loincloths are hanging on a wooden post. 'Earlier we used to have spears and swords. Nowadays, of course, they put you in jail if you have even a knife for your self-protection. Many young men prefer to learn karate these days,' he continues to enlighten me. 'Karate makes the sides of your hands into killing instruments by deadening sensation in that part. They burn the side of the hand and dip elbows in boiling salt water till all sensation is lost. But Indian-style wrestling is still superior where you can kill a man once you grapple with him. Karate is only good for long-distance fighting. Once you get in close to the opponent as in Indian-style wrestling, karate is useless.'

The Muslim *taleemkhana* does not differ substantially from the Hindu *akhara*. There will be fewer photographs and, of course, no idol of a Hindu god. It might have an *ayat* from the *Qur'an* on a wall or a coloured print of the Kaaba, Islam's holiest shrine. Comparatively speaking, with its greater profusion of religious icons, the Hindu gymnasium appears more Hindu than the more neutral *taleemkhana* appears Muslim. The Muslim training regimen is the same as the Hindu one except that the wrestlers will say the prescribed dawn prayers at home before coming to the *taleem*. They too will drink crushed nuts and crystal sugar mixed in water or milk after the training is over for the morning but, in contrast to the Hindu, eat great quantities of mutton.

It had not been easy to meet Mangal Singh. We had to go through friends of friends of friends before the meeting finally took place. Once it happened, though, Mangal Singh talked so freely and without any apparent suspiciousness or guile that I wondered why it had been so difficult in the first place. He did not quite understand what my psychological study of Hindu-Muslim violence was all about. (I confess that when I tried to explain the aims of my study to other pehlwans, I did not quite understand it myself.) He was under the impression that we might eventually want to make a movie on the subject, an impression I did not fully exert myself to correct. In any event, Mangal Singh proved to be most frank about his activities as a scourge of Muslims, perhaps also because he assumed Sahba and I were both Hindus.

The Muslim pehlwans had been open with Sahba but understandably guarded when I was also present. With Sahba they could express their bitterness and contempt for Hindus, show their pride in their role in the protection of the community from the Hindu enemy. In my presence, they became less Muslim and more inclined to express universal humanist sentiments. For instance, there was pious talk, not exactly reassuring, that if I were cut my blood would be exactly the same colour as theirs. By the end of the interviews, though, all the pehlwans were perceptibly warmer. I like to believe that this opening up was because they sensed my genuine interest in them as persons rather than being due to any typical 'shrink' 'hm-ms', phrases, or inflections. I suspect, though, that their different—although for my purposes, highly complementary—psychic agendas when talking to Sahba and to me were dictated by shifts in their own sense of identity. In other words, with Sahba, a Muslim, their self-representation was more in terms of a shared social identity. With me, a Hindu, once they felt reassured that the situation did not contain any threat, personal identity became more salient, influencing their self-representations accordingly. In any event, when we parted, promises to visit me in Delhi were made, visions of feasting in my house were conjured up, all of which I acknowledged smilingly though not without quaking inwardly at the prospect of the promise ever being kept. There were occasions in meetings with the pehlwans—for instance, when waiting for Akbar in his hotel room—where I caught myself thinking that the scholarly work of making a book out of other books was infinitely preferable to being out in the field, anxious and afraid. Besides being perpetually uncomfortable in the heat, dust, bad smells, and biting mosquitoes, I felt envious at visions of friends reading and writing in quiet air-conditioned libraries.

In the meeting with Mangal Singh, the only threat came from his generous but insistent hospitality as he pressed a glass of sugarcane juice on me, delicious but deadly, a prime vehicle for stomach disease and a possible cholera carrier. We were sitting in a room on the first floor of his house where Mangal Singh lives with his two wives. Most of the 11 rooms on this floor are empty. The ground floor has nine rooms, occupied by his widowed mother and his five brothers with their families. The rooms are in the form of a square and open out to a veranda lining a courtyard which has a tulsi (basil) plant growing in the middle. 'Not tulsi, Mother tulsi,' Mangal Singh had corrected me while demonstrating his Hindu piety at the same time. Besides a scooter and a motorcycle parked in the veranda, there was a refrigerator and a water cooler as well as some toys. Everything looked neat and tidy and freshly scrubbed. Mangal Singh had introduced us to his first wife, a shy, pretty young woman to whom he was openly affectionate. He had married again because she could not have children. 'But I actually prefer her,' he had said to the young woman's obvious pleasure. 'She looks after me well. The other one is also nice but since she is educated she doesn't look after me so well.' As with his mother, to whom he had introduced us downstairs, Mangal Singh behaved like a spoilt young boy with his wife, cracking jokes, praising her extravagantly, ordering her about, calling out to her often to reassure himself that she was not far away.

There were three other men in the room when we began the interview, the obligatory *chamchas* to amplify his statements whenever he paused for breath or effect. They provided emphasis to his statements and strove to increase their truth content by a resounding 'That is right!' to his rhetorical 'Isn't that so?' Occasionally, when he paused, they sang his praises while he looked on. smiling modestly. 'He needs good food to keep up his "manpower",' said one. 'Manpower' is said in English, the man's rough and ready translation of the Hindi word for strength. 'If he lifts his hand, all the hands in the city would rise, such is his "manpower".' They showed me the externment order served on Mangal Singh by the police and signed by the commissioner sahib himself which banished him from the city for six months in 'apprehension of inciting violence and breach of peace.' 'But I'm back after one and a half months. I got a stay from the High Court,' Mangal Singh says. The copy of the stay order is also passed on to me by a *chamcha* for my perusal. A second *chamcha* brings out a sheaf of photographs. The ones shown to me are of police torture. A subdued-looking Mangal Singh, standing in his loincloth, is bruised and the eyes puffed. He points to his left eye where the skin under it is noticeably darker. 'I have still not completely recovered from that beating,' he says with indignation, not at the beating itself but at the surrounding circumstances of which Mangal gives two versions. It seemed a few months ago, at the time of tension over the demolition of the Babri mosque, Mangal received a parcel, very probably from his Muslim enemies. It was kept in the room next to the one where we were sitting. His three-year-old son fell on it and it exploded, killing the boy. In the second version, which is also the statement he made to the police, he had stored firecrackers in the room for the children in the family. His son was playing with them and they exploded, killing the boy. 'My son dies and the motherfuckers arrest me and beat me up, claiming I was manufacturing bombs,' he says, his indignation quite convincing.

There are other occasional contradictions in Mangal's monologue which comes tumbling out at a high velocity. For instance, in talking of the wrestler's ascetic regimen, he had said that he ate exactly at eight every evening and never went out of the house after that. Yet, just before saying goodbye to us, when his wife had come out, he said, 'The poor woman makes such nice meals for me but I am so busy I never know when I will be home. I eat at all odd hours. How often she has waited up for me before she could have her own dinner!' Mangal is not exactly a liar in the sense that he wants to deceive his audience. He is an embellisher of facts, some of which may get changed to fit in with what he believes to be true at a certain time. He may also unwittingly bend the truth to project a particular image of himself. After a while, the contraditions become a part of his manic charm as I fascinatedly watch the persona he is constructing as much for himself as for us.

The first time Mangal Singh clashed with the Muslims was in 1979. The Muslims had claimed a piece of land on the specious ground that it was an old community graveyard. The man to whom the land belonged had won his case against the encroachment in the court but could not get the land vacated and came to Mangal Singh. His cause was just and Mangal agreed to help him. Mangal would never help someone who wanted illegal possession of land. He only, so to speak, expedited the notoriously lumbering machinery of the law, helped in implementing court orders which would not otherwise be carried out. Mangal settled on a sum of money for his services. Nowadays his minimum fee is a 100,000 rupees, but he takes it only after the work is done, not like some other pehlwans who take the money but refuse to do the work, daring the client to do his utmost. Mangal, on the other hand, is a man of principles.

Mangal went to the site with five of his people. They had a few knives and a couple of swords between them. The Muslims were light in number, all of them with swords and each an expert at wielding the weapon. But they were old—the oldest being almost 60—and though thorough professionals, they lacked the staying power of Mangal's much younger men. The Muslims were soon out of breath and Mangal and his men killed six of them. They put four of the corpses in an Ambassador car and threw them in different parts of the city to confuse the police. He was charged with three murders in that particular incident. He cannot tolerate *zulm*, particularly Muslim *zulm*.

The police report of the incident credits him with only one murder, of which he was acquitted because of lack of evidence. A month later, the history sheet continues, 'along with others, he assaulted Imtiaz and his parents with sticks and caused bleeding injuries to them.' Two months later, in December 1979, when riots had begun after the Rameeza Bi incident, Mangal Singh is noted to have led an armed group of 20 people who set fire to Muslim shops, attacked Muslims with sticks and knives, and pelted stones at the police. There is a succession of other brief notings over the years: assault, unlawful assembly, rioting. For a few months he was ordered to report to the police every day at eight in the morning and nine at night. But he was never convicted in the court in spite of over 40 cases registered against him by the police. Because of the intimidation of witnesses, the police say. 'Because the people love me and will not let me go to jail,' says Mangal. The police record summarizes: 'Young and energetic. Very close to the BJP MLA (Member Legislative Assembly). Has good contacts with the RSS. Also closed to the local Telugu Desam Party MLA. Tries to be close to Congress also. He is a communal element. Very active during communal disturbances and has very good following. Has become very intelligent and never exposes himself personally in crimes but uses his henchmen for creating disturbances. People of the locality very frightened and do not want to complain or become witnesses. Earns a lot of money by settling land disputes.'

Mangal Singh freely admits his political links but has a sense of outrage that he was put behind bars in the explosives case. 'I was with the Congress party for so many years. I did so much of their work. I also did the personal work of a couple of MLAs in getting their houses vacated from tenants. But then I changed over to the BJP since that is the only party defending the Hindus. And what happens? The Congress puts me in jail! No gratitude at all!'

During a riot, 'strong men' representing different localities, not all of them pehlwans, meet on almost a daily basis and decide where 'the wind is to be spread' (*hawa phailana*), a euphemism for where the killings have to take place and where they need to be stopped. For instance, it would be decided at the meeting to stop the violence in Dhulpet but start it in the old city. Mangal Singh likes to maintain a tight discipline in his own area. Once, during the riots, a mob collected spontaneously in his locality. He immediately sent a few of his boys who came back in two minutes after doing *satrol* (creating chaos). He then called in the leaders of the mob and told them, 'Never do that again without my permission.'

Although Mangal Singh enjoys recounting his violent exploits in the land business or in the political field—for instance, when he and his boys did *satrol* to the procession of a newly appointed minister at the behest of his cabinet colleague— what he is really proud of are his clashes with the Muslims in defence of the Hindus. These allow him to identify with and place himself in a long line of heroes such as Shivaji and Rana Pratap, whom he admires greatly for their armed resistance against the Muslim emperors. He tells us of the incident of a Hindu marriage procession when it was stopped in front of a mosque because it was time for the Friday afternoon prayers. An altercation took place and the bridegroom, who belonged to the Lodha community, was pushed off his horse. The incident was reported to Mangal Singh who reached the spot with a few of his men. 'Within two minutes,' he boasts, 'four of their men lay on the ground, two dead even as they fell. The others fled and the marriage procession passed the mosque.'

Mangal Singh's psychological profile shows a great resemblance to that of Akbar; the difference is that his responses are much more extreme. He believes he tries to dominate others, is very self-willed and competitive. He, too, is often sad, worries a great deal about personal problems, tends to suppress anger, and always blames himself when things go wrong. Even his choice of favourite songs reflects a preference for the sad and the sentimental. The first is a Mukesh song with the opening lyrics:

Life's road is full of tears
Someone should tell her
I have a long way to travel

The other's an old hit from a 1950s movie:

Do not forget these days of childhood
Today I am laughing
Do not make me cry tomorrow.

In spite of the dysphoric mood, Mangal feels personally potent and socially gratified. Taking into account the interview and the responses to the statements on the Giessen Test, I would surmise that the outstanding feature of Mangal's personality is a hyperactivity defending against depression, compared to Akbar's more compulsive defences. And since I am already in the comparison business, let me go further and look at the psychological profiles of all the four pehlwans. Although too small a sample for any definitive statements on the larger universe of 'strong men' who carry out the actual acts of violence in a riot, my tentative collective portrait may still be a source of hypotheses for any future psychological studies.

My first observation is that these men are not abnormal in a clinical sense. That is, they are neither psychopaths, highly neurotic, nor delinquent; their control over their violent impulses is not even greatly impaired. All of them, however, are unusually dominant and of a marked authoritarian bent. There is also a notable depressive tendency in their underlying mood, a threatened depression against which various defences are employed. Surprisingly, the depressive tendency persists in spite of the pehlwans feeling that they evoke a positive social response; that is, they are narcissistically gratified rather than frustrated by their environment.

Perhaps the need to defend against an emptying and fragmenting self, the inner experience of depression, contributes to the building up of a defensive hyperactivity wherein the cohesiveness of the self is restored and most immediately experienced through an explosion in violent action. The excitement of violence becomes the biggest confirmation that one is psychically still alive, a confirmation of one's very existence.

Psyche and Wrestling

Until now we have looked at the warriors of communal violence, the men who orchestrate the violence and who, in their younger days (and current youthful versions) were directly engaged in it, as moved by specific aspects of their religious and personal identities. Yet in Hyderabad, as well as in many other cities, where the pehlwans take a leading role in communal violence, we also need to look at their socialization as pehlwans. In other words, for a greater understanding of these warriors of religious violence, we need a close look at the culture of Indian wrestling. It may well be the development of the pehlwan's professional identity which, working in tandem with his personal and religious identities, provides us with a more complete picture of the workings of his mind. This is exemplified by an apocryphal story about Sufi Pehlwan, an old *peshawar* ('professional') who retired from the killing business after the 1979 riots. He is reported to have felt that, like everything else in India, riots too were not what they once used to be. Since each one of us interprets the world from the limited view we have of it, Sufi Pehlwan too saw the deterioration of the country through his particular professional lens. The quality of food and thus the toughness of the men's bodies had been steadily degenerating over the years. Bones had become brittle so that when one stabbed a person there was hardly any resistance to the knife blade which sliced through muscle, cartilage, and bone as if they were wet clay. Simply put, there was no longer any professional satisfaction to be obtained from a riot, and Sufi Pehlwan had turned to other, more challenging, if perhaps less exciting pursuits.

The tradition of Indian wrestling, the *malla-yuddha* of the epics, is not equally widespread. Strongest in the north Indian states of Punjab, Haryana, Delhi, Uttar Pradesh, and western Bihar, it is encountered less in the rest of the country. Although absent in most of south and central India, wrestling is quite robust in parts of Bengal and Maharashtra as well as in some erstwhile princely states such as Hyderabad where the rulers patronized the art. Wrestling in the Indian context is not just a sport but a whole way of life; it is not only a physical regimen but a moral tradition with changing political coordinates. In the felicitous phrase of the anthropologist Joseph Alter, wrestling is a 'meeting of muscles and morals'.[3]

As far as the physical regimen is concerned, there is little difference in forms and techniques of wrestling between the various parts of the country or even between Hindu and Muslim wrestlers. Waking up at dawn, the aspiring wrestler runs a few miles to build up his stamina. Ideally, he should then spend some time in contemplation (or in actual prayer in the case of the Muslim) before he makes his way to the *akhara, dangal* or *taleem*—the different names given to the wrestling gymnasium. Here he begins with a bath before donning the wrestler's habit, the *langot* or the loincloth. This is followed by the anointing of the body with oil and a collective preparation of the actual *akhara*, the approximately ten-metre-square pit. In a Hindu *akhara* there is collective invocation of Hanuman, the celibate god of wrestlers and the symbol of deepest devotion to Rama.

Wrestlers are then paired off by the guru (the *ustad* or *khalifa* in the case of Muslims) to grapple and practice moves and countermoves under the guru's close supervision and frequent instruction. After two or three hours of this *jor* (literally, 'strength'), the wrestler rolls in the earth of the pit to partake of its cooling, reinvigorating, and healing qualities and then finishes with a bath. A large hearty meal consisting of the wrestler's staple foods of clarified butter, litres of milk, and ground almonds (or chickpeas) if Hindu, meat with pistachios and almonds if Muslim (in the days when pistachios and almonds were still affordable) follows. The wrestler then has a short nap and rests for a couple of hours during the afternoon. Then it is back to the *akhara* in the early evening for another two to three hours of individual exercises to build up strength, stamina, and flexibility of joints. Besides various kinds of weight training, the core exercises are hundreds of deep knee-bends and jackknifing pushups. A bath and again a specialized meal later, the wrestler is generally supposed to be asleep by 8 or 9 p.m. so as to get up fresh and energetic at the crack of dawn to repeat the regimen the next day.

The physical regimen is part of a moral and ideological complex, and this is where Indian wrestling is similar to traditional East Asian martial arts, where physicality was inseparable from morality and skills were not independent of ethics. Here, too, traditional wrestling differs from the teaching and learning of judo, karate, or wrestling in the modern context as recreational sports, physical exercises or fighting skills. The wrestler, though very much a part of society, both looks and experiences himself as a man apart. First, there is the contrast of the bulky but muscled body to the underfed and emaciated bodies of other men in the lower-class neighbourhoods from which most wrestlers come. Besides exhibiting the outer signs of apartness, the honesty, internal and external cleanliness, simplicity, and contemplation of God which, as Alter points out, he shares with the ascetic—the sanyasin or the sadhu—who too stresses his liminality to the normal social order.[4] Of course, where the wrestler differs most strikingly from the normal man is in his advocation (like that of the ascetic) of absolute celibacy. Sexuality and, in particular, the loss of semen are concerns of high anxiety. The image of the wrestler in popular Hindi moves is generally of a strong but simple-minded rustic who goes to absurd lengths to avoid the company of women and thus any occasion for sexual excitement. As Alter tells us, for the wrestler semen is the locus of all of his strength and character. Milk, clarified butter (ghee) and almonds, the primary ingredients of a wrestler's diet, are believed to build up a store of high energy semen. Milk and ghee are also supposed to lower the body heat so that the semen is not inadvertently spilt in sleep but can perform its desired function of building bodily strength.[5]

The control of sexuality, and anxiety about sexual concerns, is the cornerstone of all conservative moralities, and the wrestler's ideological universe, with its centrality of celibacy, is very close to the most conservative parts of the Hindu and Muslim religious traditions. Like the so-called fundamentalist, the wrestler, too, is opposed to the modern entertainment forms of cinema and television where sex is so abundantly on display. He disapproves of modern educational institutions where boys and girls come into close and thus dangerous contact. He looks askance at modern fashions in clothes and bodily care which he feels are devoted to the excitement of prurient interest. In general, the wrestler's conservative morality condemns all manifestations of modernity which arouse the senses instead of calming them, which stoke the sensual fire instead of dousing its flames.

In the various philosophical and social science discourses on modernity, there is very often an absence of what many 20th century artists, writers and film-makers—not to speak of psychoanalysts—regard as its central features: the foregrounding of the biographical self and of sexuality (in its widest sense) in human subjectivity. Psychoanalysis, the study of the sexual self, is thus a pre-eminently modern discipline. The protest against the ubiquity, significance and manifestations of the sexual self is thus inevitably a basic characteristic of revivalist and fundamental rhetoric.

There is one element of the wrestling ideology which at first glance appears to run counter to the conservative label given to it. This is egalitarianism. In the *akhara* there are only bodies, without sectarian, class, and caste hierarchical distinctions. As a commentator on wrestling remarks, 'In every village everyone from the common labourer to the wealthiest person would enter the pit together. Everyone on everyone else's back with knees on necks. There was no stigma, no enmity, anger or threats. The *akhara* was a pilgrimage point of social equality; a temple of brotherly love.'[6] Until the very recent past, many *akharas* in Hyderabad were mixed in the sense that they would have both Hindus and Muslims training under a Hindu or Muslim pehlwan. Majid Khan's brother's *khalifa*, for instance, was Chintamani Pehlwan, a Hindu. In any event, although egalitarianism between men may be missing from some modern Western conservative ideologies, it can very well be a part of Hindu conservative traditions and is, of course, available in the ideology of Islam. Egalitarianism, for instance, is a point of emphasis for the deeply conservative ideologies of the RSS, the organizational vanguard in the current revival of militant Hinduism. The litmus test of revivalism and fundament-alism remains the attitude toward sex rather than power.

Morally and ideologically, the wrestler, either Hindu or Muslim, thus welcomes and feels a sense of kinship with forces in his community which oppose modernity through the revival of traditional values. The changed political coordinates of his position also make it easier for the wrestler to become an active and, given his calling, militant representative of the community. Before the independence of the country in 1947, wrestlers were traditionally patronized by Indian princes who would have court wrestlers just as they had court painters or court musicians. Akbar pehlwan's forefathers had been court wrestlers to the Nizam of Hyderabad for four generations. All the physical needs of the wrestler were taken care of by the royal patron. What the wrestler was expected to do was to concentrate on the refinement of his art and the building up of his body. In return for the patronage, the wrestlers would march on ceremonial occasions in royal processions through the streets of the capital, their magnificent physiques testifying to and reflecting on the power of the prince. They would represent the honour of the prince in their competitive bouts with wrestlers from other states—the re-creation of a legendary mode of warfare between kingdoms which has been immortalized in the Persian tale of Rustam and Sohrab.

Although some politicians did try to replace the princes as patrons of wrestling *akharas*, using wrestlers for strong-arm methods to achieve political ends, in general the wrestler had lost the morally elevated view of his calling demanded by tradition and ideology. It is in the polarization of Hindus and Muslims and in the context of religious revivalism that the wrestler is again finding a role as an icon of the community's physical power and martial prowess. Although he may still be used by the politician, by employing religious violence for his own purposes, the wrestler can again hold a cherished moral high ground and be proud of his new role as 'protector of the Muslim (or Hindu) nation'.

The traditional wrestling training, although it also graduated religious killers, did have certain advantages in structing the form of religious violence. Often, the *akharas* and the teachers had mixed Hindu and Muslim students who would never fight each other in or outside the ring and thus had a dampening influence on the battlefield enthusiasm of the two communities. The training also inculcated a strong ideology that bound the fighting and killing by certain rules of combat; where, for instance, the respect for womankind precluded a woman from being a riot victim. In Hyderabad, even now, rape is not used as a vehicle for the contempt, rage, or hatred that one community feels for the other as it is, for example, in Bosnia. As the pehlwan's traditional ideology declines and the role of the pehlwan as a channelizer of his community's violence gives way to a more brutal free-for-all, religious violence too promises to enter an era of unchecked ferocity. There are, of course, other reasons for the relative absence of rape in a Hindu-Muslim riot, including, as we shall see later, the strong moral disapproval of rape as an instrument of religious violence in both communities. Moreover, unlike in the Bosnian conflict, after a riot the Hindus and Muslims still have to live together and carry out a minimal social and considerable economic interaction in their day-to-day lives. As Mangal Singh remarked. 'A few days after the riot is over, whatever the bitterness in our hearts and however cold our voices are intially, Akbar pehlwan still has to call me and say, "Mangal bhai, what do we do about that disputed land in Begumpet?" And I still have to answer, "Let's get together on that one, Akbar bhai, and solve the problem peacefully."' Rape makes such interactions impossible and turns Hindu-Muslim animosity into implacable hatred.

As far as the warriors are concerned, their ability to get over the bitterness of the conflict to again work together further attests to their high level of ego functioning. Unlike many other members of their communities who are either unable to hate or cannot stop hating, the pehlwans have learned both how to hate and how to get over hating.[7] Killers in the service of their religious communities, they do not fit easy psychological or philosophical categories. There is no evidence, for instance, that they are psychopaths brutally trained to reject human feeling, are sexually insecure, or were abused as children. Endowed with leadership qualities and standing out from their milieu in certain aspects of character, they are not—as in Hannah Arendt's 'banality of evil' hypothesis—perfectly ordinary people with the capacity to behave as monsters.

VICTIMS AND OTHERS : I.
THE HINDUS

One of the worst hit areas in the riots was Pardiwada ('settlement of the Pardis') in Shakkergunj. Two miles from Char Minar, the centre of the walled city, Pardiwada is an enclave of about 50 Hindu houses surrounded by Muslim settlements. Before the last riot, Pardiwada had a population of about 150 families (in a family-centred culture, the population figures, too, are given in numbers of families rather than individuals) which has now dwindled to 50.

The narrow lane which branches off the main road to lead into Pardiwada meanders through Muslim mohallas where many of the houses show the religious affiliation of the owner by having a window, a door or a whole wall painted green. The access lane in generally crowded with bicycles, goats, buffaloes, and fruit vendors pushing their carts through a stream of pedestrians moving in both directions. The pedestrians are both Hindus from Pardiwada and their Muslim neighbours, and the lack of warmth between the two is palpable. A snapshot sticks in my mind: two middle-aged women, both fat, one a Hindu in a saree, the other a Muslim in an ankle-length black burqa, though with the face unveiled, walking with the same side-to-side waddle of overweight ducks, pass each other. There is no outward sign of acknowledgement as they squeeze past each other although before the riots, I am told, at least polite greetings would have been exchanged.

The small brick and cement plastered houses of Pardiwada, arranged in uneven rows, were built 30 to 40 years ago. Some of them, especially at the periphery of the *basti*, are deserted and show obvious signs of the riot: charred doors and windows, broken electric bulbs and ripped-out wires hanging loose above the chipped and pitted floors. Many have crude 'house for seal [*sic*]' signs lettered in English on their walls, as if the complex of feelings evoked in the seller by such an offer could only be dealt with in an emotionally distancing foreign language rather than in the more intimate mother tongue. They remain unsold. The Pardis believe that the prospective buyers, who are Muslim, are waiting for prices to fall further when the owners will be forced into distress sales.

The street scenes of Pardiwada, though, are cheerful enough. Since the main occupation of the Pardis is the selling of fruits and vegetables, there is a great deal of activity early in the morning when whole families are involved in sorting out and cleaning the fruits and vegetables heaped in front of the houses and loading them onto pushcarts. Many of the women have been up since three in the morning to fetch the fruit from the wholesaler, generally a Muslim, or even from the faraway Muslim-owned orchards at the outskirts of the city. These are traditional business relations which have endured through generations. They are based on trust, where the women take the fruit on credit and make the payment the next day after it has been sold. The riots have disturbed these business—and inevitably, over time, personal—relationships between the Pardis and their Muslim suppliers. The women now feel more apprehensive walking through dark and empty Muslim bazaars or gardens at this time of the morning. In any case, it is a community tradition that the women fetch the goods and the men sell them, a tradition which doubtless persists also because men find it convenient. As one of the women describing the tradition added, 'Moreover, my husband does not feel like getting up so early in the morning'.

Later in the day, once the men are gone, the teenage boys have been sent on their bicycles to sell onions, garlic, and ginger, and the older children have trooped off to school next to the Hanuman temple, Pardiwada settles down to a more easygoing pace. Free of morning household chores, the women come out to sit in front of the houses, smoking, chatting and giving baths to babies and young children while old men gather under the shade of trees to gossip or play their interminable games of cards. By one in the afternoon, the working members of the family are back as are the school children. After a lunch of rice and a vegetable curry, this is a time for relaxation and the exchange of the day's news. Children play around on the streets, generally games of marbles, and there is much casual visiting as people wander in and out of each others' houses.

Economically, the Pardis belong to the lower class. Their poverty is reflected in the garbage dump which is clean and uncluttered, with nothing more in it than shards of pottery, small strips of cloth, husks of corn, and a few rotted vegetables. Because the poor use almost everything and throw away very little, their garbage dumps are generally cleaner than those of their richer neighbours. The Pardis may be poor but they are not destitute. They seem to have enough money for simple food, clothes, and even that necessary luxury of the urban poor—a black-and-white television set. The girls and women are dressed in bright colours and wear earrings, bangles, necklaces, and large round bindis rather than small demure dots on the forehead, serenely unaware that this particular accoutrement is now a part of the urban chic of upper-class women in Delhi and Bombay. Since their economic life is critically dependent on the prices at which they buy and sell fruits and vegetables, their incomes fluctuate daily, ranging from zero on the day a Pardi does not go out to work to 100 rupees on an exceptionally good day.

Their housing, too, is decent although overcrowded, not only because of the smallness of the houses but also because of the extended nature of the Pardi family which seems to spread haphazardly in all directions like the roots of a banyan tree. In fact, in this extremely close-knit community, there is no clear-cut demarcation of one family from another. Intermarriage has been so rampant that everyone is related to everyone else. The community is divided into four clans, each deriving its name from one of the four goddesses—Chowkat Mata, Shakti Mata, Kali Mata, and Naukod Mata. Theoretically, marriages within a clan are forbidden and the marriage partner cannot be outside the other three clans; it is, however, a rule mostly observed in its violation.

The word *pardi* appears to be a distorted form of *pahadi*, 'the hill man' and the group traces its original home to the hills of Chittorgarh in distant Rajasthan in the north, inhabited by the Bhil hunting tribes. The language they speak within the community is a mixture of Marwadi and Rajasthani, although all are fluent in the Hyderabadi dialect while some also know Telugu. As skilled hunters of birds like quail and partridge and of small animals such as rabbit and barking deer, the Pardis were nomadic hunters who moved southward to Hyderabad 250 years ago. According to their lore, the Muslim king who ruled Hyderabad at the time was suffering grievously from a festering sore which did not respond to treatment. One of the king's doctors, a venerable hakim of Unani medicine, suggested that the only possible cure was the application of minced meat of a particular kind of quail which was difficult to ensnare. The king had heard of the group of Pardis who had just entered his kingdom and of their proficiency as hunters. A Pardi was summoned to the court and entrusted with the task of snaring some of these quails. The hunter executed the order and brought back several birds whose meat was minced and applied to the royal sore. The worm that was eating into the king's flesh turned its attention to the bird's meat, which was poisonous for it, and it died. The king recovered and in his gratefulness decreed that henceforth the Pardis were welcome to take up residence in the kingdom of Hyderabad. In addition, and more materially, he showed his gratefulness by giving them a large tract of land called Jalpalli, which is about ten miles from this particular Pardiwada. Here, the Pardis dug a well for drinking water, built houses, and settled down for the first time in the history of the community in a place they could call their own.

Because of the scarcity of good forests near Jalpalli and the reluctance of the younger generation to learn the arduous skills of hunting, the Pardis began to look for other sources of livelihood. From nomadic hunters they turned into daily wage labourers in the fruit orchards and vegetable farms of Muslim landlords, packing and transporting fruits and vegetables from the farms to sell in the city. Gradually, they moved from Jalpalli into Hyderabad where over the last 50 years they have created various settlements, called Pardiwadas. The whole community still assembles together in the ancestral village of Jalpalli to celebrate certain important festivals like Dussehra and Holi.

Although they are now sellers of vegetables and fruits, the tradition of hunting and the memory of the days when these nomads were considered the scourge of more settled communities are very much alive as a part of Pardi identity and cultural memory. They take a not-so-secret pride in their reputation as a violent and aggressive people. There is little shame in the 'recollections' of the men that earlier, in the days of the benefactor king, they were regarded as bandits and thieves and that, whenever a band of Pardis camped near a village for hunting, it had to report daily to the headman and the police. Generally, though, the 'outlaw hunter' is now a dark, occasionally longed-for and rarely fantasized part of the Pardi identity. It comes to the forefront only during the hunting rituals when the community assembles to celebrate its festivals in Jalpalli. In a distorted form, however, I believe it also colours their participation in riots and religious violence, which is experienced in terms of the hunter and the hunted.

The 'identity-kit' sketch the Pardis would now have others recognize as their own is of a community that is accepted as a respectable part of settled Hindu society. In their origins myth, the Pardis are intimately related to the Marwadis, India's richest and highly respected business community, who hail from the plains of the same area in Rajasthan where the Pardis roamed the rocky hills. The ancestors of the two communities were brothers; one chose business and the other hunting as his profession. In their further efforts at what the sociologist M.N. Srinivas has called the process of 'Sanskritization' the Pardis strive to emulate and adopt the manners and mores of high-caste Hindu communities in an effort to raise their ritual status.[1] The erstwhile subsistence hunters now have very strict prohibitions on the eating of beef. Drinking of liquor, too, is frowned upon, although in an earlier generation even women were regular drinkers. Some of the older women still continue to be. Marriages used to be simple affairs, with the families of the bride and the groom sitting down together with some elders of the community under a tree to decide on the arrangements and the sharing of expenses. The head of the community then conducted a simple ceremony. Today, marriages follow the more elaborate pattern of other Hindu castes. The groom's family demands and receives a dowry from the girl's side. Brahmin ritual specialists are involved in the matching of horoscopes, in determining the auspicious days, and in presiding over the elaborate wedding ceremonies.

The Pardis' Sanskritizing effort to raise their ritual status in Hindu society is paradoxically accompanied by what can only be called attempts at de-Sanskritization in the socioeconomic sphere. This is because of the reservation policy of the Indian state which seeks to benefit the historically backward and deprived sections of society through preferential quotas in school admissions and government jobs. The Pardis, who were once classified as a 'scheduled tribe' and were thus on the lowest rung of the socioeconomic totem pole (thereby having first claims on the state quotas in education and employment), have been recently reclassified as a mere 'backward caste'. The elevation has brought with it the loss of many economic benefits, and the Pardis are currently engaged in a battle with the bureaucracy to prove that their backwardness is greater than that of a backward caste and thus to recover their earlier, lower status.

With very few exceptions, anthropologists have generally not described the many reasons why a community reveals itself to an outsider. Perhaps this reserve is because many anthropologists believe that the information they receive is primarily due to their personal qualities, such as a special gift for establishing rapport with strangers, fluency in the community's spoken language, evident sympathy with its ways, or other markers of an irresistible personal attractiveness which it would be immodest to talk about in public. The community's expectations of the researcher, which both encourage and skew a community's self-revelations in a particular direction, are rarely discussed. These expectations may be frankly material, as in the case of Napoleon Cagnon's Yanomono Indians of Venezuela who expected a constant stream of presents in exchange for their cooperation in furthering the anthropologist's academic career.[2] There, the community operated according to the principle of the goose that laid the golden egg: 'If you want more eggs, be nice to the goose.' In other communities, the expectations may be linked to more nonmaterial benefits: the prestige of associating with a white sahib if the anthropologist is European or North American, or (in a more literate community) help with admission and scholarships for a relative to the sahib's university. As far as the Pardis were concerned, it was evident that their initial ambivalence toward me, the motivation both to hold back and to talk, was coloured by their preoccupation with getting themselves reclassified as a scheduled tribe. Their suspicion was of strangers who might be agents of the government, gathering data which would harm their cause, like the researcher who had come 20 years ago and on whose report the government had acted: 'For his own career, he ground a whole community into dust.' The hope, which finally triumphed over the doubt, was of my being a potential helper in their dealings with the state, given my obvious high status. The motivation of the Muslims in talking to me—or, rather of their leaders in sanctioning our conversations—was of a different kind which can be expressed in words thus: 'You want to write about us and we would like to be written about in a way which suits our political purpose of appearing as victims.' In contrast to the Pardi leaders' faintly whining, complaining tone, the leaders of the Karwan Muslim community were firmly courteous, barely betraying their slight contempt of a Hindu liberal and do-gooder whose guilt about the Muslim minority they hoped to manipulate. I was thus aware that the accounts I heard were not only self-representations of individuals and the community but were also designed to accomplish particular pragmatic actions. Thus their conversational context needed to be kept constantly in mind.

A Pardi Family

The two-storeyed house of Badli Pershad, of the Naukod Mata clan, is smack in the heart of Pardiwada. On top of the doorway, which opens into a courtyard, are two painted baked clay idols, each about a foot high. The monkey god Hanuman, with a golden mace resting on his powerful shoulder, stands on the left side, guarding with his legendary strength the inhabitants of the house from the evil forces that surround human beings. The idol of god Rama stands on the right side, with a smaller Hanuman kneeling in front of the god in his equally legendary devotion. Badli Pershad, who is about 70 years old and blind for the last five years, is usually to be found in the room to the right of the courtyard. Except for a cot, the room is empty and scrupulously clean. Its floor, made of grey paving stone, is swept and washed every morning.

Badli Pershad has four grown children, two sons and two daughters, of which his youngest son Rajesh and his family live with him. The others live separately in different parts of the city. Both his sons are college graduates who reluctantly took up the traditional family occupation of vending fruit from pushcarts because they could not find other jobs. Their feelings of bitterness and humiliation are very close to the surface. Besides his son, daughter-in-law, and two grandchildren; Badli Pershad's 90-year-old mother also lives with him. His sister, Laloo Bai, stays in a separate part of the house, occupying most of the second story, with her eldest son and his family. The kitchens are separate but on many evenings, especially in the summer when it gets very hot, the sister and her family come down to the courtyard with the food they have cooked, and both the families eat together.

This is a snapshot of the family at one particular instant in the winter of 1991, since a major feature of a Pardiwada family is its fluidity. Family members come and go and stay for varying lengths of time depending upon the impact of external events on their lives and the ebb and flow of internal family life and relationships. Badli Pershad's eldest son, Satish, lived in the same house with his family till a few months ago and moved out to a safer area after the December riot of the previous year. If his economic situation worsens, he may soon be back again. In this kind of shifting family, expanding and contracting like a giant membrane with an irregular rhythm, the only constant presence for young children is their parents (and, to some extent, their grandparents), especially the mother. Although it is both exciting and reassuring to have many caretakers who can compensate for parental shortcomings and mitigate the strong emotions aroused in a small, nuclear family, the frequent comings and goings of other adults in an extended family can also make children cling to their own parents, especially the mother, with a marked intensity as they seek to establish an intimate, enduring and trusting relationship in their inner, representational worlds—to establish 'object constancy', in psychoanalytic language. In one of my earlier writings, I had attributed the intense bond between mother and son in Hindu India solely to the vicissitudes of a woman's identity—to become a mother of a son is to finally become a woman in the eyes of the patriarchy—with all the radical improvement in her status in the family that such a transition implies.[3] I increasingly realize that the son, with his need for at least one figure to stand out clearly from a labyrinthian flux of relationships, actively furthers the mutual emotional investment of mother and son.

The experience of fluidity is not only from within the family, which constantly constitutes and reconstitutes itself, but also in relation to the wider community which, in fact, is an extended family. Badli Pershad's eldest son is married to his sister's daughter and his youngest daughter is married to one of his sister's sons. There are so many such interconnections by marriage in the Pardi community that Badli Pershad would not be surprised to discover that he was the nephew of his daughter! One of the consequences of their being such a closely knit community is the great similarity in their views and opinions on different issues and in the way they think and follow a shared logic. This can be helpful in the sense that one can be reasonably sure that even a small sample would be accurately representative of the larger community. On the other hand, it can get boring to listen to very similar responses and a shared, common discourse unenlivened by individual quirkiness.

Badli Pershad's wife, one of the economic mainstays of the family, who earned 50 to 60 rupees a day selling fruit, died in 1988. He misses her terribly. 'Her absence is unbearable at times. She used to look after all my needs. Since I cannot see, she brought me my food and medicine, took me to the bathroom. I have been a diabetic for 35 years and can only eat a restricted diet of wheat rotis and vegetables. I am not allowed to eat rice or meat. She understood that these restrictions upset me and sometimes added meat gravy to my food.

'Although my children and grandchildren are quite obedient, I feel they get tired of taking care of me to such an extent. Sometimes I think I am a major burden on them because of my lack of sight. If only I could have this [cataract] surgery, I would be more independent. My mother here, who is probably 90 years old, is still fit and healthy, and people say she is my daughter and not my mother in the way she looks after me. She brings me my food, takes me to the bathroom, bathes me, and sees to all my comforts. Even at this age, she is active and alert. When my daughter-in-law goes off to her mother's house, she does all the cooking by herself.

'I had more say in family matters when I had my eyes. My children were also younger. I was strong, worked hard, and people looked up to me to make all the major household discisions. Now I feel dependent, a burden on the family. They still respect me and are concerned about my needs and wishes. I, too, feel it is their life now and they should be allowed to do what they want to. Therefore unless someone asks my opinion I try not to force my views on others.'

The deference paid to Badli Pershad is not only perfunctory but extends to issues vital for the family's welfare. His sister and his sons want him to sell the house and move out of Pardiwada since their sense of security has diminished precipitately after the last riot. In the past, Badli Pershad had resisted the demand although he is now resigned to the move: 'This house carries memories of my youth, my wife, my children, and the good times that we spent together. Given a choice, I would not like to leave this house till I die. But under the circumstances, where we cannot hope for security or peace, I am forced to think of selling. The reason I have not done so is because the buyers are mainly Muslim who are offering very low prices for such a good house.'

Pardis and the Modern World

Badli Pershad's younger son, the 40-year-old Rajesh, is bitter that he could not find the job he feels his college education entitled him to. It is with a sense of aggrieved humiliation that he drives an auto-rickshaw to earn a living, in addition to helping out with the family's vegetable and fruit business. He has a baffled feeling of betrayal, of unkept promises, although he would be unable to say what the promises were or who made them. He blames the changing times, as do many of his friends, for this feeling of nagging dissatisfaction. Rajesh mourns the passing of an earlier era when the world was a simpler and kinder place and the bonds between the Pardis much stronger than they are today. "In Hyderabad, our *jaat* [a word denoting both a caste and a community] was once the best in the mango and grape business. No other *jaat* could even touch us. Now we compete against each other. We have become the best in the infighting business. Everyone is running after wealth, looking out only for himself. We were happier when we were together.

'In olden days after you earned 20,000 rupees, you relaxed. There was enough to eat for six months and after that we'd see. We went back to the village, lazed about, talked day and night. Now no one's desires are ever satisfied. Everyone wants more—bigger house, better food, more this, more that. It is good that a person thinks "I must progress, I must raise myself". But this raising is done by pushing someone else down. We were happier when we earned less but lived in friendship and love.

'Even the nature of our business has changed. Nowadays, it is all just calculation. Earlier, we would go into an orchard and estimate the yield of trees and come to an agreement with the owner. Most of the time the fruit would be more than the estimate and one made a little extra money. Then came these packing boxes. We do not buy the fruit on the trees any more but get it in exactly weighed boxes. You have to deal with agents, contractors, truck owners, each one measuring, weighing, calculating. There is no more of walking around in orchards in fresh air, looking up at the trees, and estimating the yield.'

Of course, a part of Rajesh's mourning for the 'good old days' may well be the normal expression of what Christopher Bollas calls a 'generational consciousness' as it gives place to the consciousness of a new generation.[4] Rajesh's nostalgic ruminations are thus also occasioned by the waning of a youthful vitality which made the world come alive at a particular time of his life. The inner feeling of the dimming of life for a whole generation then gets expressed in a sense of loss which is attributed to changes in the modernizing outside world. Many of us pass down this consciousness of loss to our young, although it is not strictly their own, and which most of them thankfully succeed in renouncing sooner or later. On the other hand, the raising of a generation's consciousness occurs precisely because of severe dislocations such as the process of modernization. Without a crisis of this historical magnitude, the demarcation between the consciousness of a preceding and a succeeding generation is not so marked; the change is not big enough to become a subject of reflection.

Rajesh's elder brother, the 45-year-old Satish, although sharing some of his brother's feelings of bitterness and disappointment—he too could not get a job in spite of his education—would confront the dislocations of modernity more actively. He is a passionate advocate of change in the community's attitudes and values. A small, intense man,whose sense of his own dignity is in constant conflict with an anxious desire to please, Satish would make the next generation a vehicle for his hopes rather than weigh it down with despair.

'You know our business is such that we cannot earn a lot of money to buy property or have savings. It is a hand-to-mouth existence. Our most valuable property is our children. So we are very careful about how we bring them up and what they will make of their lives. That is why we not only want to feed and clothe them properly but also give them the best education we can. We do not want our children to get into bad habits. Therefore I have bought a black-and-white television so that if they want to watch a film they can do it at home. Otherwise once the children are in their teens it is easy for them to fall into bad company and spoil their lives. But I know that not everyone in our community feels like this. They think that children are there for the financial support of the parents in their old age, and this is why they want to make them study and find a good job. Not for the children's sake but their own. We [indicates his wife] are not selfish like that. It is our duty to bring up the children as good people and if they feel like taking care of us in our old age then it is our good luck.

'Our people have certain fixed festivals like Bonal, Holi, and Dussehra which we have celebrated since the time of our ancestors. But now, seeing other Hindus celebrate so many festivals, our people also want to celebrate them. Festivals like Ganesh, Diwali, Ugadi are nothing but occasions for wasteful expenditure. In the name of the festival it becomes compulsory to buy new clothes, prepare good food, spend money on useless things like crackers and decorations. It is the spirit of sacredness and not the show that is important. Unfortunately, these days show and the amount of noise one can make seem to have become a sign of one's importance. And sometimes although the menfolk may not be interested in celebrating all the rituals of a festival, they may have to do so because of their wives. I am lucky that my wife shares my ideas. Many of my friends complain that they are unable to meet these expenses but have to undertake them to please their wives. These women have no thoughts of their own. They want to do everything other women do I am very particular that blind customs and useless rituals are discarded.

'Another custom I would like to change is the burial of dead bodies. I feel it is better to cremate than bury the dead. This is because space is becoming a major problem these days. Our ancestral village of Jalpalli is now only full of graves. The sad part is that these graves do not get respectful treatment from those who are alive. After a few years, the land is dug up and used for construction. Therefore I feel it is better to finish off once and for all so that there is neither a problem of space nor disrespect to the dead. Moreover, many times some of my Hindu friends have questioned me about this practice. They ask why despite being Hindus we bury the dead like Muslims. I feel very embarrassed. Now it is a mixed situation. Some families have started cremating their dead and some continue to bury them. This kind of behaviour makes you the laughing-stock of others, especially these Muslims. They are always on the lookout for our customs that are odd. This is the main difference between their religion and ours. They have fixed rules which no one can flout.

'The other thing I would like to change is our custom of marriage between members of one family. Earlier, people followed it because it ensured that all family members lived in one place. Now there is no need for such a custom because there is so much overcrowding. I feel that one must send our daughters to different families and get girls from new families because it will help us establish new relationships.'

Satish's main strategy in dealing with the dislocations caused by rapid change seems to be aimed at reducing the isolation—of the family by integrating it into a network of other families, and of the community by bringing it closer to the customs and usage of a Hindu 'mainstream'. He exemplifies the spirit of agency among the Pardis, both individual and collective. In their vigorous pursuit of community self-interest which manipulates all the levers that can influence decision-making in a modern democratic state—from preparing detailed, petitioning briefs for the bureaucracy to persistent lobbying of their elected representatives—the Pardis are by no means mere passive victims of the modernizing process.

The Night of Long Knives

The 35-year-old, plump and cheerful Lalita, Badli Pershad's eldest daughter-in-law, remembers that particular Saturday evening well. It must have been 7:30, and they were all gathered around the television set listening to the local news which comes on during the intermission of the Saturday movie. (It was *Swami Ayappa*, a religious-mythological film in the classification of Indian movies). The riots had started in another part of the walled city that morning and a curfew had been in force since five in the evening. The news announcer informed them that the curfew would be lifted for one hour the next morning so that people could go out and buy essentials such as milk and medicines. Suddenly, they heard a crowd's deep growl of '*Allah-u-Akbar*!', 'Kill! Kill!' and panicky answering shouts of 'The Mussulmans have come!' Lalita knew what to do. It was the third time since her marriage that Pardiwada had been involved in a Hindu-Muslim riot. It always happened at night. The women and older children went downstairs and started collecting stones for the men to throw at the Muslim mob. Children's school bags were emptied to serve as pouches for the stony ammunition, sarees and bedsheets were taken out and tied around the men's foreheads to prevent serious head injuries. The women could not see much whenever they looked out into the alley. There were 'hundreds' of Muslims with swords and spears, their faces covered with pieces of cloth so that only their eyes were visible. Prema, the 33-years-old daughter-in-law of Laloo Bai, Badli Pershad's sister, is certain that the attacking Muslims were not outsiders. They knew which houses belonged to the Hindus and in fact would call out the owners' names. Perhaps there were a few goondas from outside but 'the whole thing was planned by our Mussulmans here.' Prema's mother's brother was killed that evening as was her sister-in-law Kalavati, who had run out in panic to get back her four-year-old son who had slipped out of the house to see all the excitement happening outside. Both the mother and son were chopped down by sword blows before they could get back.

Kamla Bai, Badli Pershad's 'cousin' (I have given up the effort to chart more precise relationships), who lives some houses away at the outskirts of Pardiwada, had a narrow escape. Her family had just eaten and was rearranging itself before the television set when the Muslims broke into the house. She ran out with her children, pleading with the men to spare their lives. One Hindu was killed in front of her but Kamla Bai was allowed to pass through unharmed. She hid in a neighbour's house. The ration shop and the vegetable shop next to her house were looted and set on fire. 'One of my neighbours has four children who are not normal in the head. They killed her with a sword. Her head was literally in two pieces. One of the woman's relatives came out to help. They caught hold of her and asked her where her husband was. When she refused to tell, they cut off her arms and legs. She died. They broke into Ratnaram's house and killed him. His young daughter Krishnavati hid herself behind an almirah to save herself. They dragged her outside and killed her. They did not even spare old women.'

The attack on Pardiwada, which left 24 people dead, ended around eleven at night when the police arrived. The Pardis were not sure whether it was the police or a new Muslim mob disguised in police uniforms. 'Pelt them with stones,' was the general consensus on the action to be taken. 'The police would not be scared but the Muslims would run away.' More men and women now started to come out, and the alleys of Pardiwada, eerily lighted by magenta-tinged smouldering fires, began to fill with the sounds of women wailing and weeping as corpses of close relatives were discovered and mourned.

Rajesh, Badli Pershad's youngest son, was standing under a tree next to the Hanuman temple. Because of the curfew he had been playing cards with his friends, Nambre and Anto, the whole afternoon. He had just come out for a pee when he saw a group of Muslims running toward the temple with swords and tins of kerosene. Rajesh hid behind the tree, glad that he was shirtless and only wearing underwear and was thus less easy to spot in the dark. As he watched the Muslims throw lighted kerosene rags into the temple and run by to attack the house that he had just left, his only thought was that he would have died like his friends if he had not come out to ease his bladder.

For Rajesh, the Muslim attack on Pardiwada was not entirely unexpected. His Muslim friends, a couple of whom he had known since childhood, had been warning him of just such an eventuality. 'We are very worried about you,' they would say as they drank tea in a hotel. 'You are staying there, your wife and children are there. You should leave.' One day before the attack, a Muslim friend told Rajesh to go away for a few days. 'Why are you after my life?' Rajesh replied in some irritation. 'Whatever happens, will happen.' Rajesh had reported the Muslim warnings to the community elders such as Dalyan Singh, the unofficial leader of the Shakkergunj Pardis. The police had made all arrangements for their safety, Rajesh was told, and Dalyan Singh pointed to the three policemen who had been assigned to Pardiwada and with whom he was playing cards.

Running back from the temple, Rajesh met a distraught Dalyan Singh on the way. 'The Muslims have attacked from all sides,' Dalyan Singh said. 'I am trying to find the policemen.' Many Pardi men had come out. They tried to stop the attackers from entering the heart of Pardiwada by directing a barrage of stones at whichever corner a Muslim breakthrough seemed imminent. 'The men of our community are brave. We were unarmed and still did not run away from their swords and spears.' Later at night, as soon as Muslims began withdrawing from the heart of Pardiwada, Rajesh rushed to his sister's house located at the outskirts. The door was closed from inside. Rajesh banged on the door, shouted and screamed, but there was no response. "It is all over," I thought. "They are all dead. Everyone has been killed." I went up to the police inspector. They were picking up a corpse. "My sister, and her family are dead," I said. Then I saw them coming out of a neighbour's house who is a Muslim. "We are here," they said. The Muslim family had given them shelter, saved their lives.'

When the police finally arrived, Rajesh was active in helping them identify the dead bodies and gather together the injured for further transport to the hospital. This was when he saw two men bring in a seriously wounded Dalyan Singh. He had been stabbed by Jafar, the men said. Jafar was the leader of the area's Muslims and a friend of Dalyan Singh. The two had worked closely in the past, liaising with the city administration in keeping the relations between the Hindus and Muslims peaceful whenever there was communal tension in the city. (Later, it was discovered that the assassin was not Jafar but another man accompanying him.) At this time someone informed Rajesh that his 'uncle' had been killed and the body taken to Osmania hospital.

The police jeep took a long time in coming, and Rajesh offered to take some of the seriously wounded to the hospital in his auto-rickshaw. He could then also claim his uncle's body and bring it back. As he drove ot of Pardiwada around one in the morning, his adrenaline-fuelled courage evaporated. He had to pass through Muslim areas where groups of men roamed the dark streets in shadowy, menacing packs. 'I will surely die tonight,' Rajesh thought, or rather felt, in his terror. But as the headlight of the rickshaw bore down on the men, they scattered into the bylanes. They had taken it to be a police motorcycle, and Rajesh, soon cottoning on, heightened the impression by driving at full throttle while roaring threats and abuse like a real police inspector.

Osmania hospital, named after the last Nizam of Hyderabad, famed for both his wealth and his reluctance to spend it, was in total chaos. the harried doctors and staff were unable to cope with the stream of injured and dead descending on them from all over the city. Rajesh unloaded his grisly cargo on the floor of the admissions hall and hurried from one corridor to another searching for his uncle's body in the piles of corpses that were haphazardly stacked outside the wards. He did not find his uncle's body but became instrumental in saving the life of his niece, Pushpa. In one of the mounds of corpses, he saw a hand moving. As he tugged at the hand and pulled out the body, he saw it was Pushpa, who was still alive although unconscious with a severe head injury. A passing doctor was successfully importuned and cajoled into arranging for surgery, and Pushpa was saved.

Rajesh returned to Pardiwada to find the Pardis preparing to move out of their homes. 'I was against such a step and vehemently protested. To evacuate is to run away. It was a question of our self-respect. It would always stand as a shameful black mark against our community. But rumours were going around, "The Muslims have attacked here; they have attacked there." People were getting very frightened. Then Juggu and Suraj pehlwans appeared on the scene. "We have brought trucks," they said. "The *basti* must be vacated immediately." I was still unhappy but followed their instructions. My brother refused to leave. I was very angry. If everyone else was leaving what was the need for him to stay? I asked the police to help and they forced him to come with us. The trucks brought us to Gandhi Bhawan.'

It was my strong impression that the mental processing of the events of the riot is different in women. It is not only that women's memories of the riot tend to be circumscribed by what happened inside the house rather than outside and that their anxieties are centred around the danger to their children. With women, anger at Muslims is not the baffled rage I encountered among men. Women also find it easier to think and plan of moving away from their endangered homes, to leave it all behind and get on with their lives. Men seem to find it more difficult to free themselves from the impact of recent violent events, they agonize over leaving Pardiwada and the implications such a move may have for their own self-respect and the community's sense of honour. The men brood over the events of the riot more. They take the betrayal by their Muslim neighbours, who they believe helped the violent mob by identifying the Hindu houses (if they themselves were not a part of the mob), much more personally. Their sense of betrayal and perfidy is perhaps due to the fact that the men's relationships with their Muslim neighbours were more personal; some were even friends. Women's friendships were (and are) firmly within the Hindu community. With their Muslim women neighbours, the relationship was limited to the exchange of polite greetings. Women do not have to deal with the trauma of the neighbour suddenly being revealed as a deadly enemy to quite the same extent as do the men.

Although the riots have had an impact on the friendships between Hindus and Muslims, not all of these friendships, especially those that go back to childhood, have snapped completely because of the heightened conflict and violence between the communities. As an outsider, it is difficult to judge the depth of a friendship, and it may be, as studies across the borders of the other antagonistic groups such as the Protestants and Catholics in Northern Ireland, and the French and the English in Quebec have suggested, that such friendships are more illusory than real or are qualitatively different from one's friendships within one's own in-group.[5] This particular social-psychological theory predicts that such friendships can be maintained when individuals dwell upon their similarities rather than differences, avoid the divisive issue of religious affiliation, and shape their interactions so that the salience of their group membership—of one friend being a Hindu and the other a Muslim—is lowered. It appears from my observations, however, that the salience of one's religious group membership is not lowered by avoiding the issue, at least as far as deep friendship is concerned. Such an avoidance may smooth the course of fleeting Hindu-Muslim encounters that are temporary from the very outset. The maintenance of lasting Hindu-Muslim friendships, on the other hand, seems to demand (and never more so than after a riot) that the fact of friends belonging to antagonistic groups be squarely confronted before being negated as of little consequence. Rajesh, for instance, in the days following the riot, openly berated his Muslim friends for what their coreligionists had done to the Pardis. In more normal circumstances, friends seek to periodically dissipate the tension which arises from antagonistic religious affiliations by jokingly addressing each other deliberately in negative stereotypical terms such as, 'Come here, O you Hindu idolator,' 'O you Muslim violator of four wives' and so on. Such a joking relationship between friends strives to reduce the antagonism which has its source in the conflict of their religious group by acknowledging the differences while at the same time downplaying it.

Many Pardi families, including that of Satish, Badli Pershad's eldest son, moved out of Pardiwada to safer areas after the riot. Some of them have come back for reasons of both economics and sentiment. It goes without saying that they missed the homes they had grown up in. They missed the nutrients for the soul provided by the closely knit community life they had left behind to settle among strangers. They have also been unable to sell their Pardiwada houses at reasonable prices. The only interested buyers are Muslims and, though Pardis would reluctantly reconcile themselves to the idea of selling an ancestral home to a Muslim, the prices quoted are very low—the Muslim buyers content to wait till the Pardis' fear of staying on becomes greater than the wish.

The disruption in their lives caused by the riot has been considerable. 'When we all sit together to talk, certain things bring back the memories of that day, especially the sight of broken and empty houses,' says Satish. 'Even after so many months, we are very scared that it may happen again. Before we plan to celebrate any of our religious festivals on a community-wide basis, we think ten times about the likely consequences. The experience was terrifying! These days we feel a little more confident about staying here because a police picket has been permanently posted in Pardiwada. But you know the police are not very reliable. Where were they that evening? They arrived three hours after all the damage was done.

'Our business has been badly hurt. We also used to sell our stuff in Muslim areas and most of the time we went in alone. Now we are afraid to go there even in small groups. I keep on thinking about going back to the place we moved out to after the riot. But our business runs on various personal contacts which I developed over the years. To start such a business in a new locality where you neither know the people nor the place becomes difficult.'

Badli Pershad, who is resisting the family pressure to move out of the home he built 40 years ago, is naturally more sanguine about the future. 'The next riot,' he feels, 'will not occur for another five to ten years because the last riot was very severe. Both the Hindus and Muslims suffered great losses and are fully involved in repairing and trying to restart their lives. Therefore they will have neither the time nor the inclination to trouble the other community.' His children wish they could share his optimism about the force of human rationality.

For the women, the riot has had the consequence of drastically reducing their freedom of movement. 'We used to come out at night and play in small groups,' says Lalita. 'Now we can't even sit out. The policemen shoo us back.' The number of women who go out to buy fruits and vegetables from the Muslim wholesalers early in the morning has also declined. The women do not let the children venture far from their homes and have become especially watchful of the movements of young girls. 'What if Muslim boys harass one of our daughters and another riot starts?' asks Prema.

'The relations with the Muslims of our own basti have become more formal. The older ones still address us as 'daughters' and claim they did not recognize our attackers in the dark. We cannot believe them. Earlier, the Muslims used to come when we invited them for any of our community celebrations and we went whenever they invited us for theirs. When Jafar's daughter got married in Secunderabad, all of us went and helped in making the wedding arrangements. Now there are no more invitations, either from us or them.' The riots have hastened the process of Pardi differentiation and separation from their Muslim neighbours. They have given another push toward making the Pardis more Hindu, contributed to a sharper etching of Hindu and Muslim identities.

Pardis and Muslims: The Past

The Pardis recollect their shared past with the Muslims with a measure of ambivalence. They are aware that their ancestors served the Muslims as farm labourers during the latter's long rule and that they have been influenced in many ways by their erstwhile masters. The influence is evident in the way they dispose of their dead, in the many Urdu words which have crept into their dialect, for example, *valid* for father, *mazhab* for religious faith; and, till recently, in the not too seldom use of Muslim names for their children. Rajesh's wife Sakila, for instance, has a Muslim name, a fact of which he is deeply ashamed and for which he blames his illiterate in-laws who had no idea of the meaning and importance of names.

In the more recent past, Satish recalls playing football, cricket, and kabaddi as a child with Muslim boys of the neighbourhood. He visited their homes freely, as they did his, and was even friendly with their womenfolk who did not observe any purdah in front of him. Accompanying his mother on her rounds through the Muslim areas, he would carry the fruits and vegetables right inside the houses and was never made to feel unwelcome. The understanding that existed between Hindus and Muslims of the previous generation, Satish says, has disappeared in the younger one which is a hot-blooded lot. Whereas the older Muslims were tolerant, the young ones are aggressive and are provoked to violence at the slightest of pretexts. Kamla Bai agrees with the assessment, as do others, that it was easy to live together with the older generation of Muslims but it is impossible to do so with the younger who are all turning into goondas.

The· easier coexistence in an earlier era does not mean that the Pardis ever liked the Muslims or did not feel resentful toward them. The Pardi version of the history of Hindu-Muslim conflict articulated by Badli Pershad as an elder of the community, goes thus: 'The clashes between Hindus and Muslims started long ago in the period of the Nizam and his *razakars* (a marauding, unofficial army) who were very cruel to the Hindus. They used to harass our girls, rape them. This happened not only in villages but even in Hyderabad. We feared the Muslims. The rule was theirs, the king was theirs, the police were theirs, so it was hard for the Hindus to resist. We were also poor and no one supports the poor. Some Marwadis may have been well-off but the majority of Hindus was poor. The Muslims were close to the king. They were moneylenders, charging high rates of interest. Thus they were rich and the Hindus poor and though we lived together Muslims dominated the Hindus.

'We never used to mingle closely with them. Hindus feared Muslims a lot. They were very aggressive. They eat *bada gosht* (beef) which kept Hindus away from them. They used to prepare *kheer* (rice pudding) on their festival days but they cooked it in the same vessels. So we never ate even the vegetarian food they sent to our houses. People only drank tea together.

'Anyway, when the oppression of the Hindus came to the notice of our leaders in Delhi, they wanted to do something about it as the British were not going to help. After Independence all the leaders wanted Hyderabad to become a part of Hindustan but Gandhi was hesitant. So Nehru, Patel, and Rajendra Prasad felt Gandhi needed to be eliminated and had Gandhi killed. Then they could free the Hindus in Hyderabad from Muslim rule.'

Badli Pershad's account of Hindu-Muslim relations in the pre-Independence era, except for his version of the murder of the Mahatma which not every one agreed with, represents a popular consensus among the Pardis. As the historian Lowenthal has observed, it is only academic versions of the past which are variable, contested and subject to different interpretations; popular history, on the other hand, is a timeless mirror which gives accurate reflections of historical events, beyond questioning or doubt.[6]

Image of the Muslim

The two chief components of the contemporary Pardi image of Muslims are of the powerful and the animal-like Muslim. Shared alike by men and women, the image of the Muslim's power seems to be more pronounced in men. The image of the antagonist's powerfulness is certainly influenced by the Pardis' direct experience of being an embattled enclave in the walled city, surrounded by a numerically greater Muslim host. It also contains their historical memory of being serfs on the farms and estates of Muslim landlords. This image of Muslim power is in relation to the Hindus' lack of it. What is repeatedly stressed is the weak Hindus—weak because divided—rapidly losing ground against a united and purposeful nation. 'Anything happens in a Muslim community, they all become one. We don't because of our different castes. Every caste has its own customs and lifestyle.'

'We are not united. Each one is engrossed in himself. The rich try to exploit the poor. This does not happen with the Muslims. Though they have rich and poor at least at the time of prayer they are one and they all do it together at the same time. It develops unity among them. Our system is not like that. Each one goes to the temple to perform puja at his own time and in his own way and then leaves. There is no communication between us. If we could also show togetherness in our prayers, we would definitely become united and stronger than the Muslims.'

'The problem with the Hindus is that because of the number of castes they are not united. Reddys fight with Kapus, Pardis fight with Komtis, Yadavs fight with Naidus. If only they could unite like the Muslims! Muslims may be small in number but their dos and don't with regard to religion are very strict and they are forced together at least for the Friday prayer. Their leaders use these occasions to forge religious unity. I don't speak Arabic but I am told many fiery speeches are made in mosques every Friday afternoon where they talk of driving the Hindus away from Hyderabad and making their own independent Pakistan here.'

The Muslim is powerful because he is united, armed, favoured by the state in India and supported, perhaps even armed, by a state outside, Pakistan.

'Muslims have a constant supply of weapons coming from Pakistan or maybe they are locally made. They are always well-stocked. Even the poorest Muslim house will have at least a butcher's knife because they all eat meat. Hindus are not so well-equipped. If the government continues to please the Muslims and makes rules against the Hindu majority, these riots will continue forever. If processions are to be banned, both Ganesh and Muharram processions should be banned. Why is only the Ganesh procession banned? It is like blessing and protecting only one community (*sir par hath rakhna*) and behaving like a stepmother toward the other.'

'They want to dominate us. Just see how they are planning to make the old city into a Pakistan. In Hyderabad the mosques always had four minarets. But now they have started building mosques with a single minaret, just like in Pakistan. Hindus are willing to adjust but Muslims are stubborn. Our government also supports them. On Shivratri day, the markets will be closed but during Muharram they will remain open day and night. Why?'

It was strikingly apparent that the Pardis' self-identification as Hindus occurs only when they talk of *the* Muslim; otherwise the conversation is of Pardis, Lodhas, Brahmins, Marwadis, and oher castes. It seems a Hindu is born only when the Muslim enters. Hindus cannot think of themselves as such without a simultaneous awareness of the Muslim's presence. This is not so for the Muslim, who does not need the Hindu for self-awareness. The presence of the Hindu may increase the Muslim sense of identity but does not constitute it. Little wonder that Hindutva needs 'the Muslim question' for the creation of a united Hindu community and the expansion of its political base and, in fact, will find it difficult to exist without it.

In the bitter complaints directed at the government, the *mai-baap* ('mother-father') of an earlier era, the psychoanalyst cannot help but hear echoes of a collective sibling rivalry, of the group-child's envy and anger at the favouring of an ambivalently regarded sibling by the parent. This does not mean that there is no factual basis to these accusations, but only that, like many other such preceptions in the emotionally charged area of Hindu-Muslim relations, they are neither merely real nor merely psychological.

The image of Muslim animality is composed of the perceived ferocity, rampant sexuality, and demand for instant gratification of the male, and a dirtiness which is less a matter of bodily cleanliness and more of an inner pollution as a consequence of the consumption of forbidden, tabooed foods. This image is an old one, also found in S.C. Dube's 30-year-old anthropological account of a village outside Hyderabad: 'The Muslims are good only in two things—they eat and copulate like beasts. Who else except a Muslim would even think of going to bed with his uncle's daughter, who is next only to his real sister?'[7]

Badli Pershad contrasts Hindu and Muslim sexual natures explicitly: 'Muslims always had an eye for our women. This habit persists. Good thoughts and thoughts of God come into their minds only when they shout *'Allah-u-Akbar!'* Rest of the time they simply forget morality and go on sexually harassing our women. We never took a single woman of theirs. They used to take ours all the time. They were rich and the rulers and did what they wanted. We are moral (*dharmic*) and would never do such things even if rich. We treat all women as mothers and sisters. They force themselves on women; they are obsessed by women and sex. Look at all the children they produce, dozens, while we are content with two or three.'

Most Pardi women concur with these views and in fact go further in linking the outbreak of violence to the 'fact' of the Muslim's lewd sexual nature. Kamla Bai remarks, 'Muslim boys are especially prone to harass our girls. Unlike Muslim girls, we leave our women free to walk around and even go out of the *basti* if they wish to. Many times the girls are victims of very vulgar behaviour on the part of Muslim boys. If it was only kept to the verbal level, it is O.K. But the Muslims often use physical harassment. This makes our boys very angry. Sometimes these fights take on a communal colouring and in the past they have been the main triggers for the outbreak of riots.'

The Muslim animality also lies in a heedless pursuit of pleasure without any regard for the concerns and obligations which make one human. 'Their children are completely spoilt. They drink a lot. They are used to a carefree, uninhibited life. The young ones are only interested in enjoyment. Everything they do is for enjoyment. Hindus are cowards because they are worried about cultivating the land, education for their children, and so many other things. Muslims don't worry at all.'

The Pardi image of the Muslim and the arguments employed for its construction are strikingly similar to the ones used by the *sangh parivar* to attract Hindus to its cultural and political fold. (Whether this convergence of perceptions is due to the *sangh parivar's* articulation of a widespread Hindu sentiment or whether it is the *parivar's* creation through a manipulation of Hindu symbols is a question I shall discuss later.) In any event, an understanding of this component of the Hindu image of the Muslim gives us an insight into how people belonging to a vastly superior demographic majority can still psychologically experience themselves as an endangered minority.

Viewing an antagonistic group as dirty, and thus subhuman, whereas one's own cleanliness is not only humanely civilized but next to godliness, is commonplace in ethnic conflict. 'Dirty nigger' and 'dirty Jew' are well-known epithets in the United States. The Chinese regard Tibetans as unwashed and perpetually stinking of yak butter, while Jewish children in Israel are brought up to regard Arabs as dirty. In the Rwandan radio broadcasts inciting the Hutus to massacre the Tutsis, the latter were consistently called rats and cockroaches, creatures associated with dirt and underground sewers, vermin needing to be exterminated. Serbs and the Bosnian Muslims, the Turks and Kurds, and so many other groups in conflict are outraged by each other's dirtiness. Again there may be a grain of reality in some of the accusations because of a particular group's poverty, food habits, or the climatic conditions of its habitat. If the attribution of dirtiness falters against too great a discrepancy in factual reality, it will no longer be attributed to the opponent's body but to the soul. In some ways, the dirtiness is now even worse; it is a moral dirtiness which is more than skin deep. A blackness of the heart.

As a poverty-stricken community, the Pardis are not in a position to call Muslims physically dirty, an accusation which is more the province of the higher Hindu castes. One of the jokes I remember from my childhood is of the Muslim saying to the Hindu, 'You Hindus are so dirty. You have a bath today and then [now speaking in an exaggeratedly slow drawl] you will baathe agaain tomoorow. But we Muslims, we have a bath [in a rapid fire delivery] Friday-to-Friday, Friday-to-Friday!' 'The Muslims who work are dirty, others are not. We work hard to survive. So where is the time for us to appear neat and clean?' asks Badli Pershad plaintively. Muslims, however, are dirty in a more fundamental way; they eat beef.

Beef eating is the most heinous of sins among the Pardis (as it is among most Hindus), a more serious violation of the moral code than marriage to a Muslim or conversion to Islam. '*Bada gosht* (beef) is their favourite dish. If any of us even touches it he must have a bath. All Muslims eat *bada gosht*. That is why we keep ourselves away from them. We do not even drink water in their homes,' says Lalita.

'We pray to the cow because it is our (mother-goddess) Lakshmi. Hindus revere even cow dung, use it for cooking, decorating the house and for many other things. *They* eat the cow!' says Badli Pershad, his disgust palpable.

The Muslim eating and the Hindu abomination of beef creates an effective barrier between the two; it is difficult to be close to someone with whom one cannot share a meal and whose eating habits one finds disgusting.

Gandhi, Psychoanalysts and Cows

The Muslim eating of beef and thus the killing of cows has perhaps historically been the most important source of Hindu bitterness toward the Muslim. In Tipu Sultan's dominions, Abbe Dubois tells us, though Hindus witnessed the slaughter of cows without uttering loud complaint, they were far from insensible to the insult, contenting themselves with complaining in secret and storing up in their hearts all the indignation they felt about this sacrilege.[8] Pious Lingayats came up to the Abbe with tears in their eyes, imploring him to use his influence as a priest with the local Europeans to stop them from eating beef. Hindus who had been forcibly converted to Islam could not reconvert even if they had eaten beef only under duress. From the 19th century onward, Hindu revivalism has been closely associated with movements against cow slaughter.

The ferocity of Hindu emotions, chiefly disgust at the eating of beef and rage at the slaughter of cows, would automatically draw attention from psychoanalysts for whom the presence of strong emotions in a relationships implies the operation of unconscious factors. In 1924, the British army psychiatrist Owen Berkeley-Hill wrote a paper on the theme of Hindu-Muslim conflict, a paper which served as a topic for discussion at the meeting of the Indian Psychoanalytic Society in Calcutta to which Gandhi was also invited.[9] In this essay, Berkeley-Hill identifies two main hurdles in the way of Hindu-Muslim unity. The first is the Hindu's 'motherland complex' wherein the ancient cults of mother-goddesses have become associated with the ideas of woman, virgin, mother, and motherland—Bharat Mata—which the Muslims violated through their conquest of India. (The colonel does not explain why there is not such Hindu bitterness against the British for a similar 'violence'.) The second obstacle is the Muslim slaughter of cows which, Berkeley-Hill tries to establish, were once a totem animal for the Hindus (as it still continues to be for certain tribes in central and south India) and thus an object of the ambivalent feelings of cherishing and destruction which are directed against all totems. Following Freud's ideas in *Totem and Taboo*, Berkeley-Hill argues that one who violates a taboo, becomes a taboo and thus an object of detestation—more especially in the case of the Muslim because the violation of the taboo, the cow slaughter, often took place to ratify Muslim victories or show contempt for Hindu susceptibilities. The violators of a taboo are contagious and must be avoided for they arouse both envy (why should they be allowed to do what is prohibited to others?) and the forbidden desire to emulate the act. Christians and Jews, who also kill cows, do not provoke the same hostility because they do not kill cows ceremonially as do the Muslims or with a clear intention of offering insult to the Hindu. Berkeley-Hill's solution,

> . . . . in line with the fundamental ideas which underlie totemism [is that] any reconciliation between Hindus and Muslims would demand as a cardinal feature some form of ceremonial in which cows would be killed and eaten, either actually or symbolically, by Hindus and Muslims in conclave. It is quite conceivable that this killing and eating of cows could be so arranged as to fulfil every demand from a psychological standpoint without involving the death of a single animal, although in view of the great issues at stake, namely the formation of a real and permanent pact between Hindus and Muslims, the actual sacrifice of every cow in India would hardly be too big a price to pay.[10]

We do not know what Mahatma Gandhi, a strict vegetarian who shared the Vaishnava veneration of the cow, thought of this suggestion.

Even at a distance of 70 years, Berkeley-Hill's paper remains intriguing, although Freud's ideas on totemism have fallen into oblivion. I am surprised that, given the wealth of evidence and the ubiquity of Hindu worship and references to the cow as mother, Berkeley-Hill did not simply include the cow in the Hindu's 'motherland complex' but sought a separate explanation in terms of totem and taboo. Any unconscious Hindu ambivalence toward the eating of beef, which he might have observed underlying a conscious abhorrence, could then be traced back to the infant's ambivalence toward the maternal body and the breast it cherishes and would keep alive but also tears at and would destroy. But, of course, Melanie Klein had not yet formulated her theories of infant love and violence, guilt and reparation, and Berkeley-Hill, who was in charge of the Ranchi psychiatric hospital, used the theories he had available to explain his observations, though they now seem forced.

Muslim 'animality,' as expressed in dirtiness and the male's perceived aggressivity and sexual licentiousness are of course a part of human 'instinctuality' which a civilized, moral self must renounce. The animality not only belongs to an individual past—to infancy and early childhood—which needs to be transcended by the institution of a constantly endangered adult moral self, but also to the Pardis' collective past which is still a part of their folk memory. Visions from the past of themselves as aggressive hunters, killing and eating whatever animals are available (perhaps also the cow?), drinking and lazing around in the village without a thought for the future, are too dangerous to the cultural identity the Pardis are now trying to construct for themselves and others. The Muslim must be kept at a distance because that animality is too near, even within, the Pardi self.

Here, the Pardis are not different from Hindus in many other parts of India. Some years ago, while studying the phenomenon of possession by spirits in rural north India, I was struck by the fact that in a very large number of cases, 15 out of 28, the malignat spirit possessing Hindu men and women turned out to be a Muslim.[11] When, during the healing ritual the patient went into a trance and the spirit started expressing its wishes, these wishes—for forbidden sexuality and prohibited foods—invariably turned out to be those which would have been horrifying to the patient's conscious self. Possession by a Muslim spirit, then, seemed to reflect afflicted persons' desperate efforts to convince themselves and others that their imagined transgressions and sins of the heart belonged to the Muslim destroyer of taboos and were farthest away from their 'good' Hindu selves. In that Muslim spirit were universally considered to be the strongest, vilest, the most malignant and the most stubborn of the evil spirits, the Muslim seemed to symbolize *the* alien in the more unconscious parts of the Hindu mind.

The reasons why Muslims are *the* hated out-group for the Hindus (and vice versa)—rather than the Sikhs, Parsis, or Christians in India, or the 'modern West' outside the country—have not only to do with the sheer size of the Muslim minority which can thus withstand the absorptive and disintegrative pressure of the Hindu majority. They lie also in certain social-psychological axioms on scapegoating and displacement of aggression which have been systematically listed by Robert LeVine and Donald Campbell and that seem to fit the case of Hindus and Muslims to a tee:[12]

- An out-group is a target for hostility if it is a source of frustration in its own right, as Hindus have perceived Muslims to be over centuries.

- An out-group with the most disparaging images of the in-group, as Muslims have of the Hindus, and whose ethnocentrism the in-group is in a position to 'overhear,' will be the most hated.

- The out-group which is seen as the most ethnocentric, in terms of unwarranted self-esteem—the Hindu view of Muslims—will be the most hated.

- The most hated out-group will be the one which is used most as a bad example in child training. In other words, groups indoctrinate their young as to against which targets to vent their hostility.

The existence of the image of the Muslim I have described above, with all its unconscious reverberations, does not mean that a coexistence of the communities, at least in the public arena, is impossible. The hope for such a coexistence comes from many directions. First, there are many instances of Muslims and Hindus protecting each other during a riot. Bedli Pershad's own daughter and her family escaped certain death by taking shelter with their Muslim neighbour who, at some risk to his own safety, did not betray their presence to the marauding mob. Second, often enough there are acknowledgements of their common ancestry and the recognition that the two communities have to share the same physical space. 'We love our *jaat*,' says Badli Pershad, using *jaat* more in the sense of a way of life than a physical group. 'They love theirs. We should live together because we have the same blood.'

The Pardis would be willing to go even further in seeking this coexistence by accepting intermarriage with the Muslims, but they believe that here they come up against a Muslim inflexibility about matters of faith, even bigotry. Badli Pershad elaborates: 'Actually I feel marriage between Hindus and Muslims would be one method of building communal harmony. But in my opinion Hindus should never make the mistake of marrying Muslims because the Hindu is not allowed to retain his or her religion at any cost. So many of our women have got married to Muslims, either because they were in love or by force because these women were working as servants in Muslim households. None of them has been allowed to remain a Hindu or practise the Hindu religion. All of them have been converted whereas the same cannot be said of the Hindus. They are more tolerant and allow the other person to follow whatever religion he or she wants.

'We used to have a young Muslim girl coming to our house a few years ago. She was my daughter's friend. She used to spend long hours in our house. Although her family did not like her visiting us she continued to do so. She would discuss many things about Islam and the Hindu dharma with me, and one day she stated that if she marries at all she will marry a Hindu only and not a Muslim, because the Hindu religion is more humanitarian and tolerant and not as violent as Islam. She married one of our men and to this day she practises both Islam and Hinduism. She not only observes *rozas* (a month of ritual fasting), Muharram, celebrates Bakr-Id but also installs Ganesha idols in her house, celebrates Diwali and Dussehra and participates in the Holi festival along with all of us. Her children have both Hindu and Muslim names. They were living happily as a family when the mother of the girl started telling her Hindu son-in-law that he should convert to Islam. When the boy did not agree, they started threatening him. 'This is the problem with Muslims. They are so particular about their religion. Even the suggestion of conversion or practising the Hindu religion can spark off another riot.

'Unfortunately, it is more frequent for Hindu girls to marry Muslim boys. This is partly because Hindu girls are not kept in purdah like the Muslim girls and therefore come into contact with Muslim boys. We do not get even a chance to see a Muslim girl once she attains puberty. And love is such a thing that, once bitten by it, our girls seem to forget everything about their community or religion or family. They are willing to do whatever their husbands want. They get converted, their children carry Muslim names, go to *madarsas*, learn the *Qur'an* but nothing about any other religion. The tragedy is that some of the women who married Muslims 25, 30 years ago are now old and deserted by their husbands. This woman sitting here was married to a Muslim and had four children. Her husband has left her and refuses to pay a minimum maintenance. She used to earn something when she was healthier and younger. Now she is ill and goes from house to house begging for her daily food. She has no home, sleeps wherever she can, and no one treats her well. Our people don't accept her because they think it was wrong for her to marry a Muslim. That is why I think it is important to hold on to the religion of our ancestors under all circumstances. Otherwise, you not only lose the respect of your community but the other community also looks down upon you.'

It is difficult to say to what extent the Pardi attitudes toward Muslims are shared by other Hindus in Hyderabad or are generalizable to Hindus in the rest of the country. On the one hand, as victims of recent riots one may expect the Pardis to be especially bitter. On the other, they are a lower, "scheduled" caste, and we know from other studies that higher-caste Hindus evaluate Muslims much more unfavourably than the lower castes.[13]

Children's Tales

To get some impressions of the way children view and experience Hindu-Muslim confict, I adapted the 'toy construction' method used by Erik Erikson in his research on the identity development of Californian boys and girls in the 1940s.[14] Using toys such as a family, some uniformed figures, wild and domestic animals, furniture, automobiles, and wooden blocks, Erikson asked the ten-to-twelve-year-olds to imagine that the table was a movie studio; the toys, actors and props; and they themselves, movie directors. They were to arrange on the table an exciting scene from an imaginary movie. My own toys consisted of two families of dolls, each with a set of grandparents, parents, and four young children divided equally between the sexes. The dolls were identifiable as Hindu or Muslim from their dress or other markers of religious group identity: long black burqas for Muslim women, sarees and bindis for the Hindus; pyjamas, sherwanis, round caps and beards for Muslim men, dhotis, kurtas and turbans for the Hindus. In addition to the Hindu and Muslim dolls, there were the dolls of a man in a uniform with a gun slung over one shoulder, of two sinister-looking masked men in undershirts and jeans, and of a few domestic animals such as a cow, a sheep, and a dog. The dolls were placed on a stool next to a large wooden table which was used as the stage. The instructions to the child were to imagine himself or herself as a film director—the children are avid fans of popular Hindi cinema—and to construct an exciting scene for the shooting of a film, using as many or as few dolls as desired. The child was then asked to identify the dolls and after the *mise-en-scene* was over, the young director was asked to describe what was happening in the scene and why. The test, conducted in the one-room school next to the temple, aroused great excitement, and it was not easy to keep hordes of enthusiastic volunteers of all ages from pushing and shoving their way into the room to get into the action, or to stop them from shouting comments through the window which had to be kept open because of the heat. Hyderabad not being San Francisco and Pardiwada not being Berkeley, it was impossible to conduct the proceedings as a 'standardized test under controlled conditions' and therefore I will dispense with reporting my results in the proper scientific format in favour of more informal observations.

The sample consisted of 15 boys and 15 girls, ranging in age from ten to 15, with a median age of 13 for both boys and girls. The lower age limit of ten was determined by trial and error since we found that the task was not comprehensible to a child below that age—not that I had much confidence in the reported ages.

Both boys (12 out of 15) and girls (11 out of 15) made an immediate identification of the dolls as Hindu or Muslim. The three boys and two of the four girls who first identified the dolls in terms of age or gender and had to be prodded to make the religious identification, were younger children of 11 or less, confirming the findings of other studies that awareness of one's own religious affiliation and the prejudice against religious out-groups increases with age.[15] Boys typically used a large part or the whole of the stage and were generally more confident in the construction of the exciting scene than girls, who tended to start from a corner of the table and then gingerly spread out to use a bigger part of the stage, though rarely as much as the boys. The different approaches by boys and girls to the task and the use of stage space is intriguing, and some speculations accounting for gender difference are certainly in order. One could hypothesize that the different use of a public, even an exhibitionistic space, simply reflects the relative positions of boys and girls in a Pardi family where, in spite of the women's relative social freedom and economic importance, the boy is still at the centre of the stage while the girl hugs the corner. I could also speculate that the imaginative activity required by the task has an object of identification (film director) and a content (exciting theatre) that are closer to a boy's than a girl's imagination in this particular social group. Another line of argument, complementary to the other two, would hold that these particular uses of space are expressions of a broader male-female difference in patriarchal societies. The work of Luce Irigaray on women's language, especially with regard to syntax, suggests that women do not put themselves in the centre of the space they open by their utterance.[16] Their subject is hesitant, open to interaction, asking questions rather than asserting. The male subject, on the other hand, is easily dominant, at the centre of the stage, operating in terms of an expanded 'we'.

In the construction of the exciting scene, boys generally arranged Muslim and Hindu dolls in separate groups engaged in some kind of violent confrontation. The fighting between Hindus and Muslims (presented by ten of the 15 boys) is relatively absent in girls' constructions, where only three of the 15 girls staged such scenes of conflict. Girls use dolls to construct peaceful scenes from family life, even when they identify the families as Hindu and Muslim. their stories emphasize relationships between the characters, couples watching animals, and, especially, parents watching children play. Hindu and Muslim dolls are often mixed together. The excitement occurs at the periphery of the scene: a fight between the policeman and a robber, animals being chased by a goonda, a man running away from a soldier. A typical scene constructed by a 15-year-old boy has a Hindu wedding taking place at the centre of the stage, the Hindus watching the dancers. They are surrounded by four Muslims, one in each corner, two of whom are identified as goondas. The Hindu dolls move closer together for protection, wondering how to save themselves. The police doll runs away. Rather than be killed by the Muslims, the Hindus commit suicide.

A scene by a girl, a 13-year-old in this case, has Hindu and Muslim families in semi-circles next to each other, along with the animals who are an integral part of the tableau. The Hindu family is having coffee and bread. The Muslim family is saying its prayers. Small children are playing. The excitement of the scene is in a corner where a goonda is being chased by the policeman after a robbery.

The Muslim children, nine boys and nine girls from Karwan, the other location of this study, ranged in age from ten to 15 with a median age of 13 years. They did not differ from the Hindu children as far as immediate identification of the dolls as Hindu or Muslim was concerned, the younger children having more difficulty than older ones in identifying the dolls according to their religious rather than gender affiliation or according to age. Like the Hindus, the Muslim girls were shyer than the boys in their approach to the task and used less of the stage space for their constructions. As with the Hindus, less than half the Muslim children constructed scenes of violent confrontation between the communities although the distribution of the scenes between girls and boys was different from the Hindu sample. Whereas somewhat more Muslim than Hindu girls (40 per cent versus 20 per cent) constructed scenes of conflict, Muslim boys showed significantly less interest than Hindu boys in communal violence (20 per cent versus 70 per cent). It is not that violence as the source of excitement was absent from the scenes of Muslim boys. The violence in their story lines was, so to say, more traditional—between policemen and robbers or the hero and the villain, the goonda. The fantasy of Muslim boys is thus more of the Hindi film variety wherein a hero skilled in one of the martial arts such as karate rescues a damsel in distress from the unwelcome attentions of the goonda. Though the pehlwan as a hero occurs in one of the stories, I am afraid that in children's fantasy, traditional wrestling is being consigned to oblivion and is being replaced with the more modern import of karate. The fantasy of Muslim boys has not yet been overlaid by the real-life events of the riots to the same extent as in the case of the Pardi boys. I can only account for this difference by the children's actual experience of the riots. The experience of the Muslim boys from Karwan has never been as traumatic as that of the Pardi boys who have seen their homes burned and their close relatives killed by an attacking Muslim mob.

On the other hand, the dolls of the army soldier and the policeman play a greater role in the constructions of the Muslim children, either as hostile figures ('The soldier has been helping the Hindus and not Muslims') or a benign presence ('The army is telling the Hindus and Muslims not to fight'). This reflects the actual experience of the children in Karwan where police and paramilitary forces have been employed to patrol the area during a riot or to conduct house-to-house searches for hidden arms. Reflecting their experience of the riots, the Muslim children are also much less informed than the Hindu boys about the 'cause' of Hindu-Muslim confrontation; the Hindu boys often ascribe the outbreak of communal violence to the Muslims' throwing of *bada gosht* into a temple.

Two examples will give a flavour of the children's stories:

A 12-year-old boy, studying in the sixth class, immediately identifies the dolls as Hindu or Muslim. He uses all the toys and the full stage for the construction of his scene where the Hindus and Muslims are not in any kind of confrontational posture, although the Hindu dolls are clustered together on one side. He explains the scene thus: 'The animals are saying to each other, "Don't fight among yourselves. It gives other animals a chance to come in your area." The army man is telling the Hindus that they should think of their country and not trouble the Muslims. The Muslims are saying their Eid prayers. The older Muslim woman is telling other women (including the Hindu women) that a good woman always wears a veil (burqa) and they should all do so.'

A 13-year-old girl, who studied till the third class and is now a school dropout, also identifies the dolls immediately and uses all the toys for the construction of her scene which takes up half the stage. She explains: 'Hindus and Muslims are fighting. [She doesn't know why.] First, the children fight, then the adults. The soldier is saying don't fight. The Hindus brought in a goonda to attack the Muslims. The Muslims brought in a karate expert who put the goonda to flight.'

To summarize: In spite of the endemic Hindu-Muslim violence in the old city of Hyderabad, less than half the children constructed scenes of this violence in their play constructions. This number may be seen as too large or too small depending on one's own inclination to view the glass of Hindu-Muslim relations as half empty or half full. In any event, a communal orientation is present in a significant number of children between the ages of ten and 15. This orientation, however, varies with age—older children being more communal in their imagination than younger ones—and with gender—girls, especially Hindu girls, prefer to construct scenes from family life rather than from communal conflict. Scenes of Hindu-Muslim violence, when they are created, seem to express the child's unresolved anxiety in relation to his or her personal experience of the riot—for instance, the fear of imminent death at the hands of an attacking Muslim mob in the case of the Pardi boys. Unsurprisingly, the direct, personal experience of a riot as a victim is the strongest impetus to the development of religious hatred and communal imagination in a child.

In conclusion, let me note that both Hindus and Muslims do not perceive their conflict in terms of local issues but as one involving the 'essential' nature of a Hindu or Muslim which does not change over history. Such an essentialization, found in many other ethnic conflicts (such as the one between the Jews and the Blacks in New York, where local issues get linked to the perceived global nature of the 'Jew' or the 'Negro'), will always make a conflict more intractable.

5

VICTIMS AND OTHERS : II.
THE MUSLIMS

Karwan or, to give it back its original name, Karwane-Sahu ('Caravan of merchants'), was planned as a camp for traders when Hyderabad was being built. In the 17th and 18th centuries, it was a thriving commercial area with many inns, mosques, and storehouses for the convenience of merchants from all over India and abroad who camped here on their trading visits to Hyderabad. During the Qutub Shahi period, most of the Gujarati and Marwadi merchants lived here. Today, Karwan is one of the most economically backward sections of the city.

Dotted with mosques, graveyards, and dargahs, the Muslim character of Karwan is unmistakable. The shops in the cobbled streets sell cheap goods requiring low financial investment: spices, bangles, metal scrap, a small assortment of Indian sweets and savouries. There are the inevitable 'general stores' which stock most of the items needed by a poor neighbourhood from pencils for children to hair oil, packets of inferior brands of tea, and cheap detergents for the household. Some of the streets have Hindu women vegetable sellers squatting at the edges along with their young daughters. With their oiled black hair rolled into buns and their mouths stained a brick red from chewing tobacco or betel nut, the women sit behind heaps of fresh vegetables which are kept moistly glistening by frequent sprinklings of water. Cars—except for old, beat-up Ambassadors—are rare, yet the streets still manage to be clogged with pedestrians, auto- and cycle-rickshaws, bicycles, and the rattling buses of Hyderabad's road transport system.

Occasionally employed in road construction, as grave-diggers, or as kitchen helpers in large weddings, many men have only intermittent work. Others are vegetable sellers and rickshaw drivers while a few lucky ones work in the factories of the new city or at low-paid jobs in government offices. The few signs of affluence are manifested in newly built houses—'Gulf money', one is invariably told—and in restaurants on street corners owned by Muslims in city politics or in 'land business' (Majid Khan's restaurant is on one of these street corners). These eateries and the *pan* shops which stay open late into the night are places where the men like to congregate to talk and catch up with news and friends.

Rashid's family lives in one of the lanes of Kulsumpura which forms the southern part of Karwan. Rashid's house is on a lane at the edge of the Muslim quarter, the street at the back of the house separating it from the Hindu majority area. Each lane in Kulsumpura has 25 to 35 houses on either side, with a meandering ribbon of open space of varying width between them which at its narrowest permits only one bicycle to pass through at a time. The houses are generally one-room tenements with thatched or tiled roofs. They are kept scrupulously clean. The mud floor, given a fresh mud coating at least once a month, is covered with faded cotton durries or, among the poorest, with pieces of jute sacking stitched together. The access to the inside of the houses is guarded by flimsy wooden doors, barely supported at the hinges. Worn-out curtains hang at the entrance, their varying heights often permitting glimpses of the dark shapes of women and children moving inside the room. Although nominally in purdah, there are times during the day, especially at mid-morning, when one sees groups of women sitting in the doorways, chatting, chopping betel nuts into small pieces or shaving them into mottled brown slivers while they keep a watchful eye on the children playing outside. Twice a day, in the early mornings and late afternoons, at the public water tap provided by the municipal corporation, the women come to fetch buckets of water for daily use. Unlike women in Hindu areas, the Muslim women in Kulsumpura are not seen bathing their children or washing clothes at the tap, the community norms dictating that they be out in the open for as little time as possible. Yet even as they wait their turns with the bucket, the water tap becomes the women's counterpart of the restaurant or the *pan*-stall of men—a meeting place to exchange views, information, and gossip, mostly of a familial kind rather than the more political exchanges favoured by the men.

Rashid's Family

With eight years of schooling, the 55-year-old Rashid is the most educated person in his family. Nominally headed by his mother who is in her 80s, the family consists of a 65-year-old brother, a 48-year-old younger brother, a widowed sister in her late 60s, and another 38-year-old sister, all of whom live with their own families in separate households next to each other. With five to six children in each household, the extended family consists of about 30 persons.

Rashid's occupation is that of an occasional vegetable seller. Both his brothers are unemployed. The elder brother earns a little money by helping out as a cook at weddings. The younger brother runs errands for one of the 'big men' of Kulsumpura who owns a restaurant and is active in local politics. The brother-in-law drives a cycle-rickshaw and one of his nephews sells vegetables. Two others, in their early 20s, are unemployed. Unlike the Pardi women, the Muslim women only work from their homes. Rashid's younger sister sews blouses and petticoats for the neighbours, but most other women chop betel nuts to earn three to four rupees a day, a welcome addition to the family's perpetually tight budget. Except for Rashid's younger brother and a nephew, both of whom have had three years of school, all the other adults in the family are illiterate.

This situation is changing in the younger generation, at least as far as the boys are concerned. The girls are still not sent to school, much to the regret of the 14-year-old Shakira, Rashid's niece. Even Shakira, however, gets some kind of education at one of the neighbourhood institutions for young girls, opened all over the city with state support. Here, Shakira learns sewing, embroidery, Urdu, basic English, and is also taught some fundamentals of her faith. After she returns home in the afternoon, Shakira's day passes in cleaning the cooking utensils, preparing the evening meal, and looking after her younger brother. Shakira's only other outing is going to the dargah with the other women every Thursday. Like a grown-up woman, Shakira wears the veil when she goes out, a garment that needs some practice to get used to. She is an avid fan of Hindi movies but must satisfy her desire for films through television since going to the cinema with friends is strictly forbidden by the family. The other women, including Shakira's mother, chafe at the restrictions to their freedom yet accept their necessity. The women's *izzat*—their honour, so inextricably interwined with the honour of the family and the community—is much less safe out on the street after the riots. Yet even at the best of times, women had freedom of movement only after marriage and that too before the arrival of children. Although Rashid's younger sister-in-law grew up in Hyderabad, she had never seen the city's architectural glories such as the Char Minar or its main bazaars till she was married. Now, of course, the riots have further curtailed women's freedom. Some years ago at the public water tap, Shakira's mother inadvertently broke the pitcher of a Hindu woman. She was beaten by her husband for this mishap which could have raised the tensions between Hindus and Muslims to a dangerous level. After that she was forbidden to fetch the water from the tap, the errand being delegated to another woman in the family.

Early marriages, repeated pregnancies, and unremitting economic hardship have not broken the women's spirit nor exhausted their zest for life which, I suspect, is continuously renewed by a vibrant community life, especially with other women of the family. There are the many weddings and festive occasions such as the circumcision of a boy or the piercing of the nose and ears of a girl. There are the religious festivals, especially Eid, which are celebrated without regard for expense. If there is no money, it will be borrowed to buy new clothes and the goat for the festive meal. This is an extravagance needed by the poor to transcend limits imposed by the outer reality of their lives and thus regain the vitally important feeling of agency and freedom, something which those influenced solely by notions of economic rationality deplore but rarely understand. The women often offer their *namaz* together and after finishing the household chores sometimes chat and sing together till late into the night.

Another source of the women's strength lies in their religious faith. They freely admit their ignorance of Islamic tenets and traditions. None of them knows what is exactly contained in the Qur'an although a few younger ones have been taught to recite from it in Arabic without understanding the import of the words they are repeating. Their faith consists of following a simple moral code which makes them feel pious: cleanliness of body and purity of mind, respect for the aged, remembering Allah often, saying your *namaz* when the call comes from the mosque, keeping the ritual fast of the *rozas*. From a modern individualist viewpoint which stresses the woman's rights as a person rather than the duties and obligations prescribed by faith, her religious belief may contribute to the woman's feelings of integration with the community and to a personal well-being which comes from an approving conscience, and yet keep the woman imprisoned in a 'false consciousness'. The faith makes women accept their inferior status in relation to men who are deemed to be physically, mentally, and spiritually superior. It makes them only tenants rather than owners of their minds and bodies which have a more transpersonal rather than individual cast. For instance, when asked whether after giving birth to six children why she had not got her tubes tied, Rashid's younger sister replies: 'If you undergo such an operation your *namaz* is no longer legitimate. It is said in the *Qur'an* that Allah does not forgive you for this sin even on Judgement Day. On that day you will find that your face has turned black in colour. Allah does not accept your *namaz*, even the one on Eid, if you have prevented the birth of a child. My sister-in-law who had her tubes tied has stopped offering her *namaz* and is becoming unhappier by the day. All I can do is pray to Allah that He stop giving me children and bless someone else.'

Days and Nights of the Riot

To continue in the woman's voice, here of Kubra Begum, Rashid's wife: 'It was Friday. I was buying vegetables around ten in the morning when the children came running and told me that a fight had started between Hindus and Muslims. Why? I asked. They said a Muslim woman was buying vegetables when the *bhoi* (a Hindu vegetable seller) pulled at her arm and her veil and shouted at her. Perhaps she had not paid the right amount. Twenty to 25 of their men and a similar number from our side rushed to the site of the quarrel. When I saw that the men where armed with sticks and swords I hurried home and told everyone to get ready for trouble. Things were already bad with that quarrel about the Babri Masjid where many people died and which made the Hindus so angry. Then there was the attack on Majid Bhai. One knows a riot is about to start when one sees the Hindus sending away their women and their belongings.

'We did not even have lathis in our house. The women started collecting stones and stacking them in piles near the men who took up positions at the two ends of our alley. First, the Hindus started throwing stones from their side of the road. The men retaliated from our side. The police arrived. They tried to disperse the Hindus but could do so only after firing tear gas shells. At night there was again a barrage of stones from the Hindu side. We did not go out. Then there were shouts of "*Allah-u-Akbar*" and screams of "Help! Help!" None of the men went out because we all know this trick. A truckload of young Hindus dressed all in black comes to a Muslim area, gives the Muslim rallying cry and there are screams for help. Anyone who ventures out to investigate is killed and the truck drives off into the darkness of the night.

'Everything was quiet the next morning. The men went about their work. On Sunday night again there was heavy stone throwing by the Hindus. Two of my nephews received serious head injuries. I started crying, "Allah, how long must the Muslims bear this oppression!" The curfew was in force but when it was relaxed for a couple of hours more people were killed. An old woman and her grandson went out to buy vegetables. The *bhois* stabbed the boy. His name was Amjad. A rickshaw driver was killed in front of my eyes. They pulled him out of the rickshaw and knifed him repeatedly. The dust on which his body lay turned into mud from his blood.

'The curfew is the worst. If a man earns 25 rupees a day and has to feed six children, then what will the children eat if he cannot work for four days? And a curfew can go on for weeks! Last time I had enough flour for four days and we ate rotis with chillies. After that, boiled rice was all we could get for days. In the beginning people try to share but later it is every family for itself—a man is no longer a brother, nor a woman a sister.'

For women who have lost a family member in the riot, ·their faith and its traditions of mourning give both succour and structure to their grief. The journalist Anees Jung gives us a sensitive description of one such woman, Mehdi Begum, whose daughter was sick for ten days while the curfew was on. Mehdi Begum could not get medicines or milk for the daughter because the husband was unable to go to work. She blames no one for her daughter's death and attributes it to the will of Allah. 'As my child was dying I was chanting the elegy my grandfather wrote about the death of the young daughter of Imam Husain, Sakeena, who after her father's death was dragged to a prison and left alone to languish and die. My daughter's death pales in comparison.' '*Azadari*, mourning in the memory of martyred imams,' Jung comments, 'for generations has provided women like Mehdi Begum a release and lent their grief a focus.'[1] Indeed, I generally have found that women, both Hindu and Muslim, with their better-established traditions and rituals of mourning, are less bitter and more reconciled to the violent deaths of their loved ones; those who weep and mourn their losses are no longer filled with warlike anger.

The men's accounts differ from the women's in that the riot is placed in a more historical perspective and conveys less immediacy. Although so far the worst in terms of the number of lost lives and damage to property, this riot is described as part of a series—16 in the last 20 years. When the city's wholesale vegetable market was located here, Karwan was especially riot-prone as Muslims and Hindus jostled for a larger share of the business. Many Hyderabad riots began here before spreading to other parts of the city. The market has since been shifted and Karwan no longer takes the lead in communal rioting but is content to go along with the general ebb and flow of violence in the rest of the city.

The men's reports emphasize tales of masculine heroics and martial prowess in contrast to the women's anxiety about the safety of their families. With men, we hear much talk about how a small group of Muslims triumphed over a vastly superior force of attacking Hindus. Their riot stories resonate with echoes of Badr, the first battle of Islamic history, where heavily outnumbered Muslims trusting Allah and armed only with their faith succeeded against a vastly superior foe.

Another characteristic of the men's narratives is the space given to the encounters with the police. After the start of a riot, the police may descend on Kulsumpura at any time of day or night in search of hidden weapons or to recover goods reported to have been looted from their homes by the Hindus. Men of all ages, from 15 to 50, are routinely taken away for questioning so that many of them do not sleep at home at night while the curfew is on. When the police arrive, there are tense confrontations, say between a young Hindu policeman intent on entering and searching a house and a Muslim youth defending what he believes is the honour of his family. Indeed, in many towns and cities of north India, such as Meerut, the confrontation between the police and the Muslims have led to violent explosions.

Psychologically, what occurs between Hindu policemen and young Muslims is marked by the same dynamics as the encounter between white cops and black kids in the United States described by the psychoanalyst Rollo May.[2] As they come face to face, the young policeman and the Muslim youth are very much alike in their pride and their fear, in their need to prove themselves and their demand for respect. For the Hindu policeman, who additionally incorporates the state's authority and power, which he identifies with his own masculinity and self-esteem, it is essential he insist that the Muslim respect this authority. Laying hands on the other man's body, violating its intactness by rough handling without retaliation or protest, is one way of having the power over the other person acknowledged. Another way is to enter his home without invitation or permission. The Muslim youth, on the other hand, equally impelled to protect his own masculinity and honour, must resist any violation of both his body and home. It becomes imperative that even when he must bow to the policeman's superior might and tolerate the incursion into his most private space, he remain defiant. His submission should not be perceived as voluntary and under no circumstances be reflected in his eyes. This, of course, is the only kind of submission which will satisfy the Hindu policeman as the two young men proceed to become prisoners of an escalating conflict.

Babar's Children

Both men and women agree that Hindu-Muslim relations have greatly deteriorated over the last two decades, especially after the Rameeza Bi incident in 1975. The earlier participation of Hindus and Muslims in each other's festivals has all but disappeared, and ties of friendship reaching across the communities have snapped. Old Hindu friends are now only acquaintances, to be politely greeted when one passes them on the street, but one no longer stops to exchange further courtesies. The women, who meet at the public tap, are not yet as distant from each other as the men, perhaps also because they were never especially close earlier. Ghousia, Rashid's younger sister, reports Hindu women telling her: 'If you are cut the same amount of blood will come out as when we are cut. All religions are not the same but all human beings are. We wear the same clothes and it is difficult to make out who is a Hindu or Muslim if we did not wear a bindi.' The killers often ask the name of their victim before they strike because they need this additional information to make sure of the victim's religious affiliation. When there is no chance of making a certain identification by asking the man to strip and show his penis (Muslim if circumcised, Hindu if not), the marauding mobs have found other, bizarre ways of making sure of the victim's identity. A man may be first hit on the head with a lathi. If while falling he takes the name of a Hindu god or goddess, he is then stabbed if the attackers are Muslim; if the involuntary cry is 'Ya Allah!' he is spared.

The Muslims are concerned about the children who, unlike their own generation, do not even have memories of good relations with the Hindus. Whereas their own parents used to forbid them to talk in terms of, 'He is a Hindu; he is a Muslim', and instead stressed their shared humanity, today's children are acutely aware of being either one or the other from an early age.

My general impression is that Hindus are disliked and looked down upon but not passionately hated, even after so many riots. In contrast to the self-image of the Muslim who is compassionate, the Hindu is seen as cruel and without a trace of pity. 'If a Hindu woman or child walks through a Muslim street, the Muslim will let them go, thinking the fight is between men and should not involve women, children and the aged. A Hindu does not think like that. It is enough for him to see the other person is a Muslim before he strikes without regard for age or gender.

'Hindus are also cowards who can fight only when they are in a large group. Muslims are not afraid even if they are few and unarmed and their opponents have swords. Allah gives them courage and they know if they die the death will not be in vain but a martyrdom which Allah will reward in paradise.

'Hindus also have no control over their impulses and behaviour. There are no fixed times or formats to their prayers nor do their books give them instructions on how to lead a good life like the *Qur'an* does. They go to the temple any time of the day or night, ring the temple bell, and give their God instructions: "Do this for me, do that for me!" And, of course, having been slaves for thousands of years, they have no experience of governance like the Muslims. They may be more educated but they are illiterate as far as governing is concerned.'

Most of all, the Muslims feel baffled and hurt at the thought of being unwanted in the country of their birth. They seem to be struggling against a growing conviction that, irrespective of its formal Constitution, India is a Hindu country and they may be living here on Hindu sufferance. Ghousia says: 'We hear they are saying all over the country, "Go to Pakistan. Pakistan is your country, Hindustan is ours. Not a single Muslim should be seen here." They think if they harass us enough, we will leave for Pakistan. They have trains ready for our departure. We feel if we have to die, we will die here; if we have to live, we will live here.'

'*Babar ki santan, jao Pakistan* (Children of Babar, go to Pakistan)' is today one of the most popular slogans of Hindu mobs during a riot or in the preceding period of rising tension between the two communities. The crudity of the slogan should not blind us to its significance in the shaping of contemporary Hindu-Muslim relations. It reflects the Hindu nationalist's deep-seated distrust of Muslim loyalty to the Indian state and a doubt regarding Muslim patriotism if the community is faced with a choice between the country of its birth and that of its coreligionists. The slogan contains the accusation that Muslims may prove potential traitors in any conflict between their loyalty to the state and their loyalty to Islam.

Though repressed in elite political discourse, this accusation is perceived to have enough substance to arouse a sense of unease among many other Hindus who are not sympathizers of Hindu nationalism and yet subscribe to the notion of the nation-state as a definer of their political identity. The importance of this accusation as a prime irritant in Hindu-Muslim relations is also recognized by a large section of Muslims, and, as we shall later see, it evokes an emotionally charged response from the community's religious-political leadership.

Currently fuelled by events in Kashmir where a large section of the Muslim population is demanding independence or accession to Pakistan, the suspicion of Muslim loyalty to the Indian state has two main sources. First, there has been a historical tendency among upper-class Muslims (or those aspiring to higher status in the community) to stress or invent Persian, Arab, or Turkish ancestry rather than rest content with their more humble Indian origins. The tendency, more pronounced among Muslim fundamentalists, is to see themselves as superior beings from outside India who share Indian history only as the country's erstwhile rulers.

Second, as we shall again see in the next chapter, the specific Muslim history the community's conservative spokesmen would like to construct and exalt is the one shared with Muslims of the Middle East, especially the sacred history of early Islam and of the Dar al-Islam between the seventh and 15th centuries, when Islamic civilization was at its zenith and Muslims had conquered half the world. Hindu nationalists believe that only a minority of Muslims accept the Indian nation-state as a definer of their political identity and container of their loyalty. They are inclined to believe that Bernard Lewis's thesis on Muslims of the Middle East is equally applicable to the Indian context, namely, that 'there is a recurring tendency in times of crisis, in times of emergency, when the deeper loyalties take over, for Muslims to find their basic identity in the religious community; that is to say, in an entity defined by Islam rather than by ethnic origin, language, or country of habitation.'[3] The nature of the vicious circle is immediately apparent: the anchoring of Muslim identity in Islam spurs Hindu suspicion of Muslim loyalty to the nation, which makes the Muslims draw closer in the religious community for security, which further fuels Hindu distrust of Muslim patriotism, and so on.

Empirically, there is some evidence in a 25-year-old study that a situation of actual conflict between India and Pakistan is a stressful affair for Indian Muslims which makes them emotionally close ranks. Yet, in spite of increased Hindu hostility toward Muslims during the actual period of warfare, Indian Muslims do not feel any closer to their Pakistani coreligionists but in fact feel more distant toward them than in the period preceding the outbreak of hostilities.[4]

The Victim Response

Among the poorer Muslims, I was acutely aware of a weary resignation in their dislike of the Hindus. Their diatribes were often mechanical, lacking energy and that fire in the belly which leaves some hope for the transformation of various states of withdrawal into an active advocacy on one's own behalf. I wondered if there was not a repression of anger, even hate, operating here—the maintenance of repression imposing a drain on energy and depleting the aggression available for assertive action. The psychological portrait I repeatedly drew when the talk shifted from the private to the public, from the familial to collective realms, with respect to the current situation of Indian Muslims, was of the Muslim as a helpless victim of changed historical circumstances and the demands of the modern world. One of the main refrains was that since the *hukumat*—used in the sense of rule, political authority, regime—was now of the Hindus, discrimination against the Muslims was to be expected. However galling to the individual and collective sensibility of the Muslims, this was a fact of life with which one had to come to terms. A few women even took a melancholy (and I thought, masochistic) satisfaction from this turn of the historical wheel which had reversed the position of subjects and rulers and of the accustomed directions of inequality and injustice. Most, though, bemoaned the discrimination against Muslims without expressing much hope for a foreseeable change in the situation.

'The Hindu likes the Hindu and not the Mussulman,' says one woman. 'The *hukumat* is Hindu. They can now oppress us, take revenge for the thousand years of our *hukumat*.'

'They are doing *hukumat* since 40 years and will try their best to make the Mussulman weak and insignificant,' says another woman.

'Jinnah was right,' says a man who works part time for the Majlis. 'Living in a Muslim nation is the only protection from oppression by the Hindus.'

Another woman, echoing the old *mai-baap* attitude toward the state, is more plaintive: 'The *hukumat* should treat both Hindus and Muslims equally. When a mother has borne more than one child she looks at each child with equal favour.'

Rashid tries to make the abstraction of 'discrimination' more concrete by describing his own experiences. 'For 15 years I worked in the vegetable market. Then I applied for a job in the Road Transport Corporation. When I went in with my application, the clerk said, "Don't even bother to register your name. Muslims can't get a job here." I applied to at least ten other government department but the moment they heard my name they told me to go away. I finally got a job in the railways by hiding my identity and changing my name to Babu Rao. After two years when the time for promotion came they found out Babu Rao was not my real name and that I was a Muslim. I gave up after that and started working with the Majlis. I said to myself, "How can you work with the Hindus when even your name is unacceptable to them!"

'It is difficult for the Muslims to be self-employed. The Hindus control most businesses. If we ask for credit, they refuse and extend it only to members of their community. If I buy goods from them I have to pay ten rupees, but a Hindu pays only eight. Because of our poverty we cannot send our children to school. If there is only one man who earns 25 to 30 rupees a day and has eight mouths to feed, where is the money for the extra expense of school to come from?' Rashid, however, does not completely blame the modern external world for the Muslim's plight. 'Hindus are better off not only because they are favoured by the *hukumat* but also because their mothers, sisters, daughters, all work. We do not educate our women or make them work because of purdah,' he says, not in a spirit of criticism of the tenets or the loss of faith but as a pure statement of fact. Indeed, it is the loss of faith which he holds ultimately responsible for what has happened to the Indian Muslim: 'If we had unshakeable faith, then our *hukumat* would not have gone. When faith went, everything went.'

This, then, is the striking difference between the Hindu and Muslim poor: the former feel less like victims and have a greater sense of agency and mastery over the circumstances of their lives than the latter. In the victim response of the Muslims, the loss of collective self-idealization which sharply reduces self-esteem is perceived as the result of overwhelming outside forces of which they are hapless victims. The Muslim poor convey an impression of following a purposeless course, buffeted by the impact of others in a kind of social Brownian motion.[5] There seems to be a kind of institutionalized fatalism at work which makes them act as ready victims of circumstances and leaves them little ability to defend themselves against exploitation. This is not to maintain that the victim response of the Muslims in only 'in the head', without a basis in reality. Like the notion of the 'enemy', discrimination too is neither merely real nor merely psychological but a blend of the two.

Whereas the loss of collective self-idealization due to changed historical and socioeconomic circumstances evokes a depressive response among the Muslim poor, for many sensitive members of the community—including some of its writers, scholars, and artists—this loss of Muslim power and glory is explicitly mourned. The despair at the moral decay and political decline of Muslim societies, the historian Mushirul Hasan tells us, is a recurrent theme in Urdu poetry, literature, and journalism.[6] Ideally, such a mourning should clear the decks for the birth of new ideals and a more confident encounter with the future. For many, though, the mourning is never completed; its stock of narratives of loss and their elegiac mood become a part of the family heritage that is passed from one generation to the other. For these men and women, the poet Iqbal's line, 'Lightning only strikes the hapless Muslims (*Barq girti hai to bechare Mushulmanon par*)' has acquired a personal significance which has been incorporated into the social aspect of their identity. In other words, whenever a person feels, thinks, and acts as a Muslim rather than as an individual, there is a perceptible undertone of grief, a miasma of mourning in what has been called 'the Andalus syndrome'.[7] The syndrome, of course, refers to the great Muslim civilization on the Iberian peninsula that ended abruptly in the 16th century, plunging the Islamic world into gloom and leaving a yearning for its lost glory in Muslim societies on the rim of the Mediterranean, In the Indian situation, the Andalus response, I believe, is more the province of the upper and middle classes rather than of the vast number of Muslim poor. Of course, in Hyderabad, with its history bearing a striking similarity to the fate of Andalusia, especially in the abrupt ending of Muslim rule, the heartbreak is more widespread than in most other parts of the country.

Gilani Bano, a novelist from Hyderabad, is one of the more eminent Urdu writers who has tried to capture the elusive spirit of the Andalus response in her fiction. In her novel *Aiwan-e-ghazal,* she takes as her subject a slice of Muslim life just before and after 1948, the year in which Hyderabad abruptly ceased being an independent state with its own administration, ruler, and ethos, and became part of India—a country which was geographically contiguous with Hyderabad but was emotionally distant for many of its inhabitants. The title of the novel is from the name of the family mansion of an old aristocratic (nawabi) family. Literally, it also means 'the palace of the ghazal,' the ghazal more often than not being an elegy of unhappy love where the lover bemoans the loss, the inaccessibility, or the turning away of the beloved.

One of the main characters in the novel through whose eyes the events of those years are viewed is Nawab Wahid Hussain, a man in his early 50s, steeped in the ethos of a vanishing world, who is fearful and contemptuous of the change that is poised to destroy the old civilization. Wahid Hussain looks down on what he considers the crass commercialism of the modern era and deems the writing of poetry and the play of love with a favoured mistress—normally an accomplished courtesan—as the only worthwhile occupations of a civilized man. He admires his grandfather whose dead body was discovered one morning surrounded by sheets of paper covered with Urdu calligraphy while the flame in his bedroom lamp burnt low. The family had thought that the papers pertained to the affairs of the family home which the British Resident, acting on complaints of debauchery and the kidnapping of girls, had demanded for his inquiry. The papers, however, turned out to be the final drafts of 15 ghazals which the old nawab had composed throughout the night in a burst of feverish activity. With the threat of the inquiry and eventual disgrace looming over him, they were still some of the best ghazals his grandfather had ever written. Wahid Hussain ruminates on Hyderabad's fate:

> [He] opened his eyes and saw the portrait of Quli Qutub Shah on the wall opposite the portrait of the last ruler, Osman Ali. Wahid Hussain saw Quli Qutub Shah's eyes brimming with contentment as if he was searching for a ghazal or, standing on the ramparts of Golconda, lost in the dream of a beautiful city springing up on the forested land around the fort. The city he founded for Bhagmati to live in was like a garden, its magnificent buildings like lotus flowers lit with the lamps of civility and culture. He looks as if he is saying to one of his lovers, 'Prepare the festivities. The tender shoots of Urdu are coming out but we do not have much time left. Behind the hills of a few centuries, the caravans of time are moving in our direction. Soon the plunderers will fall upon us. Under the rubble of Golconda people will search for our stories. The dust particles of our fallen glory will become a diamond glittering in the crown of a queen in a distant land.'[8]

The diamond, of course, was the Kohinoor, the queen, Victoria of Great Britain.

Morality of Violence

Although they live in separate *bastis*, the inevitably close contact between Hindus and Muslims in the crowded inner city leads to interactions between the two which span the full emotional range from friendship to deadly hatred during the time of a riot. The exchanges with members of the other community which are considered to be transgressions of the group's code governing such transactions were of particular interest and invited a more systematic exploration.

In this exploration, my focus was not on questions close to the hearts of moral philosophers such as whether it was reason, reason dependent upon individual desire, religious prescription, role obligation, or a convention that was being violated by a particular action. Nor was I concerned with the religious foundations of the morality governing Hindu-Muslim relations; with what, for instance, the *Qur'an* has to say on a Muslim's various interactions with those who are outside the faith. My aim was more to understand the way people experienced these interactions and the psychological processes underlying the experiences.

It was evident from the preliminary interviews that these interactions had to be divided into two parts: those which pertain to normal, peace-time life and others which take place during a riot. In both Hindus and Muslims, riot-time interactions deviated substantially from the code that governs their actions during normal times. There are, however, as we shall see later, still a few acts that invite universal moral condemnation from both sides, independent of their temporal context—normalcy versus riot. These obligations are considered universally binding. Even within context-dependent obligations, there are interactions which are perceived as binding on one's own group and not on others; they are viewed as distinctive expressions of the community's moral qualities, uniqueness, and traditions. These obligations are perceived as objective and moral and yet not universally binding. Their violation is usually remarked upon by the phrase, 'A good Muslim (or Hindu) does not do that,' implying that the bad other may indeed do so.

Using the method developed by the anthropologist Richard Shweder who, in a series of studies, has explored the moral ideas of children and adults in India and the United States, I have attempted to examine adult Muslim and Hindu interpretations of 19 behavioural cases of Hindu-Muslim interaction in the 'Morality Interview' (*Appendix II*).[9] The first 12 cases represent different kinds of interactions in normal times while the last seven cases are descriptive of certain interactions during a riot. Examples of normal interactions are: 'A Muslim rents his house to a Hindu'; 'A Muslim girl marries a Hindu boy.' Examples of riot-time interactions are: 'Some Muslims rape a Hindu girl'; 'Some Muslims loot Hindu shops'. Further interview questions seek to elicit the respondent's view of the seriousness of the violation and the kind of sanctions it should invite.

Before discussing the results of the interviews, I need to sound a note of caution. The interactions between Hindus and Muslims had also come up during the more freewheeling conversations with some of the same respondents. I had the impression that people became 'more moral' in the situation of a structured interview using a questionnaire than they were in the unstructured setting where they were more uninhibited in the expression of violent sentiments. The 'questionnaire morality' is perhaps inclined to be more conservative than the actually lived one.

It seems, and this may be of methodological importance in the collection of psychological data, that the expression of an individual's views on subjects close to his heart becomes more and more controlled as the setting changes from an informal conversation to a formal interview to the filling in of a questionnaire, to writing for wider dissemination, and finally, to the most controlled expression of all, the enactment of views in the public arena. Differently but tentatively stated, it is perhaps less the nature of the medium in which self-disclosure is made than the imagined intimacy with the presumed recipients of our views which is important.

Our openness and honesty in revealing ourselves decreases in tandem with the degree of intimacy we believe we share with our ultimate listeners (although on rare occasions, such as an encounter on a train, we may for a time imagine sharing great intimacy with a total stranger). Writing a book for an impersonal audience is less intimate than talking to long-standing disciples; filling a questionnaire is less intimate than a friendly conversation which, in turn, is less intimate than responding to someone even closer than a friend.

The Muslim sample from Karwan consisted of ten men and ten women. The women ranged in age from 18 to 50 and all except the youngest were illiterate. The ages of the men were between 19 and 75. A couple of the men had a few years of schooling but none had finished high school. A third of them were unemployed while others worked in low paid jobs as casual labourers, vegetable sellers and auto-rickshaw drivers.

Before I discuss the morality judgments of the Muslims, there are two general remarks that need to be made. First, the idea of convention, the idea that the disapproved interactions with the Hindus could be based on a consensus within the community and are relative and alterable, is almost totally absent. Once a behaviour is seen as a violation it generally tends to be viewed starkly as a sin and it does not matter if it is done secretly or openly or whether it is permitted in other places. These interactions, except in the area of religious faith, tend to be viewed as part of a moral order, categorical, imperative and binding on all Muslims. Second, the moral code, to follow Dworkin's distinction, is duty- rather than right- or goal-based.[10] In other words, a duty like 'obedience to Allah's will as expressed in the *Qur'an*', is taken as fundamental and given priority over a right such as the 'individual's right to freedom of choice' or a goal like 'improving the welfare of the community'. The morality is traditional or customary, deeply connected to the ancestry and the narrated history of a group. The transgressions of moral ways of acting are accompanied by anxieties relating to the unexpected and the fear of narcissistic injuries such as being excluded from the group or the loss of a fantasized union with others of the community.

The statements on which there was a consensus—a consensus referring to judgements of right and wrong shared by at least 75 per cent of the sample—are the following:

Permitted Interactions
In Normal times

To have Hindu friends.
To eat with Hindus.
To work with Hindus in a factory.
To learn the Gita from a pandit.
To beat up a Hindu boy for whistling at a Muslim girl.
To beat up a Hindu who is making fun of Allah.

In Riot Time

To give shelter to a Hindu.

Wrong Interactions
In Normal Times

A Muslim girl going to the cinema with a Hindu boy.
A Muslim girl eloping with a Hindu boy.
To throw a dead cow in a temple.

In Riot Time.

To rape a Hindu girl.
To kill a Hindu woman.

Let us begin by looking at the interactions which are consensually considered wrong. In normal times, the strongest reaction is evoked by the idea of a Muslim girl going to the cinema with a Hindu boy. This is not only a serious violation of the moral code but unequivocally a sin. 'The other day we beat up one such pair,' says a 19-year-old man. 'We watched them for three days and followed them to the cinema. I slapped the girl and informed the girl's brother. He was ready to poison himself and die as he could not bear the dishonour of his sister being caught with one of their [Hindu] boys.' Almost a third of the respondents would have the girl killed, expecting the parents to quietly poison her, bury her alive or themselves commit suicide. Here, of course, our 'law' that 'expression is contingent upon its medium' also works in the reverse direction. The outrage which is being expressed in such violent words will generally be more controlled if and when it comes to concrete action. Then we can expect a beating rather than murder, wounding words, yes, but rarely the sharp stabs of a knife.

The younger Muslim women, whom I would have expected to identify more with the girl, are at one with their menfolk in considering the action a grave sin. They are, however, much less harsh in the punishment they envisage as adequate. Most would be content if the girl got a good thrashing and a couple recommend marrying the girl off against her will. In fact, the only two voices which do not consider the behaviour a sin, though it remains a serious offence, are women.

What is the culture-specific aspect of the moral code which invites such wrath on the head of a Muslim girl who goes to a movie with a Hindu boy? Pre-eminent here is a notion of the family which is not an association of individuals but a structure with differentiated roles and obligations. The structure itself is a part of and in service of a larger whole, the Muslim community. The movie-going of a Muslim girl is not an individual affair but the establishment of a particular kind of relationship with the other *qaum* which is a deadly insult to the Muslim community. Yet the ferocity of the imagined punishments arouses the suspicion that there are also some unconscious fantasies involved in this act which, for instance, are absent in the case of a Muslim girl eloping with a Hindu boy. To an outside observer, with a different moral code, the latter would seem to be a far more serious affair. Although considered a sin, the punishments for elopement are not so severe. The girl should not be readmitted to the home and should be considered dead by the community, is the general tenor of opinion in dealing with this particular 'sin'. My hunch is that going to the cinema gives rise to images of hot, hurried gropings in the darkness of its foyer, fantasies of forbidden sexuality between the pair, whereas the elopement makes sexual congress between the couple more acceptable in that it is legitimized by marriage. The girl who went to the cinema is still a part of the community, a boil which must be lanced.

Throwing a dead cow in a temple is the only violation which is not considered a sin but a minor transgression. It is wrong because it hurts the religious sentiments of the Hindus and, more rationally, can lead to outbreak of a riot. Some will content themselves with pointing out to the offender the error of his ways while others will consider handing him over to the police.

During riot time, the two consensually forbidden acts of violence relate both to Hindu women, namely, their rape and murder. In contrast, there is no consensus on the moral status of the killing of men, looting, and arson. Although both rape and killing of women are regarded as sinful, there is a hesitation, almost reluctance when it comes to punishment of the guilty. What comes to the fore here is the conflict between the perceived interests of the community and its moral codes. 'The men who have raped and killed are our own. Who will protect us if they are severely punished or handed over to the police?' expresses the nature of the dilemma. The recommended punishments range from educating the culprit, leaving it to Allah, letting the law take its course, of handing over the men to the police.

In the case of rape, there is no difference of opinion between men and women in either perception of the act or punishment of the wrongdoers. Of the two in the sample who favour the severest sanctions—castration and killing of the man—one is a man and the other a woman. During a riot, a time of danger to individual and collective survival, identification with the community outweighs all other identifications, including the identification with one's gender.

Killing and rape of Hindu women are sins because they are forbidden by Islam. This is elaborated through the idea of Islamic chivalry where a riot between Hindus and Muslims is a battle exclusively between men in defence of the honour of their *qaums*. The women are noncombatants. Weak and vulnerable, they are entitled to protection, even by men of the enemy host.

Rape of a Hindu woman, though, has some surprising twists to the nature of its sinfulness. The 75-year-old man regards rape as a sin because a Hindu woman is *haram*, forbidden to the Muslim like the eating of pork or meat of an animal not slaughtered in the ritually correct manner. Rape of a Muslim woman, on the other hand, is not a sin because she is *halal*. This view is echoed by another, much younger man, who reacts with horror to the idea of raping a Hindu woman and thereby entering the polluted and contaminating inner regions of an infidel body. In these two cases rape is not a violation of the moral code that forbids the causing of harm to another individual but the breaking of a code that decrees the preservation of one's own sanctity.

Turning to permitted interactions in normal times, there is no difficulty in Muslims having Hindus as friends. There are three sceptics, all women, who believe such friendships are no longer possible after the riots of the last decade. They mistrust the Hindu; 'Hindus are sweet outside but have poison in their hearts.'

It is also all right to eat with the Hindus. The only reservation is that since the Hindus eat *haram* foods, a Muslim might inadvertently eat something which is forbidden.

Working with Hindus in a factory does not pose any problem. It is a matter of work, of survival, and beyond the personal control of any single individual or even a community.

Learning Hindu scriptures from a Hindu priest is also not wrong. The *Gita*, too, is the voice of God in their language so it is not wrong to listen to it, opines one respondent. To do so is to gain knowledge which is pleasing to Allah, says another. It does not matter if one does so, says a third, after all a Muslim will remain a Muslim. The few dissenting voices express the fear that an exposure to unbelief (*kufar*) may corrode a Muslim's own faith.

I must confess to a mild surprise at this evidence of tolerance in matters of faith, reminding me one again not to underestimate the impact of the Hindu images from my childhood, of the Muslim as a religious fanatic. This becomes especially true if we look at the dissension on the question of a Muslim who converts and becomes a Hindu, an action I would have expected to be overwhelmingly rejected as wrong and sinful. Even the ones who condemn the conversion are reluctant to punish the offender. Others see such a conversion as a matter of personal choice. Of course, such an action is not a matter of indifference. It is an affront to the Muslim community yet does not call for its interference. Ironically, 'religious fanaticism' is less prevalent in the religious domain, in interactions at the level of faith, less than in any other area of social exchange with the Hindus. The otherwise duty-based moral code is suspended here as the individual's right to freedom of choice takes precedence over duties.

Beating up Hindu boys for whistling at a Muslim girl or for making fun of Allah are retaliations for straightforward insults to the collective honour and earn consensual approval. The qualifications are minor. In the first case, try to explain and then beat, says one man; another man will let the whistling go unpunished if the girl was out without a veil because then she has invited this unwelcome male attention. In the second case, a couple of respondents recommend forbearance in the face of this stupidity. Mostly, though, violent reprisals are fully in order, as in the case of Salman Rushdie, whose example was specifically cited by two respondents.

But during a riot, giving shelter to a Hindu is the only consensually approved action. This is viewed as a religious duty owed to Allah. It is a duty independent of one's personal feelings about Hindus in general and the individual seeking shelter in particular. It is the expression of the compassion and mercy in the heart of a good Muslim and is enjoined by Islam.

On several significant actions, the sample of 20 Muslims did not establish a consensus. The question of renting a house to a Hindu in normal times produced several reactions. The dissenter's argument is based on the pollution of the Muslims by a Hindu living among them. Hindus plaster the floors and walls with cow dung, eat pork, will perform puja where *ibadat* has been done. A few feel more strongly: 'My mother said if you give alms to a Hindu your hand will burn on Judgement Day.' It is not a sin but certainly an error to be avoided. The assenters argue that not all Hindus are bad, and there is nothing wrong with renting one's house to a good Hindu.

Dissensus existed on a number of actions if taken in riot time. Those who see setting fire to a Hindu house as a wrong act do not consider it a major violation. It is a minor offence during a riot, and the offenders should be properly counselled. Others who approve look at it as something that is inevitable during a riot.

Looting of Hindu shops is an action that produced pro and con arguments that are the same as in the case of arson.

The respondents, both men and women, are almost evenly divided on the action of killing a Hindu man during a riot. Those who consider it a sin will still not sanction any punishment by the community. Some will allow it only in retaliation. Others who consider nothing wrong with killing a Hindu in a riot liken the situation to a time of war when killing and being killed is the normal order of things.

Morality and the Hindus

The Hindu sample from Pardiwada consisted of ten men and ten women. The men ranged in age from 22 to 45 with a median age of 30 years, while the age range of women was between 20 and 59, with a median of 35 years. The Hindu women, like their Muslim counterparts, had no schooling, whereas the Hindu men were better educated than the Muslim sample, with an average of seven years of schooling. Economically, too, the Pardis, though poor, were visibly better off than the Muslims from Karwan. Most of the men were fruit vendors while two drove auto-rickshaws for a living.

Before I discuss the Hindu responses to each of the behavioural cases, there is one general observation that needs to be made. As compared to the Muslims, the Hindu respondents were much more relativistic and contextual in judging a behaviour as a transgression and more easygoing in proposing punishments for actions judged as wrong. Irrespective of age and gender, 'It all depends' was an almost reflexive response, and the individual had to be persuaded to engage further with the standard interview.

In responding to cases of interaction with the Muslims, both during normal and riot times, which were not clearly labelled as unobjectionable at the outset, the answers were almost always framed in terms of a context, temporal or spatial. The linking of the morality of an interaction with time would be typically expressed thus: 'It was wrong when times were different but it is not wrong now.' By 'different times', the person is alluding to a past golden era of individual and collective morality as compared to the degenerate Kali-yuga of today. The individual can thus convincingly state that an action is wrong in right times but right in wrong times. Similarly, demographic space seemed to be intimately involved in moral judgements, and I was often told that actions such as the beating up of a Muslim or arson and looting of Muslim shops were wrong if you lived in a Muslim majority area. This appears to have less to do with morality than with prudence and expediency unless, of course, one is willing to consider the case for an expedience-based morality. As a consequence of this contextual stance, it is understandable that the envisaged punishments by the community for wrong actions were nonexistent or weak and evoked far less emotion and righteousness than the corresponding sanctions among the Muslims against the violators of their community's moral codes.

This striking difference between Hindus and Muslims can be accounted for in religious terms. The difference in the approaches to morality may be seen as a consequence of the difference between humanist and authoritarian religions (Fromm) or between precept-based and prophetic religions (Obeyesekere).[11] In more culturalist terms, as I have discussed elsewhere, in Hindu philosophical and ethical tradition, the rightness or wrongness of a proposed action depends on the individual's *desa*, the culture in which one is born; on *kala*, the historical era in which one lives; on *srama*, the efforts required of one at different stages of life; and on *gunas*, the innate psychobiological traits which are the heritage of a person's previous lives.[12] 'Right' and 'wrong' are relative; they can emerge as clear distinctions only out of the total configuration of the four coordinates of action.

The Hindu approach to the making of moral judgements may well be a part of a basic Hindu way of thinking which the poet-scholar A.K. Ramanujan has called 'context-sensitive.'[13] Hindus, Ramanujan believes, idealize context-sensitive rather than context-free rules. Whether it is in medical matters, where the context is vital in diagnosis, prescription, and preparation of herbal medicines, or in music, where the ragas have their prescribed and appropriate times, the context-sensitivity extends even to space and time, the universal contexts, the Kantian imperatives, which in India are not uniform and neutral. Every moral rule thus has a number of exceptions, each of these additions a subtraction from any universal law so that one falls back on the universal only if one fits no context or condition (which is rare). Yet before wholly embracing the religious-culturalist explanations, as I am tempted to do, we must remember that the Pardis are not completely context bound in their moral judgements. The rape and killing of a Muslim woman are unequivocally condemned as sins, unalterable by any contextual considerations. To me, even more significant than the differences between the Hindu and Muslim approaches to morality is their similarity in the condemnation of the rape and killing of the other community's women; both groups regard these acts unalterably as sins. At an emotionally more neutral level they also share a common disapproval of acts which hurt the religious sentiments of the other community. What is most encouraging is the fact that this disapproval is often couched in terms of empathy: 'Their feelings are the same as ours and we would not like it if it were done to us.' The existence of this empathy—even if it is in a restricted sphere—demonstrates that the history of violence between the communities (which can fairly be said to have made enemies of Hindus and Muslims, at least in the poor underbelly of the city) has not yet dehumanized the enemy. There is still empathy on both sides which does not let a Muslim consider a Hindu—and vice versa—less than human and therefore a deserving prey for every imaginable brutality. Empathy with members of the other group, even when considered the enemy, defends the Other from the untrammelled aggression which can so easily be let loose against all those considered subhuman.[14]

The Hindus, as I have noted above, are far more easygoing than the Muslims in their moral judgements of interactions with members of the other community. In normal times, although a Hindu girl's elopement with a Muslim boy is consensually disapproved of, it is not considered a sin. Having Muslim friends, eating and working with Muslims, renting your house to a Muslim, learning the *Qur'an* from a Muslim priest—are all consensually permitted though some may express reservations about this conduct. The dissension is over a Hindu's conversion to Islam, a Hindu girl marrying a Muslim boy or going out with him to the cinema. The latter action, so violently disapproved of in the Muslim sample, elicits divided opinions. Its opponents would discourage such a practice because it may lead to an interfaith marriage, with all its attendant problems. Those who see nothing objectionable in the girl's action, most of them women, look at it as something which happens all the time in today's world and is not something over which one should get unduly exercised. Whether the greater Hindu permissiveness with regard to interactions with the other community is a function of the Pardis' low status in the caste hierarchy, and whether high-caste Hindus wall themselves off much more from the Muslims, as anecdotal evidence seems to suggest, is a question which can only be answered by future empirical work.

As with the Muslims, rape and killing of women of the other community during a riot, especially the former, elicited consensual condemnation—the only actions the Hindus were prepared to label as such. Similarly, giving shelter to members of the other community during a riot is not considered wrong. There is dissension over the morality of other riot-time actions such as arson, looting, and the killing of men. The riot-time morality of the Hindus is thus strikingly similar to that of the Muslims in its content, though not in the emotional intensity with which this morality is invested. The two communities share in common the commandments 'Thou shalt not kill. . . a woman' and 'Thou shalt not rape,' but the outrage associated with the transgression of these commandments is stronger among Muslims than among Hindus. Indeed, as I noted earlier, the emotional reaction of Muslims to any violation of the community's moral code of conduct is intense and especially violent in cases involving a Muslim woman's sexualized interaction with a Hindu man. In such situations, I believe, the self-representation of the community becomes identified with the woman's sexual stance in its more servile aspect, with images of being 'fucked'—not in a joyful but in a contemptuous sense—by the Hindu. To penetrate the Other, whether a woman or another group, it to be superior, powerful, and masculine; to be penetrated is to be inferior, weak, and feminine. It is a blending of the images of power and sexuality in a phallocentric vision which makes many men all over the world, for example in parts of the Middle East and Latin America, regard only the man who is penetrated by another man as a despised homosexual while the active inserter on the 'top' is considered as a 'normal' even macho male.

Violence between religious-ethic groups is then also a struggle over the assignment of gender, a way of locating the desired male and denigrated female communities. As a Hindu patient, echoing the sentiments of a few others, remarked in a session during the 1984 anti-Sikh riots in Delhi: 'It serves them right! Every one of these cunts (*chutiya*) behaves as if his prick is at full mast!'

6

A NEW HINDU IDENTITY

Great disorders lead to great devotions.
— Emile Zola

Some 15 years ago, when what is today called the Nehruvian project of a modernized secular India was still vigorous and fundamentalism was a distant gleam in the eye of an occasional imam or *mahant*, I tried to peer into the crystal ball of the future. In my conclusion to *The Inner World*, I wrote that as modernization picks up pace, individuals will increasingly seek membership in groups with absolute value systems and with little tolerance for deviation from their norms. To quote:

> 'Whereas initially the appeal of these groups may be limited to sections of society who are most susceptible to the pressures of social change— for example, youth and urbanized classes—we can expect an ever widening circle of participation as more and more people are sucked into the wake of modernization. . . . In short, we can expect an increasing destruction of the nascent, Western-style individualism as more and more individuals seek to merge into collectivities that promise a shelter for the hurt, the conflicted and the shipwrecked.'[1]

If I again take up the theme of those large social formations through which many individuals in India seek a sense of their cultural identity (a term which I prefer to the more sociological 'ethnicity'), then it is not to derive a melancholy satisfaction from any perceived prescience but to offer some psychological observations on an issue which is normally seen as the domain of political scientists and social commentators. First, to get definitional matters out of the way, by 'cultural identity' I mean a group's basic way of organizing experience through its myths, memories, symbols, rituals, and ideals.[2] Socially produced and thus subject to historical change, cultural identity is not a static affair even while it makes a decisive contribution to the enhancement of an individual's sense of self-sameness and continuity in time and space. This definition is particularly apt for the Hindutva movement—characterized by some as Hindu fundamentalism—through which a large number of Hindus today seem to be seeking a sense of their cultural identity. Let us again remember that 'fundamental' does not mean 'traditional'. As in other parts of the non-Western world, revivalism or fundamentalism in India, be it Hindu or Muslim, is an attempt to reformulate the project of modernity. Like its counterparts elsewhere, the leadership of Hindutva, for instance, has never been traditional but decidedly modern, consisting of individuals who turned their backs on their own Western education.[3] Keshav Baliram Hedgewar, the founder of the Rashtriya Swayamsevak Sangh, (RSS), the core institution and the driving force of Hindu revivalism, had his schooling in English and went on to study medicine in Calcutta. In his youth, he is reported to have felt that orthodox Hindu ritual was rather silly. His successor, Golwalkar, was the son of a civil servant, did his Master's degree in biology at Benares University and was a lecturer in zoology at the same institution before he joined the RSS.[4]

Shadows of Mourning

Haunting images of loss and helplessness among large groups of people underlie many literary and scholarly accounts of transnational historical changes. These images constitute the sombre mood with which scholars have often reflected upon the periods and processes of significant transformations in human history. When Max Weber paints the portrait of Western man in the wake of Enlightenment, we see a face aglow with the promised triumph of rationality in human affairs, yet also etched with deep shadows of mourning. From Weber's canvas, we see modern man peering out with hopeful though disenchanted eyes at a future which offers vastly greater control over nature, society and man's own destiny. Yet the portrait also conveys a palpable grief for the lost spontaneity and immediacy which the social forms and symbols of the Judeo-Christian religious tradition had built up and guaranteed.

Nearer to our own times, as we study the anthropological, psychological, and, above all, fictional accounts of another transcultural historical process, the process of modernization in the non-Western world, we again encounter the ghost of depression seated at a banquet table laid out for eagerly awaited dishes of economic development and the fruits of industrialization. Let me, then, first outline the social-psychological processes which are a consequence of modernization and which I believe are the foundation on which the edifices of the new Hindu and Muslim as well as other cultural identities in India are being constructed. These processes are, of course, not particular to India but common to most of the non-Western world.

First, population movements which take place during the modernizing process involve the separation of families and the loss of familiar neighbourhoods and ecological niches. Psychologists report and novelists describe the feelings of bereavement and states of withdrawal among those mourning for old attachments and suspicious of creating new ones. These tendencies are not only harmful for individuals but also hinder the birth of new social structures and forms while they rob community life of much of its vitality and therefore its capacity for counteracting the sense of helplessness.

With increasing globalization, migrations are no longer confined by national boundaries. Globalization, too, encroaches upon traditional group solidarities and the established relationships between different groups, whether in Cochin or Moradabad. The shifting demands of global markets for particular kinds of goods and labour make for rapid and bewildering changes in the relative status of many groups in a particular society. Whereas some groups dramatically increase their earning power (and thus claims to a higher social status) through their access to international markets in goods, services, and labour, others are as dramatically impoverished, with many forced to migrate from their traditional geographical and cultural niches.

The vast internal migrations also give rise to overcrowded living conditions in urban conglomerations, especially in the sprawling shanty towns and slums with their permanent air of transience. On the one hand, it is undeniable that urban slums, however awful they seem to middle-class sensibilities, represent to the poor a hope of escaping from deadening economic deprivation and the relatively rigid, caste-based discrimination and inequities of rural society. On the other, there is lack of cultural norms in dealing with relative strangers whose behavioural clues cannot be easily deciphered, so different from the ritualized predictability of interactions in the communities left behind in villages or small towns, which compel the person to be constantly on guard. One is in a state of permanent psychic mobilization and heightened nervous arousal.

In addition, the rapid obsolescence of traditional roles and skills as modernization picks up pace seriously dents the self-esteem—when it does not shatter it completely—of those who are confronted with simultaneous loss of earning power, social status, and identity as particular kinds of workers. For the affected and their families, especially children, there is a collapse of confidence in the stability of the established order and of the world. What looms instead is the spectre of a future which is not only opaque but represents an overwhelming threat to any sense of purpose.

The feelings of loss are not limited to the migration from geographical regions and cultural homes or to the disappearance of traditional work identities. They also extend to the loss of ancestral ideals and values. For instance, compared to what many believe was a traditionally healthy eroticism, modernity, with its popular cinema, television, fashions, the commingling of sexes in schools, colleges, and at work, is sexually decadent. 'People have lost their *brahmacharya* (celibacy), their character is destroyed and every one has become an addict of bad habits. If you cannot control your libido, you cannot be pure.'[6] Once the enlightenment values of universal equality, liberty, and fraternity, of the pre-eminence of reason and moral autonomy of the individual were formulated through the political revolutions in the non-Western world, they became a universal heritage, inevitably triumphant when in conflict with the norms and values of the local culture. In spite of the disillusionment of some postmodern Western intellectuals with the enlightenment mentality, its values continue to constitute what has been generally regarded as the most dynamic and transformative ideology in human history, closing any option of going back to pre-modern conceptions.[7] Yet the enlightenment has a dark side, too. The modernization project is riddled with its own inequities, repressions, and unfraternal conflicts. There is thus bound to be a palpable grief for the values of a lost—and retrospectively idealized—world, when in the brave new one progress often turns out to be glaring inequality, rationality becomes selfishness and the pursuit of self-interest and individualism comes to mean unbridled greed.

Secret Wounds

Whereas loss and helplessness constitute one stream of feelings accompanying the modernization process, another stream consists of feelings of humiliation and radically lowered self-worth. One source of humiliation lies in the homogenizing and hegemonizing impact of modernization and globalization, both of which are no respecters of cultural pluralities and diversities. The imperatives of economic development, which see many local cultural values and attitudes as outmoded or just plain irrelevant, are a source of humiliation to all those who have not embraced or identified with the modernization project in its totality.

For the masses, there are other occasions for blows to their self-esteem such as the increase in the complexity and incidence of bureaucratic structures, with their attendant dehumanization, which has been a corollary of development. The cumulative effect of daily blows to an individual's feelings of self-worth, received in a succession of bureaucratic and other impersonal encounters, cannot be underestimated.

For the elites of the non-Western world, there is an additional humiliation in their greater consciousness of the defeat of their civilizations in the colonial encounter with the West. This defeat is not merely an abstraction or a historical memory but one which is confirmed by the peripheral role of their countries in the international economic and political order of the postcolonial world. Their consciousness of being second-class citizens in the global order is reinforced by their many encounters with their more self-confident Western colleagues in the various international forums. An example of the role played by loss and sensed humiliation is seen in the case of those Indians, economically an elite group, who have migrated to the United States and are frequently exposed to indifference or condescension toward their cultural tradition. When they have not abjured their cultural identity altogether in what I would consider an 'identification with the aggressor' they have turned back to embrace their culture identity as Hindus, Muslims, or Sikhs with a revivalist fervour which is far in excess of their counterparts in the home country. Of course, migration itself plays a significant role in the revival of ethnic identity. Global migration, tourism, and communications confront people in a society with a foreignness of others which is unprecedented in their experience. All over the world our encounters with strangers are on a larger scale, over longer periods of time, with the strangers possessing a higher degree of strangeness, than has ever been the case before. Observation such as 'They think like that' 'They believe this' 'Their customs are like that' inevitably lead to questions which may not have been self-consciously addressed before; 'What do *we* [however that "we" is defined] think?' 'What do *we* believe?' 'What are *our* customs?' In bringing together people in close proximity, the processes of globalization paradoxically increase the self-consciousness which separates and differentiates.

The portraits of loss and helplessness may sometimes seem to be overdrawn. Human beings have a remarkable capacity for adaptation, for creating new gardens of love around them where old ones have withered. Yet before fresh psychological and social structures can emerge, there is a period— permanent for some— of apathy, chronic discontent. or rebellious rage at those who are held responsible for the loss of old social forms and ideals. Historical and social changes, working through the psychological mechanisms of loss of and humiliation, thus lead to the widespread feeling of being a victim rather than an active agent of events which are buffeting the individual and his or her group. Millions of people become patients in a broad sense, even if temporarily, patienthood being essentially a condition of inactivation. After all, *patiens*, as Erik Erikson has pointed out, denotes a state of being exposed to superior forces from within and without which cannot be overcome without energetic and redeeming help.[8]

Cultural Identity and Cure

The required energy and redemption to restore *agens*, than inner state of being which sanctions initiative and encourages purposeful activity in the outer world, is most often sought through increasing, restoring, or constructing a sense of cultural identity. Cultural groups are not only a shelter for those mourning lost attachments but also vehicles for redressing narcissistic injuries, for righting what are perceived as contemporary or historical wrongs. The question of why such 'primordial' group identities as 'Hindus' and 'Muslims' are generally preferred to identities based on class, profession, or other criteria cannot be discussed here. Perhaps the latter lack an encompassing worldview, are impoverished in their symbolic riches and devoid of that essential corpus of myths in which people have traditionally sought meaning, especially at a time when their world appears to have become meaningless.

A core attraction and vital therapeutic action of self-consciously belonging to a cultural community lies in its claim to the possession of a future which, in a state of *pateins*, is felt to be irretrievably lost. To outsiders, this future may appear to be a simplistic perspective on the world such as a promise of restoration of the perfect civil society of the ancestors, what the Hindus, for instance, call Ram Rajya. It may be the reproduction on earth of a paradise envisaged only in sacred texts. It may be the hedonistic enjoyment of more and more goods and services in a heaven presided over by a benign, supply-side God. The promise is of a future, not seen, but which 'works'.

The cultural group, which brings the 'primordiality' related to shared myths, memories, values and symbols to the fore, thus assumes a vital healing function. One of its most important aspects is to replace feelings of loss with those of love. This insight into the way groups work psychologically goes back to Freud, who postulated eros as the vital cohesive force in a group.[9] He believed the ties of love among members of a group come into existence through their emotional bond with the leader. In more technical terms, members of a group put the same object, the leader, in place of their ego ideal and consequently identify with each other. This shared idealization gives rise to the love ties which are experienced in the feelings of loyalty, *esprit de corps*, and in the more intense moments of group life, in feelings of fusion and merger. Experientially, it is a reordering and opening up of the inner world of the individual to include members of the group who, in turn, open up to include the individual in their psychological space, a mutual affirmation which lies at the heart of love. In cultural groups, the shared ego ideal may not be the figure of a single leader but many historical and mythical figures from the group's tradition, its ideals and values, and even its social and intellectual traditions.

We are all aware of the profound effect the group can have on the consolidation of a person's 'sense of identity' and in increasing the cohesiveness of the self. Even in individual psychotherapy, we often see that it is not unusual for patients in a state of self-fragmentation to achieve a firmer and more cohesive sense of self upon joining an organized group. The Nazis are not the only group who turned quasi-derelict individuals into efficiently functioning ones by providing them with the framework of a convincing world image and the use of new cultural symbols and group emblems such as shiny brown uniforms. As Ernest Wolf perceptively observes, 'It seems a social identity can support a crumbling self the way a scaffolding can support a crumbling building.'[10]

Psychology Versus Politics?

Before I look at the construction of the new Hindu identity, I would like to address the objections to a psychological approach to the subject. There are many social scientists and political analysts who would locate the enhancement of ethnicity (cultural identity in my terms) in a particular group not in social-psychological processes but in the competition between elites for political power and economic resources. In fact, this has been the dominant explanation for the occurrence of Hindu-Muslim riots and is best exemplified in the work of Asghar Ali Engineer.[11] This 'instrumentalist', as contrasted to the 'primordialist' view I advocate here, has been succinctly formulated by Paul Brass:

> In the process of transforming cultural forms, values and practices into political symbols, elites in competition with each other for control over the allegiance or territory of the ethnic group in question strive to enhance or break the solidarity of the group. Elites seeking to mobilize the ethnic group against its rivals or against the state strive to promote a congruence of a multiplicity of the group's symbols, to argue that members of the group are different not in one respect only but in many and that all its cultural elements are reinforcing.[12]

Cultural identity according to this view is not a fixed or given dimension of communities but a variable one which takes form in the process of political mobilization by the elite, a mobilization which arises from the broader political and economic environment. Brass questions the import of the primary dimensions of ethnicity in the subjective lives of individuals. Most people, he says, never think about their language at all. Millions, both in traditional and modern societies, have migrated to other countries out of choice (or necessity). And though many may have an emotional attachment to their place of birth or ancestral religion, many others have chosen to assimilate to their new societies and have lost all connection with their origins.

Brass's case for the relative insignificance of primordiality appears to be overstated. Cultural identity, like its individual counterpart, is an unconscious human acquirement which becomes consciously salient only when there is a perceived threat to its integrity. Identity, both individual and cultural, lives itself for the most part, unfettered and unworried by obsessive and excessive scrutiny. Everyday living incorporates a zone of indifference with regard to one's culture, including one's langue, ethnic origin, or religion. It is only when this zone of indifference is breached that the dimensions of ethnicity stand out in sharp relief and the individual becomes painfully or exhilaratingly aware of certain aspects of his cultural identity. The breaches in the zone of indifference, like the one which has taken place in the aftermath of the demolition of the Babri mosque, are not only made by momentous external events such as actual or threatened persecution, war, riots, and so on. Inner psychological changes at certain stages of the lifecycle may also cause these fateful incursions. Thus, for instance, youth is regarded as a period of life when issues of personal identity become crucial, when the conscious and unconscious preoccupation with the question 'Who am I?' reaches its peak. Many migrants, who have willingly chosen to thoroughly assimilate themselves into their new societies and appear to have lost all traces of their ethnic origins, are surprised to find that the issues of cultural identity have not disappeared. They have only skipped a generation as their sons and daughters, on the verge of adulthood, become preoccupied with their cultural roots as part of their quest for a personal identity.

I do not mean to imply that the instrumentalist approach is without substance. It is also not a monopoly of professional social scientists but is shared by many people in other walks of life. In Indian towns and cities where there have been riots between Hindus and Muslims, I have normally found that 'men of goodwill' from both communities invariably attribute the riots to the machinations and manipulations of politicians pursuing political power or economic advantage rather than to any increase in primordial sentiments, a perspective which is also shared by people who are far removed from the conflict. The instrumentalist theory of ethnic mobilization thus becomes an 'instigator' theory of violent conflict among religious groups. In concentrating on the instigators, it underplays or downright denies that there are 'instigatees', too, whose participation is essential to transform animosity between religious groups into violence. The picture it holds up of evil politicians and innocent masses is certainly attractive since it permits us a disavowal of our own impulses toward violence and vicious ethnocentrism. We all have different zones of indifference beyond which our own ethnocentrism, in some form or the other, will become a salient part of our identity.

The appeal of the instrumentalist or instigator theory, however, is not only that it allows us a projection of the unacceptable parts of ourselves onto "bad" politicians. Its allure is also due to a particular historical legacy of the literary elite in all major civilizations. This legacy devalues nonrational processes—what psychoanalysts call 'fantasy'—which form the basis of the primordial approach. As has been pointed out by others in a different context, the culture of fantasy lacks all meaningful status in the realm of serious public discourse which is comprised of the discussion of ideas, not shared fantasies.[13] Fantasy is regarded as primitive, primordial, before reason; it is unconscious as compared to conscious, mythic as compared to scientific, marked by the pleasures of connotation rather than the rigours of denotation. A sensitive, introspective discussion of socially shared fantasies (rather than ideas) as the moving force behind the ideals and ambitions of large groups and communities is generally not possible. Steeped in a long tradition of respect for the culture of ideas and their own professional role in its production and propagation, the scholarly elite of a society are not easily receptive to the culture of fantasy.

I do not mean to imply that the political and psychological, the instrumental and the primordial, approaches should be viewed in either/or terms. Both the approaches are complementary to each other. Whether it be the history of Hindu-Muslim relations, or the analysis of the causes of the riots between the two communities (economic-political versus social-psychological), or the explanation for the basis of emerging religious group identities ('instrumental' interests versus 'primordial' attachments), the arguments are invariably couched in a dualistic either/or mode. This, of course, is a testimony to the stronghold of the Aristotelian and Cartesian ways of thinking on modern minds. Like most shared habits, we do not recognize this kind of thinking as mere habit but take it as an unquestioned verity, as the way things 'naturally' are. Complementary thinking does not mean that 'anything goes', in a vulgar postmodernist sense. It has its own definitional constraints and boundaries; for instance, the more incompatible (not outlandish) the explanations for a phenomenon, the more complementary they will be. Complementarity is the belonging together of various possibilities of experiencing the same object differently. The wave and particle theories of light in physics, the primary and secondary processes in psychoanalysis, *mythos* and *logos* as modes of knowledge, are a few of the many examples of complementarity. Forms of complementary knowledge belong together in so far as they pertain to the same object; they exclude each other in that they cannot occur simultaneously. Complementarity is the acceptance of different possibilities and not their splitting and the exclusion of some. To describe a phenomenon complementarily is to reveal its wholeness, to understand its different aspects.[14] None of these aspects is more true than others; each is irreplaceable. In brief, the logic underlying complementary thought is not of an either/or kind but of an 'as well as' variety. Thus, without the psychological perspective to complement the political-economic one, we will have only a partial and thus dangerously inadequate understanding of the reasons for the success of political formations based on religious mobilization.

Search for Hinduness

The instrumentalist approach to ethnicidentity, however, makes an important contribution by pointing out that these identities are not fixed and immutable but more or less variable. The self-consciousness of being a Hindu today is not of the same order as at other times in India's history. What is today called 'Hinduism' has emerged through many encounters between dissenting sects professing diverse beliefs and with other, more self-conscious religions, such as Islam and Christianity.

Today, there is a new Hindu identity under construction in many parts of India, especially the northern and central states. It is a process which is undoubtedly propelled by the fact that this identity is also the basis of political mobilization by the main opposition party, the Bharatiya Janta Party (BJP). Created out of a preexisting though ill-defined and amorphous Hinduism the new identity bears only a faint family resemblance to its progenitors. Indeed, as we saw in the first chapter, some scholars argue that the sharply differentiated cultural identities of Hindus and Muslims which we encounter today, with their heightened self-consciousness, the kind of commitment they command, and the intensity with which these identities are pursued politically, are a creation of the British colonial period. They are not only a product of the colonial 'divide and rule' policies which led to the emergence of 'identity politics' but are also a consequence of the imposition of alien modes of thought on native Indian categories. The political scientist Don Miller remarks:

> By their education, legislation, administration, judicial codes and procedures and even by that apparently simple operation of 'objective' classification, the census, the British unwittingly imposed dualistic 'either-or' oppositions as the 'natural' normative order of thought. In a multitude of ways, Indians learned that one is either this or that; that one cannot be both or neither or indifferent. The significance of identity thus became a new, paramount concern . . . an orthodoxy of being was gradually replacing a heterodoxy of beings.[15]

Leaving the issue of pinpointing the time and place of birth of the new Hindu identity in the late 20th century to historians—an identity which its critics have decried as Hindu nationalism, Hindu militancy, or Hindu fundamentalism—we can only observe that this identity selects many of its symbols, myths, and images from traditional stock. The cultural values and forms it endorses have a recognizable ancestry. In its strong links with the past, this Hindu identity is neither wholly new nor completely old. It is constructed, yet also revived; it is a combination of the made and the given. The social and political forces which are self-consciously active in its constructed revival, the *sangh parivar*, have some truth on their side when they maintain that the elements of this new Hindu identity were always there; it is just that people did not see them before. The question of whether those propagating the new Hindu identity are embarked on its construction or merely on its articulation for others does not have a simple answer. The answer depends upon whether the vantage point is of an outside observer or of the insider directly engaged in the process. In any event, the political countering of this Hindu identity will involve the offer of a different Hindutva with other images, symbols, and myths of the Hindu ethos rather than any abstract concept of secularism, which for most Hindus is empty of all psychological meaning.

The Virtuous Virago

To look more closely at the constructed revival of Hindu identity, I have chosen as my text a speech by Sadhavi Rithambra, one of the star speakers for the *sangh parivar*, the prefix sadhavi being the female counterpart of sadhu, a man who has renounced the world in search of personal salvation and universal welfare within the Hindu religious worldview. It is reported that Rithambra was a 16-year-old schoolgirl in Khanna, a village in the Punjab, when she had a strong spiritual experience while listening to a discourse by Swami Parmananda, one of the many 'saints' in the forefront of Hindu revivalism.[16] Rithambra abandoned her studies and home and joined Parmananda's ashram. Soon she began travelling with her guru to religious meetings in the Hindi heartland and after a while addressed a few herself. Her oratorial talents were noticed by the political leadership of the *sangh parivar* and, after being given some training in voice modulation, she was well on her way to become the leading firebrand in the Hindu cause.

The speech I have chosen was given at Hyderabad in April 1991, a few weeks after the general election for the national Parliament and many state assemblies were announced. The speech is a standard one which Rithambra has given all over India to the enthusiastic response of hundreds of thousands of people. The political context of the speech is the bid by the BJP, the political arm of the *sangh* family, to capture power in some north Indian states in the coming elections and to emerge as the single largest party in the national Parliament. In the preceding months, the BJP had determined the country's political agenda by its mobilization of Hindus on the issue of constructing a temple to the god Rama at Ayodhya, his reputed birthplace. The construction of this temple had become an explosive and divisive issue since the designated site was already occupied by the Babri Masjid, a mosque built by Babar, the Muslim invader from Central Asia who was the founder of the Mughal dynasty that ruled over large parts of India for over 400 years. There had been much bloodshed five months earlier as many Hindus, the *kar-sevaks*, lost their lives in police firing when they attempted to defy legal orders and begin the temple construction, a step which required demolition or at least relocation of the existing mosque. The killings of unarmed Rama *bhaktas*—devotees of Rama—in Ayodhya led to a spate of riots between Hindus and Muslims in other parts of the country, including Hyderabad, a city with an almost equal proportion of the two communities and where the tension between them over the years had regularly erupted in communal violence.

The political context of the speech, the theme of temple versus mosque, the abundance of imagery and allusions in its text to the narratives of the epics *Ramayana* and the *Mahabharata*, and the person of the speaker herself are all replete with symbolic resonances, evocations, and associations. They virtually reek with a surfeit of meaning that burrows deep into the psychic recesses of the audience, going well beyond the words used as its carriers. Listening to her speak, the earlier question is once again raised: Is she an elite manipulator of Hindu cultural symbols (instrumental theory) or is she an articulator of what many Hindus feel but cannot express (primordialist viewpoint)? The answer is again not in terms of either/or but of the simultaneity of both processes. Rithambra appeals to a group identity while creating it. She both mirrors her listeners' sentiments and gives them birth. My impression is that the images, metaphors, and mythological allusions of her speech have a resonance for the audience because they also have a resonance for her. This does not imply that the speech is a spontaneous pouring out of her heart. Like an actor she has honed this particular speech through successive deliveries and knows what 'works'. It is not raw feeling but carefully crafted emotion; an epic poem rather than a scream or a shout. Rithambra's power lies less in her persuasiveness on an intellectual, cognitive plane than on the *poetic* (Greek *poiesis*—a making, shaping) that permeates her speech. It is this poetic which gives a first form to what are for her audience only vaguely or partially ordered feelings and perceptions, makes a shared sense out of already shared circumstances.[17]

As a renouncer of worldly life, a sanyasin, Rithambra conjures up the image of selflessness. Associatively, she is not a politician stirred by narrow electoral considerations or identified with partisan interest groups but someone who is moved by the plight of the whole country, even concerned with the welfare of all mankind. As an ascetic who has renounced all sexual activity, she evokes the image of the virgin goddess, powerful because virgin, a power which is of another, 'purer' world. There is also a subtle sexual challenge to the men in her audience to prove their virility (vis-à-vis the Muslim) in order to deserve her.

The key passages in the text of her speech are delivered as rhyming verses, in the tradition of bardic narration of stories from the Hindu epics. Perhaps people tend to believe verse more than prose, especially in Hindu India where the transmission of sacred knowledge has traditionally been oral and through the medium of rhymed verse. In any event, implicit in her speech is the claim to be less tainted with the corruption of language, a corruption which is widely laid at the door of the politician and which has led people to lose faith in what they hear from public platforms. It Rithambra is a politician, hers is the politics of magic that summons forces from the deep, engaging through coded ideas and ideals the deeper fears and wishes of her Hindu audiences whom she and the *sangh parivar* are determined to make 'more' Hindu. As I listened to her I was once again reminded of Milan Kundera's statement that 'political movements rest not so much on rational attitudes as on fantasies, images, words and archetypes that come together to make up this or that political kitsch.'

> Hail Mother Sita! Hail brave Hanuman! Hail Mother India! Hail the birthplace of Rama! Hail Lord Vishwanath [Shiva] of Kashi [Benares]! Hail Lord Krishna! Hail the eternal religion [*dharma*]! Hail the religion of the *Vedas*! Hail Lord Mahavira! Hail Lord Buddha! Hail Banda Bairagi! Hail Guru Gobind Singh! Hail the great sage Dayananda! Hail the great sage Valmiki! Hail the martyred *kar-sevaks*! Hail Mother India!

In ringing tones Rithambra invokes the various gods and revered figures from Indian history, ancient and modern. The gods and heroes are not randomly chosen. In their careful selection, they are markers of the boundary of the Hindu community she and the *sangh parivar* would wish to constitute today and believe existed in the past. Such a commemoration is necessarily selective since it must silence contrary interpretations of the past and seek to conserve only certain of its aspects. The gods and heroes are offered up as ego ideals, to be shared by members of the community in order to bring about and maintain group cohesion. Identity implies definition rather than blurring, solidity rather than flux or fluidity, and therefore the question of boundaries of a group become paramount. Rithambra begins the construction of Hindu identity by demarcating this boundary.

In the context of the preceding year's agitation around the construction of the Rama temple, the god Rama occupies the highest watchtower on the border between Hindu and non-Hindu. Rithambra starts by praising Rama's wife, the goddess Sita, and his greatest devotee, the monkey god Hanuman, who are then linked to contemporary concerns as she hails Rama's birthplace where the *sangh parivar* wishes to construct the controversial temple and around which issue it has sought a mobilization of the Hindus.

The 5000-year-old religion, however, with a traditional lack of central authority structures such as a church and with a diffused essence, has over the centuries thrown up a variety of sects with diverse beliefs. It is Rithambra's purpose to include all the Hinduisms spawned by Hinduism. The presiding deity of the Shaivite sects, Shiva, is hailed, as is Krishna, the most popular god of the Vaishnavas.

The overarching Hindu community is then sought to be further enlarged by including the followers of other religions whose birthplace is India. These are the Jains, the Buddhists, and the Sikhs, and Rithambra devoutly hails Mahavira, Buddha, and the militant last guru of the Sikhs, Guru Gobind Singh who, together with Banda Bairagi, has the added distinction of a lifetime of armed struggle against the Mughals. Nineteenth-century reformist movements such as the Arya Samaj are welcomed by including its founder Dayananda Saraswati in the Hindu pantheon. The Harijans or 'scheduled castes', the former 'untouchables' of Hindu society, are expressly acknowledged as a part of the Hindu society by hailing Valmiki, the legendary author of the *Ramayana* who has been recently elevated to the position of the patron saint of the Harijans.

From gods and heroes of the past, a link is established to the collective heroism of the *kar-sevaks*, men and women who in their bid to build the temple died in the police firing at Ayodhya. The immortal gods and the mortal heroes from past and present are all the children of Mother India, the subject of the final invocation, making the boundaries of the Hindu community coterminous with that of Indian nationalism.

I have come to the Hindus of Bhagyanagar [Hyderabad] with a message. The saints who met in Allahabad directed Hindu society to either bend the government to its will or to remove it. The government has been removed. On fourth April, more than two and a half million Hindus displayed their power at the lawns of Delhi's Boat Club. We went to the Parliament but it lay empty. The saints said, fill the

Parliament with the devotees of Rama. This is the next task of Hindu society.

As far as the construction of the Rama temple is concerned, some people say Hindus should not fight over a structure of brick and stone. They should not quarrel over a small piece of land. I want to ask these people, 'If someone burns the national flag will you say "Oh, it doesn't matter. It is only two metres of cloth which is not a great national loss."' The question is not of two metres of cloth but of an insult to the nation. Rama's birthplace is not a quarrel about a small piece of land. It is a question of national integrity. The Hindu is not fighting for a temple of brick and stone. He is fighting for the preservation of a civilization, for his Indianness, for national consciousness, for the recognition of his true nature. We shall build the temple!

It is not the building of the temple but the building of India's national consciousness. You, the wielders of state power, you do not know that the Rama temple is not a mere building. It is not a construction of brick and stone. It is not only the birthplace of Rama. The Rama temple is our honour. It is our self-esteem. It is the image of Hindu unity. We shall raise its flag. We shall build the temple!

Hindi is a relatively passionate language. Its brilliant, loud colours are impossible to reproduce in the muted palette of English. As the Rama temple takes shape in Rithambra's cascading flow of language, as she builds it, phrase by phrase, in the mind of her listeners, it evokes acute feelings of a shared social loss. The Rama temple, then, is a response to the mourning of Hindu society: a mourning for lost honour, lost self-esteem, lost civilization, lost Hinduness. It is the maternal and social counterpart of the individual experience of mourning. In a more encompassing formulation, the Rama birthplace temple is like other monuments which, as Peter Homans perceptively observes:

> engage the immediate conscious experience of an aggregate of egos by representing and mediating to them the lost cultural experiences of the past; the experiences of individuals, groups, their ideas and ideals, which coalesce into what can be called a collective memory. In this the monument is a symbol of union because it brings together the particular psychological circumstances of many individuals' life courses and the universals of their otherwise lost historical past within the context of their current or contemporary social processes and structures.[18]

The temple is the body in which Hindu identity is sought to be embodied.

Some people became afraid of Rama's devotees. They brought up Mandal.* They thought the Hindu will get divided. He will be fragmented by the reservations issue. His attention will be diverted from the temple. But your thought was wrong. Your thought was despicable. We shall build the temple!

I have come to tell our Hindu youth, do not take the candy of reservations and divide yourself into castes. If Hindus get divided, the sun of Hindu unity will set. How will the sage Valmiki look after Sita? How will Rama eat Shabri's berries [ber]?** Those who wish that our bonds with the backward castes and the Harijans are cut will bite dust. We shall build the temple!

Listen, Rama is the representation of mass consciousness. He is the god of the poor and the oppressed. He is the life of fishermen, cobblers, and washermen.*** If anyone is not a devotee of such a god, he does not have Hindu blood in his veins. We shall build the temple!

Marking its boundary, making it aware of a collective cultural loss, giving it a body, is not enough to protect and maintain the emerging Hindu identity. For identity is not an achievement but a process constantly threatened with rupture by forces from within and without.

Constant vigil is needed to guard it from that evil inside the group which seeks to divide what has been recently united, to disrupt and fragment what has been freshly integrated. Rithambra addresses the feeling of threat and singles out the political forces representing this threat which must be defeated at the coming battle of the ballot box.

My Hindu brothers! Stop shouting that slogan, 'Give one more push and break the Babri mosque! The mosque is broken, the mosque is broken!!' What mosque are you talking about? We are going to build our temple there, not break anyone's mosque. Our civilization has never been one of destruction. Intellectuals and scholars of the world, wherever you find ruins, wherever you come upon broken monuments, you will find the signature of Islam. Wherever you find creation, you

* Mandal refers to the reservation policy announced by the government of V.P. Singh at the height of the temple agitation. The policy sought to increase reservations in federal and state employment and admission to educational institutions for the backward castes at the expense of the upper castes.

** The sage Valmiki, reputedly a hunter belonging to a low caste gave asylum to Sita in his forest abode after she was banished by Rama. Shabri was a poor untouchable who fed berries to Rama during his exile.

*** All of them belong to the lowest castes.

discover the signature of the Hindu. We have never believed in breaking but in constructing. We have always been ruled by the maxim, 'The world is one family [*Vasudhe kuttumbkam*]. We are not pulling down a monument, we are building one.

Scholars, turn the pages of history and tell us whether the Hindu, riding a horse and swinging a bloody sword, has ever trampled on anyone's human dignity? We cannot respect those who have trod upon humanity. Our civilization has given us great insights. We see god in a stone, we see god in trees and plants. We see god in a dog and run behind him with a cup of butter. Hindus, have you forgotten that the saint Namdev had only one piece of bread to eat which was snatched by a dog. Namdev ran after the dog with a cup of butter crying, 'Lord, don't eat dry bread. Take some butter too!!' Can the Hindu who sees god even in a dog ever harbour resentment towards a Muslim?

Wherever I go, I say, 'Muslims, live and prosper among us. Live like milk and sugar. If two kilos of sugar are dissolved in a quintal of milk, the milk becomes sweet!' But what can be done if our Muslim brother is not behaving like sugar in the milk? Is it our fault if he seems bent upon being a lemon in the milk? He wants the milk to curdle. He is behaving like a lemon in the milk by following people like Shahabuddin and Abdullah Bukhari.* I say to him, 'Come to your senses. The value of the milk increases after it becomes sour. It becomes cheese. But the world knows the 'fate of the lemon. It is cut, squeezed dry and then thrown on the garbage heap. Now you have to decide whether you will act like sugar or like a lemon in the milk. Live among us like the son of a human being and we will respectfully call you "uncle". But if you want to behave like the son of Babar then the Hindu youth will deal with you as Rana Pratap and Chatrapti Shivaji** dealt with your forefathers.' Those who say we are against the Muslims lie. We are talking of the birthplace of Rama, not constructing at Mecca or Medina. It is our birthright to build a temple to our Lord at the spot he was born.

We have religious tolerance in our very bones. Together with our 330 million gods, we have worshipped the dead lying in their graves. Along with Rama and Krishna, we have saluted Mohammed and Jesus. With *Vasudhe Kuttumbkam* as our motto, we pray for the salvation of the

* Widely regarded as two of the leaders of Muslim fundamentalism in India.
** Popular embodiments of Hindu resistance to Mughal rule.

world and for an increase in fellow feeling in all human beings. We have never said, 'O World! Believe in our *Upanishads*. Believe in our *Gita*. Otherwise you are an infidel and by cutting off the head of an infidel one gains paradise.' Our sentiments are not so low. They are not narrow-minded. They are not dirty. We see the world as our family.

Here, in the construction of the Hindu identity, we see the necessary splitting that enhances group cohesion. The process involves idealizing on the one hand and scapegoating and persecutory processes on the other. What is being idealized is the Hindu tolerance, compassion, depth of insight and width of social concern. These are the contents of a grandiose Hindu group self which makes the individual member feel righteous and pure. It raises each member's sense of worth for belonging to this group.

The increase in self-esteem can be maintained only by projecting the bad, the dirty, and the impure to another group, the Muslim, with which one's own group is then constantly compared. This process is at the root of scapegoating and, as Rafael Moses reminds us, this indeed is how the original scapegoat was conceived of in religion: the animal was driven away with all the community's badness inside it so that the community of believers could remain pure and clean (like milk, I am tempted to add).[19] Of course, as a good vegetarian Hindu, Sadhavi Rithambra conceives the Muslim scapegoat not as an animal but as a lemon. As we shall see below, the Muslim is not only the object of scapegoating but also the subject of persecutory fantasies in the collective Hindu imagination.

Today, the Hindu is being insulted in his own home. The Hindu is not sectarian. How could he if he worships trees and plants! Once [the Mughal emperor] Akbar and [his Hindu minister] Birbal were going somewhere. On the way they saw a plant. Birbal dismounted and prostrated himself before the plant saying, 'Hail mother tulsi!' Akbar said, 'Birbal, you Hindus are out of your minds, making parents out of trees and plants. Let's see how strong your mother is!' He got off his horse, pulled the tulsi plant out by its roots and threw it on the road. Birbal swallowed this humiliation and kept quiet. What could he do? It was the reign of the Mughals. They rode farther and saw another plant. Birbal again prostrated himself saying, 'Hail, father! Hail, honoured father!' Akbar said, 'Birbal I have dealt with your mother. Now, let me deal with your father too.' He again pulled out the plant and threw it away. The plant was a nettle. Akbar's hands started itching and soon the painful itch spread all over his body. He began rolling on the ground like a donkey, with tears in his eyes and his nose watering. All the while he was scratching himself like a dog. When Birbal saw the condition of the king, he said, 'O Protector of the World, pardon my saying that our Hindu mothers may be innocent but our fathers are hard-bitten.' Akbar asked, 'Birbal how do I get rid of your father?' Birbal said, 'Go and ask forgiveness of my mother tulsi. Then rub the paste made out of her leaves on your body and my father will pardon you.'

I mean today that the long-suffering Hindu is being called a religious zealot today only because he wants to build the temple. The Muslims got their Pakistan. Even in a mutilated India, they have special rights. They have no use for family planning. They have their own religious schools. What do we have? An India with its arms cut off.* An India where restrictions are placed on our festivals, where our processions are always in danger of attack, where the expression of our opinion is prohibited, where our religious beliefs are cruelly derided. We cannot speak of our pain, express our hurt. I say to the politician, 'Do not go on trampling upon our deepest feelings as you have been doing for so long.'

In Kashmir, the Hindu was a minority and was hounded out of the valley. Slogans of 'Long live Pakistan' were carved with red-hot iron rods on the thighs of our Hindu daughters. Try to feel the unhappiness and the pain of the Hindu who became a refugee in his own country. The Hindu was dishonoured in Kashmir because he was in a minority. But there is a conspiracy to make him a minority in the whole country. The state tells us Hindus to have only two or three children. After a while, they will say do not have even one.'But what about those who have six wives, have 35 children and breed like mosquitoes and flies?

Why should there be two sets of laws in this country? Why should we be treated like stepchildren? I submit to you that when the Hindu of Kashmir became a minority he came to Jammu. From Jammu he came to Delhi. But if you Hindus are on the run all over India, where will you go? Drown in the Indian Ocean or jump from the peaks of the Himalayas?

What is this impartiality toward all religions where the mullahs get the moneybags and Hindus the bullets? We also want religious impartiality but not of the kind where only Hindus are oppressed. People say there should be Hindu-Muslim unity. Leave the structure of the Babri mosque undisturbed. I say, 'Then let's have this unity in the case of

---

*The reference is to a comparison between the maps of India before and after Partition.

the Jama Masjid* too. Break half of it and construct a temple. Hindus
and Muslims will then come together.

You know the doctors who carry out their medical experiments by
cutting open frogs, rabbits, cats? All these experiments in Hindu-
Muslim unity are being carried out on the Hindu chest as if he is a
frog, rabbit or cat. No one has ever heard of a lion's chest being cut
open for a medical experiment. They teach the lesson of religious unity
and amity only to the Hindus.

In Lucknow there was a Muslim procession which suddenly stopped
when passing a temple where a saffron flag was flying. The mullahs
said, 'This is the flag of infidels. We cannot pass even under its shadow.
Take down the flag!' Some of your liberal Hindu leaders and followers
of Gandhi started persuading the Hindus, 'Your ancestors have endured
a great deal. You also tolerate a little. You have been born to suffer,
take down the flag.' Luckily, I was also there. I said to the leader who
was trying to cajole the Hindus into taking down the flag, 'If I took off
your cap, gave four blows to your head with my shoe and then replaced
the cap, would you protest?' This is not just our flag, it is our honour,
our pride. Religious impartiality does not mean that to appease one
you insult the other. Hindu children were riddled with bullets in the
alleys of Ayodhya to please the Muslims. The Saryu river became red
with the blood of slaughtered *kar-sevaks*. We shall not forget.

It is true that for the strengthening of cultural identity, belief of the group members in
an existing or anticipated oppression is helpful, is not necessary. Yet for the 800 million
Hindus who are relatively more advanced on almost every economic and social criteria,
to feel oppressed by Muslims who are one-eighth their number demands an explanation
other than one given by the theory of relative deprivation. This theory, as we know,
argues that a group feels oppressed if it perceives inequality in the distribution of
resources and believes it is entitled to more than the share it receives. There is a
considerable denial of reality involved in maintaining that the Hindus are relatively
deprived or in danger of oppression by the Muslims. Such a denial of reality is only
possible through the activation of the group's persecutory fantasy in which the Muslim
changes from a stereotype to an archetype; he becomes the 'arch' tyrant. As in
individuals, where persecution anxiety often manifests itself in threats of the integrity
of the body, especially during psychotic episodes, Rithambra's speech becomes rich in
the imagery of a mutilated body. Eloquently, she conjures up an India—the motherland—

* The best known Indian mosque, located in Delhi.

with its arms cut off, Hindu chests cut open like those of frogs, rabbits, and cats, the thighs of young Hindu women burnt with red-hot iron rods; in short, the body amputated, slashed, raped. It is the use of metaphors of the body—one's own and of one's mother (India)—under assault that makes an actual majority feel a besieged minority in imagination, anchors the dubious *logos* of a particular political argument deeply in fantasy through the power of *mythos*.

They said, 'Let's postpone the mid-term elections till the Hindu's anger cools down.' I say, 'Is the Hindu a bottle of mineral water? Keep the bottle open for a while and the water will stop bubbling?' It is 900,000 years since Ravana kidnapped Sita and challenged god Rama. But to this day we have not forgotten. Every year we burn his effigy and yet the fire of our revenge burns bright. We will not forget mullah Mulayam* and his supporter Rajiv Gandhi. I have come to tell the young men and mothers of Bhagyanagar, listen to the wailing of the Saryu river, listen to the story told by Ayodhya, listen to the sacrifice of the *kar-sevaks*. If you are a Hindu, do not turn your face away from the Rama temple, do not spare the traitors of Rama.

After the incident on the ninth of November, many Hindu young men came to me. 'Sister,' they said, 'give us weapons to deal with mullah Mulayam.' I said, 'Why waste a bullet to deal with a eunuch?' Rama had become tired shooting his arrows. Ravana's one head would fall to be immediately replaced by another. Vibhishna [Ravana's brother] said, 'Lord, you will not kill this sinner by cutting off his heads. His life is in his navel.' My brother Hindus, these leaders have their lives in their chairs [of power]. Take away their power and they'll die—by themselves. They are only impotent eunuchs. When Rama was banished from Ayodhya many citizens accompanied him to the forest and stayed there overnight. In the morning, Rama said, 'Men and women of Ayodhya, go back to your homes.' The men and women went back but a group of hermaphrodites, who are neither men nor women, stayed back and asked, 'Lord, you have not given us any instructions.' Rama is kind. He said, 'In the future Kaliyuga you will rule for a little while.' These, neither-men-nor-women, are your rulers today. They will not be able to protect India's unity and integrity.

Make the next government one of Rama's devotees. Hindus, you must unite in the coming elections if you want the temple built. Hindus, if you do not awaken, cows will be slaughtered everywhere. In the

---

* The chief minister of Uttar Pradesh.

340

retreats of our sages you will hear the chants of 'Allah is Great'. You will be responsible for these catastrophes for history will say Hindus were cowards. Accept the challenge, change the history of our era.

Many say, Rithambra you are a sanyasin. You should meditate in some retreat. I tell them raising Hindu consciousness is my meditation now and it will go on till the saffron flag flies from the ramparts of the Red Fort.*

The feeling of helplessness which persecution anxiety engenders reverses the process of idealization, reveals the fragility of the group's grandiose self. The positive self-image of the Hindu—tolerant, compassionate, with special insight into the relationship between the divine and the natural worlds, between human and divine—exposes another, negative side: the specific Hindu shame and fear of being too cowardly and impotent to change the material or social conditions of life. Indeed, we should always look closely at a group's specific form of self idealization to find clues to its particular moment of self-doubt and self-hatred. What a group most idealizes about itself is intimately related to its greatest fear. For the Hindu, the positive self-image of tolerance has the shadow of weakness cleaving to it. Are we tolerant or are we merely weak? Or tolerant *because* weak?

The crumbling self, with its unbearable state of helplessness, demands restoration through forceful action. Rithambra channels this need for *agens* into a call for collective and united action in the political arena. She holds out the possibility of some kind of self-assertion through the coming electoral process where all the persecutory anti-Hindu forces, from within and without the Hindu fold, can be engaged and defeated. With this prospect, the negative self-image begins to fade, the group self becomes more cohesive. The Muslim, too, though remaining alien, becomes less demonic and more human, although still a cussed adversary.

They ask what would happen to the Muslims in a Hindu India? I tell them the Muslims will not be dishonoured in a Hindu state nor will they be rewarded to get their votes. No umbrella will open in Indian streets because it is raining in Pakistan. It there is war in the Gulf then slogans of 'Long Live Saddam Hussein' won't be shouted on Indian streets. And as for unity with our Muslim brothers, we say, 'Brother, we are willing to eat *sevian* [sweet noodles] at your house to celebrate Eid but you do not want to play with colours with us on Holi. We hear your calls to prayer along with our temple bells, but you object to our bells. How can unity ever come about? The Hindu faces this

*The symbol of political power in India.

way, the Muslim the other. The Hindu writes from left to right, the Muslim from right to left. The Hindu prays to the rising sun. The Muslim faces the setting sun when praying. If the Hindu eats with the right hand, the Muslim eats with the left. If the Hindu calls India 'Mother', she becomes a witch for the Muslim. The Hindu worships the cow, the Muslim attains paradise by eating beef. The Hindu keeps a moustache, the Muslim always shaves the upper lip. Whatever the Hindu does, it is the Muslim's religion to do its opposite. I said, 'If you want to do everything contrary to the Hindu, then the Hindu eats with his mouth; you should do the opposite in this matter too!'

After the laughter subsides, Rithambra ends by asking the audience to raise their fists and repeat aft her, 'Say with pride, we are Hindus! Hindustan (India) is ours!'

The conclusion of Rithambra's speech complements its beginning. Both the beginning and the end are concerned with the issue of drawing the boundaries of the group of 'us' Hindus. Whereas Rithambra began with a self-definition of the Hindu by including certain kinds of Hinduisms—as personified by heroes, gods and historical figures—she ends with trying to achieve this self-definition through contrasts with what a Hindu is decidedly not—the Muslim. At the start, the boundary was drawn from inside out; at the end, its contours are being marked off by reference to the 'them', the Muslims, who lie outside the psychogeographical space inhabited by 'us'. It is, of course, understood that 'their' space is not only separate and different but also devalued. In her enumeration of differences Rithambra cleverly contrives to end on a note which associates the Muslim with certain denigrated, specifically anal, bodily parts and functions.

I have suggested here that the construction/revival of the new Hindu identity in the text of Rithambra's speech follows certain well-marked turnings of the plot which are motivated, energized, and animated by fantasy. To recapitulate, these are: marking afresh the boundaries of the religious-cultural community, making the community conscious of a collective cultural loss, countering internal forces which seek to disrupt the unity of the freshly demarcated community, idealizing the community, maintaining its sense of grandiosity by comparing it to a bad 'other' which, at times, becomes a persecutor and, finally, dealing with the persecutory fantasies, which bring to the surface the community's particular sense of inferiority, by resort to some kind of forceful action.

In describing these psychological processes, I am aware that my own feelings toward the subject could have coloured some of my interpretations. This is unavoidable, especially since I am a Hindu myself, exposed to all the crosscurrents of feelings generated by contemporary events. My own brand of Hinduism, liberal-rationalist (with a streak of agnostic mysticism) can be expected to be critical of the new Hindu identity envisaged by the *sangh parivar*. Thus, to be fair (the liberal failing *par excellence*), one should add that the Hindu is no different from any other ethnic community or even nation which feels special and superior to other collectivities, especially their neighbours and rivals. This sense of superiority, the group's narcissism, its self-aggrandizement, serves the purpose of increasing group cohesion and thus the enhancement of the self-esteem of its members. Rafael Moses, reflecting on the group selves of the Israelies and the Arabs, asks: 'And is perhaps a little grandiosity the right glue for such a cohesion? Is that perhaps the same measure of grandiosity which is seen in the family and does it serve the same purpose, thereby strengthening the feeling of specialness and of some grandiosity which all of us harbour in ourselves?'[20]

The *sangh parivar* cannot be faulted for fostering a Hindu pride or even trying to claim a sense of superiority vis-a-vis the Muslim. These are the normal aims of the group's narcissistic economy. Perhaps we recoil from such aims because narcissim, both in individuals and groups, is regarded with much misgiving. A person who is a victim of passions, sexual and aggressive, may be pitied and even seen by some as tragically heroic. An individual propelled by narcissism, on the other hand, is invariably scorned as mean and contemptible. Whereas the perversions of sex may evoke sympathy, the miscarriages of narcissism, such as a smug superiority or an arrogant self-righteousness, provoke distaste among even the most tolerant. The question is not of the *sangh parivar's* fostering of Hindu narcissism (which, we know, serves individual self-possession) but of when this narcissism becomes deviant or abnormal. The answer is not easy for I do not know of any universal, absolute standards which can help us in charting narcissistic deviance or pathology in a group. One would imagine that the promotion of persecutory fantasies in a group to the extent that it resorts to violence against the persecuting Other would be deviant. Yet we all know that a stoking of persecutory fantasies is the stock in trade of all nations on the eve of any war and continues well into the duration of hostilities.

One could say that a group wherein all individual judgement is suspended and reality-testing severely disturbed may legitimately be regarded as pathological. This, however, is an individualistic viewpoint which looks askance at any kind of self-transcendence through immersion in a group. In this view, spiritual uplift in a religious assembly, where the person feels an upsurge of love enveloping the community and the world outside, would be regarded with the same grave suspicion as the murkier purposes of a violent mob. It is certainly true that transcending individuality by merging into a group can generate heroic self-sacrifice, but it can also generate unimaginable brutality. To get out of one's skin in a devotional assembly is also at the same time to have less regard for saving that skin when part of a mob. Yet to equate and thus condemn both is to deny the human aspiration toward self-transcendence, a promise held out by our cultural identity and redeemed, if occasionally, by vital participation in the flow of the community's cultural life.

It is, however, evident that it is this group pride and narcissism which have made it possible for the Hindutva forces to offer another alternative vision of

India's future as an alternate to those offered by the modernists and the traditionalists. The modernists are, of course, enthusiastic votaries of the modernization project although the Left and Right may argue over which economic form is the most suitable. Both factions, however, are neither interested in nor consider the question of cultural authenticity as important. The traditionalists, on the other hand, including the neo-Gandhians, totally reject modernity solely on the issue of cultural authenticity. The Hindutva forces have tried to offer yet another alternative by reformulating the project of modernity in a way where its instrumentalities are adopted but its norms and values are contested. The pivotal issue for them is not the acceptance of global technoscience or the economic institutions and forms of modernity but their impact on and a salvaging of Hindu culture and identity—as they define it. Cultural nationalism, though, will always have priority whenever it conflicts with economic globalism. It is apparent that such an approach to modernity will have great appeal to the emerging middle classes and sections of the intelligentsia which are committed neither to what I can only call universal modernism nor to a postmodern traditionalism.

The danger of stoking group narcissism, Hindu *garv* (pride) in our example, is that when this group grandiosity (expressed in a belief in its unique history and/ or destiny, its moral, aesthetic, technological, or any other kind of superiority vis-a-vis other groups) is brought into serious doubt, when the group feels humiliated, when higher forms of grandiosity such as the group's ambitions are blocked, then there is a regression in the group akin to one in the individual. The negative part of the grandiose self which normally remains hidden, the group's specific feelings of worthlessness and its singular sense of inferiority, now come to the fore. If all possibilities of self-assertion are closed, there is a feeling of absolute helplessness, a state which must be changed through assertive action. Such a regression, with its accompanying feeling of vulnerability and helplessness, is most clearly manifested in the sphere of group aggression which takes on, overtly and covertly, the flavour of narcissistic rage. As in the individual who seeks to alter such an unbearable self state through acts as extreme as suicide or homicide, the group's need for undoing the damage to the collective self by whatever means, and a deeply anchored, unrelenting compulsion in the pursuit of this aim give it no rest. Narcissistic rage does not vanish when the offending object disappears. The painful memory can linger on, making of the hot rage a chronic, cold resentment till it explodes in all its violet manifestations whenever historical circumstances sanction such eruptions. I am afraid Ayodhya is not an end but only a beginning since the forces buffeting Hindu (or, for that matter, Muslim) grandiosity do not lie within the country but are global in their scope. They are the forces of modernization itself, of the wonderful attractions and the terrible distortions of the mentality of Enlightenment.

It would also be easy to dismiss Rithambra's—and the *sangh parivar's*—evocation of the Hindu past from a postmodern perspective which considers every past a social construction that is shaped by the concerns of the present. In other words, there is no such thing as *the* past since the past is transformable and manipulable according to the needs of the present. Yet as the French sociologist Emile Durkheim pointed out long ago, every society displays and even requires a minimal sense of continuity with its past.[21] Its memories cannot be relevant to its present unless it secures this continuity. In a society in the throes of modernization, the need for continuity with the past, a sense of heritage, essential for maintaining a sense of individual and cultural identity, becomes even more pressing, sharply reducing the subversive attractions of a viewpoint which emphasizes the plasticity and discontinuities of the past. It is this need for a continuity of cultural memory, of a common representation of the past in times of rapid change, even turbulence, which the *sangh parivar* addresses with considerable social resonance and political success.

THE MUSLIM FUNDAMENTALIST
IDENTITY

Even though the appellation 'fundamentalist' is often used for stigmatizing particular groups, especially of Muslims, there is no other word which is a satisfactory substitute. This lies in the nature of the phenomenon itself which, with its pious passions, strong beliefs, and inflexible values, will inevitably imbue any neutral and originally descriptive term with negative or positive connotations. As a phenomenon, many hold the opinion that religious fundamentalism is an attempt by a religious community to preserve its identity by a selective retrieval of doctrines, beliefs, and practices from a sacred past.[1] Although a nostalgia for the sacred past is a hallmark of fundamentalist rhetoric, the retrieved fundamentals are very often pragmatically refined and modified. Contemporary fundamentalism is both a revival and a construction, both derivative and original.

Muslim fundamentalism in India shares some of the abiding concerns of Islamic fundamentalism elsewhere in the world but also has some distinct local flavours. As the political scientist M.S. Agwani points out, there are not one but many fundamentalisms in India of which the major varieties are associated with the names of Deoband, Nadwah, Tablighi Jamaiat, and Jamaiat-i-Islami.[2] Muslim fundamentalism is thus not monolithic but divided into factions which differ not only over the means of bringing about the desired Islamic revival but sometimes also over the preferred ends. Although they all agree that the precepts of earliest Islam, valid for all times and climes, must govern a person's private and collective life, that nationalism, secularism, and materialism are un-Islamic, and that such popular practices as saint worship at darghas (shrines) and devotional music in Muslim social and religious life are undesirable imports from Hindustan, they disagree on the desired relationship between religion and the state, or the extent of totalitarian practice needed to enforce religious orthodoxy.

For me, fundamentalism is the third Muslim response to the loss of collective self-idealizations and the fracture in self-representation brought on by historical change. If the victim is unable to hate, the fundamentalist cannot stop hating. Whereas in the Andalus syndrome the group cannot stop mourning, one of the components of fundamentalism is the phenomenon of the 'inability to mourn',[3] an emotional state where the natural process of grieving is blocked by undue anger.

Meeting the Mullahs

The men who have traditionally spearheaded the fundamentalist response of Muslim societies and who are widely regarded as representatives of Islamic conservatism are professional men of religion, the *ulema*, with various degrees of religious learning, who are also known as mullahs in Persia and India. In some ways, my encounter with the mullahs was psychologically the most difficult. The meeting itself was undemanding since besides our animating minds the encounter only involved a disembodied voice on the mullah's part and ears on mine. The mullahs— Qari Hanif Mohammad Multanwale, Syed Mohammad Hashmi, Maulana Salimuddin Shamshi, Riyaz Effendi, and others—came to me through their sermons recorded live at different times during the last decade at various mosques and reproduced in hundreds of thousands of inexpensive audiocasettes which are widely available in the Muslim neighbourhoods of Indian towns and cities.

The encounter with the mullah proved difficult on two counts. First, there was the persistence of my Hindu childhood image of the mullah as the wild-eyed man with a flowing beard who sprewed fire and brimstone every Friday afternoon in the mosque with an intent to transform his congregation into a raging mob baying for the blood of the Hindu infidel—mine. Second, the mullah's rhetoric, based on older models from the heyday of Islam in the Middle East, was unpleasantly foreign to me. Openly emotional, using the full register of the voice from a whisper to the full-throated shout, screaming and on occasion weeping as he is overtaken by religious enthusiasm, the mullah's style of public speaking (as of the Hindu zealot) was distasteful to me. My adult sensibility, influenced by psychoanalytic rationalism, recoils at the hectoring tone, the imperative voice, and the moral certainty which recognizes only the black of unbelief (*kufar*) and the white of faith and has neither time nor tolerance for the shades of grey.

Influenced emotionally by fantasies from a Hindu past and cognitively by the concepts of a Western-inspired liberalism, my first reaction to the mullah was to label him a 'fanatic', the word itself an 18th-century European coinage meant to denounce rather than describe the religious zealot. The temptation to rip open the mullah's facade of a just man gripped by religious passion to reveal the workings of other, baser motives was overwhelming. Indeed, the speeches of most mullahs, expressing contempt and indifference for everything other than the object of their passion and an unshakeable certitude in the rightness of their beliefs, seem to be verily designed for a psychoanalytically inspired hatchet job. The temptation to pathologize the mullah as an obsessional, if not psychopathic or even paranoid, had to be resisted if I wished to understand Muslim fundamentalism without resort to reductionist psychological cliches.[4] The first step in such an understanding was to listen to the mullah.

Sung in many voices and with varying lyrics, the music of the fundamentalist theme song is easily recognizable from one mullah to another. After a couple of obligatory *ayats* from the *Qur'an* in Arabic as a prelude, signifying that both the speaker and the listener are now in the realm of the sacred, the fundamentalist generally begins with a lament for the lost glories of Islam as he compares the sorry plight of Muslims today with their earlier exalted status. There may be a sizeable presence of Muslims in all parts of the globe, says one mullah, and the mosque and the *Qur'an* found in every country. Yet nowhere does one hear that Muslims are thriving, successful, or on the ascendant. A hundred and sixty million Muslims are being whipped by two-and-a-half million Jews, says another. Look at the sorry fate of Iraq, a land made sacred by the blood of the Prophet's grandsons. At one time Sultan Salah-al-din Ayubi (Saladin) commanding a force of 13,000 in the battle for Jersualem faced Richard's army of 700,000 and killed 300,000 Christians on a single day. Once, in the battle for Mecca—and the first battle of Islamic history is every mullah's preferred illustration—the Prophet with a ragtag force of 313 (a number which along with the word 'Karbala' has become the most effective symbol of political mobilization), including women, children, and old men, defeated the 1000 armed warriors of Abu Jahl, many of them on horseback, at the battle of Badr. Today, with all the oil, dollars, and weapons in the world, Muslims are slaves to the dictates of Western Christian powers even in the 36 countries of which they are the putative rulers. Once, when the Muslim saint Khwaja Moinuddin Chisti died in Ajmer, nine million *kafirs* (here, the Hindus) began reading the *kalma*, that is, became Muslims. Once, at the sight of Imam Rahimullah's funeral cortege, 20,000 Jews converted to Islam. Today, Muslims have trouble keeping their own faith alive.

The choice of historical illustrations from the early history of Islam, including their legendary elaboration, to bring home the fact of Muslim degeneration and distress in the modern world is a pan-Islamic phenomenon. Few if any civilizations have attached as much importance to history as has Islam in its awareness of itself.[5] Recognize your history (*tarikh*)!' is the common fundamentalist exhortation, in contrast to the Hindu revivalist's implied suggestion, 'Live your myth!' From the Prophet's time to the present, it has been Islam which has distinguished between self and other, between brother and stranger, between the faithful and the alien *kafir*, the unbeliever. It is therefore not surprising that in fundamentalist discourse it is the wider, Arab-centred history of Islam rather than the history of Indian Muslims through which a collective Muslim identity is sought to be shaped.

After listing the symptoms of Muslim distress, the mullahs proceed to diagnose the disease. The bad condition of the Muslims, they aver, is not due to any major changes in the outer circumstances of Muslim lives but because of a glaring internal fault: the weakening or loss of religious faith. Muslims have lost everything—political authority, respect, the wealth of both faith (*din*) and the world (*duniya*)—because they did not keep their pact with Mohammed. At one time Allah gave Muslims the kingdom of the world only in order to test whether they would continue to remain His slaves. Muslims have failed Allah's test. It was their religious zeal which made a small, unarmed group of Muslims succeed on the battlefield against overwhelming odds. (Now the mullah begins to address the listener more directly). Today, you do not respect the *Qur'an*. You do not respect the Prophet who is so pure that not a single fly came near him during his lifetime, a man whose sweat smelt more divine than shiploads of perfume. You may think of yourselves as Muslims but look into the mirror of the *Qur'an* and you will see you are not.

The Arabs lose to the Jews in Palestine because they are fighting for land, even if it is their own land. They are not fighting for Islam, for the Prophet. Sultan Salah-al-din fought for Islam and won Palestine. On the eve of the battle against Richard, he said to his soldiers: 'Paradise is near, Egypt is far.' He did not defend Islam by the sword but by his character as a Muslim. The Christians, as is their wont, used to send beautiful young women to seduce and corrupt Muslim generals, their priests assuring the girls forgiveness for all sins incurred in the service of Christianity. Saladin rejected 13 of the most beautiful Christian girls sent to his palace; in fact, the Christian women, impressed by the Sultan's steadfastness, read the *kalma*. On the other hand the Muslims lost India, not to the British, but because the last Mughal emperors like Mohammad Shah Rangile and Bahadur Shah Zafar were sunk in the quagmire of wine, women, and poetry.

After the diagnosis the physicians proceed to pathogenesis. The disease is caused by the process of modernity which the Muslim body has not resisted There is no difference today between the home of a Muslim and that of a Hindu, Jew, or Christian. The sickness of television has entered Muslim homes where families fritter away whole evenings in ungodly entertainment rather than in reading from or discussing the *Qur'an*. Some of them say, 'We watch television only for the news.' I ask, 'What news? Of murders and accidents? Is there any news to gladden the heart of the faithful? Where is the news that a Muslim country has conquered an infidel land?' People walk about the streets singing songs from movies, prostitute's songs, rather than with the *kalma* on their lips. They follow educated people who are the thieves of religion, who teach the separation of religion from life and from politics.

Muslims have now taken to these deeply offensive modern fashions. They no longer give a revered name such as Fatima, that of the Prophet's daughter, to their own daughters but prefer instead to name the little girl after some movie actress, a prostitute. Look at the Western-style trousers that men wear, with pockets in indecent places. You see man bending forward and taking out money from the hip pocket, next to the buttocks. In winter you can see them sliding their hands into the side pockets and taking out peanuts or cashews from these disgusting places and putting them in the mouth.

In olden days a ruler would never permit the presence of a woman in official rooms or at public functions. A mullah would not perform the wedding ceremony where women were present. Now some of the rulers cannot even go to the toilet without a woman. Instead of only bowing before Allah, Muslims now bow before graves of various *pirs* (holy men) who are three feet underground. No wonder

Islam is bending under the assault of *kufr*, Arabs are bowing before Jews and Christians, you before the Hindus. What is this preoccupation with worldly wealth and success? Allah says, I did not bring you into the world to make two shops out of one, four out of two, two factories out of one, four out of two. Does the *Qur'an* want you to do that? Does the Prophet? No! They want you to dedicate yourself to the faith, give your life for the glory of Islam.

The remedy suggested by the mullahs is a return to the fundamentals of the faith as contained in the *Qur'an*. The *Qur'an* is Allah's book, the light given by God to lift the darkness of mankind. Nothing can be added to or subtracted from the book. No arguments, no discussion, no objections, no asking for proof. It is eternal and unchanging. It is not like the clothes you wear which are different for summer and winter. Follow every rule of the faith, not just the ones which are convenient. It is not what you want or wish but Allah's wish that has to be complied with. It is not your likes but what is liked by the Prophet that must be done. All that is needed to live your life is contained in the examples from the life of the Prophet. All you need is faith—in Allah, the Prophet, the Book, angels, Judgement Day, paradise, and hell—and effort. If you cannot get wordly wealth without putting in an effort, how can you obtain paradise without it? Tell your daughter to offer *namaz* daily in the house; you won't be able to tell them once they are burning in hell.

Psychologically, then, fundamentalism is a theory of suffering and cure, just as modern individualism is another theory of suffering and its cure. The core of psychological individuality is internalization rather than externalization. I use "internalization" here as a sensing by the person of a psyche in the Greek sense, an animation from within rather than without. Experientially, this internalization is a recognition that one is possessed of a mind in all its complexity. It is the acknowledgement, however vague, unwilling, or conflicted, of a subjectivity that fates one to episodic suffering through some of its ideas and feelings—in psychoanalysis, murderous rage, envy, and possessive desire seeking to destroy those one loves and would keep alive—simultaneously with the knowledge, at some level of awareness, that the mind can help in containing and processing disturbed thoughts. Fundamentalism, on the other hand, identifies the cause of suffering not in the individual mind but in a historical process which, however, is not fatefully deterministic but amenable to human will and eminently reversible. Individual and collective suffering are due to a lapse from an ideal state of religious faith, and the cure lies in an effort to restore faith in one's inner life to its original state of pristine purity.

Another striking aspect of fundamentalist religious discourse is not so much its warlike anger against the enemy—the modernization process, the infidels—held responsible for the contemporary sorry state of the Muslims, but the turning of this rage inward in a collective self-recrimination and masochistic self-hate. The loss of Muslim greatness is not grieved for, a process that would pave the way for an eventual acceptance of its loss and thus enable the community to face the future without a debilitating preoccupation with the past. Instead, the loss is experienced as a persisting humiliation, a narcissistic injury to the group self which keeps on generating inchoate anger rather than the sadness of mourning. The instances from history in the mullahs' sermons are replete with sadomasochistic imagery, betraying an unconscious rage even as they seem to bemoan the lost glories of Islam. Their talk is liberally spattered with blood. Rivers of blood flow in the massacres of Muslims, fountains of the stuff spurt from the chests of children martyred to the faith. The atrocities borne by Muslims, both in modern and medieval periods, are detailed with much relish. It is not the doctors and the officers—the representatives of the modern world—who have sacrificed for the country's independence, says Quri Mohammad Hanif, but the mullahs. Detailing incidents not recorded in history books, 3000 *ulema* were laid on the road to Delhi and the British drove road rollers over their chests. Hundreds were sewn into pigskins and burnt alive. Impaling, burning at the stake, being trampled under elephant feet, and the walling in alive of early martyrs is described with an eye for gory detail. The listeners are asked to visualize the plight of the pious woman who had hundreds of nails driven into her palms and feet saying to her infidel torturer, 'You can drive a hundred nails into my tongue too and I will still take Allah's name.'

In addition to the sadomasochistic imagery, another theme in fundamentalist discourse is the inculcation of guilt. The speeches conjure up images of the ancestors regarding today's generation of Muslims with eyes full of reproach and with a 'Thou hast forsaken us!' refrain on dead lips. Skilfully reactivating the guilt vis-a-vis our parents that is our common human legacy from early childhood, fundamentalism stirs anger and guilt in a potent brew.

To trace psychological themes in Muslim fundamentalist discourse is not to reduce this discourse to psychopathology. Illness to the outsider, fundamentalism is a cure for the insider. For many Muslims with an inchoate sense of oppression and the looming shadow of a menacing future, with fractured self-esteem in the wake of historical change that saw an end to their political role and a virtual disappearance of their language, fundamentalism is an attempt, however flawed, to revive the sacred in social and cultural life, to give politics a spiritual dimension, and to recover in their religious verities a bulwark against collective identity fragmentation.

Religious Politics

To look more closely at the psychological processes involved in the fundmentalist mobilization of Muslims, I have chosen as my exemplary text a speech by Ubedullah Khan Azmi, an influential north Indian Muslim leader. Azmi, who has occupied important positions in Muslim institutions, such as the secretaryship of the Muslim

Personal Law Conference, an organization through which the conservative section of the community has zealously sought to guard its autonomy in the making and interpretation of civil laws applicable to Muslims, is what I would call a 'moderate fundamentalist'. By this I mean that, like all fundamentalists, he subscribes to the founding myth that a truly Islamic society existed only in the period of the Prophet and the first four Caliphs, and one must go back to those origins to restore the initial vitality of the community. As a moderate, however, he does not go so far as some others who advocate an opting out of or a rejection of the modern Indian political system, a *jehad* to recover the spirit of Islam's original enterprise. Informed by fundamentalist beliefs, his politics is yet politics as usual in many ways, requiring a constant adaptation to changing political realities. Like many fundamentalist leaders who must operate within secular democracies, Azmi has negotiated a degree of political influence for himself (he is a Member of Parliament) by entering into a mutually beneficial alliance with secular politicians of a mainstream political party, the Janata Dal. In such alliances, we know, fundamentalist leaders are willing to be carried along on a wave of purely socioeconomic or political resentment while they mobilize votes for their political allies by playing on religious passions and fears of their constituency, saying and doing things which the secular politician will studiously avoid.[6]

The rhetoric of fundamentalist politics attempts to seduce its target group with a sense of participation in a collectivity with a transcendent purpose, giving a higher value or meaning to life than could be given by any secular politics. The group addressed by the fundamentalist has the very satisfying feeling of being "chosen" with a sense of mission connected with a sacred purpose, sanctified by God, and superior to the adversary's mission which is not similarly blessed or is blessed by a lesser god.

My selection of this particular speech, delivered in 1985, is not because it is remarkable in any way but precisely becuase it is not. It is an ordinary speech which takes as its springboard an insignificant event, the filing of a petition by an obscure Hindu lawyer in a district court in Rajasthan seeking a ban on the *Qur'an*. Unlike Rithambra's speaking style which is modelled after Hindu bardic narration, Azmi's rhetoric is in traditional Muslim style, interspersed with Urdu couplets for an audience which likes poetical flourishes in its orators. The speech as reproduced below is necessarily abridged, though not edited to change its essential content, images, or the sequential flow of thoughts.

[I wish] I did not have to see this day. These are the offspring of Nathuram Godse [Gandhi's assassin] who are talking of banning the *Qur'an*. The children of Nathuram Godse dream of occupying the Babri mosque. Ubedullah Khan Azmi declares openly, look at the lineage of all traitors from the time of Mahatma Gandhi to that of Indira Gandhi and then look at the lineage of those who have been loyal to India from 1945 to 1985. What is the crime for which we Muslims are being punished? Our book is being banned, our personal law is being proscribed, our community's very way of life is being restricted. Beware, history may repeat itself. Balasaheb Deoras may have to read the *kalma* [i.e., become a Muslim], Atal Behari Vajpayee may have to read the *kalma*, Mister Rajiv Gandhi may have to read the *kalma*.*

> *Stars sometimes appear in the waves*
> *Khalid sometimes leads armies*
> *Every age sees the rise of Yazid*
> *Every age witnesses the birth of Shabbir.***

How much have we served this country! What have we not done to get freedom for this country! The equal rights given to Muslims under Indian law were not given as charity but because we earned them. And today they want to ban the *Qur'an*? Who led the country to independence? Everyone calls Mahatma Gandhi the father of the nation. Fine, we'll also call him that. Who killed the "father of the nation"? Nathuram Godse. Who killed Indira Gandhi? Beant Singh and Satwant Singh. Were *they* Muslims? *You* eliminated them both.

> *Even then you complain of my faithlessness,*
> *If I am not faithful, you too have not been a*
> *caretaker of my heart.*

Who did we eliminate? Let me tell you that since you call us 'Pakistanis'. When Pakistan's tanks rolled into the country then in the form of Abdul Hamid*** we destroyed eight of those tanks. Whenever the country has asked for sacrifice, Muslims have given their blood. We have protected the country at every juncture and today you are questioning our loyalty? You talk of banning the *Qur'an* which taught us to die for the country's honour. *Qur'an* gave discipline to the world. *Qur'an* gave even the lowest of the low the right to live in dignity. *Qur'an* was the first to raise its voice against caste distinctions. *Qur'an* was the first to abolish differences between high and low. *Qur'an* taught the world that man does not become great on the basis of birth but on the basis of religious virtue, abstinence, and

---

* Deoras was the chief of the RSS while Vajpayee is a prominent leader of the BJP.

** Khalid was the legendary general of the all-conquering Arab armies in the seventh century. Yazid, the first Muslim king, is the personification of evil in Islamic sacred history while Shabbir is another name for Hussain, the Prophet's grandson and Yazid's antagonist in the battle of Karbala.

*** A hero of the India-Pakistan war of 1965.

truth. To ban the *Qur'an* means to ban reality, to ban truth. These bribe-takers want corruption to continue. These libertines want the honour of women to be violated. These drunkards want the looting of India to continue. But when people come to know the *Qur'an*, when they understand *Qur'an* laws, then *Qur'an* will save both the world and the *millat* [religious community of the Muslims].

The political culture of fundamentalism, perhaps more than secular political cultures, is fundamentally a politics of imagery. The image Azmi first conjures up is of a besieged Muslim community, under attack from a vile, treacherous enemy, the Hindu nationalist. Azmi's specific technique is to project the image of a relentless attack against the central symbol of Muslim religious identity, the *Qur'an*. This citadel of the community's identity, idealized as the all-good, the all-just, the all-pure, and the source of all beneficience, is surrounded by a sea of Hindu corruption and debauchery. In contrast to a Hindu revivalist like Rithambra, who must first define and then draw up the boundaries of a Hindu community, Azmi does not need to engage in any such boundary-setting exercise. The religious-cultural identity of the Muslim *qaum* and its sense of 'us' versus 'them' has been traditionally clear-cut and relatively enduring. What Azmi attempts to do is to trigger and stoke a persecutory anxiety in his audience.

In psychoanalytic thought, persecution is an internal event, a subjective, irrational experience often equated with the pathology of paranoia. Melanie Klein has related the anxiety it generates—the feelings of disintegration—to the earliest stages of life, to the baby's experience of a depriving, frustrating breast-mother. But as Meira Likierman has pointed out, the feeling of persecution is also a normal part of the response to destructive and obstructive forces which we encounter in the course of everyday life.[7] Connecting to the individual's primitive persecution anxiety from infancy, damage, loss, deprivation, frustration are a range of events which constitute a destructive attack on our sense of identity and represent partial death. Persecution anxiety signals a situation of great danger and carries with it the fear of the group's symbolic death, an annihilation of its collective identity. It is only when this particular anxiety courses through and between members of a group, making individuals feel helpless, frightened, and paralyzed, that people become loosened from their traditional cognitive moorings and are prepared to give up previously held social, political, or economic explanations for their sense of aggrievement and become receptive to the religious critique Azmi has to offer. Persecutory anxiety is one of those strong emotions which can take people away from 'knowing' back to the realm of 'unknowing'.—from a 'knowledge' of the cause of their distress to a state where they do not know what it is that gives them suffering and pain though they *do* know that they are suffering and in pain. One antidote to this paralyzing anxiety is anger, preferably in a violent assertion that is psychically mobilizing, as Azmi continues:

Even the talk of banning the holy *Qur'an* shows what dangerous conspiracies are being hatched to damage our faith.

Awake O Indian Muslims before you disappear completely
Even your story will not find a mention in other stories.

What steps should we take under these conditions? The Muslim will not come to the court to prove the truth of the *Qur'an*. The Muslim will come out with the shroud tied to his head to protect the *Qur'an*. We will cut off tongues that speak against the *Qur'an*. We will tear off the skin of those who look askance at the *Qur'an*.

After having tried to erase previous cognitive structures through a heightening of persection anxiety and having dealt with the paralyzing fear engendered by this anxiety through fantasized violence, what the fundamentalist has before him is a newly born group without memory and with but inchoate desires. Azmi proceeds to shape the identity of this freshly minted group by offering it a series of narcissistically enhancing self-images—'This is who you are!'—particularly in relation to the elder sibling, the Hindu.

After 35 years of oppression the Indian Muslim has remained loyal to the country. If there is anyone loyal from Hindustan to *kabristan* (graveyard), then it is the Muslim. You [the Hindus] die, we die. What happens after death? You are cremated. Next, your ashes are thrown into the Ganges. Where does the river flow to? You flow from here and reach Pakistan. Ashes scattered by the wind can land anywhere. When we die, the motherland says, 'My dear son, you will not leave me to go anywhere else. If you have lived on top of me, after death you will sleep in my lap.'

There are three kinds of sons. One son, who according to the law of the land and in the light of his faith fulfils his obligations toward his parents is called *put* [son]. Another is called *suput* (good son) who not only fulfils his obligations but sacrifices his all for the happiness of the parents. The son who shoots his mother, cuts her throat, kills both his father and mother— he is called *kuput* [bad son]. Now look at the sons of this motherland and decide who is the good and who is the bad son. The Muslim who believes in *Qur'an* and calls India his own country is the *suput*. When after the formation of Pakistan there was trouble in Kashmir then it was Brigadier Usman Ali from my town of Azamgarh who was one of the first to fall to Pakistani bullets. When his twitching corpse fell to earth at the border the motherland said, 'This is my son who sacrificed himself to protect my honour.'

When Abdul Hamid stopped the Pakistani tanks which would have rolled on to Delhi and had his flesh torn to ribbons then the Indian earth said, 'This is my *suput*.' And they who killed Mahatma Gandhi, the liberator of the country, killed Indira Gandhi who sacrificed so much for the honour of the nation—what will you call them, *put, suput*, or *kuput*? You decide.'

While on the surface the whole tenor of the speech is concerned with distancing the Muslim from the Hindu enemy, on the more unconscious level it betrays the existence of an unwanted relationship with the same foe—an intimacy held at bay by disdain, even hate, but an intimacy nonetheless. Viewing oneself as the 'good son' of the mother, as opposed to the Hindu 'bad son', is an unconscious acknowledgement of their connectedness, even when this connection exists only in an unending and obsessive competition. After exorcizing doubt—including self-doubt—about Muslim loyalty to the country (vis-a-vis loyalty to the religious community outside the borders of the nation), the self-images offered to the group in the following passages are of a grandiose variety, of an exhilarating Muslim superiority. The enhancement of collective self-esteem then serves to increase the security of the group self by countering the deathly threat to its survival.

Like spokepersons of all ethnic groups in conflict around the world, Azmi's vision of Muslims and Hindus is of two groups in eternal competition to answer the question which is more civilized, stronger, and generally, better.[8] As his evidence for Muslim superiority, he offers Muslim virtues in comparison with Hindu vices. First, this superiority consists of a heightened Muslim apperception of the aesthetics of life, in the Muslim's greater resonance for sensory and sensuous experience and in greater artistic giftedness.

And you who raise slogans about Muslim loyalty, who talk of a ban on the *Qur'an*, have you ever looked at your own face in the mirror? It was the believers in the *Qur'an* who taught you the graces of life, taught you how to eat and drink. All you had before us were tomatoes and potatoes. What did you have? We brought jasmine, we brought frangipani. We gave the Taj Mahal, we gave the Red Fort. India was made India by us. We lived here for 800 years and we made India shine. In 35 years you have dimmed its light and ruined the country. A beggar will not be grateful if made an emperor. Lay out a feast for him and he will not like it. Throw him a piece of bread in the dust and he will get his appetite back. Do not force us to speak out. Do not force us to come in front of you as an enemy.

God, look at their ignorance to believe we have no words
when out of pity we gave them the power of speech.

Azmi's attempt to sharply differentiate the Hindus from the Muslims, suggesting that the Muslims consider themselves as having come to India from outside the country 800 years ago (and from a superior racial stock), is partly a consequence of the current antagonism between the two communities. In such a hostile situation, the fundamentalist exhorts the Muslims to shun contamination by any of the Hindu symbols and strive to keep their shared Islamic identity intact and pure. The fundamentalist is loath to acknowledge any Muslim similarity to the Hindu and focuses only on the differences which, he seeks to persuade those yet unconvinced, are of stubborn emotional importance.

From the relative level of sophistication of the two civilizations, the battle for superiority now shifts to the arena of power as Azmi offers up the image of a powerful Muslim nation, much stronger than the Hindu enemy.

> There is a limit to our patience and tolerance. These wicked people should understand that we can sacrifice all we have, including our lives, but not our honour. We cannot compromise the glory of the *Qur'an*. Today the whole world is in turmoil. Some madmen are disturbing the peace of the world. This is not a challenge to the 220 million Muslims of India but to the over a billion Muslims of the world. That is why I request you to remain alert. Today's tense atmosphere should make every Muslim who is still living unawares a true Muslim. They are banning the *Qur'an*. Has the time not come that you become regular in saying your *namaz* as ordained by it? They are thinking of banning the *Qur'an*. Has the time not come that you keep your *rozas* even in the heat of summer? The more they talk of banning the *Qur'an*, the more you should live according to it. Give your life a religious cast.

The secret of Muslim strength does not lie in the sheer number of Muslims all over the world, a *millat* of which the Indian Muslims are also a part, a notion of a pan-Islamic collectivity which is the stuff of the Hindu nationalist's nightmares. For the Muslims, the offer of such a collective identity helps to counteract the feeling of being an embattled minority in one particular country. The real secret of Muslim strength, however, lies in the superiority of Islam over the religion of the Hindus. Our religion makes us stronger, their divisive faith makes them weaker. Our religion is of the future, theirs mired in an outdated past. We are stronger than we think, they weaker than what they or we might believe.

> Why do they talk of a ban on the *Qur'an*? Why are they so afraid of the *Qur'an*? They are afraid because their religion is one of touchables-untouchables. *Qur'an* gives a religion of universal equality. They have no place in their hearts for their own people. Let them allow a Harijan to drink water from their wells. These high-caste people who talk of

Rama and Sita, let them first permit Harijans to enter their temples. In contrast, look at the *Qur'an*. It gives every human being a right to equality on the basis of his humanity. That is why 13,000 Harijans, 13,000 tribals, converted to Islam in Meenakshipuram in Madras. They did not know what is written in the *Qur'an*. They only knew that *Qur'an* gives people of low caste the right to sit together with people of higher castes on terms of equality. So these Harijans who have been given so many benefits by the state are ready to throw them away. We do not want benefits which give us food and clothing but which leave our hearts enslaved. We want freedom of our minds, freedom for our souls. We are prepared to tolerate slavery of every kind but not of the soul. You, enslavers of the soul, *Qur'an* liberates the soul! That is why we believe in the *Qur'an* which gives life to the soul, makes a black like Billal the chief of a fair-skinned tribe.* Today, when Muslims are being massacred everywhere, when there is talk of doing away with Muslim personal law, when the honour of our mothers and sisters is being violated, when our children are being martyred, when our very existence is unbearable to others, 13,000 Harijans chose to convert to our religion. Because man wants freedom for the soul. A bird will be unhappy even if confined in a palace of gold. Its soul craves for the freedom of the garden. Islam gives that freedom. The result is that not only in Islamic but also in non-Islamic countries, people are flocking to convert to Islam. No one is asking them or telling them to become Muslims. It is because of its teachings that people are taking refuge in the *Qur'an*.

Do you think *Qur'an* can be finished off by merely banning it? We have lived with the *Qur'an* for 1400 years. We have passed under arches of swords. We have come through the battlefield of Karbala. We have passed through the valleys of Spain, through the hills of Gibraltar, through the plains of India. We can say with pride that in spite of thousands of ordeals it has undergone, the Muslim nation remains incomparable. The love it has for the *Qur'an* is unmatched by that of any other community for its religious books. No one loves his religion more than the Muslim loves Islam. We need to maintain relationships with Muslims all over the world. We have tried and succeeded in developing these relationships. We can then deal with any challenge that comes from either inside or outside the country. Our faith grows stronger with each challenger it faces and makes us more powerful. The fox which wakes up a sleeping lion should first

---

* Billal was the black slave and a favourite of the Prophet because of his sweet singing voice.

look after its own safety. Anyone who dares to challenge the *Qur'an* should be aware that either he or his father or his offspring will have to become a Muslim.

> *It is the voice of Mohammed, the command of God, which can never be altered*
> *The world may change a thousand times, the Qur'an never.*

In summary, the psychological process involved in Muslim fundamentalist politics, which has as its goal the replacement of political, economic, and social bases of politics with a religious critique, consists essentially of two steps. First, there is an attempt to erase previous cognitive structures, as they relate to political life and issues, through the generation of a strong persecution anxiety in the group. Second, on the now relatively clean slate of the group's political psyche, the fundamentalist politician proceeds to draw a group self-portrait—offers the Muslims a collective identity—which emphasizes the community's superiority in relation to the enemy group, the nationalist Hindus. Although this superiority may have many other features, such as the strength to be derived from an identification with a larger, powerful pan-Islamic community, its core is a conviction in the inherent superiority of the group's religion, Islam, and of all its symbols. To maintain this feeling of superiority and the strength it gives to the members of the community, it is considered essential for the individual to be zealous in the observance of religious duties, accept the priority of religion in all areas of life, and to acknowledge the demands of religion as having the first call on individual loyalty.

To conclude: The reasons for the attraction of the fundamentalist identity for many Muslims are not difficult to fathom. Apart from providing a forum for resistance to perceived domination and repression, fundamentalism offers a narcissistic enhancement for a sense of self-esteem fractured by the workings of a historical fate. Besides giving a sacred meaning and transcendent purpose to the lives of the hurt, the dislocated, and the shipwrecked, fundamentalism also makes a masochistic reparation for guilt feelings possible. In defining an Other as a competitor with a deadly intent toward one's own group, fundamentalism provides a focus for undue anger and unresolved hate. Little wonder that many are willing to pay the costs of a fundamentalist identity—a considerable denial of reality, the closing of one's eyes and mind to the structures of the contemporary world, and the renunciation of a pleasure-seeking attitude in favour of a religiously disciplined life.

RELIGIOUS CONFLICT IN THE MODERN WORLD

Our times are witness to a worldwide wave of religious revival. Islam, Hinduism, Buddhism, the new religions in Japan, born-again Christians in the United States, and the Protestant sects in Latin America are undergoing a resurgence which is regarded with deep distrust by all the modern heirs to the Enlightenment. Although a secular humanist might find most manifestations of the current religious zeal personally distasteful, he or she is nonetheless aware that the revitalization of religion at the end of the 20th century constitutes a complex attempt at the resacralization of cultures beset with the many ills of modernity. As Andrew Samuels reminds us, this fragmented and fractured attempt at resacralization to combat the sense of oppression and a future utterly bereft of any vision of transcendent purpose is not only a part of the new religious fundmentalisms but also integral to the so-called left-leaning, progressive political movements.[1] One can discern the search for transcendence even in concerns around ecological issues and environmental protection where at least some of the discourse is comprised of elements of nature mysticism.

However, if we look closely at individual cases around the world, we will find that the much-touted revival is less of religiosity than of cultural identities based on religious affiliation. In other words, there may not be any great ferment taking place in the world of religious ideas, rituals, or any marked increase in the sum of human spirituality. Where the resurgence is most visible is in the organization of collective identities around religion, in the formation and strengthening of communities of believers: What we are witnessing today is less the resurgence of religion than (in the felicitous Indian usage) of communalism where a community of believers not only has religious affiliation but also social, economic, and political interests in common which may conflict with the corresponding interests of another community of believers sharing the same geographical space. Indeed, most secular analysts and progressive commentators have traditionally sought to uncover factors other than religion as the root cause of an ostensibly religious conflict. This has been as true of the anti-Semitic pogroms in Spain in the 14th century, of 16th-century Catholic-Protestant violence in France, of anti-Catholic riots in 18th-century London, as of 20th-century Hindu-Muslim riots in India.[2] The "real" cause of conflict between groups in all these instances has been generally identified as a clash of economic interests; the explanation embraces some version of a class struggle between the poor and the rich.

The danger to the material existence of an individual can indeed be experienced as an identity threat which brings a latent group identity to the forefront. This heightened sense of identity with the group provides the basis for a social cohesiveness which is necessary to safeguard the individual's economic interests. But there are other threats besides the economic one which too amplify the group aspect of personal identity. In an earlier chapter, I described the identity-threat which is being posed by the forces of modernization and globalization to peoples in many parts of the world. Feelings of loss and helplessness accompany dislocation and migration from rural areas to the shanty towns of urban megalopolises, the disappearance of craft skills which underlay traditional work identities, and the humilation caused by the homogenizing and hegemonizing impact of the modern world which pronounces ancestral, cultural ideals and values as outmoded and irrelevant. These, too are conducive to heightening the group aspects of identity as the affected (and the afflicted) look to cultural-religious groups to combat their feelings of helplessness and loss and to serve as vehicles for the redress of injuries to self-esteem.

The identity-threat may also arise due to a perceived discrimination by the state, that is, a disregard by the political authorities of a group's interests or disrespect for its cultural symbols. It can also arise as a consequence of changing political constellations such as those which accompany the end of empires. If Hindu-Muslim relations were in better shape in the past, with much less overt violence, it was perhaps also because of the kind of polity in which the two peoples lived. This polity was that of empire, the Mughal empire followed by the British one. An empire, the political scientist Michael Walzer observes, is characterized by a mixure of repression for any strivings for independence and tolerance for different cultures, religions and ways of life.[3] The tolerance is not a consequence of any great premodern wisdom but because of the indifference, sometimes bordering on brutal incomprehension, of the imperial bureaucrats to local conflicts of the peoples they rule. Distant from local life, they do not generally interfere with everyday life as long as things remain peaceful, though there may be intermittent cruelty to remind the subject peoples of the basis of the empire— conquest through force of arms. It is only with self-government, when distance disappears, that the political questions—'Who *among us* shall have power here, in these villages, these towns?' 'Will the majority group dominate?' 'What will be the new ranking order?'—lead to a heightened awareness of religious-cultural differences. In countries with multireligious populations, independence coincides with tension and conflict—such as we observe today in the wake of the unravelling of the Soviet empire.[4]

The identity-threats I have outlined above do not create a group identity but merely bring it to the fore. The group aspect of personal identity is not a late creation in individual development but exists from the beginning of the human lifecycle. Although Freud had no hesitation in maintaining that from the very first individual psychology is a social psychology as well, psychoanalysts, with their traditional emphasis on the 'body-in-the-mind', have tended to downplay the existence of the 'community-in-the-mind'.[5] They have continued to regard the social (*polis*) aspects of man's being as an overlay which compromises the wishes and needs of the self or, in the case of the crowd is destructive of individual self and identity. Erikson has been one of the rare psychoanalysts who has called for a revision of this model that differentiates so starkly betwen an individual-individual and the individual-in-mass who has no individuality at all: 'Yet that a man could ever be psychologically alone; that a man "alone" is essentially different from the same man in a group; that a man in a temporary solitary condition or when closeted with his analyst has ceased to be a "political" animal and has disengaged himself from social action (or inaction) on whatever class level—these and similar stereotypes demand careful revision.'[6]

Such revisions would begin with the idea that the inner space occupied by what is commonly called the "self"—which I have been using synonymously with "identity"—not only contains mental representations of one's bodily life and of primary relationships within the family but also holds mental representations of one's group and its culture, that is, the group's configuration of beliefs about man, nature, and social relations (including the view of the Other). These cultural propositions, transmitted and internalized through symbols have a strong emotional impact on those who grow up as members of a particular cultural group. The self, then, is a system of reverberating representational worlds, each enriching, constraining, and shaping the others, as they jointly evolve through the lifecycle. A revision of psychoanalytic notions of the self, identity, and subjectivity would also acknowledge that none of these constituent inner worlds is "primary" or "deeper", that is, there is no necessity of identity or an "archaeological" layering of the various inner worlds, although at different times the self may be predominantly experienced in one or other representational mode. It is not only the brain that is bicameral.

At some point of time in early life, like the child's 'I am!' which heralds the birth of individuality, there is also a complementary 'We are!' which announces the birth of a sense of community. 'I am' differentiates me from other individuals. 'We are' makes me aware of the other dominant group (or groups) sharing the physical and cognitive space of my community. The self-assertion of 'We are' with its potential for confrontation with the 'We are' of other groups, is *inherently* a carrier of aggression, together with the consequent fears of persecution, and is thus always attended by a sense of risk and potential for violence. (The psychological processes initiated by an awareness of 'We are', I suggest, also provide an explanation for the experimental findings of cognitive psychologists that the mere perception of two different groups is sufficient to trigger a positive evaluation of one's own group and a negative stereotyping of the other).

The further development of the social-representational world or the group aspect of identity has some specific characteristics which I have discussed in detail at various places in this book in the context of Hindu-Muslim relations. To abstract briefly: this aspect of identity is powerfully formed by the processes of introjection, identification, idealization, and projection during childhood. On the one hand, the growing child assimilates within itself the images of the family and group members. He or she identifies with their emotional investment in the group's symbols and traditions and incorportes their idealizations of the group which have served them so well—as they will serve the child—in the enhancement of self-esteem for belonging to such an exalted and blessed entity. On the other hand, because of early difficulties in integrating contradictory representaions of the self and the parents— the "good" loving child and the "bad" raging one; the good, caretaking parent and the hateful, frustrating one—the child tries to disown the bad representations through projection. First projected to inanimate objects and animals and later to people and other groups—the latter often available to the child as a preselection by the group—the disavowed bad representations *need* such "reservoirs", as Vamik Volkan calls them. These reservoirs—Muslims for Hindus, Arabs for Jews, Tibetans for the Chinese, and vice versa—are also convenient repositories for subsequent rages and hateful feelings for which no clear-cut addressee is available. Since most of the "bad" representations arise froma social disapproval of the child's "animality", as expressed in its aggressivity, dirtiness, and unruly sexuality, it is preeminently this animality which a civilized, moral self must disavow and place in the reservoir group. We saw this happening in the Hindu image of the dirty, aggressive, and sexually licentious Muslim, and we encounter it again and again in both modern and historical accounts of other group conflicts. Thus in 16th-century France, Catholics 'knew' that the Protestants were not only dirty and diabolic but that their Holy Supper was disordered and drunken, a bacchanalia, and that they snuffed out the candles and had indiscriminate sexual intercourse after voluptuous psalm singing. Protestants, on their part, "knew" that Catholic clergy had an organization of hundreds of women at the disposal of priests and canons who, for the most part, were sodomites as well.[7]

The psychological processes involved in the development of 'We are' not only take recourse to the group's cultural traditions—its myths, history, rituals, and symbols—to make the community a firm part of personal identity but also employ bodily fantasies as well as family metaphors to anchor this aspect of identity in the deepest layers of individual imagination. The "pure" us versus a "dirty" them, the association of a rival group with denigrated, often anal, bodily parts and functions, representations of one's group in metaphors of a body under attack or as a "good" son of the mother(land) while the rival group is a "bad" son, are some of the examples from Hindu and Muslim discourse which I have discussed in earlier chapters.

We must, however, also note that there are always some individuals whose personal identity is not overwhelmed by their religious or cultural group identity even in the worst phase of violent conflict. These are persons capable of acts of compassion and self-sacrifice, such as saving members of the "enemy" group from the fury of a rampaging mob even at considerable danger to their own physical safety. There are yet others—the fanatics—whose behaviour even in times of peace and in the absence of any identity-threat seems to be exclusively dictated by the 'We are' group aspect of their identity. What the social and psychological conditions are that make one person wear his or her group identity lightly whereas for another it is an armour which is rarely taken off is a question to which the answers are not only of theoretical interest but also of profound practical importance and moral significance.

Religious Identities and Violence

The development of religious identity follows the same lines through which the more global aspects of individual and group identities are also constructed. The individual track, which may be called religious selfhood, is an incommunicable realm of religious feeling which quietly suffuses what D.W. Winnicott termed 'the isolated core of the true self' requiring isolation and privacy, a core which 'never communicates with the world of perceived objects [and] must never be communicated with.'[8] In an integrated state, religious selfhood is a quiet self-experience, marked by a calmness of spirit that comes from being alone in the presence of the numinous. With its access to preverbal experience which can link different sensory modalities of image, sound, rhythm, and so on, religious selfhood deepens religious feeling and consolidates religious identity. In a state of fragmentation or threatened distintegration, religious selfhood is prey to a variety of dysphoric moods. For a few, the saints, whose religious identity constitutes the core of their being, the dysphoria can extend to the state of utter despair, the 'dark night of the soul.'

Together with religious selfhood, the "I-ness" of religious identity, we have a second track of "We-ness" which is the experience of being part of a community of believers. Religious community is the interactive aspect of religious identity. In contrast to the quietness of religious selfhood, the individual's experience of religious community takes place in an alert state. Optimally, this facet of religious identity expands the self and creates feelings of attunement and resonance with other believers. A threat to the community aspect of religious identity, however, gives birth to communalism, intolerance, and the potential for social violence. In the communal phase, the feeling of intimacy and connectedness characterizing the religious community are polluted by an ambience of aggression and persecution. Whereas both the selfhood and community facets of religious identity are only partially conscious, the change from community to communalism is accompanied and, indeed, initiated by a heightened awareness of 'We-ness', making the community aspect of religious identity hyperconscious. This awareness can be put in the form of declarations similar to the ones Oscar Patterson suggests take place in the inner discourse of an individual who, as a consequence of a shared threat, is in the process of self-consciously identifying with his or her ethnic group.[9] First, I declare to all who share the crisis with me that I am one with them—a Hindu, a Muslim. Second, from my multiple identities I choose the identity of belonging to my religious community though (paradoxicaly) I have no other choice but to belong. Third, this is my most basic and profound commitment and the one which I am least likely to abandon.

Communalism as a state of mind, then, is the individual's *assertion* of being part of a religious community, preceded by a full *awareness* of belonging to such a community. The 'We-ness' of the community is here replaced by the 'We *are*' of communalism. This 'We are' must inevitably lead to intolerance of all those outside the boundaries of the group. The intolerance, though, is not yet religious conflict since it can remain a province of the mind rather than become manifest in the outer, public realm; its inherent violence can range from a mild contempt to obsessive fantasies around the extermination of the enemy-Other rather than find explosive release in arson, rioting, and murder. The psychological ground for violence, however, has now been prepared. In mapping the sequence of religious violence from the inner to the outer terrain, I do not mean to give group psychology primacy but only precedence. Riots *do* start in the minds of men, minds conditioned by our earliest inner experience of self-affirmation and assertion.

For the outbreak of violence, the communal identity has to swamp personal identity in a large number of people, reviving the feelings of love connected with early identifications with one's own group members and the hate toward the out-group whose members are homogenized, depersonalized, and increasingly dehumanized. For social violence to occur, the threat to communal identity has to cross a certain threshold where the persecutory potential becomes fully activated and persecutory anxiety courses unimpeded through and between members of a religious group. Amplified by rumours, stoked by religious demagogues, the persecutory anxiety signals the annihilation of group identity and must be combated by its forceful assertion. Acting demonstratively in terms of this identity as a Hindu or Muslim, though, threatens members of the rival community who too mobilize their religious identity as a defence. The spiral of threats and reactive counterthreats further fuels persecutory anxiety, and only the slightest of sparks in needed for a violent explosion.

The involvement of religious rather than other social identities does not dampen but, on the contrary, increases the violence of the conflict. Religion brings to conflict between groups a greater emotional intensity and a deeper motivational thrust than language, region, or other markers of ethnic identity. This is at least true of countries where the salience of religion in collective life is very high. Religious identity, for instance, is so crucial in the Islamic world that no Muslim revolutionary has been able or willing to repudiate his religious heritage.[10] To live in India is to become aware that the psychological space occupied by religion, the context and inspiration it provides for individual lives, and its role in fostering the cultural identity and survival of different groups—Hindus, Muslims, Sikhs, Christians,

Parsis—is very different from the situation, say, in the United States. An Indian atheist cannot go along with an American counterpart's casual dismissal of religion as 'important, if true' but must amend it to 'important, even if not true.'

With its historical allusions from sacred rather than profane history, its metaphors and analogies having their source in sacred legends, the religious justification of a conflict involves fundamental values and releases some of our most violent passions. Why this is so is not only because religion is central to the vital, 'meaning-making' function of human life, causing deep disturbance if the survival of all that has been made meaningful by our religious beliefs is perceived to be under attack. Religion excites strong emotions also because it incorporates some of our noblest sentiments and aspirations—our most wishful thinking, the sceptic would say—and any threat to a belief in our 'higher' nature is an unacceptable denuding of self-esteem. Our wishful construction of human nature—that 'man is naturally good or at least good-natured; if he occasionally shows himself brutal, violent or cruel, these are only passing disturbances of his emotional life, for the most part provoked, or perhaps only consequences of the inexpedient social regulations he has hitherto imposed on himself,'[11]—is matched by our equally wishful constructions around religion. Religion, we like to believe, is about love— love of God, love of nature, and love of fellow man. Religion, we feel, is essentially about compassion and strives for peace and justice for the oppressed. Indeed, freedom from violence, an enduring wish of mankind, is reflected in various religious visions of heaven.

This construction is confronted with the reality that violence is present in all religions as a positive and even necessary force for the realization of religious goals. Religious violence has many forms which have found expression in the practice of animal or human sacrifice, in righteous and often excruciatingly cruel punishment envisaged for sinners, in the exorcism of spirits and demons, killing of witches or apostates and in ascetic violence against the self.[12] The point is, as John Bowker has vividly demonstrated, that every religion has a vision of divinely legitimized violence—under certain circumstances.[13] In the Semitic religions, we have the Holy War of the Christians, the Just War of the Jews, and the Jehad of the Muslims where the believers are enjoined to battle and destroy evildoers. In other religions such as Hinduism and Buddhism, with their greater reputation for tolerance and nonviolence, violence is elevated to the realm of the sacred as part of the created order. In Hinduism, for instance, there is a cycle of violence and peacefulness as the Kali Age is followed by the Golden Age. Buddhist myths talk of Seven Days of the Sword where men will look on and kill each other as beasts, after which peace will return and no life is taken. Although Islam (especially in its current phase) and medieval Christianity have had most violent reputations, the question as to which religions have unleashed the greatest amount of violence is ultimately an empirical one.[14] In any event, fundamentalists can unleash any violence contained in a religion even if the religion is rarely perceived to have a violent potential, as amply demonstrated by our experience of Buddhist violence in Sri Lanka and Hindu violence in India. Moreover, as Natalie Davis has observed of Catholic-Protestant violence in 16th-century France and as we saw in the case of the Hyderabad riots, so long as rioters maintain a given religious commitment they rarely display guilt or shame for their acts of violence.[15]

Rhythms of religious ritual, whether in common prayer, processions or other congregational activities, are particularly conducive to breaking down boundaries between members of a group and thus, in times of tension and threat, forging violent mobs. I have called these instruments of the community's violence 'physical' groups since the individual's experience of group identity here is through unconscious bodily communication and fantasies rather than through the more consciously shared cultural traditions. Physical groups seem to come into existence more effortlessly in religious than in other kinds of conflict.

Histories and Futures

In this book, I have attempted to contribute a depth-psychological dimension to the understanding of religious conflict, especially the tension between Hindus and Muslims. I am aware that this may be regarded by some as "psychologizing" an issue which demands social and political activism and which could well do without the introduction of psychological complexities, that 'pale cast of thought', which can only sow doubt and sap the will for unself-conscious action. In retrospect, I realize I have gone about this task in consonance with my professional identity as a clinician, though not as a psychonalyst with an individual patient but more akin to the psychotherapist with a family practice who is called upon for assistance in a disintegrating marriage. I looked at the history of the Hindu-Muslim relationship, made a diagnostic assessment of what has gone wrong, and considered the positive forces in the relationship which were still intact. At the end, it is time to weigh the possible courses of action.

The awareness of belonging to either one community or the other—being a Hindu or Muslim—has increased manifold in recent years. Every time religious violence occurs in India or in some other part of the subcontinent, the reach and spread of modern communications ensure that a vast number of people are soon aware of the incident. Each riot and its afternath raise afresh the issue of the individual's religious-cultural identity and bring it up to the surface of consciousness. This awareness may be fleeting for some, last over a period of time for others, but the process is almost always accompanied by a preconscious self-interrogation on the significane of the religious-cultural community for the sense of one's identiy and the intensity of emotion with which this community is invested. For varying periods of time, individuals consciously experience and express their identity through religious group rather than through traditional kinship groups such as those of family and caste. The duration of this period, or even whether there will be a permanent change in the mode of identity experience for some, depends on many factors, not the least on the success of revivalist and fundamentalist political and social groupings in encouraging such a switch. They do this, we saw in our analysis of the speeches by Rithambra and Azmi, by stoking the already existing persecution anxiety—its combination of aggression and fear weakening the individual sense of identity. The needed support to a weakened personal identity is then provided by strengthening its social, group aspect through an invitation to the person to identify with a grandiose representation of his or her community. The shared 'contemplation' and growing conviction of the great superiority of Hindu or Muslim culture and ways is then the required tonic for narcissistic enhancement and identity consolidation around the religious-cultural community as a pivot.

As for the future, there is more than one scenario for the likely evolution of Hindu-Muslim relations. The Hindu nationalist, who views the conflict as a product of Hindu and Muslim cultural and institutional traditions, believes the only way of avoiding future large-scale violence is a change in the Muslim view of the community's role, traditions, and institutions so that the Muslim can "adapt"—the word meaning anything from adjustment to assimilation—to the Hindu majority's "national" culture. To ask the Muslims to recognize themselves in the Hindu nationalist history of India, to expect them to feel their culture confirmed in Hindu symbols, rituals, and celebrations is asking them to renounce their cultural identity and to erase their collective memory so that they become indistinguishable from their Hindu neighbours. To be swamped by the surrounding Hindu culture has been historically the greatest fear of the Indian Muslim, articulated even by some medieval Sufis who are commonly regarded as having been closest to the Hindu ethos. Such an assimilation is feared precisely because it is so tempting, holding the promise of a freedom from fear of violence and an active and full participation in the majority culture and life, especially now when the majority is also politically dominant. The Hindu nationalist's dilemma is that the Muslims continue to decline an offer the nationalist believes they cannot refuse. The nationalist finds that the Muslim was willing to undertake the exercise in assimilation voluntarily, a highly improbable scenario, the task would involve the immensely difficult understanding of how religious-cultural traditions are transmitted and internalized and how those processes can be effectively interfered with and halted.

The secularist, who views the conflict as rooted in social-structural considerations, especially economic, is more sanguine on the future of Hindu-Muslim relations. In the long run, the secularist believes, the inevitable economic development of the country will alter social-structural conditions and thus assign the conflict, as the cliche would have it, 'to the dust heap of history' as religious identities fade and play less and less of a role in private and public life. A scepitcal note on the belief in the primacy of political and economic structures in the shaping of consciousness, however, needs to be sounded. Cultural traditions—

including the ideology of the Other—transmitted through the family can and do have a line of development separate from the political and economic systems of a society. This is strikingly apparent if one takes the case of Germany where recent studies indicate that, after living for 40 years under a radically different political and economic system, the political orientation and values of the young in relation to the family in eastern Germany are no different from those of their counterparts in the western part of the country; cultural socialization patterns within the family have survived the change in political systems relatively untouched and are stronger than the logic of the political superstructure.[16]

The optimistic realist, a breed with which I identify, believes that we are moving towards an era of recognition of Hindu-Muslim differences rather than pursuing their chimerical commonalities. We are moving toward a multiculturalism, with majority and minority cultures, rather than the emergence of a 'composite culture'. Such a multiculturalism is neither harmful nor dangerous but necessary, since it enables different religious groups to deal with the modernizing process in an active way rather than making them withdraw in lamentation at the inequities of modernization or endure it as passive victims. The problem is to ensure that one identity, Hindutva, does not dominate or assimilate other religious-cultural identities which are also embarked on the same quest as the Hindus. I can understand the validity of the nationalist call to the Hindus to find new meaning in customs, practices, and symbols of Hindu culture. But by the same logic why should this be denied to the Muslims who, too, are engaged in the same struggle to find meaning in the modern world? The realist would say that the solution is to build a state which protects the equal rights of Hindus and Muslims to be different. He believes that we must work toward building a polity which respects the beliefs of both Hindus and Muslims however odd or perverse they may seem to each other and however scornful they may be of the other community in private. Being a sceptic, he is also aware that the creation of such a public realm may be a long drawn-out affair accompanied by much tension and open conflict between the communities which will strain the social and political fabric of the country.

This realist agrees with the Hindu nationalist that clouds of violence loom over the immediate future of Hindu-Muslim relations. He is convinced, though, that achieving the desired goal of a truly multicultural policy will ultimately generate much less tension than the permanent discord which is the probable consequence of the nationalist vision. I can only hope that the violence is short-lived and that it will hasten the creation of a common, tolerant public realm. Our experience of needless suffering and cruelty can sometimes have the effect of jolting us out of accustomed ways of interpreting the world and making us more receptive to fresh ideals and new social-political arrangements. When stress and anxiety are at their greatest there is perhaps enough survival need in humans to suddenly make them reasonable. I hope the poet Theodore Roethke is right that 'In a dark time, the eye begins to see.'[17] This realist is not a cynic since unlike the latter, he still has hope. And even if the hope turns out to be illusory, he knows that, in the words of the *Mahabharata*, 'Hope is the sheet anchor of every man, When hope is destroyed, great grief follows, which is almost equal to death itself.' This applies not only to individuals but also to communities and nations.

APPENDIX I

The Giessen Test Statements

1. I have the feeling that I am relatively impatient 3210123 relatively patient
2. I think I tend to seek the company of others 3210123 avoid the company of others
3. I believe I tend to try to dominate others 3210123 to be dominated by others
4. I believe that a change in my outward circumstances would affect my emotional state very greatly 3210123 very little
5. I have the feeling that I worry about my personal problems very little 3210123 a great deal
6. I think I tend to suppress my anger 3210123 let my anger out in some way
7. I have the feeling that I care about outdoing others very much 3210123 very little
8. I feel that I am not at all shy 3210123 very shy
9. I have the impression that people are generally very satisfied with my work 3210123 very dissatisfied with my work
10. I think I tend to have very great trust in others 3210123 very little trust in others
11. I have the feeling I show my need for love very strongly 3210123 very little
12. I believe that others generally see me as strong 3210123 as weak
13. I have the feeling that it is very hard for me to make myself attractive to others 3210123 very easy for me to make myself attractive to others

14. I believe that compared with others I find it quite easy to keep my mind on one thing

3210123   very hard to keep my mind on one thing

15. I sem to find it very hard to get into high spirits

3210123   very easy to get into high spirits

16. I feel quite relaxed with the opposite sex

3210123   very awkward with the opposite sex

APPENDIX II

The Morality Interview

Nineteen Cases of Hindu-Muslim Interaction.

Normal Time Interactions

1. A Muslim (M) has many Hindu (H) friends.
2. A (M) regularly eats dinner at his (H) friend's house.
3. A (M) rents his house to a (H).
4. A (M) works in a factory where most of the workers are (H).
5. A (M) boy marries a (H) girl.
6. A (M) girl goes to a movie with a (H) boy.
7. A (M) goes to a pandit to learn the *Gita*.
8. A (M) is converted to Hinduism.
9. A (M) girl elopes with a (H) boy.
10. Some (M) boys beat up a (H) boy who was whistling at (M) girls.
11. A (M) throws a dead cow in front of a temple.
12. Some (Ms) attack some (Hs) who were making fun of Allah.

Riot Time Interactions

13. Some (Ms) beat up a (H) walking through the alley.
14. Some (Ms) rape a (H) girl.
15. Some (Ms) set fire to a (H) house in their area.
16. Some (Ms) loot (H) shops.
17. A (M) man kills a (H) woman.
18. Some (Ms) stab and kill two (H) men.
19. A (M) family gives shelter to some (Hs).

The informant's understanding of each case is sought to be elicited through a standard set of interview questions. The questions are designed to assess different features of the respondent's understanding of the morality of a particular situation.

The Standard Interview

1. Is the behaviour wrong?
2. How serious is the violence?

a. Not a violation.
b. A minor offence.
c. A somewhat serious offence.
d. A very serious offence.

3. Is it a sin?
4. What if no one knew this had been done? It was done in private or secretly. Would it be wrong then?
5. In (another city) people do (the opposite of the practice endorsed by the informant) all the time. Would (name of the city) be a better place, if they stopped doing that?
6. What if (name of informant's society) wanted to change the practice? Would it be okay to change it?
7. Do you think a person who does (the practice) should be stopped from doing that? Should he or she be punished? How?

The first question asks about the existence or nonexistence of a transgression. The second and third questions assess the perceived seriousness of the violation, should one exist. The fourth question, concerning self-regulation in absence of external monitors, tells us whether the violation is regarded as being of a moral order or a matter of convention. Questions five through seven tap the perceived universality (versus relativity) and unalterability (versus alterability) of the moral code being violated. The eighth question concerns sanctions and identifies cases where the informant believes the individual has a right to freedom of choice. In addition, the answers to this question give further clues as to the seriousness of one violation as compared to others.

NOTES

INTIMATE RELATIONS

Chapter 1

1. Richard Shweder and N. Much, "Determination of Meaning: Discourse and Moral Socialization" (Committee on Human Development, University of Chicago, 1985, unpublished).
2. Margaret T. Egnor, "The Ideology of Love in a Tamil Family" (Hobart and Smith Colelge, 1986, unpublished).
3. Oliver Sacks, *The Man Who Mistook His Wife for a Hat* (New York: Harper and Row, 1987),147.
4. Ibid., 148.
5. Robert Goldman, "The Serpent and the Rope on Stage: Popular, Literary, and Philosophical Representations of Reality in Traditional India," *Journal of Indian Philosophy* 14 (1986): 149-69.
6. As the termites say to Brahma in *Devi Bhagvata,* "Nidrabhangah kathachedo/ Dampatyoh pritibhedanam/Sisumatrivibhedasca Brahmatyasamam smrtam"(To disturb one in sleep, to interrupt a story, to separate a husband and wife as also mother and child—these things are tantamount to killing a brahmin). Cited in Vettam Mani, *Puranic Encyclopaedia* (Delhi: Motilal Banarsidas, 1985),183.
7. John A. Robinson and Linda Hawpe,"Narrative Thinking as Heuristic Process," in *Narrative Psychology: The Storied Nature of Human Conduct,* ed. T. Sarbin (New York: Praeger, 1986), 123.
8. A. MacIntyre, *After virtue* (Notre Dame, Ind.; University of Notre Dame Press, 1981), 201.
9. See Robert S. Wallerstein,"Psychoanalysis as a Science: A Response to New Challenges,"*Pyschoanalytic Quarterly* 55(1986): 414-51; M.Sherwood,*The Logic of Explanation in Psychoanalysis* (New York: Academic Press, 1968).
10. Donald Spence,"Psychoanalytic Competence," *International Journal of Psychoanalysis* 62, no. 1 (1981): 113-24.
11. For an exceptionally fine summary of object-relation view, see J.R. Weinberg and S. Mitchell, *Object Relations in Psychoanalytic Theory* (Cambridge: Harvard University press, 1982).
12. Meredith Anne Skura, *The Literary Use of Psychoanalytic Process* (New Haven: Yale University Press),178.
13. For an interesting new approach influenced by Lacan, see Peter Brooks, *Reading for the Plot* (New York: Knopf, 1984).

14. Meredith Anne Skura, *The Literary Use of the Psychoanalytic Process* (New Haven: Yale University Press, 1981).

15. Dale Boesky, 'Correspondence with Miss Joyce Carol Oates,' *International Review of Psychoanalysis* 2 (1975): 482.

Chapter 2

1. Rajinder Singh Bedi, *Ek Chadar Maili Si* (Allahabad: Neelam Prakashan, 1961).

2. Margaret T. Egnor, "The Ideology of Love in a Tamil Family" (Hobart and Smith College, 1986, unpublished), 112-13.

3. For a collection of Indian proverbs on woman, see Bharatiya Kahawat Sangraha, vol.2,ed. V. O. Narvane (Pune: Triven Sangam, 1979), 641-51. The translation of the folk sayings in this section are my own.

4. *Rig Veda* 10.145 and 10.159. Ed. F. Max Mueller (London: Oxford University Press, 1890-92).

5. *Rig Veda* 10.18.8.

6. *Ramayana* 3.57.17. Eds. G.H. Bhatt *et.al.* (Baroda: Oriental Institute, 1960-75).

7. My clinical impressions on the actual and potential sexual intimacy of the woman and the younger brother of the husband are supported by the results of at least one empirical study. Behere and Natraj found that the sexual partner of almost half of the men who admitted to premarital relations was the wife of the elder brother. See P. B. Behere and G.S. Natraj, 'Dhat Syndrome: The Phenomeno-logy of a Culture-bound Syndrome, ' *Indian Journal of Psychiatry* 26, no 1 (1984): 76-78.

8. Krishna Sobti, *Mitro Marjani* (New Delhi: Raj Kamal Prakashan, 1967).

9. Sigmund Freud, 'A Special Type of Choice of Object Made by Men' (1910), Standard Edition of the Works of Sigmund Freud (London: Hogarth Press, 1952), vol. 2, 163-76 Hereafter referred to as *Standard Edition.*

10. *The Laws of Manu,* 3.56,ed. F.Max Mueller, trans G. Buehler (Oxford Clarendon Press, 1886), 85.

11. Ibid., 9.26,332.

12. Ibid., 9.3, 328.

13. Ibid., 9.11,329.

14. Ibid., 9.12.

15. Ibid., 9.14,330.

16. Ibid., 9.15.

17. Ibid., 9.17.

18. Ibid., 9.20.

19. *Bharatiya Kahawat Sangraha,* vol 2.

20. D.W. Winnicott, *The Family and Individual Development* (London: Tavistock, 1965), 40. The original insight is, of course, by John Stuart Mill in his 1869 essay, 'The Subjection of Woman.'

22. G. Lakoff and M.Johnson, *Metaphors We Live By* (Chicago: University of Chicago Press, 1980).

Chapter 3

1. On the influence of film values on Indian culture, see Satish Bahadur, *The Context of Indian Film Culture* (Poona: National Film Archives of India, n.d.). See also the various contributions in *Indian Popular Cinema: Myth, Meaning, and Metaphor*, special ussue of the *India International Quarterly* 8, no. 1 (1980).

2. Robert J. Stoller, *Perversion* (New York: Pantheon Books, 1975), 55.

3. Sudhir Kakar, *The Inner World: A Psychoanalytic Study of Childhood and Society in India* (Delhi: Oxford University Press, 1978), chap. 3.

4. Arjun Appadurai and Carol Breckenridge, "Public Culture in Late Twentieth-Century India" (Department of Anthropology, Pittsburgh: University of Pennsylvania, July 1986, unpublished).

5. See Bruno Bettleheim, *The Uses of Enchantment* (New York: Knopf, 1976).

6. Some of these films are *Junglee, Bees Saal Baad, Sangam, Dosti, Upkaar, Pakeeza, Bobby, Aradhana, Johnny Mera Nam, Roti Kapda aur Makan, Deewar, Zanjeer, Sholay, Karz, Muqaddar Ka Sikandar*, and *Ram Teri Ganga Mali*.

7. Wendy O'Flaherty, "The Mythological in Disguise: An analysis of Karz," in *Indian Popular Cinema*, note 1 above, 23-30.

8. Sudhir Kakar and John M. Ross, *Tales of Love, Sex, and Danger* (London: Unwin Hyman, 1987), chap. 3.

9. *Mahabharata*, 5, 144.5-10. The English translation is taken from J.A.B. von Buitenen, ed. and trans., *The Mahabharata* (Chicago: University of Chicago Press, 1978), 453.

10. The psychological effects of modernization have been discussed in E. James Anthony and C. Chiland, eds., *The Child in His Family:Children and Their Parents in a Changing World* (New York: Johy Wiley, 1978).

11. Martha Wolfenstein and Nathan Leites, *Movies: A Psychological Study* (Glencoe, III.: Free Press, 1950).

12. Joyce McDougall, *Theatres of the Mind* (New York: Basic Books, 1986).

Chapter 4

1. These are the types of tales which come closest to what Luthi described as 'one-dimensional.' See Max Luthi *European Folktale: Form and Nature* (Philadelphia: Institute for the Study of Human Issues, 1982), 4-10. See also Kamil V. Zvelebil, *Two Tamil Folktales* (Delhi: Motilal Banarsidas, 1987), i.vii, for an exhaustive discussion of the formal characteristics of a similar Tamil narrative. The translations of the stories from *Kissa Tota Myna* are mine.

2. In this sense they are also what Arthur Deikman has called 'teaching stories.' See Arthur Deikman, *The Observing Self* (Boston: Beacon Press, 1982), 153.

3. Sudhir Kakar, *The Inner World: A Psychoanalytic Study of Childhood and Society in India* (Delhi: Oxford University Press, 1978), 87 ff.

4. Robert P. Goldman, 'Fathers, Sons and Gurus: Oedipal Conflict in Sanskrit Epics,' *Journal of Indian Philosophy* 8 (1978): 325-92.

5. *Mahabharata Virataparva* 2:14. Translated by P.D. Roy (Calcutta: Oriental Publishing, n.d.)

6. Zvelebil, *Two Tamil Folktales,* 131-36. A.K. Ramanujan has collected a folktale, 'The Serpent Lover,' from Karnataka, which is identical with the second part of the adventures of Princess Standing Lamp.

7. See David Will, 'Psychoanalysis and the New Philosophy of Science,' *International Review of Psychoanalysis* 13(1986): 163-74.

8. See Manfred Lurker, *Adler und Schlange: Tiersymbolik in Glauben und Weltbild der Volker* (Tubingen: 1983) and Balaji Mundkur, *The Cult of the Serpent: An Interdisciplinary Survey of its Manifestations and Origins* (Albany: State University of New York Press, 1983).

9. For a summary discussion of oedipal and pre-oedipal meanings of the snake symbolism, see Philip Slater, *The Glory of Hera* (Boston: Beacon Press, 1966), 88ff.

10. B.E.F. Beck and Peter J. Claus, eds., *Folktales of India* (Chicago: University of Chicago Press, 1986), 27.

11. Bruno Bettelheim, *The Uses of Enchantment* (New York: Knopf, 1976), 282-310.

12. Stuart Blackburn and A.K. Ramanujan, eds., *Another Harmony: New Essays in the Folklore of India* (Berkeley: University of California Press, 1986), 14.

Chapter 5

1. Oscar Lewis, *La Vida* (New York: Vintage Books, (1968), xlii.

2. B. Bernstein, *Soziale Struktur und Sprachverhalten* (Amsterdam: 1970).

3. *Mahabharata: Anusasana Parva*, translated by P.D. Roy (Calcutta: Oriental Publishing, n.d.), 325.

4. For a discussion of Jungian notions, see R.M. Stein, 'Coupling-Uncoupling: Bindung und Freiheit,' in *Analytische Psychologie* (14 (1983): 1-14.

5. Heinz Kohut, *The Analysis of the Self* (New York: International Universities Press, 1971).

Chapter 6

1. For psychoanalytic perspectives on autobiography, see Robert Steele, 'Deconstructing Histories: Toward a Systematic Criticism of Psychological Narratives,' in *Narrative Psychology*, ed. T.R. Sarbin (New York: Praeger,

378

1986). See also Erik H. Erikson, 'In Search of Gandhi: on the Nature of Psychohistorical Evidence,' *Daedalus* (Summer 1968).

2. For a discussion of Nobokov's *Speak, Memory*, see Sudhir Kakar and John Ross, *Tales of Love, Sex, and Danger* (London: Unwin Hyman, 1987), chap. 8.

3. M.K. Gandhi, *Satya no Prayoga athva Atma-Katha* (translated by Mahadev Desai as *The Story of My Experiments with Truth*) (Ahmedabad: Navjivan Prakashan Mandir, 1927), 10; henceforth referred to as *Autobiography*.

4. Ibid., 31.

5. V.S. Naipaul, *India: A Wounded Civilization* (New York: Knopf, 1976), 102-6.

6. Gandhi, *Autobiography*, 75.

7. Ibid., 69.

8. A.K. Ramanujan, 'Hanchi: A Kannada Cinderella,' in *Cinderella: A Folklore Casebook*, ed. A. Dundes (New York: Garland Publishing, 1982), 272.

9. M.K. Gandhi, *Bibi Amtussalam ke nam patra* [*Letters to Bibi Amtussalam*], Ahmedabad: Navjivan, 1960), 70.

10. Gandhi, *Autobiography*, 91.

11. Ibid., 205.

12. Pyarelal, *Mahatma Gandhi; The First Phase*, (Bombay: Sevak Prakashan). 213.

13. Ibid., 207.

14. M.K. Gandhi, *The Collected Works of Mahatma Gandhi* (Delhi: Publication Division, Government of India, 1958), vol. 3, letters of 30 June 1906 to Chaganlal Gandhi and H.V. Vohra, 352-54; henceforth referred to as *Collected Works*.

15. Ibid., 208-9.

16. Gandhi, *Collected Works*, Vol. 5, 56.

17. M.K. Gandhi, *To the Women* (Karachi: Hingorani, 1943), 49-50, 52.

18. Gandhi, *To the Women*, 194.

19. M.K. Gandhi, 'Yervada Mandir,' in *Selected Works*, Vol. 4 (Ahmedabad: Navjivan, 1968), 220.

20. Ibid.

21. M.K. Gandhi, 'Hind Swaraj,' in *Collected Works*.

22. Millie G. Polak, *Mr. Gandhi: The Man* (Bombay: Vora & Co., 1949), 63-64.

23. Gandhi, 'Yervada Mandir,' 223.

24. St. Augustine, *The Confessions*, trans. E.R. Pusey (New York: Modern Library, 1949), 227.

25. Ibid., 228.

26. Gandhi, *Autobiography*, 324.

27. Ibid., 210.

28. Ibdi., 501.

29. Ibid., 24.

30. St. Augustine, *Confessions*, 162.

31. Gandhi, *Collected Works*, vol. 37(1928), 'Speech on the Birth Centenary of Tolstoy' (10 September 1928), 258.

32. Ibid., 265.
33. Gandhi, *Autobiography*, 209.
34. Gandhi, *Collected Works*, vol. 37(1928), 258.
35. Gandhi, *Collected Works*, vol. 36 (1927-28), letter to Harjivan Kotak, 378.
36. Gandhi, 'Ek Tyag,' in *Harijanbandhu*, 22.9.35.
37. M.K. Gandhi, *Kumari Premaben Kantak ke nam patra* [*Letters to Premaben Kantak*], (Ahmedabad: Navjivan, 1960), 260-62 (my translation).
38. The best eyewitness account of Gandhi's Bengal period is by N.K. Bose, Gandhi's temporary secretary, who was both a respectful follower and a dispassionate observer: see his *My Days with Gandhi* (Calcutta: Nishana, 1953).
39. Ibid., 52.
40. Ibdi., 189.
41. In his *Key to Health*, rewritten in 1942 in the middle of another depressive phase following the widespread violence of the 'Quit India' movement and the death of his wife in prison, Gandhi had hinted at this kind of self-testing: 'Some of my experiments have not reached a stage when they might be placed before the public with advantage. I hope to do so some day if they succeed to my satisfaction. Success might make the attainment of *brahmacharya* comparatively easier.' See *Selected Works*, vol. 4, 432. For a compassionate and insightful discussion of these experiments, see also Erik H. Erikson, *Gandhi's Truth* (New York: Norton, 1969), 404.
42. Gandhi, *Kumari Premaben Kantak ke nam patra*, 16.
43. Ibid., 19.
44. Ibid., 188.
45. Ibid.
46. Ibid., 39.
47. Ibid.
48. Ibid.
49. Ibid.
50. Ibid., 190.
51. Ibid., 151.
52. Ibid., 173.
53. Ibid., 369.
54. See Mira Behn, ed., *Bapu's Letters to Mira* (1924-48) (Ahmedabad: Navjivan, 1949) and *The Spirit's Pilgrimage* (London: Longman, 1960).
55. Behn, ed., *Bapu's Letters to Mira*, 27-28.
56. R. Greenson, *The Technique and Practice of Psychoanalysis* (New York: International University Press, 1967), 338-41.
57. See Martin S. Bergman, 'Transference Love and Love in Real Life,' in J. M. Ross, ed., *International Journal of Psychoanalytic Psychotherapy* 11 (1985-86): 27-45.
58. Behn, ed., *Bapu's Letters to Mira*, 42.

59. Ibid.
60. Ibid., 43.
61. Ibid., 71.
62. Ibid., 88.
63. Ibid., 166.
64. For an elaborate description of some of these popular psychological ideas in English, see Swami Sivananda, *Mind: Its Mysteries and Control* (Sivanandanagar: Divine Life Society, 1974), chap. 28, and Swami Narayanananda, *The Mysteries of Man, Mind, and Mind-Functions* (Rishikesh: Universal Yoga Trust, 1965), chap. 19.
65. Gandhi, *To the Women*, 71.
66. G. Bose, 'All or None Attitude in Sex,' *Samiksa* 1 (1947): 14.
67. Wendy O'Flaherty, *Women, Androgynes, and Other Mythical Beasts* (Chicago: University of Chicago Press, 1980), 45.
68. See Wendy O'Flaherty, *Asceticism and Eroticism in the Mythology of Siva* (London: Oxford University Press, 1973), 55.
69. *Brahmavaivarta Purana*, 4.31, 4.32, 1.20, 4.33, 1.76; English translation abridged from O'Flaherty, *Asceticism and Eroticism in the Mythology of Siva*, 51.
70. Cited in Edward C. Dimock, Jr., *The Place of the Hidden Moon* (Chicago: University of Chicago Press, 1966), 154.
71. Ibid., 54.
72. Ibid., 156.
73. See Ramchandra Gandhi, Brahmacharya (Department of Philosophy, University of Hyderabad, 1981, unpublished), 26.
74. Thomas Mann, *Joseph and His Brothers* (London: Secker and Warburg, 1959), 719.
75. Sigmund Freud, 'Civilized Sexual Morality and Modern Nervousness' (1908), *Standard Edition*, vol. 9, 197.
76. St. Augustine, *Confessions*, 165.
77. Gandhi, *To the Women*, 81.
78. Ibid., 60.
79. Ibid., 57.
80. Polak, *Mr. Gandhi*, 34.
81. Gandhi, *To the Women*, 28-29.
82. Behn, ed., *Bapu's Letters to Mira*, 141.
83. Gandhi, *To the Women*, 102.
84. Erikson, *Gandhi's Truth*.
85. Ved Mehta, *Mahatma Gandhi and His Apostles* (New Delhi: Indian Book Co., 1977), 13.
86. D.W. Winnicott, 'Appetite and Emotional Disorder,' in *Collected Papers* (London: Tavistock Publications, 1958), 34.

Chapter 7

1. T.C. Sinha, 'Psychoanalysis in India,' *Lumbini Park Silver Jubilee Souvenir* (Calcutta: 1966), 66.

2. G. Bose, 'The Genesis of Homosexuality,' (1926) *Samiksa* 4, no. 2 (1950): 74.

3. G. Bose, 'A New Theory of Mental Life,' *Samiksa* 2 (1948): 158.

4. G. Bose, 'The Genesis and Adjustment of the Oedipus Wish,' *Samiksa* 3, no. 1 (1949): 222-40.

5. The coinage is by Clifford Geertz, who used it in the Symposium on Culture and Human Development sponsored by Committee on Human Development, University of Chicago, 5-7 November 1987.

6. Donald P. Spence, 'Narrative Smoothing and Clinical Wisdom,' in *Narrative Psychology*, ed. T. Sarbin (New York: Praeger, 1986).

7. M.K. Gandhi, *To the Women* (Karachi: Hingorani, 1943), 194 and 28-29. Karen Horney, 'The Flight from Womanhood: The Masculinity Complex in Women as Viewed by Men and Women,' in *Feminine Psychology* (New York: Norton, 1967).

8. Karl Abraham, *Dreams and Myths: A Study in Race Psychology* (New York: The Journal of Nervous and Mental Health Publishing Company, 1913), 72.

9. Sigmund Freud, 'Creative Writers and Daydreaming,' in *Standard Edition*, Vol. 9, 152.

10. Gananath Obeysekere, *Medusa's Hair: A Study in Personal and Cultural Symbols* (Chicago: University of Chicago Press, 1981).

11. Paul B. Courtright, *Ganesha* (New York: Oxford University Press, 1986), 114.

12. G. Obeysekere, *The Cult of Pattini* (Chicago: University of Chicaro Press, 1984), 471.

13. Margaret T. Egnor, *The Ideology of Love in a Tamil Family* (Hobart and Smith College, 1984, unpublished).

14. Sudhir Kakar, 'Psychoanalysis and Anthropology: A Renewed Alliance,' *Contributions to Indian Sociology* 21, no. 1 (1987), 88.

15. The Sanskrit source of the myth is the *Brahma Purana*, 81. 1—5. For an English translation see Wendy O'Flaherty, *Asceticism and Eroticism in the Mythology of Siva* (London: Oxford University Press, 1973), 203.

16. Sudhir Kakar, *The Inner World: A Psychoanalytic Study of Childhood and Society in India* (Delhi: Oxford University Press, 1978).

17. Chasseguet-Smirgel, 'Feminine Guilt and the Oedipus Complex,' in *Female Sexuality*, ed. J. Chasseguet-Smirgel (Ann Arbor: University of Michigan Press, 1964), 94—134. For traditional views, see Sigmund Freud, 'Fetishism,' *Standard Edition*, vol. 21 (1924) and 'Splitting the Ego in the Process of Defence,' *Standard Edition*, vol. 23 (1940). See also R.C. Bak, 'The Phallic Woman: The Ubiquitous Fantasy in Perversions,' *The Psychoanalytic Study of the Child*, vol. 23, 15-16.

18. Sudhir Kakar and John Ross, *Tales of Love Sex, and Danger* (London: Unwin Hyman, 1987).
19. Erik H. Erikson, *Childhood and Society* (New York: Norton, 1950).
20. Sigmund Freud, 'New Introductory Lectures on Psychoanalysis,' *Standard Edition*, vol. 22 (1922).
21. Janis Long, 'Culture, Selfobject, and the Cohesive Self,' paper presented at the American Psychological Association Meetings, August 1986.
22. Heinz Kohut, *Self Psychology and Humanities*, ed. D. Strozier (New York: Norton, 1985), 224-31.
23. Janis Long, 'Culture, Selfobject, and the Cohesive Self,' 8.

Chapter 8

1. For an exhaustive discussion of these conceptual models see A. Brittan and M. Maynard, *Sexism, Racism and Oppression*, (Oxford: Basil Blackwell, 1984).
2. Sudhir Kakar and John Ross, *Tales of Love, Sex and Danger* (London: Unwin Hyman, 1987).
3. Plato, 'Symposium' in B. Jowett, trans., *The Portable Plato*, (New York: Viking Press, 1950), p. 145.
4. See, for instance, L.H. Tessman, 'A Note on the Father's Contribution to the Daughter's Ways of Loving and Working,' in S.H. Cath *et al.*, eds., *Father and Child: Developmental and Clinical Perspectives*, (Boston: Little Brown, 1982), 219-38.

THE ANALYST AND THE MYSTIC

Chapter 1

1. N. Soderblom, *Till mystikens belysning* (Lund, 1985), cited in H. Akerberg, 'The Unio Mystica of Teresa of Avila,' in N.G. Holm, ed., *Religious Ecstasy* (Stockholm: Almqvist and Wiksell, 1981), 275-79.
2. William James, *The Varieties of Religious Experience* (New York: Longmans, Green, 1902).
3. Andrew M. Greeley, *The Sociology of the Paranormal: A Reconnaissance* (Beverly Hills: Sage Publications, 1975), 62.
4. For a psychological description of the structure of mystical experience see Committee on Psychiatry and Religion, *Mysticism: Spiritual Quest or Psychic Disorder* (New York: Group for Advancement of Psychiatry, 1976). See also H. Hof, 'Ecstasy and Mysticism,' in Holm, *Religious Ecstasy*, 243-49.
5. R.C. Zaehner, *Hindu and Muslim Mysticism* (London: Athalone Press, 1960). The authoritative work on Hindu mysticism remains S.N. Dasgupta (1927), *Hindu Mysticism* (Delhi: Motilal Banarsidas, 1987).
6. See Committee on Psychiatry and Religion, *Mysticism,* especially 782-86. For specific psychoanalytic contributions stressing the ego-adaptive aspects of the mystic experience see Paul C. Horton, 'The Mystical Experience: Substance of an Illusion,' *Journal of the American Psychoanalytic Association* 22 (1974): 364-80; David Aberbach, 'Grief and Mysticism,' *International Review of Psychoanalysis* 14(1987): 509-26.
7. Anton Ehrenzweig, *The Hidden Order of Art* (London: Weidenfeld and Nicolson, 1967).
8. Romain Rolland, *The Life of Ramakrishna* (Calcutta: Advaita Ashram, 1986), 38.
9. For the arguments against a psychoanalytic, 'scientific' study of mysticism, see Roger N. Walsh et al., 'Paradigms in Collision,' in *Beyond Ego: Transpersonal Dimensions in Psychology*, ed. R.N. Walsh and F. Vaughan (Los Angeles: Tarcher, 1980), 36-52.
10. See Peter Buckley and Marc Galanter, 'Mystical Experience, Spiritual Knowledge, and a Contemporary Ecstatic Experience,' British Journal of Medical Pyschology 52 (1979): 281-89.
11. For the case histories see P.C. Horton, 'Mystical Experience,' and Committee on Psychiatry and Religion, *Mysticism*, 799-807.
12. For a comprehensive comparison of the three see Manfred Eigen, 'The Area of Faith in Winnicott, Lacan and Bion,' *International Journal of Psychoanalysis* 62 (1981): 413-34.
13. Cited in Irving B. Harrison, 'On Freud's View of the Infant-Mother Relationship and of the Oceanic Feeling—Some Subjective Influences,' *Journal of the American Psychoanalytic Association* 27 (1979): 409.

14. Ibid.
15. J.M. Masson suggests a different passage from the writings of Ramakrishna as the source for the term 'oceanic feeling'; see his *The Oceanic Feeling: The Origins of Religious Sentiment in Ancient India* (Dordrecht: Reidel, 1980), 36.
16. Dushan Pajin, 'The Oceanic Feeling: A Reevaluation' (Belgrade, 1989, manuscript).
17. Letter to R. Rolland, 19 January 1930, in E. Freud, ed., *The Letters of Sigmund Freud* (New York: Basic Books, 1960), 392.
18. Mahendranath Gupta, *Sri Ramakrishna Vachanamrita*, trans. into Hindi by Suryakant Tripathi 'Nirala,' 3 vols. (Nagpur: Ramakrishna Math, 1988).
19. Swami Saradananda, *Sri Ramakrishna, The Great Master*, 2 vols. (Mylapore: Sri Ramakrishna Math, 1983), vol. 1, 276-77.
20. Rolland, *Life of Ramakrishna*, 22-23.
21. Saradananda, *Sri Ramakrishna*, vol. 1, 276-77.
22. Ibid., 156.
23. Ibid., 162-63.
24. Saradananda, *Sri Ramakrishna*, vol. 1, 424.
25. Gupta, *Vachanamrita*, vol. 1, 71.
26. Ibid., 301.
27. Ibid., 320.
28. Ibid., 135-36.
29. Ibid., 41.
30. Ibid., vol. 2, 241.
31. Bhavabhuti, *Uttara Rama Charita*, in *Six Sanskrit Plays* (Bombay: Asia, 1964), 368.
32. Gupta, *Vachanamrita*, vol. 1, 90.
33. S. Freud, *New Introductory Lectures* (1933), *Standard Edition*, vol. 22, 79-80.
34. Nathaniel Ross, 'Affect as Cognition: With Observation on the Meaning of Mystical States,' *International Review of Psychoanalysis* 2(1975): 79-93.
35. Gupta, *Vachanamrita*, vol. 3, 238-89.
36. Ernst Hartmann, *The Nightmare: The Psychology and Biology of Terrifying Dreams* (New York: Basic, 1984).
37. Gupta *Vachanamrita*, vol. 3, 289.
38. J.M.R. Damas Mora et al., 'On Heutroscopy or the Phenomenon of the Double,' *British Journal of Medical Psychology* 53 (1980): 75-83.
39. Gupta, *Vachanamrita*, vol. 1, 388.
40. Ibid., vol. 3, 109.
41. Ibid., vol. 1, 431.
42. Saradananda, *Sri Ramakrishna*, vol. 1, 417.
43. Octavio Paz, *The Money Grammarian*, trans. Helen Lane (New York: Seaver Books, 1981), 133.

44. For representative statements of the classical Freudian view see L. Salzman, 'The Psychology of Religious and Ideological Conversion,' *Psychiatry* 16(1953): 177-87. For the Kleinian view see Irving B. Harrison, 'On the Maternal Origins of Awe,' *The Psychoanalytic Study of the Child* 30 (1975): 181-95.

45. P.C. Horton, 'Mystical Experience.'

46. For a detailed discussion of the link and parallels between the process of mourning and mysticism see Aberbach, 'Grief and Mysticism,' 509-26.

47. S. Kakar, *Shamans, Mystics and Doctors* (New York: Knopf, 1982), chap. 5. See also Buckley and Galanter, 'Mystical Experience,' 285; P.C. Harton, 'The Mystical Experience as a Suicide Preventive,' *American Journal of Psychiatry* 130 (1973): 294-96.

48. Cited in Aberbach, 'Grief and Mysticism," 509.

49. I. Barande and R. Barande, 'Antinomies du concept de perversion et epigenese del' appetit de excitation', cited in S.A. Leavy, 'Male Homosexuality Reconsidered,' *International Journal of Psychoanalytic Psychotherapy* 11 (1985-86), 163.

50. Gupta, *Vachanamrita*, vol. 1, 388.

51. Eigen, 'Area of Faith'; 'Ideal Images, Creativity and the Freudian Drama,' *Psychocultural Review* 3 (1979): 278-98; 'Creativity, Instinctual Fantasy and Ideal Images,' *Psychoanalytic Review* 68 (1981).

52. Eigen, 'Area of Faith,' 431.

53. E. Underhill, *Mysticism* (1911) (New York: E.P. Dutton, 1961); J.H. Leuba, *The Psychology of Religious Mysticism* (New York: Harcourt, Brace, 1925).

54. A. Einstein, *Ideas and Opinions* (New York: Crown Publishers, 1954), 75.

55. Herbert Moller, 'Affective Mysticism in Western Civilization,' *Psychoanalytic Review* 52 (1965): 259-67. See also E.W. McDonnel, *The Beguines and Beghards in Medieval Culture* (New Brunswick: Rutgers University Press, 1954), 320-32.

56. Gupta, *Vachanamrita*, 3: 535-36.

57. Ibid., 107.

58. Robert Stoller, 'The Gender Disorders,' in I. Rosen, ed., *Sexual Deviation* (Oxford University Press, 1979), 109-38.

59. J.O. Wisdom, 'Male and Female,' *International Journal of Psychoanalysis* 64 (1983): 159-68.

60. D.W. Winnicott, 'Creativity and its Origins,' in *Playing and Reality* (London: Tavistock, 1971), 72-85.

61. Ibid., 85.

Chapter 2

1. Pupul Jayakar, *J. Krishnamurti: A Biography* (Delhi: Penguin, 1987), 9. Here I must add the caution contained in Brent's observation that 'In a country where there where perhaps ten million holy men, many with their own devotees,

acolytes and disciples, some of them gurus with hundreds of thousands of followers, all of them inheritors of a tradition thousands of years old, nothing tht one can say about them in general will not somewhere be contradicated in particular.' See P. Brent, *Godmen of India* (Harmondsworth: Penguin, 1973), 22.

2. For a comprehensive historical discussion of the evolution of the guru institution, on which this introductory section is based, see R.M. Steinmann, *Guru-Sisya Sambandha: Das Meister-Schuler Verhaltnis im Traditionell-en und Modernen Hinduismus* (Wiesbaden: Franz Steiner, 1986). See further W. Cenker, *A Tradition of Teachers: Sankara and the Jagadgurus Today* (Delhi: Motilal Banarsidas, 1983).

3. Cenker, *Tradition of Teachers* 41.

4. Cited in D. Gold, *The Lord as Guru* (Delhi: oxford University Press, 1987), 104.

5. Cited in Steinmann, *Guru-Sisya Sambandha*, 87.

6. Ibid., 103.

7. L. Babb, *Redemptive Encounters* (Delhi: Oxford University Press, 1987), 218.

8. *Kulanirvana Tantra*, cited in Steinmann, 103.

9. S. Abhayananda, *Jnaneshvar* (Neples, FL: Atma Books, 1989), 122-23.

10. See, for instance, Chaturvedi Badrinath, 'Sense and Nonsense about the 'Guru' Concept,' *Times of India*, 13 February 1990.

11. Steinmann, *Guru-Sisya Sambandha*, 188-89.

12. Swami Saradananda, *Sri Ramakrishna, The Great Master*, 2 vols. (Mylapore: Sri Ramakrishna Math, 1983), vol. 1, 521.

13. Jayakar, *Krishnamurti*, 4.

14. Ibid., 5.

15. Ibid., 211.

16. See S. Kakar, *Shamans, Mystics and Doctors* (New York: Knopf, 1982), chap. 5.

17. S. Kakar, *The Inner World: A Psychoanalytic Study of Childhood and Society in India* (Delhi: Oxford University Press, 1978), chap. 4.

18. See H. Kohut, *The Analysis of the Self* (New York: International Universities Press, 1971), and *The Restoration of the Self* (New York: International Universities Press, 1977).

19. Ernest Wolf, *Treatment of the Self* (New York: Guilford, 1989), 52.

20. See A. Deutsch, 'Tenacity of Attachment to a Cult Leader: A Psychiatric Perspective,' *American Journal of Psychiatry* 137 (1982): 1569-73. See also S. Lorand, 'Psychoanalytic Therapy of Religious Devotees,' *International Journal of Psychoanalysis* 43 (1962): 50-55.

21. Wolf, *Treatment of the Self*, 100.

22. S. Nacht, 'Curative Factors in Psychoanalysis,' *International Journal of Psychoanalysis* 43 (1962): 208. See also S.M. Abend, 'Unconscious Fantasy and Theories of Cure,' *Journal of the American Psychoanalytic Association* 27 (1979): 579-96.

23. Cited in Steinmann, *Guru-Sisya Sambandha*, 36.
24. Swami Satyanand Saraswati, *Light on the Guru and Disciple Relationship* (Munger: Bihar School of Yoga, 1983), 92.
25. Ibid., 77.
26. William James, *The Varities of Religious Experience* (New York: Longmans, Green, 1902), 107, 195.
27. Cited in D. Nurbaksh, 'Sufism and Psychoanalysis,' *International Journal of Social Psychiatry* 24 (1978): 208.
28. Swami Muktananda, *The Perfect Relationship* (Ganesh-Puri: Gurudev Siddha Vidyapeeth, 1983), ix.
29. Saradananda, *Sri Ramakrishna*, 454.
30. Muktananda, *Perfect Relationship*, 35.
31. Ibid., viii.
32. Christopher Bollas, 'The Transformational Object.' *International Journal of Psychoanalysis* 60 (1978): 97-107.
33. Muktananda, *Perfect Relationship*, 4.
34. Steinmann, *Guru-Sisya Sambandha*, 290.
35. Muktananda, *Perfect Relationship*, 85.
36. Babb, *Redemptive Encounters*, 173.
37. Jayakar, *Krishnamurti*, 3.
38. Cited in Steinmann, *Guru-Sisya Sambandha*, 235.
39. Ibid., 234.
40. M.L. Moeller, 'Self and Object in Countertransference,' *International Journal of Psychoanalysis* 58 (1977): 356-76.
41. S. Kakar, 'Psychoanalysis and Religious Healing: Siblings or Strangers?' *Journal of the American Academy of Religion* 53, no. 3 (1985).
42. Muktananda, *Perfect Relationship*, 37.
43. Ibid., 109.
44. Jayakar, *Krishnamurti*, 8.
45. S.L. Bady, 'The Voice as a Curative Factor in Psychotherapy,' *Psychoanalytic Review* 72 (1989): 677-90.
46. S. Kakar, *Shamans, Mystics and Doctors*, 129-30.
47. Muktananda, *Perfect Relationship*, 4.
48. Moeller, 'Self and Object,' 373.

Chapter 3

1. E.L. Meng and E. Freud, ed., *Psychoanalysis and Faith: The Letters of Sigmund Freud and Oskar Pfister* (New York: Basic Books, 1963), 117.
2. E. Jones, *The Life and Work of Sigmund Freud*, 3 vols. (London: Hogarth Press, 1957), vol. 3.
3. Sigmund Freud, *The Future of an Illusion* (1927), Standard Edition of the Works of Sigmund Freud (London: Hogarth Press, 1953-74), vol. 21. Hereafter

referred to as *Standard Edition*. Also *Civilization and Its Discontents, Standards Edition*, vol. 21.

4. S. Freud, *Obsessive Actions and Religious Practices* (1907), *Standard Edition*, vol. 9.

5. Wilhelm Reich, *The Function of the Orgasm* (New York: Argone Institute, 1942).

6. S. Freud, *Obsessive Actions*.

7. Franz Alexander, 'Buddhistic Training as an Artificial Catatonia,' *Psychoanalysis* 19(1931): 129-45.

8. J.M. Masson, *The Oceanic Feeling: The Origins of Religious Sentiment in Ancient India* (Dordrecht: Reidel, 1980).

9. P. Ricouer, *Freud and Philosophy*, trans. Denis Savage (New Haven: Yale University Press, 1970), 533.

10. Erik H. Erikson, *Young Man Luther* (New York: Norton, 1958), 264.

11. Bruno Bettelheim, *Freud and Man's Soul* (New York: Knopf, 1983).

12. Karen Horney, *Neurosis and Human Growth* (New York: Norton, 1950), 55.

13. Erich Fromm, *Psychoanalysis and Religion* (New Haven: Yale University Press, 1950).

14. A. Kaplan, "Maturity in Religion,' *Bulletin of the Philadelphia Association for Psychoanalysis* 13 (1963): 101-19; H. Guntrip, 'Religion in Relation to Personal Interaction,' *British Journal of Medical Psychology* 42 (1969): 232-33; Peter Homans, *Theology after Freud* (Indianapolis: Bobbs-Merrill, 1970).

15. Ricouer, *Freud and Phislosophy*, 548-49.

16. Jacob Arlow, 'Ego Psychology and the Study of Mythology,' *Journal of the American Psychoanalytic Association* 9 (1961): 371-93.

17. Erikson, *Young Man Luther*, 264.

18. Gregory Zilboorg, *Freud and Religion: A Restatement* (London: Chapman, 1958).

19. Meng and E. Freud, *Psychoanalysis and Faith*, 133.

20. See H.P. Jung, 'The Prototype of Pre-oedipal Reconstruction,' *Journal of the American Psychoanalytic Association* 25 (1977): 757-85; Irving B. Harrison, 'On Freud's View of the Infant-Mother Relationship and of the Oceanic Feeling—Some Subjective Influences,' *Journal of the American Psychoanalytic Association* 27 (1979): 399-421.

21. Harrison, 'Some Subjective Influences.'

22. S. Freud, *Moses and Monotheism* (1939), *Standard Edition*, vol. 23, 134.

23. Harrison, 'Some Subjective Influences.' 420.

24. Ibid., 402.

25. E. Jones, *Life and Work of Freud*, vol. 3, 392.

26. Harrison, 'Some Subjective Influences,' 418-19.

27. Peter Homans, *The Ability to Mourn* (Chicago: University of Chicago Press, 1989).

28. S. Freud, *The Psychopathology of Everyday Life, Standard Edition*, vol. 6, 2.
29. Cited in David S. Berman, 'Stefan Zweig and His Relationship with Freud and Rolland,' *Interntional Review of Psychoanalysis* 6 (1979): 85.
30. George Steiner, 'A Note on Language and Psychoanalysis,' *International Review of Psychoanalysis* 3 (1976): 257.
31. Meng and E. Freud, *Psychoanalysis and Faith*, 126.
32. W.R. Bion, *Attention and Interpretation* (London: Tavistock, 1970), 62.
33. For a survey of the various relational theories in psychoanalysis, see J.R. Greenberg and S.A. Mitchell, *Object Relations in Psychoanalytic Theory* (Cambridge, MA: Harvard University Press, 1983). For an important exploration of religion and religious experience from the viewpoint of relational theories, especially the work of Winnicott, see W.W. Meissner, *Psychoanalysis and Religious Experience* (New Haven: Yale University Press, 1984).
34. D.W. Winnicott, *Playing and Reality* (London: Tavistock, 1971), 1-25.
35. Ibid., 14.
36. Winnicott, *Playing and Reality*, 96.
37. Erikson, *Young Man Luther*, 263-64.
38. H. Kohut, *Self Psychology and the Humanities* (New York: Norton, 1985).
39. S. Kakar, 'Psychoanalysis and Religious Healing: Siblings or Strangers?' *Journal of the American Academy of Religion* 53, no. 3, (1985).
40. Ava L. Siegler, 'The Oedipus Myths and the Oedipus Complex: Intersecting Realm, Shared Structures,' *International Review of Psychoanalysis* 10 (1983): 205-14.
41. Ibid., 206.
42. Oliver Sacks, *The Man Who Mistook His Wife for a Hat* (New York: Harper and Row, 1987).
43. Bion, *Attention and Interpretation*, See also M. Milner, 'Some Notes on Psychoanalytic Ideas about Mysticism,' in *The Suppressed Madness of Sane Men* (London: Routledge, 1989), 257-71.

THE COLOURS OF VIOLENCE

Chapter 1

1. In the profession of this belief, physicists did not limit themselves to the field of natural science. In his 1929, 'Light and Life', Nils Bohr made an explicit analogy between quantum mechanics and psychology when he observed that the necessity of considering the interrelationship between the measuring instrument and the object of inquiry in physics paralleled the difficulty in psychology where the content of consciousness changed as soon as attention was directed to it; see Nils Bohr, 'Light and Life', *Nature* 131 (1933), 421-33 and 457-59.

   Wolfgang Pauli, who is regarded by many as occupying a place next only to Einstein in the hierarchy of the great modern physicists, was categorical in his conclusion that the natural sciences had taken a historically wrong turn by accepting Cartesian ideas and ways of thought engendered by Newtonian physics. The observer in modern physics, he felt, was still too separated from the phenomena observed. In so far as a content of consciousness was itself an observation, the vital question of separation of subject and object was not restricted to the narrow field of physical inquiry but was relevant for all human sciences too; Pauli, 'Phänomen und physikalische Realität', *Dialektika* 17 (1957), 36-48.

2. For a history of the city, see S.M. Alam, *The Growth of Hyderabad City—A Historical Perspective*,(Hyderabad: Azad Oriental Research Institute, 1986); D. Prasad, *Social and Cultural Geography of Hyderabad City* (New Delhi: Inter-India Publications, 1986).

3. Jean-Baptiste Tavernier, *Travels in India*, trans. V. Ball, ed. W. Crooke (1676; Delhi: Oriental Books, 1977), 122-24.

4. S.C. Dube, *Indian Village* (New York: Harper Collophon Books, 1967), 187.

5. Francois Martin, *Memoirs of Francois Martin (1670-1694)*, trans L. Vardarajan, vol. 1, p. 2 (Delhi: Manohar, 1983), 761-62.

6. *Ibid.*

7. Tavernier,127.

8. Rama Naidu,*Old Cities, New Predicaments: A Study of Hyderabad* (Delhi: Sage 1991),15.

9. Tavernier, 140.

10. Muzaffar Alam,'Competition and Co-existence: Indo-Islamic Interaction in Medieval North India', *Itinerario* 13, no. 1(1989), 51.

11. Naidu, Chap. 5.

12. The secularist view has been articulated in a host of academic and popular publications for over 50 years. Its most sophisticated proponents are a group of historians at the Jawaharlal Nehru University in New Delhi. For an older formulation of the view, Nehru's *The Discovery of India* is still one of the

of historians at the Jawaharlal Nehru University in New Delhi. For an older formulation of the view, Nehru's *The Discovery of India* is still one of the best introductions. For a recent summary, see Amartya Sen, 'The Threats to Secular India', *New York Review of Books,* 8 April 1993, 26-32. For the viewpoints of the activists, see Mehdi Arslam and Janaki Rajan, eds., *Communalism in India: Challenge and Response* (Delhi: Manohar, 1994).

13. C.A. Bayly, 'The Pre-history of 'Communalism'? Religious Conflict in India 1700-1860', *Asian Studies* 19, no. 2 (1985), 185-85.

14. This view is most forcefully advocated by Marxist and neo-Marxist historians. See, e.g, Gyanendra Pandey, *The Colonial Construction of Communalism in North India* (Delhi: Oxford University Press, 1990).

15. For some of the more recent versions of the Hindu nationalist viewpoint see Koenraad Elst, *Ayodhya and After: Issues before Hindu society* (Delhi: Voice of India, 1991); K. D. Prithipaul, 'Reason, Law and the Limits of Indian Secularism', *International Journal of Indian Studies,* July-December 1992.

16. Marc Gaborieau, 'From Al-Beruni to Jinnah', *Anthropology Today* 1, no. 3 (1985).

17. See, e.g., Tara Chand, *Influence of Islam on Indian Culture* (Allahabad: The Indian Press, 1963). For more recent formulations see Rasheeduddin Khan, ed., *Composite Culture of India and National Integration* (Simla: IIAS, 1988). See also Gyanendra Pandey, ed., *Hindus and Others* (Delhi: Viking, 1993).

18. Bayly, *op. cit.*

19. Alam, 46. See also his, 'Assimilation from a Distance: Confrontation and a Sufi Accommodation in Awadh Society', unpublished manuscript, Centre for Historical Studies, Jawaharlal Nehru University, 1992.

20. Ibid., 51.

21. Ibid., 55.

22. Abbe J. Dubois, *Hindu Manners, Customs and Ceremonies,* ed. and trans. H.K. Beauchamp (1906; Calcutta: Rupa, 1992),48.

23. Francois Bernier, *Travels in the Mogul Empire (1656-1668)* (New Delhi: S. Chand, 1972), 33.

24. Dubois, 134.

25. Erik Erikson, *Toys and Reasons* (New York: Norton, 1977).

26. Bayly, 192-95.

27. Dubois, 341-42. The Hindus' constancy to their faith in the face of Muslim oppression or blandishments is also attested to hold true in the case of north India by Alam, 48-49.

28. Ibid., 343.

29. Raymond Grew, 'On the Prospect of Global History', unpublished manuscript for the Conference on Global History at Bellagio, Italy, July 16-21 1991.

30. Ian Austin, *City of Legends: The Story of Hyderabad* (Delhi: Viking, 1991).

Chapter 2

1. Peter Marsh, 'Rhetorics of Violence' in P. Marsh and A. Campbell, eds., *Aggression and Violence* (New York: St. Martin's Press, 1982), 102-17.
2. See Larry Byron *et al.*, 'Legitimate Violence, Violence Attitudes, and Rape: A Test of the Cultural Spillover Theory', in R Prentky and V.L. Quinsey, eds., *Human Sexual Aggression: Current Prespectives,* Annals of New York Academy of Sciences, vol. 528 (New York: New York Academy of Sciences, 1988), 80-85.
3. Erik Erikson, *Identity: Youth and Crisis* (New York: W. W. Norton, 1968).
4. See Rita R. Rogers, 'International Exchange: Transference of Attitudes down the Generations', in J. Howells, ed., *Modern Perpectives in the Psychiatry of Infancy* (New York: Brunner/Mazel, 1979), 339-49.
5. Bert N.Adams and M. Bristow,"Ugandan Asian Expulsion Experiences: Rumour and Reality," *Journal of Asian and African Studies* 14(1979),191-203.
6. Ralph L. Rosnow, "Rumour as Communication: A Contextualist Approach," *Journal of Communication* 38, no. 1 (1988), 12-28.
7. Krishna Baldev Vaid, *Guzra Hua Zamana* (Delhi: Radhakrishna, 1982). 430-36; my translation.
8. Asghar Ali Engineer, *Communal Riots in Post-Independence India* (New Delhi: Sangam Books,1985).
9. Eric Hobsbawm, *Nations and Nationalism Since 1870* (Cambridge: Cambridge University Press, 1990).
10. Ashutosh Varshney, "Contested Meanings: India's National Identity, Hindu National and the Politics of Anxiety" *Daedalus* 122, no. 3 (1993), 227-61. See also Ainslee T. Embree, *Utopias in Conflict: Religion and Nationalism in Modern India* (Berkeley and Los Angeles: University of California Press,1990).
11. Varshney, 238.
12. Howard Schuman and J. Scott, 'Generations and Collective Memories', *American Sociological Review* 54 (1989), 380.
13. Maurice Halbwachs, *On Collective Memory* (Chicago: University of Chicago Press, 1992).
14. See John C. Turner, 'Towards a Cognitive Re-definition of the Social Group', in Henri Tajfel, ed., *Social Identity and Intergroup Relations* (Cambridge: Cambridge University Press, 1982); and Tajfel, 'Social Psychology of Intergroup Relation,' in W.G. Austin and S. Worchel, eds., *Annual Review of Psychology,* vol. 33, 1982.
15. Vamik D.Volkan, 'An Overview of Psychological Concepts', in V. Volkan *et al.,* eds., *The Psychodynamics of International Relationships* (Lexington: Lexington Books, 1990), 31-46.
16. Howard Stein, 'On Professional Allegiance in the Study of Politics', *Political Psychology* 7 (1986), 248. See also John Mack, 'The enemy system' in Volkan, *The Psychodynamics of International Relationships,* 57-89. Wendy Doniger

(personal communication) illustrates this dual nature of certain objects, places, people, by citing the Israeli poet Yehuda Amichai who intervened in an argument over whether Jerusalem is a symbol or a real city inhabited by real people, with the remark that Jerusalem is a symbol—but a symbol with a sewage system.

17. Sigmund Freud, 'The Taboo of Virginity' (1918), in *The Standard Edition of the Works of Sigmund Freud* (London: Hogarth Press, 1957), 11, 191-208.

18. See Natalie Z. Davis, *Society and Culture in Early Modern France* (Cambridge: Polity Press, 1987), 152-88.

19. Ikram Ali Malik, *Hindu-Muslim Riots in the British Punjab* (1849-1900) (Lahore: Gosha-i-adab, 1974), 3-5. See also Sandra Freitag, *Communalism in North India*, (Delhi: Oxford University Press, 1990). For an account of the more recent riots, see M. J. Akbar, *Riot after Riot* (New Delhi: Penguin Books, 1988).

20. Sarah J. Moore, *Rioting in Northern India* (Ph.D. diss., University of Pennsylvania, 1976), 53.

21. Phyllis Greenacre, 'Crowds and Crisis', *The Psychoanalytical Study of the Child* 27 (1972), 147.

22. See Stephen Reicher, 'The Determination of Collective Behaviour,' in Tajfel, *Social Identity and Intergroup Relations*, 40-82.

23. Moore, 62.

24. Javed Alam, 'Riots and Recent Phase of Communal Violence in Hyderabad', *Bulletin Henry Martin Institute of Islamic Studies*, Jan-March 1994.

25. Davis shows this to be one of the implicit motivations of a crowd in the case of Catholic and Protestant violence in 16th-century France.

26. Romesh C. Majumdar et al., eds., *The History and Culture of the Indian People*, vol. 5 (Bombay: Bharatiya Vidya Bhawan, 1964), 22.

27. Volkan, 'An Overview of Psychological Concepts', 44.

28. Cited in Javed Alam, 'Tradition in India under Interpreted Stress: Integrating its Claims', *Theses Eleven*, 39, 1994.

Chapter Three

1. Dieter Beckman, E. Brahler, and H.E. Richter, *Der Giessen Test*, 4th ed. (Bern: Verlag Hans Huber, 1991).

2. Samuel J. Klausner, 'Violence', in Mircea Eliade, ed., *The Encyclopedia of Religion* 15, 268-71.

3. Joseph S. Alter, *The Wrestler's Body: Identity and Ideology in North India* (Berkeley and Los Angeles: University of California Press, 1992). Much of the information on the wrestler's physical regimen and ethical attitudes is derived from this excellent study.

4. J.S. Alter, 'The Sanyasi and the Indian Wrestler: The Anatomy of a Relationship', *American Ethnologist* 16, no. 2 (1992), 317-36.

5. Ibid., 326.
6. K.P. Singh, 'Swasth Vibhagon par Kharch Bar Raha Hai, aur Nai Nai Bimariyan bhi Bar Rahi hain', *Bhartiya Kushti* 17 (1980), 21; cited in J.S. Alter, 'The Body of One Colour: Indian Westling, the Indian State, and Utopian Somatics', *Cultural Anthropology*, no. 1 (1993), 64.
7. For an elaboration of this viewpoint, see R. Gladston, 'The Longest Pleasure: A Psychoanalytic Study of Hatred', *International Journal of Psychoanalysis* 68 (1987), 371-78.

Chapter 4

1. M.N. Srinivas, *Social Change in Modern India* (Berkeley and Los Angeles: University of California Press, 1966).
2. Napoleon Chagnon, *Yanomamo: The Fierce People* (Fort Worth: Harcourt Brace, 1983).
3. Sudhir Kakar, *The Inner World: A Psychoanalytic Study of Childhood and Society in India* (Delhi: Oxford Univesity Press, 1978), chap. 3.
4. Christopher Bollas, 'Generational Consciousness', in *Being a Character: Psychoanalysis and Self Experience* (New York: Hill and Wang, 1992).
5. For a comprehensive discussion of the theory and its problems, see Thomas F. Pettigrew, 'The Intergroup Hypothesis Reconsidered', in M. Hewston and R. Brown, eds, *Contact and Conflict in Intergroup Encounters* (Oxford: Basil Blackwell, 1986), 169-95.
6. David Lowenthal, 'The Timeless Past: Some Anglo-American Historical Preconception', *Journal of American History* 75 (1989), 1263-280.
7. Dube, 187.
8. Dubois, 218.
9. Owen Berkeley-Hill, 'Hindu-Muslim Unity', in *International Journal of Psychoanalysis* 6 (1925), 287:
10. Ibid., 287.
11. Sudhir Kakar, *Shamans, Mystics and Doctors* (New York: A. Knopf, 1982), chap. 3.
12. Robert A. LeVine and Donald T. Campbell, *Ethnocentrism: Theories of Conflict, Ethnic Attitudes and Group Behaviour* (New York: John Wiley, 1972).
13. See A. Majeed and E.S.K. Ghosh, 'A Study of Social Identity in Three Ethnic Groups in India,' *International Journal of Psychology* 17 (1982), 455-63.
14. Erik Erikson, 'Womanhood and Inner Space' in *Identity: Youth and Crisis*.
15. The relevant studies are: A. Sharma and S. Anandlakshmy, 'Prejudice in the Making: Understanding the Role of Socialization', in D. Sinha, ed., *Socialization of the Indian Child* (New Delhi: Concept, 1981), 101. A.K. Singh, 'Development of Religious Identity and Prejudice in Indian Children', in A. deSouza, ed., *Children in India* (New Delhi: Manohar, 1979), 231-44. Other studies have shown a significant correlation between the parents' prejudice

and that of children, with female children tending to be more influenced by the mother's prejudices, and the fathers of prejudiced boys being significantly more authoritarian: See M.K. Hasan, 'Child-rearing Attitudes and Some Personality Traits of the Parents of Prejudiced School Children', *Manas* 24, no. 3 (1977), 1-10, and 'Parental Influence on Children's Prejudice', *Social Change* 13, no. 2 (1983), 40-46. For an overview of similar studies from all over the world in the case of ethnic groups, see Nimmi Hutnick, *Ethnic Minority identity*, (Oxford: Clarendon Press, 1991).

16. Luce Irigaray, *Je, Tu, Nous, Pour Une Culture de la Différence* (Paris: Biblio-Poche, 1994).

Chapter Five

1. Anees, Jung, *Night of the New Moon: Encounters with Muslim Women in India* (Delhi: Penguin, 1993), 59.

2. Rollo May, *Power and Inocence* (New York: Dell, 1972), 29.

3. Bernard Lewis, *The Political Language of Islam* (Chicago: University of Chicago Press, 1988), 4.

4. R.D. Meade and L. Singh, 'Changes in Social Distance during Warfare: A Study of India/Pakistan war of 1971', *Journal of Social Psychology* 90, no. 2 (1973), 325-26.

5. For an interesting description of the behaviour of various kinds of victims, see R.A. Ball, 'The Victimological Cycle', *Victimology* 1, no. 3 (1976), 379-95.

6. Mushirul Hasan, 'Minority Identity and Its Discontents: Responses and Representations', paper read at International Congress of Asian Studies, Hong Kong, August, 1993.

7. Akbar S. Ahmed, *Discovering Islam* (New York: Vistaar Publications, 1990), 158-60. See also Imtiaz Ahmed, ed., *Modernization and Social Change among Muslims* (Delhi: Manoha, 1983).

8. Gilani Bano, *Aiwan-e-ghazal* (Hyderabad, 1976).

9. See R.A. Shweder, M. Mahapatra and J.G. Miller, 'Culture and Moral Development', in J. Kagan and S. Lamb, eds., *The Emergence of Moral Concepts in Early Childhood* (Chicago: University of Chicago Press, 1987); R.A. Shweder, 'Beyond Self-constructed Knowledge: The Study of Culture and Morality', in *Merril-Palmer Quarterly* 28 (1982), 41-69; R.A. Shweder and N.C. Much, 'Determinants of Meaning: Discourse and Moral Socialization', in R.A. Shweder, *Thinking through Cultures* (Cambridge, Mass.: Harvard University Press, 1991).

10. R. Dworkin, *Taking Rights Seriously* (Cambridge, Mass.: Harvard University Press, 1991).

11. E. Fromm, *Psychoanalysis and Religious* (New Haven, Conn.: Yale University Press, 1950); G. Obeyesekere, *Medusa's Hair* (Chicago: University of Chicago Press, 1981).

12. Kakar, *The Inner World*, 37.
13. A.K. Ramanujan, 'Is There an Indian Way of Thinking?' in M. Marriott, ed., *Indian through Hindu Categories* (Delhi: Sage Publications, 1990).
14. For an elaboration on the uses of empathy see Rafael Moses, 'Empathy and Disempathy in the Political Process', *Political Psychology* 5 (1985), 135-40.

Chapter 6

1. Kakar, *The Inner World*.
2. Anthony Smith, *The Ethnic Origins of Nations* (Oxford: Basil Blackwell, 1986).
3. For a similarity in the Islamic world, see Bassam Tibi, *The Crisis of Modern Islam* (Salt Lake City: Utah University Press, 1988).
4. For brief biographies of the first and second RSS 'supremos', see Walter V. Andresen and S. Damle, *The Brotherhood in Saffron* (Delhi: Vistaar Publications, 1987).
5. The social-psychological effects of modernization have been discussed in E. James Anthony and C. Chiland, eds., *The Child in His Family: Children and Their Parents in a Changing World* (New York: John Wiley, 1978).
6. Quoted from a *sangh parivar* journal in an article, 'Women of Saffron', in *The Times of India*, February 1993.
7. See Tu Wei-Ming, 'Beyond the Enlightenment Mentality', unpublished paper given at the Second International Conference of Global History at Technical University, Darmstadt, Germany (July 1992), 4.
8. Erik H. Erikson, *Insight and Responsibility* (New York: W.W. Norton, 1964).
9. Sigmund Freud, 'Group Psychology and the Analysis of the Ego' (1921), *Standard Edition*, vol. 18.
10. Ernest Wolf, *Treating the Self* (New York: Guilford Press, 1988), 48.
11. Asghar Ali Engineer, ed., *Communal Riots in Post-Independence India*, (New Delhi: Sangam Books, 1985), 238-71.
12. Paul Brass, *Ethnicity and Nationalism* (New Delhi: Sage Publications, 1991), 15.
13. See Peter Homans, *The Ability to Mourn* (Chicago: University of Chicago Press, 1991), 309.
14. The clearest description of the concept of complementarity is by Klaus Meyer-Habich; see his 'Komplementariat', in J. Ritter and K. Gruender, eds. *Historiches Worterbuch der Philosophie* (Basel: Schwaber, 1967), 4, 933-34.
15. Don Miller, *The Reason of Metaphor* (Delhi: Sage Publications, 1991), 169.
16. For Rithambra's biographical details, see 'Virtuous Virago', *The Times of India*, 19 July 1991 and 'Hindutva by the Blood of Her Words', *The Daily*, 9 June 1991.
17. On the poetic function of rhetoric, see John Shotter, 'The Social construction of Remembering and Forgetting', in D. Middleton and D. Edwards, eds., *Collective Remembering* (London: Sage, 1990), 124.

18. Homans, 277.
19. Rafael Moses, 'The Group Self and the Arab-Israeli Conflict', *International Review of Psychoanalysis* 9 (1982), 56.
20. Sudhir Kakar, *Shamans, Mystics and Doctors* (New York: A. Knopf, 1982), chap. 3.
21. Moses, 'The Group Self', 63.
22. Emile Durkheim, *The Elementary Forms of Religious Life* (1912) (New York: Free Press, 1965).

Chapter Seven

1. See Martin E. Marty and R. Scott Appleby, eds., *Fundamentalisms and the State*, vol. 3 of The Fundamentalism Project (Chicago: University of Chicago Press, 1993), 3. For a review of scholarly discussion of and unhappiness with such terms as 'fundamentalism' and 'revivalism', see Sadik J. Al-Azm, 'Islamic Fundamentalism Reconsidered: A Critical Outline of Problems, Ideas and Approaches, Part 1', *South Asia Bulletin* 12 (1993), 93-121.
2. M.S. Agwani, *Islamic Fundamentalism in India* (Chandigarh: Twenty-first Century India Society, 1986). See also M. Ahmad, 'Islamic Fundamentalism in South Asia: The Jamaat-i-Islami and the Tablighi Jamaat', in M. Marty and R. Scott Appleby, eds., *Fundamentalism Observed* (Chicago: University of Chicago Press, 1991), 457-530.
3. For a discussion of a community or a nation's inability to mourn—in this case Germany after the Second World War—see A. Mitscherlich and M. Mitscherlich, *Die Unfähigkeit zu Trauern* (Munich: Piper Verlag, 1968). See also V. Volkan, *The Need to Have Enemies and Allies: From Clinical Practice to International Relationships* (Northvale, N.J.: Jason Aronson, 1988).
4. For a psychopathological treatment of fanaticism, see A. Haynal, ed., *Fanaticism: A Historical and Psychoanalytical Study* (NewYork: Schocken Booms, 1983).
5. Lewis, *The Political Language of Islam*, 7.
6. Marty and Appleby, *Fundamentalisms and the State*, 631.
7. Meira Likierman, 'The Function of Anger in Human Conflict', *International Review of Psychoanalysis* 14, no. 2 (1987): 143-62.
8. For a fuller discussion of competition between ethnic groups, see V.D. Volkan, D.A. Julius, and J.V. Montville, *The Psychodynamics of International Relationships* (Lexington, Ky.: Lexington Books, 1990).

Chapter Eight

1. Andrew Samuels, *The Political Psyche* (London: Routledge, Kegan and Paul, 1993), 11-12.
2. See Phillipe Wolff, 'The 1391 Pogrom in Spain: Social Crisis or Not?' *Past*

and Present 50 (1971), 4-18; George Rude, *The Crowd in History: A Study of Popular Disturbances in France and England, 1848* (New York: 1964); Janine Estebe, *Tocsin pour un massacre* (Paris, 1968). For the 'clash of economic interests' theory of religious-ethnic conflicts in South Asia see Veena Das (ed.) *Mirrors of Violence* (Delhi: Oxford University Press, 1990).

3. Michael Walzer, 'Nations and Minorities', in C. Freud, ed. *Minorities: Community and Identity* (Berlin: Springer Verlag, 1982), 219-27.

4. The leading proponent of the theory that the international environment, especially the ending of colonial rule, is responsible for ethnic conflict is D. Horowitz; see his *Ethnic Groups in Conflict* (Berkeley and Los Angeles: University of California Press, 1985).

5. Sigmund Freud, 'Group Psychology and the Analysis of the Ego' (1921), *Standard Edition*, vol. 18.

6. Erikson, *Identity: Youth and Crisis*, 46. See also Janine Puget, 'The Social Context: Searching for a Hypothesis', *Free Associations* 2, no. 1 (1991).

7. Davis, 156-60.

8. D.W. Winnicott, 'Communicating and Not Communicating Leading to a Study of Certain Opposites,' in his *The Maturational Process and the Facilitating Environment* (New York: International Universities Press, 1963), 187. For a succinct discussion of contemporary psychoanalytic thinking on self and relatedness, see Alice R. Soref, 'The Self, in and out of Relatedness', *The Annual of Psychoanalysis*, vol. 20 (1992), 25-48.

9. Oscar Patterson, 'The Nature, Causes and Implications of Ethnic Identification', in Fried, 25-50.

10. David Rapoport, 'Comparing Militant Fundamentalist Movements', in Marty and Appleby, *Fundamentalism Observed, op. cit.*, 443.

11. Sigmund Freud 'New Introductory Lectures' (1993), *Standard Edition* 22, 104.

12. See Heinrich von Stietencorn, 'Angst und Gewalt: Ihre Funktionen und ihre Bewältigung in den Religionen', in Stietencorn Ihrg.) *Angst und Gewalt: Ihre Praesenz und Ihre bewaltigung in den Religionen* (Dusseldorf: Patmos Verlag, 1979), 311-37.

13. John W. Bowker, 'The Burning Fuse: The Unacceptable Face of Religion', *Zygon* 21, no. 4 (1986), 415-38; see also Elise Boulding, 'Two Cultures of Religion as Obstacles to Peace', *Zygon* 21, no. 4 (1986), 501-18.

14. Rapoport, *op. cit.*

15. Davis, 165.

16. Hans Bertram, 'Germany—One Country with Two Youth Generations?' paper presented at the Seminar on Childhood and Adolescence, Goethe Institut, Colombo, Sri Lanka, 17-21 February 1994.

17. Cited in Kanan Makiya, 'From Cruelty to Toleration', unpublished paper read at the conference on *Religion and Politics Today*, organized by the Rajiv Gandhi Foundation, New Delhi, January 30-February 2 1994.

A NOTE FROM THE AUTHOR

In retrospect, *Intimate Relations* is a natural successor to the earlier one, *Tales of Love, Sex and Danger*. In the latter, while interpreting the legend of Radha and Krishna, I had fleetingly explored aspects of ancient and medieval Indian sexuality. Its playfulness and gravity was in sharp contrast to contemporary guilt and the shame-ridden relations between the sexes. What I tried to do in this book was to explore the contents and form of modern Indian sexual imagination as they were revealed through different kinds of collective mirrors, such as popular Hindi cinema.

The Analyst and the Mystic has its origins in the Haskell Lectures delivered at the Divinity School of the University of Chicago in the spring of 1990. In this slim volume, I return to some of the themes of another earlier work, *Shamans, Mystics and Doctors*. The new book incorporates much of what I had learnt and reflected upon in one of my areas of abiding interest—the psychology of religion.

The Colours of Violence, which takes up the theme of group identities, was perhaps the most difficult to write. Communal violence, unlike sexual love or mystical exaltations, does not allow the writer vicarious satisfaction unless, of course, he or she has highly developed sadistic impulses—which I do not. Here, the satisfaction came more from the hope of contributing a psychological perspective to one of our most important social problems. They also came from the challenge of the writing—how to maintain the psychoanalytical distance from and ironic stance on a subject which arouses so much passion.

INDEX

INTIMATE RELATIONS

Aesthetic experiences, 6-7
Ahimsa (nonviolence), 82-83
   woman as, 107-108
Alcohol, 77. *See also* Liquor
Analyst, Indian, 73. *See also* Freud,
   Psychoanalysis
Anthropology, cultural, 7
Aphrodisiac, 70. *See also* Sex charms
Ardhanari, 120
Aristotle
   on desire, 25
Augustine, St, 84, 86
Autobiography, 8
   M. K. Gandhi, 11

Balzac, Honore, 8
Barrenness, 67-68
Battle of the sexes, 14, 15, 16
Bedi, Rajinder Singh, 12
Bettelheim, Bruno, 51
Bose, Girindrasekhar, 110-112
Brahmacharya, 80, 82, 84, 90-91
   See also Celibacy, Marriage
Brother-in-law, 15, 16-17

'Castration anxiety', 50
Castration complex, 110-111, 118
Celibacy, 79, 80-81, 82-86, 88, 90, 92, 102-
   103, 106, 117
   and fasting, 84
   and food nexus, 84
   and psychic power, Gandhi on, 84
   Freud on, 105
   in women, 96, 97
   tantrik style, 104-105
Childrearing
   and flexible ego, 26
Cinema. *See also* Films
   and rape, 31-32
   and the Krishna-lover, 33
   as culture-shaper, 24-25
   audience as author, 26-27

fantasy in, 24-28
'hits', 27
prototypical love story, 28
Collective fantasy, 7
Collective meanings, 5
Collective unconscious, 25
Conception
   approved days for, 21
Cross-sexual identifications, 110-112, 113-
   114. *See also Ardhanari*
Culture, Indian. *See also* Proverbs
   its view of women, 19, 56-57
   popular mass, 54
Culture shock, 79

Desexualization, 122-123
Desire
   Aristotle on, 25
   as per the film-maker, 28
   dark face of, 121
   through liquor, 65
Dharma (faith), 63, 66
Dickens, Charles, 8
Didactic analysis, 8
Dramatization, 13
Drives, psychological, 9

Egnor, Margaret, 6, 14
Ego, 38
   Flexible Indian ego, 26
   Freudian ego in the folktale, 44
Ek Chadar Maili Si, 12, 16, 17
Erikson, Erik, 9, 109, 119
Euphemisms (sexual), 21, 68
Experiments with Truth (Gandhi) 73, 85-86

Fantasies, 5, 6, 7-8. *See also* Folktales in
   cinema, 26-27
Film. *See also* Cinema
   as daydream, 27
   as fairytale, 23, 28
   audience as creator, 30

visual landscape of, 27
Films, Hindi, 7, 24-37. *See also* Cinema
Folktales, 7, 10, 50. *See also Kissa Tota Myna,*
   38-46; *Matankamarajan Katai,* 45-49;
   Cinema, Film, Narrative, Story
   psychological function of, 38
Freud, 30, 44, 49, 86, 110-112. *See also* Jung
   Freudian mother, 44
   Indian preference for, 101
   'Object-choice', 71
Freudian theory, 9, 10, 17-18

Gandhi, Kasturbai, 74, 75, 79, 80, 91
Gandhi, M.K., 11,114
   and food, 109
   and the prostitute, 85-86
   and wet dreams, 90
   and woman, 73, 109
   as psychoanalyst, 95
   on birth-control, 91
   on mother-love, 108
   on politics and religion, 94
Gender
   boundaries, 114
   conflict, Gandhi's solution, 107
   intimacy, 23
   relations, 7-8, 67, 120, 121
   relations of Indian lower-class, 56-72. *See
   also Jodi, Pativrata,*
   marriage rivalry, 14
   superiority, 14
Ghazal, 33
Goddess, 'possession' by, 69
Goldman, Robert, 7, 45
Greenson, Ralph, 98

Heterosexual love, 37, 43. *See also* Gender
   relation, Love, Marriage
Hierarchical classification, 24
Horney, Karen, 114
Husbands, 5, 56
   serpents as, 45-46

Ichhadhari cobra, 52-61
   Nagina (film) 52-55
Incestuous tensions, 16
Indian Psychoanalytical Society, 110. *See also*
   Freud, Jung, Psychoanalysis
Infatuation, 41, 43, 46
Infidelity, 19. *see also Jodi,* Proverbs
Interpretation, 9
Intimacy

father-daughter, 32
Jealousy, 70-71, 75, 79. *See also* Battle of
   the sexes, Gender conflict
Jodi (the pair), 70-72, 144. *See also*
   Marriage, Two-person universe
Jung. *See also* Psychoanalysis
   Indian indifference to, 101
   pairing instinct, 71

Kamasutra, 21, 103
Kantak, Prema, 90, 94-97
Kapoor, Raj, 28
Karma, 62-63
Karz, 32
Kernberg, Otto, 9
*Kissa Tota Myna (The Story of the Parrot
   and the Starling),* 38-45. *See also*
   Folktales
Klein, Melanie, 9
Kleinian mother, 44
Kohut, Heinz, 9, 72, 119

Lacan, Jacques, 10
Levirate. *See Niyoga*
Liquor, 65, 67, 78. *See also* Alcohol
Literary criticism, 10
Long, Janis, 119
Love, 31, 98-100. *See also* Jealousy,
   Tenderness
   heterosexual, 46, 70
   potion, 37, 43
Lover, 5, 17, 24, 32-33, 42, 70
   Bachchan hero, 34, 36
   Karna, good-bad hero, 34-36
   Krishna-lover, 33-34, 36
   Majnun-lover, 33, 36-37
   Oedipal, 19
   Serpents as, 45-46
Lust
   Gandhi on, 86-87

Macho, 12. *See also* Battle of the sexes,
   Misogyny, Mother-son dyad
Mahabharata, 34, 46, 57
Mahler, Margaret, 9
Maila Anchal, 8
Manu, 19. *See also* Gandhi
   Laws of, 19-20
Marriage, 12-23. *See also* Celibacy,
   Jodi, Pativrata
   consensual, 58, 72
   souten, 50

Masochism, 31
Matankamarajan katai (The Story of King Matanakama), 46-49. *See also* Folktales
Maternal-feminine, 111-113. *See also* Mother
McDougall, Joyce, 37
Mira. *See* Slade, Madeline
Misogyny, 19. *See also* Proverbs, Wife-beating
Mitro Marjani, 16-18
Models, psychological, 9-10
Moksha, 79, 102
Mother
   Kleinian, 44
   -in-law, 68
Mother-son dyad, 74. *See also* Maternal-feminine
Mother-whore dichotomy, 16, 18
Movies. *See* Cinema, Films
Myths, Indian, 6, 7, 115-118. *See also* Folktales
   Tamil, 14

Nagina (film), 52-55
Naipaul, V.S., 77
Narrative, 5-8 *See also* Folktales, Story
   form, 10, 11
   form as mirror of reality, 7
   popular Indian, 38
Narratives, stock, 73
Necrophilia, 112, 114
Niyoga, 12, 13, 15
Novels, modern Indian, 8
Nudity. *See* Euphemisms

Oates, Joyce Carol, 10
Oedipal aspects, 44, 45, 50, 54, 110, 111, 116, 118. *See also* Mother-son dyad, Unfaithful mother
O'Flaherty, Wendy, 32, 103
Oneiros (the dream), 5, 37
'Oral' fears, 45
Organizing perception, 7

Passion
   as distortion, 84-86
   (sexual) as evil, 76-77
Pativrata (good woman), 57-58, 120
   See also Ardhanari, Marriage
Physical violence
   in gender relation, 58. *See also* Wife-beating

Plays, 7
Polak, Millie, 108
Post-Freudian theory, 9
Proverbs, 14, 20, 41, 44
Psyche, 28
Psychoanalysis, 5, 6-9, 21, 32, 49
   in India, 11-112
Psychoanalyst, 7, 8, 10
Psychoanalytic
   concept of sexuality, 21
   deconstruction, 73
   perspective, 8, 10
   theory of symbolism, 49-50
Psychosexuality
   in Indian marrige, 22
Psychotherapy
   of low-caste women, 22
Puranas, 20
   Brahma Purana, 21
   Vishnu Purana, 21

Ram Teri Ganga Maili (Ram, Your Ganga is Polluted), 28-32. *See also* Cinema
Ramayana, 15, 57, 87
Rape
   in films, 123
Regression, 26
Renu, Phanishwarnath, 8
Romance, 23, 70-71. *See also* Ardhanari
   Love, *Jodi,* Marriage
   absence of, 13
Ruskin, John, 79

Sacks, Oliver, 6
Self-immolation, 65. *See also* Suicide
Self-object, 72, 119
Serpent
   as lovers and spouses of humans, 45-46, 52
   as symbol, 50
   boy reborn as a snake, 39-42
   Ichhadhari cobra, 52-53
   Nagina (film), 52-55
Sex charms and spells, 15, 16. *See also* Aphrodisiac, Romance
Sex wars, 38. *See also* Battle of the Sexes
Sexual
   awakening, 122-123
   humiliation, 31
   intercourse, 20-23
   misery, 22
   mother, 122

404

politics, Indian, 5
taboos, 21
temptation, 78
Shweder, Richard, 5
Skura, Meredith Anne, 10
Slade, Madeline, 97-101
Smoking
  woman and, 67
Smritis (Law Codes), 20
Snake. See Serpent
Sobti, Krishna, 16
Son-in-law, 17
Souten (co-wife), 50. See also
  Marriage
Spence, Donald, 113
Stekel, Wilhelm, 49
Stendhal, 8
Stoller, Robert
  on fantasy, 25-26
Story, importance of, 5-8. See also Folktales,
  Narrative
Sublimation 80, 81, 88, 105-106. See also
  Love, Mother-son dyad, Passion
  Hindu theory of, 101
Suicide, 72. See also Self-immolatoion
'Superego'. See also Ego, Freud
  ideology of, 58

Tantra
  and Gandhi, 104
Tantrik, 53
Tenderness, 13. See also Love
Thematic

significance, 8
  unity, 8-9
Third ear, 30
Traditional roles, erosion of, 35
Transference (in psychoanalysis), 8
Tolstoy, Leo, 18, 81, 87
Two-person universe, 23. See also Jodi

'Ultimate' reality, 6. See also Narrative
Unfaithful mother, 122. See also Mother-son
  dyad, Oedipal

Vaishnavism, 108
Vatsayana, 21
Vedas, 15

Wife-beating, 12-13, 14, 16, 61, 68, 70.
  See also Jealousy, Marriage
Wife, serpent, 51-55
'Wild man', 13
Winnicott, Donald, 9, 22, 109
Wolfenstein and Leites, 36
Woman. See also Battle of the sexes,
  Mother, Pativrata, Proverbs
  and drinking, 65, 67
  as nymphomaniac, 44
  as seducer, 65
  essential impurity of, 20
  goodness of, 57
  purity of, in cinema, 28
  unfaithfulness of, 38

Zvelebil, Kamil, 46

THE ANALYST AND THE MYSTIC

Aberbach, David, 151
Adequatio (adequateness) principal 133-134
Affect, 147
Alexander, Franz, 178
Anxiety, 151-152. *See also* Nightmares, Separation
Arlow, Jacob, 180
Arya Samaj, 163

Babb, Lawrence, 172
Bady, Susan, 174
Basava, 168
Bernard of Clairvaux, 155
Bettelheim, Bruno, 179
Bhakti, 133, 161-162
Bhava (feeling, mood), 144, 145, 146
Bion, Wilfred, 134, 146, 153, 154, 185, 188
Bollas, Christopher, 170-171
Brahmani, Bhairavi, 141, 147
Buber, Martin, 131, 151
Buddhism, 135, 155, 178, 179
  See also Mystics, Religion

Celibacy and mystical ecstasy, 155, 156. *See also* Hallucinations, Sexuality
Chandra, 136, 137, 141. *See also* Ramakrishna
Christianity, 132, 151, 155-56, 157, 169, 184
  See also Religion, Mysticism, Visions
'Consciousness',
  altered, 133, 134
  cosmic, 132
  expanding, 132
  object of, 132. *See also* Self-realization
Creative experiencing, 134, 146, 154
  See also Bhava
Creativity, 181. *See also* Self-realization

Dabu, 172
'Darshan', 145, 186. *See also* Guru-disciple
'De-differentiation', 131, 133
Deikman, Arthur, 131
Depression, 151, 152, 175, 176, 178. *See also* Self-realization
Devi, Nirmala, 167

Ecstatic Visions, 148. *See also* Hallucinations, Nightmares, Visions
Ego psychology, 180

Ehrenzweig, Anton, 133
Eigen, Michael, 153
Einstein, Albert, 154
Erikson, Erik, 134, 154, 178, 180, 185

Fana 132, 169. *See also* Sufi
Fantasy, 187. *See also* Hallucinations
Feminine, Eternal, 181. *See also* Mother Goddess
Ferenzci, Sandor, 167
Freud, Sigmund, 133, 134, 150, 171, 172, 173, 174, 175, 177, 179
  on art, 173
  on healing, 161, 176
  on mystical motivation, 147
  on mystics, 170
  on occult, 134
  on psychical research, 174
  on Ramakrishna, 134
  on religion, 134-135, 170, 174, 175, 177, 179
  use of metaphor and analogy, 177
  works of: *Civilization and its Discontents*, 134;
  Moses and Monotheism, 182;
  'Obsessive Actions and Religious Practices', 170-171;
  The Future of an Illusion, 134-135, 170, 175
Fromm, Erich, 179

Greeley, Andrew, 131
Greenacre, Phyllis, 174
Gupta, Mahendranath, 135-136, 163
Guru-disciple relationship, 161-172, 174-176, 182. *See also* Hindu guru, Separation

Hallucinations, 146, 147, 148. *See also* Fantasy Peak experience, Self-realization, Visions
Harrison, I., 182
Hartmann, Ernst, 148
Health, mental, 132
Hindu
  guru, 160, 161, 162-166, 167
  metaphysics, 142, 143
  mysticism, 131-132, 133, 135, 140
  tradition, 161, 162, 163

Hinduism, devotional, 132, 172. *See also* Ramakrishna
Homans, Peter, 182
Horney, Karen, 179
Horton, Paul, 151
Huxley, Aldous, 136

Iconoclasm, 179-180
Infant-mother dyad, 185. *See also* Separation
'Infinite' mysticism, 131
Islam, 132, 135

James, William, 131, 169
   works of: *The Varieties of Religious experience*, 169
Jayakar, Pupul, 160, 163-164, 172
Jnaneshwara, 162, 171, 172
John of the Cross, 131, 134, 151
Jones, Ernst, 181
Judaism, 132, 179
Jung, Carl, 178-179

Kabir, 161
Kali, 138, 140, 141. *See also* Mother Goddess
Kaplan, Abraham, 180
Khudiram, 137, 138, 139. *See also* Ramakrishna
Klein, Melanie, 151, 185
Kohut, Heinz, 166, 167, 171, 185, 186
Krishna, 16. *See also* Hinduism
Krishnamurti, J., 160, 163, 164, 172

Lacan, Jacques, 134, 152, 153, 154
Leuba, James, 154

'M' *See also* Gupta, Mahendranath
Mahabhava, 132. *See also* Mystical experience
Mahler, Margaret, 152, 185
Mann, Thomas, 140, 187
   works of: *The Transposed Heads*, 140
Maslow, Abram, 132
Masson, J., 178
Master-disciple relationship, 160, 161, 173, 183
Mesmer, Franz Anton, 183
Metaphor, 187
Moeller, Michael, 175
Mother, Great, 185
Mother-child interaction, 152. *See also* Ramakrishna, Separation

Mother Goddess, 139, 140, 141, 142, 148, 149, 151. *See also* Feminine, Eternal
Muktananda, 171, 173, 175
Mystical
   cults, 131, 133, 149, 151
   ecstacy, 146. *See also* 'Oceanic feeling'
   experience, 131, 132, 133
   and creativity, 154
   illusions, 149
   insight, 133
   literature, 140
   motivation, 150, 151
   phenomena, 134
   retreat, ·133
   tradition, 131. *See also* Religion
   trance, 133
Mysticism
   affective, 144, 153, 155
   Christian, 151
   cultivated, 131
   devotional, 132, 140-141, 151
   ecstatic, 131, 134, 151, 152
   emotional, 154
   extreme, 131. *See also* 'Oceanic feeling'
   monistic, 131
   of nature, 131
   of personal life, 131
   on the infinite, 131
   soul, 131
   sporadic, 131
   Tantrik, 152
   theistic, 131
Mystics,
   Buddhist, 135, 179
   Christian, 135, 151, 155, 157, 179
   Hindu, 132, 135, 141, 142, 146, 156
   Islamic, 135
   Judaic, 179
   Taoist, 179
Mythology, 187

Nacht, Sacha, 167
Narcissism, 178, 179. *See also* Self-realization
Near-death experiences, 140
Neurotic, 179
Nightmares, 148. *See also* Regression

'Oceanic feeling', 177-178. *See also* Freud, Sigmund, Hallucinations, Ramakrishna
Oedipal father, 151, 187

Parent-child relationship,· 51, 167, 168, 173,

175. *See also* Guru-disciple relationship, Separation
Paz, Octavio, 150
'Peak experience', 131, 132. *See also* Consciousness, Cosmic, Hallucinations
Pfister, Oskar, 177, 181
Preoedipal influences, 181
Psychical research, 182, 183
Psychoanalysis, contemporary, 133
   history of, 180, 182
   and mysticism, 133, 150, 151
   and religion, 177
Puranas, 138, 162. *See also* Hinduism

Radhasoami sect, 168
Rajneesh Bhagwan, 168
Rama, 141, 142. *See also* Hinduism
Ramakrishna, 131-142
   as guru-healer, 163, 169, 170, 175
   attitude to women, 136, 137
   Bhava of, 143-145
   devotional mysticism, 143-148
   early life, 136-138
   ecstatic experience, 137, 139, 140, 141, 142, 144, 148
   femininity of, 138, 141, 157
   initial trances, 133
   mystical visions of, 139, 140, 142, 144, 145, 146, 147, 148, 149, 150
   sexual curiosity of, 136, 137
   sexuality of, 157, 158
   unmada of, 141
   visionary experience of, 145, 146, 147, 148, 149, 150
   yearning of, 150
Ramakrishna Mission, 163
Ramana Maharishi, 134
Ramkumar, 138, 139. *See also* Ramakrishna
Regression, 133, 173, 174, 176, 178
   See also Self-realization
Reich, Wilhelm, 178
Relational theories, 185
Religion, 131, 132, 133, 179
   See also Buddhism, Christianity, Hinduism, Mystics
Rituals, 180, 187
Ricouer, Paul, 178
Rolland, Romain, 133, 135, 136, 141, 182

Sacks, Oliver, 188
Samadhi, 132, 141, 142, 150. *See also* Hinduism, Ramakrishna

Saraswati, Swami Satyanand, 168, 169
satori, 132
Schizophrenia, 133
Self-object experience, 166, 168, 169-173, 175, 185
Self-psychology, 166, 167, 169, 170, 171
Self-realization, 179. *See also* Consciousness, expanding, Creativity, Hallucinations, Narcissism
Separation, 152. *See also* Infant-mother dyad, Mother-child interaction, Parent-child relationship
Sexuality and mystical experience, 155-159. *See also* Celibacy
Shankara, 161
Seigler, Ava, 187
Shakta mysticism, 141, 142. *See also* Mystics
Singh, Maharaj Charan, 168
Soderblom, Nathan, 131
Steiner, George, 184
Stoller, Robert, 157
Sufis, 132, 169

Tantra, 141, 147, 156, 160, 161, 178, 183. *See also* Mysticism
Teresa of Avila, 134, 151
Theology, dogmatic, 132. *See also* Christianity, Religion
Trances, 132
   ecstatic 133
   possession 134. *See also* Mysticism, Ramakrishna
Transsexual, secondary, 157. *See also* Ramakrishna

Underhill, Evelyn, 154
unmada (insanity), 141. *See also* Ramakrishna
Upanishads, 132, 135, 161, 163. *See also* Hinduism

Vairagya, 143
Vaishnava, 141, 144, 155. *See also* Mystics
Vedas, 160, 161. *See also* Hinduism
Virsaiva sect, 168
Vedanta, 141, 142
Vishnu, 141. *See also* Hinduism
Visions, 132, 146, 147, 148
   conscious, 147, 148. *See also* Hallucinations, Mystical illusions
   unconscious, 149, 150, 151

Waking consciousness, 131
Weber, Max, 182
Winnicott, Donald, 134, 154, 158, 167, 185
Wolf, Ernst, 167

Yoga, 132, 142. *See also* Mysticism

Zen, 132. *See also* Mystics
Zilboorg, Gregory, 181

Abdulla, Qutub Shah, 199
Advani, L.K., 236, 238
Agwani, M.S., 345
Akbar, 207, 336, 337
akhara, 247, 260, 261, 267, 268, 269. Also taleemkhana
Al Aqsa mosque, 236
Alam, Muzaffar, 208
Al-Beruni, 207
Ali, Brigadier Usman, 354
Alter, Joseph, 266, 267
Anarkali, 219
'Andalus syndrome', the, 309, 345
Arabic, 288
Arabs, 200, 202, 289, 306
Arendt, Hannah, 270
Arya Samaj, the, 332
Asaf Jah, 199, 200
assimilation, 367-368
Aurangzeb, 202, 209
Azad, Maulana Abul Kalam, 259
Azmi, Ubedullah Khan, 350-351, 367

Babar, 330, 335
Babri Masjid, demolition of, 230, 238, 263, 302
Badr, battle of, 304, 347
Bahadur Shah Zafar, 348
Bakr-Id, 294
Banda Bairagi, 260, 332
Bano, Gilani, 309
Bawan Sawadasi, 232
Berkeley-Hill, Owen, 291, 292
Bernier, Francois, 210
Bhagmati 198, 214, 310. Also Hyder Mahal
Bhagnagar, 198, 199. See Hyderabad
Bhagyanagar, 332, 339. Also Bhagnagar
Bharatiya Janta Party, the, 228, 236-237, 238-239, 256, 264, 328
Bhils, the, 273
Birbal, 336-337
Bollas, Christopher, 278
Boral, 279
Bose, Subhash Chandra, 260
boundaries, of a group, 331, 332, 334, 341, 342, 366
Bowker, John, 365
Brahmins, 200, 212, 217, 237, 260, 274, 288

British Empire, the, 259, 360
Bukhari, Abdullah, 335

Campbell, Donald, 293
caste system, the, 250
celibacy, and the Indian wrestler, 267
Cagnon, Napoleon, 275
chaku-bazi, 257
Char Minar, 199, 271, 274
Chintamani Pehlwan, 268
'chosen trauma', 238
collective belonging, 228
collective identity, 213, 225, 353, 358, 360
collective memory, 229, 333, 367
collective narcissism, 212. Also group narcissism
collective self-idealization, loss of, 308, 345
collective self-recrimination, 349
collective shame, 215
Colonialism, 206, 323, 328-329
Communalism, 206, 208, 259, 363
Complementarity, 328, 330
'composite culture', 208
conflict, and the role of religion, 364-365
Congress Party, the, 248, 264
countertransference, 198
cow, violence towards the, 232-233, 291, 297, 314
cow slaughter, movements against, 291
'creative formalization', 211
'cryptofascist', 208
cultural identity, 230, 233, 320, 323, 324, 326-327, 328, 338, 342, 344, 353, 359, 364, 366, 367, 368
cultural memory, 209, 215, 221, 238, 274, 344
cultural plurality, 323, 360
cultural psychologists, 210
cultural psychology, 205
cultures, resacralization of, 359

dangal, 267
Davis, Natalie, 236, 366
Dayanand Saraswati, Swami, 332
dehumanization, 318, 323, 364
Deoband, 345
Deoras, Balasaheb, 352
depersonalization, 231, 364

depressive tendencies, 254, 265, 266
de-Sanskritization, 274
divide and rule, policy of, 206, 329
Diwali, 279, 294
Dube, S.C., 200, 288
Dubois, Abbé, 210-211, 212, 290
Durkheim, Emile, 344
Dussehra, 234, 273, 279, 294

East India Company, the, 201
Effendi, Riyaz, 346
egalitarianism, in wrestling, 268
empathy, 196-197, 318
Engineer, Asghar Ali, 326
Erikson, Erik, 211, 221, 295, 324, 361
ethinic conflict, 289-290, 298
ethnic identity, 324
ethnicity, 325-326; as defining national identity, 228
ethnocentrism, 293, 327

'false consciousness', 302
fantasy, culture of, 327, 341, 366
Freud, S., 232, 234, 291, 292, 325, 360

Gaborieau, Marc, 206
Gandhi, Indira, 351, 352, 355
Gandhi, M.K., 216, 259, 260, 287, 291, 292, 338, 351, 352, 355
Gandhi, Rajiv, 339, 351
Ganesh Chaturthi, 234, 236, 279, 288
'generational consciousness', a, 278
Gentiles, 210
Giessen Test, the, 245, 253, 265
globalization, and effect on group solidarities, 322
Gobind Singh, Guru, 332
Golconda, 199, 214, 215, 310
Godse, Nathuram, 351, 352
Golwalkar, Guru, 321
grew, Raymond, 213
group cohesion, 336, 340, 342
group identities, 205, 324-326, 330, 359-363, 364, 366
guilt, inculcation of, 350
Gujaratis, 299
Gul Mohammad, 219-220

Halbwachs, Maurice, 229
Hamid, Abdul, 352, 355
Hanuman, Guru, 260
Hasan, Mushirul, 209

Hashmi, Syed Mohammad, 346
Hedgewar, K.B., 321
Hindu identity, 328-342, 343
Hindu-Muslim relations, according to European travellers, 210; according to Hindu nationalists, 206-208 209, 211-214, 215; according to secularists, 205-208, 209
Hindu nationalism, 329. Also Hindu fundamentalism
Hindu nationalists, 205, 206, 207, 208, 211-213, 214-215, 227, 228, 306, 353, 356, 357, 367, 368
Hindu revivalism, 206, 291, 330, 347
Hindu revivalists, 205, 229
Hindutva, 228, 237, 288, 321, 329, 342, 368
'Hinduwani' practices, 209
historical enmity, transmission of, 221
historical memory, 287
Hitler, Adolf, 260
Holi, 273, 279, 294, 340
Homans, Peter, 333
Hyderabad, decline of, 202; demographic trends in, 203; economic life of, 204; Hindu-Muslim population, 203; increasing homogenization of, 202-203; Persian influence on, 198, 200, 201, 207; plan of, 198-200; under Mughal rule, 198, 202
Hyderabadi, 200

Ibrahim, Sultan, 214
Id (Eid), 233, 298, 301, 302, 340
ideology, as defining national identity, 228
Idi Amin, 224
Indian Psychoanalytic Society, 291, 295
individual identity, 326
instrumentalist theory, of ethnic mobilization, 326-328, 330
interactions between communities, 310-319
internalization in individuality, 349
Iqbal, Mohammad, 227, 309
Islamic identity, 356
Islamic Personal Law, 230
Islamic revival, 345

Jallianwala Bagh massacre, 259
Jamaiat-i-Islami, the, 345
Jami mosque, 199
Janata Dal, the, 351
Jinnah, M.A., 207, 228, 308
Jung, Anees, 303
Jung, C., 234

Kaaba, the, 261
Kashmir, 229, 306, 337
Kayasths, 200, 203
Khatris, 203
Klausner, Samuel, 256
Klein, Melanie, 292, 353
Komtis, 287
Kripalani, Acharya J.B., 259

Lal, Sohan, 218-219
Le Bon, Gustave, 234
LeVine, Robert, 293
Lewis, Bernard, 306
Likierman, Meira, 353
Lingayats, 290
Lodhas, 258, 265, 288,

Mahmud of Ghazni, Sultan, 237, 260
Majlis, 236, 240, 244, 248, 256, 308. Also
    All India Majlis-e-Itihad-ul-Muslimeen
Malla-yuddha, 266
Mandal issue, the, 335
Marathas, 202, 245
Marsh, Peter, 220
Martin, Francois, 200, 201
Marwadis, 202, 274, 288, 299
mass psychology, 234
May, Rollo, 304
Meo tribesmen, 224
Miller, Don, 329
Mir Momin, 198
modernity, dislocations of, 278, 279
modernization, 321-324, 343, 360, 368
Mohammed Quli Qutub Shah, Sultan, 198,
    201, 214, 310
Mohammad Shah Rangile, 348
Moinuddin Chisti, Khwaja, 347
Moore, Sarah, 234
Moral codes, 310-319
Moses, Rafael, 336, 342
'motherland complex', of the Hindu, 291
Muharram procession, 233, 234, 236, 288
Mulk, Nizam ul, 202, 203, 259, 269, 283,
    286
Multanwale, Qari Hanif Mohammad, 346, 350
Multiculturalism, 203, 368
'Musalmani' practices, 209
Muslims, as the hated out-group, 292
Muslim fundamentalism, 205, 306, 335, 345-
    358
Muslim League, the, 228
Muslim Personal Law Conference, 351

Nadwah, 345
Naidus, 287
Naidu, Ratna, 202, 204
Narain Jai Prakash, 227
narcissism of a group, 342-343, 367
'narcissism of minor differences', 232
narcissistic gratification, 254, 265
narcissistic rage, 343
national identities, 228
Nehru, Jawaharlal, 205, 216, 227, 259, 287
Nietzsche, 218
noesis, 222
nonviolence, 244, 260, 365

'object constancy', 276
objective data, 209
objectivity, 198
Osman Ali, 310
Owaisi, Sultan, 241

Pakistan, 203, 207, 216, 217, 222, 224, 228,
    230, 236, 288, 306, 307, 337, 340, 352,
    355
pan-Islamism, 204, 206, 230, 347, 356-358
Pardis, intermarriages among, the, 272-273,
    276-277, 279; languages spoken by, 273;
    migration of Hyderabad, 273; Muslim
    influence on, 286; origins myths of, 273;
Parmananda, Swami, 330
Partition, 198, 216, 220, 225, 227-228, 229,
    337
Patel, Sardar Vallabhbhai, 287
Patterson, Oscar, 363
Pehlwan, in childrens' fantasies, 297; ego
    functioning of, 270; 'land business' as a
    source of income, 246, 248, 251, 256,
    263-265; role in riots, 244, 250, 257,
    263, 264-265, 269; self-image of, 245;
    socialization as, 266
persecution anxiety, 338, 340, 353-354, 357,
    364, 367
persecutory fantasy, of a religious group, 336,
    338, 341, 342, 353
Perso-Islamic domination, 200, 202
personal identity, 231, 233, 234, 261, 266,
    360, 362, 363, 364, 367
'physical group', 233, 234, 293
police, reaction to, 250, 256, 263, 284-285,
    304
pollution, Brahminical notions of, 200
Prasad, Rajendra, 287
precipitating incidents in riots, 230, 234

'pseudo secularist', 208
psychic processes, 233
psychoanalytic sensibility, 196-197
psychogeographical space, 341

Qaum, the Muslim 256, 313, 314, 353
Quli Qutub Shah, Sultan, 214
Qutub Shahi Dynasty, 214, 299

Raj, the British, 213
Rajagopalachari C., 259
Ram Lila, 238
Rama temple construction at Ayodhya, 236,
    238, 330, 332-335, 336
Ramanujan, A.K., 317
Rana Pratap, 259, 264, 335
Rashtriya Swayamsevak Sangh, 219, 230, 264,
    268, 321
Razakars, the, 259, 286
Reddys, 287
refugees, 216, 217, 221, 222
religion, as defining national identity, 228
religious identity, 205, 230, 255, 266, 285,
    306, 307, 353, 363-365, 366, 367
religious processions, disputes over, 232-233,
    236; and the issue of routes taken 235
religious selfhood, 363
religious symbols 206, 213, 236-239, 289,
    329, 357, 367
religious tolerance, 314-315
reservation policy, of the Indian State, 274
'reservoirs' 232. Also targets of
    externalization
riots, archetypes of, 232; eruption of, 229-
    231; feelings inculcated during, 225;
    hidden agenda of, 236; in Ahmedabad
    (1969), 224, 230, 233; in Hyderabad
    (1938), 259; in Hyderabad (1978), 235,
    263, 266, 305; in Hyderabad (1984), 236;
    in Hyderabad (1990), 235, 236, 239; in
    Punjab and Delhi (1886), 232; in Ranchi
    (1967), 231; and immediate tension 230-
    232, 234; and impact on friendships, 284;
    kinds of, 229; and mental processing
    among men and women, 283-284, 303;
    morality of actions during, 310-311, 312,
    313, 314, 315-316, 319; Partition, 223-
    225; role of politicians in, 327; and
    rumours, 224
Rithambra, Sadhavi, 329-342, 343, 351,
    366
Rushdie, Salman, 316

'sacred geography', 228
Samels, Andrew, 259
sangh parivar, 238, 289, 329, 330, 331, 341,
    342, 343, 344
Sanskritization, process of, 274
Sarussalam Urban Cooperative Bank, 240
scapegoating, 336
Schuman, Howard, 229
Scott, J., 229
secularism, 329, 345
secularists, 205, 206, 207, 208, 209, 227,
    228, 367
separate identities, 208-209
Sepoy Mutiny, the, 259
sexuality, control of, 268
Shahabuddin, Syed, 335
Shamshi, Maulana Salimuddin, 346
Shivaji, 259, 260, 264, 335
Shivaratri, 288
Shweder, Richard, 311
Sikhs, 219, 245, 292
Singh, Beant, 352
Singh, Satwant, 352
Singh, V.P., 334
'social identification' theory, 231
social identity, 230, 231, 232, 261, 325
Somnath, 236, 237, 238, 260
Srinivas, M.N., 274
subjective data, 209
subjectivity, 197, 208, 225, 268, 349, 361
Sufis, 208, 367

Tablighi Jamaiat, 345
taboo, 291
Tajfel, Henry, 231
taleemkahana, 246, 247, 249, 256, 261, 267
tari, 201
Tavernier, Jean-Baptiste, 199, 200, 201
Telugu culture, 200, 202, 203
Telugu Desam Party, the, 264
territory, as defining national identity, 228
Thevenot, 201
Tipu Sultan, 206, 209, 290
Tojo, Admiral, 260
totemism, 291
'toy construction' method, 295
Turks, 200, 201, 306
'two nations' theory, 207, 227

Ugadi, 279
Unani medicine, 273
Urdu, 203, 230, 231, 251, 286, 301, 309, 310

Vaid, Krishna Baldev, 225
Vajpayee, Atal Bihari, 352
Varshney, Ashutosh, 228
violence, among the younger generation,
   286; communal, 255-256, 265-266,
   269, 297, 330; and rape, 220-221, 256,
   269, 314, 318, 319; religious, 365-366,
   367; and sexual mutilation, 220-221, 225-
   226
Vivekanand, Swami, 238

Volkan, Vamik, 231, 238, 262

Walzer, Michael, 360
Weber, Max, 321
Winnicott, D.W., 363
Wodiyars, 209
Wolf, Ernest, 325

Yadavs, 287
Yadav, Mulayam Singh, 238, 339